Risk Management and Value

Valuation and Asset Pricing

World Scientific Studies in International Economics

(ISSN: 1793-3641)

Published

Vol. 1 Cross-Border Banking: Regulatory Challenges
edited by Gerard Caprio, Jr (Williams College, USA),
Douglas D. Evanoff (Federal Reserve Bank of Chicago, USA) &
George G. Kaufman (Loyola University Chicago, USA)

Vol. 2 International Financial Instability: Global Banking and National Regulation
edited by *Douglas E. Evanoff (Federal Reserve Bank of Chicago, USA),*
George G. Kaufman (Loyola University Chicago, USA) &
John Raymond LaBrosse (Int'l Assoc. of Deposit Insurers, Switzerland)

Vol. 3 Risk Management and Value: Valuation and Asset Pricing
edited by Mondher Bellalah, Jean Luc Prigent, Annie Delienne
(Université de Cergy-Pontoise, France),
Georges Pariente (Institut Supérieur de Commerce, ISC Paris, France),
Olivier Levyne, Michel Azria (ISC Paris, France) &
Jean Michel Sahut (ESC Amiens, France)

Forthcoming

Globalization and International Trade Policies
by Robert M. Stern (University of Michigan, USA)

Emerging Markets
by Ralph D. Christy (Cornell University, USA)

Institutions and Gender Empowerment in the Global Economy: An Overview of Issues (Part I & Part II)
by Kartik C. Roy (University of Queensland, Australia)
Cal Clark (Auburn University, USA) &
Hans C. Blomqvist (Swedish School of Economics and Business Adminstration, Finland)

The Rules of Globalization (Casebook)
by Rawi Abdelal (Harvard Business School, USA)

3 World Scientific Studies in International Economics

RISK MANAGEMENT AND VALUE

Valuation and Asset Pricing

Editors

Mondher Bellalah
Université de Cergy-Pontoise, France

Jean-Luc Prigent
Université de Cergy-Pontoise, France

Jean-Michel Sahut
ESC Amiens, France

Associate Editors

Georges Pariente
Institut Supérieur de Commerce Paris, France

Olivier Levyne
Institut Supérieur de Commerce Paris, France

Michel Azaria
Institut Supérieur de Commerce Paris, France

Annie Delienne
Université de Cergy-Pontoise, France

World Scientific

NEW JERSEY • LONDON • SINGAPORE • BEIJING • SHANGHAI • HONG KONG • TAIPEI • CHENNAI

Published by

World Scientific Publishing Co. Pte. Ltd.
5 Toh Tuck Link, Singapore 596224
USA office: 27 Warren Street, Suite 401-402, Hackensack, NJ 07601
UK office: 57 Shelton Street, Covent Garden, London WC2H 9HE

British Library Cataloguing-in-Publication Data
A catalogue record for this book is available from the British Library.

World Scientific Studies in International Economics — Vol. 3
RISK MANAGEMENT AND VALUE
Valuation and Asset Pricing

ISBN-13 978-981-277-073-8
ISBN-10 981-277-073-9

Typeset by Stallion Press
Email: enquiries@stallionpress.com

Printed in Singapore by World Scientific Printers

CONTENTS

INTRODUCTION

This book is devoted to selected papers from the International Finance Conference, IFC4, held during 15–17 March 2007, in Hammamet, Tunisia under the authority of the Ministry of Higher Education, Technology and Scientific Research and in cooperation with the Association Française de Finance (AFFI), Association Méditerranéenne de Finance, Assurance et Management, AMFAM, http://amfam.France-paris.org, the Network "Réseau Euro-Méditérranéen", http://remereg.France-paris.org.

The Organizing Committee from University of Cergy and ISC Paris, in collaboration with local organizers, FSEG Tunis, University of Tunis 7 November, and Universities of Sfax and Sousse and UMLT Nabeul (www.umlt.ens.tn) have done an excellent job in managing the different aspects of the conference.

We would like to thank our members of the committee and in particular our keynote speakers, Nobel Laureates James Heckman (USA) and Harry Markowitz (USA), and the main speakers such as George Constantinides (University of Chicago, USA), Dilip Ghosh (USA), Ephraim Clark (Middlesex University, UK), Gérard Hirigoyen (University of Bordeaux 4, France), and many others.

The conference attracted nearly 1,200 participants. Due to space constraints, the committee is obliged to select only some of the papers presented in the conference. In collaboration with the members of the scientific committee, the papers come from different fields covering value, volatility, and risk management in a range of areas.

We would like to thank finally the Minister of Higher Education, Technology and Scientific Research, Professor Lazhar Bououny; the Minister, Governor of the Central Bank, Toufik Baccar; the Secretary of State for

Scientific Research, Ridha Mesbah; the Tunisian Government and in particular the President Zine El Abidine Ben Ali, for his role in the success of the Fourth International Finance Conference (IFC4).

Mondher Bellalah
Conference President, President AMFAM, President of the Network REMEREG THEMA, and ISC Group, Paris.

"This conference brought together leading scholars of Economics and Finance from around the world. It provided an opportunity to exchange ideas across diverse fields. The discussions were at a high level and the setting was very beautiful. The organizers are to be praised for convening such an excellent conference."

James Heckman
Professor in Economics and the College, University of Chicago. Awarded Nobel Prize in Economic Sciences in 2000.

"I spoke to the Conference briefly via satellite. I used the fact that I was in San Diego and the Conference in Tunis to illustrate Adam Smith's observations concerning the importance of large markets. You can hardly imagine a larger market than the one which ties San Diego directly to Tunis and anywhere else in the world. You do not need video conferencing equipment to participate in this market. Frequently a cell phone will do. At first information flows, but then often goods follow. I tied this to the theme of the conference. I wish to thank the sponsors and organizers of the Conference, those who assisted me in speaking to it from San Diego, and those who asked great questions at the end of my talk."

Harry Markowitz
Professor of Finance, Rady School of Management, University of California, San Diego. Awarded Nobel Prize in Economic Sciences in 1990.

CHAPTER 1

MANAGING DERIVATIVES IN THE PRESENCE OF A SMILE EFFECT AND INCOMPLETE INFORMATION

*Mondher Bellalah**

This chapter develops a simple option pricing model when markets can make sudden jumps in the presence of incomplete information. Incomplete information can be defined in the context of Merton's (1987) model of capital market equilibrium with incomplete information. In this context, analytic formulas can be derived for options using the Black–Scholes (1973) approach as in Bellalah (1999). The option value depends upon the probability and magnitude of jumps and a continuous volatility. The model is useful in explaining the smile effect and in extracting information costs. The model can be applied to hedging strategies for different strike prices and can be used for the valuation of different types of options.[a] *It can also be used in the identification of mispriced options. Some simulations are run with and without shadow costs of incomplete information. We run some simulations to extract information costs using market data. Our model can be used to estimate information costs in different markets.*

1 Introduction

This chapter develops a simple option pricing model when markets can make sudden jumps in the presence of incomplete information. We build on Derman *et al.* (1991) modeling of jumps on the underlying asset and combine it with the Bellalah (1999) approach to include information costs.

*THEMA, University of Cergy and ISC Paris.
[a]Many thanks to Riva F, for his help in running simulations.

These costs are defined with respect to Merton's (1987) simple model of capital market equilibrium with incomplete information: investors spend time and money to gather information about the financial instruments and financial markets.

The structure of the chapter is as follows. Section 2 explains the role of information costs in asset pricing and option pricing with respect to Merton's model of capital market equilibrium with incomplete information. In Sec. 3, we present the model we use for the valuation of option prices on the S&P 500 index when prices can jump and information costs are taken into account. The results of our simulations are presented in Sec. 4. Section 5 summarizes and concludes the chapter.

2 Option Pricing in the Presence of Information Costs

Differences in information can explain some puzzling phenomena in finance such as the "home equity bias" or the "weekend effect." Information costs can also offer an explanation for limited participation in financial markets. In general, a fixed cost to participate in the stock market is viewed as summarizing both transaction (as brokerage fees) and information costs (such as the cost of understanding financial institutions, the cost of gathering information about assets, etc.).

Merton (1987) adopts most of the assumptions of the original Capital Asset Pricing Model (CAPM) and relaxes the assumption of equal information across investors. Besides, he assumes that investors hold only securities of which they are aware. This assumption is motivated by the observation that portfolios held by actual investors include only a small fraction of all available traded securities.

The story of information costs applies in varying degrees to the adoption in practice of new structural models of evaluation, i.e. option pricing models. It applies also to the diffusion of innovations for several products and technologies. The recognition of the different speeds of information diffusion is particularly important in explaining the behavior of different firms.

In Merton's model, the expected returns increase with systematic risk, firm-specific risk, and relative market value. The expected returns decrease with relative size of the firm's investor base, referred to in Merton's model as the "degree of investor recognition".

The analysis of investment opportunities can be done in a standard option framework "à la Black–Scholes" (1973). These authors derive their model under the assumption that investors create riskless hedges between options and their underlying securities. Besides, their formula relies implicitly on the CAPM.

Merton's model may be stated as follows:

$$R_S - r = \beta_S[R_m - r] + \lambda_S - \beta_S \lambda_m,$$

where

R_S: the equilibrium expected return on an asset S;
R_m: the equilibrium expected return on the market portfolio;
r: the riskless rate of interest;
R_S: $\text{cov}(R_S/R_m)/\text{var}(R_m)$;
λ_S: the equilibrium aggregate "shadow cost" for the asset S, which is of the same dimension as the expected rate of return on the asset S; and
λ_m: the weighted average shadow cost of incomplete information over all assets.

Bellalah and Jacquillat (1995) and Bellalah (1999) provide a valuation formula for commodity options in the context of incomplete information. Their analysis is based on Merton's (1987) model and can be used to extend the analysis by Derman *et al.* (1991). This is the goal of the following section.

3 Valuing Options When Markets Can Jump in the Presence of Shadow Costs of Incomplete Information

We first briefly present how to integrate market jumps in a simple way and then extend the analysis to take into account information costs.

3.1 Valuing Options When Market Can Jump

Consider the following simple model proposed by Derman *et al.* (1991). The underlying asset price at time 0 today is S. In the next instant, the underlying asset price can jump up by $u\%$ to S_u with probability w or down by $d\%$ to S_d with probability $(1 - w)$.

The probability w is expected to be close to 0 or 1. This means that either a jump up or a jump down predominates. After the first jump, the underlying asset will diffuse with constant volatility σ as in the Black–Scholes (1973) model. No other jumps will occur.

The value of any security in this model can be computed as the average of its payoffs over the scenarios where the underlying asset jumps up or down.

Hence, the option value is given by

$$\text{Option} = w\text{BS}(S_u, K, \sigma, r, \delta, T) + (1 - w)\text{BS}(S_d, K, \sigma, r, \delta, T), \quad (1)$$

where $\text{BS}(S, K, \sigma, r, \delta, T)$ is the formula by Black–Scholes (1973) and δ refers to the continuous dividend yield. This is the formula that appears in the work by Derman *et al.* (1991).

The values used for the underlying asset are:

$$S_u = S(1 + u); \quad S_d = S(1 - d).$$

The current value of the underlying asset corresponds also to an average value after a jump up and a jump down. Hence, the jump up and the jump down are related by

$$d(1 - w) = wu.$$

3.2 *Extension with Information Costs*

The extension of the jump model in the presence of shadow costs can be easily done. The value of any security in this model can be computed as the average of its payoffs over the scenarios where the underlying asset jumps up or down. This process corresponds to a continuous diffusion which is accompanied occasionally by a jump. The use of the Black–Scholes (1973) model assumes that all future variation in the underlying asset value is attributed to the continuous diffusion and none to the discontinuous jump.

The jump-diffusion process is defined by a diffusion volatility and a probability and magnitude for the discontinuous jump. The diffusion volatility characterizes the continuous diffusion. A small probability of a jump of the underlying asset price in the direction of the strike price can affect the value of an out-of-the-money option. In the presence of such a process, two options at least are necessary to extract information about the implied volatility and the implied jump. The model parameters are such that the model error, i.e. the sum of the squared difference between the model prices and the market prices for the two options are as close as possible to zero.

The same approach can be extended to allow the estimation of implied information costs from market data.

In our analysis, the option value is given by

$$\begin{aligned}\text{option} = {} & w\text{BS}(S_u, K, \sigma, r, \delta, \lambda_s, \lambda_c, T) \\ & + (1 - w)\text{BS}(S_d, K, \sigma, r, \delta, \lambda_s, \lambda_c, T), \end{aligned} \quad (2)$$

where $\text{BS}(S_u, K, \sigma, r, \delta, \lambda_s, \lambda_c, T)$ is the formula given by Bellalah (1999).

In this context, the call value is given by

$$C = S\exp((\lambda_s - \lambda_c)T)N(d_1) - E\exp(-(r+\lambda_c)T)N(d_2), \quad (3)$$

$$d_1 = [\ln(S/E) + (r + \lambda_s + 1/2\sigma^2)T]/\sigma\sqrt{T}, \quad d_2 = d_1 - \sigma\sqrt{T},$$

where

S: the underlying asset price;
E: the strike price;
λ_s: the information cost on the asset S;
λ_c: the information cost on the asset C;
T: the time to maturity;
r: the riskless interest rate; and
σ: the volatility of the underlying asset.

For a derivation of this formula, the reader can refer to Bellalah (1990, 1999).

4 The Smile Effect and the S&P 500 Index Options in the Presence of Jumps and Incomplete Information

4.1 The Smile

Consider the implied volatilities on a given day for the European-style July S&P index options expiring with a given maturity. Table 1 shows the implied volatilities and the deltas of S&P calls and puts using the Black–Scholes (1973) model.

The option maturity date is in March 2001, the index level is 1264.74, the riskless interest rate is 5.81%, and the dividend yield is 1.17%. Note that the sign $-$ refers to the put's delta and the sign $+$ refers to the call's delta.

It is important to note that options with strike prices below the index price or out-of-the-money puts with low deltas are traded at higher implied volatilities than options with strike prices above the asset price which correspond to out-of-the-money calls with low deltas. The presence of different implied volatilities for different strike prices refers to the well-known smile. This may be viewed as an "anomaly" in the Black–Scholes model since when using their formula, one must adjust the volatility as the strike price changes. Besides, the fact that implied volatilities seem to be higher for puts than calls may be a "strange" result.

Table 1: Implied volatilities and the deltas of S&P calls and puts using the Black–Scholes (1973) model.

Strike	Type	σ implied (%)	Δ (%)
950	Put	35.49	−0.37
975	Put	34.84	−0.72
1025	Put	34.72	−2.26
1050	Put	32.51	−3.68
1100	Put	31.84	−8.44
1125	Put	30.38	−11.97
1150	Put	29.80	−16.31
1175	Put	29.07	−21.45
1200	Put	28.21	−27.29
1250	Put	25.71	−40.45
1275	Call	24.28	52.42
1300	Call	24.57	45.56
1325	Call	23.65	38.96
1350	Call	22.47	32.77
1375	Call	22.02	27.13
1400	Call	21.20	22.10

4.2 Introducing Market Jumps

In fact, if market participants believe that the underlying asset is driven by a continuous random walk, then the volatility must be independent of the strike price. This strange result can be explained by the fact that market participants expect an occasionally sharp downward jump in the underlying asset price. If it were the case, then out-of-the-money puts could exhibit a higher probability of paying off than out-of-the-money calls. In this case, the smile can be explained by a jump-diffusion process.

Using the market prices of at least two options on the same underlying asset and maturity with different strike prices, the Derman *et al.* (1991) model can be used to extract the market implied volatility and information regarding the implied jumps. Knowledge about the jump probability is necessary for the estimation. As mentioned above this probability is expected to be close to 0 here as data are consistent with expectations about a downward jump. In the Derman *et al.* (1991), model, the probability is explicitly chosen by the user. We take the same approach here but we also consider the possibility for w to be endogenously determined.

Table 2: Parameter estimates using the Derman *et al.* (1991) methodology.

w (%)	d (%)	σ diffusion (%)
3	58.71	19.73
4	46.87	19.51
5	39.73	19.28
6	34.94	19.04
7	31.49	18.80
8	28.90	18.55
9	26.85	18.29
10	25.19	18.03
11	23.82	17.76
12	22.67	17.47
13	21.67	17.19
14	20.79	16.89
15	20.03	16.58

Table 3: Parameter estimates using the Derman *et al.* (1191) methodology with endogenous w parameter.

w	d	σ diffusion
15.51%	19.67%	16.43%

The calibration has been made using the 1200 and the 1250 put options as they correspond to the most liquid options given the maturity we considered. The results are given in Tables 2 and 3. In Table 2, the results are based on direct application of the Derman *et al.* (1991) methodology, i.e. the w parameter value has been explicitly chosen. We give the results for a set of reasonable values, starting from $w = 3\%$ as the algorithm was unable to achieve convergence for values less than this figure. An interesting result here is that the implied diffusion parameter is relatively insensitive to the w value which makes the model reliable even in the presence of error in w estimation by a trader. In Table 3, the w value in endogenously determined, i.e. we let the algorithm calculate the parameter values (w, δ, and σ diffusion) which best fit the market prices used for calibration. In the remainder of the chapter, we decided to restrict ourselves to this approach.

Table 4: Comparison between Black–Scholes and model prices.

Strike	Type	Market price	Black–Scholes price	Model price	Market σ (%)	Model σ (%)
950	Put	1.875	0.10	0.813	35.49	31.20
975	Put	2.625	0.21	1.587	34.84	31.90
1025	Put	5.750	0.87	4.512	34.72	32.84
1050	Put	6.375	1.59	6.746	32.51	32.98
1100	Put	12.000	4.60	12.630	31.84	32.38
1125	Put	14.500	7.28	16.194	30.38	31.64
1150	Put	18.875	11.05	20.186	29.80	30.66
1175	Put	24.000	16.13	24.719	29.07	29.49
1200	Put	30.000	22.73	30.012	28.21	28.22
1250	Put	44.125	41.07	44.140	25.71	25.71
1275	Call	54.000	54.00	54.704	24.28	24.60
1300	Call	43.625	42.98	41.540	24.57	23.62
1325	Call	32.375	33.70	30.549	23.65	22.78
1350	Call	22.500	26.03	21.727	22.47	22.06
1375	Call	15.875	19.80	14.930	22.02	21.46
1400	Call	10.250	14.84	9.907	21.20	20.96

Table 4 gives a comparison between the market price, the Black–Scholes price, and the model price,[b] and between the model implied diffusion volatility and the Black–Scholes implicit volatility. Of course, the model volatility is less than the Black–Scholes volatility as the model makes a correction for the implicit jump conveyed by the prices. Note that the model gives a partial correction for the bias one can observe when applying the Black–Scholes formula for out-of-the-money calls and puts.

4.3 *Introducing Information Costs*

We introduce information costs in the Derman *et al.* (1991) methodology. We considered information costs both on the option market (λ_c), and the underlying asset (λ_s), and ran simulations for different cost levels (from 1% to 5%). However, due to space considerations, we restrict our presentation in Fig. 1 to the most significant results. We decided to compare the model price and the market price in terms of implied volatility in order to exhibit the model ability to fit the existing smile.

[b]The input value of sigma for the Black–Scholes formula has been estimated using the 1250 at-the-money put.

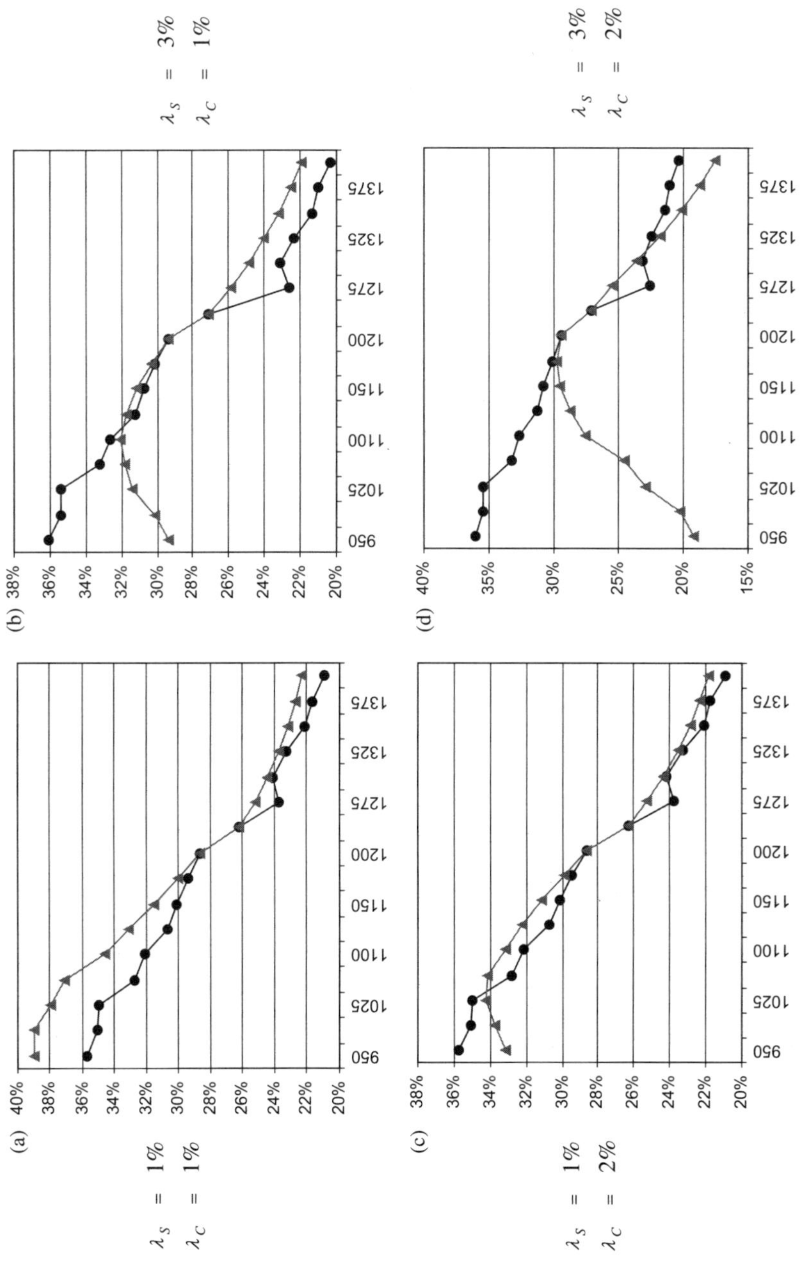

Figure 1: Comparison of implied volatility between market prices and model prices for different information cost levels.

One can notice at first glance that the introduction of information costs makes possible the production of any smile pattern (see, for example, the differences between panels a and d) which makes information costs a promising tool for explaining the volatility smile. Another striking aspect is that the information cost levels which give the best fitting ($\lambda_s = 1\%$ and $\lambda_c = 2\%$) are very close to Merton's estimates although we use a radically different approach. Thus, we can view our model as a possible (and reliable) way to extract information costs using option prices.

5 Summary and Conclusion

This chapter develops a simple model for the valuation of options in the presence of jumps and information costs. The model is an extension of the models of Derman *et al.* (1991) and Bellalah (1999). Our model has the potential to explain the smile effect. It is calibrated to market data and allows an implicit estimation of the magnitude of information costs. While our methodology and our model are applied only to index options, they can be used in different option markets.

References

Bellalah, M (1990). Quatres Essais Sur L'évaluation des Options: Dividendes, Volatilités des Taux d'intérêt et Information Incomplète, Doctorat de l'université de Paris-Dauphine.

Bellalah, M and Jacquillat, B (1995). Option valuation with information costs: Theory and Tests. *Financial Review*, August, 617–635.

Bellalah, M (1999). The valuation of futures and commodity options with information costs. *Journal of Futures Markets*, September.

Black, F and Scholes, M (1973). The pricing of options and corporate liabilities. *Journal of Political Economy*, 81, 637–659.

Derman, E, Bergier A and Kani, I (1991). Valuing index options when markets can jump. Working paper, Quantitative Strategies Research Notes, Goldman Sachs, July.

Merton, RC (1987). A simple model of capital market equilibrium with incomplete information, *Journal of Finance*, 42, 483–510.

CHAPTER 2

A VALUE-AT-RISK APPROACH TO ASSESS EXCHANGE RISK ASSOCIATED TO A PUBLIC DEBT PORTFOLIO: THE CASE OF A SMALL DEVELOPING ECONOMY

*Wissem Ajili**

This chapter deals with a delta-normal VaR application in the case of small developing economy. It assesses the exchange risk associated to the Tunisian public debt portfolio. We use daily spot exchange rates of the Tunisian dinar against the three main currencies composing the long run public debt portfolio, the dollar, the euro, and the yen. We are interested in the period from 1 January 1999 to 30 June 2006.

We firstly demonstrate that the VaR approach can be used for a small developing economy provided that time series are neither too long nor too short. For daily data, we show that the optimal length to validate the assumption normality is annual.

Secondly, we prove that the euro is the refuge value *for managing the exchange risk in the Tunisian case. Only the systematic risk measured by the calculated betas associated to the dinar exchange rate versus the euro is negative. The component VaR analysis ascertains that the Japanese yen is the main source of exchange risk for the Tunisian debt portfolio. On the contrary, the euro constitutes a* natural hedge *against this risk. The euro component VaR values are slightly negative or null.*

Finally, we demonstrate that the VaR diversification degree is stable throughout the studied period. The non-diversified VaR represents 65% of the total VaR.

*University of Paris, Dauphine.
ajiliouissem@yahoo.fr

1 Introduction

Since the middle of the nineties, the Value-at-Risk (VaR) method has become a widespread risk measure. Despite that the approach is controversial in theory, there is no doubt of the VaR success among financial practitioners and regulatory institutions mainly because of its synthetic character. The VaR provides a direct and compact appreciation of the risk level associated to an asset portfolio.

Basle Committee on banking supervision, with the "*amendment to the capital accord to incorporate market risks*" (January 1996), allows banks to use *proprietary in-house models* for measuring market risks as an alternative to a standardized measurement framework.

Increasingly banking sector operators nowadays, do use their own VaR models to manage their portfolios, with the approval of the monetary authorities. For instance, in 2001, the *Banca Commerciale Italiana* (BCI) received approval from the Bank of Italy for the use of internal market risk models using a variety of VaR methods, including parametric methods and Monte Carlo simulations for nonlinear portfolios. The approval marks the first time that an Italian bank had an internal model validated for use by the central bank.[a]

At the end of the nineties, with the public debt management reform waves, many governments have tried to adapt the VaR approach to public debt portfolio management requirements. For instance, The Danish National Bank does use the Cost-at-Risk (CaR) as an integrated risk managing approach of the sovereign debt. The work on developing and incorporating the CaR approach in the management of the domestic debt was initiated in 1997. In 2003, the CaR model was expanded to include the foreign government debt. It now comprises the domestic and foreign government debt as well as the swap portfolios.[b]

This chapter is interested in the Tunisian public debt management strategy. It makes use of the VaR approach within its parametric version to assess the exchange risk associated to the long run public debt portfolio. It is the first study that applies the VaR approach to a small developing economy.

We use daily data of the Tunisian dinar exchange rates *vis-à-vis* the three principal currencies composing the long run national debt portfolio which are the dollar, the euro, and the yen. We are interested in the period from 1 January 1999 to 30 June 2006.

[a]For further information, see the web site of the Bank of Italy: http://www.bancaditalia.it.

[b]For further information, see the web site of the Denmark National Bank: http://www.nationalbanken.dk.

We firstly demonstrate that the VaR methodology could be applied to a small developing economy. We show that the optimal daily data length is annual. The daily exchange returns of the Tunisian dinar do converge to the normal distribution when portfolios are annual. A longer time series verify less and less the normality assumption. We assume also that a 95% confidence level reduces at maximum the bias of *Leptokurtic* distributions with a *Kurtosis* excess.

Concerning the economic policies aspects of our study, the results conclude in favor of the Tunisian public debt management credibility regarding its exchange risk component. Our results are also in conformity with the World Bank recommendations (2004) related to the Tunisian public debt strategy. The dominant character of the public debt management policy in Tunisia is its prudence.

Our main conclusion is the following: the euro is the *refuge value* in managing the Tunisian public debt portfolio as only the betas associated to the Tunisian dinar exchange rate against the euro are negative.

Moreover, the component VaR analysis proves that the Japanese yen is the first risk source in the Tunisian debt portfolio followed by the American dollar. On the contrary, the euro represents a *potential hedge* against this risk. Its component VaR values are slightly negative or null.

We prove also that the diversification degree of the calculated VaR is stable throughout the studied period. The VaR associated to the Tunisian public debt portfolio are not diversified at 65% level.

The remainder of the chapter is organized as follows. Section 2 sets the VaR approach in its theoretical and empirical framework through a brief presentation of the related literature. Section 3 describes data and explains methodology, while Section 4 summarizes the main results.

2 The VaR Approach in the Literature

2.1 How to Measure Risk? A Little History

Before Markowitz, the financial risk was identified as the *correcting* factor of the anticipated return. Adjusted returns to risk were so defined in an *ad hoc* manner. The main advantage of this simple method of assessing risk is to allow an ordinal classification of investments.

Markowitz (1952, 1956) suggests as risk measures associated to investment returns the variance or the standard deviation from the means of the returns distribution. In the assets portfolio case, the risk is measured via the covariance between each pair of assets.

$$\mathrm{Cov}(X,Y) = E(X,Y) - E(X)E(Y),$$

where X and Y represent random returns.

So, the risk associated to an assets portfolio is measured through the multivariate returns distributions of all assets in that portfolio.

A multivariate distribution is characterized by both the statistical characteristics of all component random variables and the interdependence structure between these variables. Markowitz expresses the first through the two first moments of the different univariate returns distributions. He describes the second via the linear correlation coefficient of each pair of returns.

$$\rho(X,Y) = \frac{\mathrm{Cov}(X,Y)}{\left(\sigma_X^2 \sigma_Y^2\right)^{\frac{1}{2}}},$$

where σ_X and σ_Y represent respectively the standard deviations of the univariate random distributions of X and Y.

Recently, a number of studies support that the linear correlation is a good interdependence measure only in the case of the *elliptic distributions* (Szegö, 2005 among others). Consequently, the Markowitz model suits better the *elliptic distributions* with fine variances such as the t-Student and the normal distributions.

However, many other empirical essays suggest that even in the case of *non-elliptic distributions*, the standard variance–covariance model is validated with only one limit: the extreme events are under estimated (Kondor and Pafka, 2001; Putnam *et al.*, 2002; Chan and Tan, 2003 etc.).

In the sixties, the β concept as risk measure started gaining ground at the expense of the variance–covariance model. The numerical heaviness of the latter on the one hand, and the unavailability of information permitting the calculation of the variance–covariance matrix on the other hand, contribute to the β model's success.

The β as a linear dependency measure between one asset return and the market leads to the development of the two main asset pricing models, the Capital Asset Pricing Model[c] (CAPM) and the Arbitrage Pricing Theory[d] (APT). Yet, these models developed for a "*normal world*" express their limits in front of the market reality.

---

[c] See Sharpe, 1964; Lintner, 1965; Mossin, 1966 and Black, 1972.
[d] See Ross, 1976.

2.2 *The VaR — a New Risk Measure*

The multivariate models developed within a *normal framework* are, with no doubt, attractive. How a simplest tool describing two random variable combination by their respective marginal distributions and their correlation coefficient would be abandoned easily?

In the end of the nineties, new risk measures were introduced principally under the extreme events analysis influence. In this researching dynamic, the VaR concept was born.

This new risk measure was introduced to answer a relatively simple but extremely precise question: How much would be the expected loss associated to an asset portfolio, during one day, one week, or one year, with a predetermined probability?

Yet, the VaR concept has a practical origin since 1994; J. P. Morgan reveals to the shareholders that the VaR associated to their portfolio is about 15 millions of American dollars per day at 95% confidence level.

2.2.1 The VaR Models: A Small Definition

The VaR models provide an appreciation of an assets portfolio exposure degree to market risks i.e. to prices, interest rates, exchange rates, unfavorable fluctuations, etc.

The VaR models assess the maximum potential loss resulting from an unfavorable price fluctuations for a given time horizon at a specific confidence level.

A more formalized VaR definition is the following: for a given time horizon and a probability level k (with $0 < k < 1$) ; VaR_k represents the expected loss with probability $(1 - k)$. In other words, VaR_k is the maximum expected loss in a specific period with a probability level k.

The VaR_k of the random variable X is based on the k-quantile in negative sign, of the distribution function F_X:

$$\text{VaR}_k = \inf \left\{ -F_X^{-1}(k) \right\},$$

where F_X^{-1} is the inverse of the distribution function F_X.

2.2.2 The VaR Models: Different Methods

Three different VaR methods are admitted in the related literature to assess risks associated to an assets portfolio.

The first one is the delta normal method also called the standard variance–covariance model based on the financial returns normality assumption. The normal VaR uses a linear approximation of price movements (or their log). When a portfolio consists of financial instruments with linear behavior toward risks, portfolio volatility is directly calculated via the variance–covariance matrix of the risk factors.

In spite of its simplicity, the normal VaR is criticized firstly for its strong normality assumption, since financial variables usually violate this assumption. Financial returns distribution functions are characterized by both *flat tails* and *Kurtosis excess*. The normal VaR is also criticized for its inadaptability to nonlinear financial instruments such as derivatives.

The second VaR method is the non-parametric one based on the construction of a financial returns distribution with reference to historical data. Consequently, the normality assumption limit of the variance–covariance method is overcome within this second approach.

The historical approach does not formulate any a *priori* assumption on the shape of the returns distribution function. The historical VaR is an extrapolative method that assumes the future is a faithful reproduction of the past and the present. Historical data are used to identify a hypothetical density function which is employed to calculate the current or future portfolio VaR.

Yet, the non-parametric method is not so robust. Its major handicap is its high sensitivity to historical data. Within this approach, the probability that the future losses will be superior to the highest loss ever realized is null.

The third VaR method is the Monte Carlo simulation. It is based on the choice of the distribution function that fits closely the future assets prices fluctuations and the calculation of the worst loss at the 99 or 95 percentiles of the generated distribution.

Probably, the Monte Carlo simulation is the most complete VaR approach. However, the method suffers from some problems of specification. The Monte Carlo VaR is also heavy to manage since it requires doing many simulations to lead to good precise results.

In the extension of the three VaR methods, the related theoretical literature is accustomed to itemize the stress tests. These tests lead to the examination of financial variables fluctuations impact in a portfolio value. Within this approach, different prices fluctuations scenarios are identified than the assets portfolio value is evaluated under those scenarios.

The fact that a probability is attributed to each scenario, allows to the construction of a probability distribution associated to portfolio returns. The

VaR is deduced from the post-determined distribution function. The stress tests are however relatively subjective since the scenarios based on which the VaR are calculated are defined in an arbitrary way.

2.3 The VaR: Some Empirical Evidences

The VaR approach does not cease to prove itself as a quantitative risk evaluation approach. In spite of its technical limits, several empirical studies continue until now to support the VaR tool as a risk measure.

The delta normal VaR was criticized by academics mainly for its fundamental normality assumption unrealism. Paradoxically, empirical investigations persist validating the variance–covariance approach in spite of the normality assumption limit. Kondor and Pafka (2001) are interested in the paradox of the VaR success in spite of its limits. The authors attribute the VaR performance to the following two elements: (1) The choice of a very short expectation horizon (commonly one day); and (2) The method simplicity since the VaR is calculated by multiplying volatilities by a constant value determined by the chosen confidence level. In fact, when the confidence level is about 95%, the heavy *flat tails* limit characterizing *Leptokurtic* returns distributions with an excess of *Kurtosis*, does not affect or does affect little the VaR results reliability. The higher the confidence level chosen, the weighty is the *flat tail* effect and the less is the VaR results reliability.[e]

Putnam *et al.* (2002) corroborate this VaR results sensitivity to the confidence level chosen. The authors conclude that because of the *flat tails phenomena* in financial series, a 95% confidence level is empirically preferred to a 99% one.

Chan and Tan (2003) demonstrate that at the 95% confidence level the traditional stress–VaR approach performs better than the Stress–VaR approach they propose. Only with the 99% confidence level will the latter operate better. Once more, the empirical literature suggests that the *flat tails phenomena* impact is limited at the 95% confidence level.

---

[e]Technically, when the confidence level is about 95%, this implies that volatilities would be multiplied by 1.65 under financial returns normality assumptions. If on the contrary, we are interested in a slight *Leptokurtic* distribution with a *Kurtosis* equal to 5, describing better financial returns i.e. the t-Student distribution with a liberty degree equal to 7, a quantile of 5% corresponds to a standard deviation equal to (-1.60) and a standard deviation equal to (-1.65) corresponds to a quantile of 4.6%.

When we chose a higher confidence level such as 99%, the flat tails phenomena would be more significant: a quantile of 1% in the case of a t-Student distribution is about (-2.54) which is significantly diverging from the normal distribution with (-2.33) of standard deviation.

Bams *et al.* (2005) support that the exchange rate returns behavior is characterized by the *flat tails phenomena.* However, the observations in these tails are relatively reduced. Consequently, while the traditional VaR leads to an underestimation of the risk associated to extreme events, more sophisticated models which take into account the *flat tails* aspect of the financial returns distribution overestimate the risk associated to those events. In other words, models integrating *flat tails* property of financial returns distributions suffer from an over-assessment of VaR.

Empirical investigations show that the GARCH $(1, 1)$ model and the t-Student distribution allow the VaR measurements to be more appropriate to extreme events, while the normal distribution is perfectly adapted to financial returns without extreme events.

Moreover, in the VaR applications, a key role is played not only by the distribution functions, but also by the parametric values of those functions. The parametric values are calculated on the basis of historical data and this kind of data integrate worse extreme events.

Bollen and Moosa (2002) support that the VaR estimations could be biased because of the time series length or because of the methodology used to calculate volatilities. When volatilities are balance weighted, the VaR estimations are not biased for short-time series (with a length $T = 20, 60, 120$). For longer time series (i.e. $T = 240$), recent volatilities must be more weighted than the old ones in order to avoid VaR estimations bias.

Campbell *et al.* (2001) analyze the impact of non-normality on the expected returns on the one hand and on the time horizon of the selected investment portfolio on the other hand. The authors develop a selection portfolio model allowing asset allocation by maximizing the portfolio expected return under the maximum loss constraint deduced from the VaR imposed by the risk manager. The empirical validation of the model is done by using two assets: stocks and bonds in the American case. The authors conclude in favor of the VaR approach, in spite of the two limits.

Other empirical studies try to make classification between all VaR methods by comparing the results reliability degree of each one. Bollen and Moosa (2002), by comparing the parametric approach to the historical one, demonstrate that results are biased within the latter and not within the former.

Vlaar (2000) analyzes the impact of the dynamic interest rate structure upon the VaRs results reliability in the German case. Different VaRs are calculated with the historical approach, the standard variance–covariance model, and the Monte Carlo simulations. For a 10-day detention period, the best results are obtained with the joined approach, variance–covariance, and Monte Carlo.

Pritsker (2006) is interested in the historical approach limits. Firstly, he demonstrates the under-reaction of the historical VaR to conditional risk modification. He also proves the asymmetrical reaction of the method to risk variation: the measured risks increase in the case of considerable losses but not when the portfolio realizes important gains.

Nowadays, the VaR approach is criticized mainly in the case of *non-elliptic returns* distributions for the following reasons[f]:

(1) The VaR approach does not allow measuring losses in excess toward the VaR values.
(2) The VaR approach could lead to conflicting results at different confidence levels.
(3) The VaR non-sub-additivity involves that the portfolio diversification could lead to an increase of risks.
(4) The non-convexity makes impossible the VaR approach use in optimizing problems.
(5) The VaR approach is characterized by the presence of many extreme values which conduct to a non-stable VaR classification.

The VaR application in the case of developing economies is not recurrent in the related empirical literature. The developing and emerging markets characterized by both their imperfections and their heavy regulatory restrictions, do not lend themselves easily to VaR analysis.

Chou *et al.* (2006) study is one among the very rare VaR investigations, interested in the case of developing economies. The authors examine the VaR validity in Taiwan. They analyze two fundamental limits admitted in the case of developing economies: (1) The presence of price limits; and the (2) non-synchronous trading.

The first limit results fundamentally from regulatory restrictions imposed on the price fluctuations in the market. Consequently, the usual risks and returns estimators are statistically biased under such a constraint. When prices fluctuate within a pre-specified range, the portfolio value does the same, so that the risk associated to that portfolio would be artificially reduced. The VaR is biased in this case since it does not express the real risk incurred. The

[f]See Szegö (2005) among others.

second limit is related to the so-called in the non-synchronous trading literature, indeed, infrequent trading leads to spurious autocorrelations and biased returns variances estimations.

Paradoxically, the two limits characterizing developing economies do not conduct to biased VaR estimations, in the case of Taiwan. Both the alternative method proposed by Chou *et al.* (2006) and the traditional VaR (mainly the historical approach and the variance–covariance model based on naive OLS simulations) lead to statistical acceptable results.

Chou *et al.* (2006) conclude that the two limits impact is empirically reduced. The VaR is satisfactory performing even in the case of developing and emerging economies.

Finally, although the IMF and the WB[g] (2001, 2003) suggest explicitly the use of the private sector tools in managing public risks, the VaR application is still limited if not marginal in controlling risks associated to public debt portfolio.

In this chapter, we propose an exchange risk VaR modeling applied to a public debt portfolio in the case of a small developing economy: Tunisia. The empirical added value of our investigation is to apply the standard variance–covariance VaR model to a small developing economy. We test mainly, the *Leptokurtic* returns distribution with an excess of *Kurtosis* limit. In the economic side, our analysis is an *a posteriori* evaluation of the Tunisian public debt management strategy in its exchange risk component.

3 Data and Methodology

In this study, we apply the standard variance–covariance VaR model to a Tunisian representative long run debt portfolio. Indeed, the representative portfolio is a close reproduction of the sovereign debt structure. We are interested exclusively in the exchange risk resulting from the three dominating currencies in the debt portfolio: the dollar, the euro, and the yen.

Consequently, this chapter answers a very precise question: How much is the maximum potential loss associated to the Tunisian long run public debt, due to the three main currencies fluctuations, by a one-day time horizon, at a 95% confidence level?

[g]IMF: International Monetary Fund; WB: World Bank.

3.1 Data

We are interested in the three main currencies composing the Tunisian public debt portfolio, the dollar, the euro, and the yen. So, analyzing the exchange risk associated to the Tunisian national debt amounts returns to studying the three flowing exchange rates: TND/USD, TND/EUR, and TND/JPY.

Our empirical investigation deals with daily data from 01/01/1999 to 06/30/2006. The total observations number by currency is around 1950.

We use spot rates. The TND/USD and TND/EUR time series are extracted directly from *DataStream* database while the TND/JPY time series are computed using the TND/USD and USD/JPY cross exchange rates available in the database. The quotation is uncertain.

3.1.1 A Little Descriptive Statistics

The three time series statistical properties are summarized in Table A.1 (See Appendix). During the studied period, the euro *vis-à-vis* the Tunisian dinar is in average more expensive than the dollar and the yen. The exchange rate of the dinar is also more volatile versus the euro than versus the dollar and the yen.

Figure 1 illustrating the Tunisian dinar exchange rates fluctuations *vis-à-vis* the three currencies shows three different phases of evolution mainly in the case of the euro and the dollar.

(1) During 1999, the euro expressed in Tunisian dinar was more expensive than the dollar. This fact would be explained by the skepticism characterizing the euro introducing period.

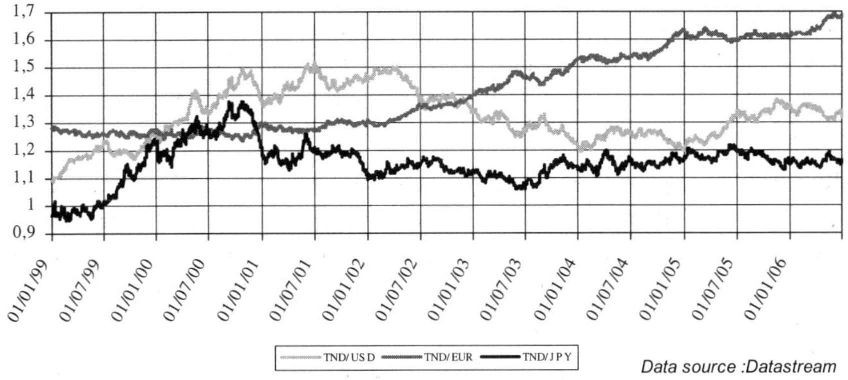

Figure 1: The Tunisian dinar exchange rates.

(2) From the beginning of 2000 to the end of 2003, the Tunisian dinar exchange rate versus the American dollar was becoming superior to the dinar exchange rate versus the euro.
(3) From 2004 to mid-2006, the dinar exchange rate *vis-à-vis* the euro took off again. The ascending tendency of the TND/EUR was going closely with a declining tendency of the TND/USD.

Figure 1 also demonstrates that during the studied period, the dinar exchange rates *vis-à-vis* the Japanese yen seems to follow the dinar exchange rates *vis-à-vis* the American dollar fluctuations.

Moreover, during the studied period from 1999 to 2006, the Tunisian dinar exchange rate *vis-à-vis* the three currencies is relatively stable. The spot rates fluctuate mainly within the (−2%, +2%) interval. The exchange rate management strategy adopted by Tunisian authorities is relatively steady. The Tunisian exchange rate seems to wave in a fixed range such as in the snake system.

The tendencies revealed by graphs would be completed via a variance–covariance analysis between the three currencies (a correlation analysis).

3.1.2 A Preliminary Correlation Analysis

The matrix of correlation between the three exchange rates could give a preliminary idea about the three variables' behaviors and their interdependence structure. In our case, the three exchange rates behavior during the period examined could be summarized in a (3×3) symmetric matrix, i.e. in three values.

The main results of the correlation analysis are the following:

Result 1: A negative correlation coefficient between the TND/USD and the TND/EUR (− 0.270). A Tunisian dinar appreciation *vis-à-vis* the dollar goes with a dinar depreciation *vis-à-vis* the euro and vice versa. The two exchange rates follow opposite tendencies.

Result 2: A negative correlation coefficient between the TND/EUR and the TND/JPY (− 0.014) significantly inferior in absolute value to that of the precedent case. When the Tunisian dinar is depreciated *vis-à-vis* the euro, it is appreciated *vis-à-vis* both the dollar and the yen, but less in the second case than in the first one and vice versa.

Result 3: The correlation coefficient between the TND/USD and the TND/JPY is not only positive but around twice in absolute value of that between the TND/USD and the TND/EUR (+ 0.534). The dinar appreciation toward dollar goes with depreciation of the euro (Result 1) and with a simultaneous appreciation in a more pronounced way toward the yen. This third result could be explained by the following status of the Japanese yen *vis-à-vis* the American dollar.

The matrix of correlation between the three exchange rates (TND/USD; TND/EUR; TND/JPY) is worth teaching about the policy of managing the exchange risk associated to the Tunisian public debt portfolio.

Consequence 1: The negative correlation between the TND/USD and the TND/EUR means that the Tunisian exchange rate *vis-à-vis* the two dominating currencies is managed to compensate the potential losses associated to the depreciation of the one throughout the gains resulting from the simultaneous appreciation of the other.

Consequence 2: The three currencies do not have the same weight in the Tunisian exchange rate management strategy. While the dollar and the euro act as *leader currencies* following opposite tendencies, the yen operates as a follower *vis-à-vis* the American dollar.

Consequence 3: The Tunisian exchange rate management strategy is characterized by its prudence since it takes into account the opposite movements of the two dominant currencies, the euro and the dollar.

The next step of the analysis is to evaluate the Tunisian exchange rate management policy viability in minimizing risks.

Calculating the correlation and the variance–covariance matrix

The correlation matrix

	TND/USD	TND/EUR	TND/JPY
TND/USD	1	–0.2700	0.5346
TND/EUR		1	–0.0141
TND/JPY			1

The variance–covariance matrix

	TND/USD	TND/EUR	TND/JPY
TND/USD	0.008758	–0.003650	0.003724
TND/EUR		0.020858	–0.000152
TND/JPY			0.005539

3.2 *Variables*

To assess the exchange risk associated to the Tunisian public debt portfolio, we use the geometric returns of the spot exchange rates evaluated in percentage (%). So we define the three following variables:

$$R_{\text{USD}} = Ln\left(\frac{\text{TND/USD}_t}{\text{TND/USD}_{t-1}}\right)$$
$$= Ln(\text{TND/USD}_t) - Ln(\text{TND/USD}_{t-1})$$

$$R_{\text{EUR}} = Ln\left(\frac{\text{TND/EUR}_t}{\text{TND/EUR}_{t-1}}\right) = Ln(\text{TND/EUR}_t) - Ln(\text{TND/EUR}_{t-1})$$

$$R_{\text{JPY}} = Ln\left(\frac{\text{TND/JPY}_t}{\text{TND/JPY}_{t-1}}\right) = Ln(\text{TND/JPY}_t) - Ln(\text{TND/JPY}_{t-1}).$$

Table A.2 summarizes the statistical characteristics of the three variables. Figures A.4–A.6 give an idea about the three exchange rates returns evolution (See Appendix). The three variables fluctuate in an interval (−1%, 1%). Only the exchange rate of the Tunisian dinar against the Japanese yen goes some times beyond this range. Yet the extreme variations of the dinar against the yen do never exceed 5% in absolute value.

3.3 *Methodology*

To assess the exchange risk associated to the Tunisian public debt, we apply the standard variance–covariance VaR. We support that the parametric method is the most appropriate one in our case since we use financial linear variables, so that the limit of the delta normal VaR non-adaptability to financial instruments with nonlinear behavior is avoided.

Concerning the financial returns non-normality limit, we assume that even our variables convergence to normality is not total; the VaR approach viability is empirically admitted despite that constraint. Indeed, Chan and Tan (2003) among others, demonstrate through daily data related to eight Asian currencies from 1992 to 1999, the normality assumption is valid even in the case of *flat tailed* distributions at the 95% confidence level.

3.3.1 A Two Assets Portfolio

The so-called delta normal method or the standard variance–covariance model assumes that all asset-prices fluctuations are normally distributed.

Under this normality assumption, the portfolio return is also normally distributed since it is a linear combination of normal variables. Consequently, a two assets portfolio VaR can be calculated from the VaR of each asset:

$$\mathrm{VaR}_P = \left[(\mathrm{VaR}_1)^2 + (\mathrm{VaR}_2)^2 + 2\mathrm{VaR}_1\mathrm{VaR}_2\rho_{12}\right]^{\frac{1}{2}}, \tag{1}$$

with

$$\mathrm{VaR}_j = Z_j k\sigma_j \text{ for } j = 1, 2; \qquad k = \begin{cases} 1.65(95\%) \\ 2.33(99\%) \end{cases};$$

Z_j is the value position of j; σ_j is the standard deviation of the asset price j fluctuations; ρ_{ij} is the correlation between the price fluctuations of the assets i and j; and $k\sigma_j$ represents the volatility of position j.

The normality assumption has the great advantage to simplify the VaR calculation since only the mean and the variance–covariance matrix are to be calculated for the different asset price fluctuations.

So, the worst loss to which a portfolio composed by normally distributed assets returns is exposed at 95% (respectively 99%) confidence level, is determined by calculating negative (unfavorable) fluctuations of prices corresponding to 1.65 (respectively 2.33) standard deviation away from the mean.

3.3.2 A More than Two Assets Portfolio

The formula (1) applied in the case of a two assets portfolio could be generalized to portfolio with n assets with $n > 2$.

So, the worst loss to which a portfolio with n assets is exposed within 95% confidence level, under the assumption of normality could be formulated in the following matrix form:

$$\mathrm{VaR}_P = \left[[\, z_1 1.65\sigma_1 \quad z_2 1.65\sigma_2 \quad \cdots \quad z_n 1.65\sigma_n \,] \times \begin{bmatrix} 1 & \rho_{12} & \cdots & \rho_{1n} \\ \rho_{21} & 1 & & \rho_{2n} \\ \cdots & & \cdots & \\ \rho_{n1} & & & 1 \end{bmatrix} \begin{bmatrix} z_1 1.65\sigma_1 \\ z_2 1.65\sigma_2 \\ \cdots \\ z_n 1.65\sigma_n \end{bmatrix} \right]^{\frac{1}{2}}. \tag{2}$$

In our investigation, we are interested in a three assets portfolio ($n = 3$) within 95% confidence level.

$$\text{VaR}_P = \left[\left[z_1 1.65\sigma_1 \quad z_2 1.65\sigma_2 \quad z_3 1.65\sigma_3 \right] \times \begin{bmatrix} 1 & \rho_{12} & \rho_{13} \\ & 1 & \rho_{23} \\ & & 1 \end{bmatrix} \begin{bmatrix} z_1 1.65\sigma_1 \\ z_2 1.65\sigma_2 \\ z_3 1.65\sigma_3 \end{bmatrix} \right]^{\frac{1}{2}}. \tag{3}$$

3.4 Application

Before calculating the VaR_P associated to Tunisian long run public debt portfolio using Eq. (3), we start with normality tests to all variables.

Empirical studies assert the normality assumption sensitivity to the time series length. The financial returns diverge more and more from the normal distribution with time series excessively long. Inversely, extremely short time series lead to biased and non-significant results. So, in the first step of our empirical investigation, we test the normality of the three exchange rates returns during the whole period studied by determining the statistical properties of what we called the global portfolio.

3.4.1 The Normality Assumption Rejection in the Case of the Global Portfolio

By global portfolio, we intend all daily data of the three currencies from 1 January 1999 to 30 June 2006. Table A.2 related to statistical properties of the three exchange rates returns reject categorically the normality assumption in the case of the global portfolio. The three distributions are severely asymmetric on the left (strictly negative *Skewness*) with an excess of Kurtosis (their respective *Kurtosis* are superior to 3).

To have an idea about the exchange rates returns correlation, we calculate also the variance–covariance matrix. The three exchange rates selected by pairs are positively correlated. Yet, this result has to be interpreted carefully since the time series are long.

The traditional measures of risk namely the return (measured by the mean) and the volatility (appreciated by the standard deviation) calculated in percentage per year (converted in the basis of 260 days per year) leads to the following results (see also Table A.4 in Appendix):

(1) On average the dinar returns against the euro and the dollar are negative during the period from 1 January 1999 to 30 June 2006 while those of the dinar against the yen are positive.
(2) On average, the dinar returns against the euro are more volatile (around 19.5% per year) than those against the dollar and the yen (respectively around 13% and 12% per year).

Figures A.4–A.6 related to daily returns of the dinar against the three currencies illustrate those results.

Consequently, we conclude that the parametric VaR is not appropriate to the dinar daily returns against the three principal currencies composing the Tunisian exterior debt portfolio during the period from 1 January 1999 to 30 June 2006.

Figure A.7 relating the empirical cumulative distribution function (cdf) of the exchange rates daily returns corroborates the normality assumption rejection in the case of the global portfolio.

The explanation of this result is based mainly on the length of the time series. For a period of $7\frac{1}{2}$ years, the historical data could not be stationary.

The returns correlation and the variance–covariance matrix (from 1 January 1999 to 30 June 2006).

Correlation matrix

	TND/USD	TND/EUR	TND/JPY
TND/USD	1	0.755368	0.582124
TND/EUR		1	0.424766
TND/JPY			1

Variance–covariance matrix

	TND/USD	TND/EUR	TND/JPY
TND/USD	6.28E − 05	7.20E − 05	3.40E − 05
TND/EUR		0.000145	3.76E − 05
TND/JPY			5.43E − 05

3.4.2 The Normality Assumption Acceptance in the Case of the Annual Portfolios

To solve the non-normality assumption problem noticed in the case of the global portfolio, we opt for a time decomposition of the starting portfolio to eight different annual portfolios. The seven first portfolios are constructed by reference to the civil year, while the last one covers the period from 1 June 2005 to 30 June 2006, so that every portfolio is composed by about 260 observations per currency.

In fact we know that the minimum length admitted in the related literature, for VaR tests, is annual and as we note that the normality convergence is increasing with the decrease in the total observations number, we choose annual decomposition of the global portfolio.

Indeed, on the one hand, the one-year minimum length is usually required by financial regulatory authorities since one-year historic data are the minimal conditions for VaR results reliability. On the other hand, tests applied to our data demonstrate that when the number of observations decreases, the financial returns distribution convergence to normality is greater.

Tables A.5–A.12 (see Appendix) and empirical cumulative distribution functions (cdf) demonstrate a best convergence of the annual portfolios to the normal distribution than the global one. Consequently, we support that, in the case of the Tunisian dinar exchange rates against the principal currencies composing the public debt portfolio, the parametric VaR is appropriate for annual portfolios. Figures A.8–A.15 also corroborate the annual portfolios convergence to the normal distribution.

3.4.3 Calculating VaR

The exchange rates returns convergence to the normal distribution in the case of the annual portfolios is the *sine qua none* condition for applying the parametric VaR. As this condition is satisfied, we can proceed to the VaR calculation.

To do that, we opt for 95% confidence level since our annual portfolios returns distributions are slightly *Leptokurtic* with a little excess of *Kurtosis*. For each of the eight annual portfolios, we proceed as follows:

First step: input data

The first step of calculating VaR deals with the three following elements:

(1) *The risk vector*

The risk associated to the three exchange rates is measured in percentage (%) through the V vector with $V = k\sigma$; k is the normal standard deviation within the 95% confidence level i.e. $k = 1.65$ and σ is the individual volatilities vector of the three exchange rates returns. In our case, the risk vector is equal to $V = \begin{pmatrix} 1.65\sigma_{USD} \\ 1.65\sigma_{EUR} \\ 1.65\sigma_{JPY} \end{pmatrix}$ with σ_j representing the standard deviation of the j position.

The examination of the different σ_j demonstrates that the three exchange rates classification by volatilities is the same for all the annual portfolios. During the last 8 years, the dinar exchange rate against the three main currencies classified from the more volatile to the less volatile is the following: the yen, the dollar, and finally the euro.

(2) *The correlation matrix*

The correlation matrix expresses the interdependence structure between the three exchange rate returns. In our case, the general characteristics of the correlation matrix are invariable throughout time. These unchanging properties could be summarized in the three following points:

(a) A negative correlation between the dinar returns against the dollar and against the euro ($\rho_{USD/EUR} < 0$).
(b) A positive correlation between the dinar exchange rate returns against the dollar and against the yen ($\rho_{USD/JPY} > 0$).
(c) Finally, a slightly negative correlation between the dinar exchange rates returns against the euro in one side and the yen in the other side corroborating the follower status of the yen *vis-à-vis* the dollar ($\rho_{EUR/JPY} <\approx 0$).

The R matrix summarizes the general characteristics of the interdependence structure between all variables:

$$R = \begin{pmatrix} 1 & \rho_{USD/EUR} < 0 & \rho_{USD/JPY} > 0 \\ & 1 & \rho_{EUR/JPY} < 0 \\ & & 1 \end{pmatrix}$$

$\rho_{i/j}$ is the correlation coefficient between i and j.

(3) *The debt flows*

The public debt flows are represented by the so-called position vector X, with

$$X = \begin{bmatrix} X_{\text{USD}} \\ X_{\text{EUR}} \\ X_{\text{JPY}} \end{bmatrix}.$$

X_j is the Tunisian external debt flow in currency j.

The position vector X represents the Tunisian long run public debt composition by currency. We choose a representative public debt flows vector with a total value of 100 millions of Tunisian dinars.

On the one hand, we know that the Tunisian long run external debt structure by currency is relatively stable during the studied period. On the other hand, we also know that the Tunisian public debt in American dollar represents 25% of the total debt portfolio, that in euro is about 23%, and that expressed in Japanese yen is around 22%.[h] The remainder is expressed in other different currencies. As we assume that the share of the Tunisian long run public debt expressed in other currencies is perfectly diversified, we presume, in consequence, that the risk associated to that public debt share is null.

In this way, the 100 million Tunisian dinars of the long run external debt is divided into 70 million exchange risky share and 30 million non-exchange risky share.

So, the vector position X expressing external public debt flows is, in our case, constant and equal to (flows are expressed in millions of Tunisian dinars):

$$X = \begin{pmatrix} 25 \\ 23 \\ 22 \end{pmatrix}.$$

The choice of a constant vector of public debt flows is justified by the stability of the by-currency structure of the Tunisian long run public debt. Moreover, and for comparative purposes, a constant by-currency public debt flows assumption allows risk management performance evaluation during the time.

Under the assumption of a constant vector position, by comparing the different calculations of VaR from one year to the other, one could evaluate the risk management performance due only to the risk factors fluctuations.[i]

[h] Data from the World Bank Report (2004) related to the public debt management strategy in Tunisia.

[i] Chan and Tan (2003) decide on a similar approach. They build a hypothetic investment portfolio with a total value of 800,000 USD. The portfolio value is divided equally between the long positions expressed in the eight Asian currencies composing the portfolio. The starting value of the portfolio is maintained constant during all the studied period from 1992 to 1997.

Second step: calculating the risk matrix

The second step of our methodology consists of the risk matrix calculation. The latter is defined as follows:

$$(kS)' R(kS) \quad \text{with } kS = \begin{pmatrix} k\sigma_{\text{USD}} & 0 & 0 \\ 0 & k\sigma_{\text{EUR}} & 0 \\ 0 & 0 & k\sigma_{\text{JPY}} \end{pmatrix}.$$

Third step: multiplying by the vector position

When it is predetermined, the risk matrix is multiplied by the vector position X to calculate the squared VaR.

$$\text{VaR}^2 = X'[(kS)'R(kS)]X,$$

so that the final number is the squared VaR. For instance, the eighth annual portfolio calculated VaR is equal to 0.2344. This result could be interpreted as follows: at 95% level confidence, the Tunisian government could lose at worst, 0.2344 millions of dinars per day, on a total external long run public debt portfolio evaluated at 100 million dinars. This loss is exclusively due to the exchange risk associated to the three composing debt portfolio main currencies fluctuations.

Fourth step: by-currency VaR decomposition

To improve our exchange risk analysis in the case of the Tunisian public debt, we extend the study to a risk decomposition by-currency, so that the concept we use is that of the *component VaR*.

The component VaR indicates how the portfolio VaR would change approximately if the component (in our case the currency) considered is deleted from the portfolio. The component VaR is also an additive measure of the portfolio risk that reflects the correlation independence between all risk factors. Components with negative sign act as hedge against the remainder risks in the portfolio. In contrast, components with positive sign are source of risk in the considered portfolio.

The component VaR is defined as follows:

$$\text{VaR}_i = \beta_i X_i \text{VaR},$$

where X_i is the individual position in currency i, VaR is the calculated global value-at-risk and β_i expresses the individual VaR contribution of each risk factor i in relation with the total portfolio risk (VaR). The β_i are also called the systematic risk of factor i *vis-à-vis* the portfolio p.

Fifth step: VaR diversification degree

The last analysis step is to compare the sum of all individual VaRs called the *non-diversified VaR* with the sum of the component VaR which corresponds to the calculated VaR or to the *diversified VaR* (integrating the interdependence structure of all assets composing the global portfolio).

All the methodology steps are reproduced for each of the eight annual portfolios.

4 Main Results

4.1 The Methodological Side

Our study demonstrates the parametric VaR applicability in the case of a small developing country such as Tunisia. Indeed, for daily exchange rates returns, the normality assumption would be validated provided that the number of observations is optimal.

Our study supports that the time series optimal length for daily data is annual. This result takes into account both convergence degree of returns distribution to normality and regulatory restrictions.

4.2 The Economic Side

Our empirical study leads to the following main conclusions:

1. A time stability of the interdependence structure between the three exchange rates

Firstly, the Tunisian exchange rate returns ***interdependence structure*** measured via the variance–covariance matrix is characterized by its ***time stability***. The correlation coefficients' signs are unchanged from one annual portfolio to another and consequently during all the studied period from 1999 to mid-2006.

Secondly, our VaR analysis corroborates the preliminary results deduced via the examination of the standard variance–covariance matrix between the three exchange rates:

(1) In the Tunisian exchange rate policy, the dollar and the euro behaves as the two ***leader currencies*** and follow opposite tendencies while the Japanese yen act as a ***follower vis-à-vis the American dollar***.

(2) The Tunisian exchange rate policy is distinguished by its prudence: the dinar exchange rate is managed in the way that the potential losses due to its depreciation *vis-à-vis* one of the two main currencies are compensated by the gains resulting from its simultaneous appreciation *vis-à-vis* the other.

2. A stable ordinal classification of the three exchange rates in return/risk terms

A Markowitz representation of the annual portfolios associating return to risk (Fig. 2) shows that, while the euro is the less risky currency in the Tunisian public debt portfolio throughout the studied period, the dollar is the highest return currency in the portfolio.

Indeed, the risk associated to the Tunisian dinar exchange rate against the euro measured by its standard deviation does not exceed 5% per year. During the same period, the dinar volatilities *vis-à-vis* the dollar are superior to 6% per year, but do never exceed those of the dinar against the yen. The dinar volatilities against the yen could reach 13% per year. *The yen is definitely the most unstable currency in the Tunisian public debt portfolio.*

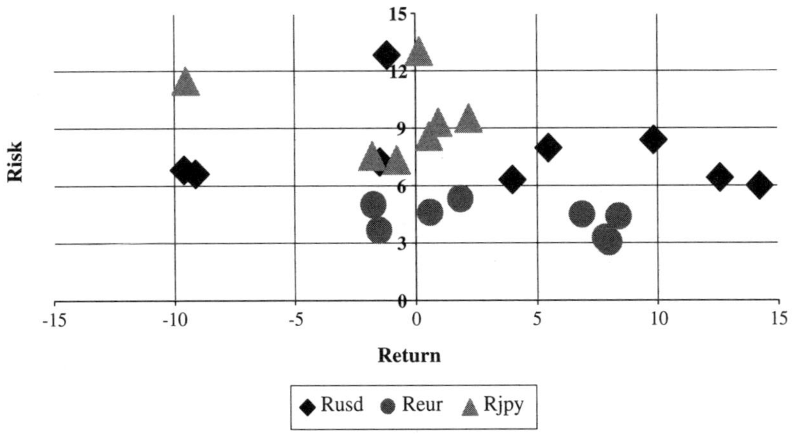

Figure 2: The by-currency return/risk (in (%) per year).

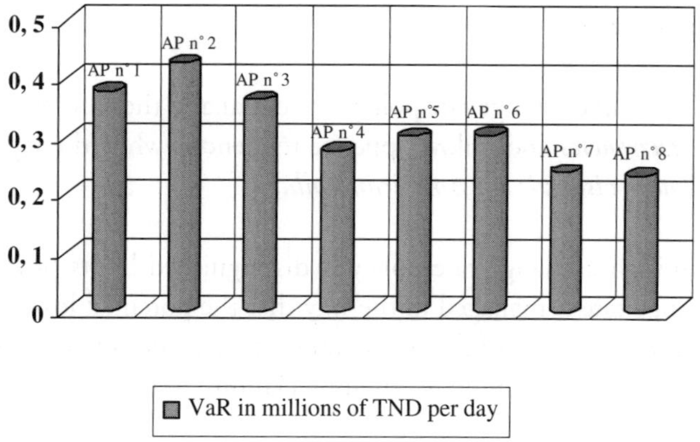

Figure 3: The calculated VaR (95% confidence level).

Concerning returns, the American dollar represents the currency with the most dispersed returns *vis-à-vis* the Tunisian dinar. The Tunisian dinar returns fluctuations against the American dollar evolve within an interval of −10% to +15% per year. The average of the dinar returns against the euro are narrower to zero with a fluctuation interval of −2% to +8% per year.

3. A Time Stability of the Calculated VaR and a Good Control of the Exchange Risk

The delta normal VaR analysis leads to results summarized in Fig. 3 related to the different calculated VaRs associated to the annual portfolios at 95% confidence level. Calculated values represent the maximum losses expressed in millions of Tunisian dinars per day associated to a 100 millions dinars public debt portfolio.

The VaR results demonstrate a good performance in managing the exchange risk associated to the Tunisian debt portfolio: *from 1999 to mid-2006, a 100 million Tunisian dinars representative debt portfolio might suffer at worse from 0.2 to 0.4 million dinars per day losses within 95% confidence level.*[j]

Moreover, from one year to the following one, the exchange risk associated to the public debt portfolio is better managed. The annual VaR are not only time-stable but also decreasing mainly after a pick in 2000 due to the incertitude characterizing the euro introduction period (see Table A.13 in Appendix).

[j]Details for VaR calculation are available.

4. The euro as a potential hedge against the exchange risk in the Tunisian public debt portfolio

The calculated betas by currency, as summarized in Table A.14 (see Appendix) and represented in Fig. 4, reveal that for all annual portfolios, only the beta of the euro are slightly negative or null. The betas associated to both the dollar and the yen are positive, but much higher in the second case. Consequently, while the euro mitigates the risk exchange associated to the Tunisian public debt portfolio, the dollar and the yen act as risk sources.

Once more, we demonstrate that the yen is the riskiest currency in the Tunisian public debt portfolio. The betas associated to that currency are not only positive but they are also superior in absolute values to all other betas.

The VaR decomposition analysis (see Table A.15 in Appendix and Fig. 5) corroborates all results ascertained until now. The yen contribution to the

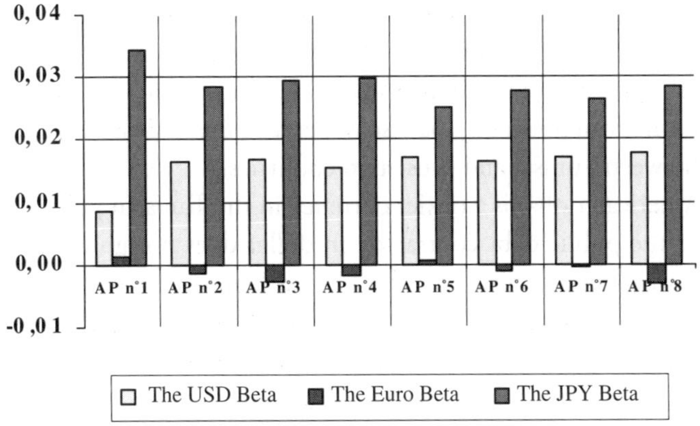

Figure 4: The by-currency betas.

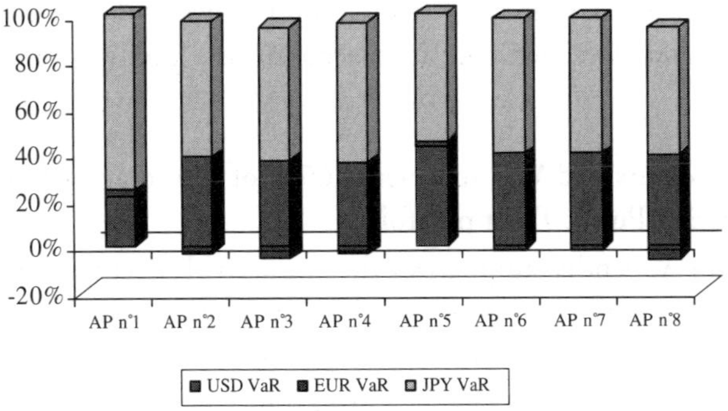

Figure 5: The calculated VaR decomposition by currency (in percentage %).

global VaR of the Tunisian public debt portfolio is on average about (+65%) while the dollar contribution is about (+40%). Finally, the euro contribution to global portfolio risk is negative and on average near to (−5%).

So, the euro may act as a hedge against the exchange risk in the Tunisian public debt portfolio. The euro relative share increase in the Tunisian public debt portfolio has a negative impact on the global risk incurred. The greater this relative share, the less is the risk associated to the public debt portfolio. Inversely, an increase in the relative share of the American dollar or the Japanese yen raises the global risk associated to the Tunisian public debt portfolio. The yen impact is yet more negative than the dollar one.

Our results are also in conformity with the World Bank (2004) recommendations expressed in the report dealing with the Tunisian public debt management strategy. The Tunisian management of the sovereign debt is globally satisfactory, yet some effort are still necessary in managing the exchange risk associated to public debt portfolio. The main reproach formulated is that the exchange risk management in the Tunisian case does ignore the "*natural hedge*" approach. The relative shares of Tunisian public debt contracted either on American dollar or Japanese yen exceed the trade flows relative shares existing between Tunisia and those two countries.

The American dollar is a riskier currency in the Tunisian public debt portfolio since the public debt contracted in dollar does not go closely with the trade flows between Tunisia and the United States. The yen does surely do the same. Yet, since its *follower status vis-à-vis* the dollar, the yen is twice threatening. The yen retransmit, in addition, some of the American risk.

The VaR decomposition analysis concludes in favor of the increase of the relative share of the Tunisian public debt in euro at the expense of those in yen than in dollar to optimize the exchange risk associated to public debt portfolio. Our recommendation is however, based only on financial analysis and does not take into account any political or institutional constraint.

5. The non-diversified VaR represents 65% of the total VaR associated to the Tunisian Public Debt portfolio

Table A.16 in Appendix summarizes the annual VaR decomposition on *non-diversified VaR* which corresponds to the sum of the individual VaR and on *diversified VaR* expressing the risk resulting from the interdependence structure between the three exchange rates. As proved in Fig. 6 related to VaR diversification degree (in percentage), the non-diversified VaR contributes to more

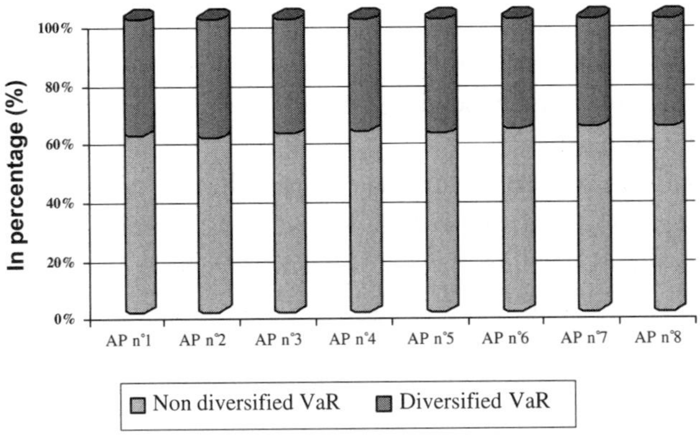

Figure 6: The annual VaR diversification degrees.

than 65% to the global VaR. Moreover, this relative share is constant during the period from 1999 to 2006.

While the sum of the individual VaR of the three currencies represents 65% of the global VaR (the non-diversified VaR), the risk associated to the interdependence structure between the three exchange rates contributes to 35% of the total annual VaR (the diversified VaR).

This result proves the management stability of both the exchange rate and the national debt policies. This stability is due to the public debt management process on itself. In fact, the Tunisian Central Bank has not only the monopole of the exchange rate management but it also intervenes actively in the management of the public debt and mainly in managing the long run public debt contracted in foreign currencies.

5 Conclusion

This first VaR application to assess exchange risk associated to a public debt portfolio in the case of a small developing economy is valuable. The Tunisian exchange rate policy built around the two dominating currencies in the World, the euro and the dollar, proves itself mainly in the public debt portfolio management area.

Our empirical results conduct not only to reduced VaR but also to time-stable VaR during 8 years with a decreasing tendency in the last 3 years. And in spite of a relatively high non-diversified VaR (around 65%), the time stability of the VaR diversification degree remains a positive signal for the credibility of the public debt management strategy.

The VaR decomposition by-currency analysis leads to the recommendation suggested by the World Bank (2004): The necessity of rebalancing the long run public debt portfolio depending on trade flows intensities between Tunisia and its different partners.

In conclusion, via only a financial approach, we succeed demonstrating that reducing global exchange risk associated to the Tunisian public debt portfolio is question of redefining the by-currency structure of that portfolio. We prove that the euro is in fact the refuge currency for managing exchange risk associated to the Tunisian public debt portfolio. This result goes together with the requirement of a "natural hedge" strategy.

Appendix

Table A.1: Data.

Series	TND/USD	TND/EUR	TND/JPY
Frequency	Daily data	Daily data	Daily data
Period	01/01/1999 06/30/2006	01/01/1999 06/30/2006	01/01/1999 06/30/2006
Total Observations Number	1956	1956	1956
Source	Datastream	Datastream	Calculating via the cross exchange rates (TND/USD, USD/JPY) extracted from datastream
Statistical properties			
Mean	1.322125	1.412505	1.154698
Median	1.318200	1.364750	1.156691
Maximum	1.517100	1.692600	1.376875
Minimum	1.089600	1.236700	0.948311
Standard deviation	0.0936100	0.144460	0.074445
Skewness	0.075884 >0 (in the right)	0.372413 >0 (in the right)	−0.099794 <0 (in the left)
Kurtosis	2.184853 <3(Platykurtic)	1.545575 <3(Platykurtic)	4.406677 >3(Leptokurtic)
Jarque-bera	56.03117	217.6145	164.5138
Probability	0.000	0.000	0.000

Table A.2: Data.

	Total observations number		
	1955	1955	1955
Statistical properties			
Variables	R_{usd}	R_{eur}	R_{jpy}
Mean	$-4.61^{E}-05$	−0.000128	$1.84^{E}-05$
Median	$7.60^{E}-05$	0.000155	$8.24^{E}-05$
Maximum	0.015888	0.012970	0.034927
Minimum	−0.292483	−0.518705	−0.152330
Standard deviation	0.007929	0.012033	0.007369
Skewness	−25.69796	−40.97097	−4.506447
	<0 (in the left)	<0 (in the left)	<0 (in the left)
Kurtosis	947.8318	1766.327	96.93317
	>3(Leptokurtic)	>3(Leptokurtic)	>3(Leptokurtic)
Jarque-Bera	729336	$2.54^{E}08$	725359
Probability	0.000	0.000	0.000

Table A.3: Return/Risk of the global portfolio (in percentage (%); per day); Period: 01/01/1999–06/30/2006.

	TND/USD	TND/EUR	TND/JPY
Return (Mean)	$-4.61^{E}-3$	−0.0128	$1.84^{E}-3$
Volatility (Standard deviation)	0.7929	1.2033	0.7369

Table A.4: Return/Risk of the global portfolio (in percentage % per year) Period: 01/01/1999–06/30/2006.

	TND/USD	TND/EUR	TND/JPY
Return (Mean)	−1.198	−3.328	0.478
Volatility (Standard deviation)	12.785	19.402	11.882

Table A.5: Annual portfolio no. 1.

Statistical properties Variables	R_{USD}	R_{EUR}	R_{JPY}
Mean	0.000546	$-6.51^{E}-05$	0.000941
Median	0.000593	0.000237	0.001258
Maximum	0.008740	0.009883	0.034927
Minimum	−0.013745	−0.010189	−0.034286
Standard Deviation	0.003746	0.003054	0.008675
Skewness	−0.537136	0.021355	−0.083378
Kurtosis	3.707949	3.786390	5.693157
Jarque-Bera	17.86295	6.693360	78.57307
Probability	0.00132	0.035201	0.0000

The correlation matrix

	R_{USD}	R_{EUR}	R_{JPY}
R_{USD}	1		
R_{EUR}	−0.331112	1	
R_{JPY}	0.255908	−0.080295	1

Return/Risk (in % per day)

	R_{USD}	R_{EUR}	R_{JPY}
Return (Mean)	0.0546	$-6.51^{E}-03$	0.0941
Volatility (Standard deviation)	0.3746	0.3054	0.8675

Return/Risk (in % per year)

	R_{USD}	R_{EUR}	R_{JPY}
Return (Mean)	14.196	−1.692	24.466
Volatility (Standard deviation)	6.040	4.924	13.988

Period: 06/01/2005–06/30/2006; Observations number: 259 per currency.

Table A.6: Annual portfolio no. 2.

Statistical properties			
Variables	R_{USD}	R_{EUR}	R_{JPY}
Mean	0.000378	$7.24^{E}-05$	$4.75^{E}-06$
Median	0.000548	0.0000	0.000249
Maximum	0.015057	0.012970	0.025049
Minimum	−0.012699	−0.009743	−0.034366
Standard deviation	0.005175	0.003276	0.008054
Skewness	−0.471269	0.344992	−0.214704
Kurtosis	4.045959	4.206075	4.286255
Jarque-Bera	21.47609	20.91588	19.92079
Probability	0.000022	0.00029	0.00047

The correlation matrix

	R_{USD}	R_{EUR}	R_{JPY}
R_{USD}	1		
R_{EUR}	−0.424129	1	
R_{JPY}	0.645525	−0.292095	1

Return/Risk (in % per day)

	R_{USD}	R_{EUR}	R_{JPY}
Return (Mean)	0.0378	$7.24^{E}-03$	$4.75^{E}-04$
Volatility (Standard deviation)	0.5175	0.3276	0.8054

Return/Risk (in % per year)

	R_{USD}	R_{EUR}	R_{JPY}
Return (Mean)	9.828	1.882	0.1235
Volatility (Standard deviation)	8.344	5.282	12.986

Period: 01/01/2000–12/31/2000; Observations number: 260 per currency.

Table A.7: Annual portfolio no. 3.

Statistical properties			
Variables	R_{USD}	R_{EUR}	R_{JPY}
Mean	0.000210	$2.37^{E}-05$	−0.000365
Median	$7.02^{E}-05$	0.000154	$1.89^{E}-05$
Maximum	0.013309	0.009353	0.031963
Minimum	−0.017504	−0.009353	−0.021217
Standard deviation	0.004922	0.002805	0.007121
Skewness	−0.152764	−0.070672	0.080375
Kurtosis	3.367357	4.095909	4.650851
Jarque-Bera	2.482756	13.27831	29.91876
Probability	0.288986	0.001308	0.0000

The correlation matrix

	R_{USD}	R_{EUR}	R_{JPY}
R_{USD}	1		
R_{EUR}	−0.558773	1	
R_{JPY}	0.513591	−0.292114	1

Return/Risk (in % per day)

	R_{USD}	R_{EUR}	R_{JPY}
Return (Mean)	0.0210	$2.37^{E}-03$	−0.0365
Volatility (Standard deviation)	0.4922	0.2805	0.7121
Return/Risk (In % per year)			

Return/Risk (in % per year)

	R_{USD}	R_{EUR}	R_{JPY}
Return (Mean)	5.460	0.616	−9.490
Volatility (Standard deviation)	7.936	4.514	11.482

Period: 01/01/2001–12/31/2001; Observations number: 260 per currency.

Table A.8: Annual portfolio no. 4.

Statistical properties			
Variables	R_{USD}	R_{EUR}	R_{JPY}
Mean	−0.000351	0.000301	$3.64^{E}-05$
Median	0.000000	0.000221	$-3.77^{E}-05$
Maximum	0.015888	0.008383	0.019107
Minimum	−0.016203	−0.006739	−0.017346
Standard deviation	0.004093	0.001998	0.005754
Skewness	−0.181410	0.0039277	−0.136469
Kurtosis	4.504631	4.8799934	3.931601
Jarque-Bera	26.05164	38.50101	10.248225
Probability	0.00002	0.00000	0.00595

The correlation matrix

$$\begin{bmatrix} & R_{USD} & R_{EUR} & R_{JPY} \\ R_{USD} & 1 & & \\ R_{EUR} & -0.581682 & 1 & \\ R_{JPY} & 0.246271 & -0.100889 & 1 \end{bmatrix}$$

Return/Risk (in % per day)

	R_{USD}	R_{EUR}	R_{JPY}
Return (Mean)	−0.0351	0.0301	$3.64^{E}-03$
Volatility (Standard deviation)	0.4093	0.1998	0.5754

Return/Risk (in % per year)

	R_{USD}	R_{EUR}	R_{JPY}
Return (Mean)	−9.126	7.826	0.946
Volatility (Standard deviation)	6.599	3.221	9.278

Period: 01/01/2002–12/31/2002; Observations number: 261 per currency.

Table A.9: Annual portfolio no. 5.

Statistical properties			
Variables	R_{USD}	R_{EUR}	R_{JPY}
Mean	−0.000370	0.000324	2.26E− 05
Median	−0.000545	0.000313	−0.000381
Maximum	0.012015	0.008535	0.016731
Minimum	−0.011103	−0.007247	−0.013434
Standard deviation	0.004243	0.002715	0.005330
Skewness	0.257070	0.000155	0.256742
Kurtosis	2.834734	3.347377	3.356622
Jarque-Bera	3.1717	1.312296	4.250438
Probability	0.204772	0.518846	0.119407

The correlation matrix

	R_{USD}	R_{EUR}	R_{JPY}
R_{USD}	1		
R_{EUR}	−0.382328	1	
R_{JPY}	0.451057	−0.105157	1

Return/Risk (in % per day)

	R_{USD}	R_{EUR}	R_{JPY}
Return (Mean)	−0.0370	0.0324	2.26E− 03
Volatility (Standard deviation)	0.4243	0.2715	0.5330

Return/Risk (in % per day)

	R_{USD}	R_{EUR}	R_{JPY}
Return (Mean)	−9.620	8.424	0.5876
Volatility (Standard deviation)	6.841	4.377	8.594

Period : 01/01/2003–12/31/2003; Observations number: 261 per currency.

Table A.10: Annual portfolio no. 6.

Statistical properties			
Variables	R_{USD}	R_{EUR}	R_{JPY}
Mean	$-5.61^{E}-05$	0.000265	$8.38^{E}-05$
Median	$-9.96^{E}-05$	0.000227	0.000368
Maximum	0.013189	0.007532	0.015731
Minimum	−0.015974	−0.007457	−0.020069
Standard deviation	0.004518	0.002757	0.005887
Skewness	0.089443	−0.069516	−0.0206938
Kurtosis	3.585966	2.806062	3.198550
Jarque-Bera	4.094638	0.621613	2.300319
Probability	0.128887	0.732856	0.31658

The correlation matrix

	R_{USD}	R_{EUR}	R_{JPY}
R_{USD}	1		
R_{EUR}	−0.514760	1	
R_{JPY}	0.343975	−0.135182	1

Return/Risk (in % per day)

	R_{USD}	R_{EUR}	R_{JPY}
Return (Mean)	$-5.61^{E}-03$	0.0265	$8.38^{E}-03$
Volatility (Standard deviation)	0.4518	0.2757	0.5887

Return/Risk (in % per year)

	R_{USD}	R_{EUR}	R_{JPY}
Return (Mean)	−1.458	6.89	2.178
Volatility (Standard deviation)	7.285	4.445	9.492

Period: 01/01/2004–12/31/2004; Observations number: 262 per currency.

Table A.11: Annual portfolio no. 7.

Statistical properties			
Variables	R_{USD}	R_{EUR}	R_{JPY}
Mean	0.000482	$-5.85^{E}-05$	$-3.03^{E}-05$
Median	0.000483	$-1.55^{E}-05$	−0.000258
Maximum	0.009389	0.006542	0.015162
Minimum	−0.011413	−0.008447	−0.012421
Standard deviation	0.003949	0.002231	0.004550
Skewness	−0.2811196	−0.223162	0.423826
Kurtosis	2.840541	3.803299	3.542578
Jarque-Bera	3.701883	9.148681	10.97313
Probability	0.157089	0.010313	0.004142

The correlation matrix

	R_{USD}	R_{EUR}	R_{JPY}
R_{USD}	1		
R_{EUR}	−0.5627610	1	
R_{JPY}	0.232492	−0.000860	1

Return/Risk (in % per day)

	R_{USD}	R_{EUR}	R_{JPY}
Return (Mean)	0.0482	$-5.85^{E}-03$	$-3.03^{E}-03$
Volatility (Standard deviation)	0.3949	0.2231	0.4550

Return/Risk (in % per year)

	R_{USD}	R_{EUR}	R_{JPY}
Return (Mean)	12.532	−1.521	−0.787
Volatility (Standard deviation)	6.367	3.597	7.336

Period: 01/01/2005–12/31/2005; Observations number: 260 per currency.

Table A.12: Annual portfolio no. 8.

Statistical properties			
Variables	R_{USD}	R_{EUR}	R_{JPY}
Mean	0.000154	0.000172	$-6.99^{E}-05$
Median	0.000266	0.000152	−0.000258
Maximum	0.008740	0.005419	0.015162
Minimum	−0.012020	−0.008447	−0.011588
Standard deviation	0.003937	0.001842	0.004693
Skewness	−0.332815	−0.140496	0.5370003
Kurtosis	3.35834	4.479330	3.662111
Jarque-Bera	6.738587	26.73611	18.77093
Probability	0.0344	0.00002	0.000084

The correlation matrix

	R_{USD}	R_{EUR}	R_{JPY}
R_{USD}	1		
R_{EUR}	−0.698520	1	
R_{JPY}	0.221129	−0.068203	1

Return/Risk (in % per day)

	R_{USD}	R_{EUR}	R_{JPY}
Return (Mean)	0.0154	0.0172	$-6.99^{E}-03$
Volatility (Standard deviation)	0.3937	0.1842	0.4693

Return/Risk (in % per year)

	R_{USD}	R_{EUR}	R_{JPY}
Return (Mean)	4.004	4.472	−1.8174
Volatility (Standard deviation)	6.348	2.970	7.567

Period: 06/01/2005–06/30/2006; Observations number: 280 per currency.

Table A.13: The calculated VaR (95% confidence level).

	Annual portfolio no.							
	1	2	3	4	5	6	7	8
VaR (in Millions of TND/Day)	0.3788	0.4272	0.3646	0.2777	0.3020	0.3042	0.2409	0.2344

Table A.14: The calculated β_i.

	Annual portfolio no.							
	1	2	3	4	5	6	7	8
USD	0.00846	0.01633	0.016866	0.0154	0.0170	0.01658	0.0173	0.0178
EUR	0.00138	−0.00153	−0.002877	−0.0018	0.0007	−0.0010	−0.0004	−0.0030
JPY	0.03438	0.02848	0.029296	0.0298	0.0252	0.02766	0.0263	0.0283

Table A.15: The by-currency calculated VaR decomposition (in percentage %).

	Annual portfolio no.							
	1	2	3	4	5	6	7	8
USD	21.12%	41%	42%	38.5%	43%	41.5%	41.5%	44.5%
EUR	3.17%	−3.5%	−6.5%	−4%	2%	−2.25%	−2.25%	−7%
JPY	75.75%	62.5%	64.5%	65.5%	55%	60.75%	60.75%	62.5%

Table A.16: The calculated VaR diversification degrees.

	Annual portfolio no.							
	1	2	3	4	5	6	7	8
The non-diversified VaR	0.585	0.630	0.567	0.451	0.471	0.504	0.412	0.402
The diversified VaR	0.379	0.427	0.364	0.277	0.302	0.304	0.241	0.234

Graphs

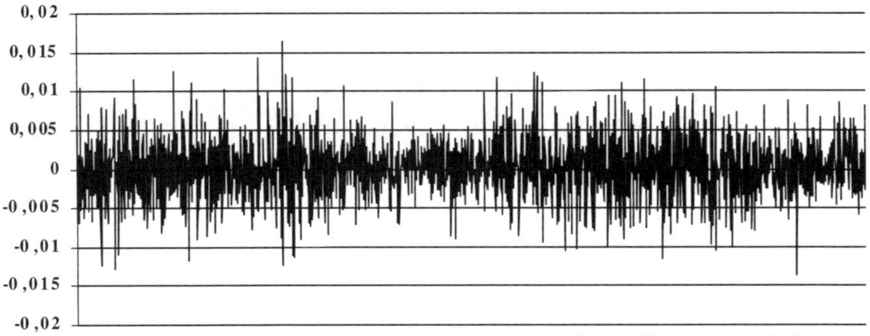

Source: The author own calculation

Figure A.1: The TND/USD fluctuations.

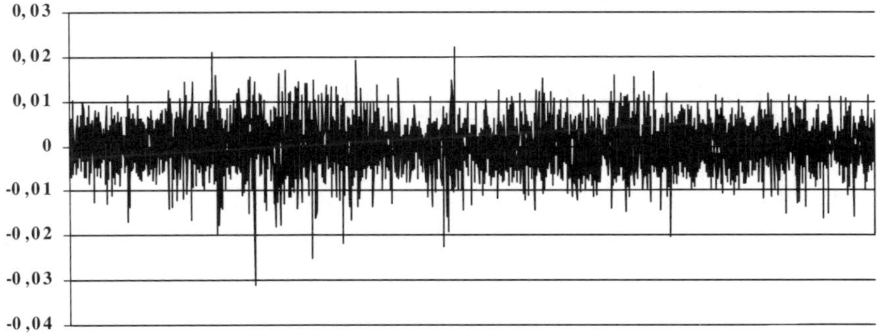

Source: The author own calculation

Figure A.2: The TND/EUR fluctuations.

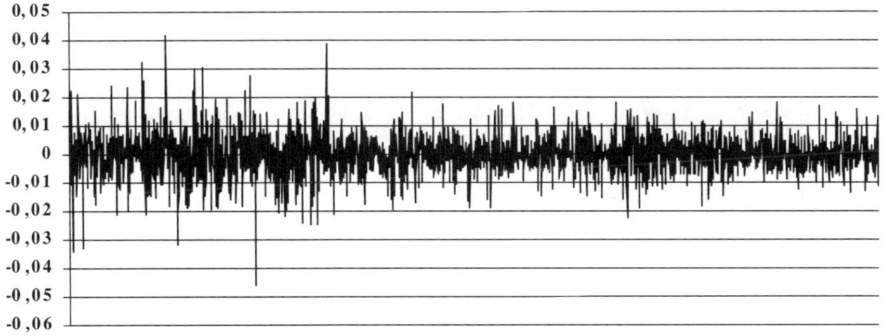

Source: The author own calculation

Figure A.3: The TND/JPY fluctuations.

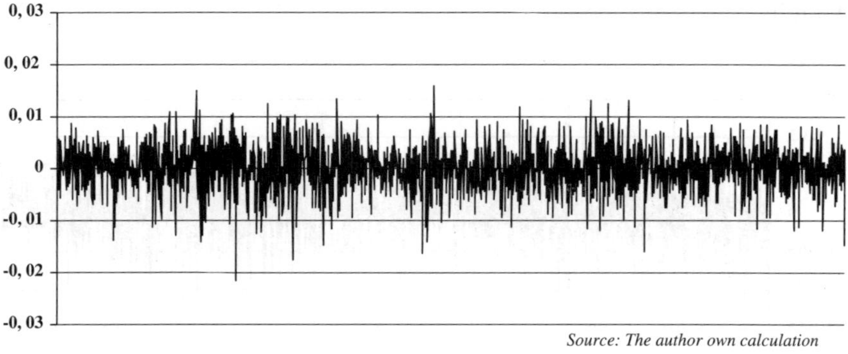

Figure A.4: The TND/USD daily returns.

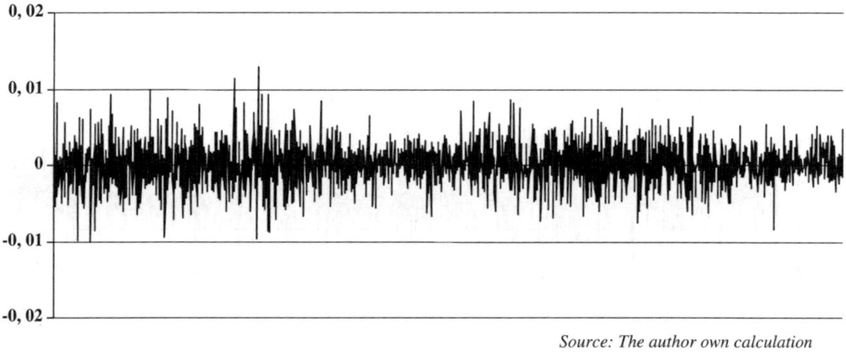

Figure A.5: The TND/EUR daily returns.

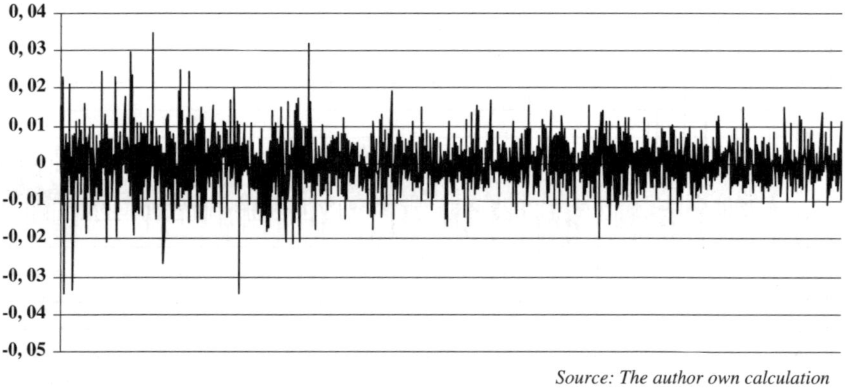

Figure A.6: The TND/JPY daily returns.

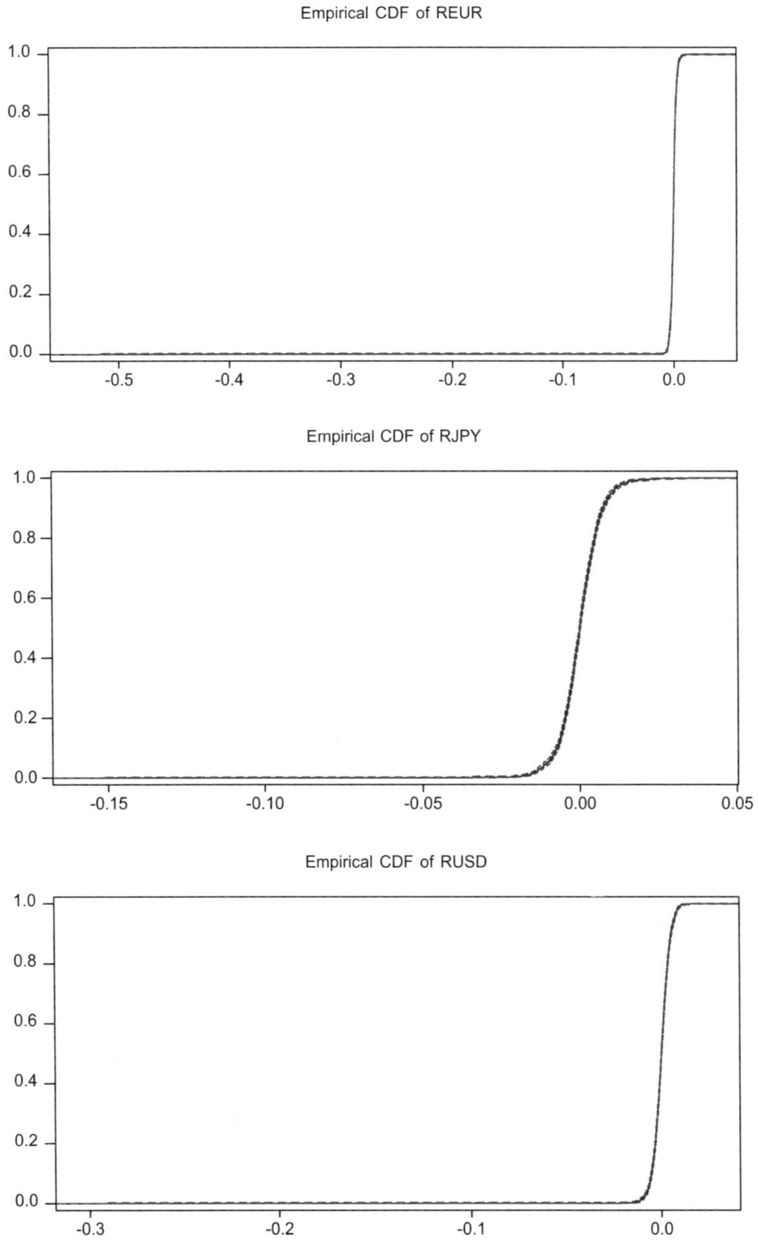

Figure A.7: The empirical cumulative distribution function (CDF). (Global portfolio)

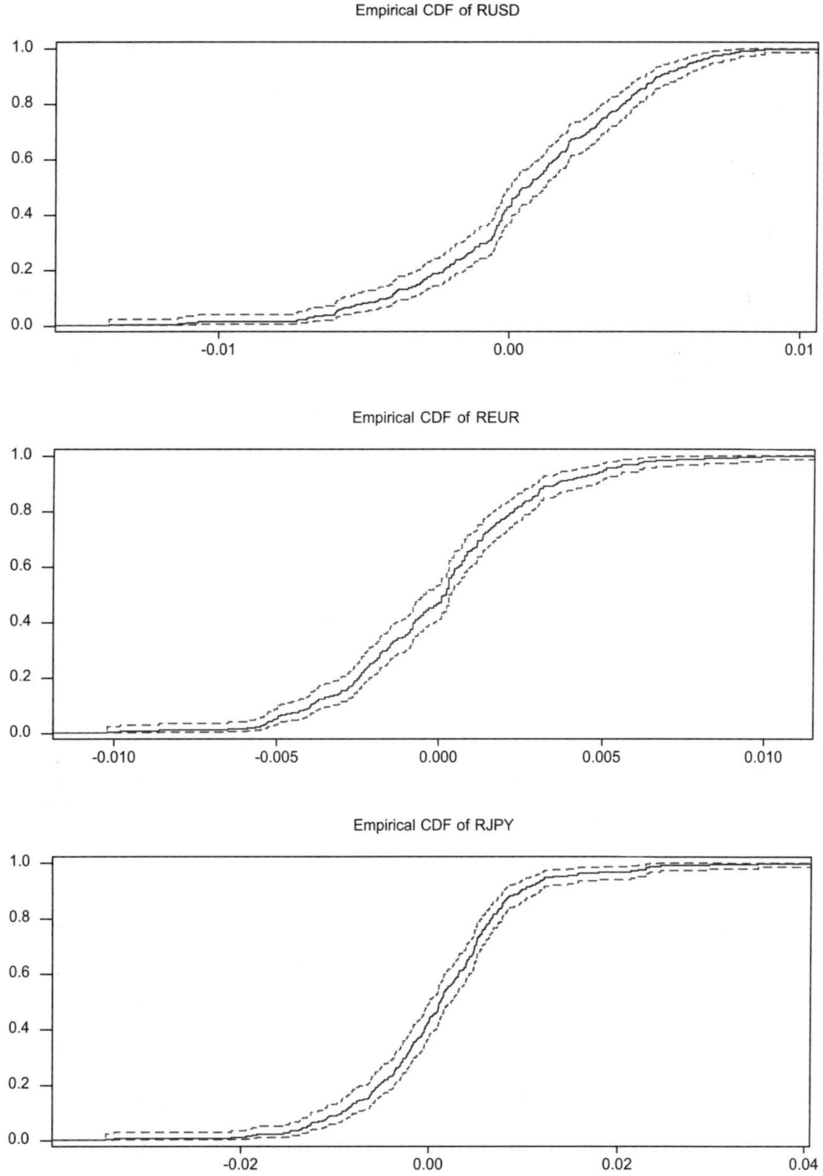

Figure A.8: The empirical (CDF) annual portfolio no. 1.

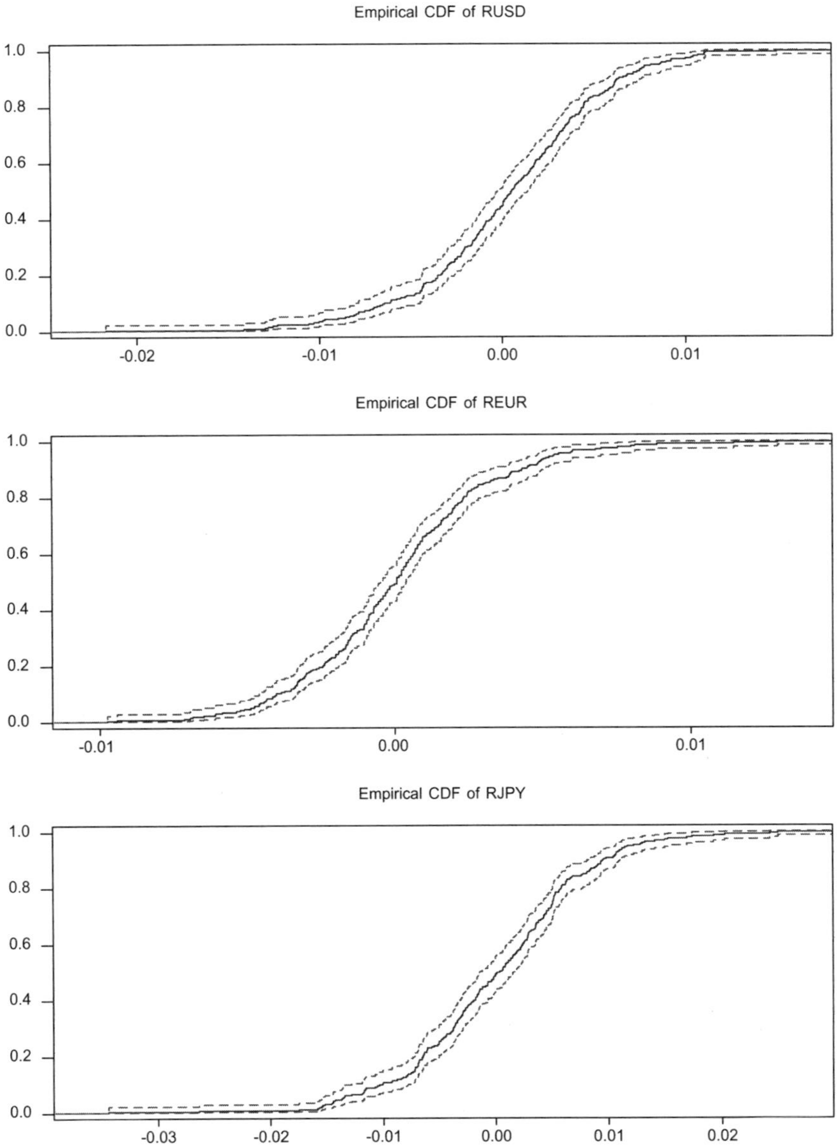

Figure A.9: The empirical (CDF) annual portfolio no. 2.

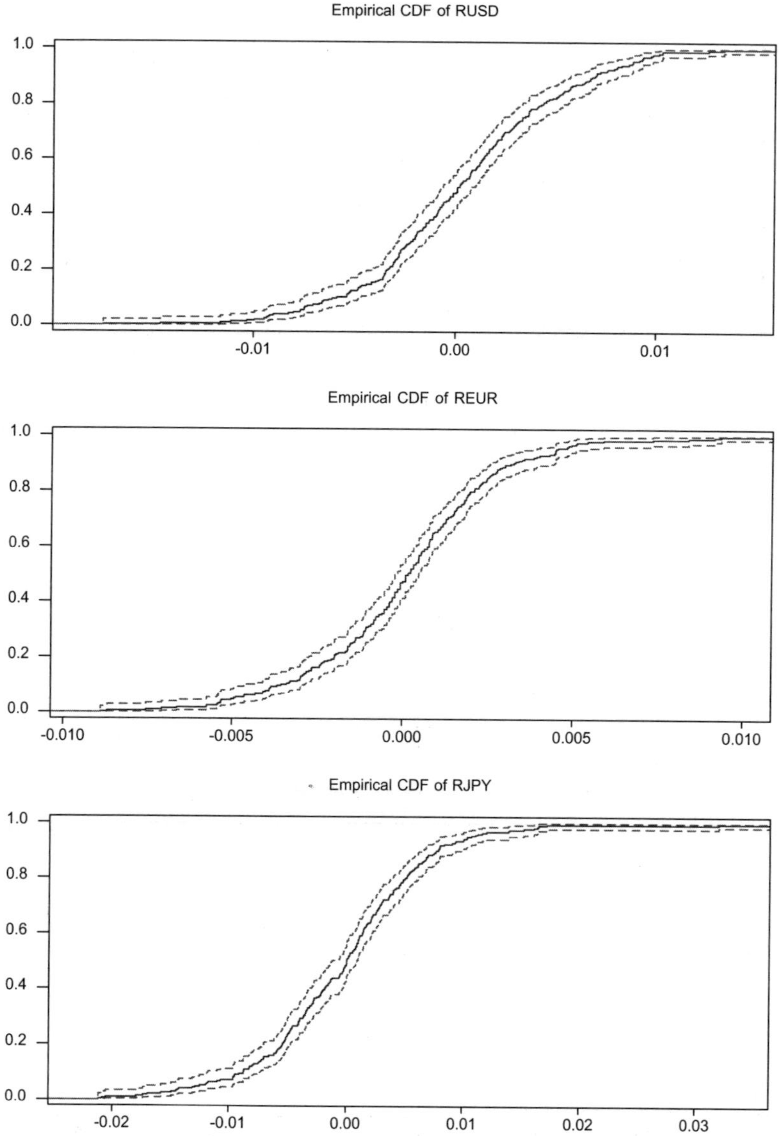

Figure A.10: The empirical (CDF) annual portfolio no. 3.

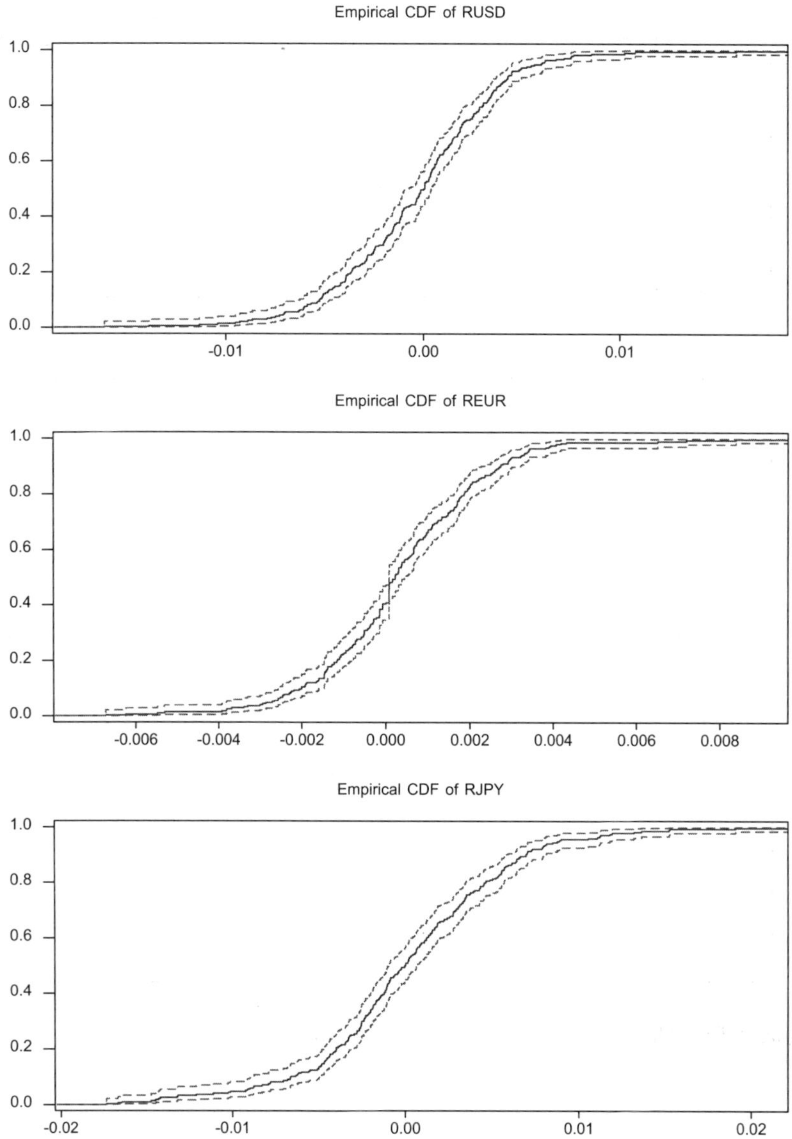

Figure A.11: The empirical (CDF) annual portfolio no. 4.

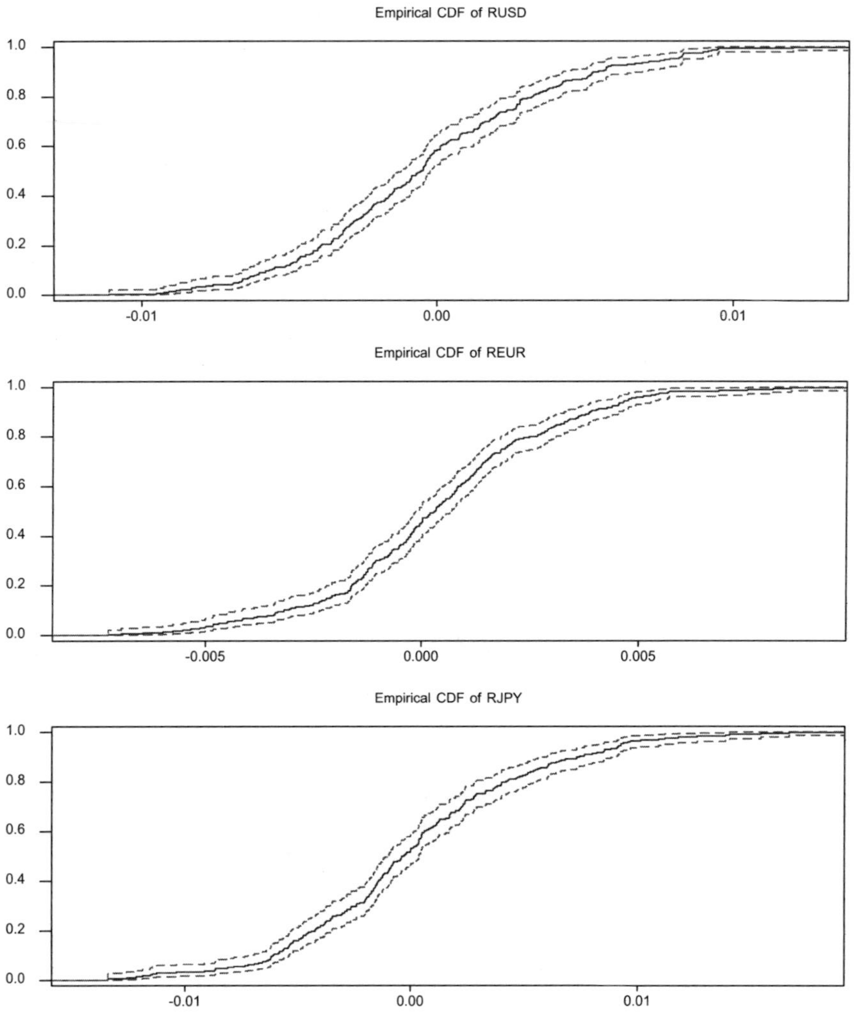

Figure A.12: The empirical (CDF) annual portfolio no. 5.

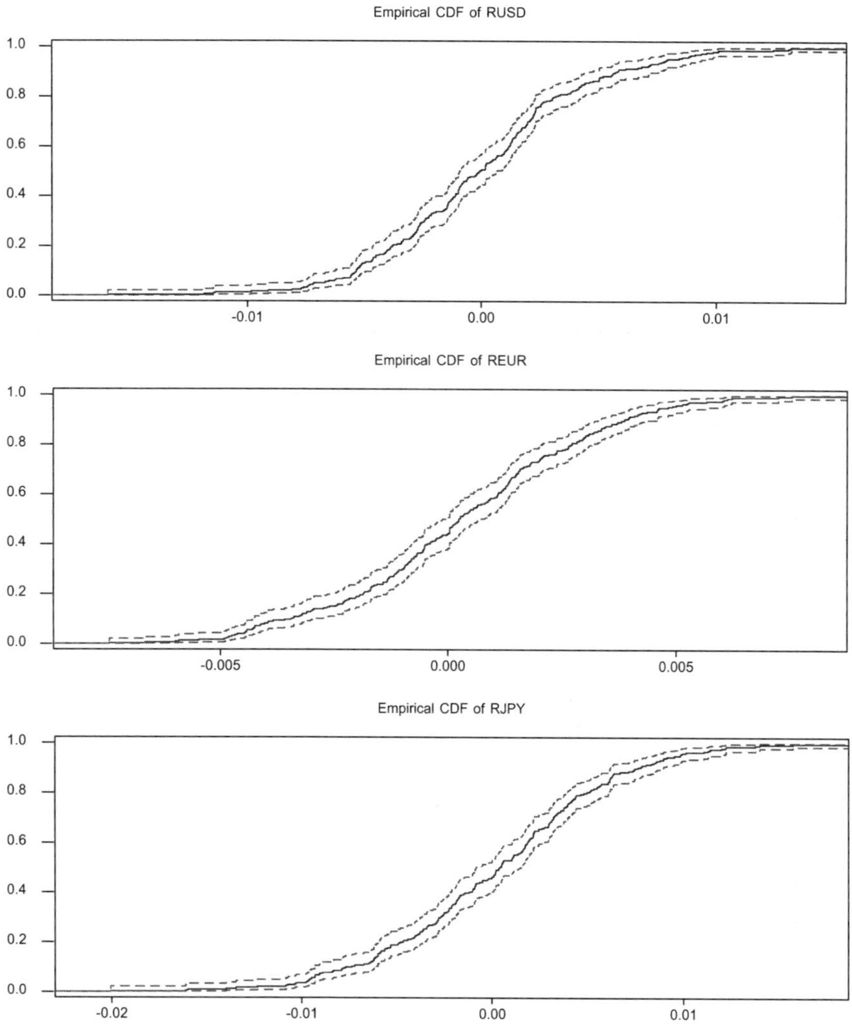

Figure A.13: The empirical (CDF) annual portfolio no. 6.

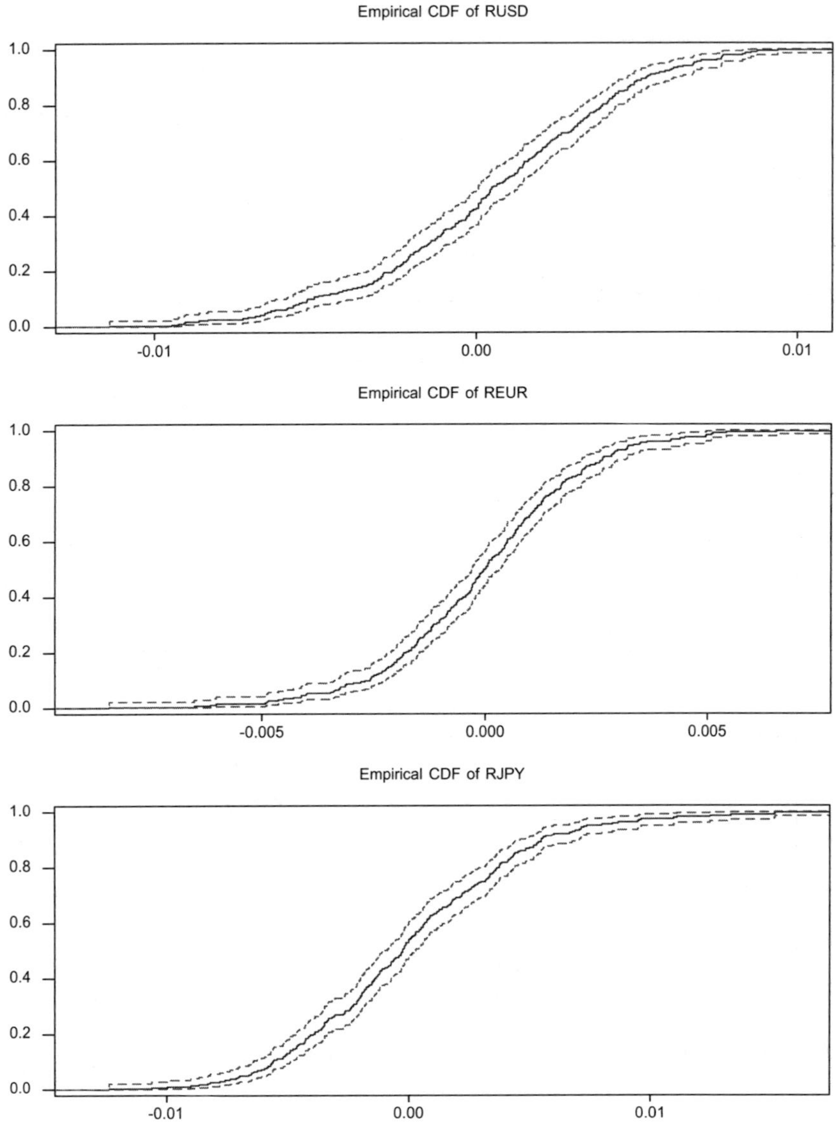

Figure A.14: The empirical (CDF) annual portfolio no. 7.

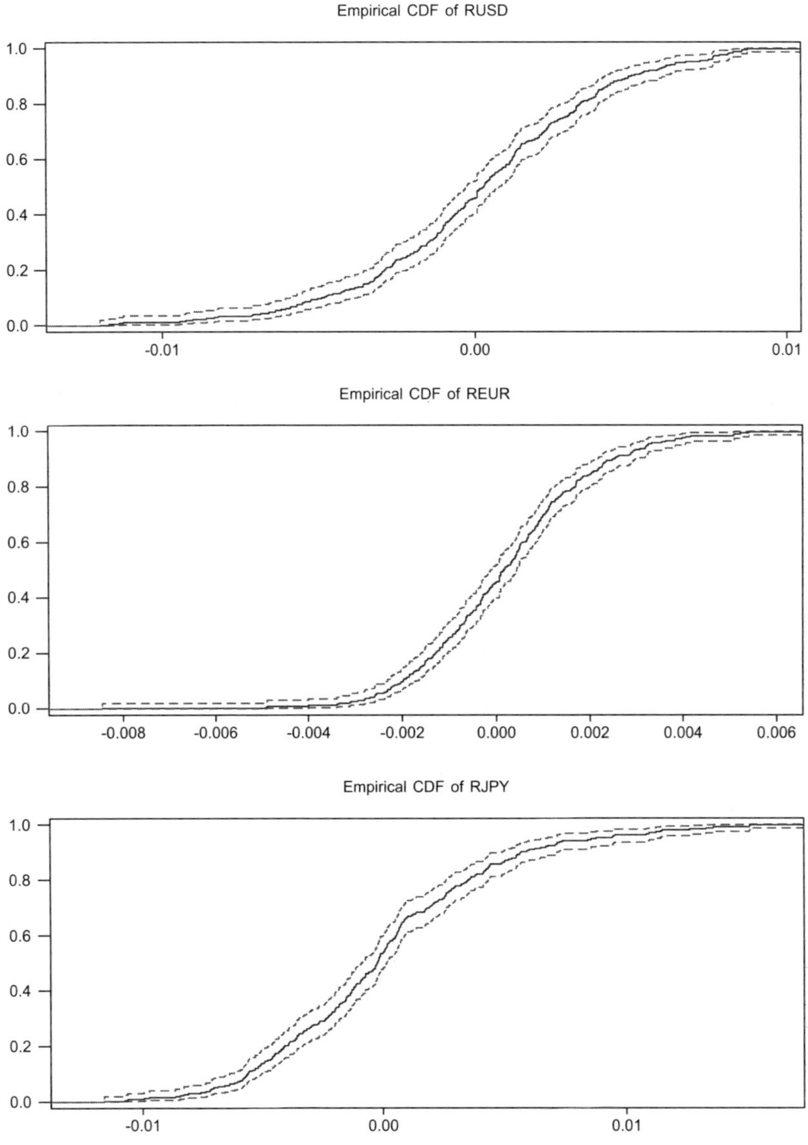

Figure A.15: The empirical (CDF) annual portfolio no. 8.

References

Bams, D, Lehnert, T and Wolff, CCP (2005). An evaluation framework for alternative VaR-models. *Journal of International Money and Finance*, 24, 944–958.

Black, F (1972). Capital market equilibrium with Restricted Borrowing. *Journal of Business*, 45, 444–454.

Bollen, B and Moosa, IA (2002). A benchmark for measuring bias in estimated daily value at risk. *International Review of Financial Analysis*, 11, 85–100.

Campbell, R, Huisman, R and Koedijk, K (2001). Optimal portfolio selection in value at risk framework. *Journal of Banking & Finance*, 25, 1789–1804.

Chan, IL and Tan, KH (2003). Stress testing using VaR approach, a case for Asian currencies. *Journal of International Financial Markets, Institutions & Money*, 13, 39–55.

Chou, PH, Li, WS, Lin, JB and Wang, JS (2006). Estimating the VaR of a portfolio subject to price limits and nonsynchronous trading. *International Review of Financial Analysis*, 15(4–5), 363–376.

International Monetary Fund and World Bank (2001, 2003). Guidelines for public debt management. Amended on 9 December 2003.

Kondor, I and Pafka, S (2001). Evaluating the riskmetrics methodology in measuring volatility and Value-at-Risk in financial markets. *Physica A* 299, 305–310.

Lintner, J (1965). The valuation of risk assets and the selection of risky investments in stock portfolios and capital budgets. *Review of Economics and Statistics*, 47, 13–37.

Markowitz, H (1952). Portfolio selection. *Journal of Finance*, 7(1), 47–62.

Markowitz, H (1956). The optimization of a quadratic function subject to linear constraints. *Naval Research Logistics Quarterly*, 3(1/2), 111–133.

Mossin, J (1966). Equilibrium in a capital asset market. *Econometrica*, 34, 768–783.

Pritsker, M (2006). The hidden dangers of historical simulation. *Journal of Banking & Finance*, 30, 561–582.

Putnam, BH, Wilford, DS and Zecher, PD (2002). A short note on the concept of risk management and VaR for asset management firms. *Review of Financial Economics*, 11, 205–212.

Ross, S (1976). The arbitrage theory of capital asset pricing. *Journal of Economic Theory*, 13, 341–360.

Sharpe, WF (1964). Capital asset prices, a theory of market equilibrium under conditions of risk. *Journal of Finance*, 19, 425–442.

Szegö, G (2005). Measures of risk. *European Journal of Operational Research*, 163, 5–19.

Vlaar Peter, JG (2000). Value at risk models for Dutch bond portfolios. *Journal of Banking & Finance*, 24, 1131–1154.

World Bank (2004). Republic of Tunisia: Strategy for public debt management. Report No. 27599-TN, January 2004.

CHAPTER 3

A METHOD TO FIND HISTORICAL VaR FOR PORTFOLIO THAT FOLLOWS S&P CNX NIFTY INDEX BY ESTIMATING THE INDEX VALUE

*K. V. N. M Ramesh**

Financial institutions face the important task of estimating the controlling of their exposure to market risk, which arises through different risk factors in their portfolio. Measurement of market risk has focused on a metric called Value at Risk (VaR). VaR quantifies the maximal amount that may be lost in a portfolio for a given period of time, at certain confidence level. For large portfolios the risk factor can be taken as an index. In this chapter, we come up with a method of estimating Historical VaR for a portfolio that reflects the S&P CNX Nifty index at any point of time. We assume that the value of index $X(t)$ is independent of time and the distribution of $X(t)$ is not necessarily Gaussian.

1 Introduction

In implementing firm-wide risk management there are two big challenges. One is to implement interfaces to all the different front-office systems, back-office systems, and databases in order to get the portfolio positions and historical market data into a centralized risk management framework. The second challenge is to use the computed VaR numbers to actually control risk and to build an atmosphere, where all participants accept the risk management system.

*Developer/Executive (Commodities), Barclays Capital Singapore, 60B Orchard Road, The Atrium@ Orchard #10-00, Singapore 238891. rameshkvnm@gmail.com.

The main contribution of this chapter is to introduce a model, which predicts the boundaries of the S&P CNX Nifty index. This can be used for calculating the VaR of a portfolio, which follows the index.

The time series of an index is a complex process. A piece of index sequence sampled over a time scale should be modeled as a non-stationary segment. This means a sequence of index values sampled over an arbitrary sampling period may be modeled as a non-stationary time sequence.

The rest of the chapter is organized as follows: Section 2 provides the literature survey. Section 3 describes the statistical modeling for VaR describing the model and approximation decisions for calculating VaR. Section 4 describes the characteristics of the index. Section 5 describes the DLF-based prediction algorithm and VaR approximation. Sections 6 and 7 explain a method to reduce the estimated VaR without forfeiting the confidence level by estimating the exact value of index in Sec. 6 and using that in estimating VaR in Sec. 7. Observations and results are discussed in Secs. 8 and 9, respectively. Section 10 gives the conclusions.

2 Literature Survey

Historical VaR is a better methodology to use if one cannot determine the distribution of his/her return series. As described in the papers given in references by Manganelli and Engle (2001), Butler and Schachter, and Fallon and Sarmiento (2004), we rank all of the past historical returns in terms of the lowest to the highest, and we compute with a predetermined confidence rate what the lowest return historically has been. This means if one had 100 past returns and wanted to know with 95% confidence what is the worst that can be done, he/she would go to the fifth data point on the ranked series and know that 95% of the time he/she will do no worse than this amount.

Historical VaR seems way too simplistic, and in fact this is the biggest criticism of the methodology. Without a distribution to help determine future returns, it is assumed that the past will exactly replicate the future, which is very unlikely in itself. The strengths of the method are that all past data have been fully incorporated in the risk calculation without the forced assumption of a normal distribution and that no variance/covariance matrix is needed to calculate the portfolio standard deviation. This avoids the risk of a changing matrix over time which is the weakness of the parametric VaR. In theory this method would be better than parametric VaR if one had enough data to fully represent all of the crisis events and changing business cycles that occurred.

One would then know exactly how the portfolio performed and how much was at risk at any period in time. This chapter addresses the pitfalls of historical VaR without foregoing its advantages over parametric VaR.

3 Statistical Modeling for VaR

VaR methodologies can be classified in terms of statistical modeling decisions and approximation decisions (Butler and Schachter). The modeling decisions are:

1. *Which risk factors to be include.* This mainly depends on the banks' business (portfolio) and availability of historical data. For smaller stock portfolios it is customary to include each stock itself as a risk factor. For larger stock portfolios, only country or sector indexes are taken as the risk factors (Longerstaey, 1996). In this chapter, we considered S&P CNX Nifty index as the risk factor assuming that the banks' portfolio reflects the instruments which are used in forming the index.
2. *How to model security prices as functions of risk factors, which is usually called "the mapping".* This is out of the scope of the chapter.
3. *What stochastic properties to assume for the dynamics of the risk factors $X(t)$.* The S&P CNX Nifty index, which is considered as the risk factor is independent of time and its distribution is not necessarily gaussian.
4. *How to estimate the model parameters from the historical data.* The model parameter considered in this chapter is the height difference correlation of the risk factor $X(t)$ which is represented as $C_2(\tau)$ in Eq. (1).

The approximation decisions are:
VaR approximation is done using the formula $kC_2(\tau)$. In this chapter, we considered $k = 10$ to have confidence level of 99% and calculated one day VaR with $\tau = 1$. To calculate n-day VaR the value of τ should be n.

4 Characteristics of Index

It is observed that the value of the index behaves like a non-stationary fractal process, which is characterized by the height difference correlation function (Fallon and Sabogal, 2004) as given in Eq. (1).

$$C_2(\tau) = \{E[(\delta X(\tau))^2]\}^{0.5} = \{E[(X(t+\tau) - X(t))^2]\}^{0.5}, \qquad (1)$$

where $X(t)$ is a fractal curve. C_2 (τ) (Fig. 1) calculates the deviation of the increments of $X(t)$ in the time scale τ. For a single-structure, non-stationary

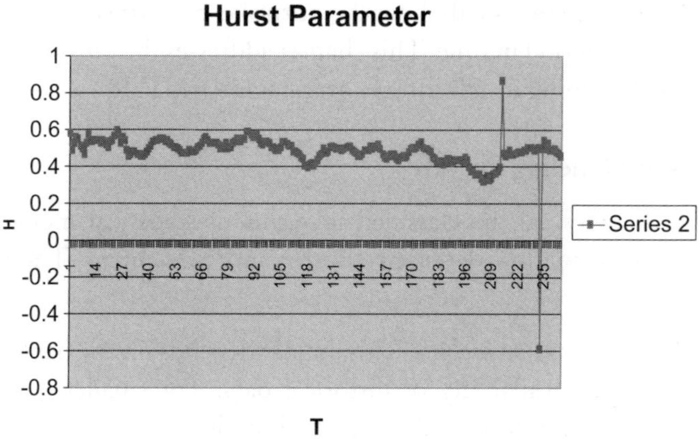

Figure 1: Hurst parameter for S&P CNX Nifty index.

fractal signal (process) $C_2(\tau)$ will have the following form:

$$C_2(\tau) \sim \tau'', \tag{2}$$

where $0 < H < 1$ is the Hurst parameter of the signal.

For a process which behaves like ideal fractional Brownian motion (fBm), if we plot log $C_2(\tau)$ versus log(τ), which will be linear over the scaling domain $\tau \in [0, +\infty)$ with slope of the plot equal to H (Fig. 2). But it is observed that the value of log$C_2(\tau)$ remains almost constant as τ increases after certain value of $\tau = \tau_s$ and remains constant between $[\tau_1, \tau_2]$.

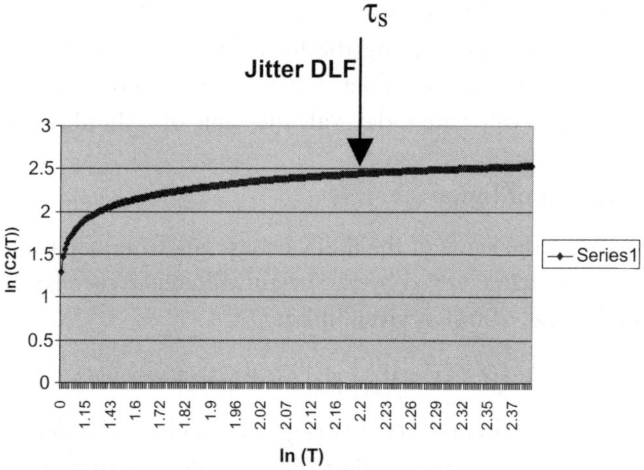

Figure 2: Jitter DLF for S&P CNX Nifty index.

This behavior is explained as below by expanding (1)

$$C_2(\tau) = \{E[X(t+\tau)^2] + E[X(t)^2] - 2E[X(t+\tau)X(t)]\}^{0.5}. \qquad (3)$$

When τ is small, C_2 (τ) behaves like fBm, which is monotonically increasing with τ. However, when τ exceeds a critical value, say $\tau > \tau_b$ a transition point occurs. At this point

$$E[X(t+\tau)^2] \gg E[X(t)^2] - 2E[X(t+\tau)X(t)].$$

So $C_2(\tau)$ is equal to the square root of moving power of the signal.

Let $X(t)$ be the closing value of the index on each day, and then $C_2(\tau)$ represents the standard deviation of the index differences (jitter) of the index value separated by a lag τ. Note that the mean jitter is zero for a stable system. We call this function as the jitter deviation-lag function (DLF) (Li and Mills, 2001).

5 DLF-Based Prediction Algorithm

The DLF curve summarizes (Fig. 3) the standard deviations of all the probability distributions as the lag varies over the measured range. According to Chebychev inequality

$$P[|\delta X(\tau)| > \delta X_b] \leq \frac{C_2(\tau)^2}{\delta X_b^2}, \qquad (4)$$

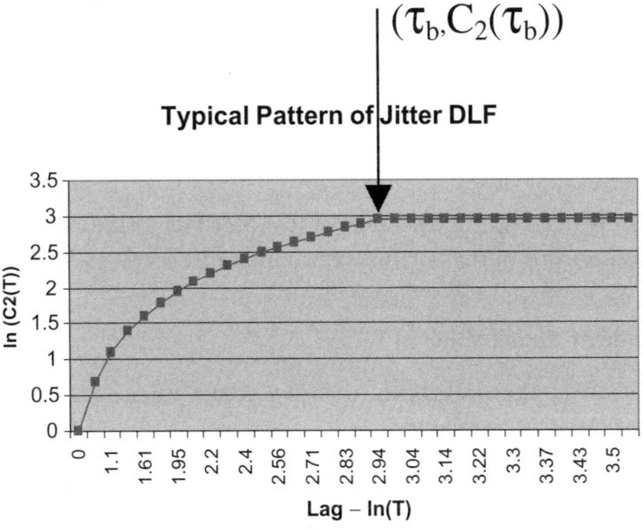

Figure 3: A typical pattern of jitter DLF.

where $\delta X(\tau)$ is the jitter of two values of the index with lag τ between them. $C_2(\tau)^2$ is the variance of the index jitter distribution function and δX_b^2 is the assumed boundary. Note that $E[\delta X(\tau)]$ is equal to zero. The Chebychev inequality means that if we take $\delta X_b = 10C_2(\tau)$ then 99% of $\delta X(\tau)$ will fall in the range $[-\delta X_b, \delta X_b]$ no matter what stationary jitter probability distribution may be. δX_b provides a jitter boundary estimate with 1% error probability.

Let $|\delta X(\tau)| = |X(t_2) - X(t_1)|$ where $t_2 = t_1 + \tau$, and take $\delta X_b = kC_2(t_2 - t_1)$, from (4), we get

$$P[X(t_1) - kC_2(t_2 - t_1) < X(t_2) < X(t_1) + kC_2(t_2 - t_1)] >= 1 - (1/k^2). \tag{5}$$

Which means that, given the index value at time $t_1 (X(t_1))$ the value at time t_2 will lie within the boundaries $X(t_1) - kC_2(t_2 - t_1)$ (lower bound) and $X(t_1) + kC_2(t_2 - t_1)$ (upper bound) with a confidence level of $(1 - (1/k^2))$*100%. Therefore, if we take the value of k as 10 then with 99% confidence level we can say that the value of the index at time t_2 will not be less than the predicted lower boundary.

5.1 *VaR Approximations*

It can be inferred that the maximum percentage of loss that the index may suffer between times t_2 and t_1 is shown in Eq. (6).

$$\frac{kC_2(t_2 - t_1)}{X(t_1)} * 100\%. \tag{6}$$

If we have a portfolio $(P(t))$ that follows (7) at any point of time then (6) also

$$P(t) = yX(t) \tag{7}$$

represents the maximum percentage of loss that the portfolio may suffer and can be taken as VaR of the portfolio at a confidence level $(1 - (1/k^2))$*100%.

6 Estimate of Actual Value of Index

We can arrive at the probability that the actual value of the index is the minimum boundary as follows:

(Max boundary − Actual value of index)/(Max boundary − Min boundary). (8)

We calculate $C_2(\tau)$ of the probability that the actual value takes minimum boundary say $C_{2p}(\tau)$. We propose the following method to arrive at the estimated value of the above mentioned probability given the previous day's value say Min_p.

Add $10^* C_{2p}(\tau)$ to previous day's value, if the resultant value ($\text{Min}_p + 10^* C_{2p}(\tau)$) is greater than "1" then subtract it from "2" and divide the result by "2" else just divide it by "2". Take this final value ($\text{Min}_{p\text{Est}}$[a]) as the probability that the index takes the calculated minimum boundary of next day. We arrive at the estimated value of the index say I_{Est}[b] as given by Eq. (9).

$$I_{\text{Est}} = (\text{Min boundary} * \text{Min}_{p\text{Est}}) + (\text{Max boundary}^*(1 - \text{Min}_{p\text{Est}})). \quad (9)$$

7 Estimate for VaR

From the above estimated index value the difference between the estimated and actual value of the index is calculated and for that $C_2(\tau)$ is computed, say $C_{2\text{var}}(\tau)$. The final estimate of the value of index for VaR is given by Eq. (10)

$$I_{\text{EstVaR}} = I_{\text{Est}} - k_{\text{var}}{}^* C_{2\text{var}}(\tau). \quad (10)$$

Finally VaR is expressed as a percentage of previous day's actual value of index, say I_p, as in Eq. (11) at a confidence level of $1 - 1/k^2_{\text{var}}$.

$$((Ip - I_{\text{EstVaR}})/I_p)^* 100. \quad (11)$$

The value of k_{var} is given by Eq. (12).

$$k_{\text{var}} = (\text{Confidence level})^*(\text{Max loss in historical data})/C_{2\text{var}}(\tau). \quad (12)$$

The above value of k_{var} given by Eq. (12) gives much better results than the expected confidence level mentioned in Eq. (12), so that we can take a still lower value to arrive at I_{EstVaR} for the confidence level mentioned in Eq. (12) (Fig. 4).

---

[a]Whenever the calculated probability repeats, for the repeated value calculation is done using the exact value (Min_p) of the previous day else the estimated value ($\text{Min}_{p\text{Est}}$) itself is used to calculate the estimated probability of the next day. It is observed that for around 30 days the values repeat.

[b]The estimated values (I_{Est}) are used for predicting the values of the index for the next four consecutive days. After that the actual boundaries are calculated using the exact value of the previous day and are used to calculate I_{Est}.

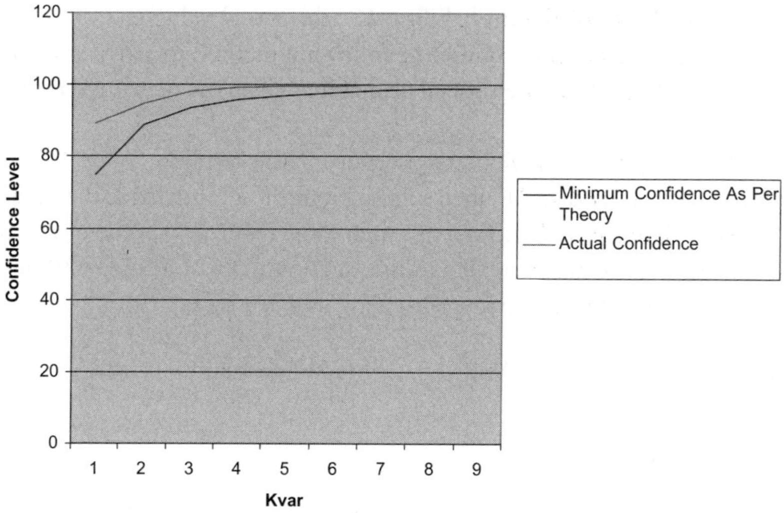

Figure 4: k_{var} vs confidence level.

8 Observations

We observed that the mean of the jitter of the index, i.e. $E[X(\tau)]$ is almost zero (around 0.6) for $\tau = 1$ and hence the system is stable. Also the $X(\tau)$ can be taken as the return on the index and hence it will be stationary.

9 Results

We did a clean back testing (assuming that the portfolio follows (7)) for every 250 days as per the BASE II norms. It is observed that the result falls in green zone (less than four violations of estimated VaR). Moreover, the average weight to be given to the max and min boundaries to obtain the exact value is nearly equal to 0.5, which means that the exact value of the index is most probably the mean of the max and min boundaries. Also it is observed that the average Hurst parameter (Fig. 1) is near to 0.5 which indicates that the future values will be similar to the historical values and $X(\tau)$ is stationary. It is observed that the actual historical VaR is misleading as it give only around 85.2% confidence but our results show 98% confidence if we take the value of k_{var} as "4". It is also observed that the estimated value of the index follows the pattern of the actual value of the index (Fig. 5). The auto-correlation (ACF) (Fig. 6) coefficient is around 0.999259666 (1.0 approx) which indicates that there is a linear dependency between the previous and the present values which is supported

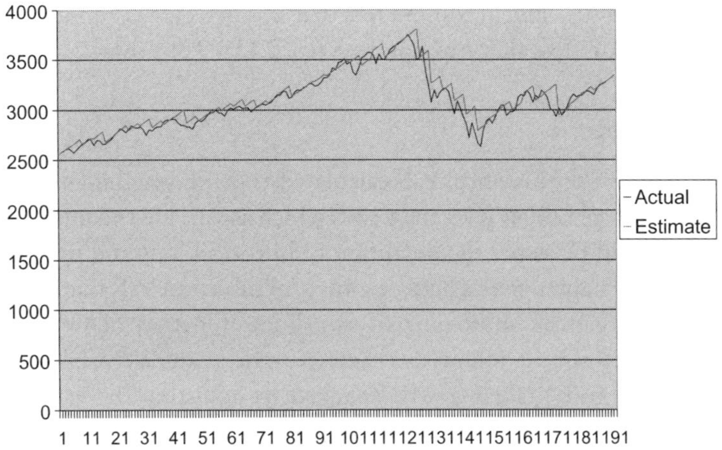

Figure 5: Actual and estimated value of the index.

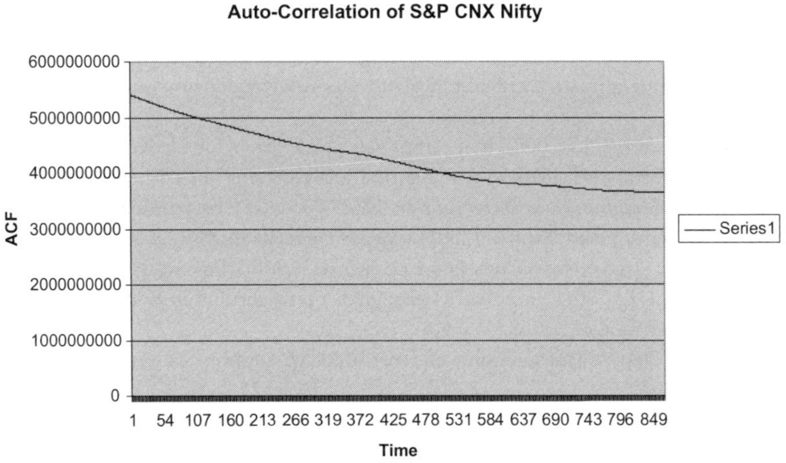

Figure 6: Auto-correlation of the index closing values.

by (Fig. 6) in which the ACF has the shape of a parabola. This shows that the index almost linearly increases with time. We also performed Kupiec's test on our VaR results for 250 trading days and the likelihood ratio (LR_{max}) is found to be 10.33 taking the lower level of confidence given by the model and by taking the higher level as 99% the likelihood ratio (LR_{min}) is found to be 1.9568. We also calculated the statistics for correct conditional coverage LR_{ind} and correct unconditional coverage LR_{cc} whose values are 9.8947 and

11.892, respectively. The maximum loss that was detected is 153.2636 points and the maximum loss that was not detected is 118.991 points.

10 Conclusions

We conclude that the historical VaR calculated as per the method described by Fallon and Sabogal (2004) gives the results which are at a lower confidence level than they should be as per the definition of historical VaR and the proposed method in this chapter gives a better estimate of historical VaR than the above. Also the index can be approximated as a linear function of time and our estimated values almost follow the same pattern as our actual values. The amount of risk to be taken can be changed by adjusting the value of k_{var}. We should take the $LR_{\min}$ value as LR_{uc} to satisfy the condition $LR_{cc} = LR_{uc} + LR_{\text{ind}}$.

References

Butler, JS and Schachter, B (1998). Estimating value-at-risk with a precision measure by combining kernel estimation with historical simulation. www.gloriamundi.org/picsresources/valueatr6.pdf.

Fallon, EC and Sabogal, JS (2004). Is historical VaR a reliable tool for relative risk measurement in the Colombian stock market? An empirical analysis using the coefficient of variation. *Cuadernos de Administracio'n, enero-junio de*, 17(27), 159–176. www.readalyc.com

Hardle, W, Kleinow, T and Stahl, G (2002). *Applied Quantitative Finance* Springer Verlag.

Hull, JC (2005). *Options, Futures and Other Derivatives*. 6th Ed. Prentice Hall.

Li, Q and Mills, DL (2001). Jitter based delay prediction algorithm in Wide-Area Networks. *Networking, IEEE/ACM Transactions*, 9(5), 578–590.

Li, Q (2001). Delay characterization and performance control. University of Delaware. www.ece.udel.edu.

Meakin, P (1998). *Fractal Scaling and Growth Far from Equilibrium*. Cambridge University Press.

Manganelli, S and Engle, RF (2001). Value-at-risk models in finance. Working Paper No. 75, European Central Bank, Working Paper Series. www.exinfm.com/training/pdfiles/variskbiz.pdf

Ramesh, KVNM and Mishra, M (2002). Performance evaluation of three round majority group membership protocol. IIT Roorkee.

Samanta, GP and Nath, GC (2003). Selecting value-at-risk models for government of India fixed income securities. http://golak.tripod.com/var_icfai.pdf.

www.nseindia.com Indices > Statistics > Historical Data of NSE Indices.

CHAPTER 4

SOME CONSIDERATIONS ON THE RELATIONSHIP BETWEEN CORRUPTION AND ECONOMIC GROWTH

Victor Dragotă[*,†], *Laura Obreja Braşoveanu*[*] *and Andreea Semenescu*[*]

There is a large volume of financial literature related to factors that could have an influence on economic growth. Some of these factors can be under the influence of corruption. The main result of this study is the evidence that there is a direct relationship between corruption and economic growth.

1 General Aspects

The factors that have an influence on economic growth could be structured, in a very general classification, as

(i) *Traditional factors*: These factors are the result of several geographical conditions or centuries of evolution and they cannot be changed easily. For example, let us suppose that someone could prove that religion has an influence on the economic growth. However, it seems very difficult to change the religion of the entire population in order to improve the economic indicators.
(ii) *Regulator factors*: These factors are sometimes the result of various speculative decisions, and moreover, they could be the result of one-man decision. For example, the fact that some countries have the regulations based on the Civil

[*]Bucharest University of Economics, Bucharest, Romania.
[†]Corresponding author. victordragota@yahoo.com; victor.dragota@fin.ase.ro; (Address: Piata Romană, no. 6, Sector 1, Room 1104, Zip Code 010374, Bucharest, Romania).

Law is the result of several political reasons, not a proof that Civil Law Regulations are better than the Common Law regulations. Moreover, in various moments, these factors could vary in time.
(iii) *Non-systematic factors*: Economic growth could be the result of some random, non-systematic factors. For example, the economic growth of one country could be the result of a military conflict nearby, which could offer the opportunity to develop certain sectors and to benefit by the decline of the direct concurrence. Of course, these factors are unpredictable, so they are very difficult to be taken into account in a general model.

The impact of these factors is individual in several cases (for example, the economic growth is determined by a higher level of natural resources or a higher level of technology), but could have joint effects, too. Taking into account only one category of factors, the results of the studies related to the economic growth could be affected. A general presentation of these factors is presented in Table 1.

This study analyses the relationship between corruption and the economic growth. Corruption could have an influence on the economic growth in various ways, which are presented below.

First, corruption could alter directly the *investors' behavior*. There are many ways the investors' behavior could be quantified. Investors' characteristics could influence the economical decisions and, finally, the economic growth. In this category, investors' characteristics could be quantified by many possible variables, from risk relative (or absolute) aversion to political orientation or religion. These factors are not easy to change even if the regulations act in this direction. In this context, corruption could have a very important impact, altering the normal entrepreneurial behavior.

In the same context, the investors' interest for financing the economy could be related to some "fashions", in Shiller's (1997) terminology. For instance, an increase of shareholders number at one moment could induce subsequent increases of their number, based on a contagion principle. In this context, different persons become investors on the capital market or banks only because it is "trendy" to do so. They try to copy the behavior of other investors independently of economical reasons: they are not interested in financial performances of the companies, but only to invest in the same activity like several other known persons. If this hypothesis could be still questioned for developed countries, it could be extremely actual for emerging markets, and especially for the countries that have adopted the market economy regulations recently.

Table 1: A general presentation of the main factors that have an influence on the economic growth.

Factors of influence	Authors	The main results
Geography, ecology, and endowment	Sachs and Warner (1997), Bloom and Sachs (1998), Gallup and Sachs (1998), Elbadawi (1999), Gallup *et al.* (1999)	This literature suggests several channels through which favorable geography and ecology could promote overall economic growth. A high share of a country's area around coastal lines or sea-navigable rivers and high economic density along the coast are important determinants of competitiveness, especially for transaction-intensive exports, such as manufactures. Moreover, a high share of non-tropical (especially temperate) regions in a country is associated with less prevalence of vector-borne diseases and high agricultural productivity. They investigate the link between geography and economic development through linkages in technology and institution
The characteristics of industries	Carlin and Mayer (2003)	There is a strong relationship between the structure of countries' financial systems, the characteristics of industries, and the growth and investments in different countries
Democracy	Helliwell (1993)	A positive effect of growth on democracy, an insignificant and negative reverse effect. He considers a positive indirect effect of democracy on the economic growth, through effects of democracy on education and investment, which compensates for the weak negative direct effect
Human and physical capital	Hall and Jones (1999)	International differences in levels of output per worker are determined by differences in human and physical capital accumulation and productivity
The structure of financial systems	Carlin and Mayer (2003)	There is a strong relationship between the structure of countries' financial systems, the characteristics of industries, and the growth and investments in different countries

(*Continued*)

Table 1: (*Continued*).

Factors of influence	Authors	The main results
Fiscal policy — government expenditures	Barro and Sala-i-Martin (1995)	Productive expenditures have a positive impact on economic growth, while non-productive expenditures have a negative effect
Fiscal policy — tax policy	Engen and Skinner (1992); Barro and Sala-i-Martin (1995)	Taxes have significant and negative effects in short and long-run on economic growth. Distorsionary taxes have a negative impact on economic growth, nondistorsionary taxes have no effect
The structure of financial markets (bank oriented versus capital markets oriented financial markets)	Levine (1997), Levine and Zervos (1998), Rajan and Zingales (1998), Beck *et al.* (2001), Arestis *et al.* (2001), Levine (2002), Beck and Levine (2002), Demirgüc-Kunt and Maksimovic (2002), Calderon and Liu (2002), Carlin and Mayer (2003)	Financial development has an impact on economic growth, or, at least, financial development is a signaling element for the economic growth
Judicial system	North (1990)	An efficient judicial system enforces contracts as an essential determinant of economic performance
Corruption	Mauro (1995), Mo (2001)	Corruption brings down private investment, reducing economic growth. The channels through which corruption affects the growth rate include investment, human capital, and political stability

The number of investors on one specific segment of the financial market could be a proxy for this "fashion". Using this variable, investors could decide investing in this component, for example, on capital market or in banks. Related to this aspect, it seems to be very important to quantify the number of years each component of financial markets had functioned normally. Hence, as long as the interest for investments is a matter of trust, a higher degree of corruption can cause a decrease of the interest in investing on financial markets. Investors could be influenced by other variables, like an increase in market indexes or in interest deposit rates offered by banks. Of course, it could be argued that decisions taken based on this information are correct, but *investments decisions are taken based on the expectations regarding future, and not on the past variable.*[a] Yet, there are other variables that could be taken into consideration in order to explain the investors' behavior, regarding their interest in investing on financial markets. For example, generous dividends or free shares for shareholders could be translated by investors as signals for a decent treatment of minority shareholders *even these decisions will not induce an increase of these minority shareholders wealth* (see again the questions related to investors' rationality, for example, De Long *et al.*, 1990). Corruption could induce the feeling that investors' interests are not respected, which could cause a decrease of the available financial resources for companies. In this context, it could be noticed that investors do not take into account the level of corruption (based on certain quantitative indicators), but the perception of the degree of corruption.

Second, it could be noticed that the "classical" assumption that *each investor is rational* does not always hold (see De Long *et al.*, 1990). For example, on the market, rational investors could be present, but, also, noise traders. In these conditions, depending on the percentage of noise traders, regulations could work or not.[b] There are several ways investors could be motivated to invest on the market. For example, if shareholders' interests are protected, they could be tempted to invest on the financial market (Glaeser *et al.*, 2003).

On the other hand, even though there are not created efficient mechanisms to insure the minority shareholders protection, these shareholders could be forced by circumstances or by the law to have a specific behavior. The situation of the communist countries confirms that, even if there is not a specific interest to insure the mechanism required by a right allocation in economy, there will be some investors interested in financing the economy, in accordance to Keynes theory (1936) regarding the marginal propensity to consume under 1. However, there is no clear evidence that minority shareholders protection represents a pre-condition of the economic growth.

---

[a]In practice, the static forte hypothesis is often used for estimations related to future, but this one is only a simplified assumption.

[b]A more profound question is what means rationality. For instance, it could be noticed that there are large differences between the Liberal and Social-Democratic Political Doctrines. However, none of these political doctrines is declared rational or irrational by the Economic Theory.

Similar considerations could be taken into account in relationship to the existence of conglomerates (see Almeida and Wolfenzon, 2006).

Considering these variables, a relationship between the investors' behavior and the development of financial primary market could be found.[c] Regarding this issue, companies are interested to acquire financial resources on financial market, in order to finance their investments projects. Depending on the financial system, financial resources are obtained mainly from banks or from capital markets. In many cases, the determinants of financial systems are historical, political, cultural, religious, etc. and each of them influences the allocation of financial resources in the economy.

However, motivations of deciders are not always related to rational perspectives, as these are defined by economical and financial theory. For example, Brau and Fawcett (2006), analyzing the motivations of Chief Financial Officers in going public by Initial Public Offers (IPO), find that their primary motivation in going public is to facilitate acquisitions.[d] The primary role of IPO seems not to be the financial resources acquirement, but the shares trade facilitation. In the same context, one important variable is the ownership structure (La Porta *et al.*, 1997, 1998, 1999). If companies are controlled by large shareholders, that could mean they decide regarding the investments projects based mainly on their own interests and not on the principles like Net Present Value, which could determine an increase of shareholders' wealth. As long as these projects are adopted mainly based on personal interest of large shareholders, the impact on economic growth is questionable.

A very close issue to this one is the "Promoter's problem" (see Mahoney, 1995), respectively, the possibility for corporate issuers to sell "bad securities" to the public. In order to facilitate the transfer of financial resources, information disclosure is very important. La Porta *et al.* (2006) noticed that in Grossman and Hart model (1980), for example, the lowest cost providers are not the investors, but the issuers, distributors, and accountants. Also, La Porta *et al.* (2006) state that "public enforcement plays a modest role at best in the development of stock markets".

Another important issue related to the financial resources transfer is represented by financial markets' regulations (see La Porta *et al.*, 2006). For example,

[c]It could be mentioned that the relationship between investors' behavior and the economic growth is interesting mainly regarding the primary financial market. The normal functioning of a secondary market represents mainly only a condition for investors to accept investing on financial market.

[d]In the same context, factors as minimizing the cost of capital or pecking order of capital have low support.

in the classical work of Coase (1960) and Stigler (1964), the optimal government policy is to leave securities markets unregulated. In the same context, issuers of securities have an incentive to disclose all available information to obtain higher prices simply because failure to disclose would cause investors to assume the worst (Grossman and Hart, 1980; Grossman, 1981; Milgrom and Roberts, 1986). The alternative hypothesis is that regulations really matter. Related to this issue, in the first case, government can standardize the private contracting framework to improve market discipline and private litigation. In the second case, as long as this standardization is not enough in order to regulate the market, a public enforcer is needed to support trade (La Porta *et al.*, 2006). Again, corruption could affect all of these mechanisms. As long as regulations matter, corruption could affect economic growth.

Third, it could be noticed that, based on the financial resources obtained from financial markets, companies could finance interesting investment projects (characterized by a positive Net Present Value). This relationship between financial systems structure, development and economic growth represents a main issue in finance (Levine, 1997; Beck *et al.*, 2001; Wachtel, 2001; Carlin and Mayer, 2003, etc.). In this context, Rajan and Zingales (1998) find that the quality of financial development promotes the growth of industries that are dependent on external finance. Moreover, Cetorelli and Gambera (2001), performing a similar test as Rajan and Zingales (1998), but using structure instead of size of financial systems, conclude that industries dependent on external finance grow faster in the presence of a concentrated banking system. In the same context, Carlin and Mayer (2003) report that there is a strong relation between the structure of countries' financial systems, the characteristics of industries, and the growth and investment of industries in different countries. Moreover, "there is a particularly strong relation between the structure of countries' financial systems and the growth of industries that are dependent on external equity and skilled labor". Even if theoretically, only attractive projects should be financed, agency problems, corruption, some lack of regulations or even a weak enforcement of the law could influence the economic growth. In this context, it could be mentioned that many recent papers conclude that overall financial development and efficiency of the legal system rather than the structure of financial system (bank versus market oriented) influence economic growth (Beck *et al.*, 2001, Levine, 2002; Beck and Levine, 2002; Demirgüc-Kunt and Maksimovic, 2002, etc.). Also, it must be mentioned that, even though they are different in form, these issues occur for developing countries, but for developed countries, too. For instance, see the problem of "perks", in Rajan and Wulf (2006) terminology, respectively, the "forms of non-monetary compensation offered to select employees".

Corruption could have an impact on all of these factors, which have an influence on the economic growth. In this context, a complete analysis should take into account the particular impact on each factor (see, for example, Mauro, 1995). In this study, we do not make a distinction between corruption, cronyism, nepotism, and *guanxi* (Khatri *et al.* (2006) for more detailed definitions of these concepts). The reason for that option is given by the available data, according to the Transparency International's annual Corruption Perception Index (see Section 3).

There is no consensus about the effects of corruption on the economic growth. For instance, certain studies suggest that corruption has a negative impact on innovative activities because innovators need government-supplied goods, but the demand for these goods is inelastic and high, hence they become primary targets of corruption (Murphy *et al.*, 1993). Moreover, the existing corruption levels are unfavorable for economic development (Gould and Amaro-Reyes, 1983; Mauro, 1995), but the actual effect of corruption on economic growth and its transmission process can be settled only empirically. However, several studies (Acemoglu and Verdier, 1998) argue that corruption might be desirable, inducing a more efficient provision of government services in the context of inefficient regulations. From this perspective, corruption improves the efficiency of an economy.

Relative to the existing literature (Mauro, 1995; Sarkar and Hasan, 2001, etc.), this study focuses only on the relationship between corruption and economic growth. This manner of analysis is explained by the fact that the corruption has an impact on many determinants of the economic growth, so it could be very difficult to separate the individual impact of all of these factors.

The paper is organized as follows. Sections 2 and 3 present the database, and, respectively, the methodology of the study. The main empirical results are depicted in Section 4. Section 5 presents the main conclusions of the study.

2 Database

The aim of this empirical study is to analyze if there is a relationship between economic growth and corruption. In this context, it could be difficult to prove if (a lack of) corruption determines the economic growth or the economic growth is a determinant factor of (the lack of) the corruption.

The variables that are usually used in the existing literature in order to quantify the economic growth are: logarithm of real gross domestic product (used by Arestis *et al.* (2001)), the gross domestic product growth rate (used by Baier *et al.* (2003)), and the gross domestic product per capita (used by King and Levine (1993)). In this study, as economic growth variable the logarithm of gross domestic product per capita was chosen. The data on the gross domestic product was selected from the International Monetary Fund database. The gross domestic product based on purchasing-power-parity (PPP) per capita was preferred in order to better reflect the cost of life and the development level for the countries in the sample.

Corruption, being a phenomenon very difficult to quantify, is represented in the study by the Transparency International's annual Corruption Perception Index (CPI). This variable was widely used in the economic literature for quantifying the corruption impact (Mauro, 1995; Sarkar and Hasan, 2001). The Transparency International Corruption Perception Index ranks countries in terms of the degree to which the corruption is perceived to exist among public officials and politicians, with a range from 0 (minimal value for the index, respectively maximal level for corruption) to 10 (maximal value for the index, minimal level for corruption). It is a composite index, drawing on corruption-related data from expert, country-analysts, and business surveys from residents and non-residents. It focuses on corruption in the public sector and defines corruption as the abuse of public office for private gain. The surveys used in compiling the CPI ask questions that relate to the misuse of public power for private benefit, for example, bribery of public officials, kickbacks in public procurement, embezzlement of public funds) or questions that check out the strength of anti-corruption policies, thereby encompassing both administrative and political corruption.

This paper develops an international empirical study on a representative sample of countries for that the Transparency International's annual Corruption Perception Index is provided. The data sample covers the period from 1995 to 2006 and contains information about 149 countries (see Appendix A), meaning 1125 records. In this study, Luxemburg was excluded from the sample because it records a very high gross domestic product per capita compared to the other records.[e] It could be noticed that the GDP/capita for Luxemburg case

[e]One possible explanation is that Luxemburg is in large extent a fiscal paradise.

has varied between USD 44,594.44 (in 1997) and USD 72,854.53 (in 2006), comparatively to the maximal value of GDP per capita of USD 44,341.9, recorded by Norway in 2006. On the other side, CPI for Luxemburg has varied between 8.4 and 9. Taking into account this country, the results of the regression would become irrelevant.

In Table 2, there is presented the situation of the countries included in the database, structured in quintiles of average GDP per capita and, respectively, average CPI (see, also, Fig. 1). Based on these values, it can be noticed that there is a relationship between corruption and economic growth. The countries with lower level of corruption record large levels of GDP per capita (one relative exception is Bhutan, but with only one record, see Appendix A). Also, generally, countries with higher degree of corruption have lower levels of GDP per capita (here, one exception is Equatorial Guinea, but again with only two records, see Appendix A).

We analyze this relationship closely in Sections 3 and 4.

3 Methodology

The variables used in this study are described in Table 3.

The analyses that have been done by asking a question in the survey about the influence of the data published in the past years on the answers given in the present survey revealed no correlation of the CPI with its past values and allow using them in a regression.

Mauro (1995) identifies the corruption also as a determinant of the industrial and the economic growth. The idea is then developed by Sarkar and Hasan (2001) who explain by a simple regression that the corruption influences negatively on the productive investment and thus the economic growth. Considering the corruption as a determinant of the economic growth, the present study expands the analysis on a worldwide sample and provides a general view on the relationship between corruption and economic growth.

Due to the characteristics of the database, with a great number of states and 12 different years, the method used for the econometric analysis was the data pool, using weighted statistics in order to emphasize the differences between the number of data for different countries, with cross-section heteroskedasticity, and residuals contemporaneously uncorrelated.

Table 2: Corruption and economic growth.

	Quintile GDP per capita (increasing →)				
	1st quintile	2nd quintile	3rd quintile	4th quintile	5th quintile
Quintile CPI (increasing ↓)					
1st quintile			Bhutan	Barbados, Botswana, Chile, Estonia, Oman, Portugal	Australia, Austria, Belgium, Canada, Denmark, Finland, France, Germany, Hong Kong, Iceland, Ireland, Israel, Japan, Malta, Netherlands, New Zealand, Norway, Singapore, Spain, Sweden, Switzerland, United Arab Emirates, United Kingdom, United States
2nd quintile		El Salvador, Jordan	Belize, Bulgaria, Colombia, Dominica, Namibia, Peru, Tunisia	Costa Rica, Czech Republic, Greece, Hungary, Kuwait, Lithuania, Malaysia, Mauritius, Poland, Seychelles, South Africa, South Korea, Trinidad and Tobago, Uruguay	Bahrain, Cyprus, Italy, Qatar, Slovenia, Taiwan

(*Continued*)

Table 2: (*Continued*)

	Quintile GDP per capita (increasing →)				
	1st quintile	2nd quintile	3rd quintile	4th quintile	5th quintile
3rd quintile	Burkina Faso, Malawi, Senegal	Egypt, Ghana, Jamaica, Lesotho, Mauritania, Mongolia, Morocco, Sri Lanka	Algeria, Belarus, Bosnia and Herzegovina, Brazil, China, Dominican Republic, Gabon, Lebanon, Panama, Suriname, Thailand, Turkey	Argentina, Croatia, Grenada, Latvia, Mexico, Saudi Arabia, Slovak Republic	
4th quintile	Benin, Central African Republic, Eritrea, Ethiopia, Madagascar, Mali, Moldova, Mozambique, Nepal, Rwanda, Tanzania, Togo, Zambia	Armenia, Bolivia, Ecuador, Guatemala, India, Nicaragua, Philippines, Vietnam, Zimbabwe	Albania, Guyana, Kazakhstan, Romania, Serbia, Swaziland, Venezuela	Libya, Russia	
5th quintile	Bangladesh, Burundi, Chad, Haiti, Kenya, Myanmar, Niger, Nigeria, Sierra Leone, Tajikistan, Uganda, Uzbekistan	Angola, Azerbaijan, Cambodia, Cameroon, Georgia, Guinea, Honduras, Indonesia, Pakistan, Papua New Guinea, Sudan	Paraguay, Turkmenistan, Ukraine	Equatorial Guinea	

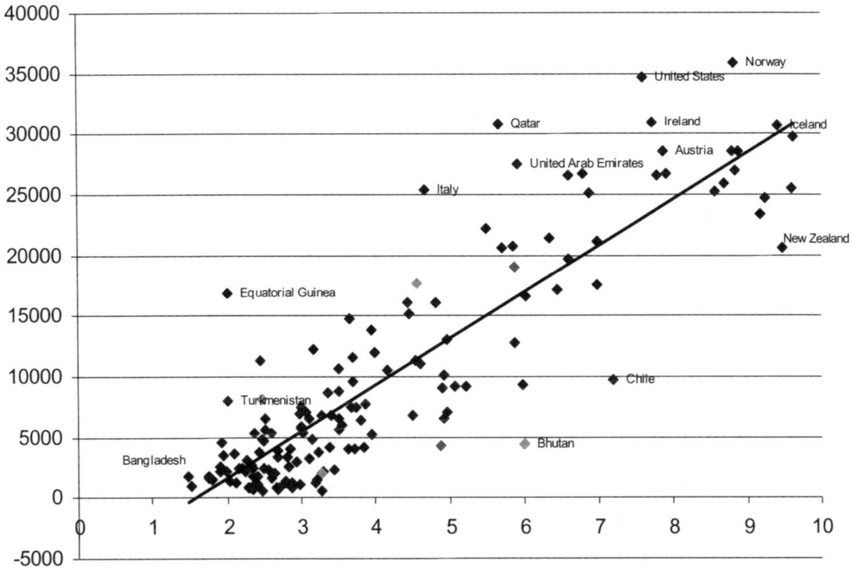

Figure 1: Corruption and economic growth.

Table 3: Variables.

Variables	Symbol	Description
Gross Domestic Product PPP per capita	GDP	Considered as an estimator for economic growth. Source: IMF database.
The logarithm of the Gross Domestic Product PPP per capita	Log (GDP)	
Corruption perception index	CPI	Considered as estimation for the corruption. Source: Transparency International

In order to present the impact of the corruption on the economic growth, the equation of the model is listed below:

$$\mathrm{Log(GDP)} = \alpha \cdot \mathrm{CPI} + \varepsilon. \tag{1}$$

The results are presented in Section 4.

4 Results

In Table 4, the results for regression (1) presented in Section 3 are provided.

Table 4: Results for regression (1).

Dependent variable	Independent variable	Intercept	
Log(GDP)	CPI	C	
	0.355143***		7.270623***
	[53.48443]		[210.6608]
R^2		0.995044	
R^2 adjusted		0.995039	
F-statistic		225,452.8***	
Durbin–Watson test		1.948119	

t-statistic in [ ].
***Coefficients in the table are significant at 1% level.
Regression (1)(weighted statistics): $\log(\text{GDP}) = 7.270623 + 0.355143 \cdot \text{CPI} + \varepsilon$.

The numerical results demonstrate that the relationship between the Corruption Perception Index and economic growth evolution is strong. However, it cannot be introduced in the regression with other common variables used to explain the economic growth such as investments, consummation propensity, and labor, because it is likely to influence these factors too. This might be an explanation for the high values of R^2 and adjusted R^2.

The result is in accordance to Mauro (1995), who shows that the corruption determines both inefficient investments that diminish the future capital of the society and inefficient allocation of the present capital that leads to a lower economic growth. The results of the regressions emphasizes that the second effect is stronger because the corruption affects mainly the present gross domestic product.

5 Conclusions

This study reveals a strong relationship between corruption, estimated by Transparency International's annual Corruption Perception Index, and economic growth, measured by the logarithm of Gross Domestic Product PPP per capita. The results are very similar to the existing literature.

Relative to the existing literature, this study is focused only on the impact of the corruption, based on a single-factor relationship. The reason for this approach is that the corruption has an impact on different variables, which have an influence on the economic growth.

Acknowledgments

This research was supported by Romanian Ministry of Education and Research — National Authority for Scientific Research (NASR) through RTD National Programme CEEX, Grant No. 1505/2006 (Module 2). Authors wish to thank to the IFC 4 Meeting participants in Yasmine-Hammamet (Tunisia, 2006), and especially to Mondher Bellalah (University of Cergy Pontoise) and Duc Nguyen (ISC Paris), for very useful comments. The remaining errors are ours.

Appendix A: GDP per capita and Corruption Perception Index.

Country	Period	No. of observation	GDP per capita[1]			CPI[2]		
			Average	Min	Max	Average	Min	Max
Albania	1999–2006	6	4762.70	3434.83	5817.57	2.47	2.30	2.60
Algeria	2003–2006	4	5322.67	6431.04	7612.46	3.02	2.60	3.10
Angola	2000–2006	6	2515.72	1868.32	3558.46	1.90	1.70	2.20
Argentina	1995–2006	12	12, 235.76	10, 470.00	14, 838.43	3.16	2.50	5.24
Armenia	1999–2006	6	3344.90	1831.53	4516.19	2.82	2.50	3.10
Australia	1995–2006	12	25, 906.73	20, 094.94	32, 127.48	8.68	8.30	8.86
Austria	1995–2006	12	28, 623.36	22, 891.04	34, 802.57	7.87	7.13	8.70
Azerbaijan	1999–2006	8	3542.00	2304.01	5895.37	1.94	1.50	2.40
Bahrain	2003–2006	4	20, 772.06	18, 780.26	22, 705.98	5.85	5.70	6.10
Bangladesh	1996–2006	7	1764.73	1268.23	2135.84	1.48	0.40	2.29
Barbados	2004–2006	3	17, 605.51	16, 825.12	18, 381.18	6.97	6.70	7.30
Belarus	1998–2006	8	6006.18	4209.54	8229.94	3.55	2.10	4.80
Belgium	1995–2006	12	26, 652.26	21, 564.50	32, 499.72	6.60	5.25	7.60
Belize	2003–2006	4	7682.17	7227.93	8054.69	3.88	3.50	4.50
Benin	2004–2006	3	1176.83	1135.05	1219.41	2.87	2.50	3.20
Bhutan	2006	1	4437.41	4437.41	4437.41	6.00	6.00	6.00
Bolivia	1996–2006	11	2447.59	2169.74	2791.23	2.49	2.00	3.40
Bosnia and Herzegovina	2004–2005	2	5833.08	5630.99	6035.18	3.00	2.90	3.10
Botswana	1998–2006	9	9356.03	6981.77	12, 131.46	5.98	5.60	6.40
Brazil	1995–2006	12	7487.95	6505.31	8917.00	3.67	2.70	4.10
Bulgaria	1998–2006	9	7448.15	5542.42	10, 003.42	3.73	2.90	4.10
Burkina Faso	2000–2006	3	1216.21	1018.33	1345.69	3.20	3.00	3.40
Burundi	2005–2006	2	758.08	739.34	776.82	2.35	2.30	2.40

(Continued)

Appendix A: (*Continued*).

Country	Period	No. of observation	GDP per capita[1]			CPI[2]		
			Average	Min	Max	Average	Min	Max
Cambodia	2005–2006	2	2466.43	2399.16	2533.71	2.20	2.10	2.30
Cameroon	1996–2006	10	2186.22	1826.31	2507.09	2.00	1.40	2.46
Canada	1995–2006	12	28, 630.44	22, 396.28	35, 778.54	8.88	8.40	9.20
Central African Republic	2006	1	1168.227	1168.23	1168.23	2.4	2.40	2.40
Chad	2004–2006	3	1526.46	1433.52	1627.01	1.80	1.70	2.00
Chile	1995–2006	12	9713.52	7423.89	12, 737.11	7.19	6.05	7.94
China	1995–2006	12	4812.22	2702.41	8004.14	3.15	2.16	3.50
Colombia	1995–2006	12	6462.01	5904.25	7645.63	3.80	2.20	4.00
Costa Rica	1997–2006	10	9097.35	7408.45	10, 747.29	4.91	4.10	6.45
Croatia	1999–2006	8	10, 643.11	8310.16	13, 062.19	3.51	2.70	3.90
Cyprus	2003–2006	4	20, 564.31	18, 907.42	22, 275.74	5.70	5.40	6.10
Czech Republic	1996–2006	11	15, 180.93	12, 814.76	19, 427.78	4.46	3.70	5.37
Denmark	1995–2006	12	29, 764.34	24, 231.08	36, 073.62	9.62	9.32	10.00
Dominica	2006	1	6843.04	6843.04	6843.04	4.50	4.50	4.50
Dominican Republic	2003–2006	4	7465.95	6998.26	8018.12	3.00	2.80	3.30
Ecuador	1999–2006	10	3735.80	3192.29	4465.63	2.44	2.20	3.19
Egypt	1996–2006	10	3729.43	2847.27	4534.82	3.23	2.84	3.60
El Salvador	1998–2006	9	4222.23	3835.83	4619.98	3.86	3.40	4.20
Equatorial Guinea	2005–2006	2	16, 966.82	16, 507.27	17, 426.37	2.00	1.90	2.10
Eritrea	2004–2006	3	855.62	850.46	858.43	2.70	2.60	2.90
Estonia	1998–2006	9	12, 737.28	9009.70	17, 802.22	5.88	5.50	6.70
Ethiopia	2000–2006	6	756.92	674.81	857.51	2.68	2.20	3.50
Finland	1995–2006	12	25, 549.07	18, 779.26	32, 822.39	9.60	9.05	10.00

(*Continued*)

Appendix A: (*Continued*).

Country	Period	No. of observation	GDP per capita[1]			CPI[2]		
			Average	Min	Max	Average	Min	Max
France	1995–2006	12	25, 125.68	20, 461.45	30, 150.37	6.88	6.30	7.50
Gabon	2004–2006	3	7056.65	6901.55	7213.68	3.07	2.90	3.30
Georgia	1999–2006	6	3049.66	2124.03	3755.29	2.27	1.80	2.80
Germany	1995–2006	12	26, 681.51	22, 316.80	31, 571.48	7.91	7.30	8.27
Ghana	1998–2006	9	2308.06	1956.13	2781.36	3.46	3.30	3.90
Greece	1995–2006	12	17, 665.82	13, 313.77	23, 518.77	4.57	4.04	5.35
Grenada	2006	1	8863.31	8863.31	8863.31	3.50	3.50	3.50
Guatemala	1998–2006	8	3897.93	3527.71	4265.80	2.68	2.20	3.20
Guinea	2006	1	2115.77	2115.77	2115.77	1.90	1.90	1.90
Guyana	2005–2006	2	4732.03	4611.91	4852.15	2.50	2.50	2.50
Haiti	2004–2006	5	1796.92	1752.06	1840.53	1.76	1.5	2.2
Honduras	1999–2006	8	2744.19	2414.06	3130.95	2.33	1.70	2.70
Hong Kong	1995–2006	12	26, 529.35	21, 275.25	35, 395.66	7.78	7.01	8.30
Hungary	1995–2006	12	13, 057.88	93, 22.29	17, 820.85	4.96	4.12	5.30
Iceland	1998–2006	9	30, 704.21	25, 624.32	37, 296.15	9.40	9.10	9.70
India	1995–2006	12	2549.41	1832.26	3550.06	2.83	2.63	3.30
Indonesia	1995–2006	12	3683.13	3084.67	4752.88	2.08	1.70	2.72
Ireland	1995–2006	12	31, 032.88	18, 900.34	42, 858.94	7.72	6.90	8.57
Israel	1996–2006	11	21, 109.03	18, 581.07	24, 357.40	6.97	5.90	7.97
Italy	1995–2006	12	25, 397.63	21, 195.46	29, 405.96	4.67	2.99	5.50
Jamaica	1998–2006	7	4059.21	3532.58	4614.62	3.71	3.30	4.00
Japan	1995–2006	12	26, 661.24	22, 719.37	31, 865.98	6.80	5.80	7.60
Jordan	1996–2006	10	4329.79	3589.06	5197.00	4.89	4.40	5.70

(*Continued*)

Appendix A: (*Continued*).

Country	Period	No. of observation	GDP per capita[1]			CPI[2]		
			Average	Min	Max	Average	Min	Max
Kazakhstan	1999–2006	8	6483.35	4138.29	9133.69	2.51	2.20	3.00
Kenya	1996–2006	10	1298.08	1170.27	1519.46	2.11	1.90	2.50
Kuwait	2003–2006	4	16, 171.88	15, 756.01	16, 592.56	4.83	4.60	5.20
Latvia	1998–2006	9	9645.37	6521.57	13, 874.60	3.70	2.70	4.70
Lebanon	2003–2006	4	6590.19	6146.37	6932.71	3.10	2.70	3.60
Lesotho	2005–2006	2	2136.27	2113.35	2159.18	3.30	3.20	3.40
Libya	2003–2006	4	11, 354.78	10, 559.88	12, 145.59	2.45	2.10	2.70
Lithuania	1999–2006	8	11, 368.77	8164.09	15, 442.91	4.55	3.80	4.80
Madagascar	2002–2006	5	859.78	750.96	964.66	2.66	1.70	3.10
Malawi	2001–2006	9	565.51	532.86	645.04	3.28	2.70	4.10
Malaysia	1995–2006	12	9210.49	7339.05	11, 914.52	5.08	4.80	5.32
Mali	2003–2006	4	1129.95	1055.29	1228.91	2.98	2.80	3.20
Malta	2004–2006	3	19, 734.41	19, 099.50	20, 364.60	6.60	6.40	6.80
Mauritania	2006	1	3205.71	3205.71	3205.71	3.10	3.10	3.10
Mauritius	1998–2006	9	11, 024.95	8496.03	13, 507.91	4.60	4.10	5.10
Mexico	1995–2006	12	8726.32	6773.16	10, 603.99	3.37	2.66	3.70
Moldova	1999–2006	8	1978.09	1449.92	2707.52	2.65	2.10	3.20
Mongolia	1999–2006	4	2031.69	1581.96	2321.79	3.28	2. 80	4.30
Morocco	1999–2006	8	4018.41	3438.48	4818.55	3.64	3.20	4.70
Mozambique	1999–2006	6	1182.55	880.21	1477.78	2.80	2.20	3.50
Myanmar	2003–2006	4	1645.69	1525.60	1752.78	1.75	1.60	1.90
Namibia	1998–2006	9	6606.62	5752.81	7854.32	4.92	4.10	5.70
Nepal	2004–2006	3	1681.88	1609.53	1760.87	2.60	2.50	2.80

(*Continued*)

Appendix A: (*Continued*).

Country	Period	No. of observation	GDP per capita[1]			CPI[2]		
			Average	Min	Max	Average	Min	Max
Netherlands	1995–2006	12	26, 991.21	21, 545.76	32, 061.85	8.84	8.60	9.03
New Zealand	1995–2006	12	20, 606.76	16, 692.33	25, 654.69	9.47	9.23	9.60
Nicaragua	1998–2006	8	3361.49	2940.96	3769.53	2.69	2.40	3.10
Niger	2004–2006	3	870.91	841.65	899.23	2.30	2.20	2.40
Nigeria	1996–2006	11	1018.01	901.42	1241.12	1.53	0.69	2.20
Norway	1995–2006	12	35, 850.98	27, 906.95	44, 341.91	8.83	8.50	9.10
Oman	2003–2006	4	16, 577.18	15, 378.62	17, 906.00	6.03	5.40	6.30
Pakistan	1995–2006	11	2167.84	1804.99	2829.52	2.25	1.00	2.70
Panama	2001–2006	6	6795.20	6119.25	7593.03	3.40	3.00	3.70
Papua New Guinea	2003–2006	4	2389.92	2317.55	2459.98	2.35	2.10	2.60
Paraguay	1998–2006	7	4601.07	4299.00	5061.40	1.91	1.50	2.60
Peru	1998–2006	9	5223.44	4577.33	6288.81	3.94	3.30	4.50
Philippines	1995–2005	11	4025.38	3392.39	4922.84	2.85	2.50	3.60
Poland	1996–2006	11	10, 516.25	7692.97	13, 797.20	4.17	3.40	5.57
Portugal	1995–2006	12	17, 149.30	13, 638.90	19, 948.54	6.44	5.56	6.97
Qatar	2003–2006	4	30, 809.28	28, 677.79	32, 595.84	5.68	5.20	6.00
Romania	1998–2006	10	6922.39	5489.64	9446.43	2.98	2.60	3.44
Russia	1998–2006	11	8181.98	5891.08	11, 904.32	2.47	2.10	2.80
Rwanda	2005–2006	2	1403.87	1379.62	1428.12	2.80	2.50	3.10
Saudi Arabia	2003–2006	4	14, 749.70	13, 615.96	15, 873.00	3.65	3.30	4.50
Senegal	1998–2006	9	1535.10	1297.38	1841.25	3.21	2.90	3.50
Serbia	2006	1	5713.49	5713.49	5713.49	3.00	3.00	3.00
Seychelles	2006–2004	3	12, 000.32	11, 838.34	12, 104.06	4.00	3.60	4.40

(*Continued*)

Appendix A: (*Continued*).

Country	Period	No. of observation	GDP per capita[1]			CPI[2]		
			Average	Min	Max	Average	Min	Max
Sierra Leone	2003–2006	4	871.74	782.29	961.77	2.28	2.20	2.40
Singapore	1995–2006	12	23, 450.65	18, 284.73	29, 742.85	9.17	8.66	9.40
Slovak Republic	1998–2002	5	11, 644.87	10, 691.02	12, 934.41	3.70	3.50	3.90
Slovenia	1999–2006	8	19, 079.18	15, 657.99	23, 159.16	5.89	5.20	6.40
South Africa	1995–2006	12	10, 163.34	8433.24	12, 760.01	4.93	4.40	5.68
South Korea	1995–2006	12	16, 081.43	11, 782.07	21, 876.57	4.43	3.80	5.10
Spain	1995–2006	12	21, 382.51	16, 011.52	27, 542.46	6.35	4.31	7.10
Sri Lanka	2002–2006	5	4119.36	3582.22	4705.18	3.38	3.10	3.70
Sudan	2003–2006	4	2474.49	2185.80	2849.34	2.15	2.00	2.30
Suriname	2004–2006	3	5649.55	5363.41	5902.49	3.50	3.00	4.30
Swaziland	2005–2006	2	5342.32	5245.38	5439.27	2.60	2.50	2.70
Sweden	1995–2006	12	24, 774.53	19, 324.66	31, 264.26	9.23	8.87	9.50
Switzerland	1995–2006	12	28, 641.97	24, 147.05	33, 793.53	8.79	8.40	9.10
Taiwan	1995–2006	12	22, 223.67	16, 161.13	29, 243.75	5.51	4.98	5.90
Tajikistan	2003–2006	4	1318.11	1117.77	1506.31	2.03	1.80	2.20
Tanzania	1998–2006	9	603.96	479.41	777.02	2.48	1.90	2.90
Thailand	1998–2006	12	6800.94	5558.94	8876.73	3.27	2.79	3.80
Togo	2006	1	1708.11	1708.11	1708.11	2.40	2.40	2.40
Trinidad and Tobago	2003–2006	4	13, 855.21	12, 056.59	16, 019.93	3.95	3.20	4.60
Tunisia	1998–2006	9	7027.50	5566.86	8808.86	4.97	4.60	5.30
Turkey	1995–2006	12	6569.32	5280.66	8384.68	3.50	3.10	4.10
Turkmenistan	2004–2006	3	8027.53	7321.46	8663.02	2.00	1.80	2.20

(*Continued*)

Appendix A: (*Continued*).

Country	Period	No. of observation	GDP per capita[1]			CPI[2]		
			Average	Min	Max	Average	Min	Max
Uganda	1996–2006	10	1296.56	1032.23	1577.14	2.38	1.90	2.71
Ukraine	1998–2006	9	5416.24	3700.81	7816.19	2.37	1.50	2.80
United Arab Emirates	2003–2005	4	27,559.26	26,870.83	27,957.08	5.93	5.20	6.20
United Kingdom	1995–2006	12	25,325.24	19,715.00	31,585.14	8.56	8.22	8.70
United States	1995–2006	12	34,687.75	27,373.10	43,236.15	7.59	7.30	7.80
Uruguay	2002–2006	9	9158.33	7818.41	11,378.20	5.23	4.14	6.40
Uzbekistan	1999–2006	8	1705.69	1453.96	1983.11	2.35	1.80	2.90
Venezuela	2003–2006	12	5573.23	4814.72	6467.17	2.51	2.30	2.80
Vietnam	1997–2005	9	2264.31	1715.92	3024.82	2.55	2.40	2.79
Zambia	1998–2006	9	818.56	693.01	973.98	2.88	2.50	3.50
Zimbabwe	2006–1998	9	2966.98	2533.69	3376.79	2.94	2.30	4.20

[1]Source: IMF database.
[2]Source: Transparency International.

References

Acemoglu, D and Verdier, T (1998). Property rights, corruption and the allocation of talent: A general equilibrium approach. *Economic Journal*, 108.

Almeida, H and Wolfenzon, D (2006). Should business groups be dismantled? The equilibrium costs of efficient internal capital markets. *Journal of Financial Economics*, 79, 99–144.

Arestis, P, Demetriades, P and Luintel, K (2001). Financial development and economic growth: The role of stock markets. *Journal of Money, Credit and Banking*, 33(1), 16–41.

Baier, SL, Dwyer, Jr GP and Tamura, R (2003). Does opening a stock exchange increase economic growth? Federal Reserve Bank of Atlanta, Working Paper 2003-36, December.

Barro, R and Sala-i-Martin, X (1995). *Economic Growth*. McGraw-Hill, Inc.

Beck, T, Demirgüc-Kunt, A, Levine, R and Maksimovic, V (2001). Financial structure and economic development: Firm, industry and country evidence. In *Financial Structure and Economic Growth: A Cross-Country Comparison of Banks, Markets and Development*, Demirgüc-Kunt, A and Levine, R (eds.), Cambridge, MA: MIT Press.

Beck, T and Levine, R (2002). Industry growth and capital allocation: Does having a market- or bank-based system matter? *Journal of Financial Economics*, 64, 147–180.

Bloom, D and Sachs, J (1998). Geography, demography, and economic growth in Africa. *Brookings Papers on Economic Activity* 2, 207–273.

Brau, JC and Fawcett, SE (2002). Initial public offerings: An analysis of theory and practice. *Journal of Finance*, 61(1) 399–436.

Calderon, C and Liu, L (2002). The direction of causality between financial development and economic growth. Central Bank of Chile, Working Paper.

Carlin, W and Mayer, C (2003). Finance, investment, and growth. *Journal of Financial Economics*, 69, 191–226.

Cetorelli, N and Gambera, M (2001). Banking market structure, financial dependence and growth: International evidence from industry data. *Journal of Finance*, 56, 617–648.

Coase, R (1960). The problem of social cost. *Journal of Law and Economics*, 3, 1–44.

De Long, JB, Shleifer, A Summers, LH and Wildman, RJ (1990). Noise trader risk in financial markets, *Journal of Political Economy*, 98, 703–738.

Demirgüc-Kunt, A and Maksimovic, V (2002). Funding growth in bank-based and market-based financial systems: Evidence from firm level data. *Journal of Financial Economics*, 65, 337–363.

Elbadawi, I (1999). Can Africa export manufactures? The role of endowment, exchange rates, and transaction costs. Policy Research Working Paper No. 2120, Development Research Group, World Bank, Washington, DC.

Engen, E and Skinner, J (1992). Taxation and economic growth. NBER Working Paper.

Gallup, JL and Sachs, J (1998). Geography and economic growth. Paper presented at the World Bank Annual Conference on Development Economics, Washington, DC, April 20–21. Available online at: http://www.worldbank.org/html/rad/abcde/sachs.pdf.

Glaeser, E, Scheinkman, J and Shleifer, A (2003). The injustice of inequality. *Journal of Monetary Economics*, 50(1), 199–222.

Gould, D and Amaro-Reyes, J (1983). The effects of corruption on administrative performance, World Bank Staff Working Paper 580, Washington DC: The World Bank.

Grossman, S (1981). The informational role of warranties and private disclosure about product quality. *Journal of Law and Economics* 24, 461–483.

Grossman, S and Hart, O (1980). Disclosure laws and takeover bids. *Journal of Finance*, 35, 323–334.

Hall, R and Jones, C (1999). Why do some countries produce so much more output per worker than others? *The Quarterly Journal of Economics*, 114 (1), 83–116.

Helliwell, J (1993). Macroeconometrics in a global economy, *American Economic Review*, 83(2), 293–299.

Keynes, JM (1936). *Theory of Employment, Interest, and Money*, Macmillan Cambridge University Press, for Royal Economic Society.

Khatri, N, Tsang, EWK and Begley, TM (2006). Cronyism: A cross cultural analysis. *Journal of International Business Studies*, 37, 61–75.

King, RG and Levine, R (1993). Finance and growth: Schumpeter might be right. *The Quarterly Journal of Economics*, 108(3), 717–737.

La Porta, R, Lopez-de-Silanes, F and Shleifer, A (1999). Corporate ownership around the world, *Journal of Finance*, 54, 471–517.

La Porta, R, Lopez-de-Silanes, F, Shleifer, A and Vishny, R (1997). Legal determinants of external finance. *Journal of Finance*, 52, 1131–1150.

La Porta, R, Lopez-de-Silanes, F and Shleifer, A (1998). Law and finance. *The Journal of Political Economy*, 106(6), 1113–1155.

La Porta, R, Lopez-de-Silanes, F and Shleifer, A (2006). What works in securities laws? *Journal of Finance*, 61 (1), 1–32.

Levine, R (1997). Financial development and economic growth: Views and agenda. *Journal of Economic Literature*, 35, 688–726.

Levine, R and Zervos, S (1998). Stock markets, banks, and economic growth. *American Economic Review*, 88, 537–558.

Levine, R (2002). Bank-based or market-based financial systems: Which is better? *Journal of Financial Intermediation*, 11, 1–30.

Mahoney, P (1995). Mandatory disclosure as a solution to agency problems. *University of Chicago Law Review*, 62, 1047–1112.

Mauro P (1995). Corruption and growth. *The Quarterly Journal of Economics*, CX(3).

Milgrom, P and John, R (1986). Relying on the information of interested parties. *Rand Journal of Economics* 17, 18–32.

Mo, PH (2001). Corruption and economic growth. *Journal of Comparative Economics*.

Murphy, K, Shleifer, A and Vishny, R (1993). Why is rent-seeking so costly to growth, *American Economic Review*, 83.

North, D (1990). *Institutions, Institutional Change and Economic Performance*. New York: Cambridge University Press.

Rajan, R and Zingales, L (1998). Financial dependence and growth. *The American Economic Review*, 88, 559–586.

Rajan, RG and Wulf, J (2006). Are perks purely managerial excess? *Journal of Financial Economics*, 79 1–33.

Sachs, J and Warner, AM (1997). Sources of slow growth in African economies. *Journal of African Economies*, 6, 335–376.

Sarkar, H and Hasan, A (2003). Impact of corruption on the efficiency of investment: Evidence from a cross-country analysis. *Asia-Pacific Development Journal*, 8(2).

Shiller, R J (1997). *Market Volatility*, 5th Ed. Cambridge, MA: The MIT Press.

Stigler, G (1964). Public regulation of the securities market. *Journal of Business*, 37, 117–142.

Wachtel, P (2001). Growth and finance: What do we know and how do we know it? *International Finance*, 4, 335–362.

CHAPTER 5

FINANCIAL RISK MANAGEMENT BY DERIVATIVES CAUSED FROM WEATHER CONDITIONS: ITS APPLICABILITY FOR TÜRKİYE

*Turgut Özkan**

Weather is the major uncontrollable factor that influences the development of agricultural and industrial products. Because there is a strong correlations between the fluctuation of production volume and the weather. Unanticipated changes of weather conditions cause important fluctuations on companies' revenues and profits. They also create evidently effects on general economic trends. Such effects have derived weather risk management concept and new financial instruments as named weather derivatives. The term weather derivatives applies to a fairly new class of weather risk management tolls that are structured like put options, call options, and swaps in the capital markets. By using a weather derivative, the company's profit levels are less dependent on foreign exchange rates as minimum incomes are projected in advance, and financial forecasts are more accruate and predictable. The strengthened risk management portfolio, combined with more transparent account, and revenue stability, also results in a lower cost of debt and makes corporate development and expansion planning easier. Weather derivatives mostly being used by developed countries are traded in the organized and OTC markets. Henceforth, they hedge lots of industries' financial statements against corrosion of weather risk, and present multi-functional advantages to users. In this article, we have analyzed the structure of weather derivatives, and discussed the applicability of these non-used financial instruments for Türkiye.

*Haliç University, Business Administration Faculty, Emekyemez Mah. Okçu Musa Cd. Şişhane Sk. No:21, Şişhane, Istanbul, Türkiye. turgut_ozkan@hotmail.com

1 Introduction

The weather condition is one of the foremost natural events that affect the revenue, the expenditure, and the market value of the firms. Apart from other natural events, variability, continuity, generality, and unpredictability of weather conditions even in the short term create almost immeasurable risks in many sectors, from real estate to natural gas and from agriculture to manufacturing industry. This unstable structure causes significant fluctuations in the revenue and profit of the firms. A firm selling oil product for warming, for instance, stockpiles according to expectations of winter conditions. Nonetheless, occurrence of a warmer season would decrease the sales volume and increase the stock expenditure per unit sales price. On the other hand, a colder season would cause insufficiency in stock levels and a negative financial position such as funding the deficient amount with higher spot price.[a]

Both situations mentioned would cause a significant financial risk. Avoiding this risk and hedging the financial structure of the firm by weather forecast using the present technology is almost impossible.

Rapidly growing, diversifying and becoming more complicated, financial derivative markets, however, enable to reduce some systematic risks to non-systematic ones. Enabling specific financial derivatives upon risk conditions and value at risk, these financial improvements make some techniques applicable to hedge the risks of the firm, emerging from the uncertainty of the variation of weather conditions.

The techniques being used by the firms exposed to these risks are classified under the name of "weather risk management". Weather risk management (WRM), and the techniques and derivatives, which arouse interest and new fields of application, are the subject matter of this essay. In this context, this chapter aims to discuss WRM's assistance on firms, the possible fields of application, the usage and the effect of derivatives on risk, and the applicability of WRM in Türkiye.

Utilizing the present literature of WRM, this chapter tries to open a discussion about this new financial instrument that is unknown in Türkiye, and to question whether it is possible to apply them within the present financial conditions of Türkiye.

[a]www.wrma.org/wrma/index.php?option=com_content&task=view&id=13&Itemid=33 (10.05.2006).

2 The Concept of Weather Risk Management (WRM)

Weather risk can be defined as the financial gain and loss,[b] or the uncertainty of cash flow and income (Cogen, 1998, p.1) that result from the volatility in the weather conditions in a certain period of time. These uncontrollable risks, which emanate from the volatility of regional weather conditions are determining economy as well as humans. For instance, it is estimated that one third of the USA economy or 3–5 trillion of it is directly influenced by weather conditions.[c,d] Moreover, some weather conditions indirectly affect the business life up to 70% of all.[e] It is seen that firms all over the world are being forced to become more sensitive to the risks and fluctuations created by weather risk particularly because of the hardening conditions of competition.[f]

Consequently, WRM aims to eliminate — partly or completely — the effects of this kind of external factors deforming financial structure or briefly, to manage the possible risks regarding them. To achieve this purpose, weather risk contract is arranged as the financial agreement between two firms, which enables to transfer the weather risk from one to another[g] (O'Hearne, 2004, p. 5).

According to the data provided from Chicago Mercantile Exchange (CME), the derivatives were firstly opened to transaction in 1997 and the amount of contracts which is 4400 in 2002 became more than 765,000 just before the end of 2005.[h,i] The derivative transactions of WRM are more intensified in the global markets of North and South America, Europe, and Asia (Clemmons, 2001, p. 2).

3 Application Fields of Weather Risk Management

Even though WRM is important for almost all sectors, main application fields consist of electricity, natural gas and energy sectors consisting in oil production and exploitation, agricultural products and agrochemicals, retailers, series

---

[b] www.guaranteedweather.com/page.php?content_id=21 (11.05.2006).

[c] www.cme.com/daily_bulletin/Section05_Underlying_Agricultural_Markets_200605.pdf (11.05.2006).

[d] www.federalreserve.gov/pubs/feds/2000/200008/200008pap.pdf, Star-McCluer. The Effects of Weather on Retail Sales, January 2000, Sf.15 (17.05.2006).

[e] www.weatherriskadvisory.com/result.php?Keywords=aviation+weather&host=www.weatherrisk-advisory. com&cat=1 (11.05.2006).

[f] www.wrma.org/wrma/library/file772.pdf (02.06.2006).

[g] www.nyc.gov/html/om/pdf/energy_task_force.pdf+%22New+York+Energy+Buyers%22&hl=tr&ct=clnk &cd=1 New York Energy Buyers Forum, 20.09.2000, Sf.10 (18.05.2006).

[h] www.prnewswire.com/cgi-bin/stories.pl?ACCT=109&STORY=/www/story/06-10-2004/0002190919 &EDATE= (11.05.2006).

[i] www.cme.com/trading/prd/env/cmeweather14270.html (11.05.2006).

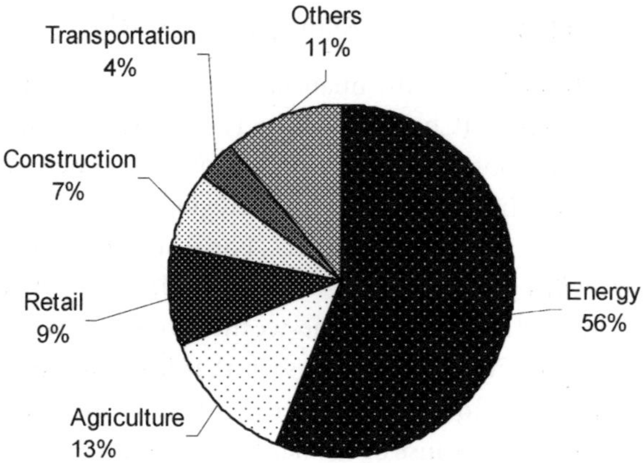

Figure 1: Industrial distribution of financial weather derivatives.

of supermarkets, transportation, construction, clothing, producers of food and beverage, medical companies, self-employed businessmen (Hull, 2006, p. 552), soft drinks including beer and ice-cream, advertising and fashion.[j,k]

Figure 1 displays the distribution of financial derivatives in respect of sectors all over the world in 2005 (O'Hearne, 2004, p. 8).

The creditors using WRM derivatives consist of insurance companies, corporate banks, investment banks, big energy companies, funds managing considerable amount portfolios, and local governments.[l]

Using WRM applications which have significant production areas and effective aspects, firms can take the following advantages:

(1) management of fluctuations of benefit affected by the weather conditions (Katsuyama, 2005, p. 4),
(2) keeping the stability of income and benefit,
  (a) improvement of conditions of competition,
  (b) increasing credibility,
  (c) reducing the capital cost,
  (d) reducing the income dependent on weather,
(3) making the benefit of capital investments,
(4) realization of budget targets (WRMA Annual Convention, 2000, p. 2),
(5) controlling the risks of pricing and production,

[j] www.wrma.org/wrma/index.php?option=com_content&task=view&id=27&Itemid=32 (15.05.2006).
[k] www.guaranteedweather.com/page.php?content_id=83 (25.05.2006).
[l] www.microfinancegateway.org/files/11437_weather_risk_rtf_format2.htm (15.05.2006)

(6) increasing and diversifying the financial portfolio,
(7) transformation of risk created by weather conditions to assets instead of liabilities (O'Hearne, 2004, p. 6),
(8) possibility of hedging particularly in the long term,
(9) possibility of creating the available, flexible, and multi-dimensional hedging product,
(10) a credible and transparent data source involving a long period (Cogen, 1998, p. 10).

4 Financial Instruments in Weather Risk Management and Differences Between Them

There are mainly two financial instruments for weather risk management:

(1) Insurance.
(2) The derivatives.

Different from the familiar insurances involving the guarantee of physical loss, weather insurances have the functions of coverage against "additional cost" or "loss from gain" that may arise from a certain weather event. Therefore, with regard to aims, involvements and usage, there are significant differences between insurances covering weather risk and the derivatives hedging the risks created by temperature, snow, rain, wind, storm, and frost. These main differences are as follows:

(1) Weather insurances provide coverage for high risk-low possibility events such as hurricane, snowfall, rainfall, and landslide. In contrast, weather derivatives hedge low risk-high possibility events which may affect incomes, expenditures, and cash flows, such as cooler summer or warmer winter than expected. For instance, in energy sector, causing idle capacity cooler summer or warmer winter than expected would lead to decrease of cash income and increase the average production cost (Cogen, 1998, p. 1).
(2) Whereas insurance payments base on the real loss, payment for weather derivatives which depends on non-physical product markets would be realized on the difference between strike price and weather indexes (Lettre, 2000, p. 3).
(3) Weather insurance bills carry on their legal status depending on the risk and the insured, whereas weather derivatives are only financial instruments dependent on risk. Therefore, while weather insurance bills are not

subject to transaction in secondary markets, weather derivatives can be purchased on a daily basis.

(4) The sole legal aim of the insurance is to guarantee the loss of the insured in kind; nonetheless, weather derivatives which are subject to transaction in organized markets can be purchased with speculation motive.

(5) While it is necessary to prove the loss for insurance, such necessity is out of question for weather derivatives which are subject to declared meteorological data.[m]

(6) Whereas the default risk of weather insurances is only subject to insurer, in weather derivatives, for instance, in forward and swap operations and particularly in OTC this risk may be subject to all the parties.

5 Derivatives Used in Weather Risk Management

The derivatives commonly used in weather risk management are swap, forward, futures, options, and exotic derivatives.[n,o] These derivatives related to WRM are more subject to transaction in over the counter (OTC) markets[p] and their date of maturity may be monthly, seasonally, annually or longer (Clemmons, 2001, p. 2).

A company that decides to hedge the weather risk can use the mentioned alternative techniques. The most preferable of these techniques is to buy an option. While a put option purchaser hedges herself against a deficit of weather such as insufficiently snowfall, a call option buyer can hedge herself against an excess amount of weather such as too much rainfall.

Apart from traditional options, weather options include "agreement levels" and "strike levels" which are based upon available historical data of past weather conditions such as temperature, rainfall or snowfall per meter square, cold or warm days. In such derivative markets, strike levels which are very significant are determined by using probability distributions, and techniques of simulation and regression (Hull, 2006, p. 553), based on the average of a data obtained in a long period as much as possible — at least a decade in the USA (Dischel, 1999, p. 5). According to this method, the strike level of the derivative which is determined in relation to the period of circulation of the

---

[m] www.nyc.gov/html/om/pdf/energy_task_force.pdf+%22New+York+Energy+Buyers%22&hl=tr&ct =clnk&cd=1 New York Energy Buyers Forum, 20.09.2000, Sf.10 (18.05.2006).

[n] www.wrma.org/wrma/index.php?option=com_content&task=view&id=27&Itemid=32 (17.05.2006).

[o] www.findarticles.com/p/articles/mi_m0BJK/is_4_15/ai_115345946 (17.05.2006).

[p] www.guaranteedweather.com/page.php?content_id=22 (17.05.2006).

derivative, and to the weather conditions or the temperature of past periods (53 weeks, for instance) is guaranteed by the dealer of the agreement. And the maturity date cash flow is calculated according to the difference between weather strike levels and real weather conditions.

The following are the concepts of "weather guarantee level" which are commonly used in applications and implemented for the derivatives:

(1) guaranteed heating degree days: HDD,
(2) guaranteed cooling degree days: CDD (Hull, 2006, p. 552),
(3) guaranteed rainfall,
(4) guaranteed snowfall,
(5) guaranteed growing degree days: GDD (Clemmons, 2001, p. 4),
(6) guaranteed freezing degree days: FDD,
(7) guaranteed melting degree days: MDD,
(8) guaranteed excess degree days: EDD (Swift, 2001, p. 16).

Figure 2 displays the distribution of the derivatives in total transaction volume in respect of weather guarantee level concepts by 2004 (Stell, 2005, p. 4).

In the following sections, basing on some concepts of weather guarantee level and some derivatives, it is exemplified how the derivatives are being used.

5.1 *Guaranteed Heating Degree Days (HDD)*

Two important meteorological concepts generally accepted and improved about temperature levels are "Heating Degree Days" and "Cooling Degree Days" (McKay, 2001, p. 7).

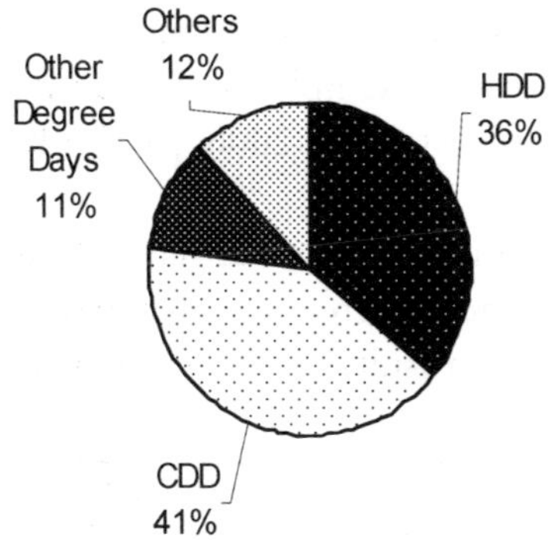

Figure 2: Productional distribution of weather derivatives.

The concept of "degree days" is a unit utilized in measuring how much of a 24 h period was cold or warm. Heating and cooling degree days are important for the comparison of the seasons of the past years and winters or summers, and for the calculation of the level of demand for energy which is crucial for many sectors. Since the heating cost is directly related with heating degree days. To find out the annual heating cost or the heating price of 1 HDD, it is sufficient to divide one year fuel cost to annual HDD.

Considering outdoor and room temperature in a certain period of time — day, month or year — HDD clarifies the intensity of cold. However, many countries use different definitions for the calculation of HDD, Eurostat offers the following method to constitute a common and comparable concept[q]:

$$\text{HDD} = \max(0, 59°\text{F} - T_{\text{m}}) \quad \text{(Hull, 2006, p. 552)}$$

$$\text{If } T_{\text{m}} \geq 59°\text{F}, \quad \text{then HDD} = 0.$$

If $T_{\text{m}} < 59°\text{F}$, weather is colder than expected or season normal (Cogen, 1998, p. 4).

In this formula accepted as index in WRM, T_{m} displays daily average temperature and 59°F (or 15°C) is the value accepted as heating threshold (65°F or 18°C in USA) by meteorological stations. From midnight to midnight, if the highest temperature of a day is 52°F while the lowest is 38°F, the average will be calculated meteorologically as $T_{\text{m}} = 45°\text{F}$. Hence, displaying the deviation from the average, HDD of that day would be 14. If T_{m} is 63°F then HDD = 0, because ($T_{\text{m}} \geq 59°\text{F}$).[r]

If it is to calculate the HDD for a certain period of time, then the formula would be as follow:

$$\text{HDD} = \max(0, 59°\text{F} - T_{\text{m}}) \times d.$$ [s]

If "d" is taken as 30 days, which displays the number of days or a certain period of time, then the data in our example would lead us to calculate HDD = 420(= 14 HDD × 30 days) (Hull, 2006, p. 552; Ruck and Polasek, 2001, p. 6).

A winter different from season normal generally affect the profitability of firms negatively. For instance, whereas a winter colder than expected increases the income of the firms selling suitable clothes for winter,[t] leading the delay of

---

[q]www.meteor.gov.tr/2006/zirai/zirai−aylikanalizler.aspx?subPg=M (31.05.2006).
[r]www.financewise.com/public/edit/riskm/weather99/wthr99−weather.htm (30.05.2006).
[s]www.meteor.gov.tr/2006/zirai/zirai−aylikanalizler.aspx?subPg=M (31.05.2006).
[t]www.wrma.org/wrma/library/file760.pdf (01.06.2006).

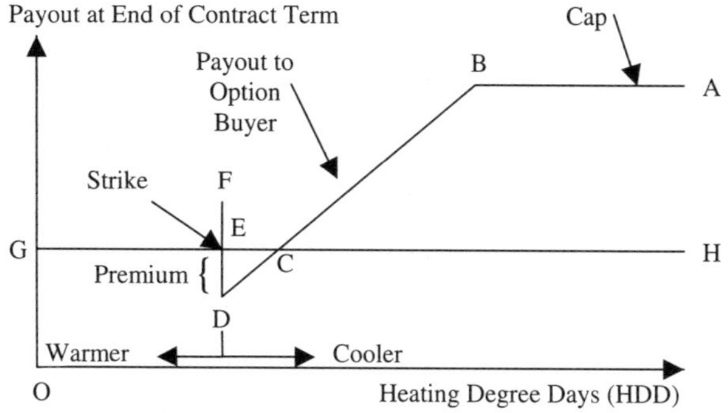

Figure 3: Heating degree days (HDD) call option.

the project and damage of the materials for a construction firm,[u] and leading a liquid fuel firm to buy fuel with a higher price from spot market, excessive cold would cause increase of costs and reduce the profitability. In other words, colder days in winter cause lesser income for construction and liquid fuel firms. To hedge the assets of the firm from such risks and outcomes, it would be a rational financial position to buy call option from Financial Weather Risk Markets.

As will be seen in Fig. 3,[v] if HDD accumulation in an option maturity date (one month, for instance) remains below the strike unit determined in option agreement, then the loss of option buyer would be as the amount option premium. Under the condition of remaining within the option term, if the accumulation of temperature becomes over the strike ($T_m < 59°F$), then option writer pays the amount agreement per temperature to option buyer. Therefore, in Fig. 3, the left side of the strike level shows the warmer and the right side of the strike level show the cooler levels.

At the option maturity date, the sum of HDDs of the agreement month is compared with strike (Strike Degree Days : SDD) (McKay, 2001, p. 10). After multiplying the sum amount of over strike with a certain tick (T), the calculated money is paid to the holder of option.

According to the data in Table 1, the amount of payment (AP) to the option holder at the end of the due (30 April 2006) is

$$AP = (ADD - SDD) \times T,$$

[u]www.wrma.org/wrma/library/file772.pdf (02.06.2006).
[v]www.wrma.org/wrma/library/file760.pdf (31.05.2006).

Table 1: HDD option (transaction summary).

Location	Konya (a city in Turkey)
Option buyer	Isıma Yakıt Dağıtım A.Ş. (an energy company in Konya)
Option seller (Writer)	Koch-Alliant Energy Co. (a company in the USA)
Type of option	Call option
Positioning	Long position
Purchasing date of option	12 May 2005
Term start	01 April 2006
Term end	30 April 2006
Strike (E) (Strike degree days: SDD)	1200 units
Thick (USD/°)F	Per every excess degree of cumulated HDD
Payout per HDD	USD 10,000
Cap (maximum payout)	USD 1,500,000
Actual degree days: ADD	1392 units
Premium (P)	USD 8000

$$\begin{aligned} \text{AP} &= (1392 - 1200) \times \text{USD}10{,}000 \\ &= \text{USD 1920 million (Hull, 2006 p. 552).} \end{aligned}$$

Yet, for the agreement includes the cap for USD 1.5 million the payment to holder of option would be no more than this amount. Thus, option holder would cover the loss after deduction of option premium (P) USD 1,492,000 (= USD 1,500,000 – USD 8000).

If cumulative actual degree days (ADD) is under 1200 units (if $T_{\text{m}} \geq 59°\text{F}$; then HDD = 0), there would be no payment and the option holder would close the option with a loss in amount of the premium paid (USD 8000).

In contrast, for the firm selling or distributing fuel or gas for heating, more warm days in the winter would cause the less income. According to calculations basing the average temperature of last 30 years, a 7.5% HDD warmer winter causes a 10% decline or a loss of USD 12,500 per HDD in incomes of such firms.[w] In such situation, there is the risk of more warm days than season normal or less cold days than a certain number. It is possible to cover the loss by buying a put option which has a floor qualification.

As will be seen in Fig. 4,[x] in this kind of a put option, if strike level (E) is 1500 and cumulative HDD is 1392 units, then the maturity date cash in-flow of option holder is

$$\text{Cash in-flow} = [(E - \text{HDD}) \times T] - P,$$

[w]www.wrma.org/wrma/library/file762.pdf (01.06.2006).
[x]www.guaranteedweather.com/page.php?content_id=78 (24.05.2006).

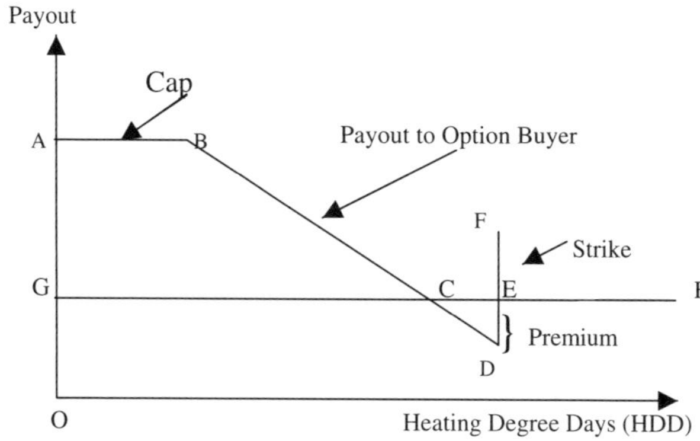

Figure 4: Heating degree days (HDD) put option.

$$\text{Cash in-flow} = [(1500 - 1392) \times \text{USD}10,000] - \text{USD } 8000 = \text{USD}1{,}072{,}000.$$

Considering the examples, it is possible to state the following equalities for call and pull options:

Call option: $\text{HDD} = \max(0, 59°\text{F} - T_{\text{m}}) \times d$ (colder than expected)
Put option: $\text{HDD} = \max(0, T_{\text{m}} - 59°\text{F}) \times d$ (warmer than expected).

5.2 Guaranteed Cooling Degree Days (CDD)

A cooler summer than expected would decrease the utilization of air-conditioner and thus the consumption of electricity. Also, the mentioned weather conditions cause a lower income and benefit for soft drink producers and dealers. Therefore, the more cool days than season normal (or a higher cumulative temperature in certain period) or the less warm days than expected constitute a significant risk for this kind of firms. It is possible to hedge the loss which may appear by a call option with floor qualification.

Figure 5[y] shows how it is possible for an option buyer to hedge this risk. If cumulative cooler degree within the contract period comes under the strike determined by the agreement, then option buyer who pays to option dealer an option risk premium as DE for the risk guaranteed has the right to get an amount for each unit under the strike. Option dealer makes the payment at

[y] www.guaranteedweather.com/page.php?content_id=798 (24.05.2006).

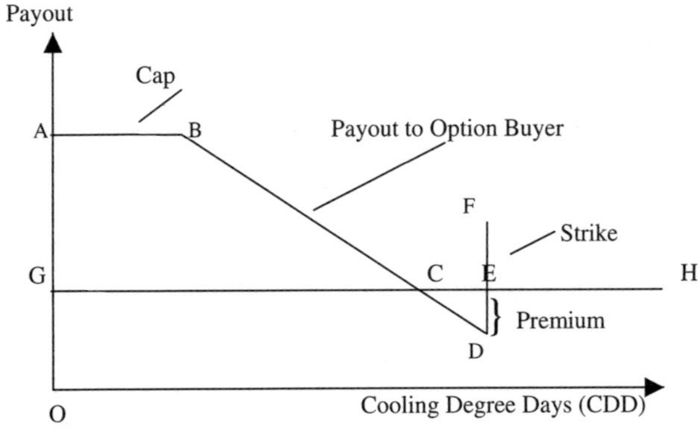

Figure 5: Cooling degree days (CDD) Call Option.

the end of the maturity date, by calculating the amount that way: cumulative cooler degree which comes under the strike multiplied with the amount determined per unit. (Cogen, 1998, pp. 3–4)

Then, it is possible to define CDD as following[z]:

Call option: $\text{CDD} = \max(0, T_m - 59°\text{F}) \times d$ (cooler than expected)
Put option: $\text{CDD} = \max(0, 59°\text{F} - T_m) \times d$ (warmer than expected).

5.3 Guaranteed Rainfall

From agriculture to tourism, rainfall both over and under the season normal considerably affect many industrial branches and the income of them. For instance, a firm producing agricultural products should acknowledge that the profit depends on productivity and a rainfall under the average would be insufficient for a well harvest. Such a farmer holds the possibility to balance the risk regarding the deficit of weather by purchasing an option including "Guaranteed Rainfall". Option dealer is to guarantee to realize a certain payment for each inch (1 inch = 2.54 cm) rainfall under the agreed amount which is necessary for the product.

Figure 6[aa] displays this kind of option used in WRM, which has a typical floor structure.

In Fig. 6, the vertical axis displays the payment levels and the horizontal shows the rainfall. Premium amount (USD 10,000, for instance) which will be

[z]www.financewise.com/public/edit/riskm/weather99/wthr99-weather.htm (30.05.2006).
[aa]www.guaranteedweather.com/page.php?content_id=82 (23.05.2006).

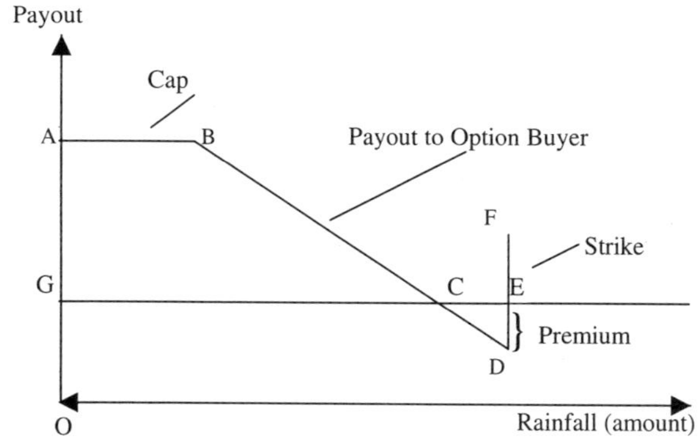

Figure 6: Rainfall option.

paid by option purchaser (farmer) is much as DE, and the line GH is used to determine the break even point, C for option buyer. If rainfall comes over the amount agreed by option, that is to say at the right side of DF limit, then option writer would not meet any payment and the loss of the option buyer would be as much as the premium she paid. If rainfall comes under the strike level, then option writer would pay the option buyer an amount by multiplying each unit rainfall agreed in option with the amount per unit. Payment will begin from the point D. The more rainfall over the guaranteed amount would lead the more payment and it would reach up to the premium level paid by option buyer at the point C. Maximum amount of payment which will be met would be limited by the point B which designates the payment cap (cap = USD 500,000, for instance). Thus, the farmer who bought the option will have the possibility to hedge the loss which may result from insufficient rainfall up to a certain amount. Therefore, the farmer paying for an insignificant premium (USD 10,000) would cover the loss up to a certain limit (USD 500,000) and would get the possibility to utilize the high leverage effect of the option.

5.4 Guaranteed Snowfall

Snowfall has a critical importance for keeping the streets open or holding the level of snow thickness in a skiing center (O'Hearne, 2005, p. 21). Therefore, it is necessary to well upon the management of risk which may cause financial loss resulting from less or more snowfall than season normal. Particularly in suburbs with limited budget, excess amount of snowfall per meter square may

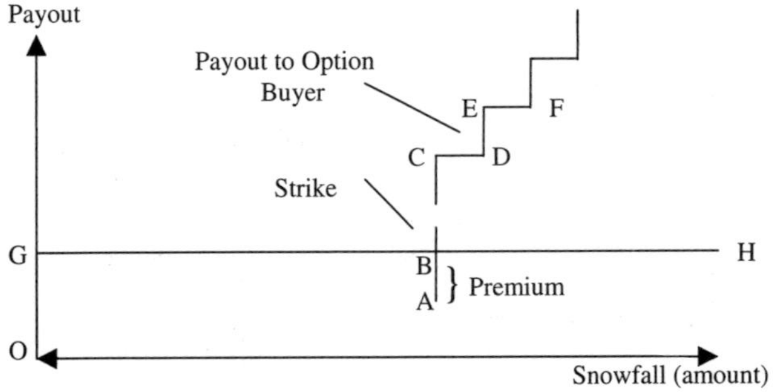

Figure 7: Snowfall option.

lead huge financial loss. Municipalities may hedge the loss emerging from excess amount of snowfall, by purchasing an option including "Guaranteed Snowfall" from OTC or from 1"Financial Weather Risk Market".

Figure 7 [ab] displays this kind of option used in WRM, which has a typical cap structure.

In Fig. 7, paying for option premium about AB, option buyer [long position] hedges herself against the risk of an excess of snowfall over the strike level determined by option. For instance, if the amount of snowfall comes over the strike level guaranteed as much as CD, then short position is to guarantee a payment to option buyer about DE.[ac]

5.5 Collar in WRM and Weather Swap

The mentioned concepts of weather guarantee level do not only hedge unilaterally the firms under risk, but they also provide a bilateral protection by financial derivatives which can be structured according to risk perception. Thus, they enable to take appropriate positions against the risk.

Combination of a long position limited with a cap and a short position limited with a floor (Saunders and Cornet, 2006, p. 743), the collars derivative which provides income guarantee (McKay, 2001, p. 15) within these limits is a significant financial instrument being used in WRM. Forcing particularly the producers and final consumers of energy to move the prices within a band determined by a contract, collar agreements hedge against the risks resulting

[ab] www.guaranteedweather.com/page.php?content_id=82 (23.05.2006).
[ac] www.wrma.org/wrma/index.php?option=com_content&task=view&id=27&Itemid=32 (02.06.2006).

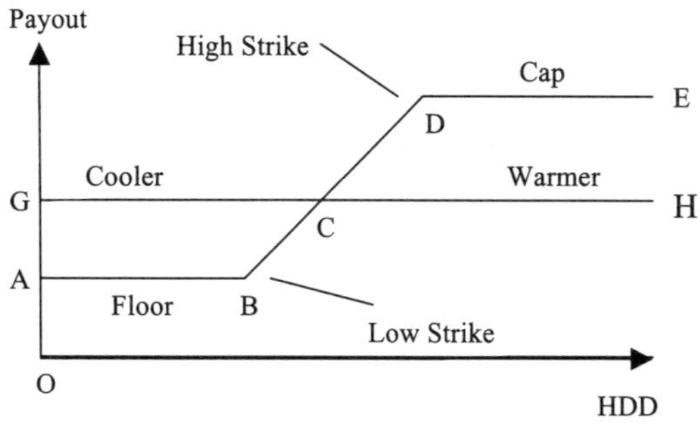

Figure 8: Collars.

from extreme volatility out of band. The collar agreements which have lower premiums in comparison with other derivatives abolish the possibility of high gain or high loss by virtue of the limit of price movement.[ad,ae]

As will be seen in Fig. 8 (Scholten, 2000, p. 5), if cumulative temperature within the option term remains below a certain floor (AB) or remains over a certain cap (DE), then the firm buying this option would experience a loss as much as the amount of option premium.[af] If cumulative temperature comes between the floor and the cap (a point on lines BD or BD+CD), then the difference between the point B (below threshold) and the point on BC (real HDD), or the difference between the point D (above threshold) and the point on CD (real HDD) is multiplied with option tick; the resulting amount is to be paid to the holder of the option.

From the viewpoint of agricultural producers, remaining below a certain threshold, delay of exceeding the threshold or coming upper the threshold, temperature can directly affect the harvest negatively. For instance, the temperature under 50°F (10°C) does not provide an appropriate environment for growth of planted products. In other words, under 50°F, the growth of product is "0". The product grows rapidly up to 93°F (34°C), whereas it cannot grow over 115°F (46°C); the product withers in 118°F (48°C) and over. Therefore, for a productive harvest the most appropriate temperature interval is accepted as between 50°F (10°C) and 86°F (30°C).[ag]

[ad] www.guaranteedweather.com/page.php?content_id=80 (24.05.2006).
[ae] www.wrma.org/wrma/index.php?option=com_ content&task=view&id=27&Itemid=32 (02.06.2006).
[af] www.guaranteedweather.com/industries/energy/research/decision.pdf (01.06.2006).
[ag] www.wrma.org/wrma/library/file775.pdf (05.06.2006).

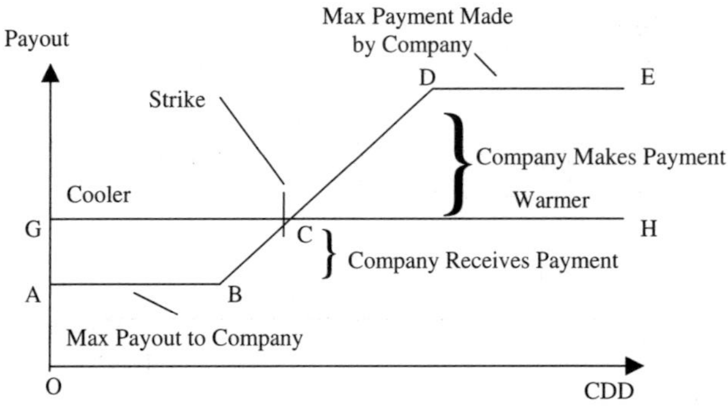

Figure 9: Wheather risk swap.

Under or over this interval consists a significant risk for agricultural producers. To hedge this risk, it is possible to take a position available for protection by utilizing several strategies against the temperature under the floor or over the cap. For instance, collar option, butterfly spreads or straddle strategies which enable such position can be used (Levich, 1998, pp. 408–411) for hedging the risk of temperature out of the band which is between below and above threshold.

However, collars seem like weather risk swap, the floors and the caps in collar states the lower and upper limits, whereas the floors and caps in swap states the limits of minimum and maximum payment which are current for the parties. In this respect, as will be seen with a comparison of Figs. 8 and Fig. 9,[ah] there is an important difference between collar and swap.

6 Applicability of Weather Risk Derivatives in Türkiye

According to the data of 2005, consisting 35% of population, 30% of total employment, 11.2% of GDP[ai] and 11.2% of exports,[aj] agriculture undoubtedly is very important for Turkish economy. However, the climatic conditions and the geography of the country consists a very suitable understructure for agriculture, the high volatility of in-season or inter-season changes increases the risks emerging from weather conditions.

Furthermore, alongside agriculture, weather conditions concern many sectors including energy, construction and health. In comparison with many

[ah]www.guaranteedweather.com/page.php?content_id=83 (25.05.2006).
[ai]www.dpt.gov.tr/sektor/sektor/htm (05.06.2006).
[aj]www.dtm.gov.tr/ead/SEKTOR/sektor.htm (05.06.2006).

other countries, for its climatic and geographical position, Türkiye's economical and industrial wavelengths are affected from weather conditions more than it is imagined. Consequently, weather risk management and the measures for controlling the weather risk are distinctly important for Türkiye.

Nonetheless, it is observed that preventive and compensative instruments which can be used in WRM are extremely limited in Türkiye with respect to other countries. It is comprehended that a significant part of necessary arrangements is about insurance sector. Also, agricultural insurances are being preferred by a small number of producers (0.51%, 0.44% and 0.74% of total production of premium other than life insurance, respectively 2003, 2004, and 2005),[ak] when compared to the size of the sector.

The only serious arrangement numbered 5363 is The Law of Agricultural Insurances (Official Gazette: 25852) which is enforced in 21.06.2005. Considering the growth of agricultural insurances up until today, it is possible to estimate that the enforced law can create an evident improvement only in medium and long term. Besides, the insurances about weather risks consist of a limited part of WRM, and the sole existence of agricultural insurances covering certain risks intensifies the limitation.

In addition, the only available exchange market for trading derivatives about WRM is İzmir Futures and Option Market (VOB) in Türkiye. VOB, the first private exchange market of Türkiye,[al] established by 24,558 numbered Official Gazette in 19.10.2001 enables to trade on limited products of the derivatives such as foreign currency, interest, index and commodity, for it has not completed the introduction period and has not been sufficiently known yet.

Therefore, it seems improbable for near future to begin trading WRM derivatives in this exchange, which are crucial for such an agricultural country and for sectors related with weather conditions. Although the data obtained from the Ministry of Environment and Forestry, General Directorate of Turkish State Meteorological Services[am] which constitutes the understructure for derivatives includes the necessary detail and period, there seems to be a long way to WRM applications in Türkiye, for financial markets are not deep enough particularly in derivatives and for informational and

[ak] www.tsrsb.org.tr/tsrsb/Istatistikler/Konsolide+Kar−Zarar+Tabloları/Teknik+Kar−Zarar+Tabloları) (05.06.2006).
[al] www.vob.org.tr/VOBPortalTur/DesktopDefault.aspx?tabid=100 (05.06.2006).
[am] www.meteor.gov.tr (05.06.2006).

institutional level to provide agriculture producers and other sectors is not accomplished yet.

7 Conclusion

It is observed that climatic changes are becoming more and more intensified with industrialization and global warming. This situation affects the economy of all the countries and directly or indirectly causes fluctuations in the incomes and benefits of many firms. In this respect, weather risk affecting almost all the sectors and all the levels of production and exploitation of individuals and firms is an element of risk should be managed, which causes the depreciation of figures of plans and budgets.

Weather risk categorized as systematic risk up till today is now among avoidable risks by virtue of the derivatives offered by constantly developing financial markets. Continuously growing since the first transaction realized in the USA, Chicago Mercantile Exchange (CME) in 1997, financial weather risk markets have reached a diversity and gravity enabling many industries from supermarket chains to transportation firms, from energy companies to ice-cream firms and to skiing centers to trade internationally.

The foremost financial products about Weather Risk Management which can be utilized in OTC markets as well the organized ones are: hedge instruments or agreements including forward, option, swap, exotic derivatives. However, there are different financial derivatives improved for any possible risk that can be created by the change of weather conditions, it is not possible to claim that they can hedge the total loss for some of the derivatives include floor and cap, and for some agreements have payment limits.

Despite this situation, the derivatives about WRM

(1) provide an effect ceasing the asymmetry of predicted-real in budgets, which is created by unexpected changes in weather conditions and thus, reduces the risks of unpredictability,
(2) limit the fluctuations of income and benefit,
(3) remove the imbalance between production and stockpile,
(4) enable the control of pricing and production risks,
(5) positively affect the firms' market prices and the credibility of their assets,

(6) cause deepening and internationally integration of the markets by increasing the diversity of products with alternatives they offered in financial markets,
(7) and consequently, contribute to the stability of general economic structure.

Despite these positive qualifications of the derivative markets about WRM, developed countries make use of these financial techniques more than developing ones, as they are new financial instruments.

In Türkiye, there is necessary legal and technical understructure, and healthy, sufficient meteorological data at international standards for application of this unknown and unused financial protection technique. İzmir Futures and Option Market (VOB) seems to have the capacity for trading this kind of derivatives. Yet, it is understood that, in Türkiye, the derivatives about WRM cannot be traded in organized or unorganized markets in a short term. For:

(1) The lack of consciousness to manage the weather risk.
(2) The lack of an argumentation or a study or a share of information on the derivatives about WRM.
(3) Since 19.10.2001, the date VOB was established, the introduction period of the derivatives which are basically subject to transaction is incomplete. It makes harder to increase the diversity of transactions and to constitute an available environment for putting this important subject which affects all economy on the agenda.
(4) Inability of financial markets to reach a potential gravity and limitations on the international integration make harder the perception, measurement and management of risk.

Consequently, one of the most effective instruments for increasing the sensitivity of financial and production vibrations toward each other and to provide a one-direction oscillation toward a channel of stability, the weather derivatives to become widespread in Turkish Financial Market primarily require a healthy and strong structure for traditional derivatives.

References

Agricultural Insurance Act, Code: 5363, Official Gazette (21.06.2005).
Clemmons, L (2001). Weather risk management. In *The Second National Conference on Scientific and Technical Data,* Dublin.

Cogen, J (1998). What is weather risk. *PMA-Power Marketing Association Magazine* (05/98).

Dischel, B (1999). Weather risk management at the frozen falls fuel company. *Applied Derivative Trading*, New York.

Dischel, B (2000). Alliant energy's use of weather derivatives. In *WRMA Annual Convention*, Paris.

Hull, JC (2006). *Options, Futures and Other Derivatives*, 6th Ed. New Jersey: Pearson Prentice Hall.

Katsuyama, M (2005). Cross-commodity wheather options to hedge energy market risks. In *WRMA 2005 Asia-Pacific Meeting*, Tokyo.

Lettre, J (2000). Weather risk management: Weather insurance, weather derivatives. Rivier College, Nashua.

Levich, RM (1998). *International Financial Markerts, Prices and Policies*. In *Finance Series*. New York: McGraw Hill Intenational Editions.

McKay, S (2001). A Practical Guide to Weather Hedging in The Canadian Electric Utility Industry, Toronto.

O'Hearne, B (2004). Earth Observation Summit. New York, USA.

O'Hearne, B (2005). Europe and Americas update strong growth — Where and why? In *2005 Asia Pacific Meeting*, Hong Kong.

Ruck, T and Polasek, J (2001). Fuel Co. case study. In *WRMA Asian Committee Meeting*, Tokyo.

Saunders, A and Cornet, MM (2006). *Financial Institutions Management: A Risk Management Approach*, 5th Ed. New York: McGraw-Hill.

Scholten, S (2000). *Weather Hedging: Utility Decision Process*. San Francisco: Vermont Gas Systems.

Stell, J (2005). *Results of the 2005 PwC Survey*. Londra: PricewaterhouseCoopers.

Swift, B (2001). Construction, ingenuity and derivatives: A profile. *Risk Management Magazine* 48(11).

CHAPTER 6

THE BASEL II FRAMEWORK IMPLEMENTATION AND SECURITIZATION

*Marie-Florence Lamy**

Securitization and credit derivatives are now commonly used by European Banks as tools in dynamic assets and liabilities management in order to optimize the allocation of regulatory capital by main activities and to increase their profitability through developing a maximum credit capacity with a more sensitive risk management.

In this chapter we wish to address the consequences of the implementation of the Basel II framework on securitizations in Europe, using data collected in QIS 5, and try to determine if it will change their utilization by European banks in their strategic allocation of capital.

We show that under the new framework, securitization does not lead to an economy in regulatory capital, and that considering the wide range of results under the Internal Rating Based approaches, we need to undertake a microeconomic analysis of the securitization portfolio of an international bank to measure the impact of the implementation of the new framework on traditional and synthetic securitizations.

1 The Role of Securitization for European Banks

In the years since 2000, securitization has become a major instrument in assets and liabilities management for European banks. Statistics show that gross issuances of credit linked notes have become significant since 2000, ABCP representing the main segment of these issuances.

*Groupe Esc Rouen, 1, rue du Maréchal Juin, BP 215, 76825 Mont-Saint-Aignan, France. Marie-florence.lamy@groupe-esc-rouen.fr

The use of securitization for originating banks aims at:

— restoring liquidity of the bank, thus hedging the liquidity risk as well as concentration risk, which is achieved by the effective cession of assets to an SPV in a traditional securitization;
— diminishing the regulatory capital amount which stems from the lending activity of the bank, representing now 8% of the exposures held by banks weighted by standard coefficients by categories of borrowers called risk weights.

Under the Basel I accord, banks have widely used traditional and synthetic securitizations in order to reduce their obligation in capital, thus enabling them to renew their lending capacity or to be able to benefit from new lending opportunities with highest margins. The choice of exposures and the securitizations structure are carefully done in order to optimize the final yield of the bank capital.

A synthetic securitization is defined in the Basel II framework (§540) as "a structure with at least two different stratified risk positions or tranches that reflect different degrees of credit risk where credit risk of an underlying pool of exposures is transferred, in whole or in part, through the use of funded (e.g. credit-linked notes) or unfunded (e.g. credit default swaps) credit derivatives or guarantees that serve to hedge the credit risk of the portfolio".

These synthetic securitizations have in the recent period become the most used instrument by European banks in their Assets and Liabilities management to reallocate capital by activities in order to maximize the bank ROC, and have largely contributed to increase the European banks' gross margins.

Although synthetic securitizations are technically burdensome and costly since the originating bank pays the excess spread though the CDS premium, they stay profitable because they allow to reduce very significantly the capital obligation by substituting the banks' risk weight of 20% to the corporate risk weight of 100%, thanks to credit swaps. The originating banks often keep the equity, i.e. the most risky tranche of credit linked notes or obligations, and may provide the collateral asset, or liquidity facilities in a repurchase agreement.

Used by banks as a major instrument in their strategic allocation of capital, the synthetic securitization funded as unfunded, have known a rapid development in Europe. This role of securitization may change with the revision of the regulatory framework by the Basel committee.

"In developing the revised framework the committee has sought to arrive at significantly more risk-sensitive capital requirements which are conceptually sound". To reach this goal the Basel II framework allows banks to use their internal risk assessments as inputs to calculate the obligation in capital and has taken into account all developments of modern finance.

The final version of the "International Convergence of Capital Measurement and Capital Standards" includes a thorough analysis of securitization mechanisms in the fourth part of Pillar one — Credit Risk — in order to correctly take their economic consequences into account.

In this chapter, we wish to address the consequences of the implementation of the Basel II Framework on securitizations using results of the 5th Quantitative Impact Study (QIS 5) and try to determine how it will change strategies of international banks in their capital allocations and dynamic assets and liabilities management.

2 The Basel II Securitization Framework and Results of QIS 5

In June 2006, the Basel II committee published the results of the fifth Quantitative Impact Study, QIS 5, which took place between October and December 2005.

This study gives the first data measuring the impact of the new framework on securitization, from 382 banks from 32 countries participating in the survey (see http://www.bis.org/bcbs/qis/qis5.htm).

The primary objective of the survey was to evaluate the potential changes on obligation in capital under the Basel II framework. The analysis of its results should allow us to measure the impact of the new framework on banks obligation in capital linked to exposures of securitization.

The new framework results in a global economy in capital required moderate for standardized approach $\approx$1.3%, but significant for foundation and advanced Internal Rating Based (IRB) approaches, for which change in total minimum capital varies from 8% to 29% according to banks categories.

Main contributors to this decrease are retail mortgages, corporate, and SME + retail portfolios.

These global results are in line with the favorable treatment of mortgages and SME financing of the new framework, and with its fundamental aim: to adjust capital requirement to the evaluation of loss expectation instead of the Basel I standards.

Traditional securitizations as well as synthetic ones unfunded, CDS, or funded by credit linked notes or obligations issuances are taken into account and operational requirements for each case are fully developed in the securitization Framework.

The three approaches for evaluating Credit Risk are applicable to securitization exposures which are either retained or held by the originating bank or resulting from investment in tranches by any bank.

2.1 Standardized Approach for Securitization Exposure

Exposures are to be weighted by given risk weight that compare to the risk weight of underlying assets as follows:

LT rating category	AAA to AA$^-$	A$^+$to A$^-$	BBB$^+$ to BBB$^-$	BB$^+$ to B$^-$	Below B$^-$/unrated
Standardized approach Corp. Banks	20	50	100	100	150/100 150
Securitization	20	50	100	350	Deduction
ST rating categories	A1/P1	A2/P2	A3/P3	Other	
Corp. and Banks	20	50	100	150	
Securitization	20	50	100	Deduction	

For retail claims most assets' risk weight is 75%, residential mortgages 35%, and commercial ones 100%; for short term exposures the securitization risk weight is the A1/P1 one.

The comparison of both treatments shows that there is no economy in capital requirement for underlying exposures rated above BB$^+$ and A3/P3, and that for low and unrated exposures the securitization treatment is highly penalizing with a risk weight of 350% instead of 100% or the obligation to deduce the below B$^-$and unrated exposures from the regulatory capital (50% off Tiers 1, 50% off Tiers 2).

The exceptions to this severe treatment are

(1) for unrated, the most senior exposure which receives a "look through" treatment — average risk weight of underlying exposures;
(2) second loss position in ABCP programs which incurs the greater of 100% and the highest risk weight in the underlying exposures;
(3) eligible liquidity facilities which are weighted at 20%, under conditions, or at the highest risk weight of underlying facilities. This 20% risk weight compares to a previous 100% risk weight when the facility was at the bank's balance sheet; thus for eligible facilities, the economy in capital required is significant 1.6% instead of 8% of exposure.

Securitization portfolio change in minimum required capital under the standardized approach in percentages.

Banks	Group 1			Group 2		
	Size	Change in MRC	Contribution	Size	Change in MRC	Contribution
G10 average	3.0	7.4	0.2	1.7	30.6	0.5
CEBS average	2.6	12.9	0.4	1.2	5.0	0.1
Non-G10 average	0.3	102.4	0.3	0.8	−18.2	−0.1

Overall, the standardized approach should result in a greater capital requirement for securitization than for the same exposures directly held in the balance sheet by banks. This is confirmed by QIS 5 results.

The size represents the ratio of exposures linked to securitization operations over the total exposures of all portfolios, and the contribution represents the impact of the change in overall required capital due to the securitization change in minimum capital requirement.

Results for the standardized approach reflect the large variety of situations covered by data; for all cases but one the MRC is higher than the present requirement in capital, which is contradictory to the fact that risk weights are smaller in the standardized approach than the Basel I ones. Exposures retained by originating banks or investment assets may be in low rating tranches, which explains large increases in MRC.

Thus averages are not very significant, and a microanalysis of each securitization portfolio appears to us as more adequate to draw a relevant conclusion.

2.2 IRB Approach for Securitization Exposures

Under the IRB approaches, banks internally rate exposures and calculate the minimum required capital for each internally rated class of its portfolio.

The securitization framework specifies that a Rating Based Approach (RBA) must be applied for rated securitization exposures, and when they are not rated, banks choose between the use of the supervisory formula to calculate risk weights and an Internal Assessment Approach (IAA) to map them, the latest method being only applicable for ABCP programs.

The maximum capital requirement is the one obtained under IRB by the underlying exposures had they not been securitized.

Risk weight assets are obtained by multiplying exposures by risk weights given in Exhibit 1, which represents versus weights presently used for the Cook ratio, a significant economy for rating above BBB$^-$ and a high penalty for below BBB$^-$.

In order to avoid a full deduction of unrated exposures off the capital, the bank should either apply the supervisory formula or use the IAA to determine their risk weights. The IAA consists in a mapping of an equivalent external rating of an eligible ECAI. The bank must satisfy operational conditions in order to use IAA, including the ability to use ECAI methodologies in developing its internal assessment.

After having estimated the internal rating through the IAA process, the bank will apply the RBA method to them. If this is not feasible the supervisory formula is used to determine directly the IRB capital charge (Exhibit 2).

Overall the IRB approach should result in an economy of required capital since unfavorable cases are capped by the maximum capital requirement of the underlying exposures had they not been securitized (see §610).

The structure of the weight scale of RBA shows that the economy in capital obligation directly depends upon the seniority of tranches held by the banks, and or of the rating of exposures retained. Thus the enhancing method resulting in leaving the originating bank with equity tranche is highly penalizing.

QIS 5 results vary largely among groups of banks.

Securitization portfolio change in MRC under most likely IRB approach (i.e. foundation on advanced according to Bank).

Portfolio	Group 1			Group 2		
	Size	Change in MRC	Contribution	Size	Change in MRC	Contribution
G10 average	2.8	0.5	0.0	1.7	−24.1	−0.4
CEBS average	2.0	8.6	0.2	1.3	−26.6	−0.4
Non-G10 average	1.3	−35.0	−0.5	1.9	−59.8	−1.2

The largest banks, Group 1 of G10 and CEBS, show as the impact of the new framework on minimum required capital linked to securitization exposures an increase 0.5%–8.6%.

For smaller banks and non-G10 banks the change is a very significant decrease of MRC, −24% to −60%.

Again these results correspond to different situations, and average results may not be significant.

The analysis by components of these increases in MRC shows that the MRC change is highly sensitive to the quality of exposures and to the proportion of unrated exposures (Exhibit 3).

As largest banks are more likely to be the originating ones, the fact that they are penalized by the new framework induces us to think that securitization no longer leads to a reduction of minimum required capital, and that each case must be carefully analyzed in order to correctly measure its effect on the obligation in capital and the capital allocation strategy of the bank.

3 Consequences of the Implementation of the Basel II Framework on Securitization

The large variation of change in minimum required capital given by QIS 5 data shows that the economy in regulatory capital given by securitization is highly dependent on the securitization structure and on the quality of the exposures held.

For synthetic securitizations, where the originating bank often retains both senior and equity tranches, global results indicate that for G10 Group 1 banks, the most concerned, the economy is small and might be questioned considering the cost and complexity of operations.

Though the limited size of the sample and the variety of structures could give misleading averages, the widespread range of detailed results indicates that a microeconomic analysis of various securitizations of a bank is needed in order to separate traditional securitizations from synthetic ones and to measure exactly for both categories the impact of securitizations on minimum capital requirement under the new framework.

It will allow us to check to what extent securitization still implies an actual significant economy of regulatory capital. As the new framework, under the IRB approaches, aims at sizing the minimum capital requirement to the expectancy of future losses linked to the nature of exposures, all securitizations which maintain the most risky exposures in the originating bank portfolio either directly or through the acquisition of equity tranche and hedges, the credit risk on others with a CDS should not result in an economy of regulatory capital versus keeping all underlying exposures.

Hence for most synthetic securitizations the benefit might be too weak to resume their use as tools in assets and liabilities management with the objective to decrease the obligation in regulatory capital, allowing the originating bank to reallocate this economy to other activities.

Exhibit 1: International convergence of capital measurement and capital standards.

615. Banks may apply the risk weights for senior positions if the effective number of underlying exposures (N, as defined in paragraph 633) is 6 or more and the position is senior as defined above. When N is less than 6, the risk weights in column 4 of the first table below apply. In all other cases, the risk weights in column 3 of the first table below apply.

RBA risk weights the external assessment represents long-term credit rating and/or an inferred rating derived from a long-term assessment

External Rating (illustrative)	Risk weights for senior positions and eligible senior IAA exposures	Base risk weights		Risk weights for tranches backed by non-granular pools
AAA	7%	12%		20%
AA	8%	15%		25%
A+	10%	18%		
A	12%	20%		35%
A−	20%	35%		
BBB+	35%		50%	
BBB	60%		75%	
BBB−		100%		
BB+		250%		
BB		425%		
BB−		650%		
Below BB-and unrated		Deduction		

RBA risk weights when assessment represents a short-term credit rating

External Rating (illustrative)	Risk weights for senior positions	Base risk weights	Risk weights for tranches backed by non-granular pools
A-1/P-1	7%	12%	20%
A-2/P-2	12%	20%	35%
A-3/P-3	60%	75%	75%
All other ratings/unrated	Deduction	Deduction	Deduction

Exhibit 2: Fifth quantitative impact study, QIS 5.

624. The Supervisory Formula is given by the following expression:

$$(2)\quad S[L] = \begin{Bmatrix} L & \text{when } L \leq K_{IRB} \\ K_{IRB} + K[L] - K[K_{IRB}] & \text{when } K_{IRB} < L \\ +(dK_{IRB}/\omega)(1 - e^{\omega(K_{RRB-L})K_{IRB}}) & \end{Bmatrix}$$

where

$$h = (1 - K_{IRB}/LGD)^{N})$$
$$c = K_{IRB}/(1 - h)$$
$$v = \frac{(LGD - K_{IRB})K_{IRB} + 0.25(1 - LGD)K_{IRB}}{N}$$
$$f = \left(\frac{v + K_{IRB}^2}{1 - h}C^2\right), \frac{(1 - K_{IRB})K_{IRB} - v}{(1 - h)I}$$
$$g = \frac{(1 - c)c}{f} - 1$$
$$a = g \cdot c$$
$$b = g \cdot (1 - c)$$
$$d = 1 - (1 - h), (1 - Beta[K_{IRB}; a, b])$$
$$K[l] = (1 - H((1 - Beta[L; a, b])l + Beta[L, a - 1, b]c)$$

625. In this expressions, $Beta[L;\ a,\ b]$ refers to the cumulative beta distribution with parameters a and at L.[a]

626. The supervisory-determined parameters in the above expressions are as follows:

$$\tau = 1000, \quad \text{and} \quad \omega = 20$$

[a]The cumulative beta distribution function is available, for example, in Excel as the function BETADIST

Exhibit 3:

Table 25: Change in minimum required capital for the securitization portfolio in per cent, G10 Group 1 banks.

	Standardised approach	IRB approach
Total risk-weighted assets; of which	−15.5	−18.5
— Risk-weighted assets rated exposures	−25.6	−18.7
— Risk-weighted assets unrated exposures	12.0	27.7
— Investors' interest early amortization	0.0	0.1
— Correction for cap	−2.0	−20.8
— Correction for provisions		6.8
Positions to be deducted	23.2	19.0
Overall change in MRC versus current	7.7	0.5

This table only includes banks for which complete QIS 5 workbooks were available.

Table 26: Change in minimum required capital for the securitization portfolio in per cent, G10 Group 2 banks.

	Standardized approach	IRB approach
Total risk-weighted assets; of which	−69.5	−62.6
— Risk-weighted assets rated exposures	−52.5	−56.2
— Risk-weighted assets unrated exposures	−16.2	5.0
— Investors' interest early amortization	0.0	0.0
— Correction for cap	−0.7	−11.4
— Correction for provisions		0.0
Positions to be deducted	79.7	45.4
Overall change in MRC versus current	10.2	−17.3

This table only includes banks for which complete QIS 5 workbooks were available.

Table 27: Change in minimum required capital for the securitization portfolio in per cent, CEBES Group 1 banks.

	Standardized approach	IRB approach
Total risk-weighted assets; of which	3.7	−5.8
— Risk-weighted assets rated exposures	−17.1	−10.1
— Risk-weighted assets unrated exposures	23.4	43.4
— Investors' interest early amortization	0.0	0.0
— Correction for cap	−2.6	−29.4
— Correction for provisions		−9.7
Positions to be deducted	17.5	13.7
Overall change in MRC versus current	21.2	7.9

This table only includes banks for which complete QIS 5 workbooks were available.

Table 28: Change in minimum required capital for the securitization portfolio in per cent, CEBS Group 2 banks.

	Standardized approach	IRB approach
Total risk-weighted assets; of which	−67.5	−60.3
– Risk-weighted assets rated exposures	−49.6	−52.3
– Risk-weighted assets unrated exposures	−16.9	−7.4
– Investors' interest early amortization	0.0	0.0
– Correction for cap	−1.0	−0.6
– Correction for provisions		00
Positions to be deducted	63.6	45.8
Overall change in MRC versus current	−3.9	−14.6

This table only includes banks for which complete QIS 5 workbooks were available.

Further Reading

Banque de France, Revue de la Stabilité Financiére (2004). Résultats de l'enquête de place française sur les instruments de transfert de risque de crédit, Juin 2004.

BIS Basel Committee on Banking Supervision (2005). International convergence of capital measurement and capital standards; A revised framework. Updated November 2005.

BIS Bas. Committee on Banking Supervision (2005). QIS 5 Results, November 2005.

BIS Bas. Committee on Banking Supervision (2004). Changes to the securitization framework, 30 January 2004.

BIS Basel Committee on Banking Supervision (2005). The role of ratings in structured finance: Issues and implications, January 2005.

Cousseran, O and Rahmouni, I (2005). Le marché des CDOs. Banque de France, Revue de la Stabilité Financière, Juin 2005.

Fédération Européenne de l'industrie bancaire Lettre à Madame Nouy (Décembre 2002).

Fitch Ratings (2005). Basel II, bottom-line impact on securitization markets, September 2005.

Hull, J and White, A (2004). Valuation of a CDO a *n*th to default without Monte-Carlo simulation. University of Turnto.

Olléon Assouan, E (2004). Techniques de marché des dérivés de crédit: les swaps de défaut, Juin (2004).

Secrétariat général de la Commission Bancaire (2002). Initial comments on the Basel II second working paper on securitization, November 2002.

CHAPTER 7

STOCHASTIC TIME CHANGE, VOLATILITY, AND NORMALITY OF RETURNS: A HIGH-FREQUENCY DATA ANALYSIS WITH A SAMPLE OF LSE STOCKS

Olfa Borsali and Amel Zenaidi†*

The purpose of this chapter is to verify whether the stochastic time change leading to a Gaussian representation of the conditional asset returns density is best represented by the number of trades. We use the same procedure then on Ané and Geman (2000) to estimate the four first moments of the latent stochastic time change/information flow that permits to recover the normality of stock returns, using a sample of LSE highly traded stocks. We are able to show empirically that the moments greater than one of the stochastic time changes coincide virtually with the moments of the number of trades. Then, we recenter the number of trades so as to have the same mean than the stochastic time change. The distribution of returns conditioned on the recentered number of trades does not correspond to the normal case. We argue that, in our data, the choice of the cumulative number of trades to represent the economic clock is not adequate. Finally, we explain why we find such results which are in line with recent empirical findings, in particular Murphy and Izzeldin (2005) and Gillemot et al. (2005).

*IHEC Carthage-Tunisia, oborsali@yahoo.fr

†a.zenaidi@planet.tn

1 Introduction

Financial markets operate in a continuous way, and transactions are made at irregular intervals so that classical financial databases, recording trades at daily and weekly frequencies, are not able to analyze the price process and to address the question of what process is directing the price movements, because they may conceal information contained in the intradaily price variations.

The availability of high frequency databases, enhanced by the technological advent, has helped researchers in investigating the empirical behavior of the trading process. For example, many researchers such as Wood *et al.* (1985) focused on volatility and volume intradaily seasonals, showing both U-shaped patterns (in the NYSE). Such regularities have led to the study of linkages between trading variables, especially volume and volatility (measured as absolute or squared price changes). In Foster and Viswanathan (1993), volatility and volume show similar intradaily patterns and are positively correlated. Karpoff (1987) reviewed empirical and theoretical research into the price change–volume relationship in financial markets and concluded that, while this relationship is positive, it is asymmetric because short positions are more costly than long positions in some financial markets. One explanation of simultaneous observations of large volumes and large price changes is their common ties to a directing process that reflects information flow. This idea is the core of the Mixture of Distributions Hypothesis, which motivates Clark (1973) in formulating a model that describes the return process as subordinated to a normal distribution, where the directing process (reflecting the different rates of information flow) is measured by the volume of transactions. Clark claimed that the observation of the market activity according to a stochastic timescale measured by the cumulative volume of transactions permits to recover the normality of stock returns. Thus, calendar time is probably not adequate to measure time in financial markets. Hence, an activity-based measure of time should be used in order to obtain desirable statistical properties of the returns distribution such as normality. In the same context, Ané and Geman (2000) showed that normality of stock returns can be recovered through a stochastic time change interpreted economically as the number of trades. In particular, they provided evidence that stochastic time change moments coincide virtually with those of the number of trades, apart from the first moment.

On the one hand, their conjecture was supported by the findings of Jones *et al.* (1994) arguing that the volume of transactions has virtually no explanatory power of the volatility when it is already conditioned on the number of trades. As a consequence, the number of trades is more likely to represent the increments of the operational time in financial markets because it is more responsible than the volume for the price movements. On the other hand, there are some empirical studies that fail in reproducing the Ané and Geman (2000) results (for example, Murphy and Izzeldin, 2005; Gillemot *et al.*, 2005; Li, 2004). These controversial results lead us to test the relevance of the number of trades as an approximation of the stochastic time change that generates a Gaussian distribution for the return process. For this purpose, we use a sample of highly traded LSE stocks over the period from 16 January 2006 to 25 January 2006. We then follow the same methodology on Ané and Geman (2000) to estimate the four first moments of the stochastic time change. Then we identify the stochastic time change through its moments and verify whether they match the moments of the number of trades. The next step concerns the construction of the return density in the new transaction time which allows us either to validate or to reject the Ané and Geman (2000) results.

The plan of this chapter is as follows. In Section 2, we present theoretical and empirical arguments that motivate rescaling financial data according to a stochastic timescale rather than a calendar timescale. Likewise, we revisit the main empirical studies highlighting that the operational time may be represented either by the number of trades or by their volume. This section gives also an insight into subordinated processes, directing processes, and stochastic time changes. Section 3 is dedicated to the study of the relative performances of the number of trades and volume in explaining the stochastic volatility, using high frequency data on some LSE stocks. In Section 4, we test whether the number of trades best defines the stochastic time change that permits to recover the normality of returns, using the method of moments introduced by Ané and Geman (2000). Finally, Section 5 summarizes our results.

2 Sampling Financial Data: Stochastic Versus Calendar Timescale

2.1 The Impact of Time on the Price Process

A vast amount of theoretical and empirical financial studies have focused on the impact of the timing of transactions on the price process. The intuition that financial markets evolve in a sporadic way, let us expect that the interval between two successive trades is likely to be of paramount importance in the price formation analysis. The question of time and its effect on prices has divided the microstructure literature, which is devoted to the study of the mechanics of price formation, into two groups.

In the first group, time *per se* plays no role on the price formation process. In particular, in the Kyle (1985) model, orders are grouped which makes the timing when individual orders arrive irrelevant for the market maker. This study claims that it is order flow and not orders timing that affects the market maker quote revisions. Similarly, according to Glosten and Milgrom (1985), orders arrive to the market in a probabilistic fashion known to the market maker. It means that the timing of trades is exogenous to the price process since it conveys no information about the true value of the asset.

In the second group of models, both the occurrence and the lack of trades are informative because they may be correlated with different aspects of information. The existence of short sale constraints in the Diamond and Verrecchia (1987) model makes non-trading intervals impart bad news because informed traders would be prevented from selling shares when they do not own them. Consequently, time is a prominent source of information for traders and the market maker. This standpoint was supported subsequently by Easley and O'Hara (1992) who found that while trades provide signals of the direction of any new information (good or bad news), the lack of trades illuminates market participants about the existence of any new information. More explicitly, informed traders exploit their private information and trade accordingly only if new information exists. Thus, long durations are likely to be associated with the absence of news arrival. Time is endogenous to the price process implying that even non-trading periods can cause quotes and prices to move.

Many empirical studies have shed light on the role played by time in the process of price dynamics. Hausman *et al.* (1992) estimated ordered probit models for transaction prices where the explanatory variable is time between the current and the last trade. Their evidence showed that time is relevant to the price formation, but it is not clear why such relationship exists. Other studies have investigated the link between durations and the price dynamics. In this respect, Engle and Russel (1994) found that duration, volume, volatility, and spread move simultaneously, which means that price-related variables depend on non-trading periods. In a further research, Engle (2000) provided empirical evidence that longer durations are matched to lower volatility and vice versa. Since time between transactions reflects trading intensity, it becomes easy to conclude that trading intensity is correlated with volatility. In Section 3 of this chapter, we investigate the relationship between contemporaneous volatility and the number of trades which may reflect the intensity of trading in a calendar time basis.

Recently, Dufour and Engle (2000) supported previous findings and showed, using a sample that consists of 18 of the most frequently traded stocks on the NYSE, that time between trades is informative, and smaller durations are mainly associated with a higher price impact of trades, and a faster adjustment to new information.

The relevance of time in the price determination leads to a very important issue: What timescale should we consider in order to understand the price formation dynamics? In fact, the observation of the price process in calendar time may disguise information reflected by intradaily price movements. Consequently, it is absolutely important to specify economically the appropriate time change that permits to understand the price dynamics. The new operational time should be linked to a trading-related variable which affects the price process.

It is also debatable what sampling frequency to choose in order to study the mechanics of price formation. If the trading process shows a similar behavior independently of the sampling frequency, it would not be profitable to consider high frequency data.

2.2 *Two Possible Representations of the Operational Time*

From the existent financial literature, we can register two trading-related variables that are mostly candidates. to represent the increments of the operational time that provide a Gaussian distribution for returns: the volume of transactions as claimed by Clark (1973) and the number of transactions as suggested by Ané and Geman (1996, 2000).

2.2.1 The Volume of Transactions

In the Clark (1973) model, daily price change or return is the sum of intradaily returns. Applying the central limit theorem, according to which the limit distribution of a random sum of random variables is asymptotically normal, it becomes easy to show that the distribution of daily returns is subordinated to the normal distribution. In other words, the distribution of daily returns is a mixture of normal distributions where the mixing variable is reflecting the information flow.

This specification comes from the fact that information is available to traders at a varying rate from one period to another, which results in different price changes during identical intervals of time. More precisely, on periods when no new information is available, trading is slow, and the price process evolves slowly. However, on periods when new information violates old expectations, trading is intensive, and the price process evolves much faster.

The mixture of distributions model formulated by Clark (1973) is basically the same than the subordinated stochastic process model. In fact, the return process can be expressed by

$$X\left(\tau(t)\right) = Y(t),$$

where

$X\left(\tau(t)\right)$ is the subordinated process (that represents the return process itself),

$Y(t)$ is the return process, and

$\tau(t)$ is the directing process and interpreted as a clock measuring the speed of evolution.

The non-normality of intradaily returns is explained by the different rates of information flow to the market. But if we succeed in sampling returns over stochastic intervals of time that contain constant quantities of information flow, it would be possible to recover the normality of returns. Clark (1973) provided evidence that the directing process of cotton futures returns is best represented by the cumulative volume of transactions. Besides, he found that the distribution of the volume is lognormal.

The main empirical finding of this study is that the distribution of returns divided by the square root of adjusted volumes presents smaller values of the kurtosis compared to that related to daily return series. Finally, the distribution of returns conditionally to the volume of transactions is virtually normal.

2.2.2 The Number of Trades

Building on the result of Jones *et al.* (1994), showing that it is the number of transactions and not their size (or volume) that generates volatility, Ané and Geman (2000) set out to determine whether it is the cumulative volume (as in Clark (1973)) or the cumulative number of trades that best defines the operational time. Hence, they introduced a stochastic time change $\Delta\tau$ rather than the directing process τ, and assumed that the return process observed in operational time has a normal distribution, which can be formulated as follows:

$$X(\tau(t))/\Delta\tau \longrightarrow N\left(\mu\,\Delta\tau,\,\sigma^2\Delta\tau\right),$$

where $X(\tau(t))$ represents the return process (it is assumed to be a Brownian motion).

Furthermore, the return process $Y(t) = X(\tau(t))$ is a normal mixture.

The idea of this study consists in identifying the stochastic time change leading to a Gaussian representation of the conditional return density through its moments.

The first six unconditional central moments of the return process $Y_t(m_i(Y_t), i= 1,\ldots,6)$ are expressed in terms of the moments of the stochastic time change $\Delta\tau(m_j(\Delta\tau(t)), j \leq i)$, mean μ, and variance σ^2 of the Brownian motion. Theoretical moment expressions are given by

$$
\begin{aligned}
m_1(Y_t) &= \mu m_1(\Delta\tau(t)),\\
m_2(Y_t) &= \sigma^2 m_1(\Delta\tau(t)) + \mu^2\, m_2(\Delta\tau(t)),\\
m_3(Y_t) &= 3\,\mu\,\sigma^2\, m_2(\Delta\tau(t)) + \mu^3 m_3(\Delta\tau(t)),\\
m_4(Y_t) &= \mu^4 m_4(\Delta\tau(t)) + 6\sigma^2\mu^2 m_3(\Delta\tau(t)) + 6\sigma^2\mu^2 m_1(\Delta\tau(t)) m_2(\Delta\tau(t))\\
&\quad + 3\sigma^4\left[m_2(\Delta\tau(t)) + [m_1(\Delta\tau(t))]^2\right], \qquad (1)\\
m_5(Y_t) &= \mu^5 m_5(\Delta\tau(t)) + 10\,\sigma^2\mu^3 m_4(\Delta\tau(t))\\
&\quad + (10\,\sigma^2\mu^3 m_1(\Delta\tau(t)) + 15\,\mu\sigma^4)\, m_3(\Delta\tau(t))\\
&\quad + 30\,\mu\sigma^4 m_2(\Delta\tau(t)),\\
m_6(Y_t) &= \mu^6 m_6(\Delta\tau(t)) + 15\sigma^6\left[m_3(\Delta\tau(t)) + 3m_2(\Delta\tau(t))\, m_1(\Delta\tau(t))\right.\\
&\quad \left.+ (m_1(\Delta\tau(t)))^3\right]\\
&\quad + 15\mu^4\sigma^2 m_5(\Delta\tau(t)) + m_4(\Delta\tau(t)) m_1(\Delta\tau(t))\\
&\quad + 45\mu^2\sigma^4\left[m_4(\Delta\tau(t)) + 2m_3(\Delta\tau(t)) m_1(\Delta\tau(t))\right.\\
&\quad \left.+ m_2(\Delta\tau(t))(m_1(\Delta\tau(t)))^2\right].
\end{aligned}
$$

The first six moments of $\Delta\tau(t)$ were estimated through the resolution of the following nonlinear optimization program:

$$
\text{Min } U = \sum_{j=1}^{k}\left[E(\exp(\beta_j Y_t))^{\text{theoretical}} - E(\exp(\beta_j Y_t))^{\text{empirical}}\right]^2
$$

under the constraints on equality $(m_i(Y_t))^{\text{theoretical}} = (m_i(Y_t))^{\text{empirical}}$.

The theoretical and empirical expressions of the moment generating function of the return process are as follows:

$$E(\exp(\beta_j Y_t))^{\text{theoretical}} \cong \exp(A\, m_1(\Delta\tau(t))) * \left[1 + \frac{A^2}{2}\, m_2(\Delta\tau(t)) + \frac{A^3}{6} m_3(\Delta\tau(t)) + \frac{A^4}{24} m_4 \Delta\tau(t))\right],$$

where $A = \beta\,\mu + \frac{1}{2}\beta^2\sigma^2$.

$$E\left[\exp(\beta_j\, Y_t)\right]^{\text{empirical}} = \frac{1}{n}\sum_{i=1}^{n} \exp(\beta_j\, Y_{t_i}).$$

Ané and Geman (2000) applied their model to high frequency transactions data from two technological stocks (Intel and Cisco), over a period of one year (from 2 January 1997 to 31 December 1997), using several timescales. They found that the moments of the stochastic time change $\Delta\tau(t)$ greater than 1 are perfectly matched by the moments of the number of trades, whereas the mean differs significantly.

According to a standard hypothesis in finance assuming that a probability distribution is defined by the knowledge of its several (usually four) moments, Ané and Geman (2000) argued that the cumulative number of trades is a good approximation of the operational time. Then, they recentered the number of trades so as to obtain a mean equal to the mean of the stochastic time change. Lastly, they constructed the distribution of returns conditionally to the recentered number of trades and found it virtually normal, which led them to conclude that the stochastic time change generating conditional normality for return process is well represented by the number of trades.

This outstanding result attracted the interest of many researchers who attempted to reproduce the Ané and Geman (2000) methodology in order to recover the normality of conditional asset returns. Recently, Gillemot *et al.* (2005) proposed to demonstrate the normality of returns in transaction time (or operational time measured by the cumulative number of trades). In contrast to Ané and Geman (2000), they found that transaction normalized return series, extracted from the same database over the same period, deviates from the normal case. Besides, Murphy and Izzeldin (2005) applied the Ané and Geman (2000) procedure to simulate data and concluded that true values of the stochastic time change moments (greater than 2) cannot be accurately recovered, which makes the method of moments controversial.

In view of these contradictory results, it would be very interesting to test the adequacy of the number of trades in approximating the stochastic time change that permits to recover normal conditional returns, using a sample of highly traded LSE stocks.

3 Empirical Analysis of the Volatility Determinants

3.1 Data

Our data is collected from Reuters and contains tick-by-tick records of bid and ask prices, volumes of transactions, and the exact moments of their occurrence, on a sample of highly traded LSE stocks, namely REUTERS, VODAFONE, LGEN, BA, HSBA, HBOS, BT, BP, and TESCO. These stocks are among the FTSE 100 index shares, which are formed by the 100 most liquid stocks in the London Stock Exchange (LSE). In addition, they correspond to various economic fields. Our study covers the period from 16 January 2006 to 25 January 2006. We construct return series Y_t[a] at 1 min intervals. Then we count the corresponding number of transactions ΔT_t and volume ΔV_t in each interval.

3.2 Empirical Evidence

In order to compare the volume and the number of trades in terms of their performance in explaining the stochastic volatility, we adopt first the Schwert (1990) procedure which provides unbiased estimates of return standard deviations. We compute volatility series expressed by $\sigma_t = \sqrt{\frac{\pi}{2}}\,|\varepsilon_t|$, where ε_t is the innovation in the following regression:

$$Y_t = \sum_{j=1}^{12} \delta_j Y_{t-j} + \varepsilon_t.$$

Second, we estimate the following three regressions (introduced by Jones *et al.* (1994)) using least square estimators.

[a] $Y_t = \mathrm{Log}\frac{P_t}{P_{t-1}}$; $P_t = \frac{a_t+b_t}{2}$, where a_t is the ask price and b_t is the bid price.

$$\sigma_t = \alpha + \beta\, \Delta V_t + \sum_{j=1}^{12} \rho_j \, \hat{\sigma_{t-j}} + \eta_t^1, \tag{2}$$

$$\sigma_t = \alpha + \gamma\, \Delta T_t + \sum_{j=1}^{12} \rho_j \, \hat{\sigma_{t-j}} + \eta_t^2, \tag{3}$$

$$\sigma_t = \alpha + \beta\, \Delta V_t + \gamma\, \Delta T_t + \sum_{j=1}^{12} \rho_j \, \hat{\sigma_{t-j}} + \eta_t^3. \tag{4}$$

Lagged volatilities are used as regressors to test persistent effects of previous volatilities.

In Table 1, we present the estimation results for stocks showing the superiority of the number of trades in explaining the stochastic volatility, namely REUTERS, VODAFONE, HSBA, HBOS, LGEN, and BA, which corroborates the results of Jones *et al.* (1994).

Now, we expose in detail the results of regressions estimation for the stock REUTERS. The same conclusions hold for the remaining stocks studied in Table 1.

In the case of REUTERS, the t-statistics for coefficients β and γ in the regression (4) are higher than 2 (they are, respectively, equal to 5.7993 and 15.1051) which implies that β and γ are statistically significant. Thus, the number of trades and the volume are both relevant for the volatility explanation.

The value of the adjusted-R^2 of regression (3) (equal to 0.2275), where the number of trades and the lagged volatilities are the sole explanatory variables of volatility, is clearly higher than value 0.1864 obtained in regression (2), where volume and lagged volatilities are the regressors of volatility. In addition, the adjusted-R^2 values of regressions (3) and (4) are very close (they are, respectively, equal to 0.2275 and 0.2344). Our results suggest that the volume has virtually no marginal explanatory power when volatility is already conditioned on the number of trades.

Moreover, the value of γ decreases slightly in regression (4) compared to its value in (3). However, the value of β decreases significantly from (2) to (4). This may indicate that the informational content of the volume is included in the informational content of the number of trades.

In the three regressions, coefficient β, reflecting the impact of traded volume on volatility, is positive which is in line with the wide range of empirical and theoretical studies supporting the positive volume–volatility relationship.

Table 1: Regressions estimation

	REUTERS			VODAFONE			HSBA		
	β	γ	$\bar{R}^2$	β	γ	$\bar{R}^2$	β	γ	$\bar{R}^2$
Regression	2.0607*E*-09		0.18646986	1.3831*E*-10		0.23339972	4.632*E*-10		0.05075537
(2)	2.0334*E*-10			1.6144*E*-11			6.9691*E*-11		
Regression		5.4177*E*-05	0.22757492		3.151*E*-05	0.23781711		1.5272*E*-05	0.05524585
(3)		3.1229*E*-06			3.2584*E*-06			1.9757*E*-06	
Regression	1.1916*E*-09	4.8918*E*-05	0.2344699	8.3159*E*-11	2.352*E*-05	0.24223293	3.212*E*-10	1.2271*E*-05	0.06051622
(4)	2.0547*E*-10	3.2385*E*-06		1.8236*E*-11	3.6913*E*-06		7.3414*E*-11	2.0862*E*-06	

	LGEN			HBOS			BA		
	β	γ	$\bar{R}^2$	β	γ	$\bar{R}^2$	β	γ	$\bar{R}^2$
Regression	1.1687*E*-09		0.2217261	9.892*E*-10		0.04433326	4.7127*E*-10		0.08203242
(2)	8.64*E*-11			2.0789*E*-10			7.4434*E*-11		
Regression		6.2608*E*-05	0.22202837		2.3544*E*-05	0.06792826		3.9054*E*-05	0.12592348
(3)		4.6116*E*-06			2.3264*E*-06			2.7314*E*-06	
Regression	8.5748*E*-10	4.6112*E*-05	0.24236965	4.7845*E*-10	2.2126*E*-05	0.06913786	2.2436*E*-10	3.6933*E*-05	0.12807048
(4)	9.1386*E*-11	4.8787*E*-06		2.1257*E*-10	2.4087*E*-06		7.4951*E*-11	2.8186*E*-06	

Standard errors for the coefficients of the regressions are presented in bold.

Table 2: Regressions estimation.

	BT			TESCO		
	β	γ	$\bar{R}^2$	β	γ	$\bar{R}^2$
Regression	5.4448E-10		0.3225	4.2446E-10		0.2632
(2)	1.0771E-10			6.4223E-11		
Regression		2.5554E-05	0.3184		2.4732E-05	0.2596
(3)		1.3681E-05			3.3825E-06	
Regression	5.2548E-10	1.4524E-05	0.3225	4.2446E-10	1.7142E-05	0.2681
(4)	1.0922E-10	1.3831E-05		6.807E-11	3.5764E-06	

Table 3: Regressions estimation.

	BP		
	β	γ	$\bar{R}^2$
Regression	1.2159E-09		−0.00301473
(2)	8.5093E-10		
Regression		9.3882E-05	−0.00329088
(3)		9.1954E-05	
Regression	1.0596E-09	6.3358E-05	−0.00316924
(4)	8.8296E-10	9.5402E-05	

Table 2 displays the results of regressions estimation for stocks having the traded volumes more efficient than the number of trades in explaining volatility.

Finally, Table 3 shows results of regressions estimation for the stock BP indicating the irrelevance of the number of trades and the volume for the volatility determination.

In the remainder of this chapter, we shed light only on the stocks having shown a better performance of the number of trades in explaining volatility, namely stocks studied in Table 1.

To ascertain whether the informational content of the transactions volume is incorporated into previous values of the number of trades, we conduct a Granger causality test. We recall that a variable y is said to be Granger-caused by x if adding lagged values of x leads to a better explanation of the current value of y. This kind of causality excludes instantaneous correlation but refers to precedence and information content.

Granger-causality is tested through the estimation of the following bivariate regressions:

$$y_t = \alpha_{10} + \alpha_{11} y_{t-1} + \cdots + \alpha_{1l} y_{t-l} + \beta_{11} x_{t-1} + \cdots + \beta_{1l} x_{t-l} + \varepsilon_t,$$
$$x_t = \alpha_{20} + \alpha_{21} x_{t-1} + \cdots + \alpha_{2l} x_{t-l} + \beta_{21} y_{t-1} + \cdots + \beta_{2l} y_{t-l} + u_t.$$

The null hypothesis is expressed as follows: x (respectively y) does not Granger-cause $y(x)$ in the first (second) regression.

Formally, the null hypothesis is couched as follows:

$$H_0 : \begin{array}{ll} \beta_{11} = \beta_{12} = \cdots = \beta_{1l} = 0 & \text{for the first regression} \\ \beta_{21} = \beta_{22} = \cdots = \beta_{2l} = 0 & \text{for the second regression.} \end{array}$$

F-statistics obtained from the regressions estimation are the Wald statistics for the null hypothesis H_0. The lag length l is picked so as to correspond to reasonable beliefs about the longest period over which one of the variables contributes to the prediction of the other variable. In our case, we have chosen a lag equal to 4. Note that our conclusions remain unchangeable even if we extend the lag length to 20.

Test results are displayed in Table 4. For stocks REUTERS, VODAFONE, LGEN, HSBA, and HBOS, we reject the null hypothesis that the number of

Table 4: Granger causality test applied to the volume and the number of trades series.

		Volume does not Granger-cause number of transactions	Number of trades does not Granger-cause volume
REUTERS	F-statistic	1.64760	4.60203
	p-value	0.15944	0.00105
VODAFONE	F-statistic	1.34702	9.13884
	p-value	0.24999	2.4E-07
LGEN	F-statistic	5.29301	6.61374
	p-value	0.00030	2.7E-05
BA	F-statistic	2.40754	1.90698
	p-value	0.04736	0.10648
HSBA	F-statistic	2.17880	11.3534
	p-value	0.06888	3.8E-09
HBOS	F-statistic	1.74804	3.29505
	p-value	0.13660	0.01053

If p-value $>$ 5%, the null hypothesis cannot be rejected.
If p-value $\leq$ 5%, the null hypothesis is rejected.

trades does not Granger-cause the volume. Therefore, the number of trades provides statistically significant information on future values of transaction volume. However, this hypothesis cannot be rejected only for stock BA.

Moreover, the hypothesis that the volume does not Granger-cause the number of trades cannot be rejected (at the 5% confidence level) in the case of four stocks among six (REUTERS, VODAFONE, HSBA, and HBOS). For LGEN and BA, current levels of volume reveal information about future values of the number of trades. To conclude, it appears that Granger causality runs one way from the number of trades to the volume for the majority of stocks (REUTERS, VODAFONE, HSBA, and HBOS) which corroborates the idea that informational content of transaction volume is included in the number of trades.

4 Testing the Relevance of the Cumulative Number of Trades as Approximation of the Operational Time

The purpose of this section is to validate or reject the conjecture of Ané and Geman (2000) that is the operational time leading to a quasi-perfect normality of returns is best represented by the cumulative number of trades.

First, we examine whether the return series observed in calendar time obeys the normal hypothesis. We compute the four first moments, the kurtosis, the skewness, and the corresponding JB statistics of the return series, and we present them in Table 5. For all the stocks studied in Table 5, the JB statistics computed for the return series is strictly higher than the critical chi-square value with two degrees of freedom at the 5% confidence level. This indicates that the null hypothesis of normality is rejected.

Second, we use the Gaussian kernel estimator to construct the empirical distributions of the stock return series. Hence, the empirical density is given by

$$f(x) = \frac{1}{nh}\sum_{i=1}^{n} K\left(\frac{x - x_i}{h}\right),$$

where n is the number of observations, x_i is observation i, h[b] is the window width, and K is the kernel estimator.

[b] We use quantity $\sigma.\left(\frac{4}{3}\right)^{\frac{1}{5}}.n^{-\frac{1}{5}}$ to approximate the window width, where σ is the standard deviation of the return series.

Table 5: Moment estimates of return series.

	REUTERS	VODAFONE	LGEN	HSBA	HBOS	BA
Number of observations	3661	3435	3280	3272	3167	3271
$m_1(Y_t)$	1.0341E-05	−1.3059E-05	−1.1944E-06	−1.0366E-05	−3.0302E-06	4.3687E-06
$m_2(Y_t)$	1.0712E-06	5.8561E-06	1.0377E-06	4.3133E-07	5.1321E-07	5.1186E-07
$m_3(Y_t)$	2.3067E-10	3.3835E-08	2.9233E-09	−1.9020E-09	−2.1985E-10	−2.3903E-10
Skewness	0.2081	2.3897	2.7666	−6.7173	−0.5985	−0.6530
$m_4(Y_t)$	1.7005E-10	2.1890E-08	2.7927E-10	4.6057E-11	2.7260E-11	1.9738E-11
Kurtosis	148.2611	638.6956	259.5007	247.7037	103.6301	75.3831
JB statistic	3218777	57875206	8995842	8188235	1334716	8188235

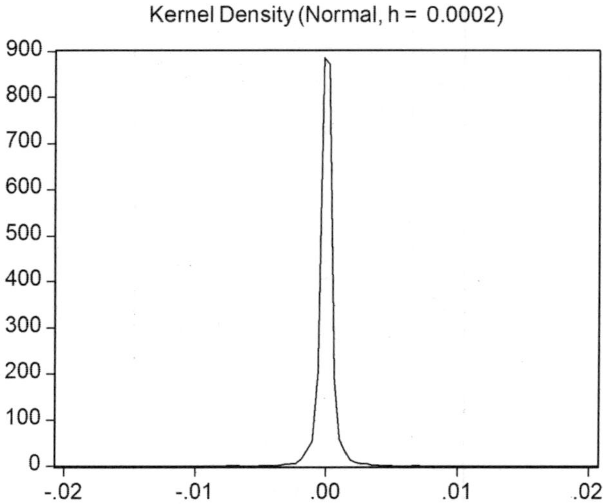

Figure 1: Empircial density of REUTERS returns.

The Gaussian kernel is expressed as follows:

$$K(x) = \frac{1}{\sqrt{2\Pi}} e^{-\frac{x^2}{2}}.$$

This choice of the kernel ensures that $\hat{f}$ is a smooth curve having derivatives of all orders and consequently ensures the existence of the four first moments of returns. The estimation results are shown in Figs. 1–6.

We note that estimated densities have fat tails because extreme observations are very large. Moreover, they are more peaked than the normal distribution, which is consistent with our earlier finding, that is, return distributions are not Gaussian.

Third, we compute the four first moments, the skewness, and the kurtosis of the number of trades' series, and we set out them in Table 6.

In our analysis, we estimate the four first moments of the stochastic time change providing normality of conditional returns using the method of moments presented in the Ané and Geman (2000) study.

We perform the optimization problem with the help of MATLAB that provides a wide variety of optimization instruments. In our case, we have to resolve a non-linear program that consists of four non-linear constraints[c] and six unknown variables. The function to minimize is also non-linear.

[c]We just consider the four first moment equations of system (1).

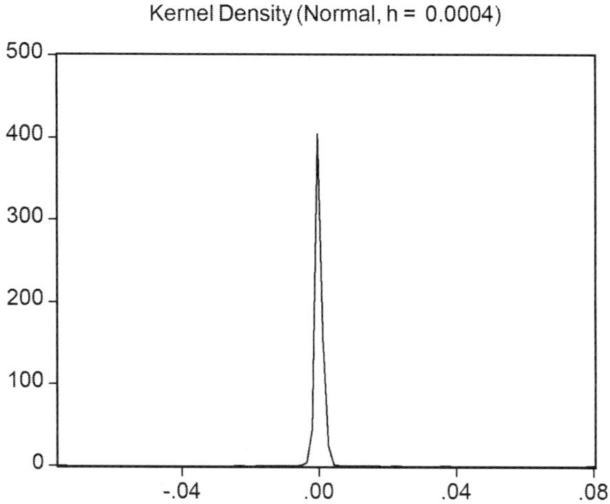

Figure 2: Empircial density of VODAFONE returns.

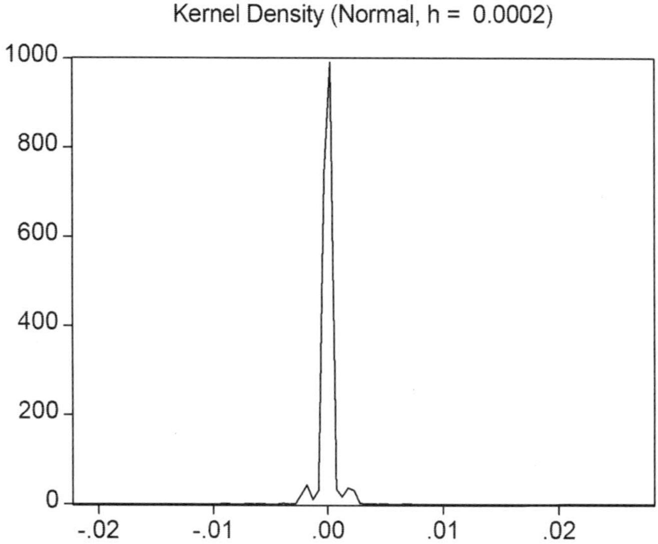

Figure 3: Empircial density of LGEN returns.

Following the Ané and Geman (2000) recommendations, we avoid very small and very large values of parameter β. Optimization results are displayed in Table 7. We notice that the moments of the stochastic time change greater than 1 are close to the moments of the number of trades. Therefore, we

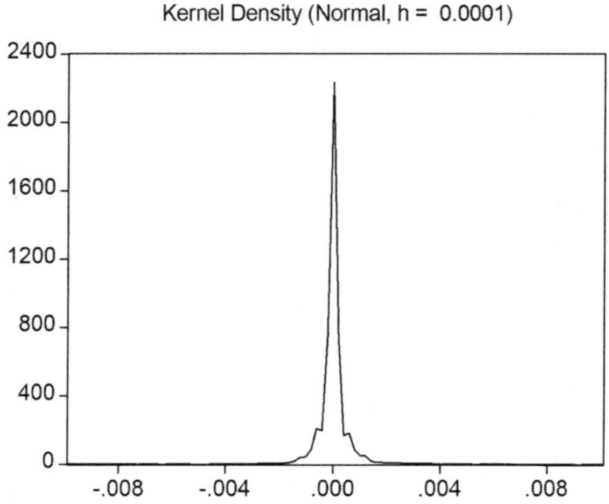

Figure 4: Empircial density of BA returns.

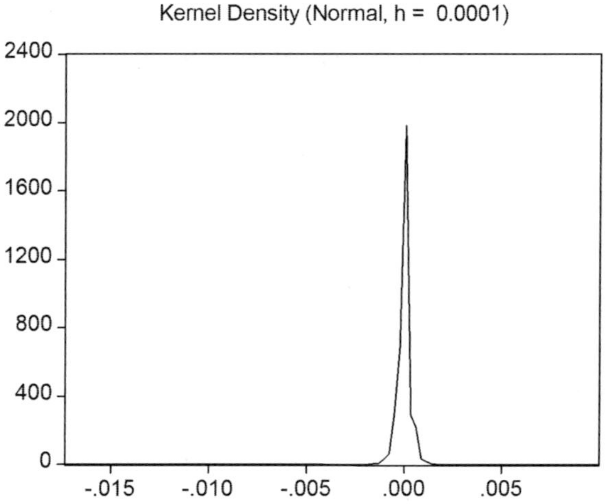

Figure 5: Empircial density of HSBA returns.

assume that the stochastic time change may be approximated by the number of transactions, up to a constant.

If this approximation is appropriate, the distribution of returns conditioned on the number of trades should be normal.[d] Then, we recenter the number of trades series so as to have a mean equal to the mean of the stochastic

[d]Ané and Geman (2000) demonstrated that $P\left(Y_t \in dy/\Delta\tau(t) = u\right) = P\left(X(u) \in dy/\Delta\tau(t) = u\right)$. Assuming that X and $\Delta\tau$ are independent, they obtained $P\left(Y_t \in dy/\Delta\tau(t) = u\right) = P\left(X(u) \in dy\right)$.

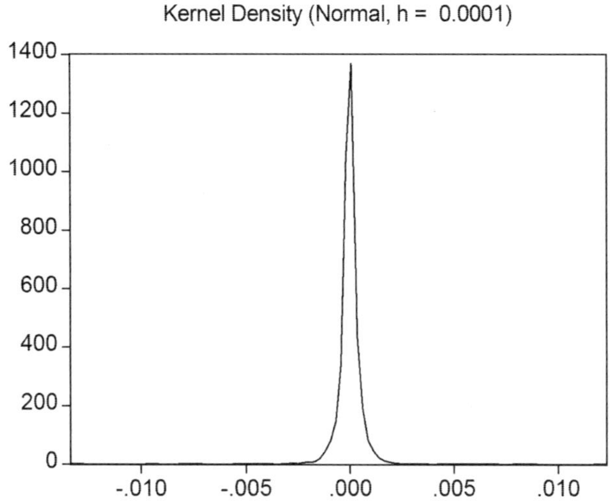

Figure 6: Empircial density of HBOS returns.

Table 6: Moment estimates of number of trades series.

	$m_1(\Delta T)$	$m_2(\Delta T)$	$m_3(\Delta T)$	Skewness	$m_4(\Delta T)$	Kurtosis
REUTERS	3.4569	28.6116	449.2305	2.9377	13,292.112	16.2548
VODAFONE	10.7983	158.8981	6089.2445	3.0427	466,075.418	18.4809
LGEN	2.4468	15.1381	200.8284	3.4128	4848.218	21.1820
BA	3.9339	24.3997	276.7601	2.2983	5988.120	10.0704
HSBA	6.4094	47.0352	835.6570	2.5929	34,085.645	15.4260
HBOS	5.0489	36.2543	744.6173	3.4143	34,717.766	26.4472

time change. Next, we construct the series of transaction normalized returns,[e] and we check their normality by computing corresponding skewness, kurtosis, and JB statistics (see Table 8).

In accordance with Gillemot *et al.* (2005), our results reveal that conditional normality of asset returns is rejected when the conditioning variable is the recentered number of trades.

On the one hand, it is likely that we fail in recovering the Ané and Geman (2000) findings because our empirical analysis is based on a relatively small

Since X is supposed to be a Brownian motion, the distribution of returns conditioned on the appropriate stochastic time change should be normal.

[e]Transaction normalized returns are returns divided by the square root of the recentered number of trades.

Table 7: Optimization results.

	μ	σ^2	$m_1(\Delta\tau(t))$	$m_2(\Delta\tau(t))$	$m_3(\Delta\tau(t))$	$m_4(\Delta\tau(t))$
REUTERS	4.7929*E*-007	2.0912*E*-007	14.306	28.624	449.01	13,292
VODAFONE	2.1725*E*-006	9.4756*E*-007	6.2956	146.32	6089	4.6608*E*+005
LGEN	−1.0229*E*-006	1.9229*E*-007	9.3041	15.296	200.05	4848
BA	1.1629*E*-006	3.265*E*-007	9.5104	25.257	200.4	5988
HSBA	2.0353*E*-007	5.7734*E*-008	23.773	59.289	800.39	34,085
HBOS	−2.7717*E*-007	4.1438*E*-008	9.8464	29.445	746.14	34,717

Table 8: Skewness, kurtosis, and Jarque and Bera statistics of transaction normalized returns series

	REUTERS	VODAFONE	LGEN	BA	HSBA	HBOS
Skewness	−0.4666	0.4657	2.3244	−0.4280	−5.1177	0.2028
Kurtosis	207.5370	718.5207	314.7928	113.8004	242.1041	156.1877
Jarque and Bera Statistic	6380030	73275807	13288974	1673317	7808567	3096619

number of observations. On the other hand, our evidence is similar to that pointed out by Murphy and Izzeldin (2005) who disagree with the Ané and Geman (2000) methodology and results. Moreover, they argue that conditional normality of returns cannot be recovered even when they use a large number of observations on simulated data from different Data Generation Processes.

5 Conclusion

This chapter is an attempt to recover the normality of returns through a timescale transformation: from calendar to operational time, with activity-related stochastic increments. This idea was introduced by Ané and Geman (2000) who succeeded in approximating the stochastic time change leading to a Gaussian representation of conditional returns, by the number of trades. Their results are consistent with the Mixture of Distributions Hypothesis approach where the mixing variable, reflecting different information flow rates, is measured by the number of trades. The non-parametric procedure that generates such results is attractive because it does not lie on any hypothesis on the probabilistic distribution of the stochastic time change, in contrast to the Clark

(1973) model, where the directing process of returns measured by the volume of trades is assumed to be lognormal.

Taking advantage of the availability of tick-by-tick data on a sample of highly traded LSE stocks, we follow the Ané and Geman (2000) methodology, but we are not able to validate the idea that the operational time is appropriately measured by the cumulative number of trades.

Our findings give support to the studies of Gillemot *et al.* (2005) and Murphy and Izzeldin (2005). The latter shows that the method of moments produces extremely inaccurate estimates of the higher moments of the stochastic time change. Alternatively, Murphy and Izzeldin (2005) claim that a bivariate mixture of distributions model (where returns Y_t and "market activity" a_t (volume, number of trades...) are independently and normally distributed, and where means and variances of both Y_t and a_t are linear on the stochastic time change $\Delta\tau(t)$) provides more precise estimates of the stochastic time change.

References

Ané, T and Geman, H (1996). Stochastic subordination. *Risk*, 9, 145–149.

Ané, T and Geman, H (2000). Order flow, transaction clock, and normality of asset returns. *Journal of Finance*, 55, 2259–2284.

Clark, PK (1973). A subordinated stochastic process model with finite variance for speculative prices. *Econometrica*, 41, 135–155.

Diamond, DW and Verrecchia, RE (1987). Constraints on short-selling and asset price adjustment to private information. *Journal of Financial Economics*, 18, 277–311.

Dufour, A and Engle, RF (2000). Time and the price impact of a trade. *Journal of Finance*, 55, 2467–2498.

Easley, D and O'Hara, M (1992). Time and the process of security price adjustment. *Journal of Finance*, 47, 577–605.

Engle, RF (2000). The econometrics of ultra high frequency data. *Econometrica*, 68, 1–22.

Engle, RF and Russel, JR (1994). Forecasting transaction rates: The autoregressive conditional duration model. NBER Working Paper No. 4966.

Foster, FD and Viswanathan, S (1993). Variations in trading volume, return volatility and trading costs: Evidence on recent price formation models. *Journal of Finance*, 48, 187–211.

Gillemot, L, Farmer, JD and Lillo, F (2005). There's more to volatility than volume. arXiv: physics/0510007 v1.

Glosten, LR and Milgrom, PR (1985). Bid, ask and transaction prices in a specialist market with heterogeneously informed traders. *Journal of Financial Economics*, 14, 71–100.

Hausman, JA, Lo, AW and Mackinlay, AC (1992). An ordered probit analysis of transaction stock prices. *Journal of Financial Economics, 31*, 319–379.

Jones, CM, Kaul, G and Lipson, ML (1994). Transactions, volume, and volatility. *Review of Financial Studies*, 7, 631–651.

Karpoff, JM (1987). The relation between price changes and trading volume: A survey. *Journal of Financial and Quantitative Analysis*, 22, 109–126.

Kyle, AS (1985). Continuous auctions and insider trading. *Econometrica*, 53, 1315–1336.

Li, Y (2004). Estimation of information time in stock returns. Working Paper, Department of Economics, Yale University.

Murphy, A and Izzeldin, M (2005). Order flow, transaction clock, and normality of asset returns: A comment on Ané and Geman (2000), Nuffield College, Oxford and Lancaster University.

Schwert, W (1990). Stock volatility and the crash of '87. *Review of Financial Studies*, 3, 77–102.

Wood, RA, McInish, TH and Ord, JK (1985). An investigation of transaction data for NYSE stocks. *Journal of Finance* 40, 723–741.

CHAPTER 8

THE BEHAVIOR OF THE IMPLIED VOLATILITY SURFACE: EVIDENCE FROM CRUDE OIL FUTURES OPTIONS

*Amine Bouden**

In this chapter, I investigate implied volatility surface patterns for call options on crude oil futures. Instead of studying the power of the large number of explanatory factors inherent in oil markets, I focus on the common characteristics of option prices. By using quadratic implied volatility functions (IVFs), I aim to establish a mapping from implied volatilities to the option's intrinsic characteristics, i.e. moneyness and time to expiration, and to test the capacity of these functions to provide a good forecast of option prices. I found that the profile of crude oil implied volatility is too complex to be fully explained by IVFs. The main aim to the chapter is to perform an econometric explanatory analysis on a high volatile market, the petroleum market.

1 Introduction

A better understanding of the empirical behavior of the implied volatility has long been of considerable interest in financial spheres. In a Black and Scholes (1973) universe, volatilities inferred from quoted option prices would be constant; unfortunately, it was found that this is not especially the case and, attractive as it may seem, this approach gives disappointing results. In the existing literature, various attempts have been made to explain departures from the Black and Scholes (1973) traditional model.[a]

*University of Paris 2 Panthéon-Assas, ERMES, CNRS, 12 Place Panthéon, 75005 Paris.
amine.bouden@u-paris2.fr.

[a]See Bates (2000) for a survey of alternative pricing models.

The so-called Smile effect is a result of an empirical observation of the option's implied volatilities across different exercise prices, with the same maturity. It typically describes an U-shaped pattern (smile), which turns to be downward sloping in some cases (skew).[b] Furthermore, it is well understood that volatility Smile is a consequence of empirical violation of normality assumption in the Black and Scholes (1973) model.[c]

The pattern of the implied volatility across time to expiration is usually referred to as the term structure of implied volatility. Nevertheless, it was found that this relationship is less explicit than the strike relationship and depends on the option market's features.

By simultaneously plotting implied volatilities across strike prices and time to expiration, we obtain the well-known implied volatility surface (IVS henceforth). As a matter of fact, the IVS is a convenient tool to illustrating discrepancies between market reality and theory. Dumas *et al.* (1998) were the first to discuss the possibility of modeling the implied volatility behavior across strike price and time to maturity. Some of the proposed functions, settled in different combinations, were successful in increasing the pricing accuracy with respect to the Black and Scholes (1973) model. Their appeal comes from their ability to capture both Smile and term structure effects in a rather simple way. They found that the implied volatility profile is non-stationary through time and that a better fit could be achieved through dynamic weekly re-estimation. They performed their analysis on the S&P 500 index options.

Using the same market data, Wang (2002) followed the same procedure, but, instead of using a weekly re-estimation, he suggests to update the implied volatility models on day-to-day basis, thereby increasing the accuracy of the estimation. He concludes that the IVS evolves dynamically over time in response to news affecting investors' beliefs.

Although much literature has focused on the IVS inferred from S&P 500 option prices, these results are not specific to this market, and similar patterns have been documented for European markets.[d]

---

[b]In the following, the pattern of implied volatilities across exercise prices will be called "Smile" regardless of its actual shape. So the expression "Smile" will refer to both smile, i.e. the U-shaped form, and skew, i.e. the monotonically decreasing form.

[c]See Rubinstein (1994) for more complete discussion of this point.

[d]Hafner and Wallmeier (2001) characterize the profile of German DAX implied volatilities and discusses the potential determinants of changes in the IVS pattern. Cassese and Guidolin (2005) analyze the structure of IVS in the Italian stock index options market, the MIB30. Duque and Lopes (2003) performed their study on a rather small market, the Portuguese market, and found evidence for both strike and time bias.

What has to be mentioned is that all these studies were performed in order to investigate the index option markets. But a question arises: what about the other financial markets? Even though we can imagine that performing such work on currency or interest rate markets would be inappropriate because of their rather simple volatility profiles, the question of knowing why practitioners have not paid more attention to extremely volatile markets, such as commodity markets, remains.

To the best of my knowledge, modeling the implied volatility has never been done on commodity markets, which appears quite surprising knowing the extremely high volatility that characterizes this type of markets.[e]

The objective of this study is twofold. First of all, I aim to study in what extent implied volatilities inferred from the crude oil options market could be explained by option's intrinsic characteristics. Second, I try to evaluate the predictive power of the implied volatility models used. The estimations are based exclusively on call options quoted on New York Mercantile Exchange (NYMEX) for the time period spanning from 5 November 2004 to 14 November 2005.

This chapter is organized as follows: the next section contains a brief summary of some institutional features peculiar to petroleum markets. Section 3 introduces the IVS and takes up the task of formally modeling its behavior. Data are described in Section 4. Finally, I present and analyze the results in Section 5. The chapter concludes with a brief summary.

2 Some Features of Crude Oil Market

Crude Oil market is the world's most actively traded physical commodity and remains an important determinant of global economic performance.

Since 1987,[f] crude oil prices fluctuate extremely causing a significantly high volatility. In September 2000, the oil price reached a peak of about $37 per barrel; it declined to less than $18 per barrel in November 2001 induced by fears inherent in the 11 September 2001 attacks. Since then, there has been an upward trend in crude oil prices exceeding $78 per barrel in August 2006 which is, up to now, the highest level ever reached. Figure 1 displays crude oil price evolution over the last 35 years.

[e]See below for more details about crude oil market's features.

[f]Since this date, crude oil prices react to the balance of demand and supply. Indeed Organization of Petroleum Exporting Countries (OPEC) abandoned the price fixing system, favoring a system in which production quotas are set based on the assessment of market's supply.

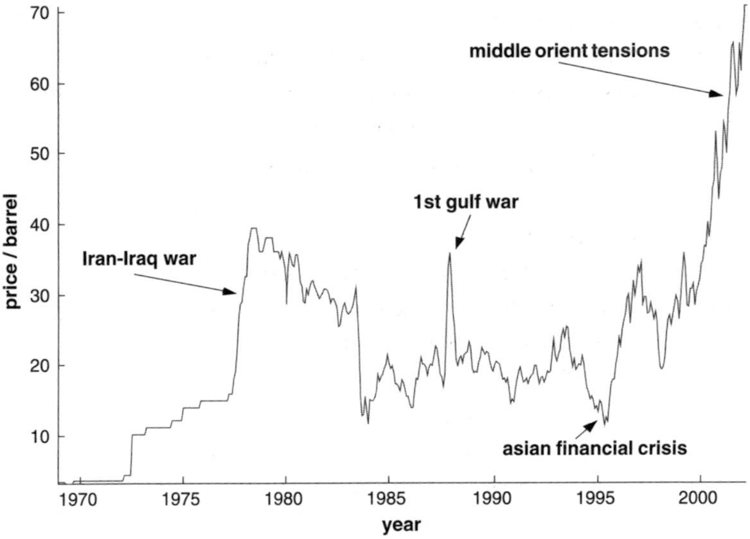

Figure 1: Evolution of crude price from January 1970 to June 2006.

Many factors have been put forward to explain these movements.[g] Market's fundamentals, those directly related to the petroleum industry such as refinery upgrading and transportation infrastructure, surging demand in emerging economies, and the available oil supply have obviously a great influence on price volatility. Daily oil prices can also get affected by shifts in traders' expectations about the future market developments. Indeed, pure speculative trading, which, in some instances, seems to carry considerable weight with some market participants, can play a great role in increasing the volatility.

Volatility generates uncertainty, and this acute uncertainty inhibits the investors. In order to achieve price fluctuations, energy derivatives have been increasingly used leading to an impressing growth of the derivatives market. Option and futures contracts are by themselves the most useful tools to manage price risk; crude oil futures contract, introduced in NYMEX in 1978, is the world's largest volume contract trading on a physical commodity with daily trading volume averaging 230 million barrels. Options offer additional flexibility in managing price risk by their ability to profit from favorable market moves. In addition to their hedging function, options are useful to infer

[g]See Lynch (2002) for a more elaborate discussion about the drivers of oil price volatility.

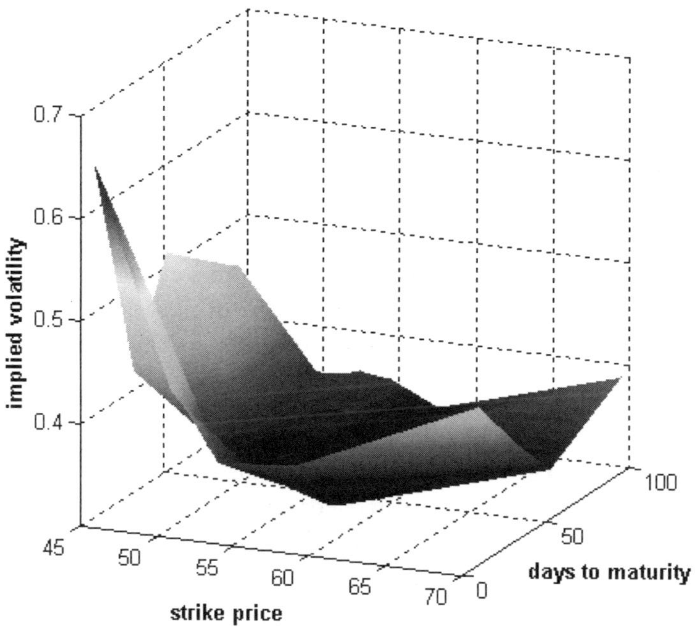

Figure 2: IVS observed on options on crude oil futures on 6 May 2005.

information about market's assessment of the future. For example, the volatility implied by the quoted crude oil option includes future expectations of price movement and thus, can be considered as a relevant indicator of the uncertainty inherent in the oil market.

3 Modeling the Implied Volatility Surface Using Implied Volatility Functions

By simultaneously plotting implied volatilities of European-style options against exercise prices and option maturities, we obtain a curve describing implied volatilities as a function of option's intrinsic characteristics. This curve is known as the implied volatility surface (IVS) (Fig. 2).

Definition: Consider a European-style option written on an asset i. For each couple (K, τ) there corresponds, at a date t, a single stochastic process $\sigma_{i,t}(K, \tau)$. Its value depends on the characteristics of the option: the exercise price K and the maturity τ.

The function $\sigma_{t,i}$: $(K, \tau) \rightarrow \sigma_{t,i}(K, \tau)$ is called implied volatility surface for the asset i at a date t.

Pricing exotic options is one of the applications of the IVS. For each underlying asset, traders estimate the IVS every day from option daily quotations. They use these estimates thereafter as a tool to price options whose prices are not directly observable on the market such as exotic options; so having an accurate IVS that reflects the traded option prices and incorporates both Smile and term structure effects proves to be crucial for pricing purposes.

In addition, the IVS estimation is useful in risk management, to the extent that it permits quantification of the risk related to a change in the volatility forecasts formulated by investors. For the sake of illustration, assume that volatility evolves randomly across time; the delta of an European call C is

$$\delta = \delta^{\mathrm{BS}} + V^{\mathrm{BS}} \cdot \frac{\partial \sigma}{\partial S},$$

where $\delta^{\mathrm{BS}}$is the delta given by the Black and Scholes (1973) model and is equal to $N(d_1)$, $N(d_1)$ being the cumulative normal distribution.

$V^{\mathrm{BS}} = \frac{\partial C}{\partial \sigma}$ is the vega of the Black and Scholes (1973) model and is equal to $n(d_1)S\sqrt{\tau}$; $n(d_1)$ being the standard normal distribution.

However, term $\frac{\partial \sigma}{\partial S}$ is difficult to quantify, and risk managers are often compelled to assume that it can be equated with $\frac{\partial \sigma}{\partial K}$ for an At-The-Money option, $\frac{\partial \sigma}{\partial S} \approx \frac{\partial \sigma}{\partial K}$. The sensitivity of the volatility to the underlying is approximated by the slope of the IVS on the exercise price.

The first attempt to model the IVS through the definition of an implied volatility function (IVF) can be traced back to 1998 (e.g. Dumas *et al.*, 1998). This function can, at least in theory, perfectly account for the profile of the Smile and for the term structure of implied volatility, at a date t.

$$\sigma_{i,t} = f(S_t, K_i, \tau).$$

However, nothing can vouch for the IVF as a good estimator of the IVS on a later date, say $t+1$: inasmuch as the IVF is sensitive to the information flow continuously arriving on the market, parameter estimates based thereupon must be regularly updated. The ensuing instability, empirically studied by Dumas *et al.* (1998), can cause acute variation in the sensitivities of hedge parameters (delta, vega), which may prove problematic for hedgers.

I propose to model the IVS using quadratic regressions that take the following form[h]:

$$\sigma = \alpha_0 + \alpha_1 X + \alpha_2 X^2,$$

where X is a state variable.

[h]The time index t is omitted for the sake of exposition's ease.

The non-linearity of the function linking implied volatilities to strike prices on the one hand, and to time to expiration on the other hand, lies behind the choice of this polynomial form, and makes the quadratic term necessary to take into account both Smile and term structure curvatures.

In the extant literature, several variables were posited to be the state variables, such as strike K (e.g. Shimko, 1993; Bates, 1995), moneyness K/F (Wang, 2002), and time to expiration τ.

The IVS could be modeled by dint of various structural forms of IVF:

$$\textbf{Model 1}: \sigma(K,T) = \alpha_0 + \varepsilon,$$

$$\textbf{Model 2}: \sigma(K,T) = \alpha_0 + \alpha_1\frac{K}{F} + \alpha_2\left(\frac{K}{F}\right)^2 + \varepsilon,$$

$$\textbf{Model 3}: \sigma(K,T) = \alpha_0 + \alpha_1\frac{K}{F} + \alpha_2\left(\frac{K}{F}\right)^2 + \alpha_3\tau + \alpha_4\tau^2 + \varepsilon,$$

$$\textbf{Model 4}: \sigma(K,T) = \alpha_0 + \alpha_1\frac{K}{F} + \alpha_2\left(\frac{K}{F}\right)^2 + \alpha_3\tau + \alpha_4\tau^2 + \alpha_5\frac{K}{F}\tau + \varepsilon,$$

where α_i is constant for $i \in [0,5]$, and ε is an error term normally distributed: $\varepsilon \to N(0,\sigma_\varepsilon^2)$.

These various forms stand in line with those proposed by Dumas *et al.* (1998) in the sense that they are limited to the option intrinsic characteristics to define the behavior of implied volatility.

Model 1, considered as the benchmark and wherein parameter α_0 measures the implied volatility of an At-The-Money option, is related to the Black (1976) model which assumes a constant volatility for all options written on the same underlying asset.

Model 2, wherein regression is performed on moneyness rather than on strike on grounds of fit, takes into account the phenomenon of Smile by testing the direct relation between implied volatility and moneyness. Since this relationship is parabolic rather than linear, the quadratic form is suited for this model. Coefficient α_2 controls for the convexity of the Smile, whereas coefficient α_1 measures how much implied volatility deviates from its At-The-Money level.

As stated previously, the shape of the Smile curve depends on the maturity of the option: the longer the time to expiration is, the less convex is the curve, and the less pronounced is the Smile effect. Furthermore, adding time to expiration as a predictor is likely to increase the precision of the IVF, and correct the fit of the cross-section of implied volatilities.

Model 3 hinges upon the same rationale but separately captures the biases related to both the option's exercise price and the time to expiration.

Model 4 combines both Smile and term structure effects through the addition of a cross term $\frac{K}{F}\tau$.

The sample selected to carry out the estimations consists of crude oil options on futures. Implied volatilities are initially derived from these options by appropriately inverting the Black (1976) pricing model.

$$C = e^{-r\tau}[FN(d_1) - KN(d_2)],$$

$$d_1 = \log\frac{\left(\frac{F}{K}\right) + \frac{\sigma^2}{2}\tau}{\sigma\sqrt{\tau}},$$

$$d_2 = d_1 - \sigma\sqrt{\tau}.$$

4 Data Description

The database used herein contains daily quotations of crude oil futures[i] and European options written on these futures contracts and traded on the NYMEX during period 5 November 2004 through 14 November 2005. The option price refers to the settlement price, i.e. the closing price determined by demand and supply. While the transaction costs are voluntarily omitted, all available strikes are considered[j] in order to take into account the options of various types, viz. At-The-Money options, In-The-Money options, and Out-of-The-Money options. Moreover, incorporating all maturities enables us to study the term structure of implied volatility.[k] To proxy for the risk

[i]For each month of the year there corresponds a different crude oil futures contract. Quotations stop three days before the 25th of the month preceding the delivery month. For example, a futures contract that expires theoretically in August will be quoted for the last time on the market on 22 July. At the expiry date, the contracts are liquidated by effective delivery which is done everywhere in the world via pipelines.

[j]Twenty strike prices are in increments of \$0.50 above and below the At-The-Money exercise price, and the next 10 exercise prices with a tick-size of \$2.50 above the highest and below the lowest existing strike prices for a total of 61 strike prices. The At-The-Money strike price is the nearest to the previous day's underlying futures contract. Strike price boundaries are adjusted according to the futures price movements. Unfortunately, these contracts are not all liquids, and quotations do not necessary appear for all exercise prices. This is why we do not have, each day, neither the same number nor the same structure of exercise prices for the same contract.

[k]It should be pointed out that we are allowed to use futures prices given that the expiration day of the futures and option contracts systematically coincide during that the expiration schedule. However, the two

free interest rate, I use the EONIA rate (Euro Overnight Interest Average) which, as typical of money market indices, represents the price of the money on the Eurozone interbank market. The rate used in Black's (1976) formula to calculate theoretically the option price is the average of the rates over the option's life period. Finally, note that all option and futures data are provided by the NYMEX, and the risk free interest rates are computed using data from the DATASTREAM database.

The sample comprises 4244 call options and 5227 put options. Since an European-style option could be exercised only on the delivery date, an analytical relationship known as Put–Call parity can be established between the price of a call option C and the price of a put option P.

$$Fe^{-r\tau} + P = C + Ke^{-r\tau}.$$

All analyses performed herein exclusively relate to European call options. Consequently, puts are replaced by calls via put–call parity, except for the 834 cases where a call and a put for the same exercise price and the same maturity are observed at the same time.

Options devoid of informative contents are excluded from the sample based on the following criteria:

— Options whose time to expiration is lower than five business days and higher than 250 business days. Short-term options have an almost null time value and therefore a very low premium. Consequently, implied volatilities extracted from these options are not significant. Long-term options are not usually exchanged, and their prices do not necessarily reflect the reality of the market.
— Quotations which violate the arbitrage limit condition for European calls:

$$C \geq \max(0; F - K).$$

— Options whose absolute value of relative moneyness $|K/F - 1|$ is higher than 25% such as very deep Out-of-The-Money or very deep In-The-Money options. Their premiums being either very low or very high, they have very limited informative contents.

Options dropped from the sample, because they meet at least one of these three conditions, amount to 2050, i.e. less than one quarter of the initial sample.

maturities are not perfectly synchronous: options expire three days before the maturity of the underlying futures contracts. This three-day shift seems not to introduce a substantial amount of noise; that is why I decided to neglect this point below.

Table 1: Number of observations and percentage of the contracts filtered of the sample according to each criterion of exclusion.

	Number of observations	Percentage %
Initial sample	8637	100
Maturity < five days	782	9
Maturity > 250 days	10	0.1
Violation of arbitrage condition	0	0
$\|(K/F) - 1\| > 25\%$	1258	14.6
Final sample	6587	76.3

Table 1 reports the number and the percentage of the quotations cleared off the database according to each exclusion criterion.

The final database is then divided into several categories according to the level of moneyness and the maturity of the option. The distinction according to moneyness is carried out in the following way: a call option is called Out-of-The-Money (OTM) if $1.02 < K/F < 1.06$; At-The-Money (ATM) if $0.98 < K/F < 1.02$; and In-The-Money (ITM) if $0.94 < K/F < 0.98$.

Moreover, the concepts of deep Out-of-The-Money (deep OTM) and deep In-The-Money (deep ITM) are defined, respectively, for $K/F > 1.06$, and for $K/F < 0.94$.

A further distinction is made between a short-term contract having a maturity that is equal to or lower than 30 days, and a long-term contract whose maturity lies between 31 and 250 days. Classification according to the level of moneyness and maturity results in 10 different categories of options as shown in Table 2.

It ensues that, for a given maturity, the pattern of implied volatilities according to moneyness exhibits a U profile. This smile is more explicit for short maturities than for long maturities.

It has been largely documented that, for a given asset, uncertainty related to the random variation thereof decreases as the expiry date of the option is drawing near. The graph in Fig. 3 provides evidence that this is not the case for crude oil futures: long-term implied volatilities are lower than those of short-term. This feature is peculiar to crude oil markets. Indeed, long-term options are not intensively exchanged on these markets; thus, recorded volumes are very low which leads to low observable volatilities. As the expiry date approaches, trading frequency becomes higher and implied volatilities increase due to the intensification of exchanges.

Table 2: Properties of the options retained in the cross-section during the sample period 5 November 2004 through 7 November 2005.

	Short-term (5–30 days)					Long-term (31–250 days)				
	Deep ITM	ITM	ATM	OTM	Deep OTM	Deep ITM	ITM	ATM	OTM	Deep OTM
Option premium	8.66	3.65	2.24	1.3	0.42	9.89	5.27	3.94	2.86	1.84
Implied volatility	0.43	0.38	0.37	0.37	0.39	0.38	0.35	0.34	0.35	0.35
Number of options	1468	431	336	217	571	1914	472	299	264	615

Note: Premiums as well as implied volatilities reported in the table are averages over the sample period considered.

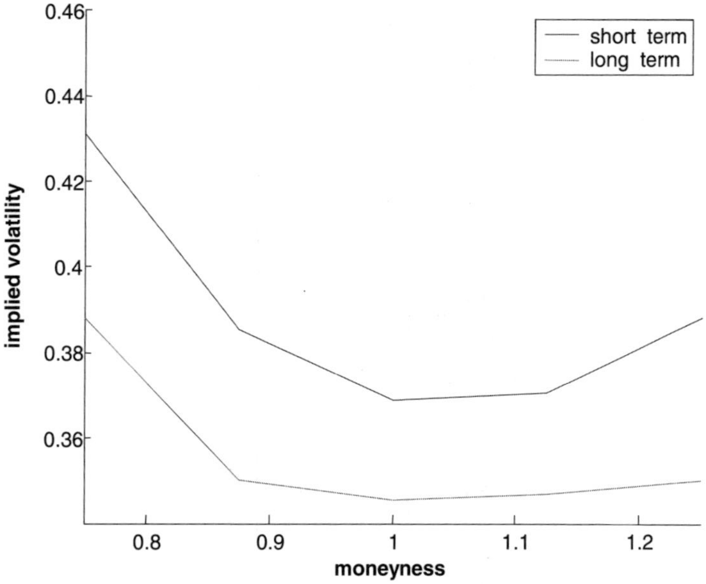

Figure 3: The Smile is more pronounced in the short-term than in the long-term
Note: All the sample estimation is according to each category of moneyness.

In addition, the bias related to the implied volatility increases as the option nears its expiry date; in other words, as the option maturity decreases, the magnitude of the smile increases: this result provides empirical support for the theoretical arguments already reported in the extant literature according to which options die smiling.[l]

With respect to underlying assets, whether relative to currencies or to equities,[m] the relationship between implied volatilities and exercise prices is too recondite to be encapsulated in a smile or a skew. This is typically the case for options on crude oil futures. Figure 4 displays a skew pattern observed on 5 October 2005 that transforms into a smile pattern two days later. The great sensitivity to all economic, financial or political information peculiar to commodity markets can most plausibly be adduced to account for this acute uncertainty that makes it difficult to imagine a standard as well as general profile for implied volatilities.

[l]See Rubinstein (1994) and EngstrÖm (2002) for more detailed discussion of this point.
[m]According to Hull (2000), the volatility pattern across exercise prices tends to be downward sloping for equity options whereas it is slightly U-shaped for currency options.

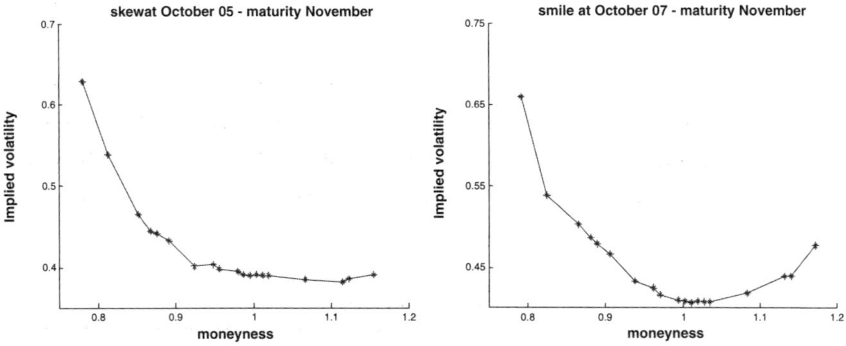

Figure 4: For the same contract, we observe two different profiles for implied volatilities on two close dates: a skew pattern on 5 October 2005 and a Smile pattern on 7 October 2005.

5 Results and Analyses

In order to identify the function that best describes the behavior of the implied volatility, each of the four regression models is estimated over all the estimation period and for all the contracts retained in the sample. For this purpose, several empirical studies had used the Ordinary Least Squares (OLS). Although, nothing ensures us that it is the appropriate method; so, it should be ascertained that the assumption underpinning the OLS estimation method is tenable, which entails checking that the residuals are normally, identically, and independently distributed with zero mean and constant variance. This can be achieved through a twofold testing procedure: first, errors independence should be tested through the errors autocorrelation test; second, variance constancy should be tested through the heteroscedasticity test.

5.1 Checking of the First Assumption: Autocorrelation of the Disturbances

There are several instruments aimed at detecting the autocorrelation in the residuals, such as the visual analysis of correlograms, the Durbin–Watson statistic, or tests pertaining to the Lagrange Multiplier (LM) tests family, among which the Breusch–Godfrey test (1988) is used herein.

The null hypothesis assumes the absence of periodic correlation until a certain order p fixed on *a priori* grounds. The alternative assumption states that the errors follow an $ARMA(r, q)$ process where the delay is such that $p = \max(r, q)$. As far as the alternative hypothesis, simultaneously the assumption of an $AR(r)$ and that of $MA(q)$ for the residuals, is concerned, this test is more robust than the classic Durbin–Watson counterpart which tests only $AR(r)$ for the residuals.

The statistic of this test is equal to $(n-p)R^2$, n being the number of observations and R^2 is the coefficient of determination. Under certain assumptions, this statistic follows the Chi-square distribution with p degrees of freedom: $\aleph^2(p)$. The application of this test on each of the four models yields the results shown in Table 3.

Table 3: Results of the Breusch–Godfrey autocorrelation test.

	Model 1	Model 2	Model 3	Model 4
Breusch–Godfrey statistic	1879.125	2410.735	1886.166	1910.442
p-value	0.0000	0.0000	0.0000	0.0000

It ensues that the disturbances are autocorrelated for all models. Thus some corrections are required to overcome this problem.

5.2 Checking of the Second Assumption: Heteroscedasticity of the Disturbances

This amounts to testing for the assumption of errors' variance constancy, or, to put it differently, to checking that the errors are identically distributed. Applying the OLS method to heteroscedastic models is not an appropriate alternative, since it would generate a skewed estimator of the variance. The White (1980) test, used herein for this purpose, assumes that the residual variance depends on the explained variable, and thus on at least one of the explanatory variables: $V(\varepsilon) = \sigma_\varepsilon^2 + \lambda\left[E(\sigma)\right]^2$.

The null assumption of homoscedasticity tests if $\lambda = 0$; on the other case, there is heteroscedasticity. The statistic of this test is $kR^2 \sim \aleph^2(k-1)$, k being the number of explanatory variables in the regression equation.

The results of this test, applied to each of the four models, are reported in Table 4.

While the test cannot be applied to **Model 1** because it does not include independent variables, it confirms the presence of heteroscedasticity for the remaining three. A key implication of these results is that the OLS estimation method is not tenable. Hence, it behooves us to consider an alternative method impervious to both autocorrelation and heteroscedasticity. Such is indeed the case of the Generalized Moments Method (GMM), inasmuch as it does not

Table 4: Results of the White heteroscedasticity test.

	Model 1	Model 2	Model 3	Model 4
White statistic	—	615.163	1149.388	1612.154
p-value	—	0.0000	0.0000	0.0000

Table 5: Regression parameters (standard deviation in parentheses) and coefficients of determination obtained with a static regression of the sample over all the time period.

	α_0	α_1	α_2	α_3	α_4	α_5	R^2
Model 1	0.3832						
	(0.0530)						
Model 2	1.5886	−2.3485	1.1189				0.2536
	(0.0345)	(0.0717)	(0.0368)				
Model 3	1.7054	−2.5009	1.1943	−0.3150	0.2679		0.4519
	(0.0297)	(0.0617)	(0.0317)	(0.0084)	(0.0114)		
Model 4	1.7208	−2.5253	1.1836	−0.4791	0.3398	0.1156	0.4952
	(0.0297)	(0.0616)	(0.0317)	(0.0272)	(0.0160)	(0.0183)	

Note: All the coefficients are significant.

impose any *a priori* pattern on the residuals. This method consists in arbitrarily fixing values for parameters to be estimated before proceeding to minimize the weighted distance between the observed value of implied volatility and its theoretical value provided by the model. This procedure is repeated until convergence. The application of the GMM[n] yields the results indicated in Table 5.

The results underscore the following observations:

— **Models 2–4** seize the Smile effect with negative coefficients α_1 (which represent the steepness of the Smile) and with positive coefficients α_2 (which represent the curvature of the Smile).

— The coefficient of determination R^2, which measures the explanatory power of the independent variables, differs largely from one model to another. It is equal to 49.52% for **Model 4**, 45.19% for **Model 3**, and 25.36% for **Model 2**. The benchmark model has a zero coefficient of determination since it is a constant function.

[n]The application of the GMM yields exactly to the same parameter estimates as well as the same coefficients of determination than the OLS method, except for standard deviations, which are higher for the former estimation technique than for the latter.

According to this metric, **Model** 4 has the best fit. The fact that this model is more accurate than **Model 3** is rather logical since it takes the same structure as **Model 3** except that it adds another explanatory variable which combines moneyness and time to expiration: $\frac{K}{F}\tau$.

Moreover, results show that the addition of maturity as a state variable proves to be necessary insofar as the explanatory power of the implied volatility was enhanced. The sign of parameters α_3 underscores the tendency of the implied volatility to decrease with the option's maturity.

These results can also be interpreted as a check of IVF stability. Indeed, a rather low coefficient of determination, which is the case for all models, suggests that static models cannot completely explain the behavior of the implied volatility and that a good fit could not be achieved through this type of estimation. This leads to infer that the IVFs are not stable over time; in other words, the volatility function estimated today cannot be the same tomorrow in the valuation formula to deduce the theoretical option premium.

Hence a too long estimation period would not be meaningful and a rather short estimation period should be called for. In order to solve this problem, Rosenberg (1999) and Dumas *et al.* (1998) propose to re-estimate each week the IVF and to compare the new coefficients of determination with those obtained following a static regression.

Following these frameworks, a weekly re-estimation of each model is performed in order to investigate the relationship between the implied volatility and its precursors. A daily re-estimation would not always be possible because of the insufficient number of observations available each day to carry out the regression; by using few observations, sampling variation may be introduced, causing a poor fit.

The estimation window is sliding and is equal to one week (five business days), whereas it was equal to the entire sample period in the first static regression. The results are summarized in Table 6.

According to the regression results, the coefficients of determination are largely higher than those obtained following the first regression. The goodness of fit is enhanced since the IVFs are updated each week. This finding must come as no surprise insofar as new market information are then taken into account from week to week in this second estimation. **Model** 4 turns out again to be the best to model the behavior of implied volatility with a coefficient of determination equal to 71.47%.

Nonetheless, a considerable portion of the implied volatility variability remains yet unexplained by intrinsic characteristics of the option (this portion

Table 6: Coefficients of determination and regression parameters obtained with a dynamic regression on five-day sliding window.

	α_0	α_1	α_2	α_3	α_4	α_5	R^2
Model 1	0.3835						
	(0.0478)						
Model 2	1.6804	−2.5192	1.1976				0.4086
	(0.2366)	(0.4963)	(0.2576)				
Model 3	1.7851	−2.5250	1.2087	−0.9576	4.9675		0.6872
	(0.1835)	(0.3614)	(0.1877)	(0.5799)	(4.4014)		
Model 4	1.8593	−2.7075	1.1940	−2.3128	7.6209	0.5880	0.7147
	(0.1843)	(0.3649)	(0.1838)	(0.7702)	(4.3466)	(0.2129)	

Note: 52 estimations were performed every week; the values referred on the table are the averages of the coefficients.

is, for example, equal to 31.28% in **Model 3** and 28.53% in **Model 4**). In order to achieve an exhaustive explanation of the structure of implied volatilities and hence that of the option premiums, other exogenous variables such as exchange volumes or transaction costs can be introduced into the IVF models.

But to the extent that my aim is to establish a mapping from the intrinsic characteristics of the option to the implied volatilities, such variables were purposely omitted that did not have a direct relation with the crude oil option market; as for this type of options, a multitude of factors[o] can purportedly influence the course of the option and thus its implied volatility.

It is worthwhile to note that regression parameters $\alpha_i, i \in [0, 5]$, while keeping the same signs, are very different from those obtained from all cross-section estimation; this is likely to corroborate the assumption according to which the IVFs are unstable over time.

These parameters are more dispersed than they were in the first estimation; this bears witness to the great heterogeneity inherent in the weekly data of options.

Of greater interest than the individual performance of each model is whether the use of IVFs increases the valuation performance compared to that of the Black (1976) model; the crucial question of how the model is able, once incorporated in a valuation formula, to provide a good estimate of the option premiums one day later needs to be addressed. A new test, this time of

[o]Besides exchange volumes and transaction costs, several factors relating to the major economic decisions or the geopolitical events which occur in the petroleum producing or exporting countries could influence the behavior of implied volatilities.

forecast, will be carried out to assess the predictive *ex ante* ability of the IVFs. The logic of our out-of-sample test is straightforward and follows two steps:

— Use the dynamic regression parameters (the window is equal to $[t-4; t]$) in order to calculate the theoretical value of the implied volatility at date $t+1$.
— The implied volatility predicted at date $t+1$ is then incorporated into the Black valuation formula in order to forecast the value of the option on that date.

This procedure is repeated each week over all the considered period for each regression model. This test allows comparing the ability of various IVFs to correctly anticipate option premiums, in compliance with forecast logic.

To assess the quality of the prediction as well as to appraise the model's out-of-sample fit, two criteria, one of analysis and the other of selection, are computed each week. Concerning the analysis criterion, I choose to work with the Mean Error (ME) which is equal to the average error between the predicted call option at date $t+1$ and that observed on the market on the same date.

$$\mathrm{ME} = \frac{1}{T}\sum_{t=1}^{T}(C_t^{\text{predicted}} - C_t^{\text{observed}}).$$

This criterion allows detecting the direction of the bias: if it is positive (negative), the theoretical model overestimates (underestimates), on average, the option premium.

The second metric is commonly used in the empirical literature to account for the adjustment quality; it is the Mean Square Error (MSE), which is the average squared deviation of the predicted option value of the market observed value. The lower this measure is, the better is the fit.

$$\mathrm{MSE} = \frac{1}{T}\sum_{t=1}^{T}(C_t^{\text{predicted}} - C_t^{\text{observed}})^2.$$

This is considered as a selection criterion in the sense that the model having the smallest MSE is selected as the best to describe the implied volatility pattern, and thus to accurately predict the corresponding option premium.

Table 7 reports, for each model, the values of the analysis criterion, ME, according to whether we place ourselves at short- or long-term, and for each category of moneyness defined above.

Table 7: Results of the out of sample test: ME on short and long terms according to different categories of moneyness.

	Short-term					Long-term				
	Deep ITM	ITM	ATM	OTM	Deep OTM	Deep ITM	ITM	ATM	OTM	Deep OTM
Model 1	0.03	−0.05	−0.10	−0.12	0.05	−0.06	−0.28	−0.30	−0.23	−0.42
Model 2	0.02	0.03	0.03	0.03	0.04	−0.13	−0.09	−0.07	−0.01	−0.17
Model 3	0.17	−0.07	−0.06	0.08	−0.96	0	0.07	0.06	0.08	0.01
Model 4	−0.02	−0.04	−0.02	0.03	0.02	0.04	0.05	0.04	0.08	0.05

ME is an average of bias calculated each day such that it will not enable us to quantify the magnitude of prediction errors, and thus to compare the models between them. Nevertheless, thanks to this first table, we will initially be able to see in which directions violations occur.

It is quite obvious that, except for some few cases, ME increases proportionally to the option maturity, whatever the structural model under scrutiny: the precision of IVF decreases as one moves away from the exercise date of the option. This result can be explained by the fact that the long-term options are not actively exchanged on the market and that their prices are somewhat biased compared to their "real" values; in this case, in addition to the option intrinsic characteristics, several criteria intervene in the assessment of long-term contracts such as investors anticipations on the evolution of the underlying, their degree of risk aversion,. . .

Furthermore, in the short run, the Black (1976) model overestimates the options near the money and underestimates the options deep ITM and deep OTM. On the other hand, in the long run, this model overestimates all the options regardless of their moneyness.

As to the other models, the direction of bias is very sensitive to the option date of expiration and moderately sensitive to its moneyness. But while **Model 2** underestimates all short-term options regardless of their moneyness, and overestimates them in the long run, **Models 3** and **4** underestimate all options in the long run; the direction of the violation is more ambiguous in the short run according to the different categories of options.

All in all, we cannot establish an ultimate clear relationship whether one specific model overestimates or underestimates the option premium; the moneyness and, to a lesser extent, the option's maturity are the principal cause of this ambiguity.

In the remnant of this study, I propose to analyze in more detail the results relating to the precision of various IVFs so as to predict the future value of the option. In so doing, the MSE is considered as the selection criterion. The results are summarized in Table 8.

Several features in Table 8 are noteworthy. First, the MSE statistic is lower in the short term than in the long term except for **Model 3** which has the worst short run forecast performance. One implication of this result is that investors agree a little more on the option value if it nears the expiry date, and the theoretical model in this case enabled us to more accurately assess the future value of the option.

Table 8: Results of the out of sample test: MSE on short and long terms according to different categories of moneyness.

	Short-term					Long-term				
	Deep ITM	ITM	ATM	OTM	Deep OTM	Deep ITM	ITM	ATM	OTM	Deep OTM
Model 1	0.01	0.02	0.05	0.03	0.01	0.09	0.13	0.17	0.11	0.15
Model 2	0.01	0.02	0.03	0.01	0.01	0.09	0.06	0.07	0.05	0.13
Model 3	1.89	0.14	0.27	0.09	11.62	0.02	0.03	0.05	0.04	0.07
Model 4	0.02	0.02	0.04	0.01	0.01	0.09	0.03	0.04	0.08	0.07

Second, in the short run, the more we approach the parity in **Models 1,2,** and **4**, the larger the error is; however, the relationship is less clear in the long-term. This can be explained by the fact that around the money and when the option nears the expiry date, the transactions intensify and exchange volumes grow sharply, so as to cause an increase in uncertainty about the exact value of the option.

Third, **Model 1** presents the worst performance of long-term forecast, which is rather logical since it conveys less information. In the short run, **Model 3** becomes the least suitable to predict the option future value. This result is all the more unexpected that this model proved to be a good fit in the former in-sample regression. The performance depletion of **Model 3** shows that a function's goodness of fit does not necessarily warrant a good quality of forecast. The presence of additional parameters such as option maturity could cause an over-fitting that penalizes the model and decreases its power with respect to short-term prediction.[p] The forecast performance of **Model 2**, which does not include the maturity variable, is better than all other models, for an MSE equal, on average, to 0.084. In the long term, the situation is quite different: the addition of the option's maturity as a predictor discriminatingly enhances the forecast precision as the models including this variable; **Models 3** and **4** are, in this sense, the best ones.

As a summary we can say that the informative value of the maturity, which is an intrinsic characteristic of the option, becomes discriminating in the long term. In the short term, the strike will suffice to correctly forecast the option price. This result seems rather logical since the influence of time until expiry date on the option price decreases monotonically as the maturity date is drawing near.

6 Conclusion

This chapter sets out to model the implied volatility behavior according to both moneyness and option's maturity using the IVFs. Having shown the instability of these functions, I suggested a re-estimation thereof each week in order to take into account the price dynamics in the modeling. The goodness of fit of these models is then largely improved, and the model including the most predictors is selected as being the best to describe the pattern of volatilities extracted from options on crude oil futures.

[p]This meets Dumas *et al.*'s (1998) results.

Once incorporated in a valuation formula, the performance of these models in correctly predicting option prices at a later date was also tested in an out-of sample test; I found that in the short term, a quadratic function of the moneyness outstrips all its counterparts with respect to forecast quality; in the long term, the models including the greatest number of predictors are the best to predict the future value of the option.

Two major results emerge from this empirical study. First, the IVF goodness of fit can be considerably improved by dynamic and continuous re-estimation of the regression parameters. Second, the use of maturity as a state variable for the construction of the IVFs can prove to be sometimes optional, especially in a forecast perspective.

However, it is clear that the profile of crude oil implied volatilities has not been fully explained by the IVFs. Indeed, I used relatively simple functions to model a rather complex variable. Generalizations of IVFs to incorporate additional state variables inherent in crude oil markets could offer promising areas to future research for a better understanding of crude oil implied volatilities.

References

Aijö, J (2003). Determinants of the volatility Smile. Working Paper, *Proceedings of the 2003 Multinational Finance Society Conference*, Montreal.

Bates, DS (1991). The crash of '87: Was it expected? The evidence from options markets. *Journal of Finance*, 46(3), 1099–1144.

Bates, DS (1995). Testing option pricing models. Working Papers, National Bureau of Economic Research, Inc.

Bates, DS (2003). Empirical option pricing: A retrospection. *Journal of Econometrics*, 116, 387–404.

Black, F (1975). Fact and fantasy in the use of options. *Financial Analysts Journal*, 31, 36–41.

Black, F (1976). The pricing of commodity contracts. *Journal of Financial Economics*, 3, 167–179.

Black, F and Scholes, M (1973). The pricing of options and corporate liabilities. *Journal of Political Economy*, 81, 637–659.

Bollen, NPB and Whaley, RE (2004). Does net buying pressure affect the shape of implied volatility functions? *Journal of Finance*, 59(2), 711–753.

Carlson, JB, Craig, BR and Melick, WR (2005). Recovering market expectations of FOMC rate changes with options on federal funds futures. Working Paper, Federal Reserve Bank of Cleveland.

Carr, P and Wu, L (2004). Stochastic skew in currency options. Technical Report, EconWPA.

Cassesse, G and Guidolin, M (2005). Modelling the MIB30 implied volatility surface. Does market efficiency matter? Working Paper, Federal Reserve Bank of St. Louis.

Chriss, NA (1996). *Black-Scholes and Beyond: Option Pricing Models*, 1st Ed. McGraw-Hill.

Cont, R (1998). Beyond implied volatility: Extracting information from option prices. Technical Report, EconWPA.

Daglish, T, Hull, JC and Suo, W (2003). Volatility surfaces: Theory, rules of thumb, and empirical evidence. Working Paper, Rotman School of Management, University of Toronto.

Dennis, P and Mayhew, S (2000). Implied volatility smiles: Evidence from options on individual equities. Working Paper, University of Virginia.

Dumas, B, Fleming, J and Whaley, RE (1998). Implied volatility functions: Empirical tests. *Journal of Finance*, 53(6), 2059–2106.

Duque, JL and Lopes, PT (2003). Maturity and volatility effects on Smiles or dying smiling. *Portuguese Economic Journal*, 2(3), 173–193.

Engstrom, M (2002). Do Swedes smile? On implied volatility functions. *Journal of Multinational Financial Management*, 12(4).

Figlewski, S (1997). *Forecasting Volatility*. Financial Markets, Institutions and Instruments, Vol. 6. Blackwell Publishing.

Godfrey, LG (1998). Tests of non-nested regression models some results on small sample behaviour and the bootstrap. *Journal of Econometrics*, 84(1), 59–74.

Hafner, R and Wallmeier, M (2001). The dynamics of DAX implied volatilities. *International Quarterly Journal of Finance*, 1, 1–27.

Haug, EG (1997). *The Complete Guide to Option Pricing Formulas*, 1st Ed. McGraw-Hill.

Heath, D and Platen, E (2004). Understanding the implied volatility surface for options on a diversified index. Research paper series, Quantitative Finance Research Centre, University of Technology, Sydney.

Heynen, R (1994). An empirical investigation of observed Smile patterns. *The Review of Futures Markets*, 13(2), 317–353.

Horan, SM, Peterson, JH and Mahar, J (2003). The behavior of implied volatility of oil futures options surrounding OPEC meetings. Working Paper, Organization of Petroleum Exporting Countries — OPEC.

Hull, JC (2005). *Options, Futures, and Other Derivatives*, 6th Ed. Prentice Hall.

Ibrahim, OF (2005). Annual oil market report 2005. Research paper series, Organization of the Petroleum Exporting Countries — Public Relations and Information Department.

Lynch, MC (2002). Causes of oil price volatility. Technical Report, 8th International Energy Forum, Osaka 2002.

Pena, I, Rubio, G and Serna, G (1999). Why do we Smile? On the determinants of the implied volatility function. *Journal of Banking and Finance*, 23(8), 1151–1179.

Rosenberg, J (1999). Implied volatility functions: A reprise. Working Paper 99-027, New York University, Leonard N. Stern School of Business.

Rubinstein, M (1994). Implied binomial trees. *Journal of Finance*, 49(3), 771–818.

Shimko, D (1993). Bounds of probability. *Risk*, 6, 33–37.

Skiadopoulos, G, Hodges, S and Clewlow, L (2000). The dynamics of the S&P 500 implied volatility surface. *Review of Derivatives Research*, 3(3), 263–282.

Taylor, S and Xu, X (1994). The magnitude of implied volatility Smiles: Theory and empirical evidence for exchange rates. *Review of Futures Markets*, 13, 355–380.

Unknown (2004). Analysis of the impact of high oil prices on the global economy. Research paper series, International Energy Agency.
Wang, S (2002). An empirical study on the implied volatility function of S&P 500 options. Working Paper, Department of Economics, Queen's University.
White, H (1980). A heteroskedasticity-consistent covariance matrix estimator and a direct test for heteroskedasticity. *Econometrica*, 48(4), 817–838.

CHAPTER 9

PROCYCLICAL BEHAVIOR OF LOAN LOSS PROVISIONS AND BANKING STRATEGIES: AN APPLICATION TO THE EUROPEAN BANKS

*Didelle Dilou Dinamona**

Many authors emphasize the procyclicity of the capital ratio to explain financial instability. The extent of the debátes leads us to question on the procyclicity of loan loss provisions (LLP). Few works were interested in the procyclical character of the policy of provisioning. However, the accounting practices as regards provisioning of the loans losses adopted by the banks can reinforce financial instability.

The objective of this contribution is to study the determinants of the procyclical behavior of loan loss provisions in response to the interrogations caused by the new regulation of Basel II. We analyze the procyclical behavior of the universal banks in the constitution of loan loss provisions. An empirical model on panel data is then adopted by the European banks of 1992–2004. The results are in conformity with those obtained in the former literature to know that the banks adopt procyclical behavior as regards provisioning. We show that when we separately consider the banks according to their degree of diversification (of the activities) the results which we obtain are different. These results enable us to have interesting conclusions like the taking into account the risk weighted asset reduces the volatility of loan loss provisions during the

CREUSET, *Université Jean Monnet*
*Centre de Recherche en Sciences Economiques de l'université de Saint-Étienne, 6 Rue Basse des Rives 42023 Saint-Etienne cedex 02.
didelle.dinamona.dilou@univ-st-etienne.fr.

cycle much more for diversified banks than for specialized banks. The findings of our research are consistent with the empirical work of Laeven and Majnoni (2003), and of Bikker and Metzemakers (2005) who show that the banks fund more the loans losses in economic downswings than in economic upswings for a whole of the OECD countries.

1 Introduction

The last 20 years were characterize by the introduction of the solvency ratios by the Basel[a] committee for the banking monitoring. The objective of the introduction of these solvency ratios is to avoid any financial instability caused by the failure of the banks. However, capital ratios (Cooke ratio and recently McDonough) were suspected to be sources of financial instability. Indeed, the capital ratios proved to be procyclical; in other words they tend to exacerbate the economic cycle. Moreover, provisioning is closely related to the cycle of the economic activity. It reduces the profits which the banks can add to their capital. The provisions are directly related to the quality of the credit banks' portfolio. Consequently, they are more sensitive to the fluctuations coming from the macroeconomic environment and the solvency of the borrowers. They are strongly procyclical because they are positively correlated with the business cycle. Borio *et al.* (2001) show that the provisions increase during the recession and that the provisions reach their maximum one year after the economy downswings.[b]

Provisioning policy is affected by specificities of each country (practical accountants, regulations, and tax policy, for example) but also by the behavior adopted by the banks. The banks create provisions for economic upswings, and they are forced to increase them in economic downswings because of a high failure rate of the borrowers and this in spite of the fall of their results. This behavior justifies the procyclical character of the provisioning policy because provisioning varies according to the economic fluctuations. During economic upswings, banks feed more the stock of provision than in economic downswings when the results are low and the capital expensive.[c]

---

[a]The Basel committee includes the governors of Central Banks and the presidents of the authorities of supervision of the G 10 countries.

[b]It is the case, for example, in Japan where the provisions increased only in the middle of year 1990, a long time after the problems of the Japanese banking structure were recognized.

[c]We suppose that loan loss provisions are stocks (of provisions) calculated by the banks each year to cover the share of the presumed existing unrecovered loan in the banks' loan portfolio. This stock could be fed by financial flows such as movements of currency entering or outgoing of the banking profits on a given date.

The progression of provisions (decrease) during the periods of weak (strong) economic growth is synonymous with a reinforcement of the cycle. The capital ratio itself was suspected to be procyclical (Turner, 2000). Several work concerning the analysis of loan loss provisions, such as Bikker and Metzemakers (2005), Bikker and Hu (2001), Cavallo and Majnoni (2001), Fonseca and Gonzalez (2005), Bouvatier and Lepetit (2006), Perez *et al.* (2006), Laeven and Majnoni (2003), Anandarajan (2005), Lobo and Yang (2001), and Dewenter and Hess (2006), approached mainly the following points: the introduction of the loan loss provisions like an integral part of the capital regulation, the amplification of the fluctuations of the credit supply induced by the capital adequacy constraint and the provisioning system, the management of loan loss provisions at the universal banks[d] and the specialized banks, and finally the use of the provisions for managing objectives and for signaling. Such approaches are valuable lesson. However, they do not integrate the impact of the diversification of the activities on the procyclical character of loan loss provisions or the respect of the risk weighted asset[e] imposed by the Basel committee.

The aim of this chapter is to determine the procyclical behavior of loan loss provisions in the European banks within the 1992–2004 period by distinguishing the banks according to their degree of diversification and by respecting the risk weighted assets as required by the Basel committee. This choice is mainly

Consequently, in the upswings period, this stock would be fed because of the high results of the banks. However, in the downswings period, this stock would not be fed any more following the fall of the results, and more still this stock would strongly decrease because banks will have to fund more (because of the very high failure rate of the borrowers).

[d]The universal banks are banks which practise several activities. They offer an exhaustive range of banking services to all the customers. The cover of the whole of the financial services would lead to savings of range and scale. At the present time in the European countries where banking consolidation is most advanced, the banking environment is structured in oligopoly of universal banks. Engaged in processes of externalization and delocalization, these banks get some of their products, either near specialized subsidiary companies, or near external suppliers. It is the case of the insurance but also for trades closer to the traditional bank, the consumer credit. In addition, Germany, Switzerland, and Austria never derogated from the concept of the universal bank since 19th century. Each bank is being entitled to cover the entirety of the banks' operations. It does not exclude the existence from the banks specialized in certain types of operations. Spain, France, the United Kingdom, and Italy performed the choice much more lately. In France, the principle of the universal bank was introduced by the banking law of 1984 which removed the traditional distinction between investment banks and deposit banks. The second banking directive of 1989 made it possible to combine deposit banks, investment banks, management of credit, financial advisory activities, and the operations related to the insurance. The law of 2, July, 1996 of "modernization of the financial activities" founded a single statute of financial intermediaries authorized to exert activity related to stock exchange.

[e]It defines as the risk measure that consists of multiplying each asset value by a factor (risk weight) that is a proxy of the (credit) risk related to the asset class. Risk-weighted assets are the denominator of the capital ratio.

explained by the fact that on the one hand the universal bank principle is very common throughout Europe and on the other hand it is supposed that the procyclicity of loan loss provisions could be reduced if the banks respect the regulatory constraint. For this purpose, we adopt a panel data approach inspired by Laeven and Majnoni (2003), and Bikker and Metzemakers (2005) using European banks data containing the individual information extracted from the data base Bankscope. Our results confirm the procyclical behavior of the banks in the constitution of the provisions of the losses. In particular, these results show that taking into account the risk weighted assets as defined by the Basel committee makes it possible to reduce the volatility of loan loss provisions during the cycle much more for the diversified banks than for the specialized banks. The chapter is organized in the following way. Section 2 examines the constitution of the provisions on a theoretical level. Adopted methodology and the data used are presented in Section 3. Section 4 analyses and discusses the principal results obtained, and the conclusion is presented in the last section.

2 Provisions: Theoretical Aspects and Procyclicity

2.1 Theoretical Aspects

The provisions are used to anticipate a probable loss. The provisions are deducted on the result of the banks to face loan losses. Provisions are deduced by anticipation from the losses which normally will occur. Provisions for depreciated credits are considered as a charge because their calculations also involve a reduction in the value of the credit net, generally by a reduction of the measured value of the loans. Dewenter and Hess (2003) add that the provisions for loan loss reduce the net profits which the banks can add in their capital. This fact reduces their capacity to increase the amount of their credits or their risk and always to satisfy the capital requirements. The provisioning gives a more faithful image of the result and banking credits (Borio and Lowe, 2001). The banks fund loan losses for two principal reasons: the first reason relates to a preoccupation with an improvement of the transparency of the balance sheet. And the second is the emphasis on the incidence of the provisioning policy on the volatility and the cyclical evolution of the earnings.

We distinguish two types of provision: general provisions and specific provisions (Cortavarria *et al.*, 2000). General provisions are used to protect from the loan losses on the bank's loan portfolio while the specific provisions are made for individually evaluated losses on loans. The specific provisions are only given when the losses are probable (Cavallo and Majnoni, 2001). With the difference of the general provisions (or discretionary) which depend partially on the expansion on credit and which are handled by the discretionary behavior of the managers, specific provisions are retrospective in nature; in other words, they reduce the risks of accounts manipulation but can amplify business cycles (Borio and Lowe, 2001; Bouvatier and Lepetit, 2006a,b). Indeed, this retrospective nature contributes to the increase of the provisions during economic downswings because of to the deterioration of the quality of the credit. The result of this fact is the increase of the variability of the accounting incomes.

In addition, the relation between LLP and equities is explained by the covering of credit risk: the conceptual framework of the credit risk management supposes that the expected losses must be covered by the provisions while the unexpected losses must be covered by the capital. If the banking earnings are not sufficient to cover the provisions, there is an erosion of the capital. Cavallo and Majnoni (2001) note that in the presence of shock, loan losses provisions make it possible to cover the expected losses while the capital makes it possible to cover the unexpected losses. They notice that the capital requirements only concern the unexpected losses and loan loss provisions do not include like component of the capital regulation. General provisions are built-in in the owners' equity of category 2 (within the limit of 1.25% of the credits balanced according to the risk) under Basel I.[f]

Borio and Lowe (2001) analyze the need for clarifying the relation between provisions and capital equities. They theoretically suggest the exclusion of the general provisions of the capital equities[g] and the determination of the provisions so as to cover the estimated amount of the net losses in the banks' portfolio. Thus, the provisions should cover the identified credit losses, and the capital should cover the unidentified credit losses. The solution suggested by the Basel committee is to anticipate and to be able to equip with the provisions for expected losses and not yet identified losses (Bank of France, 2003).

[f] The Basel committee proceeded to a revision of the treatment of the provisions for Basel II. It proposes to adjust the criteria to take into account the provisions beyond the amount which can be included in capital equities of category 2. The provisions higher than the ceiling can compensate for the capital requirements but only insofar as the share of the loss anticipated in the capital equities requirement NI also exceeds the maximum amount of the provisions being able to be included in the capital equities of category 2.

[g] The opinions are divided between the banks authorities and the banks supervisors. The researchers (in the banking field) consider that capital equities are intended to protect it from the unidentified losses rather than the losses envisaged resulting from the solvency of the borrower. Banks supervisors disagree with this opinion.

Laeven and Majnoni (2001), Bikker and Metzemakers (2005), Cavallo and Majnoni (2001), Ahmed *et al.* (1999), and Perez *et al.* (2006) confirm that loan loss provisions must be taken into account in the capital regulation. They empirically find a negative relation between the capital ratio and the loan loss provisions. Indeed, by holding risky credits, banks fund more (in the event of loss) and they are obliged to respect the capital requirements. Anandarajan *et al.* (2005) do not share this idea. They confirm the relation between the LLP and the management of the capital on the Australian banks.

Ahmed *et al.* (1999), Moyer (1990), Beatty *et al.* (1995), Collins *et al.* (1995), and Perez *et al.* (2006) show that the banks use loan loss provisions for managing their capital with an aim of satisfying the capital requirements specified by the regulators. Lobo and Yang (2001) show that banks which have a small capital ratio can increase their LLP in the intention to reduce the regulatory costs imposed by capital requirements. However, in period of recession, the capital becomes expensive and LLP are high. Banks often answer by reducing their loans. Consequently, it is difficult for banks to manage their capital by the means of LLP in period of recession.

In the analysis of the impact of the provisions on the capital, we must consider the taxes. Cortavarria *et al.* (2000) show that the deductible tax can increase the capital ratio. By supposing, for example, a rate of tax identical and a detention of the general provisions to a level for the banks of the emergent countries, the deductible tax (of the general provisions) can contribute to increase the ratio of capital and to cause a strong incentive of the banks to be subjected to the capital requirements. Conversely, a very restrictive tax policy discourages banks to fund adequately (Cavallo and Majnoni, 2001). We analyze in the following section the procyclical character of LLP.

2.2 Procyclical Aspects of Provisioning Policy

Within this framework, we analyze the procyclical behavior of LLP. It is pointed out that LLP are annual provisions made up to note the share of non-recoverability supposed in the bank's portfolio.

Indeed, the credit cycle is characterized, by a strong rise of the provisions and a contraction of the new credits in the phases of recession and during the time of growth, by a fall of the provisions and a development of the new credits (Bank of France, 2003). The banks fund only when there is a default of the borrower and that is more plausible during economic downswings. The negative relation between growth rate of the activity (CPIB) and LLP is justified by the fact that in economic upswings, banks, being very optimistic, increase their standards of credit by granting more loans and decreases the provisions for doubtful debts. For this purpose, they reduce their aptitude to suitably supervise the borrowers before granting the loans. Consequently, the asymmetry of information existing between banks and the possible borrowers in addition, increases to a level of risk of no refunding of the loans. This risk appears in the weak period of growth of the economic activity or in the period of recession where banks increase the provisions, but these provisions reduce their earnings. Banks are thus obliged to reduce their credit delivery. We find thus a tightness of credit (credit crunch) when the borrowers need liquidity. This tightness of credit accentuates the period of recession.

We suggest that it is the behavior of the banks as regards provisioning of the loans which is procyclical and not loan loss provisions themselves. The analysis of the cyclic properties of some variables relates to the amplitude of fluctuations (standard deviation) and the degree of comovement with the CPIB, which is used as measurement of the pro- or contra-cyclical character (sign). This analysis is made on the basis of the theory of the real cycle in macroeconomics.[h]

2.2.1 Cyclical Properties of the LLP

Two aspects of the evolution of the macroeconomic variables are to be retained when the statistics of the cycle are studied. First, the fluctuations of an aggregate are considered. The fluctuations of an aggregate represent the difference between the value carried out of the aggregate and the random tendency characterizing its evolution in the course of time. Second, the extent of the fluctuations of an aggregate is measured by the standard deviation expressed as a percentage difference between the value carried out of the aggregate and its random tendency. To measure the link between the business cycle and the variable concerned, two measurements are important.

First, we use the simple correlations between the CPIB and the variable concerned. Within this framework, if the correlation between LLP and CPIB is positive, then we can determine the procyclical character of the LLP. If the correlation between LLP and CPIB is negative, then we can determine the contracyclical character of LLP. The degree of comovement with CPIB is measured

[h]Work of origin on the real cycles comes from Kydland and Prescott (1982), Long and Plosser (1983), and Hansen (1985). This work is based on the whole of models seeking to establish that the optimal answers of the economic agents to shocks of real nature can produce cyclic characteristics close to those observed. Consequently, taking into account the monetary shocks is not considered to be necessary.

by the coefficients of correlation of the cyclic variations of the variable compared to the cyclic variation of CPIB. If the correlation is positive and close to 1, then we can affirm that the variable is strongly procyclical. On the other hand, if the correlation (between the variation of CPIB and the variable concerned (LLP)) is negative and close to 1, then the variable is contracyclical. Lastly, if it is close to 0, then the variables do not vary in a contemporary way with the cycle, and in this case, the variable known does not correlate with the cycle.

Second, we use the measurement of the crossed correlations to see whether there is a shift between the variables.

Within this framework, we test the degree of comovement of LLP_ASSET and CPIB.

Table 1 provides the properties of LLP and CPIB on the data of the 17 European banking structures over the period of 1992–2004. The following statistics are reproduced:

— the standard deviation (in %);
— the standard deviation of variable (in fact LLP) compared to the standard deviation of the CPIB;
— the correlation with CPIB.

The decomposition of the trend compared to the cycle is obtained by the application of the filter Hodrick and Prescott (1980). This filter makes it possible to standardize the stationarity of the data. It makes it possible to eliminate from the series the low movement's frequency. By isolating the movements from a series present between a higher limit and a lower limit of the data of a frequency or duration, this filter eliminates the movements out of the desired frequency band.[i]

Table 1: Cyclical property of LLP_ASSET.

Variable j	Standard deviation (σ_j)	$\sigma_j/\sigma_{\mathrm{PIB\_H}}$	Cor (j, PIB_H)
CPIB	0.71	1	1
LLP_ASSET	0.77	1.08	−0.076

LLP_ASSET = the ratio of loan loss provisions on the total assets. CPIB_HP = growth rate of the activity (CPIB) cleaned of the trend by the Hodrick–Prescott filter. These data are annual and relatives to the 17 countries.

[i]For more precision, see Norden (2004).

We noted that variable LLP_ASSET is negatively correlated with the CPIB. Consequently, this variable does not move in a contemporary way with the cycle. This shows that it is the procyclical behavior of the banks (because of variability of the bank earning) which justifies the procyclical character of the provisions. The procyclicity of LLP_ASSET is explained by the behavior adopted by the banks and not by the cyclical properties of LLP.

2.2.2 Credit Fluctuations and Accounting Practices

It is pointed out that the loan loss reserves are made up to cover the expected losses coming from the defaults of the borrowers or the incapacity of the borrowers to refund the interest of the loan. Of this definition, we understand well that the provisions depend enormously on the risk of credit. The increase of loan loss provisions due to the deterioration of the quality of the bank's credit portfolio can involve a fall of the banking capital if the losses are very high. Indeed, these donations are considered as an expense which decreases the value of the capital. Consequently, a bad risk management can thus have procyclical effects.

In addition, Bouvatier and Lepetit (2006a,b) show the need for the decomposition of the provisions. They highlight the two components[j]: the nondiscretionary component or nondiscretionary provisions and the discretionary component or discretionary provisions. First, it is made up to cover identified losses in the bank's portfolio (Wahlen, 1994; Beaver and Engel, 1996). Banks assimilate mainly the identification of the losses on credit to the nondiscretionary provisions, and this system is indicated of backward-looking. During economic downswings there is an increase in LLP because the default rates are high for this period. Thus, the nondiscretionary component amplifies the credit cycle and involves a misevaluation of identified losses in the portfolio. In the same way, credit risk appears as soon as the loan is granted and not only when the losses are identified during the economic downswings, which can involve a bad provisioning of the loans during the phase of growth. Thus, banks fund the loans tardily because they wait until the risks inherent in the loans are proved during economic downswings (Laeven and Majnoni, 2003). The procyclicity of LLP directly affects the capital, and earnings. Banks are

[j] According to accounting practices, we distinguish the specific provisions and the general provisions. However the literature considers the two components: discretionary and nondiscretionary components of LLP. This distinction of LLP enables us to highlight the component which is dependent on the cycle of the activity.

encouraged to grant new loans which can lead to a tightening of the credit (capital crunch) and to a stressing of the tendencies of the cycle (recession or expansion). With regard to the discretionary component of the provisions, it relates to the objectives of management. Indeed, the managers use this component for three principal reasons: to smooth their income, to manage their capital, and to signal their performance on the market. This proportion of the provisions which is used for managements' objective is not affected by the fluctuations of credit and thus by the business cycle (Bouvatier and Lepetit, 2006a).

The method of provisioning backward-looking (recording of the losses that after having intervened) amplifies the cycle of credit and thus supports a procyclical behavior because the risks of credit appear too late in the accounting system. Indeed, the provisions do not reflect the true risk of credit inherent in the bank's portfolio which from an economic standpoint exists as of the granting of the loan. Moreover, the variability of earnings and losses increases during the economic cycle. For example, during economic downswings characterized by a deterioration of the economic activity, the borrowers test more difficulties of refunding their loans, which leads banks to reinforce their provisions for doubtful debts. The provisions are proportionally made up with volumes of the loans granted by the banks. For this purpose, the increase in the provisions reduces the accounting incomes, which encourages banks to reduce their credit delivery. This restriction of the credit delivery intervenes when the borrowers have more need for liquidity, and it follows a stressing of the economic downswings. In the phase of recovery, earnings increase by the reduction in the provisions due to the general improvement of the economic situation. The increased profitability obtained by the banks leads them to soften their standards of credit and to grant loans to risky borrowers. As for the forward-looking method, it allows an adequate provisioning of the loans, and consequently it attenuates the variability of the credit cycle. This method is equivalent to a dynamic provisioning of the bank loans.

Finally, according to the selected accounting method (forward-looking or backward-looking), loan loss provisions can prove more or less procyclical. The credit cycle follows the tendencies of the cycle of the economic activity. The realization of the risks is the principal explanation. Indeed, in the phases of boom, banks try to take more risks on the basis of the trend of the economy. Indeed, banks are excessively optimistic during the high phases of the cycle.

We can say that the fluctuations of the cycle of credit in addition to the bad accounting practices (policy of provisioning) can only accentuate the procyclical behavior of banks in the constitution of loan loss provisions. We present in the following section our empirical work.

3 Methodology and Data

3.1 Data

The individual data of the banks used come from the data base Bankscope of the agency of rating Londonienne IBCA (International Credit Analysis Limited). These data relate to the details of the asset and the liability of the banking assessments harmonized, like on the income statement. The total number of the sample comprises 862 banks. They are commercial banks related to 17 countries of Europe (Austria, Belgium, Denmark, Finland, France, Germany, Greece, Ireland, Italy, Luxembourg, the Netherlands, Norway, Portugal, Spain, Switzerland, Sweden, and the United Kingdom). The choice of the only commercial banks is explained by the fact why those concentrate more on the activity of the loans and deposits. Our sample is divided into two groups: diversified banks and specialized banks. We consider that a bank is classified as diversified if the share of the non-interest incomes on the total income is higher than its median. On the contrary, it is considered as a specialized bank if the share of the incomes other than the incomes of interest is lower than its median. Consequently, the criterion of classification used is the median of the non-interest income over the total income. Under this typology we have 437 diversified banks[k] and 425 less diversified (specialized) banks over period 1992–2004 for the 17 countries.

We specify that the sample available contained at the beginning 2512 banks and 32,669 observations. To minimize the effects of measurement due to the presence of missing observations in our estimates, a filter is applied to the data, making it possible to exclude the banks whose information is not indicated over three consecutive years. With the resulting one from this process of filtering, we obtain a new sample made up of 862 banks.

In addition, we check if the explanatory variable is introduced into our equations, the ratio of loan loss provisions on the total assets (LLP_ASSET) is a homogeneous or heterogeneous variable within the 17 European countries. In other words, we check if we are confronted with homogeneity of the data

[k]After cleaning the data.

related to LLP_ASSET. For that, we carry out a test of equality of the averages on variable LLP_ASSET. For that, we break up total variability (TSS) ratio LLP_ASSET. The total variability is broken up as the sum of the interindividual variance (variability between BSS) and of the intraindividual variability (variability within WSS). The share of the interindividual variance (BSS) is stronger in total variability. We can say that there is heterogeneity of the data related to variable LLP_ASSET.[1]

The distribution of the banks available according to countries' is presented in Table A.1 of Appendix A.

3.2 *Methodology*

We consider in our estimates two categories of explanatory variables. The first relates to LLP_ASSET and the second is the volatility of LLP_ASSET. The principal equations of estimates are as follows:

$$\begin{aligned}\frac{\text{LLP}}{\text{Asset}} &= \alpha_1 + \beta_1\left(\frac{\text{Ebt}}{\text{Asset}}\right)_{it} + \beta_2\text{Pib}_{it} + \beta_3\text{R10y}_{it} + \beta_4\text{Growth\_loans}_{it} \\ &\quad + \beta_5\text{Tlta}_{it} + \beta_6\text{Eqta}_{it} + \beta_7\text{Size}_{it} + \beta_8\text{Div2}_{it} + \beta_9\text{Interact}_{it} \\ &\quad + \beta_{10}\text{Cap\_buffer}_{it} + \beta_{11}\text{Listed}_t + \varepsilon_{it}.\end{aligned}$$

LLP_ASSET volatility

$$\begin{aligned}\text{Risk\_LLP} &= \alpha_1 + \beta_1\left(\frac{\text{Ebt}}{\text{Asset}}\right)_{it} + \beta_2\text{Sh\_roa}_{it} + \beta_3\text{Ch\_eqta}_{it} + \beta_4\text{Pib}_{it} \\ &\quad + \beta_5\text{Size}_{it} + \beta_6\text{Growth\_loans}_{it} + \beta_7\text{Dpib}_{it} + \beta_8\text{Rec}_{it} \\ &\quad + \beta_9\text{Div2}_{it} + \beta_{10}\text{Tot\_capratio}_{it} + \beta_{11}\text{Listed}_t + \varepsilon_{it}.\end{aligned}$$

We estimate our model on the whole of the banks. The model is estimated with the panel data. Firstly, we carried out the estimate by the method of feasible GLS with fixed effect. Secondly, we estimated the model with delays of the endogenous. The advantage of this estimate is to take into account the provisions passed in the variable explanation of the endogenous and moreover that the potential problem of omission of the variables in the estimate reduces. We have included a first and second delay of explanatory variable LLP_ASSET.

[1]There is heterogeneity of the data if the intraindividual variability is null and the total variability is equal to the interindividual variance. Conversely, there is a perfect homogeneity of the data if the interindividual variance of the studied variable is null and the total variability is equal to the intraindividual variability.

Thus the estimated dynamic equation takes the following form:

$$\begin{aligned}\frac{\text{LLP}}{\text{Asset}} &= \alpha_1 + \beta_1\left(\frac{\text{LLP}}{\text{Asset}}\right)_{i,t-1} + \beta_2\left(\frac{\text{LLP}}{\text{Asset}}\right)_{i,t-2} + \beta_3\left(\frac{\text{Ebt}}{\text{Asset}}\right)_{it} \\ &\quad + \beta_4\text{Pib}_{it} + \beta_5\text{R10y}_{it} + \beta_6\text{Growth\_loans}_{it} + \beta_7\text{Tlta}_{it} \\ &\quad + \beta_8\text{Eqta}_{it} + \beta_9\text{Size}_{it} + \beta_{10}\text{Div2}_{it} + \beta_{11}\text{Interact}_{it} \\ &\quad + \beta_{12}\text{Cap\_buffer}_{it} + \beta_{13}\text{Listed}_t + \varepsilon_{it}.\end{aligned}$$

The introduction of the delays on explanatory variable LLP_ASSET leads us to estimate the model by the method of the generalized moments (GMM) suggested by Arellano and Bond (1991) in order to cure the correlation between the endogenous variable and the residues of the regression. This procedure of estimate includes two stages: the first consists in rewriting the dynamic model form of differences in order to eliminate the specific effects. However, this transformation generates another problem which is the correlation between the explanatory variable and the term of error. This is why in the second stage we use the instrumental variables which are made up of all the delayed variables of the endogenous variable expressed in a level to avoid any risk of autocorrelation.

However, to have robust and valid results, we carried out several tests as a preliminary. First of all, a test of Fisher was carried out to check if we are in the presence of a homogeneity or heterogeneity of the behaviors. It is a question of knowing if the European banks (resulting from our sample) have individual specificities that can induce different behaviors with regard to LLP_ASSET. For that, we confront the null assumption H0 (complete homogeneity of the behaviors) with alternative assumption HA (complete heterogeneity of the behaviors) on the basis of statistics of the test of Fisher. We reject the null assumption with a threshold of risk strongly to be mistaken in 1%. We can thus affirm that there is heterogeneity of the behaviors. Then, we tested the individual effect if it is fixed or variable by the test of exogeneity of Haussman. This test consists in testing the exogeneity of the explanatory variables compared to the error specific to the model. The null assumption of these statistics of the test is the absence of correlation between the specific error and the specific variables. The results of this test reveal the need for taking into account the effects specific to the banks. These specific effects can be related, for example, to the accounting of the non-performing loans, to tax policy etc. Then, we checked if the errors respect the good properties in fact if they are homoscedastic, and neither are correlated between the various variables by applying the test of White to the residues obtained in the regression. We point out that the test of White is based on a significant relation between the square of the residue and one or more explanatory variables in level and with the square within the same regression equation. Taking into consideration the test of White, we conclude that the heteroscedasticity is present. We corrected this heteroscedasticity by the matrix of White. Lastly, we check if the errors are correlated between them by the means of the Durbin Watson (DW) test. The autocorrelation is present, and let us correct it by the method of Newey–West.

In addition, a unit test of root was worked out for the whole of the banking series of our sample. For that, we carried out three tests of stationary to know the test of Im-Pesaran-Shin (IPS),[m] the test of Levin–Flax–Chu (LLC), and the tests of Fisher related to the data of each bank (Maddala and Wu, 1999; Choi, 2001); Fisher-type tests using ADF and PP tests (Maddala and Wu, 1999; Choi, 2001; Hadri, 1999). The results of these tests applied to our data confirm, as a whole, a rejection of the null assumption of non-stationarity to the threshold of risk of 1%. The data are stationary. The results of the tests are provided is Table A.2 of Appendix A.

4 Results

4.1 Descriptive Statistics

The statistics related to the principal variables according to the type banks (diversified, specialized) are indexed in Table 2.

We note on average that the growth of the loans for specialized banks (13.14%) is much weaker than those of the diversified banks (15.3%). This result is justified by the fact that the diversified banks (which are large banks) increase their share of market much more quickly than specialized banks because they have greater number of customers. The activity of credit (TLTA) is more important in the specialized banks (60.14% instead of 49.54% for the diversified banks). These banks are capitalized (EQTA) and hold a surplus of capital (CAP_BUFFER) higher than that of the diversified banks. Size (SIZE) of the diversified banks is larger than that of the specialized banks. It turns around 15.72 against 14.37 for the specialized banks. The share loan loss provision on the total assets (LLP_ASSET) is much weaker for the diversified banks because they are supposed to have better information on their borrowers.

[m]The H0 assumption of the IPS test is that all the series are nonstationary against the alternative assumption: only a fraction of the individual series is stationary. A probability of the test lower than 10% leads to the rejection of H0. The null assumption of the LLC test is that all the series are nonstationary against the alternative assumption: all the series are stationary. A probability of the test lower than 10% leads to the rejection of H0.

Table 2: Descriptive statistics.

Variables	N	Mean	Standard deviation	Min	Max
Specialized banks					
EBT_ASSET	1738	1.01	1.24	−19.01	12.78
CPIB	1738	2.17	1.50	−1.17	9.03
R10*y*	1738	6.06	1.88	3.15	13.54
GROWTH_LOANS	1738	13.14	32.37	−99.37	516.97
TLTA	1738	60.14	19.93	0.081	99.03
EQTA	1738	9.14	5.40	0.617	75.84
SIZE	1738	14.37	1.87	10.36	20.54
DIV2	1738	18.26	34.02	−1261.842	31.73
LLP_ASSET	1738	0.57	0.755	−6.01	11.21
INTERACT	1738	1.10	0.95	0	12.78
CAP_BUFFER	1738	7.48	8.46	−6.26	78.10
Diversified banks					
EBT_ASSET	1849	1.04	1.54	−19.04	22.90
CPIB	1849	2.33	1.61	−1.17	9.03
R10Y	1849	5.63	1.69	2.27	13.57
GROWTH_LOANS	1849	15.3	80.89	−99.91	2719.63
TLTA	1849	49.54	21.31	0.01	98.27
EQTA	1849	7.24	5.10	0.81	48.93
SIZE	1849	15.72	2.47	4.56	20.6485
LLP_ASSET	1849	0.36	0.64	−3.37	11.86
DIV2	1849	49.155	21.73	31.77	472.1466
INTERACT	1849	1.10	1.38	0	22.90
CAP_BUFFER	1849	6.04	8.01	−6.48	65.50

Of this informational advantage, we can say that the diversified banks could have fewer failed loans and constitute fewer loan loss reserves (Dewenter and Hess, 2006). The correlations between the variables is provided is Table A.3 of Appendix A.

4.2 Interpretations

4.2.1 Results Interpretation on the Whole Sample of Banks Concerning LLP_ASSET

All the coefficients have, as a whole, the excepted signs except for variable SIZE. The dummy years and dummy dates variables were introduced and then removed, because they do not improve the results. The results are provided in Table A.4 of Appendix A over period 1992–2004.

The coefficient associated to earning before tax (EBT_ASSET) is significant and has the expected sign. Indeed, banks increase their loan loss provisions when their profits are weak. This result does not confirm the assumption of the income smoothing in the majority of banks and shows that banks do not smooth their income. This result is conforming to the conclusions found by Laeven and Majnoni (2003), and Anandarajan *et al.* (2005). In addition, we can interpret this result by the fact that the banks minimize (maximize) loan loss provisions when their income are weak (high). We can note that the banks adopt an imprudent behavior with regard to the management of their provisioning policy.

The increase of loan loss provisions following the fall of the CPIB can be explained by the fact that the banks fund more in economic downswings than in economy upswings. This result confirms the procyclical character of the loan loss provisions and justifies the procyclical behavior of banks. Bouvatier and Lepetit (2006), Cavallo and Majnoni (2001), Fonseca and Gonzalez (2005), and Anandarajan *et al.* (2005) found the same results.

R10y represents the 10-year government bonds. The rate applied is a long-term interest rate. Indeed, the received interests of the banks depend on the long-term interest rates. It is noted that the coefficient which is associated to it is positive. In other words the long-term interest rate makes it possible for the banks to provide loan loss provisions.

Growth of the loans is a variable proxy of the risk (Bikker and Metzemakers, 2005) because the increase in the loans in economic upswings leads to an increase of the risk. This growth of the loans is associated to a fall of the efforts of the banks' monitoring and a deterioration of the quality of the portfolio. This variable is significant with the threshold of risk of 1%. These results are similar to those of Laeven and Majnoni (2003), and Cavallo and Majnoni (2002).

The coefficient related to the activity of credit (TLTA) is significantly positive. This means that the more the banks increase their activities of credit, the more they constitute loan loss provisions.

Variable SIZE is calculated as the logarithm of the bank's total assets. It is a control variable of banks' size but also of the phenomenon of the too-big-to-fail. The large banks tend to hold more risk. The coefficient associated with this variable is significantly negative. The larger the size of the bank is, the more the loan loss provisions decrease.

The coefficient associated to DIV2 (the share of the net interest incomes over the total income) is significantly positive. Indeed, the more the banks diversify their activities, the less they constitute loan loss provisions.

Interact has a dummy variable which takes 1 if the earning before tax is negative and zero otherwise. The coefficient associated to variable Interact is significantly positive. This result indicates that the banks increase their provisions when they cut losses and when their earnings are weak.

The coefficients associated to CAP_BUFFER and EQTA are not significant. CAP_BUFFER is introduced because it varies in a contracyclical way through the cycle. The banks are supposed to hold a surplus of capital. As for EQTA, it makes it possible for banks to absorb their unexpected losses of banks' portfolios. Thus, a more important cover of the credit by the capital makes it possible to absorb an anticipated loss.

4.2.2 Interpretation of the Results Obtained on the Diversified Banks and Specialized Banks

We find as a whole that the coefficients are significant and have expected signs. The coefficient associated with the variable with capitalization EQTA is not significant. Results are provided in Table A.4 of Appendix A.

The Listed variable is a dummy variable which takes 1 if the bank is quoted on the stock exchange and 0 if not. The sign which is associated with this variable is positive and significant. Indeed, the banks which are quoted on the stock exchange increase their loan loss provisions. This is explained by the fact that the transparency of accounting information reduced the risk of manipulation of the accounts by banks. The banks manage their policies of provisioning correctly. Consequently, they adopt a careful attitude and they reduce their procyclical behavior as regards provisioning. The nonsignificance of EQTA can be explained by the fact that diversified banks do not increase their provisions to the same level of what specialized banks do.

We find that loan loss provisions carried out in the current year are closely related to the made up loan loss provisions two years ago. These coefficients associated with the LLP_ASSET delayed one year and two years have the expected signs.[n]

4.2.3 Interpretation of the Results Obtained on the Whole Sample of Banks Concerning RISK_LLP

The results are provided in Table A.5 of Appendix A over period 1992–2004.

[n]The table of this result is not presented in this chapter but can be given if necessary.

Variable RISK_LLP indicates the volatility of loan loss provisions. We note that the coefficients associated to EBT_ASSET, CPIB, SIZE, DPIB, REC, and TOT_CAPRATIO, LISTED are significant and have the expected signs. On the other hand, GROWTH_LOANS, SH_ROA, DIV2, and CH_EQTA are not significant. DPIB represents the variation of the growth of the GDP over two consecutive years. The coefficient associated with this variable is significant and negative. This result could mean that the volatility of LLP_ASSET increases when variation of the growth of the GDP is negative. The same result is valid for REC which is a dummy variable which takes 1 if we have a weak growth of the GDP and 0 if not.

TOT_CAPRATIO which is the ratio of capital is significant. We find that the more the banks respect the ratio of capital, the more the volatility of LLP_ASSET increases. An astonishing result because of the expected effect is that the volatility of LLP_ASSET should be reduced.

The coefficient associated with variable LISTED is significantly positive. The more the banks are quoted on the stock exchange, the less variable is the RISK_LLP.

SH_ROA is the return on asset per unit of risk, and CH_EQTA represents the variation in capital over two years (T and $T+1$). The coefficients associated with these variables are not significant. Of the same DIV2, variable proxy of the diversification activities is not significant. In other words, the diversification activities do not have any impact on the risk or better on the volatility of LLP_ASSET, which is similar for the growth of loans (GROWTH_LOANS).

4.2.4 For the Specialized Banks

The coefficients associated with variables EBT_ASSET, CH_EQTA, CPIB, SIZE, GROWTH_LOANS, DPIB, REC, DIV2, TOT_CAPRATIO, and LISTED are significant. The coefficient associated with variable SH_ROA is not significant. In other words, the return on asset per unit of risk does not have impact on the volatility of LLP_ASSET for the specialized banks.

4.2.5 For the Diversified Banks

All the coefficients are significant and have the excepted signs for SH_ROA which is not significant.

All in all, the results are practically similar for the diversified banks and for the specialized banks concerning variables LLP_ASSET and RISK_LLP.

Nevertheless, the results are better for the diversified banks concerning variable RISK_LLP, because all the results are significant and have the expected signs.

We introduced thereafter into our estimates variable RWA_ASSET which is the risk weighted asset. This weighting is imposed by the regulator and is regarded as a measurement of the composition of the banks' portfolio. The introduction of this variable reduced our sample to 938 observations and restricted the period of estimate to 1992–2000. The estimate made on the total sample shows that all the coefficients are significant except for EQTA and of RWA_ASSET. The results are provided in Table A.6 of Appendix A.

Variable INTM indicates the share of the incomes of interest on the total assets. It is a variable proxy risk of the portfolio because a high interest rate should lead to a reduction in the bad quality of the portfolio. A bad quality of the portfolio generally results in bad loans. Indeed, the risky borrowers are not ready to accept the loan if the interest rate is high. We note that the coefficient associated with INTM is significantly positive. If the banks increase their incomes of interest, they could more constitute loan loss provisions.

In addition, for the estimate of variable RISK_LLP (see Table A.7) with regard to the specialized banks, we find that all the coefficients are significant except for the variation of GDP (DPIB), TOT_CAPRATIO, and LISTED. We note that the associated coefficient variable RWA_ASSET is significant and that it has the awaited sign. This coefficient is significantly positive. Indeed, if the banks balance their credits in accordance with the risks which they can take, the volatility of LLP_ASSET during the cycle is reduced. We find the same result only at the diversified banks and not at the specialized banks. We note that all the coefficients are significant for the diversified banks except for DIV2 and GROWTH_LOANS.

An increase in the return on asset per unit of risk results in a fall of the volatility of LLP_ASSET during the cycle. In the same way, an adequate weighting of the credits involves a fall of the volatility of LLP_ASSET. An improvement of CPIB (growth rate of the activity) causes an increase in the volatility of LLP_ASSET. We could explain by the fact that banks in economic upswings reduce their monitoring. We thus have an increase in asymmetry of information and rebound of the risk. The more the size of the banks the more the reduction of the volatility of LLP. This result is due to the fact that diversified banks maintain a long-term relation with their customers. They renegotiate their loans before considering them as non-performing loans. So they constitute fewer provisions compared to specialized banks, and the volatility of their LLP is reduced. More the diversified banks respect the minimal requirements of capital, the more the volatility of the LLP increases. However, if these banks remain quoted on the stock exchange, the volatility of their LLP will remain low. As for the specialized banks, we find that EBT_ASSET, SIZE, GROWTH_LOANS, DPIB, DIV2, and LISTED are significant.

RWA_ASSET, SH_ROA, and T_CAPRATIO are not significant.

5 Conclusion

Throughout this chapter, we highlighted the determinants of the procyclical behavior of the loan loss provisions within the European banks of 1992–2004. We divided the sample into the diversified banks and the specialized banks. The selected criterion is the share of non-interest income on the total incomes. The results related to the whole of the banks show that the banks increase their loan loss provisions when their profits are weak. Contrary to the conclusions made by Bikker and Metzemakers (2005) which affirm that the banks do not smooth their result. The banks behave in an imprudent way in their management of the provisions because they should increase the provisions when their profits are high. However, they fund more in economic downswings and less in economic upswings. This procyclical behavior of the banks in the constitution of loan loss provisions reinforces or exacerbates the tendencies of the cycle. The results resulting from the separate estimates show that the requirement in the transparency of accounting information reduced the risk to manipulate the accounts by the banks. The diversified banks may manage their policies of provisioning correctly. Moreover, if these banks weighted their credits according to the risks taken, they can reduce the volatility of their loan loss provisions during the cycle. Thus the procyclical behavior of the banks as regards provisioning will be reduced. As for the specialized banks, we found that the weighting of the credits according to the risks taken is not significant. This report confirms the idea according to which the Basel committee encourages the banks to diversify their credit portfolio.[o]

[o]Indeed, the calculation of capital requirements for the credit risk incurred on a loan is based on the following parameters:

— The probability of default.
— The loss given default.
— The exposure at default.
— The correlation between credits taking into account the effects of diversification potentially present in the banks' credit portfolio.

This chapter falls under the continuity of the research tasks on the call for implementation of dynamic provisioning[p] supposed to reduce the procyclical behavior of the banks as regards provisioning of the loans. The adequate weighting of the credits according to the risks as required by the Basel committee is one of the solutions suggested to reduce this procyclicity.

Appendix A

Table A.1: Distribution of the observations by country.

PAYS	Nombre de banques[1] disponibles sur Bankscope Fitch IBCA	Nombre d'observations retenues dans notre échantillon
Austria	145	31
Belgium	81	101
Denmark	93	607
Finland	13	84
France	461	955
Germany	456	108
Greece	29	25
Ireland	48	55
Italy	272	986
Luxembourg	147	119
Netherlands	73	223
Norway	21	122
Portugal	40	96
Spain	137	212
Sweden	30	124
Switzerland	270	69
United Kingdom	197	295
Total	2513	4212

[1]Commercial and cooperative banks are considered.

[p]The dynamic provisioning consists in funding the expected losses on a loan as of its granting. This accounting practice is already applied in some countries such as the United States, Spain, and Portugal. In the United States, for example, the prudential authorities use similar techniques to the dynamic provisioning founded at the same time on the evaluation of the expected and potential losses related to the banks' credit portfolio and on the constitution of the "statistical provisions" to cover them. In the same way, in Spain, the regulation concerning dynamic provisioning was reinforced by a new device which came into effect on 1, July, 2000. This device is founded either on the statistical failures recorded by each bank on the basis of internal approach of notations, or on the standard approach defined by the bank of Spain. For more details, see Bank of France (2001), bulletin no. 95.

Table A.2: Unit root test.

Panel unit root test: summary
Exogenous variables: individual effects
User specified lags at: 1
Newey–West bandwidth selection using the Bartlett kernel

Method	Statistic	Prob.[1]	Sections	Obs
Null: Unit root (assumes common unit root process)				
Levin, Lin, and Chu t^*	−110.157	0.0000	378	2493
Breitung t-stat	−5.27208	0.0000	378	2115
Null: Unit root (assumes individual unit root process)				
Im, Pesaran, and Shin W-stat	−14.4062	0.0000	378	2493
ADF-Fisher Chi-square	1218.10	0.0000	378	2493
PP-Fisher Chi-square	1880.81	0.0000	538	3413
Null: No unit root (assumes common unit root process)				
Hadri Z-stat	24.5338	0.0000	625	4212

[1]Probabilities for Fisher tests are computed using an asymptotic Chi square distribution. All other tests assume asymptotic normality.

Table A.3: Correlation.

	CAP_BUFFER	EBT_ASSET	EQTA	GROWTH_ LOANS	INTERACT
CAP_BUFFER	1	0.213	0.585	0.009	0.275
EBT_ASSET	0.213	1	0.373	0.017	0.903
EQTA	0.585	0.373	1	0.007	0.455
GROWTH_LOANS	0.009	0.017	0.007	1	0.016
INTERACT	0.275	0.903	0.455	0.016	1
LLP_ASSET	−0.134	−0.285	0.012	−0.045	−0.082
CPIB	0.026	0.053	−0.049	0.046	0.045
DIV2	−0.010	0.076	−0.085	0.040	0.071
R10Y	0.005	−0.036	−0.085	−0.021	−0.025
TLTA	−0.351	0.029	0.046	0.012	0.040
SIZE	−0.363	−0.209	−0.552	−0.014	−0.273

	LLP_ASSET	CPIB	DIV2	R10Y	TLTA	SIZE
CAP_BUFFER	−0.134	0.026	−0.010	0.005	−0.351	−0.363
EBT_ASSET	−0.285	0.053	0.076	−0.036	0.029	−0.209
EQTA	0.012	−0.049	−0.085	−0.085	0.046	−0.552
GROWTH_LOANS	−0.045	0.040	0.040	−0.021	0.012	−0.014
INTERACT	−0.082	0.045	0.071	−0.025	0.040	−0.273
LLP_ASSET	1	−0.119	−0.094	0.141	0.231	−0.140
CPIB	−0.119	1	0.011	−0.010	−0.098	0.041
DIV2	−0.094	0.011	1	−0.067	−0.273	0.129
R10Y	0.141	−0.010	−0.067	1	−0.069	0.034
TLTA	0.231	−0.098	−0.273	−0.069	1	−0.055
SIZE	−0.140	0.0413	0.129	0.0347	−0.055	1

Table A.4: RISK_LLP results (1992–2004).

	Coefficients		
Variables	Diversified banks	Specialized banks	All banks
EBT_ASSET	−0.473* (0.000)	−0.630* (0.000)	−0.61* (0.000)
CPIB	−0.038* (0.000)	−0.021* (0.000)	−0.024* (0.000)
R10Y	0.050* (0.000)	0.054* (0.000)	0.034* (0.000)
GROWTH_LOANS	−0.0001** (0.0049)	−0.001* (0.000)	−0.0003* (0.000)
TLTA	0.005* (0.000)	0.005* (0.000)	0.005* (0.000)
EQTA	−0.002 (0.2000)	0.002 (0.0851)	−0.001 (0.3798)
SIZE	−0.029* (0.000)	−0.058* (0.000)	−0.060* (0.000)
DIV2	—	—	0.0003* (0.000)
INTERACT	0.476* (0.000)	0.561* (0.000)	0.5042* (0.000)
CAP_BUFFER	−0.007* (0.000)	−0.010* (0.000)	0.0002 (0.5536)
LISTED	0.073* (0.000)	0.255* (0.000)	—
Number of observation	1849	1738	3587

Corrected values of the heteroscedasticity by the matrix of White * and ** are the significance valves at 1% and 5%. The values in parentheses indicate the thresholds of probabilities.

Table A.5: LLP_ASSET results (1992–2004).

	Coefficients		
Variables	Diversified banks	Specialized banks	All banks
EBT_ASSET	−0.073* (0.000)	−0.134* (0.000)	−0.090* (0.000)
SH_ROA	−2.34 *E*-06 (0.4814)	1.53 *E*-05 (0.7123)	1.22 *E*-07 (0.9799)
CH_EQTA	0.001* (0.4832)	0.0056** (0.0281)	0.003 (0.1801)
CPIB	0.021* (0.000)	0.04* (0.000)	0.027* (0.000)
SIZE	−0.025* (0.000)	−0.039* (0.000)	−0.024* (0.000)
GROWTH_LOANS	−3.65 *E*-07* (0.0024)	−0.0008* (0.000)	−7.08 *E*-06 (0.9270)
DPIB	0.001431** (0.0120)	−0.017* (0.0001)	−0.006**(0.0371)
REC	−0.1257* (0.000)	−0.029* (0.0000)	−0.169* (0.0001)
DIV2	—	—	−0.0001 (0.5533)
TOT_CAPRATIO	0.0009* (0.000)	0.007* (0.000)	0.0033* (0.000)
LISTED	−0.048* (0.0016)	0.024** (0.1402)	−0.0033* (0.0001)
Number of observation	1849	1738	3587

Corrected values of the heteroscedasticity by the matrix of White * and ** are the significance values at 1% and 5%. The values in parentheses indicate the thresholds of probabilities.

Table A.6: LLP_ASSET results (1992–2000).

Variables	Coefficients	Standard deviation
EBT_ASSET	−0.116* (0.0000)	0.0084
CPIB	−0.049* (0.000)	0.002
R10Y	0.0029* (0.000)	0.003
GROWTH_LOANS	−0.0001* (0.0031)	6.41*E*-05
INTM	0.0238* (0.000)	0.003
TLTA	0.0062* (0.000)	0.0002
EQTA	0.001 (0.3491)	0.001
SIZE	−0.046* (0.0000)	0.0054
DIV2	0.001* (0.0000)	0.0003
RWA_ASSET	4.64 *E*-05 (0.5394)	7.53*E*-05
CAP_BUFFER	−0.008* (0.000)	0.0015
LISTED	0.179* (0.000)	0.010
Number of observation	938	

Corrected values of the heteroscedasticity by the matrix of White * and ** are the significance values at 1% and 5%. The values in parentheses indicate the thresholds of probabilities.

Table A.7: RISK_LLP results (1992–2000).

	Coefficients		
Variables	Diversified banks	Specialized banks	All banks
EBT_ASSET	−0.0163* (0.000)	−0.104* (0.000)	−0.069* (0.000)
SH_ROA	−0.0002* (0.000)	−0.0006 (0.0870)	−0.000184* (0.000)
CH_EQTA	0.0056* (0.000)	0.003 (0.3621)	0.028* (0.0000)
CPIB	0.0096** (0.0191)	0.010 (0.1981)	0.01* (0.0007)
SIZE	−0.032* (0.000)	−0.031* (0.000)	−0.038* (0.000)
RWA_ASSET	−0.0014* (0.000)	1.74*E*-05 (0.4904)	−0.0002* (0.000)
GROWTH_LOANS	0.000157 (0.1431)	−0.001* (0.000)	2.70*E*-05** (0.0172)
DPIB	0.030* (0.000)	−0.022* (0.0000)	0.0048 (0.3402)
DIV2	—	—	0.001* (0.0000)
TOT_CAPRATIO	0.003* (0.0008)	−0.0003 (0.6104)	0.0002 (0.8194)
LISTED	−0.006 (0.4429)	0.086* (0.0000)	0.006 (0.5070)
Number of observation	469	468	938

Corrected values of the heteroscedasticity by the matrix of White * and ** are the significance valves at 1% and 5%. The values in parentheses indicate the thresholds of probabilities.

Variable Definitions

LLP_ASSET	=	loan loss provisions (LLP) on total asset (ASSET); this variable is expressed in %
EBT_ASSET	=	earning before tax (EBT) on total asset; this variable is expressed (in %)
CPIB	=	growth rate of the activity (in %)
R10Y	=	rate of government bond 10 years (in %)
GROWTH_LOANS	=	growth loans (in %)
TLTA	=	total loans on total asset (in %)
SIZE	=	logarithm of the total assets
DIV2	=	non-interest income on total revenue (in %)
CAP_BUFFER	=	capital buffer on capital ratio (in %)
EQTA	=	proxy of bank capitalization, equities on total asset ratio (in %)
CH_EQTA	=	difference over two years of EQTA
INTERACT	=	dummy variable takes 1 if the earning before tax (EBT) is positive and 0 if not
TOT_CAPRATIO	=	capital ratio (%)
RWA_ASSET	=	risk weighted asset
LISTED	=	dummy variable takes 1 if the bank is quoted in the stock exchange and 0 otherwise
DPIB	=	difference over two years of CPIB (CPIB – CPIB (−1))
REC	=	dummy variable which takes 0 if CPIB is lower than 0 and takes value 1 if the CPIB is higher than 0
ROA	=	return on asset
SH_ROA	=	return per unit of risk; the ROA on the standard deviation of the ROA
RISK_LLP	=	Standard deviation of LLP_ASSET. This variable is the square of the difference between LLP_ASSET and the mean of LLP_ASSET $\sqrt{(\text{llp\_asset}) - (\overline{\text{llp\_asset}})^\wedge 2}$
INTM	=	interest revenue on total asset.

References

Ahmed, AS, Takeda, C and Thomas, S (1999). Bank loan loss provisions: A re-examination of capital management, earnings management and signalling effects. *Journal of Accounting and Economics*, 28, 1–26.

Anandarajan, A, Hasan, I and McCarthy, C (2005). The use of loan loss provisions for earnings, capital management and signalling by Australian banks. http://www.bnet.fordham.edu/CRIF/ WorkingPapers/CRIF06002.pdf

Arellano, M and Bond, S (1991). Some tests of specification for panel data: Monte Carlo evidence and an application to employment equations. *Review of Economic Studies*, 58, 277–297.

Beatty, A, Chamberlain, SL and Magliolo, J (1995). Managing financial reports of commercial banks: The influence of taxes, regulatory capital, and earnings. *Journal of Accounting Research*, 33(2), 231–261.

Beaver, WH and Engel, EE (1996). Discretionary behavior with respect to allowances for loan losses and the behavior of security prices. *Journal of Accounting and Economics*, 22(3), 177–206.

Bikker, JA and Hu, H (2001). Cyclical patterns in profits, provisioning and lending of banks and procyclicality of the new Basel capital requirements. *Research Series Supervision*, No. 39. The Nederlandsche Bank.

Bikker, JA and Metzemakers, PAJ (2005). Banks provisioning behavior and procyclicality. *Journal of International Finance Markets*, Institutions and Money, 15(2), 141–157.

Borio, C, Furfine, C and Lowe, P (2001). Procyclicality of the financial system and financial stability: Issues and policy options. BIS Paper No. 1.

Borio, C and Lowe, P (2001). Le provisionnement en question. Rapport trimestriel de la BRI de Septembre 2001, pp. 36–49.

Bouvatier, V and Lepetit, L (2006a). Banks'procyclicality behavior: Does provisioning matter? http://mse.univ-paris1.fr/MSEPageCahier2006.htm.

Bouvatier, V and Lepetit, L (2006b). Effects of provisioning rules on bank lending: Theory and empirical evidence from European banks. Congrès de l'AFSE en 2006. http://www.afse.fr/docs/congres2006/docs2006/LEPETIT_BOUVATIER.pdf.

Bulletin de la Banque de France (2001). Une proposition pour améliorer la stabilité: le provisionnement dynamique. Novembre 2001, bulletin No. 95.

Cavallo, M and Majnoni, G (2001). Do banks provision for bad loans in good times? Empirical evidence and policy implications. World Bank Working Paper No. 2619.

Collins, J, Shackelford, D and Wahlen, J (1995). Bank differences in the coordination of regulatory capital, earnings and taxes. *Journal of Accounting Research*, 33(2), 263–291.

Cortavarria, R, Dziobek C, Kanaya, A and Inwon, S (2000). Loan review, provisioning and macroeconomic linkage. International Monetary Fund Working Paper, Working Paper 00/95.

Dewenter, K and Hess, A (2003). Are relationship and transactional banks different? Evidence from loan loss provisions and write-offs. EFMA 2004 Basel Meetings Paper. Available on SSRN http://ssrn.com/abstract= 478101.

Dewenter, K and Hess, A (2006). International evidence on relationship and transactional banks as delegated monitors. Working Paper, University of Washington.

Fonseca, A and Gonzalez, F (2005). Cross-country determinants of bank income smoothing by managing loan loss provisions. http://www.funcas.ceca.es/Publicaciones/Documentos_Trabajo.asp.

Hodrick, R and Prescott, EC (1980). Post-war US business cycles: An empirical investigation. Mimeo. Carnegie-Mellon University, Pittsburgh, PA.

Laeven, L and Majnoni, G (2003). Loan loss provisioning and economic slowdowns: Too, much, too late? *Journal of Financial Intermediation*, 12, 178–197.

Lobo, G and Yang, G (2001). Bank managers heterogeneous decisions on discretionary loan loss provisions. *Review of Quantitative Finance and Accounting*, 16, 223–250.

Maddala, GS and Wu, S (1999). A comparative study of unit root tests with panel data and a new simple test. *Oxford Bulletin of Economics and Statistics*, 61(suppl. 1), 631–652.

Moyer, SE (1990). Capital adequacy ratio regulations and accounting choices in commercial banks. *Journal of Accounting and Economics*, 13, 123–154.

Norden, S (2004). Les filtres pour l'analyse courante. *Revue d'Analyse Economique*, 80, 523–546.

Perez, D, Salas, V and Saurina, J (2006). Earnings and capital management in alternative loan loss provision regulatory regimes. Documentos de Trabajo no. 0614, Banco de Espana.

Turner, P (2000). Procyclicality of regulatory ratios? CEPA Working Papers 2000-01, Center for Economic Policy Analysis (CEPA), New School University.

Wahlen, J. (1994). The nature of information in commercial Bank loan loss disclosures. *The Accounting Review*, 69(3), 455–478.

CHAPTER 10

MARKET POWER AND BANKING COMPETITION ON THE CREDIT MARKET

*Ion Lapteacru**

This chapter presents a study of the banking competition on the credit market, taking into account the banks' market power and their probability of success. Initially, we study the banking behavior in the case of the simultaneous entry on the market and we find that the diminution of the probability of success and the raise of the number of banks reduce the credit interest rate. This is the effect of the improvement of the quality of credit portfolio and of the increase in the banking competition. Another result is that the huge difference among probabilities of success can imply the exit of the market by the banks with poor quality of credit portfolio. Then, in the case of sequential entry on the market, we analyze the role of the probability of success, i.e. quality of bank portfolio, on the gain of the market shares. Basing on Tabuchi and Thisse's (1995) paper, we show that the leader is always localizing in the center of the market, that is, where the number of clients is most important, but it can abandon the center if the follower improves considerably the quality of its credit portfolio.

1 Introduction

The banks' probability of success or the quality of their credit portfolio and their market power are two main characteristics that make an important differentiation among them and can imply a distortion of the competition on the banking market. If the banks are different regarding these two characteristics,

*LARE-efi, Université Montesquieu–Bordeaux IV, Avenue Léon Duguit, 33608 Pessac Cedex. ion.lapteacru@u-bordeaux4.fr.

they can lead different bank strategies and the banks with better quality of credit portfolio and higher market power could get more market shares. Moreover, an offensive price strategy of this kind of banks may impose the banks with lowest probability of success to exit the market and thus may reduce the level of competition.

There are many examples where it appears that banks with high probabilities of success, conducting an offensive price behavior, accelerated the bankruptcy of banks with poor quality of bank portfolio. In particular, this is the case of the emerging and developing economies in their initial stage of the opening of the financial markets, where the increased presence of foreign banks is associated with the reduction in profitability of success and interest margins for domestic banks (Claessens *et al.*, 2001), pushing them to bankruptcy or other measures to exit the market. An eloquent example is the case of the transition countries. For example, since the number of foreign banks increased from 5 to 25 in Bulgaria, from 1 to 20 in Croatia, from 1 to 23 in Romania, from 26 to 46 in Poland, and from 20 to 23 in Czech Republic during the period 1995–2000, there are a lot of domestic banks that have been liquidated. New entrants with higher chances for success, as for their know-how, management abilities, and risk and price policies, endeavor such activity areas that allow them to benefit more rapidly from these advantages. A lot of studies find that indubitable advantages of the foreign banks render them more efficiently compared to incumbent domestic ones and by that foster the competition on the banking market in transition countries (see e.g., Fries and Taci, 2005 and Bonin *et al.*, 2005). Bonin *et al.* (1998, p. 75) mention that foreign banks usually restrict their activities to those areas where they can offer a differentiated product and/or exploit cost advantages and they prefer to render financial services to multinational companies, to lend to best domestic customers, to make investment bank-ing activity. Moreover, retail banking is not a first area of interest for foreign banks. It is obvious that for these countries the competition between new entrants and incumbent banks is rather for credit market.

Foreign banks in transition countries (see e.g., Bonin *et al.*, 2000), in Latin America (see e.g., Crystal *et al.*, 2002 and Dages *et al.*, 2000), and in South-East Asia (see e.g., Jeon *et al.*, 2003, for Korea) rely more heavily on non-deposit sources of funds and their activities are more concentrated on the corporate credit market. In fact, the bank ownership does not matter such as, but only the bank health that is crucial, because, as found by Dages *et al.* (2000), domestically owned and foreign-owned banks with low problem loan ratios behave similarly in these countries. Thus, the bank strategies depend on the quality of banks' credit portfolio.

It is respectively essentially to study the banks' behavior according to their quality of credit portfolio, which also represents the bank probability of success, and to analyze the influence of the entry of new banks with higher probability of success on the situation of the incumbent banks. In this chapter we attempt to find these influences incorporating the bank behavior and bank competition in a spatial model à la Hotelling and analyzing two cases: simultaneous and sequential entries on the credit market. The first case allows observing the bank behavior according to the level of quality of credit portfolio and the level of competition on the market, and the second one establishes a framework where the impact of the entry of the higher quality bank on the behavior of the lesser quality incumbent bank may be examined.

Thus, due to our interest to study the influence of the bank's quality, expressed by the quality of credit portfolio, on the behavior of other banks, we focus our analysis on the credit market. Our choice is also based on the experience of emerging markets, where, as aforementioned, the lending sector is the target of conquest for the entrant banks with good health. Or, we recognize that such approach could be undertaken to study the bank competition on the deposit market too. Matutes and Vives (1996), for example, applying the spatial model à la Hotteling, study the competition on the deposit market and the role of the deposit insurance on the banking behavior. They find that the quality of the bank is endogenously determined by the depositors' expectations, which makes a vertical differentiation and can imply multiple equilibriums. For them, this is not the bank competition that involves a multiplicity of equilibriums but rather the coordination problem among depositors. Their results are consistent with Yanelle (1989, 1997), who studies endogenous financial intermediation with double-sided competition, that is, on the credit and deposit markets. The fragility of the banking system from the asset side has been examined by Gale (1993). He also finds multiple equilibriums resulting from the bank behavior and from the asymmetry of information existing between banks and their customers.

Aiming to study the impact of the quality of credit portfolio and of the market power on the competitive behavior of banks in the simplest and comprehensive manner, in our formalization we avoid some characteristics that determine the role of banks, such as the special function of banks to accumulate and process information, which determines the bank behavior concerning the lending. We also neglect the fact that the granting of loans could be a signal for the market concerning the quality of borrowers. Other elements that are studied in recent literature on banking, such as moral hazard, adverse selection, screening and monitoring costs, switching costs, and winner's curse problem (Shaffer, 1998), are excluded from our analysis. The effects of these banking market imperfections are weakened when banks are too different concerning the quality of their credit portfolio, which determine the probability of success of the banks.

The formulation of our model follows closely the approach of Tabuchi and Thisse (1995), which study how the firms choose their location as the result of their price behavior. Or the aim of this chapter is to analyze the modification of the banks' price behavior in function of their probability of success and their market share that is determined by their location on the credit market. In our model, the banks located closer to the center of the market have more customers, because they dispose better qualities than other banks. In consequence, a spatial model is an appropriate approach to analyze bank behavior and bank competition. In such model the concept of distance is usually used, which implies the transport cost to go to bank. This type of cost is a kind of opportunity cost. The customer will choose the bank for which the opportunity cost is lesser, that is, the bank characteristics suit him the most. Thus, the concept of distance in a spatial model takes into account the differences existing among banks. These differences can characterize the banking activity (the credit qualities, balance sheet mismatches), the relationship between bank and her clients (quality of proposed services, branch network), the banking governance (management skills, structure of the shareholders), etc. All these characteristics can explain, for example, why some banks have a market power and others not.

The rest of the chapter is composed as follows. Section 2 introduces the spatial model, where customers are distributed in a triangular form and banks are distributed uniformly. Section 3 analyzes the influence of the banks' probability of success and market power on their behavior if they enter simultaneously on the credit market. Section 4 examines the way in which the banks are located, respectively their market share, and choose the credit interest rates if a new bank enters on the market. This study is made in a framework of the sequential entry on the market and the conditions under which the new better quality bank makes another bank to exit the market are also established. Section 5 concludes.

2 Model

Our approach is based on the spatial model à la Hotelling, excepting the fact that the clients are gathered around a center. This different distribution of customers allows a discrimination of the banks in function of their location on the market: the bank being in the center is the bank with the best qualities (or the most developed bank) and which gains most of the clients. The localization on the market represents the perception that clients have *vis-à-vis* the banks. Approaching to the center, the bank improves its characteristics and more and more clients will go to this bank and in consequence her market share will increase.

2.1 Distribution of the Banks and Clients

Let us consider that there are $n+1$ (n could take value 0) banks uniformly and discretely distributed on the one-unit market with the dimension [0; 1] and that clients are continuously distributed according to the triangular density function $f(x) = 2 - 4|x - 0.5|, \forall x \in [0; 1]$ (Fig. 1). The big and the small points represent respectively the banks' and clients' distribution.

According to the clients' distribution function, the model is symmetric: the behavior of the banks located on the first half of the market [0; 0.5) is the same as that of the banks located on the second half (0.5; 1]. Thus, only the behavior of the banks located on the first half of the market will be studied.

2.2 Bank Problem

Collecting deposits in order to finance the firms' projects, the banks choose the credit interest rate that maximizes their profit, taking also into account

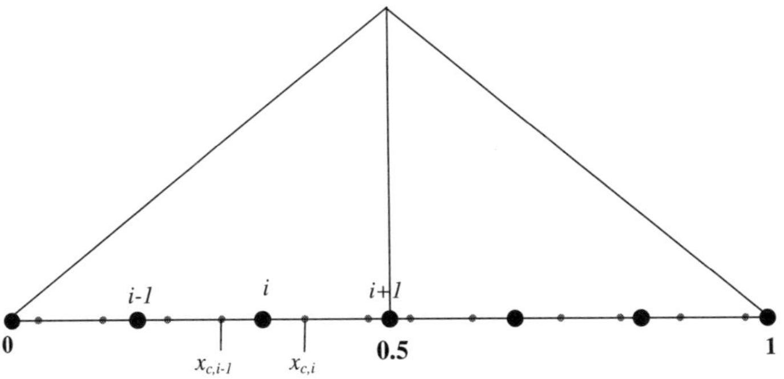

Figure 1: Distribution of the banks and clients.

their investment in the riskless asset. Supposing that the banks have the same marginal cost, the profit of bank i is

$$\pi_i = \left(\mathrm{pr}_{c,i} r_{c,i} - m_c\right) n_{c,i} + r_s S_i - \left(r_{d,i} + m_d\right) n_{d,i}, \tag{1}$$

where $n_{c,i}$ and $n_{d,i}$ represent the shares on the credit and deposit markets, respectively; $r_{c,i}$ and $r_{d,i}$ are the credit and deposit interest rates, respectively; r_s means the return on riskless asset; m_c and m_d are the marginal costs of lending and deposit services, respectively; S_i is the share of the investments in the riskless asset; and $\mathrm{pr}_{c,i}$ represents the probability of success, which also describes the quality of credit portfolio.

We suppose that the banks are *price takers* on the risk-free investments market; as a consequence interest rate r_s is the same for all banks. The bank $i$maximizes the profit function (Eq. (1)) under the following budget constraint:

$$n_{c,i} + S_i = n_{d,i}. \tag{2}$$

3 Bank Behavior in the Case of Simultaneous Entry on the Market

In order to find the influence of the banks' probability of success and of their location on the bank behavior, the framework of simultaneous entry on the market is applied. Initially, we determine the expressions of the banks' market share in function of their locations. Then, we examine the behavior of the banks in function of their probabilities of success.

3.1 Determination of the Market Shares

As aforementioned, the analysis of the bank behavior is made into spatial model framework. This approach implies to use the concept of "transport cost", which can be explained as an opportunity cost to go to the bank. This cost can be expressed by the time and money spent, by the nature of services offered to depositors, the quality of service, etc. Otherwise, the opportunity cost is lesser in the economy with well-developed banking sector and it is higher if the networks of banking transactions are rudimentary.

We take the quadratic form for the transport cost function. The transport cost incurred by the client located at point $\hat{x}$ choosing the bank located at point x_i is $t\left(\hat{x} - x_i\right)^2$, where t is the distance coefficient and, alongside with the number of banks, expresses the level of competition on the market. The quadratic form does not change much the results, but allows a greater sensitivity regarding the locations of the banks. Many studies use the quadratic form for the transport cost function.[a] In fact, a greater sensitivity of clients implies a fiercer competition on the banking market. Moreover, basing on the Caplin and Nalebuff 's (1991) paper, Tabuchi and Thisse (1995, p. 216) show that, in the case of the triangular distribution of the clients, the quadratic form of the transport cost insures the existence of the equilibrium.

The transport cost and the credit interest rate influence the firms' decision to choose a bank. The marginal clients are indifferent to which bank to go if the total costs are equal. These clients determine the market share of each bank, because they are situated on the border of market segment of each bank. For marginal client, which has no preference between the bank i and the bank $i+1$, the equality of total costs gives

$$r_{c,i} + t(x_{c,i} - x_i)^2 = r_{c,i+1} + t(x_{i+1} - x_{c,i})^2,$$

where $x_{c,i}$ is the location of the marginal client i and x_i is that of the bank i, (see Fig. 1). As a result, the location of the marginal client i, which indicates also the market border between the bank i and the bank $i + 1$, is

$$x_{c,i} = \frac{r_{c,i+1} - r_{c,i}}{2t(x_{i+1} - x_i)} + \frac{x_{i+1} + x_i}{2}. \tag{3}$$

According to the distribution function of the clients, the market share of the bank i is

$$n_{c,i} = \int_{x_{c,i-1}}^{x_{c,i}} f(x)dx,$$

where

$$n_{c,i} = 2(x_{c,i} - x_{c,i-1}) + 2[(0.5 - x_{c,i})^2 - (0.5 - x_{c,i-1})^2], \quad \text{for } x_{c,i} \leq 0.5, \tag{4a}$$

$$n_{c,i} = 2(x_{c,i} - x_{c,i-1}) - 2[(x_{c,i} - 0.5)^2 + (0.5 - x_{c,i-1})^2], \quad \text{for } x_{c,i-1} \leq 0.5 \text{ and } x_{c,i} \geq 0.5, \tag{4b}$$

$$n_{c,i} = 2(x_{c,i} - x_{c,i-1}) - 2[(x_{c,i} - 0.5)^2 - (x_{c,i-1} - 0.5)^2], \quad \text{for } x_{c,i-1} \geq 0.5. \tag{4c}$$

3.2 *Different Bank Strategies*

The banks maximize their profit in respect to their credit interest rate. They are uniformly distributed and this distribution is fixed according to the bank

[a]For example, Economides (1989), Tabuchi and Thisse (1995), Mai and Peng (1999).

located in the center, i.e. at the point $x = 0.5$.[b] Taking into account the symmetry of the model, for a market composed by $n+1$ banks, we study only the behavior of the first $n/2+1$ banks. Let note the bank located in the center by the bank $n/2$. In consequence, $x_{n/2} = 0.5$. Moving to left, the rank of the bank diminishes (see Fig. 1) and the first bank is bank 0, whose position is determined by the point x_0.

According to the uniform distribution of the banks, there is equal distance among them expressed by $d = x_{i+1} - x_i$. Expressing the locations of the banks by those of the bank 0, we have $x_i = x_0 + i * d$ and, according to the Eq. (3), the location of the marginal client is

$$x_{c,i} = \frac{r_{c,i+1} - r_{c,i}}{2 \times t \times d} + \frac{2x_0 + d\,(2i+1)}{2}.$$

Due to the bank maximization problem, the interest rates proposed by banks are

— for the bank located at the point x_0[c]

$$r_{c,0} = \frac{2}{3}\left[\frac{r_{c,1}}{2} + \frac{d^2 t + d \times t - d^2 t \times n}{2} + \frac{m_c + r_s}{\mathrm{pr}_{c,0}}\right]; \tag{5a}$$

— for the bank located at the point $x_i < 0.5$[d]

$$r_{c,i} = \frac{1}{2}\left[\frac{r_{c,i+1} + r_{c,i-1}}{2} + d^2 t + \frac{m_c + r_s}{\mathrm{pr}_{c,i}}\right]; \tag{5b}$$

— and for the bank located in the center, that is, at the point $x_{n/2} = 0.5$

$$r_{c,n/2} = \frac{1}{6\mathrm{pr}_{c,n/2}}\left\{A + \sqrt{A^2 - 12\mathrm{pr}_{c,n/2}\,(B + C)}\right\}, \tag{5c}$$

where

$$A = 2(m_c + r_s + 2\mathrm{pr}_{c,n/2} r_{c,n/2-1} + 2 \times d \times t \times \mathrm{pr}_{c,n/2}(d-1)), \tag{6a}$$

$$B = 2(m_c + r_s)(d \cdot t(d-1) + r_{c,n/2-1}) + d^3 t^2 \mathrm{pr}_{c,n/2}(d-2) + \mathrm{pr}_{c,n/2} r^2_{c,n/2-1}, \tag{6b}$$

$$C = 2 \times d \times t \times \mathrm{pr}_{c,n/2} r_{c,n/2-1}(d-1). \tag{6c}$$

[b] We further explain why for a triangular distribution of the clients there is always a bank which is located in the center.

[c] We have the same result for the bank located at the point x_n.

[d] We have the same result for the bank located at the point $x_i > 0.5$.

(More explanations on the determination of the expressions for the interest rates are presented in Appendix A (A.1)).

From the obtained results, one may deduce two important observations.

The first observation is that if the banks are homogeneous, i.e. the quality of credit portfolios is the same ($\mathrm{pr}_{c,i} = \mathrm{pr}_c$, for $\forall i$), and $d = 0$, there is a perfect competition on the banking market. From Eqs. (5a)–(5c) and (6a)–(6c), for $d = 0$, the interest rates are:

— for the bank located at the point x_0,

$$r_{c,0} = \frac{2}{3}\left[\frac{r_{c,1}}{2} + \frac{m_c + r_s}{\mathrm{pr}_{c,0}}\right]; \tag{7a}$$

— for the bank located at the point $x_i < 0.5$,

$$r_{c,i} = \frac{1}{2}\left[\frac{r_{c,i+1} + r_{c,i-1}}{2} + \frac{m_c + r_s}{\mathrm{pr}_{c,i}}\right]; \tag{7b}$$

— and for the bank located in the center, that is, at the point $x_{n/2} = 0.5$,

$$r_{c,n/2} = \frac{2}{3}\left[\frac{r_{c,n/2-1}}{2} + \frac{m_c + r_s}{\mathrm{pr}_{c,n/2}}\right]. \tag{7c}$$

The equality of the probabilities of success involves an identical behavior of the banks. In the Appendix A (A.2) we show that if $\mathrm{pr}_{c,i} = \mathrm{pr}_c$, then

$$r_{c,i} = \frac{m_c + r_s}{\mathrm{pr}_c}, \quad \text{for } \forall i \in [0; n]. \tag{8}$$

The second observation is that the bank strategies depend on the competition on the banking market, expressed by the distance among banks and by the number of banks. The raise of the number of banks and respectively the reduction of the distance between two neighboring banks foster the competition diminishing the interest rates.

3.3 Analysis of the Bank Behavior

We will analyze the behavior of the banks within a framework where there is always a bank located in the center, which has the highest pat of the market. In the first part of this point, the locations of the banks are fixed and the banks operate without moving alongside of the market. The smallest bank, the bank 0, is located at the point $x_0 = 0$ and the biggest bank, the bank

$n/2$, is located in the center, $x_{n/2} = 0.5$. In the second part of this point, we suppose that the banks are also different according to their probability of success. In consequence, their reactions on the fluctuations of the quality of credit portfolio have repercussions not only on the interest rate but also on their location on the market, which means that some banks could exit the market if their qualities are too bad.

Solving simultaneously Eqs. (5a)–(5c), we find the equilibrium interest rates for different values of probability of success $\mathrm{pr}_{c,i}$ and of coefficient t. In the first case, we analyze the market by supposing that the banks are identical regarding the quality of their investments. According to the results of simulations (Table C.1), the bank that has the biggest share beneficiates from a highest market power offering highest interest rate. The credit interest rate of this bank, like the interest rates of all banks, decreases with the increase in the number of banks and becomes identical with the interest rate on the market with perfect competition (calculated by Eq. (8)), that is, when n equal to infinity.

The credit quality, expressed by the probability of reimbursement, has also an important role in the determination of the interest rate. The improving of the credit quality diminishes the interest rates for all banks. As for the local market power, expressed by the coefficient t, its increase raises the interest rates.

Or, we have another situation where the banks are different regarding their probabilities of success. Let us take an example of 11 banks on the market ($n = 10$). If we apply different probabilities of success, we find that some banks cannot remain on the market. According to the results of simulations presented in the left side of Table C.2(a), one may observe that, excepting for the biggest bank, the bank 5, the location of the banks does not respect the market border principle, i.e. $x_{c,i-1} \leq x_i \leq x_{c,i}$, which means that the banks move alongside the market. Their location is modified until the market border principle is respected (the right side of Table C.2(a)). The results suggest that, thanks to the improving in the credit quality, the banks located near the center have the possibility to reduce more their interest rates than other banks (to compare with the results of Table C.1 with $n = 10$ and $t = 0.1$), fostering the competition on the market. Not all banks can withstand this higher competition and some of them are liquidated. As a result, the reduction of the number of banks hampers the competitive behavior on the market. This is why the banks 0, 1, and 2 exit the market and the remaining banks have the possibility to increase their interest rates (to compare the right side with the left side of Table C.2(a)). Moreover, due to the difference between the probability of success of bank 3 and that of the banks 4 and 5, bank 3 loses a part of her clients to the benefice of two others (to compare with the results of Table C.1 with $n = 4$ and $t = 0.1$). Bank 4 gains more, because she is the direct competitor of bank 3. Another characteristic of this presentation is that bank 4 proposes an interest rate which is lower than that offered by bank 3, and it is higher than the interest rate offered by bank 5. This result is different to that presented in Table C.1. (for $n = 4$, $t = 0.1$, and $p_{rc} = 0.75$). An obvious explanation is the bad credit quality of bank 3 compared to that of bank 4, which is also lower than that of bank 5 analyzed in Table C.1. In consequence, bank 3 compensates the slump of the credit quality by an increase in the interest rate.

Supposing that the most developed bank increases the quality of her credit portfolio and respectively her probability of success till 1, all banks apply the same strategy consisting to reduce their interest rates as a result of more intensive competitive pressures. As in precedent case, some banks are obliged to exit the market (see the left side of the Table C.2.(b)). Moreover, bank 3 loses a more clients and her market share becomes close to zero. While bank 3 is off-market located, banks 4 and 5 increase their interest rates (see the right side of Table C.2.(b)). A strong raise of the probability of success of the bank 5 doubles her market share. She has 80% of the market, compared to her first competitor who has only about 10.5%.

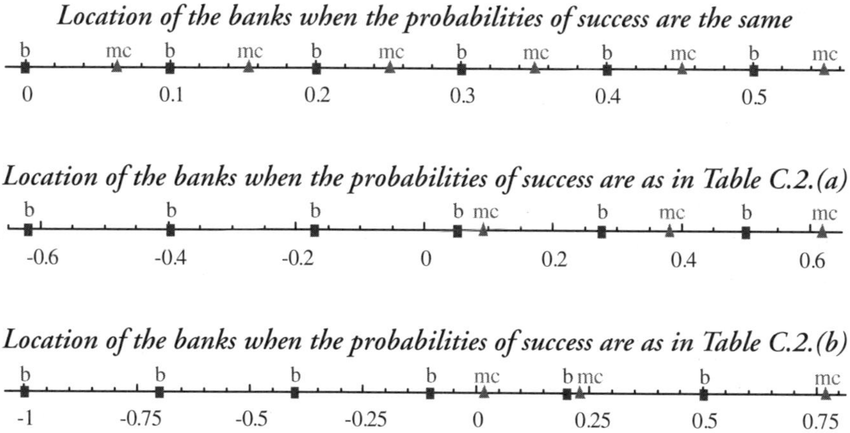

Figure 2: Locations of the banks and marginal clients.

Basing on the results of Tables C.1, C.2.(a), and C.2.(b), a diagrammatic presentation is proposed in Fig. 2, where "b" indicates the location of the banks and "mc" the location of the marginal client.

4 Bank Behavior in the Case of Sequential Entry on the Market

As in the Tabuchi and Thisse's (1995) paper, we describe a game with three stages. The first two stages represent a game à la Stackelberg for the location of the banks, while the third stage is a game of simultaneous choice of the interest rates.[e]

We study a market of two banks, where bank 1 enters the first on the market.[f] We analyze the case $x_2 < x_1$, but the results are the same for $x_1 < x_2$.

4.1 Determination of the Locations and the Choice of the Interest Rates

In order to study the bank behavior in the case of the sequential entry on the market, we apply the same approach as in the precedent section. The location of the marginal client is determined by the Eq. (3) which, in this case, takes the following form:

$$x_c = \frac{r_{c,1} - r_{c,2}}{2t\,(x_1 - x_2)} + \frac{x_1 + x_2}{2}. \tag{9}$$

For a market with only two banks, we have $n_{c,1} + n_{c,2} = 1$. By construction of the model, the marginal client is located between these two banks and more to the right than the bank 2, i.e. $x_2 \leq x_c \leq x_1$. In order to make easy the notations, we note $n_{c,2} = n_c$. According to Eqs. (1) and (2), the profit of the bank $i = 1,\ 2$ becomes

$$\pi_1 = \left\lfloor \mathrm{pr}_{c,1} r_{c,1} - m_c - r_s \right\rfloor (1 - n_c\,(x_c)) + \left\lfloor r_s - r_{d,1} - m_d \right\rfloor n_{d,1}, \tag{10a}$$

$$\pi_2 = \left\lfloor \mathrm{pr}_{c,2} r_{c,2} - m_c - r_s \right\rfloor n_c\,(x_c) + \left\lfloor r_s - r_{d,2} - m_d \right\rfloor n_{d,2}. \tag{10b}$$

The profit maximizing banks will choose the interest rate and the location on the market that maximize their profit. For this reason, to make possible the comparison between the profits of the banks, in the profit equations we

[e]The results do not change if the banks initially enter on the market and then propose their interest rates.

[f]The same analysis is valid if there are three banks on the market, because, how we will see, the first bank is always located in the center. In consequence, the model takes a symmetric form studied in the precedent section. The third bank follows the same strategy as that of the second one and its location would be symmetric to that of the second bank, i.e. at the point $x_3 = 1 - x_2$.

take away the terms which do not describe the banking behavior on the credit market, i.e. the latest terms of Eqs. (10a) and (10b). These profit functions are differentiable and the first order conditions for the equilibrium interest rates are

$$\frac{\partial \pi_1}{\partial r_{c,1}} = \mathrm{pr}_{c,1}(1 - n_c(x_c)) - \frac{\lfloor \mathrm{pr}_{c,1} r_{c,1} - m_c - r_s \rfloor \frac{\partial n_c}{\partial x_c}}{2t(x_1 - x_2)} = 0, \quad (11a)$$

$$\frac{\partial \pi_2}{\partial r_{c,2}} = \mathrm{pr}_{c,2} n_c(x_c) - \frac{\lfloor \mathrm{pr}_{c,2} r_{c,2} - m_c - r_s \rfloor \frac{\partial n_c}{\partial x_c}}{2t(x_1 - x_2)} = 0. \quad (11b)$$

Solving simultaneously Eqs. (9), (11a), and (11b), we obtain the equilibrium interest rates and the location of the marginal client in function of the location of the banks x_1 and x_2. By introducing them into Eqs. (10a) and (10b), we find the profits of the banks, which depend only on x_1 and x_2.

$$\pi_1^*(x_1, x_2) = \frac{2t \cdot \mathrm{pr}_{c,1}(x_1 - x_2)[1 - n_c(x_c)]^2}{\frac{\partial n_c}{\partial x_c}}, \quad (12a)$$

$$\pi_2^*(x_1, x_2) = \frac{2t \cdot \mathrm{pr}_{c,2}(x_1 - x_2)\, n_c^2(x_c)}{\frac{\partial n_c}{\partial x_c}}. \quad (12b)$$

After the choice of the interest rate, the banks establish their location that maximizes their profit functions, expressed by Eqs. (12a) and (12b) for bank 1 and bank 2, respectively. By construction of the model, bank 2 is a "*follower*" and responds to the choice made by bank 1. Noting by $x_2 = R(x_1)$ the response function of bank 2 to the location decision made by bank 1, the location of banks is determined by the following first order conditions:

$$\frac{d\pi_1^*}{dx_1} = \frac{\partial \pi_1^*}{\partial x_1} + \frac{\partial \pi_1^*}{\partial x_2}\frac{dR}{dx_1} = 0, \quad (13a)$$

$$\frac{\partial \pi_2^*}{\partial x_2} = 0. \quad (13b)$$

The response function is derived from Eq. (13b), that is, more exactly, from the following equation:

$$-\frac{n_c(x_c)}{\frac{\partial n_c}{\partial x_c}} + 2(x_1 - x_2)\frac{\partial x_c}{\partial x_2} - \frac{(x_1 - x_2)\, n_c(x_c)\, \frac{\partial^2 n_c}{\partial x_c^2}\frac{\partial x_c}{\partial x_2}}{[\frac{\partial n_c}{\partial x_c}]^2} = 0. \quad (14)$$

As for market share of bank 2, n_c is measured according to the location of the marginal client:

— if $x_c \leq 0.5$, then $n_c = 2x_c^2$; and (15a)
— if $x_c > 0.5$, then $n_c = 4x_c - 2x_c^2 - 1$. (15b)

Obtaining the response function $x_2 = R(x_1)$, the profit of bank 1, $\pi_1^*(x_1, R(x_1))$, is a function only of her location. We can thus determine where the bank 1 will be located in order to maximize her profit; and this location is the center of the market (see the proof in Appendix B).

4.2 Simulations and Results

In order to study the behavior of the banks and taking into account the complexity of equations to solve, we found the results by simulations (Table D.1). Initially, we make simulations supposing that the marginal client is located on the first half of the market, i.e. $x_c \leq 0.5$, and applying the Eq. (15a) for the market share of bank 2. When the location of the marginal client goes beyond the center, i.e. $x_c > 0.5$, the solutions are not real and we use Eq. (15b).[g]

From the obtained results we can make the following observations:

(1) Bank 2, the "*follower*" is "off-market located". Being very different of bank 1, or not so developed, and having a lower probability of success, bank 2 is disadvantaged.
(2) Rising the probability of success of bank 2, the difference between the banks decreases and thus the competition is amplified, and the two banks must reduce their interest rates. The market share of bank 2 increases to the detriment of that of bank 1.
(3) If the quality of credit portfolio of bank 2 is much better than that of bank 1, then the later can abandon the center. In other words, the bank 2 becomes more effective (for $t = 0.1$, $\text{pr}_{c,1} = 0.75$ and $\text{pr}_{c,2} = 0.98$, bank 1 is obliged to be off-market located) and gains respectively more and more clients. Her profit increases and that of bank 1 decreases. Since the probability of success of bank 2 is much higher than that of her

[g]In this case, the location of bank 1 is found by trial. This is the only possibility, taking into account the complexity of equations to solve.

competitor, the two banks increase their interest rates: bank 1, due to the losses of market share, and bank 2, thanks to the amplified market power.

(4) If the quality of credit portfolio of bank 1 is too bad, bank 2 needs a less significant improvement of the credit quality in order to draw aside the *leader* from the center of the market.

(5) The latest observation is that if the coefficient t is too important, i.e. local market power of bank 1 is too high, bank 2 could never draw aside bank 1 from the center of the market. The amplified market power allows *leader* to keep its position.

5 Conclusion

We have analyzed the banking behavior within a spatial model à la Hotelling. The triangular form of the distribution of the clients allowed us to make discrimination among the banks according to their location.

In the case of the simultaneous entry on the market, our results show that the increase in the probabilities of success of the banks contributes to the diminution of the credit interest rates. The reduction of the market power, expressed by the increase in the number of banks and by the decrease in the transport cost, produces the same effect.

The fact that there are different probabilities of success amplifies the differences among banks. Assigning higher probabilities of success to the banks located near the center, we find that the smallest banks are obliged to exit the market. All these imply an increase in the credit interest rates.

Within a sequential entry framework, as in the Tabuchi and Thisse's (1995) paper, we show that the first bank will always choose the center of the market, i.e. the position where she has most clients. On the other hand, the reaction of the second bank depends much on the difference which exists between the quality of her credit portfolio and that of her competitor. As this difference decreases, the second bank gains the market shares to the detriment of the first bank and the competition increases, reducing thus the interest rates. At the moment when this difference is in favor of the second bank, which obtains considerable market shares, the first bank is drawn aside from the center. The abandon of the center can be explained by the fact that the qualities of this bank have been surpassed by those of the second bank. However, for high values of market power, the first bank can always keep her position on the market.

Appendix A. Several Explanations for the Model Resolution

A.1 *Determination of the Credit Interest Rates*

The first order condition for the maximization of the profit (1) under the budget constraint (2) requires that the bank i proposes the following interest rate:

$$r_{c,i} = -\frac{n_{c,i}}{\frac{\partial n_{c,i}}{\partial r_{c,i}}} + \frac{m_c + r_s}{\mathrm{pr}_{c,i}}. \tag{A.1}$$

— For the banks located at the point $x_0 \leq 0$, $x_{c,i-1} = 0$ and according to the Eq. (4a):

$$n_{c,0} = 2x_{c,0} + 2\left\lfloor \left(0.5 - x_{c,i}\right)^2 - 0.25 \right\rfloor \text{ and } x_{c,0} = \frac{r_{c,1} - r_{c,0}}{2 \times t \times d} n + \frac{2x_0 + d}{2}.$$

Introducing it in Eq. (A.1), we obtain Eq. (5a).

— For the banks located at the point $x_i < 0.5$, there is any particularity. The substitution of Eqs. (3b) and (4a) in Eq. (A.1) gives the result (5b).

— Using Eq. (4b) and the symmetric relations evocated in the text, for the bank located in the center, the first order condition presents the following result:

$$r_{c,n/2} = \frac{1}{6\mathrm{pr}_{c,n/2}} \left\{A \pm \sqrt{A^2 - 12\mathrm{pr}_{c,n/2}\,(B + C)}\right\},$$

where A, B, and C are expressed by Eqs. (6a)–(6c), respectively. However, the second order condition is respected only by Eq. (5c).

In the determination of Eqs. (5a)–(5c) and as a result of Eqs. (6a)–(6c), we have taken into consideration the symmetry of the model ($r_{c,n/2-i} = r_{c,n/2+i}$) and the uniform distribution of the banks, with the first bank located at the center of the market. In consequence, we have $x_0 = 0.5 - d * n/2$.

Let us mention that the expression under the square root of Eq. (5c) is always positive. After some mathematical transformations, we obtain that

$$\begin{aligned} A^2 - 12\mathrm{pr}_{c,n/2}\,(B + C) &= (m_c + r_s - \mathrm{pr}_{c,n/2}(r_{c,n/2-1} + d \cdot t \cdot (d - 1)))^2 \\ &\quad + 3\mathrm{pr}^2_{c,n/2} d^2 t^2 > 0. \end{aligned}$$

A.2 *Demonstration of the Market of Perfect Competition*

Equations (7a) and (7b) are obtained imposing the condition $d = 0$ for Eqs. (5a)–(5c). But, the analytical demonstration of the result (8) is very difficult. We will analyze a particular case, $n = 6$, for example:

$$r_{c,0} = \frac{2}{3}\left[\frac{r_{c,1}}{2} + \frac{m_c + r_s}{\mathrm{pr}_c}\right], \tag{A.2}$$

$$r_{c,1} = \frac{6}{11}\left[\frac{r_{c,2}}{2} + \frac{4}{3}\cdot\frac{m_c + r_s}{\mathrm{pr}_c}\right], \tag{A.3}$$

$$r_{c,2} = \frac{22}{41}\left[\frac{r_{c,3}}{2} + \frac{15}{11}\cdot\frac{m_c + r_s}{\mathrm{pr}_c}\right]. \tag{A.4}$$

$$r_{c,3} = \frac{2}{3}\left[\frac{r_{c,2}}{2} + \frac{m_c + r_s}{pr_c}\right] \tag{A.5}$$

The solution of this system is $r_{c,0} = r_{c,1} = r_{c,3} = \frac{m_c+r_s}{pr_c}$. This solution implies that banks behave identically and characterizes a perfect competitive behavior. Moreover, if we take into consideration only the elements of profit function that influence the bank behavior on the credit market, i.e. $\pi_i = \left(\mathrm{pr}_{c,i} r_{c,i} - m_c - r_s\right) n_c$, then this profit equal zero for $r_{c,i} = \frac{m_c+r_s}{\mathrm{pr}_c}$, for $\forall i = \overline{0, n}$. All these findings relate a perfect competition on the credit market if $d = 0$ and if the banks have the same quality of the credit portfolio.

Appendix B. Determination of the Location of Bank 1

The analysis is divided into two parts. In the first part, we analyze the case when $x_1 \geq 0.5$ and in the second one when $x_1 \leq 0.5$. In the first case x_c is always lesser than or equal to 0.5. The location of the marginal client in the center means that the banks divide the market into two equal parts. The least moving of this client to right, i.e. $x_c > 0.5$, reduces the market share of bank 1. In consequence, having the possibility to choose her location first, bank 1 will choose her position so that x_c is always lesser than or equal to 0.5. For the same reason, in the second case, x_c is always bigger than or equal to 0.5.

In two cases one must find x_c in function of x_1 and x_2. Then, thanks to Eq. (13b), the response function $x_2 = R(x_1)$ is determined. These equations will be substituted in Eq. (12a) and this later equation will be analyzed.

(1) For the first case, $x_1 \geq 0.5$, we have

$$x_c = \frac{X_1 \pm \sqrt{8Y_1^2 + X_1^2}}{8Y_1}, \tag{B.1.a}$$

where

$$X_1 = \text{pr}_{c,1}\text{pr}_{c,2}t\left(x_1^2 - x_2^2\right) - (m_c + r_s)\left(\text{pr}_{c,1} - \text{pr}_{c,2}\right) \text{ and} \tag{B.2}$$
$$Y_1 = \text{pr}_{c,1}\text{pr}_{c,2}t\,(x_1 - x_2)\,.$$

Analyzing Eq. (B.1.a), we have that the solution $x_c = \frac{X_1 - \sqrt{8Y_1^2 + X_1^2}}{8Y_1}$ is always lesser than 0, which is impossible because the marginal client must be located on the market. In consequence, the marginal client is located at the following point

$$x_c = \frac{X_1 + \sqrt{8Y_1^2 + X_1^2}}{8Y_1}. \tag{B.1.b}$$

In order to find the response function $x_2 = R(x_1)$, we introduce Eq. (15a) in Eq. (14) and the first equation is solved with respect to x_2. As a result, we have

$$x_2 = \frac{9x_1}{8} \pm \frac{K_1}{8\sqrt{B_1}} \pm \frac{1}{2}\left[\frac{81x_1^2}{8} + \frac{A_1 + B_1\left(2 - 19x_1^2\right)}{2B_1} - \frac{\sqrt{B_1}}{K_1}\left(\frac{729x_1^3}{8} + \frac{x_1\left(9A_1 + 2B_1\left(1 - 45x_1^2\right)\right)}{B_1}\right)\right]^{\frac{1}{2}} \tag{B.3.a}$$

where

$$K_1 = \sqrt{72A_1 + B_1\left(16 + 9x_1^2\right)}, \quad A_1 = (m_c + r_s)\left(\text{pr}_{c,1} - \text{pr}_{c,2}\right) \text{ and}$$
$$B_1 = \text{pr}_{c,1}\text{pr}_{c,2}t. \tag{B.4}$$

The different simulations for different values for the probabilities of success show that the condition $x_2 < x_c < x_1$ is always respected only for

$$x_2 = \frac{9x_1}{8} - \frac{K_1}{8\sqrt{B_1}} - \frac{1}{2}\left[\frac{81x_1^2}{8} + \frac{A_1 + B_1(2 - 19x_1^2)}{2B_1} - \frac{\sqrt{B_1}}{K_1}\left(\frac{729x_1^3}{8} + \frac{x_1(9A_1 + 2B_1(1 - 45x_1^2))}{B_1}\right)\right]^{\frac{1}{2}} \tag{B.3.b}$$

Taking into account that the location of bank 2 and the profit of bank 1 depend on the probabilities of success, we analyze graphically the profit of bank 1 for two different values of the probability of success $\mathrm{pr}_{c,1}$ and we draw the figures in function of x_1 and $\mathrm{pr}_{c,2}$. Since, according to Eqs. (B.4) and (B.3.b), the response function is symmetric in respect with the probabilities of success, it is not necessary to draw these graphics in function of $\mathrm{pr}_{c,2}$ for different values of $\mathrm{pr}_{c,1}$. The values of other parameters are the following: $m_c = 0.03$; $r_s = 0.05$; and $t = 0.1$.

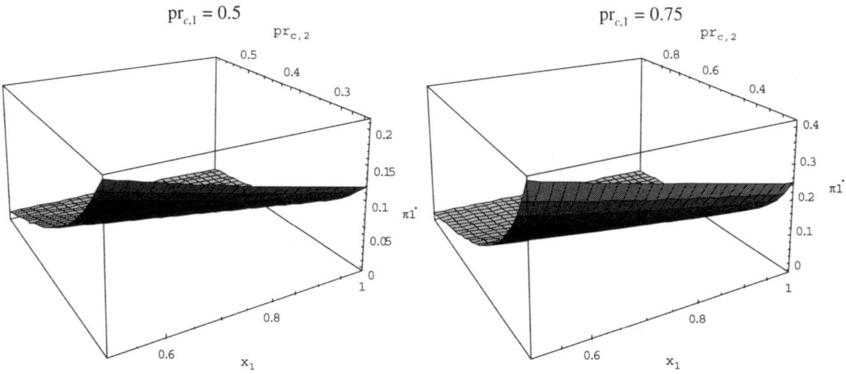

According to the above figures, for all values of $\mathrm{pr}_{c,2}$ the bank 1 maximizes her profit if she is located in the center of the market, i.e. at the point $x_1 = 0.5$.

(2) For the second case, $x_1 \leq 0.5$, we have $x_c \geq 0.5$ and the configuration of the model changes: $x_2 > x_1$ and n_c becomes the market share of bank 1. Applying the same procedure as in Sec. 4.1, we find

$$x_c = \frac{X_1 + 6Y_1 \pm \sqrt{(X_1 + 6Y_1)^2 - 8Y_1(2X_1 + 3Y_1)}}{8Y_1}, \qquad \text{(B.4.a)}$$

where X_1 and Y_1 represent Eq. (B.2).

According to Eq. (B.4.a), we find that the solution $x_c = \frac{X_1+6Y_1-\sqrt{(X_1+6Y_1)^2-8Y_1(2X_1+3Y_1)}}{8Y_1}$ is always higher than 1 and thus does not corroborate with the construction of the model, because the marginal client must be located on the market as bank 2 has a market share. In consequence, the location of the marginal client is expressed by

$$x_c = \frac{X_1 + 6Y_1 + \sqrt{(X_1 + 6Y_1)^2 - 8Y_1(2X_1 + 3Y_1)}}{8Y_1}. \qquad \text{(B.4.b)}$$

Solving a similar system to the precedent case, the response function of bank 2 to the location of bank 1 is found to be

$$x_2 = \frac{9x_1 - 1}{8} \pm \frac{K_2}{8\sqrt{B_1}} \pm \frac{1}{2}\left[\frac{(9x_1-1)^2}{8} + \frac{A_1 + B_1(3 + 2x_1 - 19x_1^2)}{2B_1} + \frac{\sqrt{B_1}}{K_2}\left(\frac{(9x_1-1)^3}{8} + \frac{9A_1(1-x_1) - B_1(90x_1^3 - 27x_1^2 + 8x_1 + 3)}{B_1}\right)\right]^{\frac{1}{2}} \qquad \text{(B.5.a)}$$

where $K_1 = \sqrt{72A_1 + B_1\left(25 - 18x_1 + 9x_1^2\right)}$. The different simulations show that the condition $x_1 < x_c < x_2$ is always respected only for

$$x_2 = \frac{9x_1 - 1}{8} + \frac{K_2}{8\sqrt{B_1}} + \frac{1}{2}\left[\frac{(9x_1-1)^2}{8} + \frac{A_1 + B_1(3 + 2x_1 - 19x_1^2)}{2B_1} + \frac{\sqrt{B_1}}{K_2}\left(\frac{(9x_1-1)^3}{8} + \frac{9A_1(1-x_1) - B_1(90x_1^3 - 27x_1^2 + 8x_1 + 3)}{B_1}\right)\right]^{\frac{1}{2}} \qquad \text{(B.5.b)}$$

Making the same graphical analysis as in the precedent case, we obtain that bank 1 maximizes her profit only if she is located in the center of the market (see the figures below). This is the expected result since the model is symmetrical in respect to the center. The values of the parameters are the same: $m_c = 0.03$; $r_s = 0.05$; and $t = 0.1$.

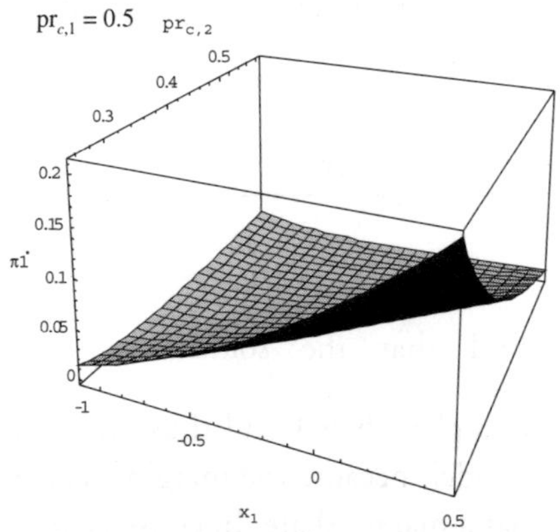

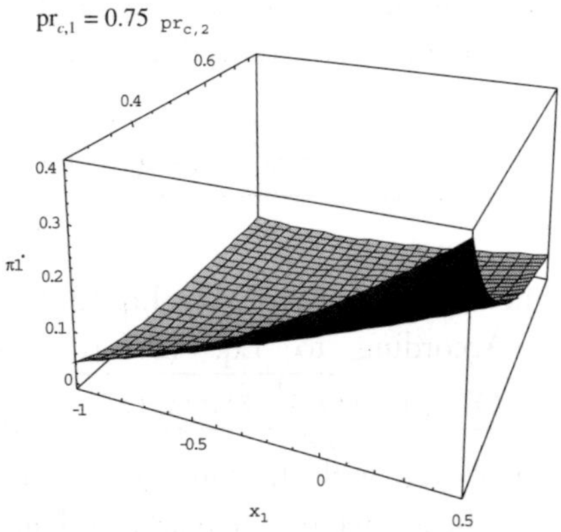

Appendix C. Results of the Simulation for the Simultaneous Entry Case

Table C.1: Equilibrium interest rates and the market shares of the banks ($\mathrm{pr}_{c,i} = \mathrm{pr}_c, m_c = 0.03, r_s = 0.05$).

Location of the banks	Market share of the banks	Equilibrium interest rates								
		$t = 0.1$			$t = 0.3$			$t = 0.5$		
		$\mathrm{pr}_c = 0.5$	$\mathrm{pr}_c = 0.75$	$\mathrm{pr}_c = 1$	$\mathrm{pr}_c = 0.5$	$\mathrm{pr}_c = 0.75$	$\mathrm{pr}_c = 1$	$\mathrm{pr}_c = 0.5$	$\mathrm{pr}_c = 0.75$	$\mathrm{pr}_c = 1$
$n = 4$										
0	0.0509	0.1640	0.1107	0.0840	0.1720	0.1186	0.0920	0.1799	0.1266	0.0999
1	0.2507	0.1657	0.1124	0.0857	0.1772	0.1238	0.0972	0.1886	0.1353	0.1086
2	0.3968	0.1664	0.1131	0.0864	0.1792	0.1258	0.0992	0.1919	0.1386	0.1119
$n = 10$										
0	0.0080	0.1606	0.1073	0.0806	0.1619	0.10857	0.0819	0.16317	0.10984	0.08317
1	0.0392	0.1609	0.10757	0.0809	0.16271	0.10937	0.08271	0.16451	0.1112	0.08451
2	0.0789	0.16097	0.10764	0.08097	0.16292	0.10959	0.08292	0.16487	0.1115	0.08487
3	0.1197	0.16099	0.10766	0.0810	0.16299	0.10965	0.08299	0.16498	0.11164	0.08498
4	0.1613	0.16100	0.10767	0.08101	0.16302	0.10969	0.08302	0.16503	0.1117	0.08503
5	0.1858	0.16103	0.10770	0.08103	0.16309	0.10976	0.08309	0.16515	0.1118	0.08515

(Continued)

Table C.1: (*Continued*)

Location of the banks	Market share of the banks	Equilibrium interest rates								
		$t = 0.1$			$t = 0.3$			$t = 0.5$		
		$\text{pr}_c = 0.5$	$\text{pr}_c = 0.75$	$\text{pr}_c = 1$	$\text{pr}_c = 0.5$	$\text{pr}_c = 0.75$	$\text{pr}_c = 1$	$\text{pr}_c = 0.5$	$\text{pr}_c = 0.75$	$\text{pr}_c = 1$
$n = 20$										
0	0.0020	0.16016	0.10683	0.08016	0.16048	0.10714	0.08048	0.16079	0.10746	0.08079
1	0.0098	0.16023	0.10689	0.08023	0.16068	0.10734	0.08068	0.16113	0.10779	0.08113
2	0.0197	0.16024	0.10691	0.08024	0.16073	0.10740	0.08073	0.16122	0.10789	0.08122
3	0.0298	0.16025	0.10691	0.08025	0.16075	0.10741	0.08074	0.16124	0.10791	0.08124
4	0.0399	0.16025	0.10692	0.08025	0.16075	0.10742	0.08075	0.16125	0.10791	0.08125
5	0.0500	0.16025	0.10692	0.08025	0.16075	0.10742	0.08075	0.16125	0.10792	0.08125
6	0.0600	0.16025	0.10692	0.08025	0.16075	0.10742	0.08075	0.16125	0.10792	0.08125
7	0.0700	0.16025	0.10692	0.08025	0.16075	0.10742	0.08075	0.16125	0.10792	0.08125
8	0.0801	0.16025	0.10692	0.08025	0.16075	0.10742	0.08075	0.16125	0.10792	0.08125
9	0.0904	0.16025	0.10692	0.08025	0.16075	0.10742	0.08075	0.16126	0.10792	0.08126
10	0.0965	0.16025	0.10692	0.08025	0.16076	0.10743	0.08076	0.16127	0.10794	0.08127

Note: The interest rates on the perfect competitive market are: $r_c = 0.16$ for $\text{pr}_c = 0.5$; $r_c = 0.10667$ for $\text{pr}_c = 0.75$; and $r_c = 0.08$ for $\text{pr}_c = 1$.

Table C.2(a): Equilibrium interest rates and the market shares when probabilities are different, except for banks 4 and 5 (t =0.1).

	Left side					Right side			
i	$pr_{c,i}$	$r_{c,i}$	x_i	$x_{c,i}$	Profit maximization	$r_{c,i}$	x_i	$x_{c,i}$	$n_{c,i}$
0	0.55	0.14190	0	−0.356	No	—	−0.62	—	—
1	0.6	0.13378	0.1	−0.312	No	—	−0.396	—	—
2	0.65	0.12457	0.2	−0.162	No	—	−0.172	—	—
3	0.7	0.11633	0.3	0.043	No	0.11635	0.052	0.0922	0.0170
4	0.75	0.11018	0.4	0.394	Yes	0.11314	0.276	0.3811	0.2734
5	0.75	0.10907	0.5	0.606	Yes	0.11283	0.5	0.6189	0.4191

Note: "Yes" ("No") means that the profit maximization principle is (is not) respected. The left side of the table provides the results issuing from simulations. Then, they are selected, according to profit maximization and border market ($x_{c,i} > x_i$) principles, and presented in the right side of the table.

Table C.2(b): Equilibrium interest rates and the market shares when probabilities are different and it is highest for bank localized at the center (bank 5) (t =0.1).

	Left side					Right side			
i	$pr_{c,i}$	$r_{c,i}$	x_i	$x_{c,i}$	Profit maximization	$r_{c,i}$	x_i	$x_{c,i}$	$n_{c,i}$
0	0.55	—	−0.62	—	No	—	−1	—	—
1	0.6	—	−0.396	—	No	—	−0.7	—	—
2	0.65	—	−0.172	—	No	—	−0.4	—	—
3	0.7	0.11539	0.052	0.0491	Impossible case	0.11485	−0.1	0.0189	0.0007
4	0.75	0.11024	0.276	0.2085	Yes	0.11299	0.2	0.2297	0.1048
5	1	0.10219	0.5	0.7915	Yes	0.10577	0.5	0.7703	0.7890

Note: "Yes" ("No") means that the profit maximization principle is (is not) respected. The left side of the table provides the results issuing from simulations. Then, they are selected, according to profit maximization and border market ($x_{c,i} > x_i$) principles, and presented in the right side of the table. "Impossible case" signifies that border market principle is not respected even if it the profit maximization one is verified.

Appendix D. Results of the Simulation for the Sequential Entry Case

Table D.1: Bank 1 enter the first on the market.

$pr_{c,2}$	$r_{c,1}$	$r_{c,2}$	x_1	x_2	x_c	$n_{c,1}$	$n_{c,2}$	π_1^*	π_2^*
$t = 0.1$ and $pr_{c,1} = 0.75$									
0.25	0.6874	0.3580	0.5	−1.6685	0.1752	0.9386	0.0614	0.4088	0.0006
0.50	0.3213	0.1971	0.5	−0.8663	0.2714	0.8527	0.1473	0.1373	0.0027
0.75	0.2033	0.1407	0.5	−0.443	0.3608	0.7397	0.2603	0.0536	0.0066
0.95	0.1443	0.1122	0.5	−0.1062	0.4618	0.5735	0.4265	0.0162	0.0113
0.97	0.1368	0.1088	0.5	−0.0460	0.4830	0.5333	0.4667	0.0121	0.0119
0.98	0.1388	0.1722	1.27	0.3825	0.6382	0.2618	0.7382	0.0063	0.0655
1	0.1391	0.1762	1.30	0.3910	0.6445	0.2527	0.7413	0.0061	0.0714
$t = 0.1$ and $pr_{c,1} = 0.5$									
0.25	0.6155	0.3580	0.5	−1.4370	0.1962	0.9230	0.0770	0.2120	0.0007
0.5	0.2567	0.1940	0.5	−0.443	0.3608	0.7397	0.2603	0.0358	0.0044
0.59	0.1890	0.1617	0.5	−0.0360	0.4867	0.5263	0.4737	0.0076	0.0073
0.60	0.1923	0.2286	1.299	0.3911	0.6444	0.2529	0.7471	0.0041	0.0428
0.75	0.1930	0.2729	1.634	0.4884	0.7124	0.1655	0.8346	0.0027	0.1040
1	0.1932	0.3194	1.894	0.5507	0.7534	0.1217	0.8783	0.0020	0.2103
$t = 0.5$ and $pr_{c,1} = 0.75$									
0.25	1.0627	0.5039	0.5	−0.7950	0.2840	0.8387	0.1613	0.6013	0.0074
0.5	0.7106	0.3355	0.5	−0.5461	0.3355	0.7748	0.2252	0.3510	0.0198
0.75	0.5901	0.2768	0.5	−0.443	0.3608	0.7397	0.2603	0.2682	0.0332
0.95	0.5379	0.2512	0.5	−0.3940	0.3736	0.7208	0.2792	0.2331	0.0443
1	0.5279	0.2464	0.5	−0.3843	0.3762	0.7169	0.2831	0.2265	0.0471

References

Bonin, J, Mizsei, K, Szekely, I and Wachtel, P (1998). *Banking in Transition Economies: Developing Market Oriented Banking Sectors in Eastern Europe*, Cheltenham, UK — Northampton, MA, USA; Edward Elgar.

Bonin, J, Hasan, I, Wachtel, P (2005). Bank performance, efficiency and ownership in transition countries. *Journal of Banking and Finance*, 29, 31–53.

Caplin, A and Nalebuff, B (1991). Aggregation and imperfect competition: On existence of equilibrium. *Econometrica*, 59, 25–59.

Claessens, S, Demirgüç-Kunt, A and Huizinga, H (2001). How does foreign entry affect domestic banking markets? *Journal of Banking and Finance*, 25, 891–911.

Crystal, JS, Dages, BG and Goldberg, LS (2002). Has foreign bank entry led to sounder banks in Latin America? *Current Issues in Economics and Finance*, 8, 1–6.

Dages, BG, Goldberg, LS and Kinney, D (2000). Foreign and domestic bank participation in emerging markets: Lessons from Mexico and Argentina. *Federal Reserve Bank of New York Economic Policy Review*, (September), 17–36.

Economides, N (1989). Symmetric equilibrium existence and optimality in differentiated product markets. *Journal of Economic Theory*, 47, 178–194.

Fries, S and Taci, A (2005). Cost efficiency of banks in transition: Evidence from 289 banks in 15 post-communist countries. *Journal of Banking and Finance*, 29, 55–81.

Gale, D (1993). Informational capacity and financial collapse. In *Capital Markets and Financial Intermediation*, C Mayer and X Vives (eds.), pp. 117–148. Cambridge, UK: Cambridge University Press.

Jeon, Y, Miller, S and Natke, P (2003). Do foreign bank operations provide a stabilizing influence in Korea? Working Paper 2004-21, University of Connecticut.

Mai, Ch-Ch and Sh-K Peng (1999). Cooperation vs competition in a spatial model. *Regional Science and Urban Economics*, 29, 463–472.

Matutes, C and Vives, X (1996). Competition for deposits, fragility, and insurance. *Journal of Financial Intermediation*, 5, 184–216.

Shaffer, S (1998). The winner's curse in banking. *Journal of Financial Intermediation*, 1(4), 359–392.

Tabuchi, T and Thisse, J-F (1995). Asymmetric equilibria in spatial competition. *International Journal of Industrial Organization*, 13, 213–227.

Yanelle, M-O (1989). The strategic analysis of intermediation. *European Economic Review*, 33, 294–304.

Yanelle, M-O (1997). Banking competition and market efficiency. *Review of Economic Studies*, 64, 215–239.

CHAPTER 11

EARLY WARNING DETECTION OF BANKING DISTRESS — IS FAILURE POSSIBLE FOR EUROPEAN BANKS?

*Anissa Naouar**

The aim of this paper is to predict banking distress resulting from capitalization problems in order to justify the viability of Prompt Corrective Actions in Europe. In particular, I examine the impact of the "safety net" and the role of rating agencies through negative credit watches, using a binomial logit model in order to predict European commercial banks capital stress and to test the contribution of institutions and regulatory factors. I also study the impact of concentration and moral hazard generated by deposit insurance on banking stability. My results are in line with previous findings in the literature and demonstrate not only a negative influence of institutional and regulatory factors on European banking systems' distress probability but also a significant role for the rating agencies. In addition, the quality of national regulatory frameworks including supervision restrains considerably moral hazard and excessive risk taken by European commercial banks.

0 Introduction

Advanced detection of individual banking fragility is supposed to ease the setting-up of prompt corrective actions to avoid the risk of failure and the resulting contagion (systemic risk). Methods used by the supervisors to evaluate the financial health of banks are subject to severe critics regarding their ability to estimate the problems. Indeed, till the end of the nineties, these methods were mainly based on balance sheet data and financial ratios. On

*EconomiX — UMR 7166, 200, avenue de la république, 92000 Nanterre Cedex, France Anissanaouar@yahoo.fr

another note, the majority of the papers developed in this field concentrated on major events such as banks' failures — declared by the public authorities — in the US or in emerging markets. Some article that studied the emerging markets case focused on the impacts of regulatory frameworks and institutional actions, as in some cases, these could exacerbate risk taking and increase a bank's failure probability. La Porta *et al.* (1997, 1998, 2000), for instance, focused on the impacts of juridical and institutional environments on shareholders' protection as well as on the nature and the efficiency of capital market. Their main findings pointed out this environment as major determinant of corporate governance and risk appetite. Barth *et al.* (2000) focused on the relationship between different regulatory frameworks and banks' performances and stability. They find that the former affects the latter negatively in the case of banking activities restrictions. Hussain and Wihlborg (1999) and Mitton (2002) find that weak corporate governance amplified the Asian crisis of 1997–1998. This paper aims to answer for two questions: firstly, I propose a failure prediction framework for European banks, and secondly, I raise some questions that have not been yet asked in the previous literature on the European case. In this sense, I build an early warning model based on capitalization levels using a set of balance sheet indicators (CAMEL) and qualitative variables reflecting private and public interventions as explanatory variables. I also examine the impact of moral hazard that results from deposit insurance and banking concentration on European banks' distress detection.

To my knowledge, to date, there is only one study that focused on distress detection on a panel of European banks. This study uses both balance sheet data and market data to explain the probability of rating downgrade (Tarazi *et al.*, 2003).[a] In this sense, I focused my work on the prediction of capital movement of mid-sized banks rather than treating the question of banking failure prediction.[b] This methodological choice facilitates the application of a prompt corrective action. In this respect, I focused on predicting banking distress and the role of institutional and regulatory issues through the information contained in dynamic data movements rather than a point in time observation.

The paper is organized as follows: in Sec. 1, I present an overview of the methods and the sets of data used in my estimation. Section 2 focuses on

[a]Two other studies conducted by Gropp and Vulves (2002, 2005) and Brossard *et al.* (2006) have looked for detecting the difficulty of European banks but used only market indicators.

[b]Failure is often the results of an authority decision rather than the immediate consequence of market forces (Kane, 1989).

descriptive statistics of the sample used. In Sec. 3, I perform some empirical estimation and present my main findings and the last section concludes.

1 General Presentation of the Method and the Data Used

The approach used in this paper consists in the identification of the contribution of balance sheet indicators in predicting solvency ratios' deterioration and the study of the stability of their effects given institutional, regulatory (supervision and central bank), and private (rating agencies negative credit watches actions) role in different European country included in the sample used.

1.1 Bank Distress Identification

The ultimate goal consists in predicting the deterioration of banks' capital ratios, which are approximated by the decline of regulatory capital ratio below a given threshold considered as sufficiently low to result in a corrective action from a bank's senior managers or supervisors. This methodology is justified by the fact that there is a few number of banks that are officially in default in Europe. This relationship is modeled through a logit[c] model commonly used to analyze binary qualitative variables — takes either 0 or 1 value depending on the event. This model is as appropriate as more complex models such as non-parametric models — Trait Recognition Analysis (TRA).[d]

Y^*_{it} denote the dependant binary variable. However, I focus on modeling the probability that $P(Y_{it} = 1)$ takes the value 1. Then I assume that the value of this probability is determined according to the following process, whereby Y^*_{it} is not observable:

$$Y_{it} = 1 \text{ if the bank is undercapitalized, then } Y^*_{it} > 0.$$

$$Y_{it} = 0 \text{ if the bank is well capitalized, then } Y^*_{it} \leq 0.$$

Y^*_{it} is modeled linearly through a set of explanatory quantitative variables X_{it} and qualitative variables Q_{it} as follows:

$$Y^*_{it} = \alpha X_{it} + \beta Q_{it} + \varepsilon_{it}$$

i stands for the bank j at given date "t".

[c]The choice of the logit method rather than the probit one is motivated by the non-equality of frequency in the simple (under-capitalized banks and well-capitalized banks)(Maddala, 1983). We have realized many estimations of the logit model: firstly to identify the effects of balance sheet variables, then institutional and regulatory factors in every country and secondly to identify the same effects on a global European scale in order to derive the implications of national regulation and the viability of a single pan-European regulation.

[d]Jagtiani *et al.* (2003).

The probability of the event ($Y_{it} = 1$) takes place is equivalent to the case where the residual factor ε_{it} is smaller than $\alpha X_{it} + \beta Q_{it}$. In this case:

$$P(Y_{it} = 1) = P(Y_{it}^* > 0) = F(\alpha X_{it} + \beta Q_{it})$$
$$= \exp[(\alpha X_{it} + \beta Q_{it})/(1 + \exp \alpha X_{it} + \beta Q_{it})].$$

where F is the logistic distribution function.

In order to maximize the quality of the model, I focus, in the first step, on choosing the best explanatory variables of banks' capital ratio deterioration using a stepwise process. Each variable is subject to tests based on its specific contribution in the explanation of Y_{it} and this process is expected to help the identification of the most appropriate set of variable. Once this set is determined, the next step consists in identifying, on the one hand, ratings agencies' role and on the other hand, the impact of regulation and institution using the same stepwise approach as for the first step.

2 Sample

I used a sample of 134 commercial banks located in 11 European countries in the following:

Country	FR	ALL	IT	ESP	UK	PB	IRL	PRG	BLG	GRC	AUT	Total
Number of banks	25	15	20	12	19	15	5	4	8	6	5	134

Balance sheet and profit and loss statements were collected from Bankscope for the period 1998–2005[e] while institutional and regulatory variables were collected from the World Bank database and using the paper of De Caprio *et al.* (2001). I choose to focus only on the rating action made by Standard & Poor's as a result of its leading status on this market. These actions were collected from Ratings Direct.

2.1 Dependant Variable

The model used focus on two states: well capitalized banks versus under capitalized banks with the last state denoting banking distress that is, under normal

[e]The choice of this starting data is explained by the fact that, officially, the year 1998 represents an important step marking the euro passage: the countries members of the EMU are identified by the European committee, the ECB government is nominated, the first stage of euro passage is accomplished and the official exchange rates between the different European money are fixed.

condition, predicted by the supervisors. In each of the retained countries, the sample is divided as follows[f]:

- Undercapitalized banks with capital ratios below the first quartile $Q1$.
- Well-capitalized banks with capital ratios above the third quartile $Q3$.

The choice of this threshold is partly explained by the fact that European banks keep in general a capitalization ratio above 4% for Tier 1 and above 8% for total regulatory capital ratio as per Basel committee recommendations. In order to test for the robustness of the model, I have also distinguished between banks with capital ratios above and below the median ($Q2$). The table below presents the different capital ratios distribution quartiles in each country over the period 1998–2004.

Country	$Q1$	$Q2$	$Q3$
FR	9.1	10.16	11.4
GR	9.4	10.5	12.06
IT	8.7	9.85	11.1
SP	9.1	10	10.8
UK	11.5	13.15	14.52
PB	10.1	10.6	12.4
IRL	10.16	11.1	11.8
PRG	9.37	10.55	11.45
BLG	10.7	12	13.05
GRC	9.72	12.35	14.77
AUS	9.95	10.7	11.35
Total	9.68	10.9	12.02

2.2 *Explanatory Variables*

X_{it}: This set of variables is constructed from the balance sheet and P&L data and consists of the generally used variables in the CAMEL methodology. The table below summarizes the variables retained in this paper as well as the assumptions regarding their expected effect on the probability of a bank being in distress.

Balance sheet data can either be taken in form of Direct level or in form of ratios in the equation. Previous studies have mostly used ratios

[f]In previous studies ran on the American banks, some authors qualify a well capitalized bank such a bank that satisfy a ratio Tier 1 of at least 5.5%: a threshold that coincide with the regulatory standards in USA in 1980. Jagtiani *et al.* (2000, 2003) and Estrella *et al.* (1995, 2000)) have find that this level is a good proxy for detecting the bank fragility first signs.

Financial ratios

Category	Title	Definition	Description of the expected effect
C[g]	Tier 1	Common equity/risk weighted assets	(+ / −) a high level of equity allows the bank to absorb un-anticipated shocks. A low level of equity could be compensated by a high amount of sub-debt issues
	DSUB	Subordinated debt/assets	(+ / −) banks that issue high amounts of subordinated debt could or not exhibit higher ratios of non-performing loans/total loans than those of their competitors and thus a higher of lower probability of a sistress
A[h]	PRVCB	Provisions/gross loans	(+ / −) an increase of provisions could be considered as resulting from a potential increase in non-performing loans. At the same time, provisions increase could be interpreted as an increase in the buffer the bank can use to cover asset quality problems
M	DOTREV	Provisions/net interest income	(+) we anticipate a positive relationship between this variables and the bank's overall financial health. The more the ratio is high and the less the bank is efficient
	DOPRO	Operating expenses/operating income	(−) this ratio measures the loans coverage by short term funds. A high ratio represents a good loan coverage
E	PRFIN	Loans/ST financing	(−) Profitability affects negatively the probability of trouble. The more a bank is profitable, the less it is vulnerable
L	ROA INTAM	Net result/total assets Net interest income/average assets	(−) The more the bank has liquid assets, the more it can weather any pressure on liquidity. (The ratio Liquid assets to deposits is much more appropriated)
	ALD	Liquid assets/total deposits	This ratio translates the bank's intermediation rate (the ability to transform customer deposits into loans). A negative sign signify that the more a bank can offers loans using only some deposits, the least is its defaulting risk
	CDRF	Total loans/customer deposits	(+) a high sensitivity of the bank to financial market movements reflects an increase of its risk portfolio and of the likelihood of trouble

(*Continued*)

(*Continued*)

Category	Title	Definition	Description of the expected effect
S	SNB	Market sensitivity measured by the market beta (beta > 1 imply a strong sensitivity of the bank's stocks to market variation).	(+ / −) a significant contribution of market related income to total income could leave the bank vulnerable to market movements
	RSM	Market sensitive income/total income	(+ / −) this variable allows for contagion's control (via Interbank market) and allows the isolation of potential discipline role of depositors
	DINT	Interbank deposits/total assets	(+ / −) market concentration should have positive effects according to the too big to fail theory (Mishkin, 1999; Pollin, 2006). It could also have a negative effect as it allow dominant banks to protect their profitability.
CONC[i]		Market concentration	

[g]Banking capitalization is generally measured by two indicators: shareholders equity/total assets and total capital ratio (Shareholders equity + hybrid equity + subordinated debt)/total assets. European banks issue subordinated debt particularly to enhance their capital adequacy ratio (cf. Sironi, 2001). Indeed, some banks state that they issue sub-debt only if there is a positive effect on capital adequacy ratio. Thus, we distinguish between two ratios of capital adequacy (Tier 1 and Tier 2). There are some particular cases where the bank issues a high amount of sub-debt with limited capital base. Sub-debts allow also the detection of minimal *ex post* market discipline.

[h]Empirical study has been limited as data is observed on a yearly basis and because of the limited amount of information of some asset classes (such as the level of non-performing loans that are supposed to anticipate the ratio of loses on credits coverage).

[i]The concentration is a relevant question approached in the theoretic and empirical literatures mainly regarding its impact on the stability (assumption of concentration/stability vs. concentration/fragility). Among authors that support the first assumption, Diamond (1984), Ramakrishnan and Thakor (1984), Boyd and Prescott (1986), Williamson (1986), and Allen (1990) who confirm the fact that in concentrated markets, large banks tend to be more diversified and than would be less fragile than in markets with a great number of small banks. Allen and Gale (2000, 2004) have concluded that banking systems with many small banks are more sensitive than concentrated markets and that these last ones are easier to supervise. Beck *et al.* (2006) have used a data base of 69 countries during the 1980–1997 period to demonstrate that national banking concentration, banking regulation, and institutions are negatively influence the probability of systemic banking crises.

In contrary, another point of view stipulates that concentrated structures augment banking fragility. Boyd *et al.* (2000) and Caminal and Matutes (2002) argued that market power and the banking stability ignore bank individual comportment motivated by an excessive risk taking and non-rationing credits generating bank fragility. For more details, see Carletti and Hartmann (2003) and Boyd and De Nicolo (2006).

(Gunther *et al.*, 2001; Curry *et al.*, 2002). This approach appears adequate when dealing with important events such a bank failure. In this paper, I am trying to predict the medium term evolution of the banks' financial health. This implies that the absolute level of the ratios could be meaningless for us while the variation of each ratio could be important. Thus, a firm can benefit from a satisfactory situation (good levels of book ratios) but at the same time, the evolution of its financial ratios could be negative[j] and this could be reported only through the study of the medium term evolution of these ratios. I assume $C_{it} = \Delta R_{it} = R_{it} - R_{it-1}$, the variation of the balance sheet ratio R_{it}. The empirical findings of the previous literature seem to be unanimous about the role of individual data in predicting banking distress. Nevertheless, there are limited studies on the impact of institutional and regulatory factors on banks' insolvency especially in Europe. Thus, I try to focus on this question through the introduction of regulatory and institutional variables that constitute a sort of "safety net" for banks and through the impacts of different supervisory systems and regulatory disciplines on the prediction of European banks' distress. The focus is finally diverted toward the role of rating agencies through negative credit watch actions in helping the anticipation of European banks' distress. This variable is set to reflect the rating agencies' reaction, which could result in a supervisory process. The actions made by Standard & Poor's are used in this study as this agency enjoys a solid leading position on capital markets. This is expected to provide a measure of banks' solidity as viewed by the private actors. Table A.4 presents some criteria used by Standard & Poor's in its rating process. There are some articles in the previous literature that focused on the implication of ratings actions on stock prices[k] (cf. Followill and Martell, 1997; Barron *et al.*, 1997; Goyeau *et al.*, 2000; Heude and Blanc, 2004; Damak, 2006). Some articles focused also on distress situations described approximated by a rating downgrade (cf. Gropp *et al.* 2002, 2005; Tarazi *et al.* (2003); Brossard *et al.* 2006). I focus only on short term negative announcement (the placement of the rating under watch negative or downgrade) regardless of the

[j]This approach is adopted from the study realized by Tarazi *et al.* (2003) on the European banking difficulty detection.

[k]For instance, Heude and Paget-Blanc (2004) have studied the impact of different rating actions on the French equity market. The main result is the denunciation of the lack of informational content of the rating actions and the impossibility of using them as a tool for investment policies.

Regulatory and private actions.

Symbol	Designation	Effect description	Source
Sup	BC role of supervision	0 None	Aglietta M (1999) Barth *et al.* (2002) and ECB (2006)
RBC		1 limited role the expected effect may be 2 principal role (+) or (−)	
OBP	Does the supervision agency has the authority to oblige the constitution of provisions to cover present or potential losses?	(−) 0 NO 1 YES	World Bank
JURD	Does the supervisor intervene beyond a determined threshold of solvency?	(−) 0 NO 1 YES	
ROB	Role of other banks in helping the bank in distress.	(−) 0 none 1 important role	World Bank
IASRD[1]	Deposit insurance index impacts, which is expected to reflect moral hazard.	1 if there is an explicit deposit insurance 0 if not (+) or (−) effect	World Bank
	Coverage variation		
VCOUV	*COA*: Do depositors benefit from coinsurance?	0 NO 1 YES	Demirgüç-Kunt K and Detragiache E (2002, 2007)
	LCOUV: coverage limitation or amount of coverage authorized	0 limited (−) 1 not limited	
	COUVME: foreign deposits eligibility to insurance	1 YES (+) or (−) effect 0 NO	World Bank

(*Continued*)

(*Continued*)

Symbol	Designation	Effect description	Source
	COUVDI: *Interbank deposits eligibility to insurance*	1 YES 0 NO	
VFIN	*Financing variation*	1 if *ex ante* 0 if *ex post*	
	PRIM: If the prime is fixed *ex ante* (regularly) or *ex post* (occasionally)		
	SFIN: Agency financing sources	0 if bank only 1 if bank and government (+) or (−) effect 2 if government only	
MNG	Agency management	0 public 1 Joint (+) or (−) effect 2 private	
MSSAN*	Rating agencies Negative watches	This variable allows the detection of rating agencies role in the detection of banking distress. If the effect is positive, the rating agencies do not improve the flow of information already available. If not, the rating agencies provide shareholders and supervisors with information that can be taken into account in setting up a prompt correction.	

[1]This index of deposit insurance is determined according to Demirgüç-Kunt and Detragiache (2002, 2007) approach in which the first test consists in determining if a dummy that takes the value 0 or 1 for the presence of explicit deposit insurance has a significant coefficient. However, this approach constraints all deposit insurance schemes type to have the same effect on the probability of meeting banking problems. In practice, such impact must be different according to the type of insurance system. Mainly, a limited coverage should, reduce the hazard moral. Similarly, in a financed system, the guaranties should be more credible than that it would be when the system is not financed, than inherent hazard moral would be stronger and bank runs risk weaker.

To take these differences into account, we construct alternative variables of deposit insurance constructed around a hazard moral index in which the simple dummy variable is replaced by each refined variable (according to the financing type, financing sources, management, etc.).

number of notches for downgrade as the main aim of this study is to focus on the informational content of the rating action compared with accounting data.

3 Descriptive Analysis

The sample includes major European banks. The sample used for each country is designed such as that the smallest bank accounts for at least 1% of the sample's cumulative total assets using 2004 data. This limitation is set to ignore very small banks in the sample. In addition, banks with capital ratios of more than 20% were excluded from the sample. The examination of the sample leads to a certain number of conclusions, including:

- Capital ratios are on average higher than the minimal prudential requirements of 8% for all European countries included in the sample. There are some countries (Spain, Belgium, Greece, and Austria), where this rule is not applicable without any action from the supervisor.
- Subordinated debt/total assets ratio reflects the quality of the bank capital. This ratio is very low in Europe. Indeed, sub-debts account for 2.48% of total assets on average. In addition, sub-debt issues are usually made by large banks.[m]
- Non-performing loans' provisions to gross loans ratio is high for Italy and limited for the Netherlands.
- The cost of risk (measured by provisions to net interest income) is high for Italy and limited for Belgium.
- Operational expenses account for about 61.84% on average of the operational income. This ratio is high for the Netherlands and small for Spain.
- Average return on assets reaches 1.64% and is high for Germany and limited for Greece.
- Net interest income/average assets reach 2.1% on average.
- Interbank deposits account for a small portion of total assets except for Austria and Belgium which have a high portion of Interbank deposits on their balance sheet.

[m] Some authors consider the subordinated debt policy as a requirement that comes to complete the capital standards. Other partisans confer to the subordinated debt a much important role, assuming that it can be a substitute to the shareholders equities.

Banks distribution of the capital ratio level (K) according to the quartiles.

Banks number	GR		FR		IT		SP		UK		PB	
	$K < Q_1 = 9.4$	$K \geq Q_3 = 12.06$	$K < Q_1 = 9.1$	$K \geq Q_3 = 11.04$	$K < Q_1 = 8.7$	$K \geq Q_3 = 11.1$	$K < Q_1 = 9.17$	$K \geq Q_3 = 10.82$	$K < Q_1 = 11.5$	$K \geq Q_3 = 14.52$	$K < Q_1 = 9.6$	$K \geq Q_3 = 12.4$
98	6	9	4	21	5	15	4	8	4	15	5	10
99	3	12	5	20	4	16	2	10	1	18	3	12
00	5	10	6	19	6	14	4	8	3	16	6	9
01	3	12	5	20	6	14	3	9	2	17	4	11
02	4	11	5	20	2	18	2	10	2	17	2	13
03	3	12	6	19	1	19	2	10	3	16	0	15
04	1	14	6	19	1	19	3	9	4	15	0	15

Banks number	IRL		PRG		BLG		GRC		AUS		EUROPE	
	$K < Q_1 = 8.16$	$K \geq Q_3 = 12.8$	$K < Q_1 = 9.37$	$K \geq Q_3 = 11.45$	$K < Q_1 = 10.7$	$K \geq Q_3 = 13.08$	$K < Q_1 = 8.72$	$K \geq Q_3 = 17.77$	$K < Q_1 = 9.95$	$K \geq Q_3 = 11.35$	$K < Q_1 = 9.68$	$K \geq Q_3 = 12.2$
98	1	4	1	3	3	5	1	5	2	3	35	99
99	1	4	1	3	1	7	1	5	1	4	28	106
00	1	4	2	2	2	6		5	2	3	33	101
01	2	3	3	1	1	7	1	5	1	4	19	1115
02	3	2	0	4	0	8	1	6	0	5	16	118
03	1	4	0	4	0	8		6	0	5	20	114
04	0	5	0	4	1	7	0	5	1	4	15	121
							0					
							1					

Distribution of negative watches announced by rating agencies (MSSAN).

Number of negative watches	ALL	FR	IT	ESP	UK	PB	IRL	PRG	BLG	GRC	AUT	Total
98	3	2	3	1	6	2	0	1	1	0	2	21
99	4	4	1	3	4	2	2	1	0	0	0	21
00	2	0	2	4	2	1	0	1	0	0	2	14
01	1	2	2	2	1	5	0	1	1	1	2	18
02	4	4	5	3	3	2	3	2	4	2	1	33
03	5	4	1	0	2	1	1	0	0	0	0	15
04	5	5	4	3	1	2	1	2	1	0	0	24

Banks included in the sample enjoy satisfactory financial ratios on average. However, these ratios could change dramatically as shown by the variation during the 1998–2004 period.

4 Empirical Results

Logit regression was applied to all the binary variables on a stand-alone basis in order to measure the informational content of each variable and to retain the best ones in the final model. The role of regulatory and institutional variables were estimated then. In this respect, I tried to identify the safety net impact and the implication of deposits insurance complex index, which may materialize the exposure of the banks to moral hazard. The results are shown in Table A.5 in Appendix A. Estimations were performed for each country and then at the European level. This allows a comparison between the different European countries taking into account their own institutional scheme and to judge on the degree of homogeneity of European banking system and the viability of a prompt corrective action by a "mega" European regulator. Individual contributions of financial ratios in the explanation of a bank's capital deterioration are detailed in Table A.6 in Appendix A. significant negative contribution of equity ratio in the explanation of total capital degradation suggests that total capital ratios decrease was preceded by improved Tier 1 capital ratio and vice versa. The ratio Tier 1 is negatively significant in all countries except for United Kingdom and Austria.

This result can be explained by a high amount of general provisions constituted by the majority of banks in the sample. Besides, the balance sheet exam show an increase in the shareholders equities during the period 1998–2004 for almost banks. For the case of United Kingdom and Austria, the prediction of banking distress may be much more explained by the others financial indicators.

The subordinated debt issuance represents an additional source of banking capitalization. The positive contribution of the subordinated debt/assets ratio suggests that decreases of solvency ratios were preceded by negative evolutions on the subordinated debt issuance, mainly in France, United Kingdom, Netherlands, Portugal, and Greece. Moreover, this indicator is insignificant mainly in less concentrated markets. In Europe, a decrease of subordinated debt issuance contributes to the capital deterioration. In fact, a decrease in subordinated debt amount could exhibit a much important risk profile and than a decreased performance.

The asset quality ratio approximated by the provisions on non-performing loans/gross credits contributes significantly to the explanation of future capital ratio decreases. This result may be interpreted by the increase of European commercial banks risked portfolios. Also, the balance sheet exam of the banking balance sheets shows that this ratio variation during 1998–2004 was negative in some banks which amplifies the probability of facing financial difficulties.

The provisions/net interest income ratio is less significant in explaining future capital degradations.

The management quality has a mitigated effect. The lost-income ratio is significant only on the Netherlands, Belgium, and Austria.

The asset profitability has a negative significant effect mainly in large countries. But the ROA ratio is more significant than the net interest income/average assets. This result can be interpreted by a good earning quality of European banks.

The banking liquidity has a negative significant effect in most of the countries. The expected sign of the variation in the liquidity ratio measured by the fraction of liquid assets/total deposits and refinance is justified by the fact that the ratios decreases are generally preceded by liquidating a fraction of bank assets.

Market sensitivity is also significant in the majority of banking systems. The more the income is sensitive to market risk the more the bank is weakened. Its negative effect in France and United Kingdom can be explained by the fact that banks in these countries degage an important market share due to financial operations that procures them a better financial health.

We present in Table A.7 of Appendix A, the contribution of the accounting indicators of banking capital deterioration. Our estimations are run only on the significant variables of the basic model.

When integrated together, a number of accounting indicators have lost their explicative power. The shareholders equity ratio variation still significant to explain total capital degradation as indicator of bank solidity. The decrease of subordinated debt issuance, that represents in part a substitute of shareholders equity and a certain market discipline,[n] no more explains the future degradation of European banks solvency mainly in less concentrated countries. Thus, social capital and reserves (components of Tier 1) constitute in my

[n]In this case, the transmitted information to the market permits a better evaluation of risk profiles and submits banks to a discipline as every risk increase is sanctioned by a higher cost on liabilities. This market risk evaluation can serve as signal to supervisors and contributes to the amelioration of defaulting prevention mechanism.

sense more flexible instruments to preserve the bank viability than the subordinated debt mainly because they could absorb portfolio credit looses in most cases. These elements represent thus ideal components of economic capital. In return, subordinated and others elements of complementary capital (except general provision for non-performing loans) are unavailable to compensate loses suffered by solvent banks but still certainly very interesting as banking financing source and also as additional cushion for the insurance fund in case of failure.[o]

In summary, the balance sheet indicators retained for predicting European banking difficulty are: Tier 1 capital ratio, asset quality defined as provisions on non-performing loans/gross loans, profitability defined as return on assets, and market sensibility defined as market sensible income/total income.

At this stage, we have also identified the negative watches impact on undercapitalization prediction in each country. Ours results show that in almost all countries, except Ireland, Greece, and Belgium, these actions negatively influence the prediction of capital ratio degradation. In the first case rating would bring new information on the short term bank situation that could be explored by shareholders and supervisors to take corrective actions in a preliminary stage.

Finally, banking concentration in Europe has a negative effect on the probability of capital banking deterioration. Thus, my results confirm the concentration/stability hypothesis that suppose that an increase in banking concentration improve market power, permits the bank higher earnings and than reduces the distress probability.

After having studied the individual influence of each financial indicator and then taken together in each country, we try in the next step to identify the supplementary impact of regulatory variables, rating agencies and taken into account the market concentration on detecting banking distress in Europe. We proceed by selecting the optimal sub-group of explicative financial variables of the prior estimation which are summarized in the first column of the table below.[p]

The results are more significant than those of the origin model (informational criteria AIC and SC). Thus, the introduction of public sector impact (CB, supervisory agency, deposit insurance, and banking solidarity) and the

[o] In fact, Sironi (2001, p. 257) has argument in favor of the exclusion of subordinated debt from regulatory capital definition mainly for banks that use internal allocation capital models.

[p] A thinner selective process that takes into account colinearity problems between different indicators has conducted to the same optimal sub-group of explicative variables whatever the predictive horizon.

		Model 1 (CAMELS)		Model II (CAMELS + Regulation and rating agencies actions)	
		Coefficients	*P*-value		*P*-value
Tier 1 ratio	ΔTier1	−2.61*	0.012		
Asset quality ratio	ΔPRVCB	0.024*	0.004	0.002*	0.033
Earning ratio	ΔROA	−0.043	0.021	−0.024*	0.043
Market sensibility ratio	ΔRSM	0.08*	0.028	0.265*	0.017
Concentration	IHH	−0.514*	0.021	−0.274*	0.014
Supervision impact	RBC	—		−0.567**	0
	OBP	—		−0.484*	0.02
Law impact	JURD	—		−1.876**	0.0031
Deposit insurance impact	VCOUV	—		−0.753**	0.0012
(IASRD)	VFIN	—		0.276**	0.0034
	MNG	—		0.165*	0.045
	⇒IASRD	—		0.874**	0.0031
Rating agencies impact	MSSAN	—		−0.2602*	0.021

private sector influence (negatives watches) have improved the explicative power of the model. In fact, the qualitative variables that constitute the national public sector role are of negative expected sign. First, the CB implication in the supervision process reduces the probability of under-capitalization. Thus, unless the central bank does not centralize banking supervision in the majority of European banks, still have a preponderant role in exercising a pressure on distressed bank.

Moreover, when the supervisory agency can oblige provisions constitution to cover actual and potential losses also reduces the probability of capital degradation and incites banks to double efforts on capital improvement. Nevertheless, in some countries like Germany, Italy, and the Netherlands, this law is not applied, which makes banks in these countries responsible of their risk taking decisions.

The fact that the law imposes an intervention beyond a certain solvency capital ratio reduces the probability that capital ratio decreases. This action is a kind of prompt alert to banks on difficulty to make readjustment of their capital. Beyond hazard moral problems that could be caused by such a law (there is always a lender of last resort), it generates more financial stability on European banking system. Thus, this law that only exists in Spain and Austria must conserve its "constructive ambiguity" to conserve the regulation efficiency.

Finally, the banking solidarity enforces the safety net of banking in difficulty. This supporting action very present in France, Germany, and Italy creates a sort of discrimination between the commercial banks in different European countries.

All these results permit to conclude that the existence of a strong safety net reduces the probability that a European commercial bank is under capitalized. However, given the relations complexity and national supervision system divergences, as shown Table 8 of Appendix A, it is necessary that national supervisory authorities collaborate in order to contain an eventual systemic risk. A mega European supervisor could well fulfil this function in the aim of a prompt corrective action towards banks on difficulty.

Given the fact that the deposit insurance system is explicit in all European countries of simple considered, we have constructed a complex indicator of deposit insurance that takes into account different characteristics such variations in coverage, in financing, and in management that are specific to every country and study its effect on European banking stability.

The results taking into account the dummy of deposit insurance that distinguishes different coverage degrees show a significant negative effect on the bank difficulties probability. This conclusion confirms the previous literature that stipulates a limited coverage reduces the banking excessive risk taking and the hazard moral. Nevertheless, the deposit insurance financing system has a positive effect on the probability that commercial banks face difficulties. This conclusion can be justified by the fact that when deposits insurance agency is in part financed by the government such as for Italy, the Netherlands, Portugal, Belgium, and Austria, this creates a supplement security for banks and incite them to take more risky positions. Results are more significant when we integrate the financing type (*ex ante*, *ex post*) and the prime risk sensibility.[q]

The deposit insurance agency management does not have any effect on the probability of facing future financial problems.

[q]This result can be explained by the fact that in most considered countries, the prime on deposit insurance is risk neutral and paid *ex ante*, which constitute a supplement guaranty for banks.

In sum, the interactions of different components of insurance systems permit to conclude their negative effect on banking difficulties probability. In fact, the existence of explicit limited insurance system has reduced risk taking. As shown in the construction of our simple, there is a deposits insurance coverage limitation and that more than the half of systems (6/10) are financed by banks which guaranties a certain regulatory discipline. In consequence, the insurance deposits drawbacks have been reduced by limiting the coverage extend in almost all countries and by making banks participate themselves in the fund financing.

Finally, the rating agencies have a significant role in Europe. In fact, negative watches performed by rating agencies reduce the probability of European banks undercapitalization. In other words, the rating agencies would have the ability to diffuse information that shareholders or debt holders cannot necessary collect because of their expertize shortage or the costs of informational research. Also, these private information contained in banking balance sheets could be used by national supervisors for a better banking monitoring and then avoid them to take frequent on-site inspections.

4.1 Lessons and Conclusions

Problem of solvency is the most vulnerable element of prudential system in promoting integration. I have demonstrated that the insolvency prediction is influenced by the financial ratios evolutions. It is negatively influenced by the Tier 1 ratio, the good profitability, banking concentration and positively by the asset quality and the income market sensibility.

The national supervisor's behavior is characterized, as shown, by loses allowance as far as they support also banks that exhibit critical threshold solvency and that must be subject of harder restrictions on activity (such the case of same Italian and Spanish banks). The presence of such security net including features that encourage hazard moral and risk taking could open the doors to the regulator laxity. That is why; some supervisors have adopted the "constructive ambiguity" arm and restrictions on insurance deposit systems that suggest the prime sensibility to risk and coverage limitation.

A solution to the hazard moral behavior could consist on limiting the insured deposits access for banks that have suffered substantial degradation on their risk profile and constraining large banks to issue subordinated debt more frequently.

This new way for satisfying capital requirements relies on market mechanisms rather than on formal capital requirements.

This discipline imposed by the market (subordinated debt issuance) should be facilitated by the role played by rating agencies that are assumed to transmit the private information contained in banks balance sheets. In fact, my study advanced the role that rating agencies can play in predicting, trough their negative watches, a bank disease. Moreover, they can facilitate the regulator task and than contribute to the regulatory discipline efficiency. Nevertheless, the major feedback of such market discipline is the fact that it can introduce supplementary rigidities in the actual regulatory systems, which are not really compatibles with the actual safety net flexibility.[r]

Moreover, European banking supervision is not deployed at the financial markets euro zone. It still narrowly national and decentralized, but also there are multiples of national supervisory models. These disparities can engender discriminations in European banks treatment and discourage European financial integration. Thus, the diversity of national laws on banking difficulty apprehension, resolution proceeds and the weakness of purely European legal system could strongly increase the systemic resolution of international large banks and conglomerates in case of distress.

That is why the enforcement of supervisory authorities' collaboration should be drawn by the insaturation of a pan European mega supervisor able to put in coherence the national laws on banking failures to maintain the European banking stability via prompt corrective actions. Those recommend (1) the definition of a critical capital ratio on its beyond the closure is imperative, (2) Banking classification on different categories relatively to the capitalization ratio and (3) prompt actions enumeration that can or must be applied to banks facing a capital degradation.

5 Conclusion

In this paper, I have performed a binomial logit model in order to study the factors that could affect the probability of future capital distress using a sample of 134 commercial European banks. My results show that both national regulatory and institutional framework and rating agencies actions help the

[r]Under the actual regulatory system, that is, in the absence of explicit subordinated debt policy (SDP), banks have the privilege to choose library the precise moment of their intervention in the primary market. In these conditions, market discipline is easy to bypass. In fact, banks have sufficient flexible means that permit them to substitute less risk sensible resources (as insured deposits) to subordinated debt, mainly when their financial conditions are deteriorated. A SDP mashed obligatory would prevent these behaviours by constraining banks to be continually submitted to the investor's vigilance. By this way, market forces will be active when the bank risk profile starts to be degraded.

prediction of future banks' distress. In addition, my findings show that market discipline is weak in Europe and this is the result of the presence of a strong safety net. They said, to enhance competition among European banks, regulators should take out some protections that result in risky behaviors of some banks in opposition to the objective of the safety net. Having said that, depositors' protection and offsetting systemic risks should not be interpreted as survival guarantee measures. European central banks have, however, intervened in the past allowing failing banks to continue to run their businesses despite their status. In order to manage these negative effects, regulators have to stop systematic recapitalizations of troubled institutions and to allow the natural mechanism of the market to lead to the absorption of the failing bank by other players. Finally, the presence of a mega regulator should allow institutional frameworks alignment among different European countries and to set up more strict prompt corrective actions to protect the stability of European banks.

Appendix A

Table A.1: Principal supervisory systems of banking sector in Europe.

	Country					
	Germany	France	Netherlands	Italy	United Kingdom	United States
System name and objective	BAKIS	ORAP	RAST	PATROL	RATE	CAMELS
	Financial ratios and group analysis	Rating system	Bank risk evaluation	Rating system	Bank risk evaluation	Rating system
Supervision authority	German Federal Supervision	Commission bancaire	Netherlands Bank	Bank of Italy	Financial Services Authority	Federal Reserve System FDIC OCC
Total used ratios	47 ratios	14 ratios	13 ratios	5 ratios	9 ratios	6 ratios
Banking activity aspects	Number of retained ratios in the model					
1. Asset quality	18 ratios	4 ratios	1 ratio	1 ratio	1 ratio	1 ratio
2. Solvability	1 ratio	2 ratios	—	1 ratio	1 ratio	1 ratio
3. Profitability	10 ratios	3 ratios	—	1 ratio	1 ratio	1 ratio
4. Liquidity	2 ratios	1 ratio	1 ratio	1 ratio	1 ratio	1 ratio
5. Market risk	16 ratios	1 ratio	3 ratios	—	1 ratio	1 ratio
6. Management and control	—	3 ratios	3 ratios	1 ratio	3 ratios	1 ratio
7. Other citeria		5 ratios operational risk, Strategic, informatique and technologic, legal, of reputation	—	—	Business risk	—

Table constituted from different annexes of Sahajwala and Van Den Bergh (2000).

Table A.2: Summary of EWS methodological models.

Author	Variables	Statistic method
Altman and Narayanan (1977)	• Net operational revenue/gross operational revenue • Net situation/total assets • Immobilized assets/total assets • Result/total assets • Total loans/total savings • Loans/total savings • FHLBB advanced part[1]/net situation	Discriminant analysis
Martin (1977)	• Equity/risked assets • Expenses/operational revenue • Commercial loans/total loans • Total net revenue/total assets	Logit
Avery and Hanweck (1984)	• Log of total assets less non-performing loans provisions • After tax total revenue/total assets • Equity + provisions on non-performing loans/total assets • Total loans — provisions on non-performing loans/total assets • Industrial and commercial loans/total loans • Deposits growth rate • Bank market share	Logit

(*Continued*)

Table A.2: (*Continued*)

Author	Variables	Statistic method
Pantalone and Platt (1987)	• Net result/total assets • Stocks/total assets Total loans/total assets Total commercial loans/total loans • Residential constructions growth rate	Logit
Godlewski (2003)	• Stocks/total loans • Net revenue • Net interest margin • Net revenue/total assets • Liquid assets/total assets • Total loans/total deposits	Probit
Soledad *et al.* (2001)	• Equity/weighted assets • Non-performing loans/total loans • Hypothecary loans/total loans • Credit concentration indicators (by sector and by client) • Return/total assets • Expenses/total assets • Service quality • Liquidity and liquidity equivalent/total assets	Panel

[1]Federal Home Loan Bank Board.

Table A.3: Institutional architecture of banking supervision in Europe.

Country	Number of authorities responsible for supervision	Inclusion of the CB in the supervision	Intervention forms of CB in the supervision			
			Central Bank is the banking supervisor	The Central Bank is not the bank supervisor		
				Central Bank is involved in the management of the banking supervisor	Central Bank has supervisory tasks or responsibilities	Formal mechanism for cooperation and sharing information
BE	1[1]	YES	NO	YES NO	YES	YES
DK	1	NO	NO	NO	YES	NO
DE	1	YES	NO		YES	YES
GR	3	YES	YES			
ES	3	YES	YES	YES		
FR	4[2]	YES	NO	NO	YES	YES
IE	1[3]	YES	NO		YES	YES
IT[4]	3	YES	YES	NO		
LU	2	NO	NO		NO	NO
NL[5]	2	YES	YES	YES		
AT	1	YES	NO		YES	NO

(*Continued*)

Table A.3: (*Continued*)

Country	Number of authorities responsible for supervision	Inclusion of the CB in the supervision	Intervention forms of CB in the supervision			
			Central Bank is the banking supervisor	The Central Bank is not the bank supervisor		
				Central Bank is involved in the management of the banking supervisor	Central Bank has supervisory tasks or responsibilities	Formal mechanism for cooperation and sharing information
PT	3	YES	YES			
FI	2	YES	NO	YES	NO	YES
SV	1	YES	NO	YES	NO	NO
UK	1	YES	NO		NO	NO[6]

Source: ECB (2006). Recent supervisory structures in the EU members states.

[1]The existing two supervisory institutions have merged in an unique supervisor called "la commission bancaire, financière et des assurances (CBFA)" in January 2004.

[2]Many institutions are incorporated in the supervisory body. The number "4" includes "la Commission Bancaire, l'Autorité des Marchés Financiers (AMF) — the result of the merger of "la Commission des opérations de bourse (COB), le Conseil des marchés financiers (CMF) et le Conseil de discipline — le Comité des Etablissements de Crédit et des Entreprises d'Investissement (CECEI) et le Comité consultatif de la législation et de la réglementation financières (CCLRF)".

[3]The single supervisory authority (IFSRA) is a central bank component but is independent of it and responsible for the date to date different financial services supervision. The central bank government reserves the right of designing an official, if he desires, to financial institutions inspection.

[4]The regulation and supervision of the financial system are shared by four different authorities: Bank of Italy, National Commission for the Society and the Bourse, the Supervisory Institute of Insurance (ISVAP), and the Supervisory Commission of Pension Funds (COVIP).

[5]In 2004, an institutional reform in the Netherlands has aimed at the merger of the Nederlandsche Bank and Pensions and Insurance Supervisory Authority Foundation (The Pensioen-en Verzekeringskamer) in charge of the prudential supervision of financial institutions. while the Autoriteit Financiële Markten (Authority for the Financial Markets — AFM) is responsible for monitoring the proper conduct of business and the transparency and accuracy of the information available on the market.

[6]The Bank of England (BoE) and the Financial Services Authority (FSA) work occasionally for each others, which might be considered as a form of resource sharing.

Table A.4: S&P banking rating criteria.

I. Qualitative analysis
   1. Economic risk[1]
      - Economy size and strengths and weaknesses checkup and implications on bank situation
      - Economy real growth rate compared to the monetary supply real growth rate and to the credit growth rate.
      - Savings and investment dynamic and motivation determinants of abroad investments as well as the sensibility to these motivations.
      - The economy degree of opening (up to which point, its growth is correlated with the growth of neighboring economies)
      - Position on the business cycle as well as on the GDR minimal and maximal variations
      - Structural problems and eventual solutions
      - Political stability
   2. Industrial risk
      - Banking system structure (number of banks, relative size of banks, bancarization degree of the population (approximated by the number of box offices devised by total population) and anticipated changes (Mergers and acquisitions)
      - Intermediation rate
      - Aggregated assets quality
      - Equity market development degree
      - Politic influence on decision making
      - Non-performing loans part in the balance sheet
   3. Client Portfolio
      - Client kinds and banking services price sensibility
      - Bank and clients relationship
      - Portfolio quality
   4. Regulatory structure
      - Degree and quality of supervision, degree of independence of regulatory organism, communication structure between bankers and regulators, track of same historic assistance of the regulator to a bank on difficulty, systemic crises management.
      - Deposit Insurance system existence
      - Government philosophy in term of regulation and deregulation
   5. Shareholding
      - Government participation in the banking system and effects on the competition.
      - Privatization degree of interbank system
      - Shareholders ability to support banking development by capital injection
      - Equity invested quality: Tier 1 and/or Tier 2

(*Continued*)

Table A.4: (*Continued*)

6. Banking services supply
   - Diversification (products, clients, geography)
   - Equilibrium between credit supply and non-funded business
7. Competitive position
   - Bank share market, competitive position advantages (such as pricing power) or disadvantages and comparison Peer to Peer
   - Competitive pressures Kind and characteristic: competition price vs. competition out of price
   - Penetration degree of foreign competitors in the systems
   - Disintermediation degree and evolution in time, as well as its effects on the banking system
8. Management and strategy
   - Organizational structure (centralization, decentralization)
   - Management quality (efficiency, dependence on key character, continuity, independence)
   - Efficiency and risk aversion in the strategy direction
   - Governance and managerial independence
   - Public and private financial information quality mainly accounting practices and financial transparency
9. Risk taking and managing
   - Credit risk : Credit supply process, power delegation and degree of control and client situation and repayment persistency, concentration by type of clients, provisions on classified loans.
   - Market risk: Market fundamentals control, risk aversion and strategy, control tools adaptability, stress testing, major mistakes during the 5 last years
   - Activity risk coverage policy

II. Quantitative analysis

10. General ratios (annual evolution)
    - Total balance sheet
    - Total weighted balance sheet (solvency ratio denominator)
    - Loans
    - Clients deposits (unless interbanking deposits)
    - Total capital stock
    - Net banking return (NBR)
    - Exploitation expenses
    - Exploitation gross result
    - Provisions
    - Before tax result and net result

(*Continued*)

Table A.4: (*Continued*)

11. Capitalization
    - Capital adequacy (comparison with prudential requirements), equity/total balance-sheet
    - prudential ratios (Cooke and McDonough), equity/total loans
    - Access degree to capital source
12. Profitability
    - Net interest income (margin tendency and ability to volume maintaining), net interest/average assets
    - Intermediation net return (less interest), part in the total return, sources diversity and continuity Commissions et other returns/average assets
    - Exploitation expenses (level and tendency in relation to the agencies network evolution) compared to the NBR.
    - NBR/average assets and NBR/average weighted assets, exploitation gross result/average assets, net result/average assets
13. Liquidity
    - Deposits (unless interbank deposits)/total liabilities
    - Short term Liquid assets and ability to generate funds in the case of crisis.
    - Loans/Client deposits (monetary creation coefficient)
14. Asset quality
    - Provisions/average loans
    - Non-performing loans/loans
    - Provisions/non-performing loans

Source: S&P (2005b).

[1]The economic risk is the subject of a score, maintained confidential, attributed by bank analysts. This score reflects the economic situation potential impact on the banking system mainly on credit growth, its quality and the banking system liquidity. In addition to the industrial risk (we intend systemic risk which is the object of a score), bank analyst determines a maximal note for the counterparty ratings, independently of sovereign rating.

Table A.5: Sample principal characteristics during the period 1998–2004.

Percentage	German			France			Spain		
	Mean	Min	Max	Mean	Min	Max	Mean	Min	Max
Tier 1 ratio	6.84	4.12	13.30	8.08	4.40	17.70	7.01	2.10	11.70
Solvency ratio	11.05	7.70	17.50	10.45	7.60	18.80	9.74	4.10	12.96
Subordinated debt/total assets	1.63	0.12	3.26	1.53	0.00	4.20	1.70	0.00	5.31
Non-performing loan provisions/Gross loans	2.44	0.59	8.28	3.94	0.020	11.42	2.08	1.00	3.96
Provisions/net interest income	25.20	−59.12	93.62	18.75	−38.76	90.00	14.32	0.69	45.95
Operational expenses/operational income	65.40	17.80	109.95	68.74	34.49	111.17	53.65	5.06	75.75
ROA	−1.16	0.211	1.45	0.90	−0.24	8.58	0.95	0.43	1.96
Net interest income/average assets	1.18	0.30	6.34	2.01	−0.92	9.44	2.58	0.75	4.68
Interbank assets/total assets	0.23	0.20	1.78	0.25	0.21	4.93	0.22	0.067	0.79
Concentration indice Herfindhahl[2]	1696.8	—	–	2910.62	–	—	2821.42	—	—
	United Kingdom			Italy			The Netherlands		
	Mean	Min	Max	Mean	Min	Max	Mean	Min	Max
Tier 1 ratio	9.02	5.50	13.40	7.91	4.30	17.80	8.79	4.80	16.80
Solvability ratio	13.25	7.31	19.10	10.21	7.60	16.00	11.58	5.70	19.90
Subordinated debt/total assets	2.34	0.00	5.53	2.09	0.00	4.90	1.99	0.00	4.43
Non-performing loan provisions/Gross loans provisions	1.82	0.01	4.15	4.01	0.00	11.39	1.41	0.00	3.18
Provisions/net interest income	10.15	−3.88	10.15	21.15	3.98	87.64	17.47	−36.59	159.22
Operational expenses/operational income	56.54	31.68	83.92	67.58	30.58	100.9	72.29	29.42	109.04
ROA	1.07	−0.21	2.80	0.51	−1.74	1.52	0.56	−1.16	2.33
Net interest income/average assets	2.46	0.60	8.08	2.58	1.40	4.04	1.50	0.26	2.90
Interbank assets/total assets	0.12	0.033	1.80	0.18	0.07	0.56	0.26	0.022	0.79
Concentration indice Herfindhahl	4562			3714			2710		

(*Continued*)

Table A.5: (*Continued*)

Percentage	Portugal			Austria			Belgium		
	Mean	Min	Max	Mean	Min	Max	Mean	Min	Max
Tier 1 ratio	7.30	5.70	9.20	6.46	3.20	8.20	7.75	3.80	10.60
Solvability ratio	10.46	8.10	13.51	10.45	6.80	12.78	11.90	6.90	17.70
Subordinated debt/total assets	2.16	0.23	4.39	1.61	0.00	3.27	2.32	0.00	5.01
Non-performing loan provisions/Gross loans provisions	2.75	2.00	3.99	2.81	2.21	3.23	2.02	0.34	2.98
Provisions/net interest income	22.23	15.13	50.20	21.51	1.12	46.40	6.06	−81.85	37.13
Operational expenses/operational income	60.10	41.99	74.11	63.89	51.12	74.07	73.53	51.80	118.18
ROA	0.76	0.10	2.14	0.42	0.19	1.19	0.63	−0.62	2.71
Net intérêt income/average assets	2.32	0.94	3.73	1.67	0.88	2.49	1.47	0.34	3.54
Interbank assets/total assets	0.24	0.053	0.53	23.29	8.38	39.36	19.63	4.74	59.05
Concentration Indice Herfindhahl	3893			3574			3639		

This index is used as control for differences in the banking market structure in Europe. This index, named IHH, is calculated as the sum of the squared market share of all the banks in the sample. Generally, market concentration is weak when IHH is lower than the level 1000. It is medium when it varies between 1000 and 1800 and high when it is more than 1800.

Impact of each regulatory variable and of rating agencies on national and European banking difficulty prediction.

		ALL	FR	IT	ESP	UK	PB	IRL	PRG	BLG	GRC	AUT	EU
SUP	RBC		—	—	—	—	—	—	—	—	—	—	−0.60**
	p-value												0.02
	OBP	—	—	—	—	—	—	—	—	—	—	—	−1.05***
	p-value												0.010
JURD	—	—	—	—	—	—	—	—	—	—	—	—	−0.385*
													0.082
ROB	—	—	—	—	—	—	—	—	—	—	—	—	−0.54***
													0.00
IASRD	VCOUV	—	—	—	—	—	—	—	—	—	—	—	−4.24***
	p-value												0.003
	VFIN	—	—	—	—	—	—	—	—	—	—	—	−5.67***
	p-value												0.010
	MNG	—	—	—	—	—	—	—	—	—	—	—	0.46***
	p-value												0.000
MSSAN	*p*-value	−0.73**	−1.46***	−1.39***	0.25*	−1.16	−1.872**	−0.009	−1.79	−1.94	−0.06	−0.008	1.118
		0.011	0.009	0.01	0.061	0.23	0.013	0.132	0.097*	0.068*	0.262	0.214	0.21
CONC		—	—	—	—	—	—	—	—	—	—	—	−0.51**
													0.03

(—) The regulatory variable impact is only determined at a global task.
The Huber White estimation method of estimated coefficient variances et covariances is used. The asterisks *, ** and *** indicate risk levels at 10, 5 and 1% respectively.
The different statistic values are not reported here.

Table A.6: Individual influence of the different variables on banking difficulty probability.

		GR	FR	IT	SP	UK	ND	IRL	PRG	BLG	GRC	AUS	EU
Capital ratios	Δ Tier 1	**−0.109***	**−0.07***	**−0.31***	**−0.47****	−0.055	**−0.22*****	**−0.061***	**−0.36****	**−0.049***	**−0.244****	1.467	**−0.08****
	P-value	0.047	0.060	0.07	0.011	0.64	0.012	0.087	0.016	0.08	0.032	0.40	0.061
	Δ DSUB	0.87	**−0.015***	0.22	0.40	**−0.47****	**−0.83***	−0.792	**−0.273***	0.56	**−0.378****	0.856	**−0.097***
	P-value	0.24	0.096	0.143	0.271	0.04	0.09	0.18	0.065	0.161	0.047	0.443	0.089
Asset quality ratio	Δ PRVCB	**0.236****	**0.02***	**0.03***	**0.01***	**0.101***	**0.01****	**0.218***	**0.020***	**0.011****	**0.121****	**0.007***	**0.001***
	P-value	0.031	0.096	0.07	0.066	0.070	0.039	0.062	0.068	0.044	0.012	0.086	0.052
	Δ DOTREV	**0.059***	**0.089****	−0.04	0.54	0.616	**0.42*****	2.46	**0.427***	0.601	0.207	**1.684***	0.082
	P-value	0.099	0.044	0.73	0.34	0.142	0.017	0.150	0.063	0.166	0.577	0.096	0.157
Management quality ratio	Δ DOPRO	0.043	0.001	0.01	0.06	0.017	**0.01***	0.038	0.022	**0.903*****	−0.014	**0.07****	0.01
	P-value	0.75	0.195	0.41	0.30	0.64	0.084	0.532	0.836	0.001	0.664	0.035	0.29
	Δ PRFIN	−0.236	0.01	−0.03	0.01	0.47	−0.055	-0.22	−0.061	0.273	−0.56	−0.013	−0.378
		0.137	0.46	0.723	0.66	0.11	0.218	0.112	0.2387	0.656	0.161	0.435	0.154
Profitability ratio	Δ ROA	**−0.06****	**−0.59****	**−0.61*****	**−1.13***	**0.366****	**−0.95***	0.126	−0.24	0.463	−0.41	-6.03	**−0.206***
	P-value	0.0321	0.046	0.017	0.065	0.020	0.08	0.917	0.860	0.537	0.364	0.190	0.079
	ΔINTAM	−0.26	−0.118	**−1.16***	−0.29	−0.107	**−2.28****	−1.297	2.25	−0.395	0.587	1.755	0.307
	P-value	0.23	0.701	0.055	0.62	0.83	0.05	0.540	0.105	0.787	0.96	0.308	0.103

(*Continued*)

Table A.6: *(Continued)*

		GR	FR	IT	SP	UK	ND	IRL	PRG	BLG	GRC	AUS	EU
Liquidity ratio	Δ ALD	−0.038	0.015	0.03	0.03	0.015	−0.00	0.148	**−0.181***	0.006	0.059	−0.02	0.008
	P-value	0.159	0.373	0.34	0.20	0.53	0.86	0.088	0.062	0.847	0.206	0.805	0.32
	Δ CDRF	**−0.01***	**−0.041***	**−0.023***	**−0.13***	**−0.014***	**−0.070****	**−0.29***	0.107	**−2.28****	**−0.01****	**−0.03***	−0.01**
		0.056	0.052	0.08	0.06	0.064	0.043	0.062	0.83	0.05	0.046	0.07	0.03
Market sensibility ratio	Δ SNB	1.791	**1.087****	1.3	0.91	**2.00****	0.91	0.04	0.54	0.616	0.015	0.00	0.95
	P-value	0.19	0.040	0. 305	0.12	0.0215	0.27	0.73	0.34	0.142	0.53	0.86	0.132
	Δ RSM	**0.179*****	**−1.087****	**0.013*****	**0.42***	**−0.46***	**0.02***	**0.03***	**0.01***	0.06	**0.017***	**0.01***	**0.427***
		0.019	0.034	0.005	0.017	0.075	0.096	0.07	0.066	0.30	0.064	0.084	0.068
Interbank debt/assets	Δ DINT	0.001	1.0488	3.44	0.32	1.82	5.67	24.84	1.11	0.085	0.334	0.11	**0.021***
	P-value	0.93	0.3897	0.19	0.46	0.102	0.13	0.260	0. 380	0.117	0.196	0.123	0.0618

Huber–White estimation method of estimated coefficient variances and covariances is used. *, ** and *** indicate risk levels at 10%, 5% and 1%, respectively. The different statistic values are not reported here.

Table A.7: Accounting variables contribution to the bank difficulty prediction.

		GR	FR	IT	SP	UK	PB	IRL	PRG	BLG	GRC	AUS	EU
Capital ratios	Δ Tier 1	**−0.77***	**−0.26***	—	**−0.35***	—	**−0.26***		**−0.128***	**0.765***	**−0.207***	—	**−2.61***
	P-value	0.013	0.021		0.025		0.013		0.035	0.058	0.042		0.012
	Δ DSUB				—	—	—	—	**−0.32***	—	—	—	0.18
	P-value	—	—	—					0.041				0.116
Asset quality ratios	Δ PRVCB	**−0.01***	—	**−1.34***	**0.55***		**0.082***	**0.253***	**−0.010***	**0.010***	**0.098***	**0.07***	**0.024***
	P-value	0.047		0.03	0.02		0.018	0.037	0.04	0.045	0.02862	0.020	0.004
	Δ DTREV	—	**−0.017***	—	—	**−0.12***		—					
	P-value		0.043			0.0 33							
Management quality ratios	Δ DOPRO	**0.011***	—	—	—	**0.007***	**0.0235***	—					
	P-value	0.041				0.041	0.0139						
	Δ PRFIN	—	—	—	—			**0.011***	**−0.040***	**0.086***		**−0.08***	
	P-value							0.0171	0.034	0.039		0.035	
Profitability ratio	Δ ROA		**−0.027***	**−0.054***	**−0.041***		**4.0721****	**0.58***	**−0.187****				**−0.043***
	P-value		0.016	0.031	0.032		0.0055	0.048	0.01				0.021
	Δ INTAM	—	—	**−1.30***	—		—	—					
	P-value			0.04									

(Continued)

Table A.7: *(Continued)*

		GR	FR	IT	SP	UK	PB	IRL	PRG	BLG	GRC	AUS	EU
Liquidity ratio	Δ ALD	−0.27*	—	−0.075*	—		—	—					
	P-value	0.014		0.046									
	Δ CDRF	—				−0.154*	—	−0.125		−0.06*	−0.035	−0.07*	
	P-value					0.044		0.124		0.0407	0.148	0.034	
Market senbility	Δ SNB		—		—		—	—					
	Δ RSM	1.81*	−1.14**	1.4**	0.795*	−2.003**	—	—	1.4**		0.820**	0.275*	0.08*
	P-value	0.018	0.002	0.0030	0.045	0.002			0.0031		0.0091	0.031	0.028
MSSAN		−0.73*	−1.46**	−1.39*	0.25*	−1.16	−1.872**	−0.009	−1.79*	−1.94*	−0.06	−0.008	−1.118*
	P-value	0.041	0.009	0.03	0.031	0.23	0.013	0.132	0.097	0.068	0.262	0.214	0.011
CONC		—	—	—	—	—	—	—	—	—	—	—	−0.51**
													0.021

The Huber–White estimation method of the coefficient variances and covariances is used. * and ** indicate here risk levels of 5% and 1%, respectively. The different statistic values are not reported here.

Table A.8: Characteristics of supervision systems in the different European countries of the sample.

	GR	FR	IT	SP	UK	PB	PRG	IRD	GR	BLG	AUS
Insurance deposits system Explicit 1 Implicit 0	1	1	1	1	1	1	1	1	1	1	1
Establishment date	1966	1980	1987	1977	1982	1979	1992	1989	1993	1974	1979
coassurance Yes 1 No 0	1	0	1	0	1	0	0	1	0	0	0
Coverage limit Ł High 1 Weak 0	0 90% deposits	0 70,000	1 103,300	1 20,000	0 100% First 2000£, 90% of next 33,000	1 20,000	1 25,000	1 20,000	1 20,000	1 20,000	1 20,000
Foreign money deposits coverage Yes 1 No 0	1	0	1	1	0	1	1	0	0	0	0
Interbank deposits coverage Yes 1 No 0	0	0	0	0	0	0	0	0	0	0	0

(*Continued*)

Table A.8: (*Continued*)

	GR	FR	IT	SP	UK	PB	PRG	IRD	GR	BLG	AUS
Financement With 0 Without 1	1	0	0	1	0	0	1	1	1	1	0
Financement source Bank alone 0 Bank Government 1 Government alone 2	0	0	1	0	0	1	1	0	0	1	1
Banking prime *Ex ante* 1 *Ex post* 0	1	1	0	1	1	0	1	1	1	1	0
Prime risk sensibility Yes 1 No 0	1	1	1	0	0	0	1	0	0	1	0
Management Public 0 Joint 1 Private 2	0	0	0	0	2	0	0	0	1	1	1

(*Continued*)

Table A.8: (*Continued*)

	GR	FR	IT	SP	UK	PB	PRG	IRD	GR	BLG	AUS
CB role in the supervision None 0 Limited 1 Principal 2	1	1	2	2	1	2	2	2	2	0	1
Others banks role None 0 Important 1	1	1	1	0	0	0	0	0	0	0	0
Intervention beyond a certain threshold (law) Yes 1 No 0	0	0	0	1	0	0	0	0	0	0	1
Supervisory agency obliges looses provision constitution Yes 1 No 0	0	1	0	1	1	0	1	1	1	1	1

References

Aglietta, M (1999). A lender of last resort dor Europe. CEPII, document de travail No. 99–12.

Ahumada, A and Bulnevich, C (2001). Some measures of financial fragility in the Chiliean banking system: An early warning indicators application. Banking Financial Integration and International Crisis. Central Bank of Chile.

Allen, F and Gale, D (2000). Financial contagion. *Journal of Political Economy*, 108, 1–33.

— (2004). Financial intermediaries and markets. *Econometrica*, 72, 1023–1061.

Altman and Narayanan (1997). Business failure classification models: An international survey in *International Accounting*, Choi, DS (ed.), New York.

Altman and Saunders (1998). Credit risk measurement: development of the last 20 years. *Journal of Banking and Finance*, V21.

Altman, E (1968). Financial ratios, discriminant analysis and the prediction of corporate bankruptcy. *Journal of Finance*, V23.

Barth, JR, Caprio, Jr G and Levine, R (1999). Financial regulation and performance: Cross country evidence. Working Paper, World Bank.

Barth, JR, Caprio, Jr G and Levine, R (2000). Banking systems around the globe: Do regulation and ownership affect performance and stability? Working Paper, World Bank.

Barth, JR, Caprio, Jr G and Levine, R (2001). The regulation and supervision of banks around the World a new database. Working Paper, World Bank 23.

Barth, JR, Nolle, DE, Phumiwasana, T and Yago, G (2002). A cross-country analysis of the bank supervisory framework and bank performance. Economic and Policy Analysis Working Paper 2, O_ce of the Comptroller of the Currency (O.C.C.).

Basel Committee on Banking Supervision (2002). Supervisory guidance on dealing with weak Banks. *Report of the Task Force on Dealing with Weak Banks* (March).

Beaver (1966). Financial ratios as predictors of failure in Empirical Research in Accounting: Selected Studies. *Journal of Accounting Research*, 4.

Beck, T, Demirgüc-Kunt, A and Levine, R (2006). Bank concentration, competition, and crises: First results. *Journal of Banking and Finance*, 30, 1581–1603.

Bell, J and Pain, D (2000). Leading indicator models of banking crises: A critical review. Financial Stability Review, December, Bank of England.

Berger, AN, Herring, RJ and Szegö, GP (1995). The role of capital in financial institutions. *Journal of Banking and Finance*, 19, 393–430.

BIS (2006). Recent initiatives by Basel-based committees and the financial stability forum. *BIS Quarterly Review*,

Blöndal, S and Christiansen, H (1999). The recent experience with capital flows to emerging market economies. OECD-Paris.

Blum, J (1999). Do capital adequacy requirements reduce risks in banking? *Journal of Banking and Finance*, 23, 755–771.

Bongini, P, Claessens, S and Ferri, G (2000). The political economy of distress of East Asian financial institutions. Policy Research Working Paper No. 2265, World Bank.

Boyd, J and Prescott, E (1986). Financial intermediary coalitions. *Journal of Economic Theory*, 38(2), 211–232.

Boyd, JH and Nicolo, GD (2006). The theory of bank risk taking and competition revisited. *The Journal of Finance*, 60(3), 1329–1343.

Brossard, O, Ducrozet, F and Roche, A (2006). An early warning model for EU banks with detection of the adverse selection effect. Présenté dans le cadre du Groupement de Recherches du CNRS "Economie monétaire et financière" à l'Université Paris X NANTERRE.

Bruno, PF (2000). Les déterminants des faillites bancaires dans les pays en développement: Cas des pays de l'union économique et monétaire ouest-africaine. Cahier du CRDE, Université de Montréal.

Calomiris, CW and Powell, A (2000). Can emerging market bank regulators establish credible discipline? The Case of Argentina, 1992–1999. Working Paper, World Bank.

Caminal, R. and Matutes, C (2002). Can competition in the credit market be excessive? UFAE and IAE Working Papers 527.02.

Caprio, G and Klingebiel, D (1996). Bank insolvencies: Cross-country experience. Working Paper, World Bank.

Caprio, Jr G and Levine, R (2002). Corporate governance in finance: Concepts and international comparison. Working Paper, World Bank.

Carletti, E, Hartmann, P and Spagnolo, G (2003). Bank mergers, competition and liquidity. Working Paper Series 292, European Central Bank.

Chauveau, C-B (2002). La supervision du secteur bancaire en Europe: l'apport des modèles quantitatifs. Document de travail Banque de France.

Cole and Gunther (1998). Predicting banking failure: A comparaison of on- and off-site monitoring systems. *Journal of Financial Services Research*, 13.

Curry, TJ, Elmer, PJ and Fissel, GS (2002). Regulator use of market data to improve the identification of bank financial health. FDIC Working Paper.

Damak, M (2006). Implications des systèmes de notation sur les cours boursiers. Thèse de doctorat en Sciences de Gestion, Université de Paris II, Panthéon Assas.

DeMarzo, PM and Michael, F (2004). Optimal long-term financial contracting with privately observed cash flows. Working Paper, Stanford University.

Demirgüç-Kunt, A (1989). Deposit-institution failures: A review of empirical literature. Economic Review 25, Federal Reserve Bank of Cleveland.

Demirgüc-Kunt, A and Detragiarche, E (1999). Does deposit insurance increase banking system stability? An empirical investigation. World Bank Policy Research. Working Paper No. 2247.

Demirgüc-Kunt, A and Detragiarche, E (2000). Monitoring banking sector fragility: A multivariate logit approach. *The World Bank Economic Review*, 14(2), 287–307.

Demirgüc-Kunt, A, J-Kane, E and Laeven, L (2007). Determinants of deposit-insurance adoption and design. NBER Working Paper No. 12862,

Descrochers and Fisher, K (2002). Corporate governance and depository institutions failure: The case of an emerging market economy. CIRPEE Working Paper No 01-02, Université de Laval.

Diamond, D (1984). Financial intermediation and delegated monitoring. *Review of Economic Studies*, 51, 393–414.

Diamond, D and Dybvig, P (1983). Bank runs, liquidity and deposit insurance. *Journal of Political Economy*, 91(3), 401–419.

Diamond, D and Dybvig, P (2000). Bank runs, deposit insurance, and liquidity. *Federal Reserve Bank of Minneapolis Quarterly Review*, 24(1), 14–21.

Distinguin, E, Rous, P and Tarazi, A (2006). La prédiction des détériorations financières des banques. Quel est l'apport de l'information de marché. *Revue Economique*, 57.

ECB (2006). *The European Central Bank: History, Role and Functions.* (2nd ed.)

Estrella, A (1995). A prolegomenon to future capital requirements. *Economic Policy Review*, 1(2), 1–12.

Estrella, Park and Prestiani (2000). Capital ratios as predictors of bank failure. *Federal Reserve Bank of New York Economic Policy Review*, 1(2).

Followill, RA and Martell, T, (1997). Bond review and rating change announcements: An examination of informational value and market efficiency. *Journal of Economics and Finance*, 21, 75–82.

Gaytan, A and Johanson, Ch (2002). A review of the literature on early warning systems for banking crises. Working Paper No 183, Central Bank of Chile.

Godbillon, B and Dietsch, M (1997). La règle de fermeture des banques. L'intérêt de l'ambiguïté constructive. *Revue Économique*, 48(3) 707–718.

Godlewski, Ch (2003). Modélisation de la prévision des défaillances bancaires :une application aux banques des pays émergents. Document de travail LARGE, Université Robert Schuman Strasbourg.

Gonzalez-Hermosillo, B (1999). Determinants of *ex ante* banking system distress: A macro–micro empirical exploration of some recent episodes. Working Paper 33, International Monetary Fund.

Goyeau, D, Sauviat, A, Tarazi, A (2001). Marché financier et évaluation du risque bancaire. Les agences de notation contribuent-elles à améliorer la discipline de marché? *Revue Economique*, 52, 265–283.

Gropp, R, Vesala, J and Vulpes, G (2006): Equity and bond market signals as leading indicators of bank fragility. *Journal of Money, Credit and Banking*, 38(2).

Gropp, R., Lo Duca, M and Vesala, J (2006). Cross-border bank contagion in Europe. ECB Working Paper No. 662.

Gunther, J, Levonian, M and Moore, R (2001). Can the stock market tell bank supervisors anything they don't already know. *Federal Reserve Bank of Dallas Economic and Financial Review.*

Heude, FA and Paget-Blanc, E (2004). Les annonces de rating: Impact sur le rendement des actions cotées sur Euronext-Paris. *Banque & Marchés*, No 70, mai–juin.

Hoenig, T (1999). Financial regulation, prudential supervision, and market discipline: Striking a balance. Presented to the Conference: Lessons from Recent Global Financial Crises. Federal Reserve Bank of Chicago.

Hussain, Q and Wihlborg, C (1999). Corporate insolvency procedures and bank behaviour: A study of selected Asian economies. Working paper No. 135, International Monetary Fund.

Jackson, HE (2002). The role of credit rating in the establishment of capital standards for financial institutions in a global economy. SSRN.

Jagtiani, J, Kolari, J, Lemieux, C and Shin, G (2000). Predicting inadequate capitalization: Early warning system of bank supervision. *Emerging Issues Series*, Federal Reserve Bank of Chicago, September.

Jagtiani, J, Kolari, J, Lemieux, C and Shin, G (2003). Early warning models: Simpler could be better. Economic Perpectives No 3, Federal Reserve Bank of Chicago.

Kaminsky, Lorenzo and Reinhart (1998). Leading indicator of currency crisis. IMF Staff Paper.

Kane, EJ (1989). Policy implications of structural changes in financial markets. *American Economic Review*, 73.

Kliger, D and Sarig, O (2000). The information value of bond ratings. *The Journal of Finance*, 55, 2879–2902.

Kolari, G, Shin and Caputo (2000). Predicting large US commercial bank failures. Economic and Policy Analysis Working Paper. Office of the Comptroller of the Currency number.

La Porta *et al.* (1997). Legal determinants of external finance. NBER Working Paper No. 5879.

La Porta, R, Lopez-de-Silanes, F and Shleifer, A (1998). Law and finance. *Journal of Political Economy*, 106, 1113–1155.

La Porta, R, Lopez-de-Silanes, F, Shleifer, A and Vishny, RW (2000). Investor protection and corporate governance. *Journal of Financial Economics*, 58, 3–27.

L'AMF: L'impact de la notation. 31 January 2006.

Linciano, N (2004). The reaction of stock prices to rating changes. SSRN.

Liu, Seyyed and Smith (1999). The independent impact of credit rating changes — The case of Moody's rating refinement on yield premiums. *Journal of Business Finance and Accounting*, 26, 337–363.

L1ewellyn, D (2002). An analysis of the causes of recent banking crises. *The European Journal of Finance*, 8, 152–175.

Maddala, GS (1983). Limited-dependent and qualitative variables in econometrics. *Econometric Society Monographs*, No.3. Cambridge: Cambridge University Press.

Madiés, P (2001). Coassurance des depots et panique bancaire: une étude expérimentale: WP 01-05.

Martin, D (1977). Early warning of bank failure. *Journal of Banking and Finance*, 1, 249–276.

Mishkin, F (1999). Financial consolidation: Dangers and opportunities. NBER Working Paper 6655, National Bureau of Economic Research.

Mitton, T (2002). A cross-firm analysis of the impact of corporate governance on the East Asian financial crisis. *Journal of Financial Economics*, 64(2), 215–242.

Pollin, JP (2006). La régulation bancaire face au dilemme du "TOO BIG TO FAIL": mécanismes et solutions. Présenté au sein des Journées de l'AFSE Strasbourg.

Ramakrishnan, R and Thakor, A (1984). Information reliability and a theory of financial intermediation. *Review of Economic Studies*, 51, 415–432.

Rojas-Suarez (2001). Rating banks in emerging markets: What credit rating agencies should learn from financial indicators. Working Paper of Institute of International Economics Février.

Sahajwala and Van der Bergh (2000). Supervisory risk assessment and early waring systems. Basel Committee of Banking Supervision Working Papers No 4, December, BIS.

Santos, JA (2001). Bank capital regulation in contemporary banking theory: A review of the literature. *Financial Markets, Institutions and Instruments*, 10, 41–84.

Schwarcz, S (2002). Rating agencies in global market regulation. SSRN.

Scialom (2005). Pur une approche holiste du filet de sécurité financière dans l'union européenne: quelques arguments.

Shen, Ch (2002). Prediction of bank failures using macro- and micro-data. Working Paper, National Cheng Chi University.

Shim, U (2006). Dynamic prudential regulation: Is prompt corrective action optimal? BIS Working Papers No. 206.

Sinkey, JF Jr (1975). A multivariate statistical analysis of the characteristics of problem banks. *Journal of Finance*, 30, 21–36.

Sironi, A (2001). An analysis of European banks' SND issues and its implications for the design of a mandatory subordinated debt policy. *Journal of Financial Services Research*, 20(2–3), 233–66.

Tang, H, Zoli, E and Klytchnikova, I (2000). Banking crises in transition economies: Fiscal costs and related issues. Policy Research Working Paper.

Thomas, A (2000). Econométrie des Variables Qualitatives. Dunod.

Thomson, JB (1991). Predicting bank failures in the 1980s. Economic Review 27, Federal Reserve Bank of Cleveland.

Thomson, JB (1992). Modeling the bank regulator's closure option: A two step logit regression approach. *Journal of Financial Services Research*, 6, 5–23.

Wakeman, LM (1984). The real function of bond rating agencies. In *The Modern Theory of Corporate Finance*, Jensen, MC and Smith, Jr CW (eds), New York: McGraw-Hill Inc.

Williamson, SD (1986). Costly monitoring, financial intermediation, and equilibrium credit rationing, *Journal of Monetary Economics*, 18(2), 159–179.

Wimboh, S (2001). The determinants of problem banks in Indonesia: An empirical study. Working Paper Bank Indonesia.

CHAPTER 12

PORTFOLIO DIVERSIFICATION AND MARKET SHARE ANALYSIS FOR ROMANIAN INSURANCE COMPANIES

*Mihaela Dragotă**, *Cosmin Iuliu Şerbănescu**,† *and Daniel Traian Pele**

The Romanian insurance market is very heterogeneous and, in this context, for the year 2005, three different insurance companies could be identified having together 50% from total gross written premiums. January the first was the starting point of future development, since Insurance Supervision Commission had already been informed on foreign insurers' intentions to provide financial services on this market. The main goal of this study was to analyze the determinants for the Romanian insurance companies' market share and its relationship with the degree of concentration and the most important finding was that the Romanian market is an oligopoly.

1 Some Considerations about the Romanian Insurance Market

Romania joined the European Union on 1st January 2007. This important step will determine a lot of implications, both for the Romanian economy, in general, and for the insurance field of activity, in particular. Even if Romanian business environment for the last few years has improved and this trend is also visible in the insurance industry, the development must continue, to be harmonized, at least, with other EU countries.

*Bucharest University of Economic Studies, Romania.
†Corresponding author. serbanescucosmin@yahoo.com

Compared to these countries, on the one hand, and with other East European ones, on the other hand, the Romanian insurance market finds itself at the beginning of the road. The steady growth of the Romanian market, even bigger than the EU 25, is based on a relative measure, but should also be analyzed in absolute values. As an example, the gross written premiums for the first semester of 2006,[a] have reached the level of 641 million euros (by extrapolation a total year amount of about 1300 million euros), while Slovenia has attained 1190 million euros. But the population of this country represents the 10th part of Romania's population.

The drifts of the Romanian insurance market are finally provided by mergers which already took place or are in course, the continuing process of bank insurance and the increasing insurance intermediaries.

2 The Most Important Goals of the Study

This study is structured in three main parts, in order to analyse the Romanian insurance market for the financial year 2005. The input data were provided by the Insurance Supervision Commission (ISC) yearly reports, which were improved from one period to another, with more and more information. The analysis was made generally for P&L insurance market, but the first study consists of a comparative analysis of non-life and life insurance.

The first study explores the correlations between different financial variables, such as gross written premiums, net written premiums, technical provisions, equity, claims, number of authorized classes, and the financial result.

The second study investigates the degree of concentration for the Romanian insurance market in order to classify the insurance companies; the most used variable was the market share.

The third part consists a principal component analysis in order to understand the factors that contribute to the variability in this market.

3 The Input Data

Some of the variables used for the first study were provided by ISC, such as equity, gross written premiums, financial result and number of authorised insurance classes. Also, some variables were determined by the authors from the ISC reports.

The second study had as principle variable the market share for each P&L insurance company, determined a ratio between gross written premiums

[a] www.csa-isc.ro

subscribed by each company and total gross written premiums (for the entire insurance industry).

The variables used for the P&L insurance classes in the principal component analysis are equity, financial result, number of authorized insurance classes, gross claim reserve, net claim reserve, and unearned premium reserve.

4 The Methodology of the Study

The first study used the Pearson correlation coefficients matrix as the statistical support of the static analysis.

The second study take into account the different measures for the degree of concentration on a competitive market:

(1) *Concentration ratio* (*CR*)[b] represents a simple and usual measure for the degree of concentration of a certain market, in our case for the insurance industry. The computation is done by adding the market shares of the most important three or four insurance companies, especially those with best financial results.

Lesueur (2004) said that "a market is called to be a monopoly if the demand is atomized". The Romanian insurance industry could not be considered as a monopoly at that moment, for any specific insurance class, because of the last years steady development. Though, an example of monopoly market could be provided at the end of the nineties: ING Nederlanden was the only insurer offering a new, and, at the same time, special product, the so-called *unit-linked* life insurance.

Oligopoly is based on a situation defined by an insurance market with a few operating insurers. From this point of view, the Romanian insurance market is an oligopoly. All databases confirm this status illustrated in Tables 1–3:

Table 1: Market share for the Romanian insurance industry (P&L insurance).[c]

Number of companies	Market share
Four companies (Allianz-Tiriac, Asirom, Omniasig, and Unita)	57.8%
Eight companies (Allianz-Tiriac, Asirom, Omniasig, Unita, Ardaf, Asiban, Astra, and BCR Asigurari)	83.57%

[c]www.1asig.ro
www.xprimm.ro

[b]O'Sullivan, A and Sheffrin, SM (2004). *Economics: Principles and Tools* (4th ed.). Prentice Hall.

Table 2: Market share for the Romanian insurance industry (life insurance).[c]

Number of companies	Market share
One company (ING Life Insurance)	37.85%
Eight companies (Allianz-Tiriac, Asirom, Omniasig, Unita, Ardaf, Asiban, Astra, and BCR Asigurari)	88.09%

[c]www.1asig.ro
www.xprimm.ro

Table 3: Market share for the Romanian insurance industry (P&L and life insurance).[c]

Number of companies	Market share
Five companies (Allianz-Tiriac, Asirom, Omniasig, ING, and Asiban)	57.75%

[c]www.1asig.ro
www.xprimm.ro

(2) *Herfindahl index* (*Herfindahl–Hirschman index or HHI*): HI (Brown and Warren–Boulton 1988), represents a measure for the degree of market competition. The values of this index lie between 0 and 1, a lower value meaning an aggressive competition on the market, and a value closer to 1 revealing a monopoly market. The minimum value of the index, $1/n$, is obtained when the market shares of the insurance companies are equal, and the maximum value shows a monopoly case.

Since the variation interval of the *Herfindahl index* depends on the number of insurance companies, a *Normalized Herfindahl index* will be used, with values between 0 and 1:

$$H_* = \frac{H - 1/n}{1 - 1/n} \in [0, 1],$$

where n is the number of insurance companies and H is the *Herfindahl index*, stated above.

(3) *Shannon informational entropy*: This represents a measure for the degree of concentration of a distribution. If the following discreet distribution for the random variable X: $\begin{pmatrix} X_1 & X_2 \cdots X_n \\ p_1 & p_2 \cdots p_n \end{pmatrix}$ is considered, where $p_i = \Pr(X = X_i)$, $0 \leq p_i \leq 1$ and $\sum_{i=1}^{n} p_i = 1$, the *Shannon informational entropy* could be defined as follows: $H(X) = -\sum_{i=1}^{n} p_i \log_2 p_i$. This variable could take values in the interval $[0, \log_2 n]$, the minimum value proving the maximum concentration level.

This measure for the degree of concentration was used in other international studies, too. At this moment, the study of Hoskisson *et al.* (1993) could be mentioned who concluded that the measures of diversification are highly correlated with the measures of performance used. They applied these concepts to the large multi-product firms in US, using the entropy as a measure of portfolio diversification.

Kochhar and Hitt (1998) examined the relationship between corporate strategy and capital structure, specifically the diversification and financing strategies for 180 large manufacturing firms trading on the American NYSE. They used entropy to measure the total level of diversification, taking into account the proportion of sales in each business segment.

In order to investigate the behavior of the companies playing in general insurance market we have done several regression analysis, trying to explain a key element, like *market share* or *gross written premiums*, based on the other variables available for the study, such as number of insurance classes, equity, return on equity, gross claim technical provision, and unearned premium reserve. Unfortunately, all the conclusions of the regression analysis had low statistical significance, due to the high correlation level between the variables involved and the discrepancies between the various companies acting on the market.

A principal component analysis was performed in order to reduce the measurement of the factorial vector, which determined the market share of insurers. As the variables related to the insurance companies are highly correlated, a classical regression model is difficult to apply. Using principal component analysis, we will identify only the main factors causing variability of market share among insurers.

5 Empirical Results

5.1 The Pearson Correlation Coefficients for P&L and Life Insurance

Table 4 illustrates the results of our first case study, meaning the values of the correlation coefficients for the P&L insurance classes.

The correlation analysis for the year 2005, revealed the following conclusions:

(A) Correlation between the gross written premiums and the financial result (0.1629)

For the year 2005, the correlation coefficient suggests a direct but weak correlation. The possible explanations are related to the level of the paid claims. A higher level of claims might determine, as a strategy, a higher level of gross

Table 4: Correlation coefficients between the financial variables for P&L insurance classes.

Year	2005
Gross written premiums/financial result	0.1629
Equity/financial result	−0.2705
Number of classes/gross written premiums	0.8295
Number of classes/equity	0.5444
Number of classes/gross paid claims	0.5862
Reinsurance underwriting/financial result	−0.089
Number of classes/financial result	−0.11053

written premiums, but the unpredictable claims' dynamics had determined the weakness of this correlation.

(B) Correlation between equity and the financial result (−0.2705)

The result is normal because the level of equity is not a guarantee for an appropriate level of the financial result. The Insurance Supervision Commission (ISC) decided to increase the level of equity for the Romanian insurance companies, probably because of the greater stability, the image of a stable company, but some significant events could generate, even for the important insurers, a non-suitable level of the financial result.

(C) Correlation between the number of classes and the gross written premiums (0.8295)

A strong correlation could be observed between these two variables, maybe too strong for an emergent market, as the Romanian one. Another argument for the emergent quality of the Romanian insurance market is the statistics revealing that only 4% of the whole number of buildings is insured. This strong and direct correlation could mean that the greater the portfolio diversification is, the bigger the level of gross written premiums will be. The incomes seemed to be greater not by "capturing" one or few classes, but by taking control on a larger number of insurance ones.

(D) Correlation between the number of classes and equity (0.5444)

The result was not very surprising; however, the level was too low. It is not a reflex response to increase the equity when the number of insurance classes increased. On one hand, some Romanian insurance companies (e.g., Nationala), had four classes with an issued capital of 25 billions ROL, and, on the other hand, other companies (e.g., Petroas) had 15 billions ROL equity for seven classes.

(E) Correlation between the number of insurance classes and the gross paid claims (0.5862)

For the year 2005, the correlation coefficient revealed a strong link, as the result is, somehow, reasonable since the level of gross paid claims increased every time when ISC approved new insurance classes. The analysis must be performed for a minimum of 10 years together with the correlation between the number of classes and the financial result, since both theory and practice proved that the risk will be diminished and the portfolio will be diversified through the number of insurance classes.

(F) Correlation between the reinsurance underwriting and the financial result (−0.089)

Reinsurance is a complex activity, with both sides of acceptance and ceded for reinsurance. Our study analyzed only the ceded reinsurance, due to the lack of information. The level of correlation coefficient revealed a very weak correlation between the two variables, very closed to independent. Some possible explanations could be (1) the accepted for reinsurance, which was not taken into account and (2) the reinsurance contracts with unfavorable terms for reinsured, with over dimensioned claims.

(G) Correlation between the number of insurance classes and the financial result (−0.1105)

As in the previous case, the correlation revealed almost two independent variables. The possible explanations are the following:

- The possession of more insurance classes, with an outstanding financial result from P&L (e.g. Allianz-Tiriac, BCR Insurance, and Omniasig Vienna Insurance Group).
- The possession of more insurance classes, with a suitable financial result (e.g. Ardaf, Asitrans, and City Insurance).
- The possession of more insurance classes, with un-appropriate financial results (e.g. Asiban, Asirom, Astra, BT Transilvania Insurance, Garanta, Generali, and Interamerican).
- The practice of less insurance classes with a suitable financial result (e.g. Asimed, Asito Kapital, Gerroma, and Nationala).

Table 5: Correlation coefficients between the financial variables for life insurance classes.

Year	2005
Gross written premiums/financial result	0.7943
Equity/financial result	0.2621
Number of classes/gross written premiums	0.469
Number of classes/equity	0.293
Number of classes/gross paid claims	−0.106
Reinsurance underwriting/financial result	0.278
Number of classes/financial result	0.1687

- The practice of less insurance classes with an un-appropriate financial results (e.g. Irasig and Medas).

To conclude, the financial management affects the financial result, and not the number of insurance classes.

Table 5 illustrates the results of the empirical study for *life insurance.*

The correlation analysis for the year 2005 revealed the following conclusions:

(1) Correlation between the gross written premiums and the financial result (0.7943)

As far as life insurances are concerned, their features could be taken into account. First of all, the moment in time could influence the financial result. It is well known that for the life insurance contract, the premiums are paid at this moment, and the most important part of the payments will be made 25 years later (on average). Of course, some unexpected cash outflows could appear from the insured company, but the amounts are not so significant.

The two types of insurance — life and non-life — had different treatment analyzed through the financial results and the most important variable is the maturity of these types of contracts. After a few years, the dissimilarities could be diminished.

(2) Correlation between equity and the financial result (0.2621)

The correlation between these two variables is direct but weak due to their peculiar circumstances: on one hand, the companies with a great level of equity and negative financial results, and on the other hand, the companies with small equity and with important net profits. Anyway, the level of the correlation coefficient could not express a significant relationship between the two variables.

(3) Correlation between the number of classes and the gross written premiums (0.4692)

The result is consistent with the developing stage for the Romanian life insurance companies. Since this is an emergent market, the weak correlation between the two variables could be explained. Most of the insurers had only one class of life insurance, the maximum of four classes was used only by three companies in the year 2005. One of these three companies has the first position from the gross written premiums' point of view.

(4) Correlation between the number of classes and equity (0.1441)

If we consider two companies with a single life insurance class, but with big equity (Asirom and Unita) and, also, some companies with the four agreed classes with the biggest equity (Aviva with 571 billions ROL and ING with 450 billions ROL), these important positions could be explained by the fact that the level of equity depends on the total insurance classes accepted by ISC. So, the result was normal and it defined accurately the relationship of the actual developing stage of the Romanian insurance market. The correlation is weak because, with the above-mentioned exceptions, there are companies with less equity and a great number of insurance classes (e.g. Ardaf had four classes with an issued capital of 175 billions ROL, Grawe, with three classes had a capital of 36 billions ROL and Asiban, with one class had a capital of 190 billions ROL).

(5) Correlation between the number of classes and the gross paid claims (−0.106)

It is a weak and negative correlation and it is easy to find out explanations, if the sample will be analyzed in detail. For example, Asirom, with only one class had a very high level of the gross paid claims (above 62 billions ROL), which mainly explains the financial loss at the end of the year 2005. Moreover, some of these companies with one life insurance class had a very low level of paid claims (such as BT Life Insurance and Garanta).

On the other hand, the conditions are almost the same for the companies with many accepted classes. Sara Merkur had a lower level of the gross paid claims, but it had financial loss at the end of 2005. Aviva had a small amount of claims, too, but it had profit in the same period and ING and Omniasig had big claims with big financial results, too.

(6) Correlation between reinsurance underwriting and the financial result (0.278)

The correlation is direct but not very strong. The result reflected the special cases of the companies with losses at the end of the year and with no reinsurance covering. However, the reinsurance is a necessary but not sufficient condition for the companies to be profitable.

(7) Correlation between the number of classes and the financial result (0.1687)

There has been a direct, but weak correlation, which revealed, from an analytical point of view, the existence of some insurers with one class and big profits (e.g. Asiban or BCR Insurance), and of some companies with a lot of insurance classes but with financial losses (e.g. ARDAF).

5.2 The Analysis of the Concentration Level for the P&L Insurance Market

The first step is to identify the determinants for the market share of all P&L insurance companies. For the year 2005, this market was very heterogeneous and three different insurance companies could be identified (Allianz Tiriac, Asirom, and Omniasig), which together had 50% from total gross written premiums, as observed in the box plot in Fig. 1.

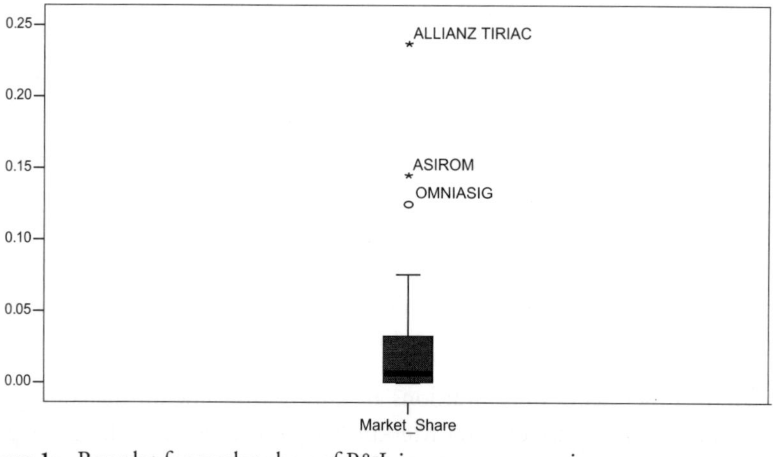

Figure 1: Box plot for market share of P&L insurance companies.

Based on the histogram analysis (Fig. 2), the distribution of market share was abnormal and, moreover, this conclusion was sustained by the level of variables presented in Table 6.

The database of P&L insurance companies showed that 75% of them had a market share lower than 3.16% , indicating the absence of homogeneity. This conclusion is also sustained by the greater value of the variation coefficient.

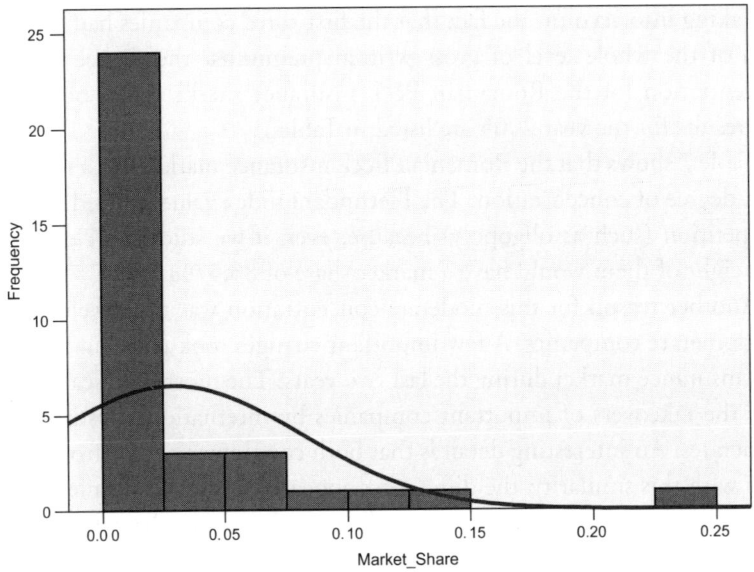

Figure 2: Histogram of market share for P&L insurance companies.

Table 6: The market share distributions features.

Indicator	Value
Mean	2.94%
Median	0.65%
Quartile 1	0.05%
Quartile 3	3.16%
Standard deviation	5.18%
Sample variance	0.0027
Kurtosis	7.54
Skewness	2.60
Range	23.72%
Minimum	0.0000021%
Maximum	23.72%
Coefficient of variation	1.76

Table 7: Concentration measures for P&L insurances market.

Concentration measure	Value	Conclusion
Concentration ratio — three firms	0.51	Oligopoly
Herfindhal index	0.12	Moderate concentration
Shannon Entropy	3.55	Moderate concentration

Taking into account the fact that the first three companies had more than 50% of the whole level of gross written premiums, the degree of market concentration for the Romanian P&L insurance market must be analyzed. The results for the year 2005 are listed in Table 7.

Table 7 shows that the Romanian P&L insurance market had a medium to great degree of concentration. The Herfindahl index value showed a medium competition (such as oligopoly) because, even if we studied 34 companies, only eight of them would have a market share of 83.57% .

Another reason for this moderate concentration was the development of conglomerate companies. A few important changes took place on the Romanian insurance market during the last two years. The most significant of them were the takeovers of important companies by international insurance conglomerates. An interesting detail is that both conglomerates are from Austria. Even with this similarity, the differences appeared at a more detailed analysis: one of the conglomerate organizations kept the Romanian brands: Omniasig, Unita (a simple merging), while the other one took the option of merging by absorption.

The first conglomerate is Vienna Insurance Group (VIG), former Wiener Stadtische Group. The Austrian insurer took over Omniasig, Unita (two of the main Romanian insurers), Omniasig Life and Agras. In 2005, Omniasig was the third most important P&L insurer, with a total amount of gross written premiums of 421.607.612 RON (123,638,596 Euro) and a market share of 12.48%. Unita had also an important leading position (the seventh) and a market share of 7.07% .

Grazer Wechselseitige Versicherung (GRAWE) is the second conglomerate, operating in Romania under GRAWE Romania. The Romanian branch took over SARA MERKUR in March 2006 and both conglomerates reached an important position in 2006. After three quarters of 2006, the financial results were outstanding. Omniasig (now a member of Vienna Insurance Group) reported gross written premiums of 366.955.640 RON, that means a growth (compared to the previous year) of more than 25% . Meanwhile, the loss ratio decreased to 53.13% . The previous loss ratio (before Omniasig became part of VIG) was of 40% . There was a similar situation for the second conglomerate: the merger, Grawe Romania, succeeded to improve its loss ratio from 3.09% to less than 1% .

This important financial aspect was also emphasized by King (1975) in one of his studies. It is extremely possible that the separated insurance companies would record a smaller loss ratio than the conglomerate organizations.

We could also rely on the fact that the bigger the companies are, the better the services provided will be. Whenever an insurer succeeds to subscribe new policies, it must expect to pay claims in the future. Moreover, if the insurer did not pay the claim because of an internal problem, its financial distress will affect the entire insurance industry and the confidence in this economic branch will decrease. In this context, Forbes (1970) conclusion could be mentioned — "the surviving company usually absorbs all of the rights, powers, and liabilities of the merged corporation" and this is the moment when the insurance company will develop a successful method the new owner will take advantage of. In fact, the bigger the merged insurance company, the more efficient the "mother company" becomes.

5.3 Portfolio Diversification and Market Share — An Empirical Study for the Romanian P&L Insurance Market

The Insurance Supervisory Commission approved 18 classes on the Romanian P&L insurance market. There is a heterogeneous insurance market in this field, too; some of the insurers had contracts from one insurance class, and others had subscribed policies in 14 insurance classes, as illustrated in Fig. 3.

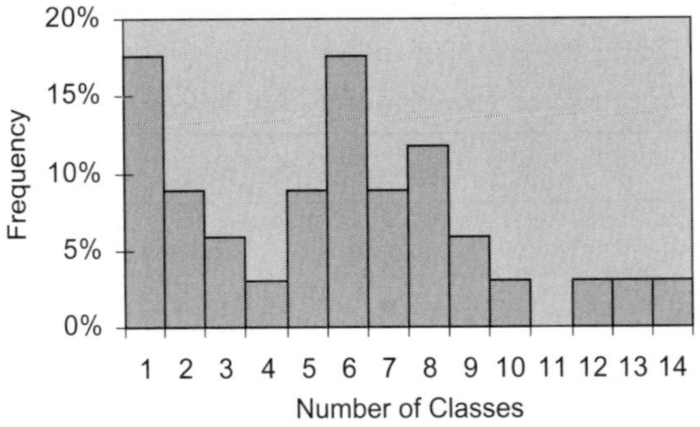

Figure 3: The distribution of P&L insurance classes per number.

In this context, it could be interesting to find out the relationship between the degree of portfolio diversification and the market share. The weights of gross written premiums were determined for each insurance company and for each insurance class from the sample in total amount of this variable, for the entire P&L insurance market. The probability vector was obtained for each company i, where $i = \overline{1, n}$, $w_i = (w_i^1, w_i^2, ..., w_i^{m_i})$ and m_i represents the number of classes for each insurance company.

Then we measured the degree of concentration of the portfolio through Shannon entropy; thus for each company i, where $i = \overline{1, n}$, the entropy level is $H_i = -\sum_{j=1}^{m_i} w_i^j \log_2 w_i^j$. A simple linear regression model was fitted to analyze the relationship between the degree of concentration of the portfolio and the market share:

$$\mathrm{MS}_i = \alpha + \beta H_i + \varepsilon_i,$$

where MS_i represents the market share for each company's i, H_i is the Shannon entropy, and ε is the residual term with zero mean and constant variance.

The results of the regression model of the entire P&L market were synthesized in Table 8.

The slope of the regression line was statistically significant, with a confidence level of 95%, but the value of Durbin–Watson statistics indicated the presence of autocorrelation in errors. Moreover, the lower value of R^2 showed a weak explanatory power of the model. The model was re-estimated after removing from the sample the two outliers in terms of market share (Allianz Tiriac, and Asirom) that cumulate almost 40% from the market. The most important results are presented in Table 9.

After the re-estimation of the simple regression model the results are slightly improved; the value of R^2 showed that the model explained almost 25% of the total variation of the market share. The Durbin–Watson statistic sustained

Table 8: Shannon's entropy on regression of market share (1st model).

	R	R^2	Adjusted R^2	Std. error of the estimate	Durbin–Watson
Panel A: Regression statistics	0.390	0.152	0.126	0.705767	1.371

Panel B: Coefficients table

	Coefficients	t	Sig.
(Constant)	−0.9	−0.518	0.608
Entropy	2.7	2.397	0.023

Table 9: Shannon's entropy on regression of market share (2nd model).

	R	R^2	Adjusted R^2	Std. error of the estimate	Durbin–Watson
Panel A: Regression Statistics	0.499	0.249	0.224	2.68384	2.019

Panel B: Coefficients table

	Coefficients	t	Sig.
(Constant)	−0.879	−0.871	0.391
Entropy	1.973	3.155	0.004

this result. The ANOVA table certificated the validity of the model; moreover, both coefficients were statistically significant; there was a direct relationship between the portfolio degree of concentration and the market share. Since the portfolio is less concentrated (or more diversified) we can expect a higher market share. From Fig. 4, we could agree that residuals distribution can be approximated as a normal distribution (Figs. 5 and 6).

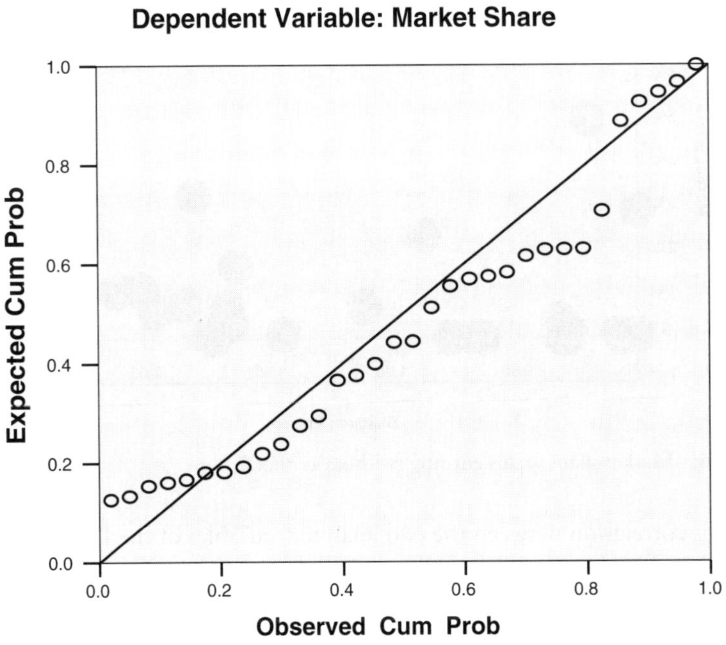

Figure 4: Normal probability plot of the second regression model.

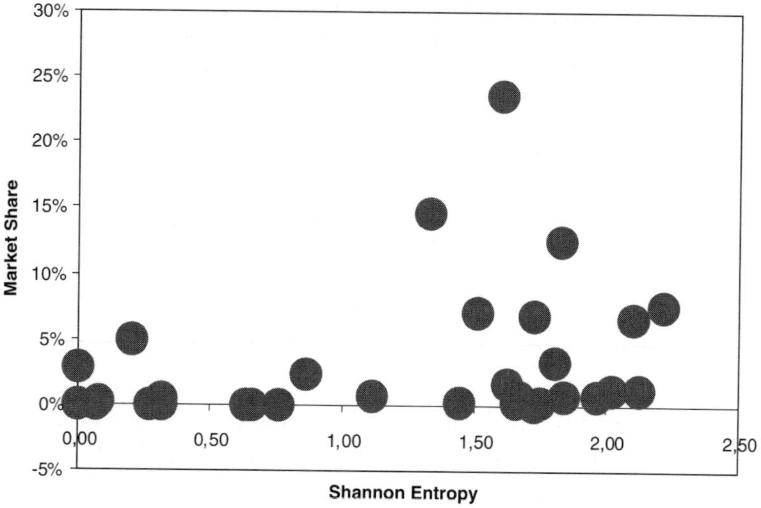

Figure 5: Market share versus entropy (entire market).

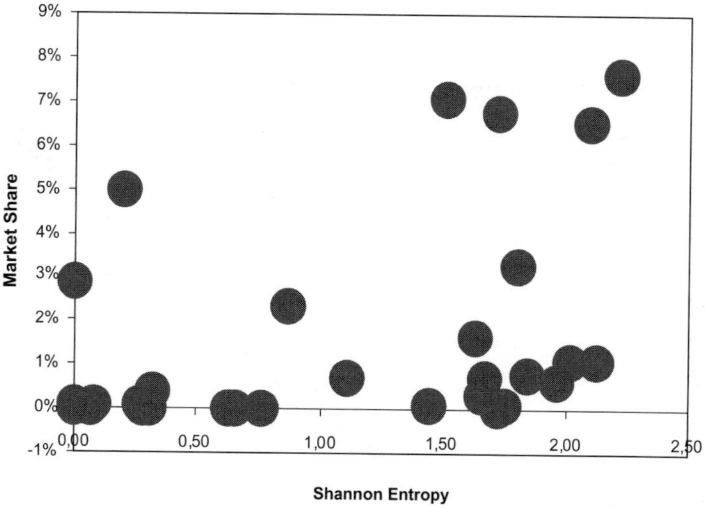

Figure 6: Market share versus entropy (without outliers).

This correlation between the two analyzed variables of the P&L insurance market could have more financial explanations, such as:

- a sign of aggressive marketing policies of the Romanian insurance companies, which have tried, for the last few years, to conquer a greater market share and the most appropriate manner was to extend their portfolio. At this point, the portfolio diversification could be taken into account, analyzed through the number of classes in which the insurers accepted their risk exposure. The Romanian insurer's business philosophy could be considered to act as follows: the more the classes underwritten, the more recognized the insurance company will be on the market;

- a prudent portfolio management policy, according to the following principle: the bigger the number of classes accepted by an insurance company, the less the risk exposure and the financial distress probability;
- a normal result for an emergent market. Since the Romanian insurance industry is still growing, each insurer, authorized for another class, will have many clients. This is the so-called "one stop shop" marketing policy.

5.4 Principal Components Analysis of the Market Share of the P&L Insurance Companies

The principal component analysis was realized in order to understand the determinants of the market variability. The variables considered in this study were transformed according to the standard methodology of this type of analysis in order to achieve the maximum number of factors which could explain the dissimilarities between P&L insurance companies.

Table 10 shows the proportion of the explained variance for each variable considered, into an individually and cumulative analysis.

Table 10: Proportion of variance explained by initial and transformed factors.

Component	Initial eigenvalues			Extraction sums of squared loadings		
	Total	Percentage of variance	Cumulative %	Total	Percentage of variance	Cumulative %
1	4.791	68.441	68.441	4.791	68.441	68.441
2	1.409	20.132	88.573	1.409	20.132	88.573
3	0.570	8.143	96.716			
4	0.132	1.891	98.607			
5	0.061	0.874	99.481			
6	0.027	0.390	99.871			
7	0.009	0.129	100.000			

Table 11: Correlation matrix between the initial variables and principal components.

	Component	
	1	2
Financial result	0.075	0.968
Paid claims	0.974	0.046
Number of insurance classes	0.663	−0.272
Gross claim technical provision	0.961	0.203
Net claim technical provision	0.979	0.132
Unearned premium reserve	0.959	0.175
Equity	0.772	−0.555

As Table 10 showed, two is the optimum number for principal components. These two factors explained almost 89% of these fluctuations. Table 11 presents the correlation coefficients for each of these two components.

The first factor is highly correlated to paid claims, gross claim technical provision, net claim technical provision, unearned premium reserve, and medium correlated to equity and number of insurance classes. This first factor contributed with 68% to the total variability on the market. Taking into account the characteristics of this synthetic factor and the correlations with the initial variables, we defined it as *risk exposure*. *The second factor*, which contributes with 20% to total variability, has captured, mainly, the action of financial results.

A regression model was used in order to explain the variation of market share as a function of these two factors.

As shown in Fig. 7, a linear regression model of market share on the risk exposure could be estimated. Since the variables derived from principal component analysis are standardized, the market share must also be standardized, following the formula:

$$\mathrm{MS}_{\mathrm{std}} = \frac{\mathrm{MS} - \mu}{\sigma},$$

where $\mu = 0.031$ and $\sigma = 0.053$ are the sample mean and standard deviation for the market share.

Two regression models were used, whose main results are presented below:

$$\text{Model 1:} \quad \mathrm{MS}_{\mathrm{std}} = \beta_0 + \beta_1 F_1 + \varepsilon,$$

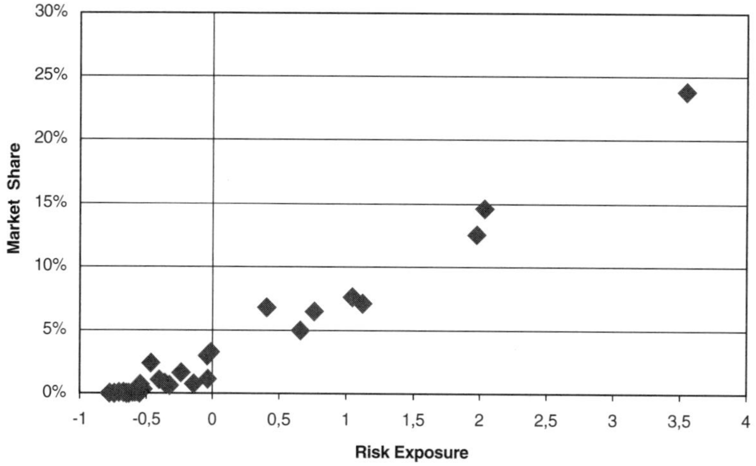

Figure 7: Scatter plot of market share versus risk exposure.

where ε is the residual term and F_1 is the main factor described as a result of the principal component analysis (risk exposure).

According to the data presented in Table 12, Panel A, this model explained 96% of standardized market share variation. The hypothesis of residuals autocorrelation could be rejected.

A second model was re-estimated, taking into account the influence of the second factor.

$$\text{Model 2:}\quad \text{MS}_{\text{std}} = \beta_0 + \beta_1 F_1 + \beta_2 F_2 + \varepsilon,$$

Table 12: Regression of standardized market share on risk exposure (1st model).

	Model	R	R^2	Adjusted R^2	Std. error of the estimate	Durbin–Watson
Panel A:						
Regression statistics	1	0.983(a)	0.967	0.966	0.18541	1.750

Panel B: Coefficients table

Model		Coefficients	t	Sig.
1	(Constant)	0.000	0.000	1.000
	Factor 1	0.983	29.525	0.000

Table 13: Regression of standardized market share on the two factors (2nd model).

	Model	R	R^2	Adjusted R^2	Std. error of the estimate	Durbin–Watson
Panel A: Regression statistics	2	0.989	0.977	0.976	0.15624	2.247

Panel B: Coefficients table

Model		Coefficients	t	Sig.
2	(Constant)	0.000	0.000	1.000
	Factor 1	0.983	35.038	0.000
	Factor 2	0.102	3.640	0.001

where ε is the residual term and F_1, F_2 are the two factors described as a result of the principal component analysis.

According to the decision rules of Durbin–Watson test, the hypothesis of residuals autocorrelation could be rejected. The second model used the data better than the first model, so two factors explaining market share of companies from general insurance market could be identified (Table 13).

6 Conclusions and New Directions of the Study

The Romanian insurance market is, still, very heterogeneous due to two main reasons, firstly, the relative low power of purchase and secondly the still growing market. As we stated before, it is enough to be authorized for another insurance class to attract more clients. Two possible explanations are the low-price policy and the "one stop shop" policy.

The values obtained revealed the great power of absorption of the Romanian market. The correlation coefficients especially proved the fact that Romania is still waiting for the big insurers from outside the country. January the first is the starting point of future development, because ISC has already been noticed of the intentions of foreign insurers to provide financial services on this market.

One of the most important variables used in this study was the number of insurance classes which was correlated with other financial indicators. A highly statistical positive significance was achieved between the number of insurance classes and the gross written premiums, for both P&L and life insurance. This result is consistent with the conclusions of the regression model of market share on portfolio diversification degree, measured by Shannon entropy. Moreover, this statement underlined the quality of the Romanian insurance market as an emergent one.

Moreover, there is a significant positive correlation between the number of classes and the gross claim paid for the P&L insurance, which explained, somewhat, their diversification policy. This result is sustained by the conclusions of the principal components analysis and the aggressive marketing policy remained as an additional argument for the Romanian insurance market.

The legal background, from the equity point of view, was amended several times in order to correlate the Romanian regulations with the EU ones. The minimum level of equity was determined on three different stages, without counting the exact number of classes: P&L insurance without compulsory third party liability; compulsory third party liability and life insurance.

This was the reason why the direct correlation between those two variables was, also, medium. In fact, if an insurer is authorized for one or five classes he might choose the same level of equity.

Using the concentration measures described in Chap. 4, the conclusion is that the Romanian insurance market is an oligopoly.

As the principal component analysis has shown, the more attention is paid to the financial variables such as paid claims, gross claim technical reserve or unearned premium reserve, the more you can expect to gain market share.

As future directions of the study, the followings could be mentioned: (1) the extensions of these analyses for the life insurance classes; (2) a study from the insured persons' perspective, as a consumer point of view; (3) an analysis of other variables which influence the Romanian insurance companies market share, such as advertising expenditures; (4) a dynamic analysis, as to be able to confirm or to reject the conclusions of this static analysis; (5) an international study, at EU level, at least, to bring in the Romanian insurance market, with its features.

References

Brown, DM and Warren-Boulton, FR (1988). Testing the structure–competition relationship on cross-sectional firm data. Discussion Paper 88-6, Economic Analysis Group, US Department of Justice.

Forbes, SW (1970). Growth performances of nonlife insurance companies: 1955–1966. *The Journal of Risk and Insurance*, 37(3), 341–360.

Forbes, SW (1971). Rates of return in the nonlife insurance industry. *The Journal of Risk and Insurance*, 38(3), 409–422.

Hoskisson, RE, Hitt, MA, Johnson, RA and Moesel, DD (1993). Construct validity of an objective (entropy) categorical measure of diversification strategy. *Strategic Management Journal*, 14(6), 215–235.

King, A (1975). The market performance of diversified and non-diversified organizations within the P-L insurance industry. *The Journal of Risk and Insurance*, 42(3), 471–493.

Kochhar, R and Hitt, MA (1998). Linking corporate strategy to capital structure: Diversification strategy, type and source of financing. *Strategic Management Journal*, 19(6), 601–610.

Lee, SH and Urrutia, JL (1996). Analysis and prediction of insolvency in the property-liability insurance industry: A comparison of logit and hazard models. *The Journal of Risk and Insurance*, 63(1), 121–130.

Lesueur, JY (2004). *Microéconomie*: Edition Vuibert.

Makki, S and Somwaru, A (2001). Evidence of adverse selection in crop insurance markets. *The Journal of Risk and Insurance*, 68(4), 685–708.

O'Sullivan, AM and Sheffrin, S (2004). *Economics: Principles and Tools*, 4th Ed. Prentice Hall Pub.

Yamori, N (1999). An empirical investigation of the Japanese corporate demand for insurance. *The Journal of Risk and Insurance,* 66(2), 239–252.

CHAPTER 13

ON THE CLOSED-END FUNDS DISCOUNTS/PREMIUMS IN THE CONTEXT OF THE INVESTOR SENTIMENT THEORY

*Ana Paula Carvalho do Monte** and
Manuel José da Rocha Armada†

The existence of closed-end funds discounts/premiums, although an issue largely studied, it is still puzzling both academics as well as practitioners. As it is well known, they result from the difference between the value of the shares of the fund, determined by the market, and their net asset value (the market value of the securities held by the fund, less the liabilities). Taking into account that the closed-end fund shares are traded on the stock exchange, as well as the assets included on their portfolios, no discrepancies would be expected (at least theoretically) between the market value of the funds and their net asset values, since the market should be able to adjust and correct the prices, due to the fact that the information is widely diffused.

In attempt to explain this "puzzle" several theories have been suggested. On one hand, those based on rational factors, such as: potential tax liabilities due to unrealized capital gains, the dividend policy, the fund portfolio composition, agency costs and management performance and, on the other hand, those based on behavioral factors, such as the investor sentiment theory. This latter framework, at least theoretically is, in our view, the one that seems to better explain almost all the features of the "puzzle", trying not only to explain

*Escola Superior de Tecnologia e de Gestão de Bragança, Campus de Santa Apolónia–Apartado 134, 5301-857 Bragança, Portugal. apmonte@ipb.pt

†Escola de Economia e Gestão — Universidade do Minho, Gualtar 4710 BRAGA, Portugal. rarmada@eeg.uminho.pt

the existence of discounts but also the existence of premiums and their behavior among the funds themselves and over time.

In this context, we developed our research trying to explain the existence and persistence of the discounts/premiums. We also investigate the correlation between the discounts/premiums of those funds among themselves and each other over time, the mean reversion of the discounts/premiums, as well as the predictability power of the fund shares and of the net asset value returns. It was also our objective to search for the relevance of the investor sentiment theory in order to explain the discounts/premiums, so that we used Brauer's (1993) methodology and the signal extraction technique of French and Roll (1986). We also carried out (as far as we know, for the first time) a panel data analysis in order to check how much of the discounts/premiums variability is due to the presence of "noise traders".

This research was based on a sample of North-American closed-end funds, which invest mainly on stocks and/or bonds traded on the NYSE or on the AMEX, during the period from January 1987 to June 1999 (inclusive). The data was collected from the Wiesenberger database.

From the results that we got, we noticed that there seems to exist an indication of the presence of "noise traders" on the closed-end funds market which, in turn, seems to confirm the assumptions of the investor sentiment theory: the discounts/premiums were positively correlated, were mean reverted and had some predictability power in terms of fund share returns but not so much in relation to their net asset value returns. Nevertheless, we observed that the estimated proportion of the variance of standardized weekly discounts changes, explained by the investor sentiment on the total period studied, was only 8.6% . Also, the results from the panel data analysis seem to suggest the relatively low importance of the investor sentiment theory to explain those discounts/premiums.

1 Introduction

As the price of the closed-end fund shares and its net asset value (NAV) are determined independently, they can diverge from each other and, as a consequence, we can observe either discounts or premiums, being the first ones the most common and persistent form, in recent years (Dimson and Minio-Koserski, 1998; Elton *et al.*, 1998; Klibanoff *et al.*, 1998). Nevertheless, taking into account that the closed-end fund shares are traded on the stock exchange, as well as the assets on their portfolios, no discrepancies would be expected (at least theoretically) between the market value of the funds and their NAVs. Besides the fact that the funds are frequently traded at discount, they vary from fund to fund, in the same period, and along the time. The flotation of the discounts follow, in general and closely, the market cycles and the launch of new funds happens in general during the phase in which the majority of the existing ones are at premium or at discount.[a] These new funds, usually, are placed in the market at premium but, surprisingly, this is going to be diluted, becoming at discount or at reduced premium (Lee *et al.*, 1990).

Another intriguing aspect is the behavior of the discounts when an open-ending operation is announced. In general, in such situation, it can be observed that the price of the fund tends to converge to its NAV, deeply reducing the discount. Afterwards, and until the operation effectively takes place, the discount still reduces, approaching zero, in most of the cases.[b] We should point out, however, that the conflicts between the administration and the stockholders can obstruct and impede an open-ending operation (Brauer, 1984; Barclay *et al.*, 1993). In case the managers do not own significant participations in the fund, they will tend to resist to the operation because they can loose their jobs or certain privileges (for example, pecuniary benefits). The large stockholders, and the blockholders, can also resist, even if the operation can benefit them in terms of excess returns, because they may prefer to maintain their private benefits (Barclay *et al.*, 1993).

On the other hand, several authors (among others, for example, Cheng *et al.*, 1994; Pontiff, 1995; Arak e Taylor, 1996a; Sias, 1997b) detected excess returns in relation to funds sold at high discount/premium as a result of implemented certain strategies having concluded that the discount/premium is mean reverting, at least in the short period. Given this apparent market inefficiency, it would be expected that the rational investors would try to take advantage of this opportunity and would implement arbitrage strategies. However, Pontiff (1995) concluded that those investors did not succeed to implement completely effective strategies. Consequently, the actual discount/premium of the fund containing information on the future discount/premium would also contain information which would allow forecasting fund returns (Pontiff, 1995; Cheung *et al.*, 1997).

[a] See, for example, Weiss (1989) and Levis and Thomas (1995).

[b] According to Brickley and Schallheim (1985), the temporal pattern of the decline on the discounts is probably due to the reduction of the uncertainty about the effectiveness of the operation, i.e. if the fund will (or will not) be restructured.

In attempt to explain the "puzzle" some theories were suggested. On one hand, perhaps the most common type of explanations, are those that are based upon rational factors, such as, the potential tax liabilities for the fund's unrealized capital gains, the dividend policy, the composition of the fund's portfolio, agency costs and management performance, among others. On the other hand, are those which are based upon behavioral factors like the investor sentiment theory.

The first set of theories tries to explain the existence of the discounts, but not always the premiums or of the behavior of these at the time of an initial public offering (IPO) or of an open-ending operation. However, there are some factors, so called rational, which seem to have economic and statistical relevance for explaining the cross-sectional behavior of the discounts/premiums, such as the characteristics of the fund's portfolio composition (the existence of restricted assets, illiquid or foreign), the dividend policy, the unrealized capital appreciation, and agency costs.

The other set of theories, the investor sentiment theory (for example), seems to consider almost all the pieces of the "puzzle" trying, not only, to explain the existence of discounts but also of the premiums as well as their behavior among funds and along time. Nevertheless, it is also not exempt of criticism, the main ones being related with the fact of being able to fully explain the variation of the discounts/premiums of the closed-end funds, an indicator of the investor's sentiment, and if this is (or not) a factor of systematic risk.

Within this context, we carried out our research trying to explain the existence and persistence of the discounts/premiums, having the De Long, Shleifer, Summers and Waldmann model (1990) as the starting point. Having a deep relation with our main objective, we investigated the correlation among the discounts/premiums and of these for each fund over time, the existence (or not) of mean reversion for discounts/premiums as well as of their weekly changes, and also their predictive power on the fund's share returns as well as of their NAV returns. Finally, in order to investigate about the relevance of this theory for the explanation of the discounts/premiums, we applied the Brauer's (1993) methodology as well as the signal extraction technique of French and Roll (1986), carrying out also a panel data analysis (to the best of our knowledge for the first time) for checking how much of the variability of the discounts/premiums is due to the presence of noise traders.

This chapter is structured in the following way: first, we expose the investor sentiment theory and its applicableness to the closed-end funds, evidencing the implications of this in the behavior and explanation of the discounts/premiums. After, we exhibit the methodology used to determine the relevance of this theory in the explanation of the variability of the discounts/premiums, as well as the several methods and statistical techniques such as the panel data analysis. On the fourth section, we describe the sample and define the variables used in the study. On the fifth section, we expose and analyze the results and, at last, we present the conclusions as well as some suggestions that are indicated for future research.

2 The Investor Sentiment Theory and Its Applicability to the Closed-End Funds

The investor sentiment theory is based on the notions of rational and informed investor versus non-rational and less informed investor (the "noise traders") as well as the way that this latter type of investors affects the asset prices. De Long *et al.* (1990) formalized such a theory, having presented a model of asset valuation upon these type of investors which do not act in a rational way, creating additional risk for the assets they hold.

According to these authors, there are two types of investors in the market: the rational investors and the noise traders. The first ones, which they designated by sophisticated investors,[c] form their expectations based on information concerning the intrinsic value of the assets. They form rational expectations. The second ones, the noise traders, who do not have access to inside information, frequently form biased expectations about the asset prices. It can even be said that they act in an irrational way, as their expectations are not based on the assets' fundamental value but on the misleading information obtained from pseudo-signals of the market.[d] The optimistic or pessimistic noise traders' opinion makes the assets resale price become unexpected. As a result, the assets can be undervalued or overvalued. This unpredictability is worsened by the fact that the noise traders' opinion could change (or become even more extreme) during the period of the strategy implementation, creating an additional risk to rational investors[e] — the "noise traders risk", which

[c]These investors have access facilitated to all sources of information, including the inside information–private information, that is why their expectations are unbiased.

[d]These investors form their expectations on "(...) pseudo-signals from technical analysts, stockbrokers or economic consultants, and irrationally believe that these signals carry information" about the assets' întrínsíc value (De Long *et al.*, 1990:706). For this reason, their expectations are biased and, in general, reflect their optimism or pessimism in relation to the asset prices.

[e]These investors can select aggressive arbitrage strategies to explore the assets' mispricing but due to the noise traders' risk they are not able to drive asset prices to their fundamental values because, in general, they are risk averse.

limit their performance as arbitrageurs. Consequently, asset prices can diverge significantly from their intrinsic values, albeit there is no fundamental risk (De Long *et al.*, 1990).

In this model, De Long *et al.* (1990) consider that the investors can invest in two asset types: assets without risk, that pay a real fixed dividend, r, which supply is perfectly elastic and risky assets which also pay a real fixed dividend, r, like the riskless assets but which supply is inelastic, i.e. the supplied quantity is fixed and normalized at one unit, that is why their price varies along time. According to the authors, the variation in the risky asset prices is mainly due to the misevaluation made by noise traders. So, the risky assets price is given, in equilibrium, by the equation:

$$P_t = 1 + \frac{\mu\left(\rho_t - \bar{\rho}\right)}{1+r} + \frac{\mu\bar{\rho}}{r} - \frac{(2\gamma)\,\mu^2\sigma_\rho^2}{r\,(1+r)^2}, \tag{1}$$

where

$P_t \equiv$ the price of the risky assets, in period t;
$r \equiv$ fixed real dividend;
$\gamma \equiv$ absolute coefficient of risk aversion;
$\mu \equiv$ percentage of "*noise traders*" in the market;
$\rho_t \equiv$ non informed investor — "*noise traders*" sentiment, that is, their optimism or pessimism relatively to the asset prices, where $\rho_t \sim N\left(\bar{\rho}, \sigma_\rho^2\right)$.

This equation represents the equilibrium risky assets price where the price depends on exogenous parameters of the model (the technological parameters, r, and the behavioral parameters, γ) plus the public information regarding the actual and future sentiment of the noise traders, i.e. the misperception (sentiment) about these asset prices by the noise traders, ρ_t, at moment t.

This model can be applied to the closed-end funds' pricing and it may explain the existence, variance, and persistence of their discounts/premiums, if we consider that the closed-end fund's NAV is equivalent to the riskless asset of the model, since its fundamental value is easily calculated,[f] and the fund shares are equivalent to a risky asset. In this manner, the notion of noise traders can explain the "closed-end funds' puzzle" as the fund shares are subject to the "noise traders sentiment" which is systematic and correlated among the funds[g] (De Long *et al.*, 1990).

[f]Closed-end funds pay a dividend equivalent to the sum of the dividends paid by the stocks in its portfolio; hence the market price of the fund should be equivalent to the sum of its portfolio market price.
[g]The noise traders risk has to be systematic to be evaluated by them because the idiosyncratic risk, since it is diversifiable, it is not priced by the model.

When investors are optimistic about closed-end funds, they force the fund prices to a superior level relative to its fundamental value, therefore the discounts decrease or become premiums. When the investors are pessimistic, the opposite is observed, discounts increase. Then, investors are subject to two types of risk: the risk from holding fund's portfolio (similar to the fundamental risk) and the risk of the resale price (equivalent to the "noise trader risk"). The resale price risk comes from the uncertainty in relation to the investor sentiment at the moment that they need to sell the fund, i.e. at that moment the discount might widen. If the sentiment is systematic, that is, if it affects all funds and other assets, then the associated risk should be rewarded. Due to this, closed-end funds have to sell, on average, at discount to reward the associated noise traders' risk (Lee *et al.*, 1990; Shleifer and Summers, 1990). Hence, closed-end funds sell, on average, at discount because discounts fluctuate and investors require an additional return for bearing the risk of fluctuating discounts (Shleifer and Summers, 1990). Lee *et al.* (1991) point out that discounts/premiums changes reflect not the aggregated effect of investor sentiment change but the differential effect of the clientele that invest in closed-end funds relatively to the clientele that invest in the underlying assets of portfolio's funds.[h]

Lee *et al.* (1991) call attention to a set of empirical implications for the pricing of closed-end funds as a consequence of the investor sentiment shifts as well. One of the implications is related by the fact that discounts/premiums simultaneously vary across funds as it reflect widespread changes in investor sentiment. Hence, with reference to De Long, Shleifer, Summers and Waldmann model (1990), theoretically, discounts/premiums changes have to be stochastic because, if discounts/premiums are constant, it would be quite easy to implement arbitrage strategies, even for short investment horizons and, therefore, discounts/premiums would decrease.

Another implication of this theory is regarding to new funds being placed in the market when the sentiment is positive (optimistic), that is, when the seasoned funds are traded at low discount or even at premium.[i]

In addition, the investor sentiment theory tries to explain why fund's price rises when an open-ending operation is announced and why discounts are

[h] As De Long, Shleifer *et al.*, model require different clienteles, Lee *et al.* (1991) have assumed that noise traders probably invest more in closed-end funds than in its portfolio's underlying assets.

[i] Several empirical research papers corroborate this fact. See, for example, Weiss (1989), Peavy (1990), Levis and Thomas (1995), among others.

reduced and afterwards eliminated when the open-ending operation happens.[j] As it is known that the fund will be reorganized or liquidated, investors can buy the fund shares and short sell the underlying assets (begin an arbitrage strategy to explore the remainder discount) because that strategy will be certainly lucrative, i.e. the risk of having to sell the fund while the discount is even widen no longer exists. The (small) discount that, eventually, still exists after the announcement of this operation, can be easily explained by the transaction costs of the arbitrage strategy[k] or by some rational explanations of discounts/premiums (e.g. agency costs, tax liabilities on unrealized capital gains, among others), as is pointed out by Lee *et al.* (1991).

The majority of empirical research papers which intend to test this theory applied to closed-end funds discounts/premiums are based on De Long *et al.* model (1990), although, sometimes, they use different econometric methods to test its implications (e.g., Lee *et al.*, 1990; Lee *et al.*, 1991; Abraham, Elan & Marcus, 1993; Brauer, 1993; Chen, Kan & Miller, 1993; Chopra *et al.*, 1993; Hardouvelis *et al.*, 1993; Bordutha *et al.*, 1995; Kramer and Smith, 1995; Frankel and Schmukler, 1996; Elton *et al.*, 1998; Klibanoff *et al.*, 1998, among others). Notice, as well, that most of these papers are anchored in samples of "country funds". This may be due to the fact that these researches were done at the same time as the launch and development of this type of funds.

As far as we know, only Brauer (1993) attempted to measure the relevance of the investor sentiment theory concerning the explanation of the closed-end funds discounts/premiums variability, despite the critics that are done due to the use of "proxies" to identify the presence of noise traders in the market as given by the signal extraction technique of French and Roll (1986). Brown (1999) also tried to identify the presence of noise traders in the closed-end funds' market, but does not show a method to measure the relevance of this to the explanation of the existence and variability of the discounts/premiums.

[j]This fact is supported by, among others, Brauer (1984; 1988), Hardouvelis *et al.* (1993), Cheng *et al.* (1994), Pontiff (1995), Arak and Taylor (1996a; 1996b), Frankel and Schmuckler (1996), Sias (1997a) and, Cheung *et al.* (1997).

[k]An arbitrage strategy is never totally exempted of risk and costless (Lee *et al.*, 1990).

3 The Relevance of the Investor Sentiment Theory, Applying the Defined Methodology for the Effect

3.1 The Methodology of Brauer (1993)

Brauer (1993) developed a methodology which intends to measure the relevance of the investor sentiment to the pricing of closed-end funds and to the explanation of its discounts/premiums variability. This is based on the De Long, Shleifer, Summers and Waldmann model (1990) and the signal extraction technique of French and Roll (1986).

Therefore, considering that the De Long, Shleifer, Summers and Waldmann model (1990) implies that the price return of the closed-end funds shares is subject to an additional source of variation — the change in the noise traders sentiment about the fund price returns in relation to the returns of its portfolio's underlying assets, Brauer (1993) infer a model to predict the standardized variance of the discounts/premiums change in the closed-end funds over time,[1] that is given by the following expression:

$$\hat{\mathrm{Var}}\left(\Delta\tilde{D}_t\right) \cong \frac{\mathrm{Var}\left(\tilde{n}_t\right)}{\left[1+\mathrm{E}\left(\tilde{r}_{P_t}\right)\right]^2}. \tag{2}$$

In that

$\hat{\mathrm{Var}}\left(\Delta\tilde{D}_t\right) \equiv$ Estimated variance of standardized discounts/premiums change, over time.
$\mathrm{Var}\left(\tilde{n}_t\right) \equiv$ Variance of the price return of the fund shares due to "*noise trading*".
$\mathrm{E}\left(\tilde{r}_{P_t}\right) \equiv$ Expected value of NAV returns.

Where the standardized discounts/premiums change over time (a random variable) is given by the expression

$$\Delta\tilde{D}_t = \frac{\Delta\tilde{d}_t}{d_{t-1}+1}. \tag{3}$$

As

$\Delta\tilde{d}_t \equiv$ Discounts/premiums change of the period $t-1$ for the period t (random variable).
$d_{t-1} \equiv$ Discount/premium of the period.

[1]To verify the demonstration of this deduction consult Monte (2000) and Brauer (1993).

The expression (2) is the operational form of the De Long, Shleifer, Summers and Waldmann model (1990) prediction about the variance of discounts changes over time. According to Brauer (1993), the assessment of this approach requires the estimate of two statistics E $(\tilde{r}_{P_t})$ and Var $(\tilde{n}_t)$, for a closed-end fund. Assuming that the fund's NAV is random walk, i.e. it is identical and independently distributed (i.i.d.), then E $(\tilde{r}_{P_t})$ can be estimated by the mean weekly rate of return on the fund's portfolio, which is represented by $\bar{r}_{P_t}$. The estimate of Var $(\tilde{n}_t)$, the variance of the rate of return of the fund's stocks price due to noise trading, can be achieved, according to the author, through the signal extraction technique used by French and Roll (1986).

According to French and Roll (1986), long term returns are less affected by the noise traders sentiment than short term returns because the misevaluation induced by the noise traders activity tends to revert (it is mean reverting) sooner or later. So, if daily returns are independent, the returns for longer holding periods should be equal to the accumulated daily returns within that period. But if daily returns are correlated to each other and across time[m] due to noise traders' activity, subsequently the longer holding periods' variance will be smaller than the variance of cumulated daily returns (French and Roll, 1986).

The French and Roll signal extraction technique[n] that intend to, specifically, identify the fraction of the daily return variance caused by the information, which they represent as V_6, consists in several steps. First, compute the average daily rate of return for each subperiod of two years of the sample (the authors use a total period of 20 years). The second step comprises the sum of the squared deviations around that average. After, under the assumption that the daily returns are serially independent, estimate the implied six-month variance by dividing the sum of the squared deviations by four, since each two year subperiod contains four semesters. Finally, divide the actual variance of six-month return for the subperiod by the implied variance. In order to measure how much the daily return is affected by noise, the assumption of the serial independence will be violated by the presence of negative autocorrelation and the observed six-month variance will be smaller than the cumulated daily variance (Brauer; 1993). French and Roll (1986) determine the lower and upper bound of the relative variance error. The upper

[m] If there is positive autocorrelation among daily returns, then it is not, obviously, independent.

[n] French and Roll (1986) analyzed three possible theories to explain the variance of the daily rate of return of the assets, during normal business hours and out of this schedule: the theory of information, the theory of noise trading and the theory of bid-ask spread. These theories are not mutually exclusive; they could explain together the daily asset prices volatility (French and Roll, 1986).

bound[o] is given by the difference between one and the ratio of six-month variance[p] (the ratio between the variance of the daily information component and the total daily return variance). The lower bound[q] is given by a third of the difference between one and the ratio of the six-month variance plus two-thirds of the first order autocorrelation of the daily return.

When, Brauer (1993), applied this methodology to variance of the discounts/premiums change of the closed-end funds using weekly rates of return of the funds and considering the ratio of the actual-implied six-month variance as representative of the fraction of the weekly return variance due to the incorporation of the information, having represented it as V_6^*. Taking into account that, the De Long, Shleifer, Summers, and Waldmann model (1990) claims that $\tilde{r}_{St} = \tilde{r}_{Pt} + \tilde{n}_t$, where $\tilde{r}_{St}$ is the weekly return of the fund shares prices, as a result, according to Brauer (1993), $\left[\left(1 - V_6^*\right) \text{Var}\left(\tilde{r}_{S_t}\right)\right]$ represents an estimate of $\text{Var}\left(\tilde{n}_t\right)$ for the weekly return. Thus, considering Eq. (2), the estimated variance of the discounts/premiums change is given by

$$\hat{\text{Var}}\left(\Delta\tilde{D}_t\right) \cong \frac{\left(1 - V_6^*\right)}{\left(1 + \bar{r}_{P_t}\right)^2} \text{Var}\left(\tilde{r}_{S_t}\right). \tag{4}$$

3.2 *Additional Delineation of the Research*

Bearing our objective in mind, we will try to explain the existence and persistence of the discounts/premiums in the context of the investor sentiment theory, testing some of its implications in the behavior of closed-end fund discounts/premiums (namely, the correlation among the discounts/premiums across funds and along time, the discounts/premiums and its weekly change mean reversion, as well as its predictive power on the fund share price return and its NAV). It is also our goal to investigate about the relevance of the investor sentiment theory for the explanation of the discounts/premiums variability.

Thus, we design our research in two phases. In the first phase, we start by determining the correlation of the weekly discounts/premiums levels across the funds in the sample, the correlation of the weekly discounts/premiums changes, applying the Pearson correlation coefficient, attempting to test whether the discounts/premiums are positively correlated. Next, we analyze the behavior of the time series of the discounts/premiums levels and

---

[o] Assuming that the variance of bid-ask spread error is null (French and Roll, 1986).
[p] Represent as V_6, as we have already mentioned.
[q] Assuming that the daily return components are serially independent (French and Roll, 1986).

its weekly changes to confirm if these are stationary. For this purpose, we will carry out the classic tests of unit root, i.e. the stationarity tests: Augmented Dickey–Fuller test and Phillips–Perron test on these variables. The number of lags is determined by Akaike Information Criterion (AIC). Finally, in order to test the predictive power of the discounts/premiums,[r] we consider the relationship between the cumulated share price return of the funds and discounts/premiums, as well as the cumulated NAV return of the funds and its discounts/premiums, through the following regressions:

$$\sum_{k=1}^{K} \mathrm{RFND}_{i,t-k} = \alpha^{f}_{i,t} + \beta^{f}_{i,t}\mathrm{DISC}_{i,t} + e^{f}_{i,t}, \tag{5}$$

$$\sum_{k=1}^{K} \mathrm{RVPL}_{i,t-k} = \alpha^{v}_{i,t} + \beta^{v}_{i,t}\mathrm{DISC}_{i,t} + e^{v}_{i,t}, \tag{6}$$

where

$\sum_{k=1}^{K} \mathrm{RFND}_{i,t-k}$ ≡ The cumulated share price returns of the fund i.
$\sum_{k=1}^{K} \mathrm{RVPL}_{i,t-k}$ ≡ The cumulated NAV returns of the fund i.
$\mathrm{DISC}_{i,t}$ ≡ The discount/premium of the fund i, in the period t.
α_i e β_i ≡ The fund-specific intercept and slope coefficients, respectively.
K ≡ The cumulative return horizon of investment (as suggested by Hardouvelis *et al.*, 1993, horizons of one, four, and thirteen weeks are used).

To correct the heteroskedasticity problem we use the method of White (1980) for one week investment horizon of return, and the method of Newey–West (1987), for investment horizons of four and thirteen weeks.[s]

Regarding the underlying advantages of using panel data analysis, in particular to this type of surveys (despite its limitations[t]), which characterize the

[r]Considering that the investor sentiment theory also claims that discounts/premiums contain information concerning future returns.
[s]These methods can be automatically applied when the univariate regression is considered by the least square method, using the statistical package *EViews*. The method of White (1980) presupposes that the residuals of the estimated equation are serially uncorrelated, while Newey–West method (1987) proposes a covariance matrix estimator that is consistent with the presence of both heteroskedasticity and autocorrelation of unknown form. For investment horizons of one period, these methods are identical.
[t]About this subject see, for example, Jorge (1997), Baltagi (1995), Hsiao (1986) and Hausman and Taylor (1981).

phenomenon considering its individual and time-series characteristics, we test as well the predictive power of the discounts/premiums on the fund returns and NAV returns using this technique, as far as we know for the first time in this type of research. We achieve the following procedures: test the homogeneity of the coefficients — to test whether the parameters of the model are homogeneous (across individuals and through the time), covariance analysis and model of error component is used — to test the heterogeneity of the interception and homogeneity of the slope. If it is not rejected, it is still applied the conditional test of the interception homogeneity as the slope is homogeneous, i.e. the Hausman[u] test is applied to determine if we should use the fixed effects model or the random effects model.

After having tested these implications of the investor sentiment theory in the behavior of closed-end funds discounts/premiums (and of its changes), we pass to the second phase of the research where we investigate on the relevance of this theory in the explanation of the discounts/premiums variability. Consequently, we apply the methodology of Brauer (1993) and the signal extraction technique of French and Roll (1986), as follows:

1st step — Calculate the standardized weekly discounts/premiums changes, considering the expression (3), and compute its descriptive statistics as mean, standard deviation, skewness, kurtosis, autocorrelation with lags of one, two, three, and four weeks and the standard error of the 1st order autocorrelation.

2nd step — Determine the mean weekly fund price returns for each two years subperiod of the 12 years sample total period (which represent six subperiods in the total) and the sum of the square deviations around each mean, in each subperiod and for each fund.

3rd step — Estimate the implied six-month variance by dividing the sum of the square deviations by four.[v]

4th step — Compute the actual — implied six-month variance ratio through the division of the actual (observed) six-month variance by the implied six-month variance, as calculated in the previous step.

5th step — Calculate the "great mean" by averaging the actual — implied variance ratio among all the funds, in each period, and divide

[u]See, e.g. Hausman (1978), Hausman and Taylor (1981), Holly (1982), Hsiao (1986), Arellano (1993), and Baltagi (1995).

[v]This is the number of semesters in the two years subperiod.

this by the total number of subperiods (average for period of the implied variance average ratio for fund).

6th step — Compute the estimated standardized weekly discounts/premiums changes variance, regarding expression (4), as V_6^* represents the "great mean", calculated in the previous step; $\bar{r}_{P_t}$ is the weekly mean fund NAV return in the subperiod or period and $\mathrm{Var}(\tilde{r}_{S_t})$ is the variance of the fund shares price return (trade-to-trade) in the subperiod or period.

7th step — Calculate the estimated proportion of the standardized weekly discounts/premiums changes variance explained by the presence of noise traders (and, consequently, for the investor sentiment theory), dividing the estimated variance (calculated in the previous step) by the observed standardized weekly discounts/premiums changes variance in the sample subperiod or period.

To test the robustness of the results, we analyze the relationship between the observed and estimated variance of standardized weekly discounts/premiums changes as well as the relationship between the observed variance of the standardized weekly discounts/premiums changes and the specific-value of $(1 - V_6^*)$ for each fund.[w] The generic linear regression models are, respectively:

$$\mathrm{Var}(\Delta\tilde{D}_t)_{i,t} = \phi_{0i,t} + \phi_{1i,t}\mathrm{Va\hat{r}}(\Delta D_t)_{i,t} + \varepsilon_{i,t} \tag{7}$$

$$\mathrm{Var}(\Delta\tilde{D}_t)_{i,t} = \varphi_{0i,t} + \varphi_{1i,t}\left(1 - V_6^*\right)_{i,t} + \varepsilon_{i,t}, \tag{8}$$

where

$\mathrm{Var}(\Delta\tilde{D}_t)_{\mathrm{i,t}}$ ≡ Actual variance of the standardized weekly discounts/premiums changes.

$\mathrm{Va\hat{r}}(\Delta D_t)_{i,t}$ ≡ Estimated variance of the standardized weekly discounts/premiums changes.

$(1 - V_6^*)_{i,t}$ ≡ Proportion of the variance of the shares price return of the fund attributed to the noise trading, specific to each fund.

$\phi_{0rmi,t}; \phi_{1i,t}$ e $\varphi_{0i,t}; \varphi_{1i,t}$ ≡ Linear regression coefficients.

$\varepsilon_{i,t}$ ≡ Random error.

We use panel data analysis to improve the resulting information of these linear regressions (as best of our knowledge for the first time for this effect).

[w]This value represents the proportion of the fund shares return variance due to the noise trading (as it was estimated by the signal extraction technique of French and Roll, 1986), i.e. the portion of the variance that is not attributable to the information.

4 Description of the Sample and Definition of the Variables

The data was obtained from Wiesenberger closed-end funds database, which we selected a sample of 41 closed-end investment funds traded in the New York Stock Exchange (NYSE) and/or in the American Stock Exchange (AMEX), that invest mainly in North American, specialized or diversified stocks and/or bonds — excluding the "country funds" and the "municipal bonds funds", during the period 2 January, 1987–18 June, 1999 (inclusive), with a minimum of 104 observations. The fund to be included should have a report of, at least, two years of publication either of its quotations (price of the fund) or of its NAV. Nonetheless, it is not a primordial feature for this research, as we have no intention of evaluating the performance of these funds, the selected sample does not suffer of the survivorship bias problem because the sample has funds that stopped existing during the sample period and others that started in the meantime.

In Table A.1, we list the funds contained in the sample. With reference to the empirical research done by other authors, namely Brauer (1984) and Peavy (1990), we made two adjustments in the time-series of the sample. Hence, the first 24 observations were not considered (equivalent to six months) after the date of IPO of the fund because, as Peavy (1990) claims, discounts tend to increase in the weeks after the fund IPO which could cause a bias in the results. On the other hand, we did not include those observations of the six months previous to the open-ending operation date because discounts tend to decrease during the period previous to the open-ending operation announcement, as supported by Brauer (1984) research.[x] The number of observations in Table A.1, is relative to the effective number of observations, previously corrected by these adjustments.

The variables in study are defined like this:

$RFND_t$ — The price return of the fund shares, in continuous capitalization that is calculated as: $RFND_t = \ln[P_t + D_t] - \ln[P_{t-1}]$,
where

$P_t \equiv$ fund Price, at the end of the week t (closing price)
$D_t \equiv$ total dividend distributed by the fund at the end of the week t ($=$ distribution of income and capital gains)

$RVPL_t$ — NAV returns of the fund, in continuous capitalization, specified as: $RVPL_t = \ln[V_t + D_t] - \ln[V_{t-1}]$,

[x]Thus, some funds lost some observations due to these adjustments.

where

$V_t \equiv$ net asset value, at the end of the week t;
$D_t \equiv$ total dividend distributed by the assets that composes the fund portfolio, at the end of the week t.

The cumulated return, for four and 13 weeks, either for fund return or its net asset value, is calculated by the sum of the weekly return to the proposed cumulated investment horizon.

DISC_t — Discount/premium, in percentage:

$$\text{DISC}_t = \frac{P_t - V_t}{V_t} \times 100$$

$\Delta\text{DISC}_{i,t+1}$ — Discount/premium change, which is given as: $\Delta\text{DISC}_{i,t} = \text{DISC}_{i,t} - \text{DISC}_{i,t-1}$

Although we do not plan to analyze the results in this section, we think that is important to emphasize (see Table A.2) that discounts/premiums vary over this period. The higher mean discount was at 1988 (−8.45%) and the higher premium in 1992 (0.44%).

5 The Results and Their Analysis

5.1 The Discounts/Premiums Correlation

One of the assumptions of the investor sentiment theory, applied to the closed-end funds discounts/premiums, claims that discounts/premiums are positively correlated among them (Lee *et al.*, 1990). Therefore, we test the null hypothesis that the closed-end funds discounts/premiums are not correlated, using the Pearson coefficient of determination.

We have confirmed that more than half (71%) of the correlation coefficients are positive (see Table A.3), and about 88% of these are statistically significant. As a consequence, this is suggestive that the closed-end funds discounts/premiums are correlated to each other and they tend to move together. The same result is found in relation to the weekly discounts/premiums change.[y]

These results are consistent with the results of Lee *et al.* (1991) as well as Cheung *et al.* (1997). Since these results seem to confirm one of the implications of the investor sentiment theory which predicts that closed-end

[y]The results of these tests can be requested to the authors.

funds discounts/premiums (and discounts/premiums change) are driven by the investor sentiment, and so they are likely to vary together.

5.2 The Stationarity of the Discounts/Premiums

The stationarity analysis becomes important because if the discounts/premiums reflect the investor sentiment, since, concerning the investor sentiment theory, the sentiment is mean reverting, then the discounts/premiums should be mean reverting as well. The hypothesis of unit root of the discounts/premiums level as well as weekly discounts/premiums change is tested applying the classic tests of Augmented Dickey–Fuller (ADF) and Phillips–Perron (PP) test,[z] integrated in the EViews package.[aa]

By ADF test (see Table A.4), at a significance level of 5% or 10% , it is not possible to conclude whether the discounts/premiums tend to be stationary or not. By PP test, at a significance level of 5% , or even 10% , the hypothesis that the proportion of funds with non-stationary discount/premium is 50% is rejected, which shows that discounts/premiums seems to be stationary.

It is even found that the series of the weekly discounts/premiums change are stationary for most of the funds.[ab]

5.3 The Predictive Power of the Discounts/Premiums on the Net Asset Value Return and of the Share Price Return of the Funds

The discounts/premiums mean reversion implies that the actual discount/premium should contain information on future discount/premium and, consequently, we can estimate future returns. As the discounts/premiums change reflect, roughly, the difference between the funds return and its underlying assets returns,[ac] the discounts/premiums will be correlated whether with the fund share price returns (hereafter fund return, for simplicity), or with its NAV return.

[z]Once the graphic representation of the series of the variable discounts level was not very clear with relationship to its behavior and as no economics reasons seems to exist that justify the inclusion of the tendency in the closed-end funds, we had just considered the test regression with constant.

[aa]The ADF test is not very powerful, as Stwart and Gill (1998:239) as well as Pindyck and Rubinfeld (1998:51) say, that is why its capacity to detect the absence of unit roots, when it does not exist, is reduced. It just allows us to reject the hypothesis that the variable is not random walk.

[ab]In the stationarity analysis, we have applied, in the same way, the two classic tests, the ADF test and the PP test whose results can be requested to the authors.

[ac]Mainly if we consider that the distribution of dividends is not very significant.

To study the discounts/premiums predictive power on future fund return as well as of its NAV, we used panel data analysis and we have computed cumulated returns for investment horizons of one, four, and 13 weeks, as it is suggested by Hardouvelis *et al.* (1993:18). So, as to test the homogeneity of the regression coefficients, we estimated regressions (5) and (6), as defined in the Sec. 3.2, resulting from there the appropriate Covariance model.

Analyzing Table A.5, it is shown that, in most cases, and for any investment horizon (K), closed-end funds discounts/premiums are positively correlated with fund return, that is, an increase in the discount/premium level compel to a consequent increase in the fund return. As K enlarges, β_i^f increases, this is statistically significant for more than 50% of the funds, at a significance level of 5% .

These results corroborate other empirical research on this subject (e.g. Hardouvelis *et al.*, 1993:19) and imply that closed-end funds discounts/premiums might predict fund returns, as investor sentiment is a component of the fund price, corroborating the hypothesis that discounts/premiums are positively correlated with the fund return.

The discounts/premiums have less predictive power on NAV returns. Although, the majority of the closed-end funds discounts/premiums are negatively correlated with the cumulated NAV return (see Table A.6), only some funds present β_i^v negative and statistically significant, as a consequence, occasionally, closed-end funds discounts/premiums contain information on the future NAV return.

The fact that discounts/premiums have some predictive power on fund return but less obvious on NAV return can be justified, in part, by the difference of clienteles that invest in the closed-end funds and in its underlying assets. The majority of closed-end funds are traded by small investors — noise traders — while funds' underlying assets can be traded by institutional investors (more informed and that act in a more "rational way"), reducing the weight of the noise traders on these assets (Lee *et al.*, 1991). Accordingly, the influence of the noise traders on the fund's portfolio price is less significant, in that case the discounts/premiums have little predictive power on the NAV return.

Next, we impose the condition of total homogeneity of the coefficients (whether of the interception or the slope). Those regressions constitute the Simple model. This hypothesis is rejected, at any significance level and investment horizon considered — see Table A.7. So, we try to investigate if the heterogeneity of the coefficients can be attributed to the slope or to the interception, testing the hypothesis H_2: the homogeneity of the slope and the heterogeneity of the interception (the slope is common but the interception is variable). Therefore, we estimate the Intra-individuals model. As it is shown in Table A.7, the F_2 test is not significant which is not possible to reject H_2. Then, we want to know if the heterogeneity is coming of the interception, testing H_3: the interception is homogeneous as the slope. At any significance level, H_3 is rejected, as a consequence, the interception is heterogeneous even the slope is homogeneous (see Table A.7).

In this manner, we should use the fixed effects model as regression model to represent the predictive power of the discounts/premiums on the cumulated fund return as well as its NAV returns (see Table A.8). Those models show that discounts/premiums have some predictive power on the (future) funds return as well as on its NAV return given that the slope is statistically significant in both cases.

5.4 The Investor Sentiment Theory as Explanatory Factor of the Discounts/Premiums Variance

After having tested some of the implications of the investor sentiment theory, namely, the positive correlation among the discounts/premiums (the discounts/premiums covariance), the discounts/premiums stationarity and the discounts/premiums predictive power on fund return or on NAV return, it is intended to test now the relevance of this theory in the explanation of the existence and persistence of the discounts/premiums, assuming that it explains a part of the discounts/premiums variance.

For this study, we analyzed the period from 2/01/1987 to 31/12/1998 and we only included funds in which the difference between the number of observations of the time series of the fund return and the ones of the NAV return is less than 1% of the total observations. So, we eliminated in these series the observations that are not synchronized.[ad] We impose these limitations since the Brauer (1993) methodology as well as the French and Roll (1986) technique imply that identical number of observations is used in the fund return as of NAV return.

Considering the expression (3), the standardized discounts/premiums change is computed and its mean, standard deviation, skewness, kurtosis, autocorrelation with lags of one, two, three, and four weeks as

[ad]As a result, the following funds are eliminated from the initial sample of 41 funds: ALM, CET, CIM, CNN, CTF, EGX, EIS, FT, HU, IIS, JHI, MRF, PEO, RIF, and VIN.

well as the standard error of the 1st order autocorrelation[ae] are calculated. Notice that all funds of the sample have negatives 1st order autocorrelation coefficients,[af] which is consistent with the results of Brauer (1993) and Bonser-Neal *et al.* (1990). According to these authors, given a negative 1st order autocorrelation coefficient of weekly discounts/premiums change this is an indicator of the presence of noise traders, like French and Roll (1986; 15) say.[ag]

Afterwards, we calculate the "great mean"—V_6^*, which result was of 0.929, what means that, according to the signal extraction technique of French and Roll, 92.9% of the closed-end fund shares rate of return variance is due to the rational answer of the investors to the information emitted for the market and 7.1% of that variance is just due to the noise. For this reason, a small portion of the fund shares variance can just be explained by the investors' irrational behavior and, as consequence, investor sentiment is likely to have low significant weight in the mispricing of the assets. Our results are slightly superior to the Brauer (1993) results which was $V_6^* = 0.947$ and the portion of the return variance explained by the noise of 5.3% .

At last, we calculate the estimated — observed weekly standardized discounts/premiums change variance ratio. The estimated weekly standardized discounts/premiums change variance is calculated by the expression (4), having used the ratio between the weekly mean fund NAV return and the fund shares return variance. These results are summarized in Table A.9. The first value of this table corresponds to the estimated variance in relation to observed weekly standardized discounts/premiums change variance ratio. The second value corresponds to the number of observations used in the calculation of the previous ratio, for each fund and in each period. The last two lines of this table correspond, respectively, to the weighed average of the estimated to observed variance ratio, weighed by the number of observations in each period, for all the funds and to the number of total observations of the period.

[ae]These results can be obtained directly by the authors.

[af]According to Brauer (1993) and Bonser-Neal *et al.* (1990), the negative 1st order autocorrelation in the weekly discounts/premiums is due to the nonsynchronous trading between fund stocks and their respective underlying assets, above all to the smallest trade frequency of the closed-end funds stocks.

[ag]In agreement with the investor sentiment theory (under the hypothesis of presence of noise traders), fund shares returns should be autocorrelated, while its pricing errors would be corrected in long run, as these corrections would generate negative autocorrelations (French and Roll, 1986:15). On the other hand, according to these authors, due to the fact that each closing trade may be executed at any price within the bid/ask spread, the negative 1st order autocorrelation can be induced by this type of mispricing, mainly if these measurement errors are independent from day to day.

Taking the last value of the ratio in Table A.9, corresponding to the total period analyzed, the percentage of the observed weekly standardized discounts/premiums change variance over time, explained by the investor sentiment theory, for all the funds in the sample is around 8.55%, slightly superior to the 6.77% achieved by Brauer (1993:211).

Dividing the total period in study in three subperiods (1987–1990, 1991–1994, and 1995–1998), the period from 1987 to 1990 was the one that showed the largest percentage (9.65% , approximately) of the observed weekly standardized discounts/premiums change variance, explained by the investor sentiment theory. Analyzing fund to fund, it is shown that the model can explain, in the best of hypotheses, about 12% of the weekly standardized discounts/premiums change variance of the funds ADX, GAB, SBF, and TY. The remaining funds present equal or lower percentages than 11.5% , having found the smallest percentage in the case of the fund BKT (5.69%), in the period from 1987 to 1998. Analyzing by subperiod, and across funds, it is realized that the model allows the explanation, at the most, around 15% of the weekly standardized discounts/premiums change variance of the fund GAB, in 1987–1990. But in the period of 1991–1994, the highest percentage that the model can explain is only 10.8% , approximately (for the case of the fund TY).

These results suggest that, although the presence of noise traders in the closed-end funds sector can influence and justify the discounts/premiums existence, no more than 9%, roughly, of the variance of the discounts/premiums changes would be explained by presence of noise traders. Like Brauer (1993), we cannot confirm that the investor sentiment has a lot of relevance on the explanation of the discounts/premiums variability.

Using the panel of observations connected with the 26 funds in the sample, during the three subperiods in that the time horizon was distributed (1987–1990, 1991–1994, and 1995–1998), we test the robustness of our results. Consequently, we analyze the relationship between the observed standardized discounts/premiums weekly change variance and the estimated one, set out of the generic linear regression model (7) as defined in Sec. 3.2. Based on the generic linear regression model (8), we analyze the relationship between the standardized discounts/premiums weekly change variance (observed) and the specific value of each fund $(1 - V_6^*)$ — the portion of the fund return variance that is not caused by the information.

In first place, we have estimated the simple linear regression model, i.e. that with both homogeneous coefficients (whether the interception or the slope are not variable with the time and of fund to fund). After that, we have estimated the specific linear regressions to each fund, which constitute the covariance model.[ah]

Taking the sum of the squares of the residuals of each model, we have tested H_1: total homogeneity of the coefficients. Consistent with the statistics of F_1 test, in both situations, we reject the null hypothesis since F_1 is significant, at a significance level of at least 1.5% — see Table A.10. Hence, we have tested the hypothesis H_2: homogeneity of the slope and heterogeneity of the interception. Therefore, we have considered the fixed effects model. The results of the F_2 test do not allow us, in both situations, to reject the null hypothesis H_2. Like so, we carry out the conditional test of hypothesis H_3: interception homogeneity given the homogeneity of the slope. In this case, for the first situation, the hypothesis is rejected, at a significance level of fence 3.5%, and for the second situation the hypothesis is not rejected, at a significance level of at least 10%.

Thus, the model of fixed effects, according to the results of the tests, is the most suitable to specify the relationship between the observed weekly standardized discounts/premiums change variance and the estimated one — see Table A.11. The pooled regression or the simple model is, in accordance with the results of the tests, the most suitable to specify the relationship between the observed weekly standardized discounts/premiums change variance and the specific value of each fund $(1 - V_6^*)$ — see Table A.11.

Analyzing the relationship between the observed weekly standardized discounts/premiums change variance and the estimated one, the results suggest that, on average, funds with larger estimated standardized discounts/premiums weekly change variance might have larger observed variance. This correlation is statistically significant. The high R_2 (determination coefficient), in addition to the significant coefficient, suggest that the ratio between both variances tends to be quite stable from fund to fund and over the time. Only about 9.1% of the observed variance is not explained by the implied variance.[ai] Even the high coefficient of determination, we cannot infer that noise trading explains a substantial portion of the weekly standardized discounts/premiums change

[ah]These procedures were followed in the two situations in study.

[ai]If the ratio between the estimated variance and the observed variance of weekly standardized discounts/premiums change variance is exactly 8.55% to all the funds, the regression slope would be the inverse, that is to say, 11.696 with t-statistical infinite and the determination coefficient would be equal to one.

variance of the funds. Considering that the approximate expression (4) is used to determine the estimated weekly standardized discounts/premiums change variance and we use the same value V_6^* for all funds, these results reflect strong correlation between the observed weekly standardized discounts/premiums change variance and the variance of the fund weekly return, which suggest that funds with more volatile share prices also have larger discounts/premiums variability.

In relation to the second relationship, it was verified, in average, that funds with higher proportion of return variance explained by the presence of noise traders is likely to have higher observed weekly standardized discounts/premiums change variance. But this positive correlation is not statistically significant and the determination coefficient ($R_2 = 1.65\%$) is not very high. However, our results do not diverge from those achieved by Brauer (1993). His coefficients are not significantly positive, as well. Even so, his coefficient of determination is slightly superior — around 5%. We believe that these results match with the relative low relevance of the investor sentiment theory, in quantitative terms, on the explanation of the variability of the discounts/premiums as they demonstrate such a low explanatory power.

The results of these linear regressions corroborate those previously achieved. subsequently, the proportion of the weekly discounts/premiums change variance as explained by the presence of noise traders is small, so the investor sentiment theory, although can have some explanatory power in relation to both the persistence and existence of the closed-end funds discounts/premiums (our study confirmed the regularity of some of its implications as predicted by the theory), it scarcely can explain a small part of this "puzzle".

6 Conclusions and Suggestions for Future Research

This research is based on the investor sentiment theory as conceptual framework to explain the existence and persistence of the discounts/premiums, because we believe it to be the most extensive one, i.e. which theoretically explains the facts "*sui generis*" related to the behavior of the closed-end funds discounts/premiums, explaining not only the persistence of the discounts/premiums, but also, the reason for, at certain times, funds being traded at premium.

Moreover we tested some implications of this theory regarding discounts/premiums behavior (its correlation, stationarity and if they contain information about the fund future return and/or its NAV returns). We tried to confirm, as well, if this theory is relevant to the explanation of the discounts/premiums variability (there is little research on this). Most of the research papers published till the moment were only focused on finding empirical evidence concerning the investor sentiment theory in the explanation of the discounts/premiums existence and persistence, testing some implications of De Long, Shleifer, Summers and Waldmann model (1990) in the discounts/premiums behavior. Only Brauer (1993) tried to measure its relevance. Still to be pointed out to test the discounts/premiums predictive power we have used panel data analysis, which still have not been applied by the published researches up to the moment, as best of our knowledge.

The results presented in the previous sections allow us to confirm some of the investor sentiment theory underlying implications concerning to the discounts/premiums behavior, requiring that noise traders are present in the closed-end funds market. However, when we analyze the relevance of this theory to the explanation of the weekly standardized discounts/premiums change variance, we verify that the investor sentiment theory can only explain 8.6% of that variance. This result is confirmed by the panel data analysis. We have analyzed the linear correlation between the observed weekly standardized discounts/premiums change variance and the estimated variance as well as between the observed variance and the proportion of the fund return variance explained by the noise trading. Like Brauer's (1993) study, we do not find empirical evidence that allows us to announce, definitely, that investor sentiment theory explains great part of the discounts/premiums variance (regardless of our results being slightly more optimistic).

Though, this research presents as main limitation the fact of using a methodology, so-called indirect, to determine the influence of the noise traders in the discounts/premiums variance, which is based on the ratio of the implied to observed fund return variance as indicator of the investor sentiment, resulting from this, as it is evident, deviations in relation to what would be expected. The fact that the results were not very satisfactory regarding what would be expected might have to do with the limitation of the applied methodology,[aj] even though we found some evidence that noise traders are present in this market. These results also imply that there must be other

[aj] No one can deny, taking into consideration the results obtained in the present study and in other researches (e.g. Neal and Wheatley 1998; Elton *et al.*, 1998; Frankel and Schmukler 1996; Hardouvelis *et al.*, 1993; Brauer, 1993; Chen *et al.*, 1993; Chopra *et al.*, 1993; Lee *et al.*, 1990; 1991, among others) that noise traders are in the market and they influence it, increasing prices volatility (e.g. Brown, 1999).

factors that joint with the one now analyzed will better explain this puzzle. One of those factors may be related with limits of arbitrage and the performance of the arbitrageurs. Shleifer and Vishny (1997) postulate that there are limitations to the arbitrage (such as, transaction costs, financial restrictions, agency costs, among other) that difficult the arbitrageurs activity. This inhibits them of implementing perfect strategies and, as a consequence, the quick adjustment of the market prices is not verified. Such limits might allow that the irrational investors affect fund prices for more time than desired. As the discounts/premiums persist, it would be interesting to study why the arbitrageurs are notable to implement with total success its strategies as well as if they are really present in the closed-end funds market. It would still be important to study if there is a relationship between the arbitrageurs "impotence" in leading to converge the fund prices to NAV (that may be one of the reasons of the closed-end funds discounts/premiums persistence) and the investor sentiment.

Also to be noticed that the studies that, up to the moment, were disclosed concentrate the attention in a restricted group of factors, studying them a lot of times in an isolated way, and they rarely make the study with the combination of several and different factors, above all the factors of rational nature with non-rational ones — said behavioral factors. Future developments might try to find methodologies that combine these two factor types, namely the investor sentiment theory and the limits of arbitrage, as explanation of the discounts/premiums. Another investigation path will be to analyze the investor sentiment comparing to the investors' appetence[ak] for open-end investment funds (potentials competitors of the closed-end funds) with the time that new funds are placed on the market, and the evolution of the seasoned one (namely the behavior of its discounts/premiums) since it has been verified that new funds, that try to offer different investment policy (objectives) from the seasoned one, appeared when the other closed-end funds were at premium or at reduced discount.

[ak]The investors' appetence for open-end funds (the demand for open-end funds) may be measured by the liquid acquisition of participation units — the difference between the number of acquired units and redeemed units.

Appendix

Table A.1: Funds contained in the sample.

Fund name	TICKER	IPO date	Sample period	No. Obs.
Adams express company	ADX	01/10/29	2.01.1987–18.06.1999	650
Allmerica securities trust	ALM	28/02/73	2.01.1987–18.06.1999	650
ACM managed income fund	AMF	03/10/88	4.11.1988–18.06.1999	531
Bergstrom capital corporation	BEM	25/04/68	2.01.1987–18.06.1999	650
Baker fentress & company	BKF	01/01/71	2.01.1987–18.06.1999	650
BlackRock income trust	BKT	29/07/88	5.08.1988–18.06.1999	543
Blue chip value fund	BLU	02/04/87	1.05.1987–18.06.1999	609
Central securities	CET	01/10/29	2.01.1987–18.06.1999	650
CIM high yield securities	CIM	18/11/87	4.12.1987–18.06.1999	580
Clemente global growth fund	CLM	01/07/87	31.07.1987–8.06.1999	596
CNA income shares	CNN	15/05/73	2.01.1987–18.06.1999	650
Counsellors tandem securities fund	CTF	01/10/86	2.01.1987–15.11.1996	641
Duff & Phelps utilities income	DNP	28/01/87	6.02.1987–18.06.1999	621
Engex	EGX	20/11/68	2.10.1987–18.06.1999	612
Excelsior income shares	EIS	30/05/73	2.01.1987–18.06.1999	651
Franklin universal trust	FT	23/09/88	30.09.1988–8.06.1999	534
Gabelli equity trust	GAB	14/08/86	2.01.1987–18.06.1999	650
General American investors	GAM	30/01/27	2.01.1987–18.06.1999	650
Templeton global income Fd	GIM	24/03/88	1.04.1988–18.06.1999	561
CIGNA high income shares	HIS	10/08/88	2.09.1988–18.06.1999	539
Hampton utilities trust	HU	08/03/88	1.04.1988–5.08.1994	307
Morg Stan D Witter income sec	ICB	06/04/73	2.01.1987–18.06.1999	650
CIGNA investment securities	IIS	24/01/73	2.01.1987–18.06.1999	650
John Hancock investors trust	JHI	29/01/71	2.01.1987–18.06.1999	650
Scudder global high income fund	LBF	31/07/92	31.07.1992–8.06.1999	335
Mentor income fund	MRF	30/12/88	6.01.1989–18.06.1999	521
Putnam dividend income fund	PDI	21/09/89	6.01.1989–18.06.1999	482
Petroleum and resources corp.	PEO	30/01/29	2.01.1987–18.06.1999	650
Pacholder fund	PHF	23/11/88	2.012.1988–8.06.1999	526
Putnam master income trust	PMT	28/12/87	1.01.1988–18.06.1999	574
Pilgrim prime rate trust	PPR	12/05/88	3.04.1992–18.06.1999	377
Cohen & Steers realty income fund	RIF	23/08/88	20.09.1988–8.06.1999	539
Salomon Brothers fund	SBF	24/09/29	2.01.1987–18.06.1999	650
Source capital	SOR	24/10/68	2.01.1987–8.06.1999	650
Tuxis corporation	TUX	08/11/96	6.12.1996–25.12.1998	83
Tri-continental corporation	TY	31/12/29	2.01.1987–18.06.1999	650
Liberty all-star equity fund	USA	24/10/86	2.01.1987–18.06.1999	638
Vestaur securities	VES	30/11/72	2.01.1987–18.06.1999	650
Van Kampen income trust	VIN	21/04/88	20.03.1987–8.06.1999	556
Zweig fund	ZF	03/10/86	2.01.1987–18.06.1999	640
Zenix income fund	ZIF	27/04/88	6.05.1988–18.06.1999	556
Zweig total return fund	ZTR	22/09/88	4.11.1988–18.06.1999	530

Table A.2: Characterization of the sample to the "fund discount/premium" variable, during the period 2/01/1987–18/06/1999.

Year	Mean	Stdev	Max	Min	No obs.	No of funds
1987	−5.98	9.63	17.25	−43.82	1048	23
1988	−8.45	10.40	14.75	−35.95	1374	30
1989	−6.51	10.04	17.92	−32.82	1855	38
1990	−7.09	9.08	20.52	−28.29	2005	39
1991	−4.02	8.78	28.21	−30.42	2026	39
1992	0.44	9.62	29.32	−27.91	2062	40
1993	−0.24	9.38	32.40	−26.58	2121	41
1994	−3.49	9.99	22.02	−31.73	2087	41
1995	−6.22	9.36	18.10	−31.97	2080	40
1996	−6.57	9.28	16.08	−31.02	2074	40
1997	−5.31	9.87	23.63	−34.05	2028	39
1998	−3.60	9.39	52.44	−28.50	2028	39
1999	−5.10	10.02	28.16	−27.48	975	39
Total	−4.58	9.90	52.44	−43.82	23763	41

Table A.3: Correlation between weekly discount/premium level (in %) of the closed-end funds.

	Weekly Discounts/Premiums		
	Pearson Correlation Coefficient		
	Mean	Maximum	Minimum
Weekly Discounts/premiums	0.188	0.878	−0.767
	Frequency of the coefficient signal		
	Positive	Negative	Total
	583	237	820
	(514)	(181)	(695)

Note: The values in parenthesis correspond to the number of Pearson correlation coefficients significant for a level of 5% (bilateral).

Table A.4: Synthesis of the tests results of the unit root tests in the discount/premium variable of the closed-end investment funds.

Test	N.S.[1]	No of funds that				ET[2]	
		Reject Ho		Do not reject Ho			*p*-value
	1%	10	(24%)	31	(76%)	3.2796	(0.0005)
ADF	5%	14	(34%)	27	(66%)	2.0303	(0.0212)
	10%	21	(51%)	20	(49%)	−0.1562	(0.5621)
	1%	19	(46%)	22	(54%)	−0.4685	(0.3197)
PP	5%	26	(63%)	15	(37%)	1.7179	(0.0429)
	10%	32	(78%)	9	(22%)	3.5920	(0.0002)

Note:
[1] Significance level.
[2] Z Test — test to the binomial proportion, for a sample of great dimension, considering the null hypothesis that the number of non-stationary funds is 50% .

Table A.5: Statistics — summary of the predictive power of the discounts/premiums on the fund return (accumulated).

No of funds with	$N = 1$				$N = 4$				$N = 13$			
	Freq.	%	ET[1]	p-value	Freq.	%	ET[1]	p-value	Freq.	%	ET[1]	p-value
$\beta_i > 0$	40	97.6	13.9944	0.00000	35	85.4	11.7002	0.00000	33	80.5	10.7825	0.00000
$\beta_i \leq 0$	1	2.4	−3.9001	0.99995	6	14.6	−1.6059	0.94585	8	19.5	−0.6882	0.75435
β_i significant												
10%	29	72.5	8.9472	0.00000	22	55.0	5.7354	0.00000	26	65.0	7.5707	0.00000
5%	26	65.0	7.5707	0.00000	16	40.0	2.9824	0.00143	23	57.5	6.1942	0.00000
1%	19	47.5	4.3589	0.00001	7	17.5	−1.1471	0.87433	14	35.0	2.0647	0.01947
$\beta_i > 0$ and significant												
10%	12	30.0	1.1471	0.12567	19	47.5	4.3589	0.00001	18	45.0	3.9001	0.00005
5%	15	37.5	2.5236	0.00581	24	60.0	6.6531	0.00000	21	52.5	5.2766	0.00000
1%	21	52.5	5.2766	0.00000	33	82.5	10.7825	0.00000	26	65.0	7.5707	0.00000

Note: [1]ET — test statistics: Z test to the binomial proportion of a sample of great dimension and the respective test value (p-value).

Table A.6: Statistics — summary of the predictive power of the discounts/premiums on the NAV return (accumulated).

No of funds with	$N = 1$				$N = 4$				$N = 13$			
	Freq.	%	ET[1]	p-value	Freq.	%	ET[1]	p-value	Freq.	%	ET[1]	p-value
$\beta_i < 0$	34	82.9	4.2167	0.00001	24	58.5	1.0932	0.13715	20	48.8	−0.1562	0.56205
$\beta_i \geq 0$	7	17.1	−4.2167	0.99999	17	41.5	−1.0932	0.86285	21	51.2	0.1562	0.43795
β_i significant												
10%	18	43.9	−0.7809	0.78256	7	17.1	−4.2167	0.99999	14	34.1	−2.0303	0.97883
5%	16	39.0	−1.4056	0.92007	3	7.3	−5.4661	1.00000	10	24.4	−3.2796	0.99948
1%	13	31.7	−2.3426	0.99043	1	2.4	−6.0908	1.00000	2	4.9	−5.7784	1.00000
$\beta_i > 0$ and significant												
10%	18	43.9	−0.7809	0.78256	4	9.8	−5.1537	1.00000	11	26.8	−2.9673	0.99850
5%	17	41.5	−1.0932	0.86285	2	4.9	−5.7784	1.00000	7	17.1	−4.2167	0.99999
1%	13	31.7	−2.3426	0.99043	1	2.4	−6.0908	1.00000	2	4.9	−5.7784	1.00000

Note: [1]ET- test statistics: Z test to the binomial proportion of a sample of great dimension and the respective test value (p-value).

Table A.7: Summary of the results of the panel data analysis — hypothesis tests.

		A	B
$H_1 : \alpha_1 = \alpha_2 = \cdots = \alpha_N \wedge \beta_1 = \beta_2 = \cdots = \beta_N$			
$K = 1$	F_1	127.92	117.03
	(p-value)	(0.00)	(0.00)
$K = 4$	F_1	125.52	111.96
	(p-value)	(0.00)	(0.00)
$K = 13$	F_1	119.60	75.22
	(p-value)	(0.00)	(0.00)
$H_2 : \alpha_1 \neq \alpha_2 \neq \cdots \neq \alpha_N \wedge \beta_1 = \beta_2 = \cdots = \beta_N$			
$K = 1$	F_2	−2.20	−1.34
	(p-value)		
$K = 4$	F_2	−2.30	−3.22
	(p-value)		
$K = 13$	F_2	−4.32	−6.04
	(p-value)		
$H_3 : \alpha_1 = \alpha_2 = \cdots = \alpha_N \wedge \beta_1 = \beta_2 = \cdots = \beta_N$			
$K = 1$	F_3	260.34	236.88
	(p-value)	(0.00)	(0.00)
$K = 4$	F_3	255.69	229.75
	(p-value)	(0.00)	(0.00)
$K = 13$	F_3	247.26	159.60
	(p-value)	(0.00)	(0.00)

Note: A — About fund return; B — About NAV return.
Being the test statistics given by:

$$F_1 = \frac{(\mathrm{SSR}_{MS} - \mathrm{SSR}_{MC})/(N-1)(M+1)}{\mathrm{SSR}_{MC}/NT - N(M+1)},$$

$$F_2 = \frac{(\mathrm{SSR}_{MI} - \mathrm{SSR}_{MC})/M(N-1)}{\mathrm{SSR}_{MC}/NT - N(M+1)},$$

$$F_3 = \frac{(\mathrm{SSR}_{MS} - \mathrm{SSR}_{MI})/(N-1)}{\mathrm{SSR}_{MI}/(NT - N - M)},$$

where

$\mathrm{SSR}_{MC} \equiv$ Residual sum of squares of the covariance model.
$\mathrm{SSR}_{MS} \equiv$ Residual sum of squares of the simple model.
$\mathrm{SSR}_{MS} \equiv$ Residual sum of squares of the intra-individuals model

$N \equiv$ number of funds in the sample;
$M \equiv$ number of the explanatory variables;
$NT \equiv$ number of panel totals observations.

Table A.8: Fixed effects model (homogeneity of the slope and heterogeneity of the interception).

	About fund return	About NAV return
$K = 1$	$\sum_{k=1}^{K} \text{RFND}_{i,t-k} = \alpha_i^f + 0.0299\ \text{DISC}_{i,t}$ (7.6129) [0.0000]; $R_a^2 = 0.0069$	$\sum_{k=1}^{K} \text{RVPL}_{i,t-k} = \alpha_i^v - 0.0178\ \text{DISC}_{i,t}$ (−6.5975) [0.0000]; $R_a^2 = 0.0063$
$K = 4$	$\sum_{k=1}^{K} \text{RFND}_{i,t-k} = \alpha_i^f + 0.0378\ \text{DISC}_{i,t}$ (4.7902) [0.0000]; $R_a^2 = 0.0053$	$\sum_{k=1}^{K} \text{RVPL}_{i,t-k} = \alpha_i^v - 0.0274\ \text{DISC}_{i,t}$ (−4.1217) [0.0000]; $R_a^2 = 0.0120$
$K = 13$	$\sum_{k=1}^{K} \text{RFND}_{i,t-k} = \alpha_i^f + 0.0581\ \text{DISC}_{i,t}$ (4.0243) [0.0001]; $R_a^2 = 0.0108$	$\sum_{k=1}^{K} \text{RVPL}_{i,t-k} = \alpha_i^v - 0.1004\ \text{DISC}_{i,t}$ (−7.5505) [0.0000]; $R_a^2 = 0.0280$

Note: α_i^f e α_i^v, represents the interception coefficient of the model, is variable from fund to fund. The value among curved parenthesis corresponds to the *t*-statistical of the coefficient and the right parenthesis to its *p*-value.

Table A.9: The estimated proportion (ratio) of the estimated variance in relation to observed weekly standardized discounts/premiums change variance of the closed-end investment funds, for the period of 2/1/1987–31/12/1998.

Funds	1987–1990	1991–1994	1995–1998	1987–1998
ADX	0.1190	0.0806	0.1754	0.1187
	206	205	208	619
AMF	0.0747	0.0649	0.0635	0.0675
	88	209	208	505
BEM	0.0714	0.0710	0.0639	0.0698
	206	209	208	623
BKF	0.1308	0.0679	0.0903	0.0984
	208	209	208	625
BKT	0.0336	0.0708	0.0694	0.0569
	100	209	208	517
BLU	0.0934	0.0732	0.0684	0.0798
	164	209	208	581
CLM	0.0775	0.0726	0.1268	0.0915
	153	207	208	568
DNP	0.0775	0.0842	0.0550	0.0717
	176	207	208	591

(*Continued*)

Table A.9: (*continued*)

Funds	1987–1990	1991–1994	1995–1998	1987–1998
GAB	0.1516	0.0844	0.1005	0.1157
	208	209	208	625
GAM	0.1429	0.0988	0.1002	0.1225
	208	209	208	625
GIM	0.0715	0.0775	0.0721	0.0740
	118	205	208	531
HIS	0.0678	0.0783	0.0776	0.0736
	96	205	208	509
ICB	0.0740	0.0790	0.0715	0.0755
	208	209	208	625
LBF	0.0000	0.0753	0.0671	0.0683
	0	101	208	309
PDI	0.0605	0.0693	0.0663	0.0667
	39	209	208	456
PHF	0.0810	0.0531	0.0767	0.0644
	83	207	208	498
PMT	0.0685	0.0762	0.0821	0.0753
	131	209	208	548
PPR	0.0000	0.0669	0.0649	0.0657
	0	143	208	351
SBF	0.1410	0.0937	0.1138	0.1198
	198	207	208	613
SOR	0.0917	0.0730	0.0812	0.0822
	208	209	208	625
TY	0.0926	0.1075	0.2671	0.1182
	204	209	208	621
USA	0.1444	0.0728	0.0956	0.1095
	195	209	208	612
VES	0.0725	0.0797	0.0694	0.0743
	208	209	208	625
ZF	0.0851	0.0727	0.0899	0.0821
	197	209	208	614
ZIF	0.0716	0.0681	0.0720	0.0712
	111	205	208	524
ZTR	0.0677	0.0594	0.0697	0.0644
	85	207	208	500
Weighed	0.0965	0.0759	0.0904	0.0855
mean	3798	5234	5408	14440

Table A.10: Hypotheses Tests–covariance analysis.

	1st Regression	2nd Regression
H1: Total homogeneity of the coefficients		
F_1	3.05882	2.16761
p-value	0.001471	0.000473
H2: Slope homogeneity and interception heterogeneity		
F_2	1.32	1.30
p-value	0.22367	0.128579
H3: Interception homogeneity given the slope homogeneity		
F_3	1.82	1.14
p-value	0.035432	0.312345

Note:
where: 1st Regression

$$\left(\Delta\tilde{D}_t\right)_{i,t} = \phi_{0i,t} + \phi_{1i,t}\hat{\text{var}}\left(\Delta D_t\right)_{i,t} + \varepsilon_{i,t},$$

2nd Regression

$$\text{var}\left(\Delta\tilde{D}_t\right)_{i,t} = \varphi_{0i,t} + \varphi_{1i,t}\left(1 - V_6^*\right)_{i,t} + \varepsilon_{i,t}.$$

Table A.11: Linear regressions relative to the general models (7)–(8).

1st Regression	2nd Regression
Fixed effects model (slope homogeneity and interception heterogeneity)	Simple model —*pooled regression* (total homogeneity of the coefficients)
$\text{var}\left(\Delta\tilde{D}_t\right)_{i,t} = \phi_{0\text{i},t} + 12.20241\ \hat{\text{var}}\left(\Delta D_t\right)_{i,t}$	$\text{var}\left(\Delta\tilde{D}_t\right)_{\text{i,t}} = 0.000286 + 0.001177^*\left(1 - V_6^*\right)_{i,t}$
(13.25977)	(1.4625)
$R^2 = 0.908327$ [0.0000]	$R^2 = 0.016511$ [0.2535]
$\text{SSR}_{mi} = 1.01E - 06$	$\text{SSR}_{ms} = 2.16E - 05$

Note: $\phi_{0i,t}$, represents the model interception coefficient, variable from fund to fund. The value among curved parenthesis corresponds to the t-statistical of the coefficient and the right parenthesis to its p-value.

References

Abraham, A, Elan, D and Marcus, AJ (1993). Does sentiment explain closed-end fund discounts? Evidence from bond funds. *Financial Review*, 28(4), 607–616.

Arak, M and Taylor, D (1996a). Optimal trading with mean-reverting prices: Switching between foreign stocks and closed-end country funds. *Applied Economics*, 28(9), 1067–1074.

Arak, M and Taylor, D (1996b). Risk and return in trading closed-end country funds: Can trading beat holding foreign stocks?. *The Quarterly Review of Economics and Finance*, 36(2), 219–231.

Arellano, M (1993). On the testing of correlated effects with panel data. *Journal of Econometrics*, 59, 87–97.

Baltagi, BH (1995). *Econometric Analysis of Panel Data*, Chichester: John Wiley & Sons.

Barclay, MJ, Holderness, CG and Pontiff, J (1993). Private benefits from block ownership and discounts on closed-end funds. *Journal of Financial Economics*, 33, 263–291.

Bonser-Neal, C, Brauer, G, Neal, R and Wheatley, S (1990). International investment restrictions and closed-end country fund prices. *The Journal of Finance*, 45(2), 523–547.

Bordurtha, JN, Kim, D and Lee, CMC (1995). Closed-end country funds and US market sentiment. *Review of Financial Studies*, 8, 879–918.

Brauer, GA (1984). Open-ending closed-end funds. *Journal of Financial Economics*, 13, 491–507.

Brauer, GA (1988). Closed-end fund shares' abnormal returns and the information content of discounts and premiums. *The Journal of Finance*, 43(1), 113–127.

Brauer, GA (1993). Investor sentiment and the closed-end fund puzzle: A 7 percent solution. *Journal of Financial Services Research*, 7(3), 199–216.

Brickley, AJ and Schallheim, JS (1985). Lifting the lid on closed-end investment companies: A case of abnormal returns. *Journal of Financial and Quantitative Analysis*, 20(1), 107–117.

Brown, GW (1999). Volatility, sentiment, and noise traders. *Financial Analysts Journal*, 55(2), 82–90.

Chen, N-F, Kan, R and Miller, MH (1993). Are the discounts on closed-end funds a sentiment index? *The Journal of Finance*, 48(2), 795–800.

Cheng, A, Copeland, L and O'Hanlon, J (1994). Investments trust discounts and abnormal returns: UK evidence. *Journal of Business Finance & Accounting*, 21(6), 813–831.

Cheung, CS, Kwan, CCY and Lee, J (1997). The noise trader hypothesis: The case of closed-end country funds. *Reserch in Finance,* AH Chen (ed.), 15, 115–136.

Chopra, N, Lee, CMC, Shleifer, A and Thaler, RH (1993). Yes, discounts on closed-end funds are a sentiment index. *The Journal of Finance*, 48(2), 801–808.

De Long, B, Shleifer, A, Summers, L and Waldmann, R (1990). Noise trader risk in financial markets. *Journal of Political Economy*, 98, 703–738.

De Long, JB, and Shleifer, A (1992). Closed-end fund discounts. *The Journal of Portfolio Management*, 46–53.

Dimson, E and Minio-Koserski, C (1998). Closed-end funds: A survey. LBS, forthcoming in *Financial Markets, Institutions & Instruments*, 79.

Elton, EJ, Gruber, MJ and Busse, JA (1998). Do investors care about sentiment. *The Journal of Business*, 71(4), 477–500.

Frankel, JA and Schmukler, SL (1996). Country fund discounts, asymmetric information and the Mexican crisis of 1994: Did local residents turn pessimistic before international investors? NBER Working Paper No 5714, 43.

French, K and Roll, R (1986). Stock return variances — The arrival of information and reaction of traders. *Journal of Financial Economics*, 17, 5–26.

Hardouvelis, GA, La Porta, R and Wizman, TA (1993). What moves the discounts on country equity funds?. NBER Working Paper No 4571, 76.

Hausman, JA (1978). Specification tests in econometrics. *Econometrica*, 46(6), 1251–1271.

Hausman, JA and Taylor, WE (1981). Panel data and unobservable individual effects, *Econometrica*, 49(6), 1377–1398.

Holly, A (1982). A remark on Hausman's specification test. *Econometrica*, 50(3), 749–759.

Hsiao, C (1986). Analysis of panel data. Econometric Society Monographs No. 11, Cambridge: Cambridge University Press.

Jorge, SMF (1997). Determinantes da Estrutura de Capitais: um Caso Português — 1990 a 1995. Dissertação de Mestrado; Escola de Economia e Gestão da Universidade do Minho, Braga.

Klibanoff, P, Lamont, O and Wizman, T (1998). Investor reaction to salient news in closed-end country funds. *The Journal of Finance*, 35(2), 673–699.

Kramer, C and Smith, RT (1995). Recent turmoil in emerging markets and the behavior of country-fund discounts: Renewing the puzzle of pricing of closed-end mutual funds. IMF Working Paper, WP/95/68, 26.

Lee, CMC, Shleifer, A and Thaler, RH (1990). Closed-end mutual funds. *Journal of Economic Perspectives*, 4(4), 153–164.

Lee, CMC, Shleifer, A, and Thaler, RH (1991). Investor sentiment and the closed-end fund puzzle. *The Journal of Finance*, 46(1), 75–109.

Levis, M and Thomas, DC (1995). Investments trust IPO's: Issuing behavior and price performance evidence from London Stock Exchange. *Journal of Banking & Finance*, 19(8), 1437–1458.

Monte, APC (2000). Sobre os Discounts/Premiums dos Fundos de Investimento Fechados no Contexto da Teoria do Sentimento do Investidor. Dissertação de Mestrado, Escola de Economia e Gestão da Universidade do Minho, Braga.

Monte, APC and Armada, MJR (2000). Sobre os Discounts/Premiums dos Fundos de Investimento Fechados: uma digressão sobre os quadros conceptuais que explicam a sua existência. Working paper No 7/2000, Núcleo de estudos em Gestão, Universidade do Minho, Braga.

Newey, WK and West, KD (1987). A simple, positive semi-definite, heteroskedasticity and autocorrelation consistent covariance matrix. *Econometrica*, 55(3), 703–708.

Peavy, J (1990). Returns on initial public offerings of closed-end funds. *Review of Financial Studies*, 3, 695–708.

Pindyck, RS and Rubinfeld, DL (1998). *Econometric Models and Economic Forecasts*, 4th Ed., Economic Series, McGraw-Hill International Editions.

Pontiff, J (1995). Closed-end premia and returns implications for financial market equilibrium. *Journal of Financial Economics*, 37, 341–370.

Shleifer, A and Summers, LH (1990). The noise trader approach to finance. *Journal of Economic Perspectives*, 4(2), 19–33.

Shleifer, A and Vishny, RW (1997). Limits of arbitrage. *Journal of Finance*, 52, 33–55.

Sias, RW (1997a). Price pressure and the role of institutional investors in closed-end funds. *The Journal of Financial Research*, 20(2), 211–229.

Sias, RW (1997b). The sensitivity of individual and institutional investors expectations to changing market conditions: Evidence from closed-end funds. *Review of Quantitative Finance and Accounting*, 8, 245–269.

Stwart, J and Gill, L (1998). *Econometrics*, 2nd Ed., Oxford: Prentice Hall, Europe.

Weiss, K (1989). The post-offering price performance of closed-end funds. *Financial Management*, 57–65.

White, H (1980). A heteroskedasticity-consistent covariance matrix estimator and a direct test for heteroskedasticity. *Econometrica*, 48(4), 817–838.

CHAPTER 14

WHY HAS IDIOSYNCRATIC VOLATILITY INCREASED IN EUROPE?

*Jean-Etienne Palard**

This paper documents the evolution of idiosyncratic volatility across a sample composed by the main 250 European listed companies between 1987 and 2003, and investigates the corporate determinants. We estimate two measures of financial volatility based on the decomposition of CAPM and on the model of Campbell et al. (2001). We show that both the industry-level and the firm-level volatilities have increased significantly between 1987 and 2003, whereas the market-level component has stayed relatively stable over the sample period. Then, we try to explain this phenomenon by exploring the corporate determinants of this increase. Similarly to Dennis and Strickland (2005), the results of panel data regressions show that the growth of idiosyncratic volatility is significantly correlated with the volume of stocks traded, the movement of corporate refocusing and the reinforcement of institutional investors in the ownership structure of European listed firms.

1 Introduction

Standard asset pricing models suggest that only systematic risk should be priced in stock returns since idiosyncratic risk can be eliminated without almost any costs by diversification. That is why idiosyncratic risk should bear no risk premiums in stock returns. In addition, early seminal works in finance (Markowitz, 1952; Lintner, 1965; Black and Scholes, 1973) assumes that the

*University of Montesquieu Bordeaux IV IRGO — Institut de Recherche en Gestion des Organisations, 35 Avenue Abadil, 33100 Bordeaux, France.
palard@u-bordeaux4.fr

volatility of equity returns is known and constant. However, these assertions have been criticized by some significant theoretical papers, which show that idiosyncratic volatility does play a pricing role and by a growing empirical literature that documents an increase of firm-level volatility in the long run in US stock markets mainly. There are several reasons to be interested in the evolution of firm-specific risk and to explore why this component changes over time.

Theoretically, the role of firm-specific risk in the dynamic of assets prices can be justified by the fact that some investors cannot hold an optimal combination of the market portfolio and a free-risk asset for some exogenous reason. Levy (1978) and Merton (1987) propose an extension of CAPM by integrating some information asymmetries and find that idiosyncratic risk can be priced. For Constantidines (1986), the pricing role of residual risk is due to transaction costs that limit investors' access to different compartments of financial markets and restrict the possibilities of arbitrage. Another set of theoretical papers is based upon the existence of non-trading assets that affect asset allocations. Two different types of assets have been examined in the literature: human capital assets (Mayers, 1976) and non-trading activities (Heaton and Lucas, 2000; Rampini, 2004). More recently, Barberis and Huang (2001) develop a dynamic model of asset pricing where investors are risk-averse with the decrease of their portfolio's value. Their model fetches up to a positive relation between the market portfolio expected return and idiosyncratic risk.

Empirically, it is by now a common observation that the volatility of the aggregate market is not constant but changes over time. Recently, there have been some renewed attempts to re-examine the relations between the idiosyncratic risk and the stock return. First, Campbell *et al.* (2001) (CLMX) observe that the measure of aggregate idiosyncratic volatility constructed from US data on NYSE/AMEX/NASDAQ, corresponding to firm-level components that cannot explained by market nor by industry-level volatility, has a significant upward trend over the period from July 1962 to December 1997, whereas market and industry risks have changed little over time. This result has been confirmed by several others papers such as Philippon (2002), Hirt and Pandher (2005), Bennett and Sias (2005) or Ferreira and Laux (2007). Second, Goyal and Santa-Clara (2003) report that the equal-weighted idiosyncratic volatility is positively and significantly related to future stock market returns using monthly US data over the period from July 1962 to December 1999, although market volatility has negligible predictive power. Third, Malkiel and Xu (2003) investigate the behavior of idiosyncratic volatility and find that idiosyncratic volatility is useful in explaining cross-sectional expected returns.

They also discover that returns from constructed portfolios directly co-vary with idiosyncratic risk hedging portfolio returns. However, Guo and Savickas (2004) and Marsh and Frazzini (2005) show that, even so idiosyncratic risk has significantly increased in the US and UK stock markets, this assertion seem not to be true in Germany, France, Switzerland or in Italy. Moreover, Bali *et al.* (2005) find the results observed by Goyal and Santa-Clara (2003) are no longer true when the period is extended from July 1962 to December 2001. Nevertheless, the consensus on the pricing role of idiosyncratic volatility among financial economists seems to be strong.

In the line of those first empirical findings, another stream of researches have tried to explain the determinants of idiosyncratic volatility upward. Vuolteenaho (2002) suggests that the increase in aggregated firm-specific risk can be explained by the volatility of discount rates, the upward in the volatility of expected future cash flows and the increase in the covariance between these factors. For Bennett and Sias (2005), three factors are primarily responsible for the upward trend in estimated value-weighted firm-specific risk: the growth of "riskier" industries, the increased role of small stocks in the market, and the decline in within-industry concentration. Moreover, their analysis demonstrates that when these three factors are combined it largely explains the upward trend in firm-specific risk over the past three decades. Ferreira and Laux (2007) study the relationship between measures of corporate governance policy and idiosyncratic risk in stock returns. They show that low quality governance is associated with low levels of idiosyncratic risk, low trading activity, and low efficiency between corporate investments. Poor-quality earnings reporting, in contrast, are associated with high levels of idiosyncratic risk and low efficiency of corporate investment. Using Japanese data from 1975 to 2003, Chang and Dong (2005) show that both institutional herding and firm earnings are positively related to idiosyncratic volatility. They also find that the dispersions of change in institutional ownership and return-on-asset move together with the market aggregate idiosyncratic volatility over time. Their results suggest that investor behavior and stock fundamentals may both help explain the time-series pattern of market aggregate idiosyncratic volatility.

However, we can address three major critics to those empirical studies relating to the determinants of idiosyncratic volatility. The first limit is about the set of control variables: the researchers generally do not take into account the results from previous papers. In this Caper, we control volume, size, and variation of return on equity. The second limit deals with the non-constant number of selected firms used to measure the evolution of idiosyncratic volatility over time. We can indeed suppose that financial risk of new listed companies is higher because their product markets are actually less mature. In this paper, we have selected a steady sample of the main 250 European listed companies with financial data from 1987 to 2003 collected from *Datastream* and *Worldscope*. The last critic we can address is that the studies are usually more focused on cross-section data regressions rather than on time-series panel data regressions.

In this paper, we refer to the recent paper of Dennis and Strickland (2005). We investigate three main hypotheses concerning the upward in idiosyncratic volatility over the past two decades. In the time-series, they find that firm-level volatility is positively related to increased firm focus, leverage, and increased institutional ownership. Furthermore, the explanatory power of market-model regressions has decreased over the sample period (1980–1997) and is negatively related to institutional ownership, increased firm focus, and leverage. Our results confirm the studies of Campbell *et al.* (2001) and Goyal and Santa-Clara (2003), for instance, as we observe an upward of monthly idiosyncratic volatility in Europe between 1987 and 2003 based on two measures of firm-specific risk constructed from CAPM and CLMX model decompositions. Inversely, market volatility and industrial-level risk have remained fairly stable over the sample period. We also document that firm-specific risk explain more than 70% of the total variance of monthly stock returns. Using firm fixed-effects regressions, we find that the annual measures of firm focus, leverage and institutional ownership are significantly related to the increase of both CAPM and CLMX measures of idiosyncratic firm volatility, but only on the restrained sample period (1988–1998). Indeed, the results are not statistically significant for the whole sample period because of data estimation problems induced by jumps of financial volatility.

2 Hypotheses

In this paper, we assume that idiosyncratic volatility is driven by shifts in the corporate structure of European listed companies. As indicated by Dennis and Strickland (2005), we focus on three types of changes: modification in the portfolio of firm's segments activities, change in financial leverage, and reinforcement of institutional ownership.

2.1 Corporate Focus

As Lubatkin and Chatterjee (1994) pointed out, if we suppose that a multi-segment company can be modeled as a portfolio of different assets and the correlation between return to each asset is less than 1, the standard portfolio theory predicts that divesting one or more segments will increase the level of idiosyncratic risk of equity returns (Markowitz, 1952). Of course, as the correlation between segments approaches one, the increase in volatility from focusing in fewer segments approaches zero. For Black and Scholes (1973), the equity stake in a multi-segment firm can be viewed as a call option on a portfolio of different business segments. In other words, the more a company is focused on few segments of activities the higher is firm-specific risk.[a]

The issue of corporate refocusing has received a considerable attention both in the strategic management and the corporate finance literature. The stream of studies have mainly focused on the antecedents, the process, and the consequences of that type of strategy (Johnson, 1996). Two major results can be outlined.

On the one hand, the movement of corporate refocusing seems to have been deep during the eighties and the nineties both among American and European companies. For instance, Markides (1995) finds that the number of SIC codes (*Standard Industry Classification*) with two (SIC2) and for activities (SIC4) of S&P 500 index has decrease steadily between 1985 and 1993. Comment and Jarrel (1995) observe also an important upward between 1978 and 1992 in the number of US listed firms with only one segment of activity and in revenue-based and EBIT-based Herfindahl index. More recently, Devogelaer (2003) shows from a panel of 400 hundred European listed firms that the movement corporate refocusing in Europe has been particularly strong during the nineties in comparison to the former decade.

On the other hand, refocusing strategies seem to improve financial performance. Markides (1992), Comment and Jarrel (1995), and Desai and Jain (1999) find a strong support that US and UK stock markets reacts positively to corporate refocusing announcements. The daily abnormal returns swing to between +1.27% and +2.89%. Moreover, the papers of John and Ofek (1995) and Berger and Ofek (1999) report that refocusing programs are one of the categories of divestments that increase financial return in the long run.

[a]However, Dennis and Strickland mentioned that "*when this effect is examined in the context of the entire stock market, it does not necessarily have to be the case that each firm has to divest segments and increase focus to get an increase in the volatility of the average stock in the market*". If old firms remain relatively diversified but new firms are created that have a focus in only one or two segments, the volatility of the average firm in the market will increase due to the creation of new, more focused firms.

Market and accounting measures of performance are positively linked to firm focus. Gilson *et al.* (2001) explain this benefit by the fact that financial analysts upgrade more focused firms.

Nevertheless, this last result support the first hypothesis mentioned above since financial theory predicts a positive relationship between risk and return: the more performing is a company the higher level of risk the firm is supposed to bear. That is why we can assume that an increase in idiosyncratic volatility is positively correlated with the movement of corporate refocusing.

2.2 *Leverage*

The effect of leverage on financial risk has been quite well documented since the seminal theoretical work of Hamada (1972) to precise the CAPM framework in the context of levered companies. As the volatility of equity return depends on the level of debt, he shows that the beta of a firm which carries a high level of debt is mechanically higher because of the leverage effect. This assertion can be expressed in the following way, where β^* is the beta of an unlevered company and β corresponds to levered company: $\beta = \beta^* + \beta^*[(1-t)L]$. The factor L measures the leverage effect given by the ratio debt on equity (D/S) and t is the tax rate. The systematic risk of a levered firm can be decomposed into two elements: β^* is a measure of business risk common to levered or unlevered firms and $\beta^*[(1-t)L]$ is a measure of financial risk. Although the emphasis is put on idiosyncratic financial risk in this paper, argumentation remains the same. We present a simple model developed by Figlewski and Wang (2000), which is also reported in Dennis and Strickland (2005).

Suppose that the value of a firm is equal to V_t at the date t, equity market value is equal to S_t and debt market value is equal to D_t. Then asset value at the date t is equal to: $V_t = S_t + D_t$. Furthermore, as Black and Scholes (1973) pointed out, if we consider that the debt component of a levered firm consists of a single T-year zero-coupon bond, the equity stake can be modeled as a T-year call option on the assets of the firm. Since the equity position is a levered position on the firm's assets, the volatility of the firm's equity returns is greater than the volatility of the asset's returns by a leverage multiple. Thus, any change in the value of debt can be captured by a change in the value of equity. This impact can be written in the following form:

$$\Delta V_t = V_{t+1} - V_t, \tag{1}$$

$$\Delta V_t = [S_{t+1} + D_{t+1}] - [S_t + D_t], \tag{2}$$

hence

$$\Delta V_t = \Delta S_t, \quad \text{because we suppose } \Delta D_t = 0.$$

Therefore, if we consider the relative variation of equity $(\Delta S_t / S_t)$, we obtain:

$$\frac{\Delta S_t}{S_t} = \frac{\Delta V_t}{S_t} = \frac{\Delta V_t}{V_t} \cdot \frac{V_t}{S_t}, \tag{3}$$

$$\frac{\Delta S_t}{S_t} = \frac{\Delta V_t}{V_t} \cdot \frac{S_t + D_t}{S_t} = \frac{\Delta V_t}{V_t}\left[1 + \frac{D_t}{S_t}\right], \tag{4}$$

hence

$$\frac{\Delta S_t}{S_t} = \frac{\Delta V_t}{V_t}[1 + L_t], \tag{5}$$

where $L_t = \frac{D_t}{S_t}$.

The ratio L_t corresponds to the leverage effect. Considering Eq. (5) from a standard deviation analysis, we have

$$\sigma_{S_t}^2 = \sigma_{V_t}^2[1 + L_t]. \tag{6}$$

By doing the static comparative of Eq. (6), we obtain the following expression:

$$\frac{\partial \sigma_{S_t}}{\partial \sigma_{V_t}} > 0 \quad \text{and} \quad \frac{\partial \sigma_{S_t}}{\partial L_t} > 0. \tag{7}$$

This last expression implies that the volatility of equity value σ_{S_t} is a positive function of both assets volatility σ_{V_t} and financial leverage L_t. So, we can assume that an upward of leverage provokes an increase in idiosyncratic volatility. Empirically, Schwert (1989) observes that the correlation between volatility and leverage variations are statistically significant.

2.3 *Institutional Ownership*

The last hypothesis is related to the transformation of ownership and control in Europe during the last two decades. The potential impact of those changes is based on two main stylized facts: block holding trades from institutional investors affect both market liquidity and assets prices and institutions tend to herd together.

A series of recent papers have documented the transformation of ownership and control of European corporations since the beginning of the eighties. The most important change is due to the reinforcement of institutional investors in the ownership structure of both public and private companies. Gompers and Metrick (2001) underline that the category of institutional investors is not homogeneous. It regroups banks, insurance companies, private and public pension funds, mutual funds, and hedge funds. Becht and Rok (1999) study the structure of block shareholdings in Europe. They find that the concentration of shareholder is particularly high in continental Europe relative to US and UK. They also report that the large controlling shareholders have diminished in southern Europe. Faccio and Lang (2005) analyze ownership and control of 5232 corporations in 13 western European countries. They find that financial and large firms are more likely to be widely held whereas non-financial and small firms are more likely to be family-controlled. They find more particularly that the percentage of shares controlled by institutional investors has grown continuously especially in the UK, in the Netherlands, and in Belgium where widely held firms are more important. From a panel of the largest 100 firms in the five major European economies, Kirchmaier and Grant (2005) confirmed the results reported by Thomsen and Pedersen (2002). They show that between 1994 and 2001, the percentage of institutional investors' control has increased steadily from 14% to 19%. Obviously, this movement cannot explain by itself the upward of idiosyncratic volatility. The institutional hypothesis is based on two main empirical results.

A first set of studies show that large blocks of shares traded by institutional investors have a considerable impact on both market liquidity and asset prices. Gompers and Metrick (2001) document the properties of institutional trades. They find that institutional ownership of stocks has nearly doubled from 1980 to 1995. Besides, the quantity of trading activity has increased considerably more among institutions than among individual investors over. Nielsen (2004) investigates institutional investors' demand for stock characteristics both in America and in Europe. He finds that institutional investors on the aggregate level prefer large and liquid stocks even if the demand is not homogeneous. Thus, banks, mutual funds, and insurance companies have a strong demand for large and liquid stocks contrary to private and public pension funds that do not have a preference for liquidity.

Given that institutions trade frequently, several authors have investigated whether this trading moves prices. Chan and Lakonishok (1995) study the daily transactions from 37 institutions over a 30 months period between July 1986 and December 1988. They find that market impact and trading costs are related to firm capitalization and institutions' size behind the trade.

They show that money managers with high demand for immediacy tend to be associated with larger market impact. Nosfinger and Sias (1999) find that increases in institutional ownership are associated with positive abnormal returns. In addition to moving prices, there is evidence that institutional ownership also contributes to volatility. Sias and Starks (1997) distinguish between the hypothesis that institutions buy stocks and then their prices increase (price pressure/informed institutions) and the hypothesis that a stock's price increases and then institutions buy it (positive feedback trading). They reject the positive feedback trading hypothesis in favor of the hypothesis that institutions trade because they possess superior information, and these trades move prices. Chakravarty (2001) compare the price impact of different type of trades. He finds that the impact of medium sized trades is much more significant on asset prices than small trades or large trades. Furthermore, he demonstrates that most of the price movement can be explained by institutions breaking large packages of trades into a series of medium sized trades.

A second set of both theoretical and empirical papers focus on herding behavior from institutional investors. Several models in the literature try to provide motives for the herding behavior of institutional managers. In all of these models, the herding results in an inefficient equilibrium, where the private information that the managers have is not fully impounded in the observable market prices. These models are based on the following hypotheses: asymmetric information hold by managers and sequentially revealed to the market (Froot *et al.*, 1992, Conrad *et al.*, 2002) and reputation on labour market (Scharfstein and Stein, 1990). Recent empirical papers tend to prove that institutional investors have a strong propensity to herd in financial markets. Dennis and Strickland (2002) condition on an event of a positive or negative market return greater than 2% in magnitude and find that stocks with higher institutional ownership have a greater absolute value of return than stocks with lower institutional ownership, which is consistent with herding on the part of institutions. Griffin *et al.* (2003) use a 10 month proprietary database that indicates whether trades are coming from individuals or institutions. They find a strong contemporaneous correlation between changes in institutional ownership and stock returns on a daily level.

The herding hypothesis has been tested into two papers. By conducting a cross-sectional analysis on the determinants of the changes of idiosyncratic risk, Dennis and Strickland (2005) find that changes in idiosyncratic volatility are positively related to changes in institutional ownership. The results reported suggest that a one standard deviation change in institutional ownership results in a 75% increase in idiosyncratic volatility. Furthermore, after controlling the changes in institutional ownership, they find that changes in ownership of equities by mutual funds are positively related to changes in idiosyncratic volatility. Using Japanese data from 1975 to 2003, Chang and Dong (2005) show that both institutional herding and firm earnings are positively related to the increase in idiosyncratic volatility. They also find that the dispersions of change in institutional ownership and return-on-asset move together with the market aggregate idiosyncratic volatility over time. However, they reject the hypothesis that institutional investors herd toward stocks with high idiosyncratic volatility and systematic risk.

Therefore, we can assume from the above argumentation that the increasing role of institutional investors in the financial markets and the corporate governance of European companies can be associated with a higher level of idiosyncratic volatility.

3 Sample, Measures and Data

3.1 Sample Selection

Instead of analyzing European markets as a whole to measure the evolution of idiosyncratic volatility, we have selected from *Worldscope* the most important companies listed in Europe in the eight main stock markets: Belgium, France, Germany, Italy, The Netherlands, Spain, Switzerland, and United Kingdom. The main advantage to work with a fix sample of company is to control the number of firms. Then we do not introduce any bias related to different risk characteristics of new listed companies. Indeed, we can assume that new firms are more volatile and focused on their core business and less levered than more mature firms.

We used the same procedure selection as described in Lins and Servaes (1999) for the period 1987–2003. In the initial sample, we have picked out all the non-financial and service companies whose turnover and market capitalization were, respectively, more than 100 M$ at 200 M$ as of 31 December 1987. This first sample was amounted to 455 companies. From this first sample, we have eliminated all the firms with missing activity or accounting information, delisted companies over the time period, firms listed on another market, and all listed subsidiaries of another selected company. The procedure of sample selection is summarized in Table 1. The final sample is composed of 250 companies whose main characteristics are the following: 63 German corporations (25%), 14 Belgian companies (6%), 12 Spanish firms (5%),

Table 1: Sample selection summary. The table reports the procedure of selection for the whole sample of European listed companies collected from *Worldscope*. The final sample amounts to 250 firms from the eight main stock markets in Europe: Belgium, Germany, France, Italy, the Netherlands, Spain, and Switzerland.

	Belgium	Germany	France	Italy	The Netherlands	Spain	Switzerland	United Kingdom	Echantillon Total
Initial sample in 1987	22	104	82	38	35	26	43	105	455
• Sectors SIC 0010-5900 firms									
• Turn. > 100 M & Mkt Cap > 200 M									
Multiple *SIC* Codes in *Worldscope*	(2)	(17)	(3)	(5)	(2)	(5)	(3)	(41)	(78)
Delisted firms	(2)	(6)	(8)	(3)	(2)	(2)	(4)	(10)	(37)
Double listing firms	(2)	(6)	(5)	(3)	(2)	(3)	(3)	(5)	(29)
Financial holdings	(1)	(4)	(4)	(2)	(2)	(1)	(2)	(2)	(18)
Listed subsidiaries	(1)	(8)	(9)	(2)	(3)	(3)	(3)	(14)	(43)
Total	14	63	53	23	24	12	28	33	250

53 French corporations (21%), 23 Italian firms (9%), 24 Dutch companies (10%), 33 UK corporations, and 28 Swiss firms (11%).

3.2 Measures and Data

3.2.1 Idiosyncratic Volatility: IV

We measure idiosyncratic volatility from CAPM and CLMX decompositions. This couple of measures is also reported in the papers of Bennett and Sias (2005), Bali *et al.* (2005), Comin and Philippon (2005), Dennis and Strickland (2005) or Irvine and Pontiff (2005).

- IV_CAPM

(1) *The model*
If we consider the market model equation used by Stapleton and Subrahmanyam (1983) to test the CAPM, the excess return R_{it} in comparison with the risk-free rate of a stock i at the date t can be estimated in the following way:

$$R_{it} = \alpha_i + \beta_i R_{mt} + \varepsilon_{it}, \quad \text{which is equivalent to:}$$

$$R_{it} = \alpha_i + \frac{\sigma_{im}}{\sigma_m^2} R_{mt} + \varepsilon_{it}, \tag{8}$$

where R_{mt} is the market excess return, σ_{im} is the covariance between security i and the market return (i.e. $\sigma_{im} = \text{Cov}(R_{it}, R_{mt})$), and σ_{mt}^2 is the market return variance: $\sigma_{mt}^2 = \text{Var}(R_{mt})$.

The variance of the return R_{it}, wrote down σ_{it}^2, is a measure of total risk at the date t:

$$\sigma_{it}^2 = \beta_i^2 \cdot \sigma_{mt}^2 + \sigma_{\varepsilon_{it}}^2 + 2\beta_i \cdot \text{Cov}\left(R_{mt}, \varepsilon_{it}\right). \tag{9}$$

Even so, the CAPM theory suggests that the market return and the residual components of risk are not correlated: $\text{Cov}(R_{mt}, \varepsilon_{it}) = 0$. Thus, idiosyncratic risk, $\sigma_{\varepsilon_{it}}^2$, that is, a measure of the residual component of risk is equal to:

$$\sigma_{\varepsilon_{it}}^2 = \sigma_{it}^2 - \beta_i^2 \cdot \sigma_{mt}^2. \tag{10}$$

The market variance has been measured annually from the evolution of daily returns R_{mt} at the day s — such as $s \in t$ — from two distinct market indexes: the main national market index and the MSCI Europe index. Thus, the market variance $\hat{\sigma}^2_{mt}$ is equal to:

$$\hat{\sigma}^2_{mt} = \sum_{s \in t} (R_{ms} - \mu_m)^2, \tag{11}$$

where μ_t is the annual average of the market index.

Equivalently, $\hat{\sigma}^2_{it}$ has been estimated as follows:

$$\hat{\sigma}^2_{it} = \sum_{s \in t} (R_{is} - \mu_i)^2. \tag{12}$$

Based on the daily returns R_{it} — day s during the month t, such as $s \in t$ — collected in *Datastream*, the individual measure of volatility $\hat{\sigma}^2_{it}$ has been evaluated for the whole sample of 250 European listed companies each month from January 1987 to December 2003. Individual betas β_i are annual betas evaluated from daily market and individual stock returns.

(2) *Estimation*

Then, the estimation of idiosyncratic volatility IV_CAPM$_{it}$ for a stock i during the month t is equal to:

$$\hat{\text{IV}}\_\text{CAPM}_{it} = \sigma^2_{\hat{\varepsilon}_{it}} = \hat{\sigma}^2_{it} - \hat{\beta}^2_{it} \cdot \hat{\sigma}^2_{mt}. \tag{13}$$

We have also measured the monthly weighted-average IV_CAPM$_t$ for the entire sample of 250 European companies:

$$\hat{\text{IV}}\_\text{CAPM}_t = \sum_{i=1}^{N_i=250} w_{it}(\varepsilon^2_{it}), \quad \text{where} \sum_{i=1}^{N_i=250} w_{it} = 1. \tag{14}$$

- IV_CLMX

(1) *The model*

We begin by reviewing the CLMX return decomposition (Campbell *et al.*, 2001). In a CAPM framework, industry j's excess return in period t can be expressed as:

$$R_{jt} = \beta_{jm} R_{mt} + \tilde{\varepsilon}_{jt}, \tag{15}$$

where β_{jm} is industry j's sensitivity to the market return R_{mt} and $\tilde{\varepsilon}_{jt}$ is the portion of the return that is uncorrelated with the market portfolio. The variance of

Eq. (15) partitions the total risk of industry j into market and industry-specific components:

$$\operatorname{Var}\left(R_{jt}\right) = \beta_{jm}^2 \cdot \operatorname{Var}\left(R_{mt}\right) + \operatorname{Var}\left(\tilde{\varepsilon}_{jt}\right). \tag{16}$$

Estimating such a decomposition, however, requires estimation of industry sensitivities to the market (β_{jm}). CLMX propose a clever alternative that circumvents the need for these estimates by assuming unit market betas and focusing on the weighted-average variance across industries.

In this simplified framework, the return for industry j is expressed as

$$R_{jt} = R_{mt} + \varepsilon_{jt}. \tag{17}$$

Substituting in for R_{jt} from (15) and solving for the industry-specific residual yields:

$$\varepsilon_{jt} = \tilde{\varepsilon}_{jt} + \left(\beta_{jm} - 1\right) R_{mt}. \tag{18}$$

The variance of R_{jt} in (17) may be expressed as

$$\begin{aligned} \operatorname{Var}\left(R_{jt}\right) &= \operatorname{Var}\left(R_{mt}\right) + \operatorname{Var}\left(\varepsilon_{jt}\right) + 2\operatorname{Cov}\left(R_{mt}, \varepsilon_{jt}\right), \text{ then} \\ \operatorname{Var}\left(R_{jt}\right) &= \operatorname{Var}\left(R_{mt}\right) + \operatorname{Var}\left(\varepsilon_{jt}\right) + 2\left(\beta_{im} - 1\right)\operatorname{Var}\left(R_{mt}\right). \end{aligned} \tag{19}$$

Equation (19) reintroduces the market sensitivity, β_{jm}, into the simplified decomposition. However, taking the weighted-average across industries yields a beta-free decomposition of average industry volatility (because the weighted-average beta equals one):

$$\begin{aligned} \sum_j \left[w_{jt} \cdot \operatorname{Var}\left(R_{jt}\right)\right] &= \operatorname{Var}\left(R_{mt}\right) + \textstyle\sum_j \left[w_{jt} \cdot \operatorname{Var}\left(\varepsilon_{jt}\right)\right], \\ \sum_j \left[w_{jt} \cdot \operatorname{Var}\left(R_{jt}\right)\right] &= \sigma_{mt}^2 + \sigma_{\varepsilon t}^2, \end{aligned} \tag{20}$$

where $\sigma_{mt}^2 \equiv \operatorname{Var}\left(R_{mt}\right)$ and $\sigma_{\varepsilon_{jt}}^2 \equiv \sum_j w_{jt} \cdot \operatorname{Var}\left(\varepsilon_{jt}\right)$ are the value-weighted average of industry-specific volatility.

Thus, CLMX decompose the total risk of a single security into market, industry, and firm-specific components. Specifically, they express the excess return for security i (in industry j) at time t as a function of industry returns:

$$R_{ijt} = \beta_{ij} R_{jt} + \tilde{\eta}_{ijt}. \tag{21}$$

Substituting in Eq. (8) for R_{jt} yields:

$$R_{ijt} = \beta_{ij}\beta_{jm} R_{mt} + \beta_{ij}\tilde{\varepsilon}_{jt} + \tilde{\eta}_{ijt}, \tag{22}$$

where $\tilde{\eta}_{ijt}$ is the firm-specific residual (assumed orthogonal to R_{mt} and $\tilde{\eta}_{ijt}$). As a result, firm i's sensitivity to the market is given by $\beta_{mt} \equiv \beta_{ij}\beta_{jm}$ and firm i's return can be expressed as

$$R_{ijt} = \beta_{im} R_{mt} + \beta_{ij}\tilde{\varepsilon}_{jt} + \tilde{\eta}_{ijt}. \tag{23}$$

A decomposition of the variance of security i's return expressed in (22) involves both market and industry betas:

$$\mathrm{Var}\left(R_{ijt}\right) = \beta_{im}^2 \cdot \mathrm{Var}\left(R_{mt}\right) + \beta_{ij}^2 \cdot \mathrm{Var}\left(\tilde{\varepsilon}_{jt}\right) + \mathrm{Var}\left(\tilde{\eta}_{ijt}\right). \tag{24}$$

Assuming unit industry sensitivities ($\beta_{ij} = 1$, $\forall i \in j$), the return on i is given by

$$R_{ijt} = R_{jt} + \eta_{ijt}. \tag{25}$$

By isolating the residual risk η_{ijt} from this last expression and combining expressions (17) and (23), we obtain:

$$\begin{aligned}
\eta_{ijt} &= \left(R_{ijt} - R_{jt}\right) = \left(\beta_{im} R_{mt} + \beta_{ij}\tilde{\varepsilon}_{jt} + \tilde{\eta}_{ijt}\right) - \left(\beta_{jm} R_{mt} + \tilde{\varepsilon}_{jt}\right), \\
\eta_{ijt} &= \left(R_{ijt} - R_{jt}\right) = \tilde{\eta}_{ijt} + \left(\beta_{jm} - \beta_{jm}\right) R_{mt} + \left(\beta_{ij} - 1\right)\tilde{\varepsilon}_{jt}, \qquad (26) \\
\eta_{ijt} &= \tilde{\eta}_{ijt} + \left(\beta_{ij} - 1\right) R_{jt}.
\end{aligned}$$

From Eq. (23), the variance of R_{ijt} can be written as

$$\begin{aligned}
\mathrm{Var}\left(R_{ijt}\right) &= \mathrm{Var}\left(R_{jt}\right) + \mathrm{Var}\left(\eta_{ijt}\right) + 2\mathrm{Cov}\left(\tilde{\eta}_{ijt}, R_{jt}\right), \text{then} \\
\mathrm{Var}\left(R_{ijt}\right) &= \mathrm{Var}\left(R_{jt}\right) + \mathrm{Var}\left(\eta_{ijt}\right) + \left(\beta_{ij} - 1\right)\mathrm{Var}\left(R_{jt}\right) \qquad (27)
\end{aligned}$$

which again results in an expression involving factor sensitivities. However, because the weighted-average industry beta equals one, these sensitivities are eliminated when computing the weighted-average across stocks in industry j:

$$\sum_{i\in j}\left[w_{ijt}\cdot \mathrm{Var}\left(R_{ijt}\right)\right] = \mathrm{Var}\left(R_{jt}\right) + \sum_{i\in j}\left[w_{ijt}\cdot \mathrm{Var}\left(\eta_{ijt}\right)\right],$$
$$\sum_{i\in j}\left[w_{ijt}\cdot \mathrm{Var}\left(R_{ijt}\right)\right] = \mathrm{Var}\left(R_{jt}\right) + \sigma^2_{\eta_{ijt}}, \tag{28}$$

where w_{ijt} is security i's weight in industry j at time t and $\sigma^2_{\eta_{ijt}}$ is the weighted-average firm-specific volatility across firms in industry j. Taking the weighted average of Eq. (27) across industries and substituting in from (19) yields an expression for aggregate volatility:

$$\begin{aligned}\sum_j\left[w_{jt}\sum_{i\in j}\left[w_{ijt}\cdot \mathrm{Var}\left(R_{ijt}\right)\right]\right] &= \sum_j\left[w_{jt}\cdot \mathrm{Var}\left(R_{jt}\right)\right] \\ &\quad + \sum_j\left[w_{jt}\sum_{i\in j}\left[w_{ijt}\cdot \mathrm{Var}\left(\eta_{ijt}\right)\right]\right], \\ &= \mathrm{Var}\left(R_{mt}\right) + \sum_j\left[w_{jt}\cdot \mathrm{Var}\left(\varepsilon_{jt}\right)\right] \\ &\quad + \sum_j\left[w_{jt}\cdot \mathrm{Var}\left(\eta_{jt}\right)\right], \\ &= \sigma^2_{mt} + \sigma^2_{\varepsilon t} + \sigma^2_{\eta t},\end{aligned} \tag{29}$$

where $\sigma^2_{\eta t} \equiv \sum_j\left[w_{jt}\sum_{i\in j}\left[w_{ijt}\cdot \mathrm{Var}\left(\eta_{ijt}\right)\right]\right]$ is the weighted-average variance of that portion of the return that is uncorrelated with market return R_{mt} and industry return R_{jt}. Thus, average total risk can be decomposed into the three components: market risk $\left(\sigma^2_{mt}\right)$, industry-specific risk $\left(\sigma^2_{\varepsilon t}\right)$, and firm-specific risk $\left(\sigma^2_{\eta t}\right)$.

(2) *Estimation*

Following CLMX, we subtract the risk-free rate from raw returns and estimate market risk in month t as the sum of that month's squared demeaned daily value-weighted market returns:

$$\mathrm{MKT}_t = \sigma^2_{mt} = \sum_{s \in t} (R_{ms} - \mu_{mt})^2, \tag{30}$$

where R_{ms} is the value-weighted market return on day s in month t and μ_m is the mean market of return *MSCI Europe Index* over the entire sample period (1987–2003). The market return on day s is calculated as the weighted average across all firms with returns on day s, using weights based on beginning of month market values.

Then, as our sample is composed only by industrial firms, we use *MSCI Europe Sector Index* classification industrial classification ($j = 1, \ldots, 10$) to measure the industry-specific risk for industry j in month t is estimated as

$$\sigma^2_{\hat{\varepsilon}_{jt}} = \sum_{s \in t} \left(R_{js} - R_{ms}\right)^2, \tag{31}$$

where R_{js} is the return of *MSCI Europe Sector Index* j on day s in month t and R_{ms} is the market return on day s in month t. The value-weighted-average variance (IND_t) for the 10 different sectors selected is equal to:

$$\mathrm{IND}_t = \sum_{j=1}^{10} \left(w_{jt} \cdot \sigma^2_{\hat{\varepsilon}_{jt}}\right), \tag{32}$$

where industry weights w_{jt} are based on beginning of month industry market values.

Similarly, the firm-specific risk for firm i in industry j in month t is estimated as

$$\hat{\mathrm{I}}\mathrm{V\_CLMX}_{ijt} = \sigma^2_{\hat{\eta}_{ijt}} = \sum_{s \in t} \left(R_{is} - R_{js}\right)^2. \tag{33}$$

The firm-specific risk of industry j is defined as the value-weighted average firm-specific risk of companies within that industry:

$$\hat{\mathrm{I}}\mathrm{V\_CLMX}_{jt} = \sigma^2_{\hat{\eta}_{jt}} = \sum_{i=1}^{N_{ij}} \left(w_{ijt} \cdot \sigma^2_{\hat{\eta}_{ijt}}\right), \tag{34}$$

where N_{ij} is the number of securities in industry j.

Similarly, the estimated firm-specific risk across all stocks selected in our sample of 250 listed firms is given by

$$\begin{aligned}\text{FIRM}_t = \hat{\text{I}}\text{V\_CLMX}_t &= \sum_{j=1}^{10}\left(\omega_{jt}\cdot\sigma^2_{\hat{\eta}_{jt}}\right)\\ &= \sum_{j=1}^{10}\omega_{jt}\sum_{i=1}^{N_{ij}}\left(\omega_{ijt}\cdot\sigma^2_{\hat{\eta}_{ijt}}\right)\\ &= \sum_{i=1}^{250}\left(\omega_{it}\cdot\sigma^2_{\hat{\eta}_{ijt}}\right).\end{aligned} \tag{35}$$

3.2.2 Firm Focus, Leverage, and Institutional Ownership

- Firm Focus: FOCUS

The level of corporate focus has been estimated by the turnover-based Herfindahl index constructed from *Worldscope* segment data. For each firm, *Worldscope* reports the annual number of SIC codes (SIC2 and SIC4) and the breakdown of turnover and revenue by segment of activities.

The Herfindahl index of a firm i in year t is defined as follows:

$$\text{FOCUS}_{it} = \sum_{j=1}^{n}\left[\frac{T_j}{\sum_{j=1}^{n} T_j}\right]^2, \tag{36}$$

where T_j is the segment j turnover from a firm with n segments. The panel mean (median) of the variable FOCUS reported in Table 5 is equal to 0.5265 (0.4991).

- Leverage and debt maturity: LEV and DLT

The financial structure has been estimated from two proxies: leverage and debt maturity. The leverage ratio (LEV) is defined as the book value of total net debt divided by the market value of equity. The debt maturity ratio (DLT) is defined as the book value of long term debt divided by the book value of total assets. The panel mean of LEV and DLT reported in Table 5 are, respectively, 37.71% and 13.81%.

- Institutional ownership: IOWN and MFUND

We have collected institutional ownership data for the whole sample of 250 European firms from three databases — *Dafsaliens* available in *Amadeus11.0*, *Bloomberg*, and *Factset* — and cross-verified our data sample. Working with three different sources of data has been completely necessary since, contrary to the US legislation, the data on ownership structure are not available in an unified database for European listed companies.[b] Kirchmaier and Grant (2005) observe that "*ownership data is inherently unreliable and the use of a single data source — as in the case for most papers in the field — limits the generalizability of the results.*" In cases where both sources showed identical results, we assumed that the data was correct. In the case of discrepancies, we consulted other sources including regulatory listings, public statements, news sources, and industry analysts.

Two measures of institutional ownership have been estimated. The variable IOWN is defined as the percentage of a firm's outstanding shares held by institutional investors (banks, insurance company, pension fund, and mutual fund) on the last day of each year. The variable MFUND is defined as the ratio of mutual fund ownership to total institutional ownership. The panel mean of IOWN and MFUND reported in Table 5 are 23.08% and 5.40%.

3.2.3 Control Variables

Three types of control variables have been estimated.

We first take the daily volume VOL of shares traded. VOL is measured as the annual percentage of a firm's outstanding shares traded within a day. This variable has been introduced for two major reasons. On the one hand, Schwert (1989) and Chordia *et al.* (2001) have found that aggregated market volatility is positively associated with the volume of trades. On the other hand, Nosfinger and Sias (1999) have reported that institutional investors tend to hold larger and more liquid stocks than other types of investors so as to limit the impact of their trade on stock prices volatility.

Second, we use the decimal logarithm of annual turnover to control firm size (SIZE). Three main reasons have motivated the choice of inserting this variable in the regressions. First, firm size is positively associated with the level

[b]Securities Act Amendment of 1975 requires that institutional investors report their portfolio holdings to the Securities and Exchange Commission (SEC) on a quarterly basis. This type of requirement is still not available in Europe.

of institutional ownership since institutional investors have a preference for liquid assets. Second, size is correlated with the degree of firm focus. Eventually, size is also correlated with the level of leverage as larger firms have a better access to the public debt markets.

Third, control variable is a measure of accounting volatility. We have measured this variable from a 5-year moving variance of ROE (VAROE):

$$\text{VAROE}_{it} = \frac{1}{5}\sum_{t=-2}^{t=+2}\left(\text{ROE}_{it} - {}^{+2}_{-2}\,\overline{\text{ROE}_i}\right)^2, \qquad (37)$$

where ${}^{+2}_{-2}\overline{\text{ROE}_i}$ is the 5-year average of ROE for a firm i computed during the dates $t = -2$ and $t = +2$.

Marsh and Frazzini (2005) find that the non-anticipated variation of ROE computed from I/B/E/S dataset is positively correlated with the increase of idiosyncratic volatility. Comin and Philippon (2005) report that both turnover and ROA variation are significantly correlated with the increase of the residual component of risk computed from CAPM. Chang and Dong (2005) observe on Japanese stock markets that firm earnings are positively related to idiosyncratic volatility.

3.3 Regression Methodology

We have relied on the model proposed by Dennis and Strickland (2005) to test hypotheses concerning the explanatory power of firm focus, leverage, and institutional ownership on the evolution of idiosyncratic volatility. We use the following fixed effects model:

$$\begin{aligned}\text{IV}_{it} = {} & \alpha_i + \alpha_1\text{VOL}_{it} + \alpha_2\text{SIZE}_{it} + \alpha_3\text{VAROE}_{it} + \alpha_4\text{FOCUS}_{it} \\ & + \alpha_5\text{LEV}_{it} + \alpha_6\text{DLT}_{it} + \alpha_7\text{IOWN}_{it} + \alpha_8\text{MUTF}_{it} + \varepsilon_{it}, \qquad (38)\end{aligned}$$

where i indexes the firm, t indexes the year and IV is either the firm's idiosyncratic volatility computed from CAPM and CLMX decomposition of risk.

The main advantage of fixed effect models is to focus on temporal effects as fixed firm effects are absorbed by the intercept term α_i in Eq. (38). Then, this model is equivalent to another model with one intercept for all firms, but where the dependent variable and each independent variable are *de-meaned* by subtracting the respective within-firm time-series annual average of each variable:

$$\begin{aligned}\left(\mathrm{IV}_{it}-\overline{\mathrm{IV}_{i}}\right) &= \alpha_0+\alpha_1\left(\mathrm{VOL}_{it}-\overline{\mathrm{VOL}_{i}}\right)+\alpha_2\left(\mathrm{SIZE}_{it}-\overline{\mathrm{SIZE}_{i}}\right)\\ &\quad+\alpha_3(\mathrm{VAROE}_{it}-\overline{\mathrm{VAROE}_{i}})+\alpha_4(\mathrm{FOCUS}_{it}-\overline{\mathrm{FOCUS}_{i}})\\ &\quad+\alpha_5(\mathrm{LEV}_{it}-\overline{\mathrm{LEV}_{i}})+\alpha_6(\mathrm{DLT}_{it}-\overline{\mathrm{DLT}_{i}})\\ &\quad+\alpha_7(\mathrm{IOWN}_{it}-\overline{\mathrm{IOWN}_{i}})\\ &\quad+\alpha_8(\mathrm{MUTF}_{it}-\overline{\mathrm{MUTF}_{i}})+\varepsilon_{it}. \qquad (39)\end{aligned}$$

This removes cross-sectional variation of the average value of each variable and allows us to focus on the time-series.

4 Results

The descriptive statistics of all the variables included in the regressions are reported in Table 2. We first notice that the annual mean of IV_CAPM, which is equal to 0.0089, is greater than the mean of IV_CLMX, which is 0.0077. This difference can be explained by the fact that the effect of industry-level variance is fully integrated in the measure of IV_CAPM. We also observe that 0.29% of the total outstanding shares is traded each day. This figure is very close to the percentage of 0.33% reported by Dennis and Strickland (2005) on the US security markets. We can last mention that the average turnover of European firms (SIZE) is equal to 2513 M€ with a huge difference between the maximum (141,351 M€) and the minimum (200 M€) level of turnover over the panel. The results of time-series are reported in Table 3 for all the variables. The evolution of corporate focus measured by the revenue-based Herfindahl index has increased constantly until 1998 underlying a movement of business refocusing among European companies. Since 1999, the variable FOCUS has decreased irregularly implying a comeback to certain form of strategic diversification. The percentage of control by institutional investors has grown up continuously from 1987 through 2003. We can also notice an upward, though irregular, of the variables VOL, VAROE, and SIZE.

First, we analyze the increase of idiosyncratic volatility in Europe and document the econometric properties of IV_CAMP and IV_CLMX for the period 1987 through 2003. Second, we present the main results concerning the determinants of this increase for three different types of period.

Table 2: Summary statistics.

	Variable									
	IV_CAPM	IV_CLMX	VOL	SIZE	VAROE	FOCUS	LEV	DLT	IOWN	MFUND
Mean	0.009	0.008	0.003	3.400	0.063	0.526	0.377	0.138	0.231	0.054
Median	0.006	0.005	0.003	3.335	0.028	0.499	0.326	0.117	0.208	0.046
Maximum	0.271	0.301	0.025	5.150	6.709	1.000	11.758	1.252	0.980	0.287
Minimum	−0.039	0.000	0.000	2.301	0.000	0.150	−8.763	0.000	0.005	0.000
Std. Dev.	0.016	0.018	0.002	0.591	0.171	0.217	0.322	0.116	0.133	0.040
Observations	4250	4250	4250	4250	4250	4250	4250	4250	4250	4250

The table presents summary statistics for the variables used in our analysis. The variables are measured annually over the period 1997–2003. For each variable, we provide means, medians, minimums, maximums, and standard deviation. IV_CAPM is the sum of the squared errors from firm-level CAPM regressions. IV_CLMX is the firm-level measure of idiosyncratic risk from the CLMX-model regressions. VOL is the annual mean of daily volume expressed as a percentage of outstanding shares. SIZE is the logarithm of annual turnover expressed in millions of euros. VAROE is the five-year rolling mean variance of ROE. FOCUS is the annual sales-based Herfindahl index. LEV is the book value of net debt divided by the market value of equity. DLT is the book value of long-term debt divided by the book value of total assets. IOWN is the percentage of outstanding shares held by institutional investors. MFUND is the percentage of mutual funds in the ownership to total institutional ownership.

Table 3: Times series trends.

Year	IV_CAPM	IV_CLMX	VOL	SIZE	VAROE	FOCUS	LEV	DLT	IOWN	MFUND
1987	0.0165	0.0142	0.0024	3.1304	0.0537	0.4594	0.2222	0.1369	0.0771	0.0202
1988	0.0077	0.0061	0.0036	3.1848	0.0701	0.4738	0.3519	0.1315	0.0871	0.0247
1989	0.0053	0.0039	0.0021	3.2410	0.0489	0.4854	0.3493	0.1349	0.0917	0.0296
1990	0.0080	0.0075	0.0025	3.2799	0.0509	0.4991	0.3311	0.1372	0.1065	0.0326
1991	0.0058	0.0057	0.0029	3.3053	0.0489	0.5114	0.5138	0.1442	0.1218	0.0402
1992	0.0070	0.0059	0.0025	3.3266	0.0546	0.5154	0.4148	0.1409	0.1224	0.0438
1993	0.0092	0.0067	0.0027	3.3336	0.0563	0.5362	0.4118	0.1389	0.1346	0.0532
1994	0.0071	0.0070	0.0026	3.3623	0.0610	0.5439	0.3129	0.1312	0.1454	0.0555
1995	0.0079	0.0068	0.0023	3.3935	0.0533	0.5518	0.3012	0.1280	0.1554	0.0619
1996	0.0070	0.0074	0.0024	3.4130	0.0595	0.5610	0.3302	0.1271	0.1685	0.0601
1997	0.0078	0.0059	0.0025	3.4716	0.0577	0.5848	0.2759	0.1233	0.1780	0.0678
1998	0.0100	0.0093	0.0031	3.4885	0.0658	0.6099	0.2953	0.1259	0.1838	0.0667
1999	0.0083	0.0081	0.0036	3.5270	0.0743	0.5275	0.3567	0.1344	0.1964	0.0693
2000	0.0114	0.0110	0.0033	3.5940	0.0939	0.5123	0.3860	0.1381	0.2181	0.0726
2001	0.0137	0.0090	0.0031	3.6243	0.0951	0.5395	0.4539	0.1487	0.2167	0.0759
2002	0.0094	0.0087	0.0036	3.6127	0.0794	0.5150	0.4337	0.1603	0.2166	0.0749
2003	0.0083	0.0071	0.0038	3.6009	0.0499	0.5272	0.4966	0.1696	0.2075	0.0689

The table contains the annual mean values of the variables used in our study for each year. IV_CAPM is the sum of the squared errors from firm-level CAPM regressions. IV_CLMX is the firm-level measure of idiosyncratic risk from the CLMX-model regressions. VOL is the annual mean of daily volume expressed as a percentage of outstanding shares. SIZE is the logarithm of annual turnover expressed in millions of euros. VAROE is the five-year rolling mean variance of ROE. FOCUS is the annual sales-based Herfindahl index. LEV is the book value of net debt divided by the market value of equity. DLT is the book value of long-term debt divided by the book value of total assets. IOWN is the percentage of outstanding shares held by institutional investors. MFUND is the percentage of mutual funds in the ownership to total institutional ownership.

4.1 The Increase of Idiosyncratic Volatility in Europe

4.1.1 Graphical Analysis

In Fig. 1, we plot monthly measures of market variance (MKT) computed from daily data for the period 1987 through 2003. MSCI Europe Index is directly available in *Datastream*. The daily return of Europe 250 Sample Index is constructed from the weighted-average return of European listed companies that compose our sample. We also report in Fig. 2 shows the 12-months moving average of both MKT and IND. As what popular discussions seem to suggest about the evolution of stock market, we find no systematic trend in the dynamics of market volatility. Although Fig. 2 shows huge spikes of market

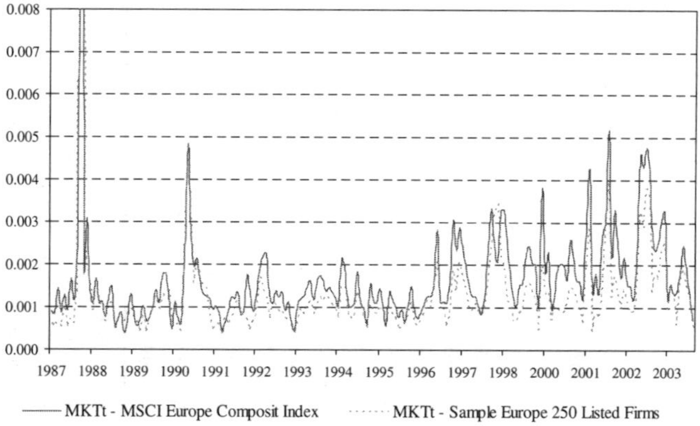

Figure 1: Monthly measure of market volatility (MKT_t).

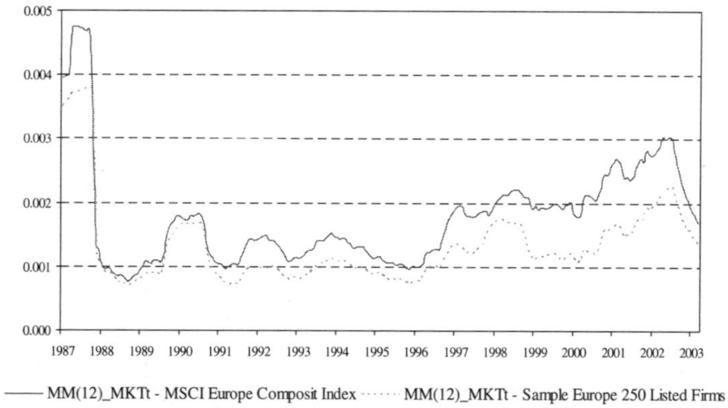

Figure 2: 12 months moving average of market volatility (MKT_t).

volatility during the crash of October 1987 and during Internet bubble in the early 2000s, market volatility does not seem to increase over time. Therefore, this results confirm the findings reported by Schwert (1989), Campbell *et al.* (2001), Malkiel and Xu (2003) or Guo and Savickas (2004).

In Fig. 3, we plot monthly measure of industry-level variance (IND) computed from Eq. (32). In Fig. 4, we report 12-months moving average of sector-level variance. Compared with market volatility, industry volatility is slightly lower on average. As for MKT, there is a slow moving component and some high frequency noise. However, conversely to former studies reported above, we do observe a noteworthy upward in the evolution of IND assessed from daily returns from MSCI Sector Indexes. The figures exhibit huge

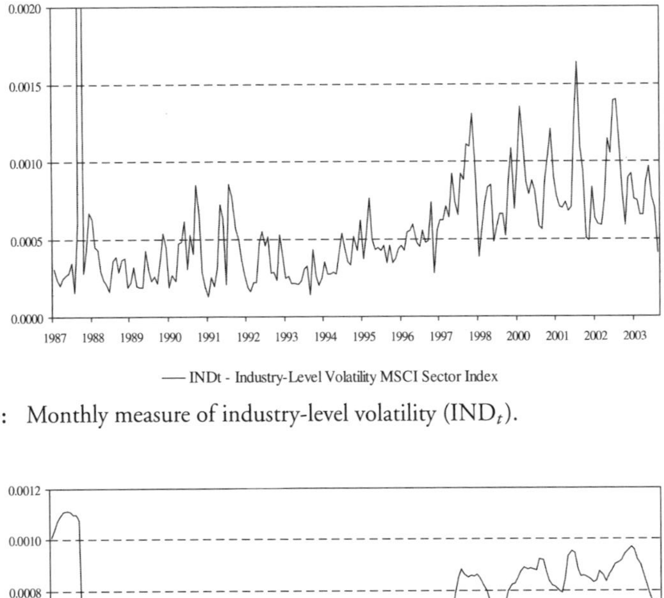

Figure 3: Monthly measure of industry-level volatility (IND_t).

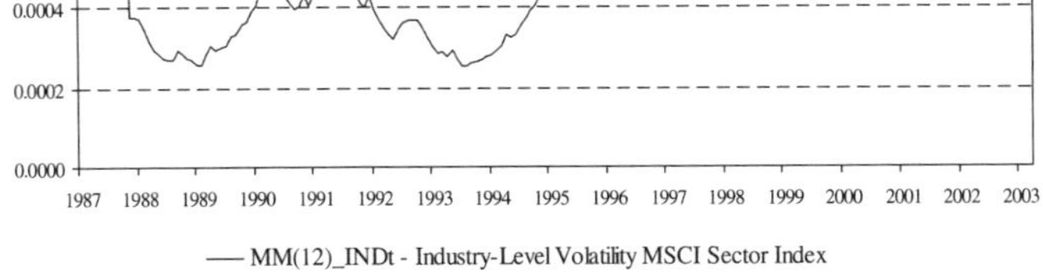

Figure 4: 12 months moving average of industry-level volatility (IND_t).

spikes of industrial volatility during the crash of October 1987 and during the Internet bubble in the early 2000s and a relative increase over time.

In Figs. 5 and 6, we plot monthly measures of idiosyncratic variance from CAPM and CLMX decompositions. IV_CAPM and IV_CLMX are computed for each stock from previous variables and daily returns available in *Datastream*. The first striking feature is that idiosyncratic volatility is much higher than the market-level and the industry-level volatility. This implies that

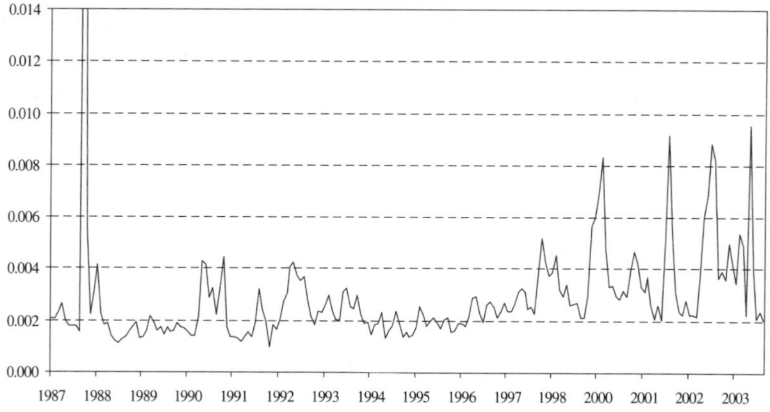

Figure 5: Monthly measure of residual volatility (IV_CAPM$_t$).

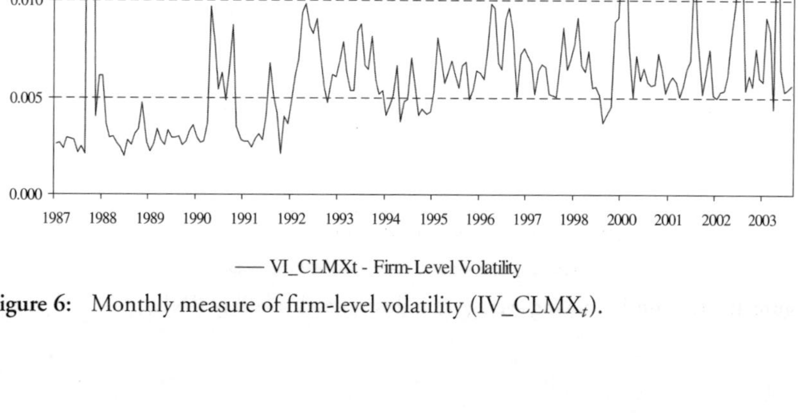

Figure 6: Monthly measure of firm-level volatility (IV_CLMX$_t$).

IV is the largest component of the total volatility of an average firm. The second major feature is the upward overtime of the measures of idiosyncratic volatility (IV_CAPM and IV_CLMX) (Fig. 7). The increase of IV_CLMX over the sample period is particularly strong as we can observe in Fig. 8 that reports the 12-months weighted-average. The level of idiosyncratic volatility in the early 2000s (0.075) has increased more than twice as the level in 1988 (0.032). The

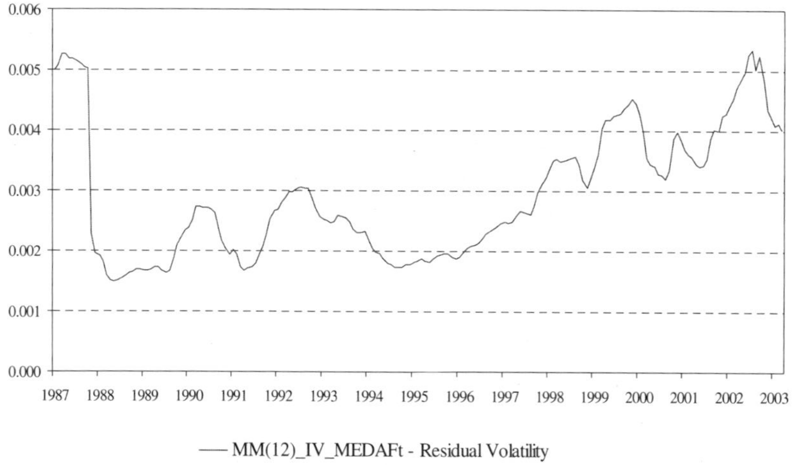

Figure 7: 12 months moving average of residual volatility (IV_CAPM$_t$).

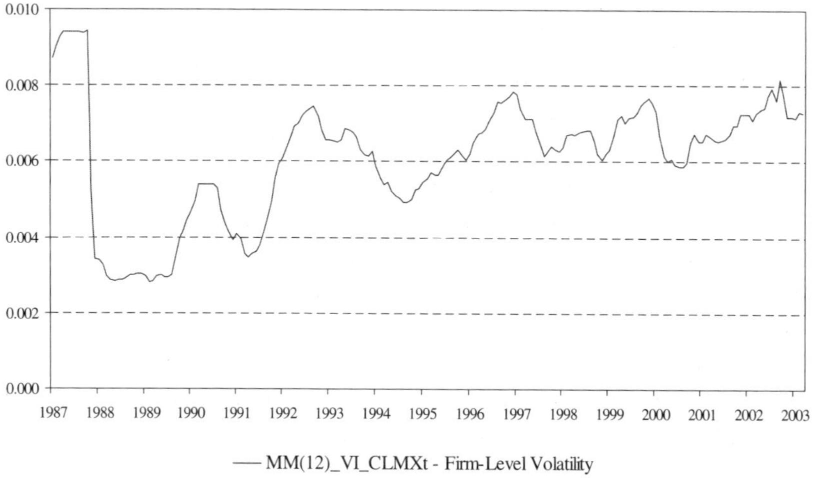

Figure 8: 12 months moving average of firm-level volatility (IV_CLMX$_t$).

effect of the crash in October 1987 and the Internet bubble in the early 2000s has also been very strong since we observe high pikes during those two periods. We can infer from this evolution that the tendency of decorrelation between market return and individual security returns has been important. Thus, our results tend to confirm the findings reported in the studies of Campbell *et al.* (2001), Bennett and Sias (2005), Comin and Philippon (2005) or Dennis and Strickland (2005) for US stock markets, Marsh and Frazzini (2005) for UK, and Guo and Savickas (2004) for Germany, France, and Italy.

It is evident from the four volatility plots that the all measures tend to move together. The effect of the crash of October 1987 and the Internet bubble is particularly strong. This raises the issue that those events may have a significant outcome on the assessment of volatility measures and then distort some of the results. That is why we use in the following sections three types of data: raw data (1987–2003), post-crash 1987 data with and without Internet bubble.

4.1.2 Deterministic Trend of Idiosyncratic Volatility (IV)

We use the same methodology developed by Campbell *et al.* (2001) to test the hypothesis of an upward of idiosyncratic volatility (IV). As all these series exhibit high level of serial correlation, which raises the possibility of the presence of unit roots, an important question is to know whether the trend is stochastic or determinist.

Table 5 shows descriptive statistics and linear trend of monthly measures of volatility constructed from daily returns. The mean of MKT is equal to 0.00176 implying an annual standard deviation of 14.53%. The mean value of IND is lower: it equals to 0.00059 standing for an annual standard deviation of 8.41%. The means of IV_CAPM and IV_CLMX amount, respectively, to 0.00293 and 0.00604 implying an annual standard deviation of 18.75% and 26.92%. As pointed out by Campbell *et al.* (2001), these numbers imply that over the whole sample the share of systematic risk that is due to the market variance is only about 21% whereas residual risk that is due to idiosyncratic variance is more than 70%. Therefore, industry and particularly firm-level volatility are the main components of the total volatility of an average firm.

Table 6 reports autocorrelation coefficients for the four measures of volatility using both the raw data and the post-crash 1987 data. Because the crash had an enormous impact on all the four measures of volatility, the autocorrelation coefficients are much larger when the data do not include the crash.

Table 4: Correlation between variables.

	IV_CAPM	IV_CLMX	VOL	SIZE	VAROE	FOCUS	LEV	DLT	IOWN	MFUND
IV_CAPM	1.000									
IV_CLMX	−0.032	1.000								
VOL	0.021	−0.012	1.000							
SIZE	−0.041	−0.009	0.006	1.000						
VAROE	0.010	−0.004	0.082	−0.036	1.000					
FOCUS	−0.019	−0.010	−0.058	−0.126	0.026	1.000				
LEV	0.014	−0.002	0.091	0.089	0.057	0.021	1.000			
DLT	0.015	−0.005	0.080	0.079	0.016	0.079	0.528	1.000		
IOWN	0.021	−0.034	0.058	0.279	0.032	−0.038	−0.003	0.041	1.000	
MFUND	0.012	−0.021	−0.006	0.238	0.038	0.040	−0.009	−0.015	0.776	1.000

The table presents the structure of correlation between exogenous and endogenous variables. The variables are measured annually over the period 1997–2003. For each variable, we provide means, medians, minimums, maximums, and standard deviation. IV_CAPM is the sum of the squared errors from firm-level CAPM regressions. IV_CLMX is the firm-level measure of idiosyncratic risk from the CLMX-model regressions. VOL is the annual mean of daily volume expressed as a percentage of outstanding shares. SIZE is the logarithm of annual turnover expressed in millions of euros. VAROE is the five-year rolling mean variance of ROE. FOCUS is the annual sales-based Herfindahl index. LEV is the book value of net debt divided by the market value of equity. DLT is the book value of long term debt divided by the book value of total assets. IOWN is the percentage of outstanding shares held by institutional investors. MFUND is the percentage of mutual funds in the ownership to total institutional ownership.

Table 5: Descriptive statistics of monthly volatility.

	Raw data				Post-crash 1987 data			
	MKT	IND	IV_CAPM	IV_CLMX	MKT	IND	IV_CAPM	IV_CLMX
Mean . 10^2	0.176	0.059	0.293	0.604	0.163	0.056	0.280	0.587
Médian . 10^2	0.135	0.049	0.234	0.560	0.135	0.050	0.235	0.574
Maximum . 10^2	3.098	0.878	3.418	5.235	0.519	0.164	0.955	1.644
Minimum . 10^2	0.040	0.013	0.097	0.199	0.040	0.013	0.097	0.199
Std. Dev. . 10^2	0.224	0.065	0.265	0.424	0.089	0.030	0.150	0.230
Linear Trend . 10^5	0.210	0.201	0.614	0.886	0.393	0.154	0.610	1.002
Observations	204	204	204	204	192	192	192	192

The table presents descriptive statistics of monthly volatility constructed from daily data. MKT is the market volatility constructed from Eq. (30), IND is the industry-level volatility constructed from Eq. (32), IV_CAPM is residual volatility constructed from Eq. (7) and IV_CLMX is firm-level volatility constructed from Eqs. (33)–(35). All measures are value-weighted variances.

Table 6: Autocorrelation structure of monthly volatility measures.

Autocorrelation	Raw data				Post-crash 1987 data			
	MKT	IND	IV_CAPM	IV_CLMX	MKT	IND	IV_CAPM	IV_CLMX
ρ_1	0.120	0.137	0.241	0.385	0.621	0.786	0.689	0.625
ρ_2	0.089	0.074	0.105	0.053	0.428	0.622	0.468	0.432
ρ_3	0.034	0.104	0.095	0.059	0.280	0.552	0.364	0.367
ρ_4	−0.004	0.084	0.072	0.029	0.247	0.507	0.222	0.289
ρ_5	0.021	0.062	0.026	−0.023	0.243	0.496	0.197	0.225
ρ_6	−0.008	0.050	0.029	−0.040	0.246	0.461	0.191	0.195
ρ_{12}	0.019	0.098	0.082	0.038	0.304	0.549	0.363	0.265

The table presents the autocorrelation structure of monthly volatility measures constructed from *daily data*. MKT is the market volatility constructed from Eq. (30), IND is the industry-level volatility constructed from Eq. (32), IV_CAPM is residual volatility constructed from Eq. (7) and IV_CLMX is firm-level volatility constructed from Eqs. (33)–(35). All measures are value weighted variances.

As pointed out by Bennett and Sias (2005), we can observe that the resonance of autocorrelation, evaluated by the coefficients p_i from order 1 to 12, is statistically much weaker with raw data than with the second type of data.

We employ augmented Dickey and Fuller (1979) p-tests and t-tests based on regressions of time series on their lagged values and lagged difference terms that account for serial correlation. The results of unit root tests based on monthly measures of MKT, IND, IV_CAPM, and IV_CLMX are reported in Table 7. The null hypothesis of unit roots is rejected at the level of 5% for all the four measures tested. When we look at the coefficients of the determinist trend, our results confirm the importance of the coefficients of IV_CAPM and IV_CLMX are statistically higher than those of MKT and IND.

In this first part, we have extended the studies of Campbell *et al.* (2001) and Bennett and Sias (2005) to European securities. Our results confirm the hypothesis of an increase of idiosyncratic volatility underlined graphically. In addition, we find that firm-specific risk stand for the most part of the total variance of an average stock. In the following section, we will focus on the determinants of the both measures of idiosyncratic volatility: IV_CAPM and IV_CLMX. So, why has firm-level volatility increased in Europe over time?

4.2 Results from Panel Data Regressions

The model estimated from Eq. (39) has been tested considering the whole panel of 250 European listed firms. The results are shown in Table 8 for three types of data. The model in the first column includes all independent variables tested with raw data for both measures of idiosyncratic volatility IV_CAPM and IV_CLMX. The models in the second and third columns include all independent variables tested with and without the effect of Internet bubble.

Generally speaking, we observe that the coefficients of exogenous variables are not stable through time since both the value and the level of significance change considerably in relation to data. For instance, in the first regression tested from IV_CAPM, the coefficient of FOCUS is not significant with the raw data and the post-crash data. Inversely, the parameter becomes significant for the data corresponding to the period 1988–1998. Actually, only the control variables VOL and SIZE are globally significant at the level of 5% for all types of data. Consequently, the results reported in Table 7 do not support the hypotheses exposed above for the whole period 1987–2003.

However, we find strong results when the data do not include the two pikes of volatility related to the crash of October 1987 and the Internet bubble. Thus,

Table 7: Unit roots ADF tests on monthly measures of volatility.

	Raw data				Post-crash 1987 data			
	MKT	IND	IV_CAPM	IV_CLMX	MKT	IND	IV_CAPM	IV_CLMX
ADF Tests with intercept								
t-test	−8.681	−8.775	−8.271	−8.787	−5.693	−4.501	−5.454	−5.727
F-statistic	79.345	76.368	61.266	46.375	23.460	11.377	17.389	22.966
Lag order	2234				243			5
ADF Tests with trend and intercept								
Linear trend . 10^5	0.210	0.201***	0.614**	0.886**	0.393***	0.154***	0.610***	1.002***
t-test	−8.705	−9.234	−8.544	−9.072	−6.990	−6.641	−6.717	−7.010
F-statistic	52.988	54.337	42.624	32.414	21.467	15.640	16.829	21.061
Lag order	1212				231			3

The table reports unit-root tests for monthly volatilities series constructed from daily data. MKT is the market volatility constructed from Eq. (30), IND is the industry-level volatility constructed from Eq. (32), IV_CAPM is residual volatility constructed from Eq. (7) and IV_CLMX is firm-level volatility constructed from Eqs. (33)–(35). All measures are value weighted variances. The unit root tests are based on regressions that include a constant or a constant and a time trend. The critical value for the Dickey–Fuller p-tests are −8.00 when a constant is included in the regression and −21.5 when a constant and a linear trend are included. The 5% values for the t-test are 2.87 with a constant and 3.42 with a constant and a deterministic trend. The number of lags is determined by the general to specific method recommended by Campbell and Perron (1991).

*,** ,*** significant at the level of 0.10, 0.05 et 0.01.

Table 8: The corporate determinants of idiosyncratic volatility.

Variables	Idiosyncratic volatility (IV)					
	IV_CAPM			IV_CLMX		
	Raw data	Data post-crash 1987	Data post-crash 1987 and Internet bubble	Raw data	Data post-crash 1987	Data post-crash 1987 and Internet bubble
Intercept	0.712***	0.578***	0.368***	0.317***	0.675***	0.436***
	(0.020)	(0.040)	(0.023)	(0.034)	(0.037)	(0.031)
VOL	0.305***	0.330***	0.245***	0.353***	0.474***	0.286***
	(0.068)	(0.062)	(0.042)	(0.042)	(0.034)	(0.052)
SIZE	−0.315	−0.501*	−0.575**	−0.215**	−0.297**	−0.260**
	(0.237)	(0.278)	(0.293)	(0.103)	(0.148)	(0.125)
VAROE	0.070*	0.053*	0.033	−0.018	0.037	−0.033
	(0.040)	(0.031)	(0.041)	(0.038)	(0.032)	(0.049)
FOCUS	0.138	0.136	0.207***	0.079	0.116	0.216**
	(0.106)	(0.091)	(0.074)	(0.099)	(0.096)	(0.098)
LEV	−0.061	0.071	0.099*	0.052	0.067*	0.110***
	(0.092)	(0.088)	(0.054)	(0.040)	(0.037)	(0.034)
DLT	−0.003	−0.005	−0.002	−0.003	−0.006	−0.011
	(0.013)	(0.016)	(0.013)	(0.027)	(0.020)	(0.016)
IOWN	0.029*	0.029**	0.043***	0.042	0.041	0.056**
	(0.015)	(0.014)	(0.016)	(0.038)	(0.030)	(0.027)

(*Continued*)

Table 8: (*Continued*)

Variables	Idiosyncratic volatility (IV)					
	IV_CAPM			IV_CLMX		
	Raw data	Data post-crash 1987	Data post-crash 1987 and Internet bubble	Raw data	Data post-crash 1987	Data post-crash 1987 and Internet bubble
MFUND	−0.003	0.003	−0.013	0.005	0.007*	0.006*
	(0.004)	(0.006)	(0.009)	(0.003)	(0.003)	(0.004)
Number of observations	4250	4000	2750	4250	4000	2750
Adjusted R^2	0.165	0.183	0.205	0.137	0.149	0.234
Fischer test (p-value)	< 0.001	< 0.001	< 0.001	< 0.001	< 0.001	< 0.001
Hausman test (H-value)	14.883*	16.352*	26.701***	12.865	15.161*	21.870***

The table reports coefficients and standard errors estimates from a fixed-effect regression. The values of adjusted R^2, *Fischer p-test* and *Hausman* statistics (*H-test*) are also reported. The estimated model is based on three types of data from the sample of 250 European listed firms: raw data, post-crash 1987 data and internet bubble. IV_CAPM is the sum of the squared errors from firm-level CAPM regressions. IV_CLMX is the firm-level measure of idiosyncratic risk from the CLMX-model regressions. VOL is the annual mean of daily volume expressed as a percentage of outstanding shares. SIZE is the logarithm of annual turnover expressed in millions of euros. VAROE is the five-year rolling mean variance of ROE. FOCUS is the annual sales-based Herfindahl index. LEV is the book value of net debt divided by the market value of equity. DLT is the book value of long term debt divided by the book value of total assets. IOWN is the percentage of outstanding shares held by institutional investors. MFUND is the percentage of mutual funds in the ownership to total institutional ownership.

*,** ,*** significant at the level of 0.10, 0.05 and 0.01.

it corresponds to a restrained period 1988–1998 reported in the third column. The five variables that relate directly to our three hypotheses are FOCUS, VOL, DLT, IOWN, and MFUND.

The coefficient of the variable FOCUS is positive and significant at the level of 5% for both IV_CAPM and IV_CLMX. The value of t-statistic is, respectively, equal to 2.78 and 2.21. Consistent with modeling a firm as a portfolio of business segments, the positive and statistically significant coefficient on Herfindahl indicates that an increase in a firm's focus, as measured by the revenue-based Herfindahl index, is associated with an increase in firm-level volatility.

Besides, we find the correlation that higher leverage is associated with higher idiosyncratic volatility. The coefficients are positive and significant at the level of 5%. An idiosyncratic shock to the value of the firm's assets is increased by a factor LEV and passed through to the equity returns: $\sigma_{S_t}^2 = \sigma_{V_t}^2[1 + L_t]$. Even so, the variable DLT measuring debt maturity is not significant.

Last, surprisingly, only the variable IOWN related to institutional ownership is positive and statistically significant at the level of 5%. This is consistent with the herding-based hypotheses outlined in Sec. 2. In return, the variable MFUND related to mutual fund ownership is not significant at the level of 5%. In other words, we find that the fraction of institutions that are not mutual funds is important in explaining the increase in a firm's idiosyncratic volatility through time. Therefore, contrary to the findings reported by Dennis and Strickland (2002), we cannot predict that mutual funds' managers are more subject to herding than other institutional investors.

The control variable SIZE is what we would expect: through time, as a company gets larger and more mature, its idiosyncratic volatility decreases. Furthermore, as turnover in the firm's shares increases, measured by the variable VOL, its idiosyncratic volatility increases. It takes trading volume to move prices and create volatility. However, the variability of ROE (VAROE) is not significant what is not consistent with the findings of Marsh and Frazzini (2005).

5 Robustness Checks

The results reported in the third column of Table 8 related to the period 1988–1998 can be biased by some endogenous elements. Then, we carry out some robustness checks based on usual tests to be sure that the determinants of idiosyncratic volatility upward are statistically robust. Then, we estimate another model to check if the cross-sectional changes of idiosyncratic volatility are still linked with the changes of the independent variables.

5.1 *Usual Tests*

Though the results in Table 8 are statistically significant, they could be driven by correlation among the independent variables or by specific definitions for the independent variables. As pointed out by Dennis and Strickland (2005), to be sure that our results are still robust, we estimate model (39) while controlling for correlation among the independent variables and using alternative definitions of the independent variables.

As institutional investors prefer large firms and liquid stocks, we could expect a strong correlation effect between all the independent variables and the variable IOWN. The correlation of institutional ownership with VOL and SIZE may indicate that the results obtained from the first model could be contaminated by proxy effects. To address this issue, we orthogonalize the independent variables with the variables in the following order: constant, SIZE, VOL, and IOWN. While the magnitudes of the coefficient estimates differ from those presented in Table V, the sign and significance of the coefficients are unchanged. In the interest of brevity, the results are not tabulated.

We also estimate the model (39) by testing alternative specifications of the independent variables in order to control the robustness of the regression specification. We replace the variable FOCUS measured from revenue-based Herfindahl index with for-digit SIC codes. We also replace the variable LEV based on the market value of equity with the book value of total assets. Finally, we substitute the change in institutional ownership with a dummy variable equal to 0 if IOWN < 0 and 1 otherwise. For brevity, the results are not reported. The coefficients reported are still quantitatively and qualitatively similar to those obtained from the original specification reported in Table 8.

5.2 *Cross-Sectional Changes in Idiosyncratic Volatility*

Our ambition is now to determine the cross-sectional determinants of idiosyncratic volatility changes over time. One approach would be to regress the level of idiosyncratic volatility on the proportion of all the independent variables. This is problematic since some variables may covary with other ones. For instance, institutional investors may prefer larger securities, more liquid stocks, and more focused companies. One possible solution is to regress the lagged change in idiosyncratic volatility on the changes on all independent variables.

To determine the cross-sectional relations between the significant exogenous variables exhibited in the first model and idiosyncratic volatility, we estimate the following cross-sectional regression:

$$\Delta \mathrm{IV}_{it} = \alpha_i + \alpha_1 \Delta \mathrm{VOL}_{it} + \alpha_2 \Delta \mathrm{SIZE}_{it} + \alpha_3 \Delta \mathrm{FOCUS}_{it} + \alpha_4 \Delta \mathrm{LEV}_{it} + \alpha_5 \Delta \mathrm{IOWN}_{it} + \xi_{it}.$$

Table 9 presents the results of two different specifications for the period 1988–1998. The model in the first and in the second column reports, respectively, the determinants of the changes of ΔIV_CAPM and ΔIV_CLMX. We find

Table 9: The corporate determinants of idiosyncratic volatility.

Variables	Change in idisosyncratic volatility (IV)	
	IV_CAPM	IV_CLMX
Intercept	0.329***	0.165***
	(0.038)	(0.022)
VOL	0.417***	0.537***
	(0.160)	(0.143)
SIZE	−0.082	−0.099
	(0.058)	(0.077)
FOCUS	0.017*	0.056***
	(0.010)	(0.011)
LEV	0.003	−0.014
	(0.003)	(0.020)
IOWN	0.051*	0.118***
	(0.021)	(0.022)
Number of observations	2750	2750
Adjusted R^2	0.010	0.058
Fischer test (*p*-value)	<0.100	<0.001

The table reports coefficients and standard errors estimates from a fixed-effect regression. The values of adjusted R^2 and *Fischer p-test* are also reported. The estimated model is based upon post-crash 1987 data for the period 1988–1998 from a sample of 250 European listed firms. IV_CAPM is the sum of the squared errors from firm-level CAPM regressions. IV_CLMX is the firm-level measure of idiosyncratic risk from the CLMX-model regressions. VOL is the annual mean of daily volume expressed as a percentage of outstanding shares. SIZE is the logarithm of annual turnover expressed in millions of euros. VAROE is the five-year rolling mean variance of ROE. FOCUS is the annual sales-based Herfindahl index. LEV is the book value of net debt divided by the market value of equity. DLT is the book value of long term debt divided by the book value of total assets. IOWN is the percentage of outstanding shares held by institutional investors. MFUND is the percentage of mutual funds in the ownership to total institutional ownership.
*, **, *** significant at the level of 0.10, 0.05 and 0.01.

that the changes in idiosyncratic risk are strongly correlated with the variation of volume exchanged each day. The coefficient for VOL is, respectively, 0.417 and 0.537 and equality of the coefficient and zero is rejected with a *t*-statistic of 3.601 and 4.756. The variation of the variables FOCUS and IOWN are also strongly correlated with the changes of firm-level volatility. The parameters reported in the regressions are significant at a level of 1% for ΔIV_CLMX whereas the coefficients are not significant to explain the variation of IV_CAPM. However, changes in SIZE and LEV do not covary with the changes of idiosyncratic volatility (ΔIV).

6 Conclusion

In this paper, we have tried to extend the model of Campbell *et al.* (2001) related to the evolution of idiosyncratic risk on an original sample of 250 European listed firms. We have used the MSCI Europe Index which is a composite index for the whole European stock markets to compute the residual components of financial volatility. Our results show a strong increase of both industry-level and firm-level volatility. Then, we examine the time-series and cross-sectional determinants of this upward. In the time-series, we find that the increase in idiosyncratic volatility is positively related to increased firm focus, leverage, and institutional ownership. Besides, idiosyncratic risk is also strongly and positively correlated with the volume of outstanding shares traded within a day and the size of companies. However, we find surprisingly no correlation with debt maturity and the percentage of mutual fund ownership. We also carry out a cross-sectional analysis of the determinants of the changes of idiosyncratic volatility. We find that in the cross-section, changes in idiosyncratic volatility are positively related to changes in focus and institutional ownership.

Acknowledgement

I am grateful to Gérard Hirigoyen (IRGO) for his insightful supervision and to Narjess Boubakri (HEC Montréal) for her help and encouragement.

References

Bali, GT, Gakici, N, Yan, X and Zhang, Z (2005). Does idiosyncratic rick really matters? *Journal of Finance*, 60, 1234–1262.

Barberis, N and Huang, M (2001). Mental accounting, loss aversion and individual stock returns. *Journal of Finance*, 56, 1247–1292.

Becht, M and Rok, A (1999). Blockholdings in Europe: An international comparison. *European Economic Review*, 43, 1049–1056.

Bennett, J and Sias, R (2005). Why has firm specific risk increased over time? *Review of Financial Studies,* 17, 334–366.

Berger, P and Ofek, E (1999). Causes and effects of corporate refocusing programs. *Review of Financial Studies,* 12, 311–345.

Black, F and Scholes, M (1973). The valuation of options and corporate liabilities. *Journal of Political Economy,* 81, 637–659.

Campbell, JY, Lettau, M, Malkiel, B and Xu, Y (2001). Have individual stocks become more volatile? An empirical exploration of idiosyncratic risk. *Journal of Finance*, 56, 1–43.

Chakravarty, S (2001). Stealth trading: Which traders' trades move stock prices? *Journal of Financial Economics*, 61, 289–307.

Chan, L and Lakonishok, J (1995). The behavior of stock prices around institutional trades. *Journal of Finance*, 50, 1147–1174.

Chang, E and Dong, S (2005). Idiosyncratic volatility, fundamentals and institutional herding: Evidence from the Japanese stock market. Working Paper, New York: Columbia University, 29.

Chordia, T, Roll, R and Subrahmanyam, M (2001). Market liquidity and trading activity. *Journal of Finance*, 56, 501–547.

Comin, D and Philippon, T (2005). The rise in firm-level volatility: Causes and consequences. *NBER Twentieth Annual Conference on Macroeconomics*, MIT & NBER, New York, 44.

Comment, R and Jarrel, A (1995). Corporate focus and stock returns. *Journal of Financial Economics,* 37, 67–87.

Conrad, J, Johnson, K and Wahal, S (2002). The trading of institutional investors: Theory and evidence. *Journal of Applied Finance,* 12, 134–179.

Constantidines, G (1986). Capital market equilibrium with transactions costs. *Journal of Political Economy,* 94, 842–862.

Dennis, P and Strickland, D (2002). Who blinks in volatile markets, individuals or institutions? *Journal of Finance*, 57, 1923–1949.

Dennis, P and Strickland, D (2005). The determinants of idiosyncratic volatility. Working Paper, University of North Carolina, Chapell Hill, 37.

Desai, A and Jain, P (1999). Firm performance and focus: Long run stock market performance following spin-offs. *Journal of Financial Economics,* 44, 75–101.

Devogelaer, D (2003). *European Refocusing Throughout Nineties.* PhD, Applied Economics, University of Leuven, Faculty of Economics and Applied Economics, Leuven, Belgium, 345.

Dickey, D and Fuller, W (1979). Distribution of the estimators for autoregressive time series with a unit root. *Journal of the American Statistical Association,* 74, 427–431.

Faccio, M and Lang, L (2005). The ultimate ownership of western European corporations. *Journal of Financial Economics,* 66, 342–388.

Ferreira, M and Laux, P (2007). Corporate governance, idiosyncratic risk and information flow. *Journal of Finance,* 62(2), 951–989.

Figlewski, S and Wang, X (2000). Is the "leverage effect" a leverage effect? Working Paper, NYU, Stern Business School, New York, 43.

Froot, K, Scharfstein, D and Stein, J (1992). Herd on the street: Informationnal inefficiencies in a market with short-term speculation. *Journal of Finance*, 47, 1461–1484.

Gilson, S, Healy, P, Noe, C and Palepu, K (2001). Corporate focus and the benefits from more specialized analyst coverage. *Journal of Financial Economics,* 59, 413–440.
Gompers, P and Metrick, A (2001). Institutional investors and equity prices. *Quarterly Journal of Economics,* 116, 229–259.
Goyal, A and Santa-Clara, P (2003). Idiosyncratic risk matters! *Journal of Finance,* 58, 975–1007.
Griffin, J, Harris, J and Topaloglu, S (2003). The dynamics of institutional and individual trading. *Journal of Finance,* 58, 2285–2320.
Guo, H and Savickas, R (2004). Aggregate idiosyncratic volatility in G7 countries. Working Paper # 36, Washington: Washington University, 41.
Hamada, RS (1972). The effects of capital structure on the systematic risk of common stocks. *Journal of Finance,* 27, 435–452.
Heaton, J and Lucas, D (2000). Portfolio choice and asset prices: The importance of entrepreneurial risk. *Journal of Finance,* 55, 1163–1198.
Hirt, G and Pandher, G (2005). Idiosyncratic risk and return across S&P500 stocks. Working Paper, DePaul University, 44.
Irvine, P and Pontiff, J (2005). Idiosyncratic return volatility, cash flows, and product market competition. Working Paper, Carroll School of Management, Boston College, Boston, 53.
John, K and Ofek, E (1995). Asset sales and increase in focus. *Journal of Financial Economics,* 37, 105–126.
Johnson, R (1996). Antecedents and outcomes of corporate refocusing. *Journal of Management,* 22, 439–483.
Kirchmaier, T and Grant, J (2005). Corporate ownership structure and performance in Europe. Working Paper, London School of Economics, 36.
Levy, C (1978). Equilibrium in an imperfect market: A constraint in the number of securities in the portfolio. *American Economic Review,* 68, 643–658.
Lins, K and Servaes, H (1999). International evidence of the value of corporate diversification. *Journal of Finance,* 54, 2215–2240.
Lintner, J (1965). The valuation of risks assets and the selection of risky investments in stock portfolios and capital budgets. *Review of Economics and Statistics,* 47, 13–37.
Lubatkin, M and Chatterjee, S (1994). Extending modern portfolio theory into the domain of corporate diversification: Does it apply? *Academy of Management Journal,* 37, 109–136.
Malkiel, B and Xu, Y (2003). Investigating the behavior of idiosyncratic volatility. *Journal of Business,* 76, 613–645.
Markides, C (1992). Consequences of corporate refocusing: *Ex ante* evidence. *Academy of Management Journal,* 35, 398–412.
Markides, C (1995). *Diversification, Refocusing and Economic Performance,* 1st Ed. Cambridge: MIT Press, 345.
Markowitz, H (1952). Portfolio selection. *Journal of Finance,* 7, 77–91.
Marsh, I and Frazzini, A (2005). Idiosyncratic volatility in the US and UK equity markets. *NBER Twentieth Annual Conference on Macroeconomics,* Yale University & NBER, New York, 37.
Mayers, D (1976). Non-marketable assets, market segmentation and the level of asset prices. *Journal of Financial and Quantitative Analysis,* 11, 1–12.

Merton, R (1987). A simple model of capital market equilibrium with incomplete information. *Journal of Finance*, 42, 483–510.
Nielsen, K (2004). Institutional investors and the market for corporate governance in Europe. Working Paper, University of Copenhagen, Copenhagen, 32.
Nosfinger, J and Sias, R (1999). Herding and feedback trading by institutional and individual investors. *Journal of Finance*, 54, 2263–2299.
Philippon, T (2002). Corporate governance and aggregate volatility. Working Paper # 56, MIT, Cambridge, 36.
Rampini, A (2004). Entrepreneurial activity, risk and the business cycle. *Journal of Political Economy,* 112, 433–477.
Scharfstein, D and Stein, J (1990). Herd bahavior and investment. *American Economic Review,* 80, 465–479.
Schwert, GW (1989). Why does stock market volatility change over time? *Journal of Finance,* 44, 1115–1153.
Sias, R and Starks, L (1997). Institutional and individuals and the turn of the year. *Journal of Finance,* 52, 897–923.
Stapleton, R and Subrahmanyam, M (1983). The market model and capital asset pricing theory. *Journal of Finance*, 38, 1637–1642.
Thomsen, S and Pedersen, T (2002). Ownership structure and economic performance in the largest European companies. *Strategic Management Journal,* 21, 689–705.
Vuolteenaho, T (2002). What drives firm level stock returns? *Journal of Finance*, 57, 263–264.

CHAPTER 15

DEBT VALUATION, ENTERPRISE ASSESSMENT AND APPLICATIONS

*Didier Vanoverberghe**

The interactive impact of the leverage effects of debt, of taxes, of the risk of bankruptcy and the generation of free cash flow, on the enterprise value, is a constant concern for business leaders in order to make investments and financial decisions. We will focus on that topic throwing a new light on recent theoretic developments in the framework of: cost information, cost of bankruptcy, tax savings, coupons, and principal payments of the debt.
In this framework, this chapter:

- *provides the equity value as a Call of the enterprise value on the debt increased by the coupons effects and the risk of bankruptcy effects;*
- *demonstrates that the values of the different assets have stochastic drifts μ and volatilities σ;*
- *gives the values of these rates;*
- *provides an adjusted CAPM and an instantaneous Beta which is stochastic and time-dependent, that better fits with the current reality;*
- *make the link between the various models studied of which the usual model is of the financial analysts Discounted Cash Flow (DCF).*

1 Introduction

Before building our models, it is important to recall briefly some fundamentals of corporate valuation. In this respect, a number of major milestones have marked the history of corporate valuation. One will naturally cite the research

*Ingénieur général des Télécommunications.
didier-vanoverberghe@wanadoo.fr

of Franco Modigliani and Merton Miller which stands:

— neutrality of dividend policy (when there is sufficient return on investment) (1961);
— the relative neutrality of capital structure (1958, 1963, 1977).

The impact of bankruptcy costs therefore calls for other developments. Therefore, by forming the hypothesis that corporate debt may be seen as an asset derivative, Merton, R, Black, F and Scholes, M used options theory to value corporate debt.

Various models have been built keeping and demonstrating the equality between the Betas ratio and the elasticity ratio (debt to debt-free assets elasticity ratio), so Cox *et al.* (1979), starting from a binomial equities model obtained this Merton's equality.

Theoreticians of Costs of Information — Leland and Bellalah — have added numerous enhancements by integrating the cost of information (due to imperfect information) and continued the work by integrating all these factors.

In the framework of the Leland model they calculated the enterprise value with constant coupons but not any reimbursement of the principal.

While continuing in the same perspectives this chapter, ambitions to go further in a time-dependent framework.

(1) Firstly, starting from the principle that for a growing asset value, the value of debt tends toward a non-zero value we illustrate on a simple case that the instantaneous volatility of debt thus becomes a random variable and so for the drift. The elasticity thus differs with the Betas ratio.

If we assume that the volatility is constant we obtain a new differential equation that supplements the Merton's equation. Solving the system of the two equations leads to unsuitable solutions. By this way we demonstrate that the drifts μ and the volatilities σ become random variables.

In order to have a base of comparison we use the Leland's model (independent from time: the repayment of debt principal is pushed away) that we complete by costs of information and factor of scale to have a risk of bankruptcy which increase with the coupon. We deduct the various values from it (debt, stockholders' equities, and company) and the stochastic volatility and drift.

(2) Secondly, we are interested to integrate the time factor with coupons and significant debt. We take the space of certain values (risk neutral

probability) and we calculate then the value of the stockholders' equities, of the debt and the company within the framework of a geometrical Brownian model, with the hypothesis of a constant coupon of debt. The formula of valuation of stockholders' equities has to move closer a Call of the value of company on the debt which integrates the coupons effects. The Leland's model — similar to a case of coupon of debt without final repayment of the principal — which we complete by a hypothesis of scalability, serves as a base of comparison.

We give then the stochastic formulas of the drift and of the volatility. We finally propose the model of consistent adjusted CAPM.

(3) As an application we take back the Leland model conclusions in order to integrate them into a classic Discounted Cash Flow (DCF) valuation model used by financial analysts which can include more complete factors of evolutions of the activity and the environment of a company.

Throughout the chapter we will note:

V_S — The equity value (Stock value).
V_d — The value of the debt.
V_E — The value of the Enterprise (adds the two previous ones).

V is the underlying value of the activity of the company excepting bankruptcy effects debt effects and tax saving effects (it corresponds to value of the after taxes EBIT where capex replaces the amortizations).

In other words the enterprise value of company V_E includes that of the activity plus the tax savings minus the costs of bankruptcy:

$$V_E = V + TS - BC.$$

We will symbolize a definition by $\equiv$.

Throughout the chapter we will make the following assumptions:

A1: There are a sufficient number of investors with comparable wealth levels so that each investor believes that he can buy and sell as much of an asset as he wants at the market price.
A2: There exists a riskless asset paying a known constant interest rate r.
A3: Trading takes place continuously and there are no problems with indivisibilities of assets.
A4: There is absence of arbitrage (except possible cost of information effects where we mention it).

A5: There is tax savings risk of bankruptcy; we consider a firm whose activities have value V which follows a geometric Brownian diffusion process:

$$dV = \mu_V * V * dt + \sigma_V * V * dW,$$

where the drift μ_V and the volatility σ_V are deterministic (even constant) and where W is a standard Brownian motion. The stochastic process of V is assumed to be unaffected by the financial structure of the firm, because we take the case where any cash outflows will be financed by the selling stock (Leland, 1994).

2 Stochasticity of Drift and Volatility for the Debt and Equity and Enterprise Values

2.1 *On Debt/Assets Elasticity*

Assuming that the value of a company's debt is expressed as follows:

$$V_d = D_\infty + k * V^{-y} \quad \text{(for example, Leland model)},$$

where V is a random variable representing the value of the debt-free asset, we can deduce that when V becomes infinite

$$D_\infty = \frac{Rd_0 * D_0}{r},$$

where the numerator represents the interest paid on the debt and the denominator represents the Risk Free (plus the cost of information if factored in).

The elasticity

$$\Omega_d = \frac{V}{V_d} * \frac{\partial V_d}{\partial V} = \frac{-y * k * V^{-y}}{D_\infty + k * V^{-y}}$$

is therefore a random variable depending on V, and subsequently we must renounce to the equality $\Omega_d = \frac{\beta_d}{\beta_V}$.

2.2 *Approach Using a Simple Case of a Derivative $F(V)$ with Zero Distribution*

Let us express the value of the asset in the shape of a geometrical Brownian motion:

$$dV = \mu_V * V * dt + \sigma_V * V * dW,$$

where μ_V and σ_V are supposed to be non-stochastic, and let $F(V)$ be a derivative, which accordingly verifies the Itô formula:

$$dF = \frac{1}{2} * \sigma_V^2 * V^2 * \frac{\partial^2 F}{\partial V^2} * dt + \frac{\partial F}{\partial V} * dV.$$

We can define its geometric parameters by:

$$dF = \mu_F F dt + \sigma_F * F * dW.$$

Note $\overset{0}{X} = \frac{\partial X}{\partial V}$ for all X, and we retain:

$$\sigma_F * F = \sigma_V * V * \overset{0}{F},$$

the equality between elasticity and volatilities ratio. We may therefore proceed to partially derive this equality with respect to V, which gives us:

$$\sigma_V^2 * V^2 * \overset{00}{F} = (\sigma_V * V * \overset{0}{\sigma_F} + (\sigma_F - \sigma_V) * \sigma_F) * F.$$

Hence,

$$\frac{dF}{F * dt} - \frac{dF}{F * dt} = \frac{1}{2} * (\sigma_V * V * \overset{0}{\sigma_F} + (\sigma_F - \sigma_V) * \sigma_F) + \mu_V * \frac{\sigma_F}{\sigma_V} - \mu_F = 0,$$

or

$$\mu_F = \mu_V * \frac{\sigma_F}{\sigma_V} + \frac{1}{2} * (\sigma_V * V * \overset{0}{\sigma_F} + (\sigma_F - \sigma_V) * \sigma_F).$$

Besides, we can also apply the lemma of Itô:

$$dF = \frac{1}{2} * \sigma_V^2 * V^2 * F_{VV} dt + F_V * dV + F_t dt$$

using

$$dV = rVdt + \sigma_V * V * \left(dW_V + \frac{\mu_V - r}{\sigma_V} dt \right)$$

$$= rVdt + \sigma_V * V * dW_V^Q$$

and also for F:

$$dF = rFdt + \sigma_F * F * (dW_V + \frac{\mu_F - r}{\sigma_F} dt)$$

$$= rFdt + \sigma_F * F * dW_F^Q,$$

where Q is the risk neutral probability (which allows leaving expected values to obtain certain values). We deduct from it:

$$\frac{1}{2} * \sigma_V^2 * V^2 F_{VV} + rV * F_V + F_t = rF$$

(which is the risk neutral Itô formula in the risk neutral space, known as the Merton's formula) and using the equality between the volatilities ratio and the elasticity:

$$dW_F^Q = \frac{\mu_F - r}{\sigma_F} dt + dW_V = dW_V^Q = \frac{\mu_V - r}{\sigma_V} dt + dW_V$$

which leads to the equality of the risk premium volatility ratio between V and its derivative:

$$AOA_V \equiv \frac{\mu_V - r}{\sigma_V} = \frac{\mu_F - r}{\sigma_F}.$$

This Sharpe ratio shows an absence of opportunity of arbitration between a derivative and its underlying value in regards to the volatility. (Note: For another demonstration see the riskless portfolio built Merton, 1974.)

We still have:

$$\mu_F = \mu_V * \frac{\sigma_F}{\sigma_V} - r * \frac{\sigma_F}{\sigma_V} + r.$$

Therefore,

$$\left(r + \frac{1}{2}\sigma_V * \sigma_F\right)(\sigma_V - \sigma_F) = +\frac{1}{2}\sigma_V^2 * V * \sigma_F^0.$$

By using AOA_V we get:

$$\left(r + \frac{1}{2}\sigma_V * \sigma_F \frac{AOA_V}{AOA_V}\right)(AOA_V\sigma_V - AOA_V\sigma_F) = +\frac{1}{2}\sigma_V^2 AOA_V * V * \sigma_F^0,$$

$$\left(r + \frac{1}{2}\sigma_V * \frac{\mu_F - r}{AOA_V}\right)(\mu_V - \mu_F) = +\frac{1}{2}\sigma_V^2 * V * \mu_F^0.$$

In particular, we deduce that when the volatility of the derivative is not stochastic, the solution is: $(\sigma_V = \sigma_F)$ (and it is V) or $\left(\sigma_F = -\frac{2r}{\sigma_V}\right)$ and $\mu_F = r\left(1 - \frac{2AOA}{\sigma_V}\right)$. $\Big($in this case $\left(\sigma_F = -\sigma_V \frac{2r}{\sigma_V^2}\right)$ to remind the case of Leland's model studied later$\Big)$.

Furthermore,

$$\overline{\mu_F} = \mu_V * \frac{\overline{\sigma_F}}{\sigma_V} + \frac{1}{2} * (\sigma_V * E(V * \sigma_F^0) + E((\sigma_F - \sigma_V) * \sigma_F)).$$

Note: In the case where the volatility of the derivative is deterministic one finds the usual equality between elasticity and ratio of the betas.

2.3 *Case of a Derivative with Constant Volatility and with Constant Distribution (Not Proportional)*

2.3.1 Differential Equations to be Verified

We are interested in a derivative volatility of which constant $y = \Omega_F$ (as an example of the type

$$F(V,t) = D - D_\infty = k * V^{-y}).$$

Let us start with

$$dV = (\mu_V - c_V) * V * dt + \sigma_V * V * dW.$$

We are held in a case where the payment for the holders of securities is financed by selling stock (cf. Leland) in a way that the activities of the firm are not affected by the financial structure and thus $c_V = 0$.

The dynamics of the firm activities (without bankruptcy and tax savings) is given by:

$$dV = \mu_V * V * dt + \sigma_V * V * dW.$$

Similarly, for a derivative we take

$$dF = (\mu_F * F - C_F)dt + \sigma_F * F * dW.$$

Therefore,

$$\frac{\sigma_F}{\sigma_V} = \frac{V}{F} * \frac{\partial F}{\partial V} = Cte = \Omega$$

is thus a constant that we withdraw out of the equality stemming from Itô and from the geometrical shape. Therefore,

$$E\left(\frac{dF}{F * dt} - \frac{dF}{F * dt}\right) = E\left(\frac{1}{2} * \sigma_V^2 * \frac{V^2}{F} * \frac{\partial^2 F}{\partial V^2} + \frac{1}{F}\frac{\partial F}{\partial V} * \mu_V * V - \mu_F + \frac{C_F(V)}{F} + \frac{1}{F}\frac{\partial F}{\partial t}\right).$$

Thus (cf. Appendix A.1),

$$\frac{1}{2} * \sigma_V^2 * V^2 * \frac{\partial^2 F}{\partial V^2} + r * V * \frac{\partial F}{\partial V} - rF + E\left(\frac{C_F(V)}{F} + \frac{\partial F(V,t)}{F\partial t}\right) * F = 0.$$

Furthermore, with AOA_V we get the Merton equation:

$$\frac{1}{2} * \sigma_V^2 * V^2 \frac{\partial^2 F}{\partial V^2} + rV \frac{\partial F}{\partial V} + \frac{\partial F}{\partial t} = rF - C_F$$

which corresponds to the writing of the Itô formula in the risk neutral probability.

In case of non-stochastic volatility one thus has two equations which must be verified. We can summarize them in the following system:

(i) $\frac{1}{2} * \sigma_V^2 * V^2 \frac{\partial^2 F}{\partial V^2} + rV \frac{\partial F}{\partial V} + \frac{\partial F}{\partial t} = rF - C_F,$

(ii) $C_F + \frac{\partial F(V,t)}{\partial t} = a(t)F.$

2.3.2 Resolution of the System of Two Differential Equations (cf. Appendix A.2)

We show (cf. Appendix A.2) that if constant C is non-zero or if $\frac{\partial F(V,t)}{\partial t}$ is non-zero, then the various non-coarse solutions (V) are the following ones:

(a) $C_F \neq 0$ and $\frac{\partial F(V,t)}{\partial t} = 0$. Thus, $F = \frac{C_F}{r}$ is a certain equivalent value, that would mean being able to pay the debt infinitely without the risk of bankruptcy.

(b) $C_F \neq 0$ and $\frac{\partial F(V,t)}{\partial t} \neq 0$. Therefore,

$$F = \frac{C_F}{r} + (A + B_1 V^{y_2}) \exp rt$$

or

$$F = -C_F t + B_1 V^{y_1} \quad \text{with } y_1 = \frac{-2r}{\sigma_V^2}.$$

Furthermore, in the simple case of debt without coupon, we have to obtain the formula of Black and Scholes for the value of stockholders' equities: a Call of the enterprise value on the debt. Thus, in this general frame there is no solution adapted to the constant volatility of the return on the capital.

The drift μ_F and the volatility σ_F of a time-dependent derivative distributing a non-zero coupon are stochastic (similarly in the presence of cost of bankruptcy).

2.3.3 Case of an Invariant Derivative ($F_t = 0$) Distributing a Coupon

We shall find their stochastic drift and volatility (cf. Appendix B.1).

$$\frac{1}{2} * \sigma_V^2 * V^2 \frac{\partial^2 F}{\partial V^2} + rV \frac{\partial F}{\partial V} + \frac{\partial F}{\partial t} = rF - C_F = r\left(F - \frac{C_F}{r}\right).$$

We define

$$F' \equiv F - \frac{C}{r}.$$

Therefore

$$dF = dF' = d(KV^{y_1}).$$

We get

$$\frac{1}{2} * \sigma_V^2 * V^2 \frac{\partial^2 F'}{\partial V^2} + rV \frac{\partial F'}{\partial V} = rF'$$

which is simply resolved as: $F' = k_1 V^{y_1}$ with solution $y_1 = \frac{-2r}{\sigma_V^2}$ ($y_0 = 1$ is not kept because it diverges more for V.

Therefore, $F = \frac{C_F}{r} + KV^{y_1}$

$$AOA_V = \frac{\mu_V - r}{\sigma_V} = \frac{\mu_F - r}{\sigma_F}$$

$$\sigma_{F'} = \sigma_V y_1$$

and

$$\mu_{F'} = r + \left(\frac{\mu_V - r}{\sigma_V}\right)\sigma_{F'} = r + (\mu_V - r)y_1$$

Note: We do not use boundary conditions.

Furthermore,

$$\sigma_F = \sigma_{F'} \frac{F'}{F} = \sigma_{F'} \frac{F - \frac{C}{r}}{F} = \sigma_V y_1 \frac{F - \frac{C}{r}}{F}$$

is stochastic.

$$\mu_F = r + \frac{\mu_V - r}{\sigma_V}\sigma_F = r + (\mu_V - r)y_1 \frac{F - \frac{C}{r}}{F}$$

is stochastic too. we can also note:

$$\mu_F = r + AOA_V \sigma_{F'} \frac{F'}{F}.$$

We obtain:

$$dF = \left(\left(r + (\mu_V - r)y_1 \frac{F - \frac{C}{r}}{F}\right) F - C\right) dt + \left(\sigma_V y_1 \frac{F - \frac{C}{r}}{F}\right) FdW,$$

the formula which brings to light the stochastic drift and volatility.

One will retain that it is thus interesting to shift F by removing certain equivalent value of the coupons to pass to F' which is inevitably a martingale, and the valuation of which is then simple, and we get back to F.

Let us generalize this approach in the case of a time-dependent derivative.

2.3.4 General Case $F(V, t)$ (cf. Appendix B.2)

Let us define $F' \equiv F - \frac{C}{r}$. We have

$$\begin{aligned} dF &= (\mu_F F - C)dt + \sigma_F F dW, \\ dF' &= \mu_{F'} F' dt + \sigma_{F'} F' dW, \\ AOA_V &= \frac{\mu_V - r}{\sigma_V} = \frac{\mu_F - r}{\sigma_F} = \frac{\mu_{F'} - r}{\sigma_{F'}}, \quad \text{and} \\ dF &= dF'. \end{aligned}$$

And the lemma of Itô pulls that

$$\sigma_{F'} F' = \sigma_V V \frac{\partial F'}{\partial V} = \sigma_V V \frac{\partial F}{\partial V} = \sigma_F F,$$

$$\sigma_F = \sigma_{F'} \frac{F'}{F} = \sigma_{F'} \frac{F - \frac{C}{r}}{F},$$

$$\mu_F = r + \frac{\mu_V - r}{\sigma_V}\sigma_F = r + \left(\frac{\mu_V - r}{\sigma_V}\right) \sigma_{F'} \frac{F - \frac{C}{r}}{F}.$$

2.3.5 General Equation with Costs of Information

We suppose that drifts and volatilities can be stochastic, and we take the deterministic costs of information.

$$dV = (\mu_V - c_V) * V * dt + \sigma_V * V * dW$$

or simply

$$\begin{aligned} dV &= \mu_V * V * dt + \sigma_V * V * dW, \\ dF &= (\mu_F * F - C_F)dt + \sigma_F * F * dW \\ 0 &= (dF - dF)/dt \\ &= \frac{1}{2} * \sigma_V^2 * V^2 F_{VV} + F_V * (\mu_V - c_v)V - \mu_F F + C_F + F_t. \end{aligned}$$

We shall use AOA_V with costs of information:

$$AOA_V = \frac{(\mu_{F'} - \lambda_{F'}) - r}{\sigma_{F'}} = \frac{(\mu_V - \lambda_V) - r}{\sigma_V} = \frac{(\mu_F - \lambda_F) - r}{\sigma_{F'}}.$$

We have $\lambda_F = \lambda_{F'}$ (cf. demonstration Proposition 3, Appendix B)

$$\sigma_{F'} * F' = \sigma_V * V * F'_V = \sigma_V * V * F_V = \sigma_F * F.$$

Therefore,

$$\begin{aligned} f &= \frac{1}{2} * \sigma_V^2 * V^2 F_{VV} + (r + \lambda_v - c_v + \mu_V - r - \lambda_v) * V * F_V + F_t \\ &= (r + \lambda_F + \mu_F - r - \lambda_F)F - C \\ f &= \frac{1}{2} * \sigma_V^2 * V^2 F_{VV} + (r + \lambda_v - c_v)V * F_V \\ &\quad + (\mu_V - r - \lambda_v) * V * F_V + F_t \\ &= (r + \lambda_F)F + (\mu_F - r - \lambda_F)F - C \end{aligned}$$

or

$$\begin{aligned} (\mu_V - r - \lambda_v) * V * F_V &= AOA_V \sigma_v * V * F_V = AOA_V * \sigma_F F \\ &= (\mu_F - r - \lambda_F)F. \end{aligned}$$

Thus,

$$\frac{1}{2} * \sigma_V^2 * V^2 F_{VV} + (r + \lambda_v - c_v)V * F_V + F_t = (r + \lambda_F)F - C$$

$$\frac{1}{2} * \sigma_V^2 * V^2 F_{VV} + (r + \lambda_v - c_v)V * F_V + F_t = (r + \lambda_F)\left(F - \frac{C}{r + \lambda_F}\right).$$

We find the generally given equations without using Beta but only AOA_V; they thus have a more general feature.

We note furthermore that the differential equations being linear for the vector $(V, F, C) \to \lambda(V, F, C)$ we can make a hypothesis of scalability.

2.4 Calculation of the Value of Stockholders' Equities in the Case of Fixed or Proportional Costs of Bankruptcy to a Trigger Value (Leland's Model)

We take back here the approach of Leland, that means a resolution in the case of time independence, which can justify itself in at least two different cases:

A1 — Very long maturity of the debt such that the return of the principal has a value close to zero and can be thus ignored

A1bis — An alternative time-independent environment is when, at each moment, the debt matures but is rolled over at a fixed interest rate (or fixed premium to a reference risk-free rate) unless terminated because of failure to meet a minimum value. This environment bears resemblance to some revolving credit agreements.

We complete the model by introducing the costs of information.

We thus have (in a risk neutral probability or after transformation of the derivative):

$$\frac{1}{2} * \sigma_V^2 * V^2 F_{VV} + (r + \lambda_v - c_v)V * F_V = (r + \lambda_F)\left(F - \frac{C}{r + \lambda_F}\right).$$

Then

$$F' \equiv F - \frac{C}{(r + \lambda_F)}.$$

We have the equality of the partial derivatives and thus:

$$\frac{1}{2} * \sigma_V^2 * V^2 F'_{VV} + (r + \lambda_v - c_v)V * F'_V = (r + \lambda_F)F',$$

and therefore (cf. Appendix B, Proposition 3),

$$\lambda_F = \lambda'_F.$$

Thus,

$$F = kV^{y_1} + \frac{C}{(r + \lambda_F)}$$

with

$$y_1 = \frac{-\left(r + \lambda_V - \frac{\sigma_V 2}{2}\right) - \sqrt{\left(r + \lambda_V - \frac{\sigma_V{}^2}{2}\right)^2 + 2 * \sigma_V{}^2 * (r + \lambda_F)}}{\sigma_V{}^2}$$

$$\left(\text{without costs of information } y_1 = -\frac{2r}{\sigma_V^2}\right).$$

We gave in Sec. 2.3.3 the shape of the drift and volatility.

We complete Leland's model by taking a hypothesis of scalability that allows to keep a bankruptcy possibility even if V grows if the debt (coupons) grows so much.

Indeed, if we add the hypothesis of linearity of the model (idem of scalability), we have

$$F_{\lambda * C_D}(\lambda * V) = \lambda * F_{C_D}(V)$$

and thus, $\lambda(C_D) = \lambda * C_D$ (linear); therefore for

$$\lambda = \frac{1}{C_D},\ F_1\left(\frac{V}{C_D}\right) = \frac{1}{C_D} F_{C_D}(V).$$

By replacing and by multiplying by λ (and making $= 0$), we obtain an almost identical differential equation for F_1. This hypothesis is made in order to show the fact that when the debt grows the risks effect of default also grows (even in the case or V grows if thc debt grows just as much). According to Modigliani and Miller (1958), the value of the company being equal has that of assets (stockholders' equities and debt) plus the tax savings and minus the costs of bankruptcy:

$$V_E(V) = V + TB(V) - BC(V).$$

Let V_B be the value of the assets of the company when the bankruptcy is declared with the cost of bankruptcy, $\alpha * V_B + K$.

Let us calculate the cost of bankruptcy,
$BC(V)$:

$$BC(V) = [\alpha * V_B + K] * \left(\frac{V}{V_B}\right)^{y_1},$$

or with the scalability:

$$BC(V) = [\alpha * V_B + K_B] * \left(\frac{V}{C_D V_{1,B}}\right)^{y_1}.$$

We notably have a cost of bankruptcy which increases when the coupon grows because the exhibitor is negative. If the coupon grew as much as V then the cost of bankruptcy does not reach zero any more when V believes infinitely.

For the debt V_d we define

$$F' = V_d' = V_d - \frac{C_D}{r + \lambda_F};$$

$$\frac{1}{2} * \sigma_V^2 * V^2 F'_{VV} + (r + \lambda_V) * V * F'_V = (r + \lambda_{F'})F';$$

$$\mu_{F'} = r + (\mu_V - r)y_1 = r\left(1 - \frac{2 * AOA}{\sigma_V}\right).$$

We thus have under scalability hypothesis:

$$V_d = \left(\frac{C_D}{r + \lambda_F} + \left[(1 - \alpha) * V_B - K_B - \frac{C_D}{r + \lambda_F}\right] * \left(\frac{V}{C_D V_{1,B}}\right)^{y_1}\right).$$

For the tax savings $TB(V)$ the boundaries give:

$$TB(V) = \tau * \frac{C_D}{r + \lambda_F}\left(1 - \left(\frac{V}{C_D * V_{1,B}}\right)^{y_1}\right),$$

and therefore the enterprise value:

$$V_E(V) = V + TB(V) - BC(V),$$

$$V_E = V + \tau * \frac{C_D}{r + \lambda_F} - \left(\tau * \frac{C_D}{r + \lambda_F} + \alpha * V_B + K\right) * \left(\frac{V}{V_B}\right)^{y_1}.$$

Because for stockholders' equities we have $V_S = V_E - V_d$. Therefore,

$$V_S = V - (1-\tau) * \frac{C_D}{r+\lambda_F} + \left((1-\tau) * \frac{C_D}{r+\lambda_F} - V_B\right) * \left(\frac{V}{C_D V_{1,B}}\right)^{y_1}.$$

We note that the costs of bankruptcy on the company are assumed by the bondholder and not by the shareholder.

3 Assets Values in the Presence of Costs of Bankruptcy and with Debt Coupons

We take a rather additional case of that of the Leland's although more general under certain aspects. We keep the hypotheses of financing the net coupons by sale of shares.

3.1 Calculations of the Value of the Debt

We will be under risk neutral probability, keeping the costs of bankruptcy stemming from the approach of Leland because they can be seen as a derivative without distribution, thus undated of maturity; this corresponds to the idea that the past is less significant toward the costs of bankruptcy than the current value of the company.

One defined the underlying V as being the value of a company without bankruptcy; we have:

$$V_E(t) = V(t) + TS(V) - BC(V),$$

where $BC(V) = B_{V_B} * (\frac{V_B}{V})^y$ with $V_B = D + v_b$ and $y = -y_1 = \frac{2r}{\sigma^2}$ if there is no costs of information;

We have:

$$V(T) = V(t) * \exp\left(\left(r - \frac{1}{2}\sigma^2\right)(T-t) + \sigma_V b^Q\right).$$

To simplify the notation we can put:

$$\Psi = \left(r - \frac{1}{2}\sigma_V^2\right)(T-t) + \sigma_V b^Q,$$

$$G(t) = \text{SumCoupon}(T) = \frac{C}{r}(\exp r(T-t) - 1),$$

where the last term corresponds to the paid coupons.

The risks of bankruptcy are assumed by the bondholder and we have:

$$V_S(t) = \exp -r(T-t) IE^Q([V(T) + TS(V) - BC - (D + G - BC)]^{++}),$$

where ++ means $V(t) \geq V_B$,

$$\begin{aligned} &IE^Q([V(T) - (1-\tau)G(t) - D]^{++}) \\ &= \int_{-\infty}^{+\infty} [V(T) - (1-\tau)G(t) - D]^{++} \\ &\quad * \frac{1}{\sqrt{2\pi(s-t)}} \left(\exp - \left(\frac{b^{Q^2}}{2(s-t)}\right)\right) db^Q. \end{aligned}$$

And we define

$$n' = -\frac{b^Q}{\sqrt{s-t}}, \quad n_b' = \frac{\ln\left(\frac{V_t}{D+v_b}\right) + \left(r - \frac{1}{2}\sigma_V{}^2\right)(T-t)}{\sqrt{T-t}}, \quad \text{and}$$

$$n_b = n_b' + \sigma\sqrt{T-t}.$$

We obtain the Value of stockholders' equities:

$$\begin{aligned} V_S(t) = V(t) * N(n_b) - (1-\tau)\frac{C}{r}(1 - \exp - r(T-t))N(n_b') \\ - \exp - r(T-t)) * D * N(n_b'). \end{aligned}$$

In other words,

$$\begin{aligned} &IE^Q([V(T) - D]^{++}) \\ &\quad = E^Q\left([V(t)\exp\Psi - D - v_b + v_b - (1-\tau)\text{SumCoupon}]^{++}\right) \\ &\quad = E^Q\left([V(t)\exp\Psi - (D + v_b)]^+ + [v_b - (1-\tau)\text{SumCoupon}]^{++}\right), \end{aligned}$$

or still in the form of Call:

$$\begin{aligned} V_S(t) = \text{Call}(V, D + v_b, T, t) + \exp - r(T-t) * v_b * N(n_b') \\ - (1-\tau)\frac{C}{r}(1 - \exp - r(T-t))N(n_b'). \end{aligned}$$

Note: When $D = 0$ and $v_b = 0$, we find the usual formula of the call when we have a debt *in fine* (without coupons). When $D = 0$, we must take into account the coupons effects (v_b is supposed to be small).

The tax savings are worth:

$$TS(V) = \tau \frac{C}{r}(1 - \exp - r(T - t))N(n'_b).$$

For the debt value we have:

$$V_d(t) = V_E(t) - V_S(t)$$

$$V_d(t) = V(t)(1 - N(n_b)) + \frac{C}{r}(1 - \exp - r(T - t))N(n'_b)$$

$$+ \exp - r(T - t) * D * N(n_{b'}) - B * \left(\frac{D + v_b}{Vt}\right)^y,$$

which can also take a shape consisting notably of the value of the enterprise minus a Call and other complement.

$$V_d(t) = V(t) - \text{Call}(V, D + v_b, T, t) + \frac{C}{r}(1 - \exp - r(T - t))N(n'_b)$$

$$- \exp - r(T - t) * v_b * N(n'_b) - B * \left(\frac{D + v_b}{V(t)}\right)^y,$$

$$TS(V) = \tau \frac{C}{r}(1 - \exp - r(T - t))N(n'_b),$$

and

$$V_E(t) = V(t) + \tau \frac{C}{r}(1 - \exp - r(T - t))N(n'_b) - B * \left(\frac{D + v_b}{V(t)}\right)^y.$$

3.2 Example for Particular Cases or in the Limits

3.2.1 Limits When $V \to \infty$

(1) $V \to \infty$ alors $N(n) \to 1$

$$BC(V) \to 0 \quad V_E(t) \sim V(t) + TS(V)$$

$$V_S(t) = V(t) - (1 - \tau)\frac{C}{r}(1 - \exp - r(T - t))$$

$$- \exp - r(T - t) * D$$

$$V_d(T) \sim \frac{C}{r}(1 - \exp - r(T - t)) + \exp - r(T - t) * D.$$

(2) When $t \to T$ if $V \to \infty$ then $N(n) \to 1$

$$BC(V) \to 0 \quad V_E(T) \sim V(T)$$
$$V_S(T) \sim V(T) - D \quad V_d(T) \sim D.$$

3.2.2 Limits at the Beginning of Bankruptcy

$$t \to T \text{ if } V \to V_B^- \text{ then } N(n) \to 0$$
$$BC \sim BV_E(B) = V_B - B \quad V_S(B, T) = 0.$$
$$V_d(B, T) = V_B - B.$$

We find the values at the boundaries given by Leland:

	BC =	TB(V) =	Vs =	Vd =	Ve =
Leland					
V = Vb	B	0	0	$Vb - B$	$Vb - B$
V = infinite	0	Taxrate $*$ C/r	Vs without banruptcy	C/r	V+taxRate$*C/r$
Our Model					
V = Vb	B	0	0	$Vb - B$	$Vb - B$
V = infinite	0	Taxrate $*$ *Coupons*	Vs without banruptcy	(*Coupons* + *dept*) sure actualized	V+ taxRate$*$ *Coupons*

3.2.3 Without Risk of Bankruptcy

$$BC(V) = 0 \quad \text{et } V_B = 0 \quad V_E(t) = V(t)$$
$$V_s(t) = V(t) * N(n_D) - (1 - \tau)\frac{C}{r}(1 - \exp - r(T - t)N(n'_D))$$
$$- \exp - r(T - t) * D * N(n'_D).$$

It is as a Call corrected by the distribution of the coupon. If there is no distribution of coupon we find the usual formula of a Call.

3.2.4 When we push away the term of the Refund $T \to \infty$

We suppose that: $V_0 \gg v_b$:

$$V_E(t) = V(t) + \tau\frac{C}{r} - B * \left(\frac{v_b}{V(t)}\right)^y,$$

$$V_S(t) = V(t) - (1 - \tau)\frac{C}{r},$$

$$V_d(t) = \frac{C}{r} - B * \left(\frac{v_b}{V(t)}\right)^y.$$

For $t = 0$:

$$V_d(t = 0) = \frac{C}{r} - B * \left(\frac{v_b}{V(0)}\right)^y = D.$$

3.3 *Approached Case of Coupons Guaranteed by the Assets*

3.3.1 Hypothesis of Guarantee of the Coupons on the Assets

Let us work on an approximate case where the coupons are supposed to be paid whatever happens, including by paying them off by selling the assets, which will thus be decreased so far (if there is bankruptcy).
On the other hand we choose v_b very small.

We then retain the solutions securing totally the following coherences:

$$\begin{aligned} V_S(t) &= \mathrm{Call}(V, D + v_b, T, t) + \exp - r(T - t) * v_b * N(n'_b) \\ &\quad - (1 - \tau)\frac{C}{r}(1 - \exp - r(T - t); \\ V_d(t) &= V(t) - \mathrm{Call}(V, D + v_b, T, t) + \frac{C}{r}(1 - \exp - r(T - t) \\ &\quad - \exp - r(T - t) * v_b * N(n'_b) - B * \left(\frac{D + v_b}{V(t)}\right)^y; \\ V_E(t) &= V(t) + \tau\frac{C}{r}(1 - \exp - r(T - t) - BC(V), \end{aligned}$$

where we shall suppose $N(n'_b)$ (the v_b coefficient) to be approximately constant locally and to be a weak term.

3.3.2 Calculation of the Differential of the Debt Value

The value of the debt is a compound of the value of all the assets without risk of default, a call, a cost of bankruptcy, and a function of time.

We define $V'_d \equiv V_d - \frac{C}{r}$. We notice by deriving simply V'_d the differential equation without second member.

For calculations cf. Appendix C:
We find

$$dV_d = (rV_d - C)dt + \sigma_d V_d db^Q.$$

The volatility is stochastic and we get:

$$\sigma_d V_d = \sigma_V (V - VN(n_b) - y_1 BC(V))$$

and the drift is stochastic and time-dependent is given by

$$\mu_d = \mu_V - (\mu_V - r) * \left(\frac{\exp - r(T-t) * D * N(n'_b) + G(t) - (1 - y_1)BC(V)}{V_d}\right);$$

$$\frac{\beta_d}{\beta_V} = \frac{\overline{\sigma_d}}{\sigma_V} = IE(\varepsilon_{V_d,V}) = IE\left(\frac{V(1 - N(n_b)) - y_1 BC}{V_d}\right)$$

$$= 1 - IE\left(\frac{G(t) + D \exp - r(T-t)N(n'_b) + (y_1 - 1)BC}{V_d}\right).$$

3.3.3 Calculation of the Differential of the Equity

We have for valuation of stockholders' equities:

$$V_S(t) = \text{Call}(V, D + v_b, T, t) + \exp - r(T-t) * v_b * N(n'_b)$$
$$- (1 - \tau)\frac{C}{r}(1 - \exp - r(T-t)).$$

Let us take

$$V'_S(t) \equiv V_S + (1 - \tau)\frac{C}{r}.$$

We take as an approximation:

$$V_S(t) = \text{Call}(V, D + v_b, T, t)$$
$$+ \exp - r(T-t) * v_b * N(n'_b) - (1 - \tau)G(t).$$

We find:

$$\sigma_S V_S = \sigma'_S V'_S = \sigma_{\text{Call}}, \text{Call} = \sigma_V VN(n_b).$$

And for the drift:

$$\mu_S = \mu_V + (\mu_V - r)$$
$$* \frac{(\exp - r(T-t) * (D) * N(n'_b) + (1 - \tau)\frac{C}{r}(1 - \exp - r(T-t))}{V_S}$$

and

$$\frac{\beta_S}{\beta_V} = \frac{\overline{\sigma_S}}{\sigma_V} = IE(\varepsilon_{V_S,V}) = IE\left(\frac{VN(n_b)}{V_S}\right)$$
$$= 1 + IE\left(\frac{(1-\tau)G(t) + D\exp - r(T-t)N(n_b')}{V_S}\right).$$

And

$$dV_S = (\mu_S V_S + (1-\tau)C)dt + \sigma_S V_S dW,$$

which corresponds to the hypothesis of financing cash out (after tax coupons) by selling shares.

3.3.4 Calculation of the Differential of the Enterprise Value

$$V_E(t) = V(t) + TS(V) - BC(V).$$

We define:

$$V_E' \equiv V - \tau\frac{C}{r}$$

and we get (cf. Appendix C):

$$dV_E = (\mu_E V_E - \tau C)dt + \sigma_E V_E dW.$$

We have

$$TS(V) = \tau\frac{C}{r}(1 - \exp - r(T-t)).$$

$$\sigma_E' V_E' = \sigma_V V - \sigma_{BC} BC = \sigma_V (V - y_1 BC) = \sigma_E V_E$$

and

$$\mu_E = \mu_V + (\mu_V - r)\frac{-\tau G + (1-y_1)BC}{V_E}$$

is stochastic and time-dependent.

Moreover, we have

$$dV_E = (\mu_E V_E - \tau C)dt + \sigma_E V_E dW.$$

It is necessary to note that we supposed the market has drift and volatility non-stochastic.

As a result of the enterprise Beta calculation (see Appendix C), we get:

$$\frac{\beta_E}{\beta_V} = \frac{\overline{\sigma_E}}{\sigma_V} = IE(\varepsilon_{V_E,V}) = IE\left(\frac{V - y_1 BC}{V + \tau G(t) - BC}\right)$$
$$= 1 - IE\left(\frac{\tau G(t) + (y_1 - 1)BC}{V + \tau G(t) - BC}\right).$$

Note: In first approach, in time t, if we work with certain equivalent values (risk neutral values) we can keep the formula simplified without IE, and we have values then in time t.

3.4 *Adjusted CAPM: A-CAPM*

In order to achieve our approach we suggest applying all the previous results to the whole market.

We note M^0 the market (except bankruptcy and tax savings effects) which translates the only fluctuations due to the activity and the market; we hence have a link of the same nature as for the valuation of the activity of a company and the enterprise value. Therefore, we have:

$$\mu_E(t) - r = (\mu_V - r)\frac{(V_E - \tau G_E + (1 - y_1)BC_E)}{V_E}$$
$$= (\mu_V - r)\frac{(V - y_1 BC_E)}{V_E}.$$

Because of the CAPM, we have:

$$\mu_V - r = \beta_V(\mu_{M^0} - r).$$

Therefore,

$$\mu_E(t) - r = \beta_V(\mu_{M^0} - r)\frac{(V_E - \tau G_E + (1 - y_1)BC_E)}{V_E}$$
$$= \beta_V(\mu_{M^0} - r)\frac{(V - y_1 BC_E)}{V_E}.$$

We thus obtain:

$$\mu_E(t) - r = \beta_V(\mu_{M^0} - r)\frac{(V - y_1 BC_E)}{V_E}.$$

We then obtain the adjusted CAPM:

$$\mu_E(t) - r = \widetilde{\beta}_E(t)(\mu_{M^0} - r)$$

with adjusted Beta defined by

$$\widetilde{\beta}_E(t) \equiv \beta_V \frac{(V - y_1 BC_E)}{V_E}.$$

Furthermore for the market we have:

$$\begin{aligned}\mu_M(t) - r &= (\mu_{M^0} - r)\frac{(M - \tau G_M + (1 - y_1)BC_M)}{M} \\ &= (\mu_{M^0} - r)\frac{(M^0 - y_1 BC_M)}{M},\end{aligned}$$

and thus we get the apparent CAPM:

$$\mu_E(t) - r = \beta_V \frac{(V - y_1 BC_E)/V_E}{(M^0 - y_1 BC_M)/M} * (\mu_M(t) - r).$$

If we want to connect a share to the market we have:

$$\mu_E(t) - r = \tilde{\beta}_{\text{apparent}}(t) * (\mu_M(t) - r),$$

where the apparent Beta is:

$$\tilde{\beta}_{\text{apparent}}(t) = \beta_V \frac{(V - y_1 BC_E)/V_E}{(M^0 - y_1 BC_M)/M}.$$

(Note: We cannot assimilate this corrective to a cost of information: $\lambda_E^1 = (\mu_V - r)\frac{-\tau G_E + (1 - y_1)BC_E}{V_E}$; the costs of information, more general than this double effect bankruptcy/tax savings, must be again added.)

4 Value of the Debt and the Value of the Company in a Homogeneous Model DCF

(See calculations in Appendix D.)

4.1 Principle of the Second Model: Homogeneous DCF

A difficulty of the Discounted Cash Flow (DCF) model is in the evaluation of the debt; whether it is for its updating or for the valuation of the risk (thus the Beta) which is necessary to be associated to it.

In so doing, we propose a model where all the variables will be independently updated according to two axes: the time by means of Risk-free r (interest rate of the Treasury Bonds) and the annual risk connected to the probability to realize or not the profit in one year (that leads to three different risks: risk for the company, for the shareholder, for the debt).

We shall take a hypothesis of annual probability of bankruptcy. In other words to resolve the system we separate the updating in two parts, the risk effect and the time:

$$\mu_F = (\mu_F - r) + r.$$

Firstly, we have to obtain a certain equivalent value by updating with $\mu_F - r$, and secondly it remains only to actualize the time. This approach is similar to the use of a risk neutral probability.

Example of Free Cash Flow (FCF) with growth g and price of the risk i:

$$V_E = \sum \frac{FCF_0 * (1+g)^n (1-i)^n}{(1+r)^n} = \frac{FCF_1}{r+i-g} = \frac{FCF_1}{wacc-g};$$

the certain equivalent of FCF is $FCF_0 * (1+g)^n (1-i)^n$.

4.2 *Enterprise Valuation*

We built a model where debt interests costs are issued from risk of bankruptcy.

As a preliminary remark it must be pointed out that for reasons of simplification, the following calculations start from a FCF approach using amortizations instead of investments, assuming that knowledgeable readers will transpose the following equations using the exact definition of FCF.

We define the risk of not going bankrupt annually as $(1-\theta_d)$.

We have two cases to add:

— if no bankruptcy:

$$\begin{aligned}(1-\theta_d)^n \mathrm{FCF}_n \\ &= (1-\theta_d)^n * (EBIT_n - \mu_{d,n} D_n) * (1-t) + (1-\theta_d)^n * \mu_{d,n} D_n;\end{aligned}$$

— if bankruptcy:

$$(1-(1-\theta_d)^n) * \mathrm{FCF}_n = 0.$$

This therefore gives:

$$\begin{aligned}\mathrm{FCF}_n = & \left[(1-\theta_d)^n * (EBIT_n - \mu_{d,n} D_n) * (1-t)\right] \\ & + \left[(1-\theta_d)^n * \mu_{d,n} D_n\right].\end{aligned}$$

In other words,

$$\mathrm{FCF}_n = \left[(1-\theta_d)^n * EBIT_n * (1-t)\right] + \left[(1-\theta_d)^n * t * \mu_{d,n} D_n\right].$$

We must also factor in corporate risk, so let io be the zero-debt corporate risk.

This gives:

$$\mathrm{FCF}_n * (1-i)^n = EBIT_n * (1-t) * (1-io)^n * (1-\theta_d)^n + (1-\theta_d)^n * t * \mu_{d,n} D_n,$$

where i represents corporate risk; we therefore have:

$$\mathrm{FCF}_n * (1-i)^n = (1-t) * (1-\theta_d)^n (EBIT_n * (1-io)^n - \mu_{d,n} D_n) + (1-\theta_d)^n * \mu_{d,n} D_n,$$

$$\mathrm{FCF}_n * (1-i)^n = \left[\mathrm{DIV}_n * (1-a)^n\right] + \left[\mathrm{Fin}C * (1-\theta_d)^n\right],$$

where a represents the risk for the shareholder and DIV represents distributable dividends.

We can thus implement the DCF model in this way provided we determine θ_d, which, we shall do at the end of the section.

To achieve a resolution, we must therefore now formulate two equations:

— the equation of the values by discounting all parts using risk-free r: $V_E = V_S + V_d$;
— the equation of the expected or average flows (obtained by derivation of the previous equation; in the case of the continuous model, if $V_i = V_{0,i} * \exp(\mu_i * t)$ we get $\frac{dV_i}{dt} = \mu_i * V_i$; therefore, $\mu_E * V_E = \mu_S * V_S + \mu_d * V_d$. In the discrete model, we demonstrate the same thing by taking the annual variation from each of these values. This derivative, of course, applies to all equalities between values. The two above-mentioned axes look thus:
for the company — $V_E = \sum \frac{\mathrm{FCF}_n * (1-i)^n}{(1+r)^n}$;
for debt — $V_d = \sum \frac{\mu_n * D_n * (1-\theta_d)^n}{(1+r)^n}$.

We define α by:

$$V_d = (1-\alpha) * V_d^0 \quad \text{with} \quad V_d^0 = \sum \frac{\mu_n * D_n}{(1+r)^n},$$

where V_d^0 is the value of the risk-free debt without future risk of bankruptcy. Similarly,

$$\mathrm{FCF}_n^0 * (1-io)^n = EBIT_n * (1-t) * (1-io)^n$$

depends only of the activities and not of the financing. We can also define:

$$V' = k * V$$

where V is the value of the company without debt nor risk of bankruptcy (we should have named it V^0 to have a homogeneous notation but, it is named V in the previous Modigliani Miller and Leland models).

$$V' = \sum \frac{\mathrm{FCF}_n^0 * (1 - i_0)^n (1 - \theta_d)^n}{(1 + r)^n},$$

$$V = \sum \frac{\mathrm{FCF}_n^0 * (1 - i_0)^n}{(1 + r)^n}.$$

We now have:

$$V_E = V_S + V_d' = V' + t * V_d \quad \text{and}$$

$$V_S = V' + (t - 1) V_d.$$

$$V' = V_E - tV_d = V_S + (1 - t) * V_d.$$

So we obtain the deleveraged and without bankruptcy WACC:

$$\mu_V = \frac{(\mu_S - \mu_d) V_S + (1 - t) * rV_d}{V_E - t * V_d}$$

which is different from

$$\mu_{V'} = \frac{\mu_S V_S + (1 - t) * \mu_d V_d}{V_E - t * V_d}$$

and is different from

$$WACC \equiv \frac{\mu_S V_S + (1 - t) \mu_d V_d}{V_E}$$

which includes tax savings effects factor in V_E.

We can now describe the different equations derived from the following flows:

$$\mu_E * V_E = \left[(\mu_V + \theta_d) * V' - (1 - t) * (r + \theta_d) * V_d\right] + (r + \theta_d) * V_d$$

[a dividend portion minus the debt effect decreased by the tax effect] + a part link to the debt.

$$\mu_E * V_E = (\mu_V + \theta_d) * V' + t * (r + \theta_d) * Vd = \mu_S * V_S + (r + \theta_d) * V_d.$$

Let us now calculate μ_S:

$$\mu_S = \mu_V + \theta_d + (1-t) * \frac{V_d}{V_S} * (\mu_V - r).$$

Similarly for μ_E:

$$\mu_E = r + \theta_d + (\mu_V - r) * \left(1 - t * (1-\alpha) * \frac{V_d^0}{V_E}\right).$$

We can thus see directly how α limits the beneficial impact of taxes on corporate value.

Let us express the link between β_d and β_e and the lever:

$$\beta_V = \frac{\beta_S * V_S - \theta_d * \left(\frac{V_S}{(Rm-r)}\right)}{V'} = \frac{\beta_S - \beta_d}{1 + (1-t) * \frac{V_d}{V_S}}.$$

Note: From the first model we deduce a variable behavior of β_S thus defined.

Let us express the link between β_d and β_V and V_E:

$$\beta_V = \frac{(\beta_S - \beta_d) * \left(1 - \frac{V_d}{V_E}\right)}{1 - t * \frac{V_d}{V_E}}.$$

4.3 Enterprise Valuation in the Case of Constant Interests of Debt and Growth

To better appreciate the proposed model, we resolve it in the trivial case where interests of the debt are approximately held constant and where growth in FCF is estimated using the constant g. As usual the Debt is considered constant.

V_d represents the resale value of the debt.

— thus for a coupon $\mu_{d,0} * D$ constant we have:

$$V_d \approx \frac{\mu_{d,0} * D}{(r + \theta_d)};$$

— if $\mu_{d,0} = (r + \theta_d)$, then $V_d = D$;
— and if the asset value grows infinitely, we obtain

$$V_d = V_d^0 = \frac{\mu_{d,0} * D}{r} = \frac{C}{r} \quad \text{and} \quad \theta_d = 0.$$

We also see the fact that there is no random opportunity that is creating wealth, since risk offsets profitability and, in that homogeneous (similar) manner for both debt and shareholders' equity.

$$
\begin{aligned}
V_E &= V' + t * V_d \\
V_d &= \sum \frac{\mu_d * D * (1-\theta_d)^n}{(1+r)^n} = \frac{\mu_d * D}{(r+\theta_d)} * (1-\theta_d) \\
V' &= \sum \frac{(EBIT(1-t)) * (1-io)^n (1-\theta_d)^n * (1+g)^n}{(1+r)^n} \\
&= EBIT(1-t)\frac{(1-io)*(1+g)*(1-\theta_d)}{(1+r)-(1-io)(1+g)(1-\theta_d)}; \\
V &= \sum \frac{(EBIT(1-t)) * (1-io)^n * (1+g)^n}{(1+r)^n} \\
&= EBIT(1-t)\frac{(1-io)*(1+g)}{(1+r)-(1-io)(1+g)}; \\
V &\approx \frac{EBIT(1-t)}{\mu_V - g}
\end{aligned}
$$

depends only on the activity.

This leads to (see Appendix D)

$$\frac{V_E}{1-\theta_d} = \frac{\mu_V - g}{(\mu_V - g + \theta_d)} * V + t * \frac{\mu_d * D}{(r+\theta_d)}.$$

Note: We obtain $V_e \leq V + t * D$ because the coefficients are less than 1. Let

$$a = \mu_V - g;$$

hence,

$$
\begin{aligned}
&\frac{V_E}{1-\theta_d} = \frac{a}{(a+\theta_d)} * V + t * \frac{\mu_d * D}{(r+\theta_d)}, \\
&V_E * (a+\theta_d) * (r+\theta_d) = (1-\theta_d) * (a * V * (r+\theta_d) \\
&\quad + t * \mu_d * D * (a+\theta_d)).
\end{aligned}
$$

We can therefore generate a second degree equation in θ_d (which could constitute an initial approach for interpolating the risk, but it is, in a way, self-referential).

Let us look for a formula that approaches the value of shareholders' equity in the case of constant debt and growth g of FCF.

$$\frac{V_E}{1-\theta_d} = \frac{\mu_V - g}{(\mu_V - g + \theta_d)} * V + t * \frac{\mu_d * D}{(r+\theta_d)};$$

$$V_S = V' + (t-1)V_d;$$

$$V_S = (1-\theta_d) * \frac{\mu_V - g}{(\mu_V - g + \theta_d)} * V - (1-t) * \frac{\mu_d * D}{(r+\theta_d)};$$

$$V_S = (1-\theta_d) * \left(1 - \frac{\theta_d}{(\mu_V - g + \theta_d)}\right) * V - (1-t) * \frac{\mu_d * D}{(r+\theta_d)}.$$

Hence,

$$V_S = V - (1-t) * \frac{\mu_d * D}{(r+\theta_d)} - \theta_d * V * \left(1 + \frac{(1-\theta_d)}{(\mu_V - g + \theta_d)}\right)$$

which constitutes the formula for valuing capital in this DCF model.

This can be compared with that of the first mode, although the bankruptcy assumption used is different.

4.4 Reintroducing the Bankruptcy Risk Derived from the First Model in the DCF Model

We place ourselves in the classic case of pricing the assets of a company using the DCF method with constant debt but increasing growth.

We therefore start with:

$$V_d = \frac{\mu_d * D}{(r+\theta_d)} * (1-\theta_d) = \frac{C_D}{(r+\theta_d)} * (1-\theta_d).$$

Moreover, the equations of the first model gave:

$$V_d = C_D * \left(\frac{1}{r+\lambda_D} - k * \left(\frac{V}{C_D}\right)^{\overline{\Omega}}\right),$$

where

$$\overline{\Omega} = -y < 0.$$

(Note: In this case we can determine optimum debt.)

We look for θ_d by equalizing the two values. As a way of simplifying the presentation we solve the equations without factoring in information costs.

$$\frac{1}{(r+\theta_d)} * (1-\theta_d) = \frac{V_d}{C_D} = \frac{1}{r} - k * \left(\frac{V}{C_D}\right)^{-y};$$

therefore,

$$\theta_d = \frac{r}{\left(1+\frac{1}{r}\right) * \frac{\left(\frac{V}{C_D}\right)^{+y}}{k} - 1}.$$

We must now determine k and y.

One solution is to take the values at two instants (we could use a similar solution using any interpolation method if we have more than two relevant, recent values); in t_1:

$$k = \left(1+\frac{1}{r}\right) * \frac{\theta_{d1}}{r+\theta_{d1}} * \left(\frac{V_1}{C_{D_1}}\right)^{+y};$$

hence,

$$\theta_d = \frac{r}{\frac{(r+\theta_{d1})}{\theta_{d1}} * \left(\frac{V * C_{D1}}{C_D * V_1}\right)^{y} - 1}. \quad (1)$$

In t_2, we will have θ_{d2}; hence,

$$\left(\frac{C_{D1} * V_2}{C_{D2} * V_1}\right)^{y} = \frac{(r+\theta_{d2})}{\theta_{d2}} * \frac{\theta_{d1}}{(r+\theta_{d1})}.$$

We can therefore proceed by correlating the logarithms if we have several values, or if we only have two, we may select:

$$\overline{\Omega} = -y = \frac{\left(\ln\frac{(r+\theta_{d1})}{\theta_{d1}} - \ln\frac{(r+\theta_{d2})}{\theta_{d2}}\right)}{\ln\left(\frac{V_2}{C_{D_2}}\right) - \ln\left(\frac{V_1}{C_{D_1}}\right)}.$$

4.5 Enterprise Valuation in the Case of Constant Debt and Growth

In order to study a very simple case we first hold the trivial assumption that interest rates of the debt are adjusting immediately for all the amount of debt.

We reused all the preceding conclusions by assuming the particular case of constant risk of bankruptcy where $\mu_d = (r + \theta_d)/(l - \theta_d)$ and thus defining V_d by:

$$V_d = \frac{\mu_d * D}{(r + \theta_d)} * (1 - \theta_d) = D$$
$$\mu_d * Vd = \mu_d * D$$

We consequently have:

$$V_E = V_S + V_d = V_S + D = V' + t * D$$

and

$$V_S = V' + (t - 1) * D$$

The market value of the debt to be taken into account is then closer to its book value. Then

$$\begin{aligned} \mu_E * V_E &= \mu_S * V_S + \mu_d * D \\ &= (\mu_V + \theta_d) * V' + t * \mu_d * D. \end{aligned}$$

The market equity value becomes approximatively:

$$V_S = V - (1 - t) * \frac{D}{(1 - \theta_d)} - \theta_d * V * \left(1 + \frac{(1 - \theta_d)}{(\mu_V - g + \theta_d)}\right).$$

If the risk of bankruptcy is small we obtain the optimum debt, in particular the moment when tax benefits equal bankruptcy by:

$$\theta_d^* = (\mu_V - g)\left(\frac{1}{(1 - tD/V(\mu_V - g - 1))} - 1\right)$$

and optimum $V = V(D)$ solving formula 1 with this previous equality.

4.6 Corporate DCF Model in Case of Constant Debt

If we throw an eye on the most generic case of equations presented formerly in Sec. 4.2 but in the case where debt interest rate are adjusting only for the part of the debt being refinanced. Therefore, we keep all the equations stated in Sec. 4.2, V_d defined as equal to

$$V_d = D * \sum \frac{\mu_{d,n} * (1 - \theta_{d,n})^n}{(1 + r)^n},$$

where $\theta_{d,n}$ could be issued from Sec. 4.4.

That allows to build a model integrating the agenda of refinancing debt.

5 Conclusions

From this chapter, the following several conclusions could be drawn:

(1) To guarantee all the coherence in the valuation of company within the framework of costs of bankruptcy and of tax savings and debt (principal and coupons) we demonstrated that the drifts and the volatilities are stochastic and depend on time.
(2) Observed Betas are inevitably stochastic, and it is necessary to have an adjusted CAPM, starting from values of activity (that means without the effects of tax savings and risk of bankruptcy).
(3) We restored the usual expressions of the values of assets under a shape which completes the usual approach of stockholders' equities as a call of the value of the company on the debt, by integrating the effects of the debt coupons and of the costs of bankruptcy.
(4) A part of these elements is rather easy to implement in DCF current models which help financial analysts to situate the corporation closer to its economic environment.

Appendix A: Case of Deterministic Volatility

A.1 Supplementary Differential Equation Connected to Deterministic Volatility

The dynamics of the i firm without bankruptcy and tax savings effects is given by:

$$dV = \mu_V * V*dt + \sigma_V * V*dW.$$

Similarly for the derivative let us start by:

$$dF = (\mu_F * F - C_F)dt + \sigma_F * F*dW,$$

thus,

$$\frac{\sigma_F}{\sigma_V} = \frac{V}{F} * \frac{\partial F}{\partial V} = Cte = \Omega.$$

Under the risk neutral probability

$$dV = r * V*dt + \sigma_V * V*dW^Q,$$

$$dW^Q = dW + \frac{\mu_V - r}{\sigma_V}dt$$

and we have

$$AOA_V\colon \frac{\mu_V - r}{\sigma_V} = \frac{\mu_F - r}{\sigma_F},$$

$$dF = \left(\left(r + (\mu_V - r)\frac{\sigma_F}{\sigma_V}\right)F - C_F\right)dt + \sigma_F * F{*}dW,$$

$$dF = \left(\left(r + (\mu_V - r) * \frac{V}{F}\frac{\partial F}{\partial V}\right)F - C_F\right)dt + \sigma_F * F{*}dW,$$

$$dF = (r{*}F - C_F)dt + \sigma_F * F{*}dW + (\mu_V - r){*}V\frac{\partial F}{\partial V} * dt,$$

$$dF = (r{*}F - C_F)dt + \sigma_F * F{*}dW + \frac{\mu_V - r}{\sigma_V} * \sigma_V V\frac{\partial F}{\partial V} * dt,$$

$$dF = (r{*}F - C_F)dt + \sigma_F * F{*}dW^Q.$$

Because $\frac{\mu_V - r}{\sigma_V} = \frac{\mu_F - r}{\sigma_F}$, μ_F is also non-stochastic (we shall note that this last equality which gives the absence of opportunity of arbitration for and underlying its derivative remains true with stochastic values).

Let us return in usual probability by supposing the deterministic volatility:

$$\frac{V^2}{F} * \frac{\partial^2 F}{\partial V^2} = \Omega(\Omega - 1)$$

are thus constants that we can go out of the equality stemming from Itô and from the geometrical shape, thus:

$$E\left(\frac{dF}{F{*}dt} - \frac{dF}{F{*}dt}\right) = E\left(\frac{1}{2} * \sigma_V^2 * \frac{V^2}{F} * \frac{\partial^2 F}{\partial V^2} + \frac{1}{F}\frac{\partial F}{\partial V} * \mu_V * V \right.$$
$$\left. - \mu_F + \frac{C_F(V)}{F} + \frac{1}{F}\frac{\partial F}{\partial t}\right).$$

Therefore,

$$\frac{1}{2} * \sigma_V^2 * \frac{V^2}{F} * \frac{\partial^2 F(V,t)}{\partial V^2} + \mu_V * \frac{V}{F} * \frac{\partial F(V,t)}{\partial V}$$
$$- \mu_F + E\left(\frac{C_F(V)}{F} + \frac{\partial F(V,t)}{F\partial t}\right) = 0.$$

And by multiplying by F:

$$\frac{1}{2} * \sigma_V^2 * V^2 * \frac{\partial^2 F(V,t)}{\partial V^2} + \mu_V * V * \frac{\partial F(V,t)}{\partial V} - \mu_F * F + E\left(\frac{C_F(V)}{F} + \frac{\partial F(V,t)}{F \partial t}\right) * F = 0.$$

By using AOA_V we get:

$$\frac{1}{2} * \sigma_V^2 * V^2 * \frac{\partial^2 F(V,t)}{\partial V^2} + \mu_V * V * \frac{\partial F(V,t)}{\partial V} - \frac{\mu_V - r}{\sigma_v} * \sigma_F F - rF + E\left(\frac{C_F(V)}{F} + \frac{\partial F(V,t)}{F \partial t}\right) * F = 0,$$

thus,

$$\frac{1}{2} * \sigma_V^2 * V^2 * \frac{\partial^2 F}{\partial V^2} + r * V * \frac{\partial F}{\partial V} - rF + E\left(\frac{C_F(V)}{F} + \frac{\partial F(V,t)}{F \partial t}\right) * F = 0.$$

A.2 Resolution of the System of Two Differential Equations

In case of non-stochastic volatility we have two equations which must be verified:

(i) $\frac{1}{2} * \sigma_V^2 * V^2 \frac{\partial^2 F}{\partial V^2} + rV \frac{\partial F}{\partial V} + \frac{\partial F}{\partial t} = rF - C_F$,

(ii) $C_F + \frac{\partial F(V,t)}{\partial t} = a(t) F$.

We are going to demonstrate that if C is constant non-zero or if $\frac{\partial F(V,t)}{\partial t}$ differs from zero, there is not a solution of this system adapted to the valuation of enterprise; we shall deduct from it that when the coupon is constant the only solution is that the volatility is stochastic and therefore the drift.

(a) $C_F \neq 0$ and $\frac{\partial F(V,t)}{\partial t} = 0$; therefore, $F = \frac{C_F}{a(t)}$ and (i) $F = \frac{C_F}{r}$ would mean being able to pay the debt infinitely without risk of bankruptcy.

(b) $C_F \neq 0$ and $\frac{\partial F(V,t)}{\partial t} \neq 0$, then

$$\frac{1}{2} * \sigma_V^2 * V^2 F_{VV} + rVF_V + (a(t) - r)F = 0$$
$$C_F + F_t = a(t)F,$$

(i) if $a(t) = 0$

$$F_t = -C_F$$
$$F = -C_F t + G(t)$$
$$\frac{1}{2} * \sigma_V^2 * V^2 G_{VV} + rVG_V - rG = 0$$
$$F = -C_F t + B_1 V^{y_1} \quad \text{with } y_1 = \frac{-2r}{\sigma_V^2} \quad \text{or} \quad y_1 = 1.$$

In the general case we cannot retain for the assets these infinitely decreasing t solutions.

(ii) if $a(t) = r$

$C_F + F_t = rF$; therefore, $F = \frac{C_F}{r} + L(V) \exp rt$

$$\frac{1}{2} * \sigma_V^2 * V^2 L_{VV} + rVL_V = 0.$$

Therefore, $L = A + B_1 V^{y_2}$ avec $\frac{1}{2} * \sigma_V^2 * y(y-1) + ry = 0$. Thus $y_2 \left(\frac{1}{2} * \sigma_V^2 * y_2 + r - \frac{1}{2} * \sigma_V^2\right) = 0$.

$$F = \frac{C_F}{r} + (A + B_1 V^{y_2}) \exp rt.$$

(iii) if $a(t) \neq r$

$$\frac{1}{2} * \sigma_V^2 * V^2 F_{VV} + rVF_V + (a(t)_t - r)F = 0;$$

therefore, $F = B_1(t)V^{y1} + B_2(t)V^{y2}$ with y solution of

$$\frac{1}{2} * \sigma_V^2 * y^2 + \left(r - \frac{1}{2} * \sigma_V^2\right) y + (a(t) - r) = 0,$$

and

$C_F + F_t = a(t)F$, let us take $I_t = a(t)$ incompatible solutions.

Appendix B: Approach Leading to Stochastic Volatilities

B.1 Case of a time-invariant derivative with $F_t = 0$ and coupon distribution

(1) General case

Let $F \equiv A + KV^{y1}$ with non-zero A and K.

We define $F' \equiv F - A = KV^{y1}$, thus we have $dF = dF' = d(KV^{y1})$.

We are looking for

$$dF = (\mu_F F - C)dt + \sigma_F F dW,$$

such as F verifies:

$$AOA_V = \frac{\mu_V - r}{\sigma_V} = \frac{\mu_F - r}{\sigma_F}.$$

The Itô lemma for $dF' = d(KV^{y1})$ leads to:

$$\sigma_{F'} = \sigma_V \frac{V}{F'} \frac{\partial F'}{\partial V} = \sigma_V y$$

is a constant volatility.

$$\frac{1}{2} * \sigma_V^2 * V^2 \frac{\partial^2 F'}{\partial V^2} + \mu_V V \frac{\partial F'}{\partial V} = \mu_{F'} F'.$$

Thus

$$\frac{1}{2} * \sigma_V^2 * V^2 \frac{\partial^2 F'}{\partial V^2} + (r - \mu_V - r) V \frac{\partial F'}{\partial V} = (r + \mu_{F'} - r) F'.$$

Because

$$AOA_V\colon \frac{\mu_V - r}{\sigma_V} = \frac{\mu_{F'} - r}{\sigma_{F'}},$$

$$\frac{1}{2} * \sigma_V^2 * V^2 \frac{\partial^2 F'}{\partial V^2} + rV \frac{\partial F'}{\partial V} = rF'$$

and therefore, $\frac{1}{2} * \sigma_V^2 * y_1(y_1 - 1) + ry_1 = r$, which leads to $y_1 = \frac{-2r}{\sigma_V^2}$ or $y_0 = 1$ and $F' = k_0 V + k_1 V^{y_1}$, but we will only study the case where $y_1 = \frac{-2r}{\sigma_V^2} \neq 1$.

Thus, $\sigma_{F'} = \sigma_V y_1$ and

$$\mu_{F'} = r + \left(\frac{\mu_V - r}{\sigma_V}\right) \sigma_{F'} = r + (\mu_V - r) y_1.$$

Similarly for F:

$$\sigma_{F'} F' = \sigma_V V \frac{\partial F'}{\partial V} = \sigma_V V \frac{\partial F}{\partial V} = \sigma_F F,$$

$$f = \frac{1}{2} * \sigma_V^2 * V^2 \frac{\partial^2 F}{\partial V^2} + \mu_V V \frac{\partial F}{\partial V} = \mu_F F - C.$$

We use the equality of the derivatives, therefore:

$$f = \frac{1}{2} * \sigma_V^2 * V^2 \frac{\partial^2 F'}{\partial V^2} + (r - r + \mu_V) V \frac{\partial F'}{\partial V} = rF' + (\mu_V - r) V \frac{\partial F}{\partial V}$$
$$= \mu_{F'} F - CrF' + \frac{(\mu_V - r)}{\sigma_V} \sigma_V V \frac{\partial F}{\partial V} = \frac{(\mu_F - r)}{\sigma_F} \sigma_F F + rF - C.$$

Thus, using AOA_V equality:

$$F = F' + \frac{C}{r}.$$

Note: We do not use a boundary condition to find this.

Moreover,

$$\sigma_F = \sigma_{F'} \frac{F'}{F} = \sigma_{F'} \frac{F - \frac{C}{r}}{F} = \sigma_V y_1 \frac{F - \frac{C}{r}}{F}$$

is stochastic.

$$\mu_F = r + \frac{\mu_V - r}{\sigma_V} \sigma_F = r + (\mu_V - r) y_1 \frac{F - \frac{C}{r}}{F}$$

is stochastic too.

We can resume all this in:

$$\mu_F = r + AOA_V \sigma_{F'} \frac{F'}{F}$$

which is a more general formula, that we shall use afterwards.

In a risk neutral probability we thus have:

$$dF' = r{*}F'dt + \sigma_{F'} * F'{*}dW^Q$$

$$dW^Q = dW + \frac{\mu_V - r}{\sigma_V} dt = dW + \frac{\mu_{F'} - r}{\sigma_{F'}} dt$$

$$dF' = r{*}F'dt + \sigma_{F'} * F' * \left(dW + \frac{\mu_{F'} - r}{\sigma_{F'}} dt \right)$$

$$dF' = \mu_{F'} * F'dt + \sigma_{F'} * F'{*}dW.$$

Therefore,

$$\mu_{F'} = r + (\mu_V - r)y = r\left(1 - \frac{2{*}AOA}{\sigma_V}\right),$$

$$F' = F'_0 \exp\left(\left(\mu_{F'} - \frac{\sigma^2_{F'}}{2}\right)t + \sigma_{F'} W\right),$$

$$F' = F'_0 \exp\left(\left(r + (\mu_V - r)y - \frac{\sigma^2_{F'}}{2}\right)t + \sigma_{F'} W_t\right),$$

$$F = \frac{C}{r} + \left(F_0 - \frac{C}{r}\right)\exp\left(\left(r + (\mu_V - r)y - \frac{\sigma^2_{F'}}{2}\right)t + \sigma_{F'} W_t\right),$$

$$dF = (\mu_F F - C)dt + \sigma_F F dW = dF'$$
$$= \mu_{F'} F' dt + \sigma_F F dW,$$
$$(\mu_F F - C) = \mu_{F'} F' = \mu_{F'}\left(F - \frac{C}{r}\right).$$

Then,

$$\mu_F = \mu_{F'} + \frac{C - \mu_{F'}\frac{C}{r}}{F}.$$

For F', we indeed have:

$$\frac{1}{2} * \sigma_V^2 * V^2 \frac{\partial^2 F'}{\partial V^2} + rV\frac{\partial F'}{\partial V} = rF'.$$

And therefore,

$$\frac{1}{2} * \sigma_V^2 * V^2 \frac{\partial^2 F}{\partial V^2} + rV\frac{\partial F}{\partial V} = r\left(F - \frac{C}{r}\right)$$

which is the differential equation in risk neutral probability. We can also verify directly that:

if $F \equiv \frac{C}{r} + KV^{y1}$ then with Itô:

$$dF - \sigma_V V\frac{\partial F}{\partial V}dW = \left(\frac{1}{2} * \sigma_V^2 * y_1(y_1 - 1) + \mu_V y_1\right) kV^{y_1} dt$$
$$= \left(\frac{1}{2} * \sigma_V^2 * y_1(y_1 - 1) + (\mu_V - r + r)y_1\right) kV^{y_1} dt.$$

Seen that

$$\frac{1}{2} * \sigma_V^2 * y_1(y_1 - 1) + ry_1 = r$$

$$= (r + (\mu_V - r)y_1)kV^{y_1}dt = \mu_{F'}kV^{y_1}dt = \mu_{F'}\left(F - \frac{C}{r}\right)dt$$

$$= (\mu_F F - C)dt. \quad \text{CQFD}$$

$$dF = \left(\left(r + (\mu_V - r)y_1\frac{F - \frac{C}{r}}{F}\right)F - C\right)dt$$

$$+ \left(\sigma_V y_1 \frac{F - \frac{C}{r}}{F}\right)FdW.$$

B.2 More General Case $F(V, t)$

Choosing $F' \equiv F - A$ a derivative where A does not depend on V.

We are looking for:

$$dF = (\mu_F F - C)dt + \sigma_F F dW$$

$$dF' = \mu_{F'}F'dt + \sigma_{F'}F'dW$$

such as F verify the AOA_V equality:

$$AOA_V = \frac{\mu_V - r}{\sigma_V} = \frac{\mu_F - r}{\sigma_F} = \frac{\mu_{F'} - r}{\sigma_{F'}}.$$

We have $dF = dF'$.

The Itô lemma implies that:

$$\sigma_{F'}F' = \sigma_V V\frac{\partial F'}{\partial V} = \sigma_V V\frac{\partial F}{\partial V} = \sigma_F F,$$

$$\frac{1}{2} * \sigma_V^2 * V^2 F'_{VV} + \mu_V V F'_V + F'_t = \mu_{F'}F'.$$

Because AOA_V:

$$\frac{\mu_V - r}{\sigma_V} = \frac{\mu_{F'} - r}{\sigma_{F'}},$$

$$\frac{1}{2} * \sigma_V^2 * V^2 F'_{vv} + rVF'_v + F'_t = rF'.$$

Similarly for F:

$$f = \frac{1}{2} * \sigma_V^2 * V^2\frac{\partial^2 F}{\partial V^2} + \mu_V V\frac{\partial F}{\partial V} + F_t = \mu_F F - C$$

$$q = \frac{1}{2} * \sigma_V^2 * V^2 \frac{\partial^2 F}{\partial V^2} + rV \frac{\partial F}{\partial V} + F_t = rF - C.$$

If we use the equality of the derivatives:

$$\begin{aligned} q &= \frac{1}{2} * \sigma_V^2 * V^2 \frac{\partial^2 F'}{\partial V^2} + rV \frac{\partial F'}{\partial V} + F'_t \\ &= rF' = rF - C. \end{aligned}$$

Therefore,

$$\begin{aligned} F &= F' + \frac{C}{r} \\ \sigma_F &= \sigma_{F'} \frac{F'}{F} = \sigma_{F'} \frac{F - \frac{C}{r}}{F} \\ \mu_F &= r + \frac{\mu_V - r}{\sigma_V} \sigma_F = r + \left(\frac{\mu_V - r}{\sigma_V} \right) \sigma_{F'} \frac{F - \frac{C}{r}}{F}. \\ dF &= (\mu_F F - C)dt + \sigma_F F dW = dF' \\ &= \mu_{F'} F' dt + \sigma_F F dW, \end{aligned}$$

$$(\mu_F F - C) = \mu_{F'} F' = \mu_{F'} \left(F - \frac{C}{r} \right).$$

Therefore,

$$\mu_F = \mu_{F'} + \frac{C - \mu_{F'} \frac{C}{r}}{F}.$$

If we take the case of Call we indeed have volatility and a stochastic drift but we keep a deterministic AOA_V because there is no distribution

$$\frac{\tilde{\mu}_{\text{Call}} - r}{\tilde{\sigma}_{\text{Call}}} = \frac{\mu_V - r}{\sigma_V} \quad \text{with} \quad \tilde{\sigma}_{\text{Call}} = \frac{V * N(d_1)}{\text{Call}}$$

and consequently,

$$\tilde{\mu}_{\text{Call}} = r + \frac{\mu_V - r}{\sigma_V} \tilde{\sigma}_{\text{Call}},$$

$$\frac{1}{2} * \sigma_V^2 * V^2 \text{Call}_{VV} + r * V * \text{Call}_V + \text{Call}_t = r\text{Call}.$$

Appendix C: Derivatives with Distribution

C.1 Asset Values and Their Volatilities

Proposition 1 (without costs of information): If F is a derivative of V such as: $dF = (\mu_F F - C)dt + \sigma_F F dt$ verifying AOA_V then, $F' = F - \frac{C}{r}$ verifies AOA_V (and reciprocally).

Because $dF' = dF = \text{Itô}(F) = \text{Itô}(F')$, F' is a derivative of V and $dF' = \mu_{F'} F' dt + \sigma_{F'} F' dt$ and $\sigma_{F'} F' = \sigma_F F$, therefore we have

$$\mu_F F - C = (\mu_F - r + r)F - C \overset{AOA_V}{=} (r + AOA_V * \sigma_F)F - C$$

thus:

$$\mu_{F'} F' = \mu_F F - C = AOA_V * \sigma_{F'} F' + r\left(F - \frac{C}{r}\right)$$
$$\mu_{F'} F' = \mu_F F - C = rF' + AOA_V * \sigma_{F'} F' \text{CQFD.}$$

Proposition 2 (without costs of information): If F_1 and F_2 are two derivatives which verify AOA_V, then $F = F_1 + F_2$ is a derivative verifying AOA_V.

We generalize for n derivatives.

Demonstration for the not coarse cases (which are evident):

$$dF = (\mu_{F_1} F_1 + \mu_{F_2} F_2)dt + (\sigma_{F_1} F_1 + \sigma_{F_2} F_2)dt,$$
$$dF = \mu_F F dt + \sigma_F F dt,$$
$$\mu_F = \frac{(\mu_{F_1} F_1 + \mu_{F_2} F_2)}{(F_1 + F_2)} \quad \text{and} \quad \sigma_{F_1} = \frac{(\sigma_{F_1} F_1 + \sigma_{F_2} F_2)}{(F_1 + F_2)},$$
$$\mu_F - r = \frac{(\mu_{F_1} F_1 + \mu_{F_2} F_2) - r(F_1 + F_2)}{(F_1 + F_2)} \sigma_F$$
$$= \frac{AOA_V \sigma_{F_1} F_1 + AOA_V \sigma_{F_2} F_2}{(F_1 + F_2)} = AOA_V \sigma_F.$$

Proposition 3 (with costs of information): If F is a derivative of V such as

$$dF = (\mu_F F - C)dt + \sigma_F F dt$$

and verifies AOA_V, let us take $F' \equiv F - \frac{C}{r + \lambda_F}$, then $\lambda_F = \lambda_{F'}$

demonstrates

$$AOA_V = \frac{(\mu_{F'} - r - \lambda_{F'})}{\sigma_{F'}F'}F' = \frac{(\mu_F - r - \lambda_F)}{\sigma_F F}F,$$

therefore $(\mu_{F'} - r - \lambda_{F'})F' = (\mu_F - r - \lambda_F)F$.

Because

$$\mu_{F'}F' = \mu_F F - C \quad \text{and} \quad F' = F - \frac{C}{r + \lambda_F}$$

$$(r + \lambda_{F'})F' + C = (r + \lambda_F)F' + C. \quad \text{CQFD}$$

We can add in complement to this proposition:

$$\begin{aligned}
\mu_V - \lambda_V &= r + AOA_V * \sigma_V \\
dV &= \mu_V Vdt + \sigma_V Vdt \\
&= (\mu_V - r - \lambda_V + r + \lambda_V)Vdt + \sigma_V VdW, \\
dV &= (r + \lambda_V + AOA_V * \sigma_V)Vdt + \sigma_V VdW \\
&= (r + \lambda_V)Vdt + AOA_V * \sigma_V)Vdt + \sigma_V VdW, \\
dV &= (r + \lambda_V)Vdt + \sigma_V V(AOA_V dt + dW).
\end{aligned}$$

Let us take

$$dW^Q = (AOA_V dt + dW),$$

thus

$$dV = (r + \lambda_V)Vdt + \sigma_V VdW^Q$$

in risk neutral probability with costs of information.

Similarly:

$$dF = (\mu_F F - C)dt + \sigma_F Fdt = ((r + \lambda_F)F - C)dt + \sigma_F FdW^Q$$

$$dF' = \mu_{F'}F'dt + \sigma_{F'}F'dt = (r + \lambda_{F'})F'dt + \sigma_{F'}F'dW^Q$$

Application 1 (without cost of information)

The value of the debt is a compound of the value all the assets without risk of default, a call, cost of bankruptcy and a function of time:

$$V_d = V - \text{Call} + H(t) - BC$$

$$H(t) \equiv \frac{C}{r}(1 - \exp - r(T - t)) - \exp - r(T - t))*v_b * N(n'_b).$$

Thus if we define:

$$H'(t) = H(t) - \frac{C}{r}.$$

$$dH(t) = \left(r\frac{C}{r}(1 - \exp - r(T-t)) - r\exp - r(T-t)) * v_b \right) dt,$$

$$dH(t) = (rH - C)dt = dH' = rH'dt,$$

$$\begin{aligned} dV_d &= (rVdt + \sigma_V V db^Q) - (r\mathrm{Call}(V)dt + \sigma_{\mathrm{Call}}\mathrm{Call}(V)db^Q) \\ &\quad + (rH(t) - C)dt - (rBC(V) * dt + \sigma_{BC}BC(V)db^Q), \\ dV_d &= r\left(V - \mathrm{Call}(V) + H(t) - BC(V) - \frac{C}{r}\right) dt \\ &\quad + \left(\sigma_V V * \frac{\partial V}{\partial V} - \sigma_V V\frac{\partial \mathrm{Call}(V)}{\partial V} - \sigma_V V\frac{\partial BC(V)}{\partial V}\right. \\ &\quad \left. + \sigma_V V\frac{\partial H(t)}{\partial V}\right) db^Q. \end{aligned}$$

We find well

$$dV_d = (rV_d - C)dt + \sigma_V V\frac{\partial V_d}{\partial V}db^Q.$$

Thus

$$dV_d = (rV_d - C)dt + \sigma_F V_d db^Q.$$

The volatility is stochastic and gives by

$$\sigma_d V_d = \left(\sigma_V V - \sigma_V V\frac{\partial \mathrm{Call}(V)}{\partial V} + \sigma_V V\frac{\partial BC(V)}{\partial V}\right).$$

This leads to

$$\begin{aligned} \sigma_{V_d} V_d &= (\sigma_V V - \sigma_V VN(n_b) - \sigma_V y_1 BC(V)), \\ \sigma_d V_d &= (\sigma_V V - \sigma_V V * N(n_b') - \sigma_V yBC(V)), \\ \sigma_d V_d(db^Q - db) &= (\sigma_V V - \sigma_V V * N(n_b) - \sigma_V yBC(V))(db^Q - db) \\ &= \left(\sigma_V V\left(\frac{\mu_V - r}{\sigma_V}\right) - \sigma_{\mathrm{Call}V}\mathrm{Call}\left(\frac{\mu_{\mathrm{Call}} - r}{\sigma_{\mathrm{Call}}}\right)\right. \\ &\quad \left. - \sigma_{BC}BC(V)\left(\frac{\mu_{BC} - r}{\sigma_{Bc}}\right)\right)dt \end{aligned}$$

$$= (V(\mu_V - r) - \text{Call}(\mu_{\text{Call}} - r) - BC(V)(\mu_{BC} - r))dt$$
$$dV_d - \sigma_{V_d} V_d db = (V\mu_V - \text{Call}\mu_{\text{Call}} - BC(V)\mu_{BC} + rH - C)dt.$$

We have:

$$V_d = V - \text{Call} + H(t) - BC.$$

We define

$$V_d' \equiv V_d - \frac{C}{r} = V - \text{Call} - BC + H(t) - \frac{C}{r}$$
$$H'(t) = H(t) - \frac{C}{r} = -\left(\frac{C}{r} + v_b * N(n_b')\right) \exp -r(T-t)$$
$$dH'(t) = rH'(t)dt.$$

We deduct from it:

$$\sigma_d' V_d' = \sigma_V V - \sigma_{\text{Call}}\text{Call} - \sigma_{BC} BC = \sigma_d V_d,$$
$$\mu_d' = r + AOA_V * \frac{\sigma_V V - \sigma_V V * N(n_B) - \sigma_V y_1 BC}{V_d'},$$

and

$$\mu_d = r + AOA * \frac{\sigma_V V - \sigma_{\text{Call}}\text{Call} - \sigma_{BC} BC}{V_d},$$
$$\mu_d = r + AOA_V * \frac{\sigma_V V - \sigma_V V * N(n_B) - \sigma_V y_1 BC}{V - \text{Call} - BC + G(t)},$$
$$\mu_d = r + (\mu_V - r) * \frac{V - V * N(n_B) - y_1 BC}{V - \text{Call} - BC + G(t)},$$

and because

$$V_d(t) = V(t)(1 - N(n_b)) + G(t) + \exp$$
$$- r(T-t) * D * N(n_b') - B * \left(\frac{D + v_b}{V(t)}\right)^y.$$

This leads to:

$$\mu_d = \mu_V - (\mu_V - r) * \left(\frac{\exp -r(T-t) * D * N(n_b') + G(t) - (1 - y_1)BC(V)}{V_d}\right).$$

Application 2: Calculation of the derivative of the equity.

We have for valuation of the equity:

$$V_S(t) = \text{Call}(V, D + v_b, T, t) + \exp - r(T - t) * v_b * N(n'_b) - (1 - \tau)\frac{C}{r}(1 - \exp - r(T - t).$$

We define $V'_S(t) = V_S + (1 - \tau)\frac{C}{r}$.

We take as an approximation:

$$V_S(t) = \text{Call}(V, D + v_b, T, t) + \exp - r(T - t) * v_b * N(n'_b) - (1 - \tau)G(t).$$

Because

$$\sigma_S V_S = \sigma'_S V'_S = \sigma_{\text{Call}}\text{Call} = \sigma_V VN(n_b),$$

using AOA_V:

$$\mu_S - r = AOA_V * \frac{\sigma_S V_S}{V_S} \quad \text{and} \quad \mu_S = r + AOA_V * \frac{\sigma_V(V*N(n_b))}{V_S}$$

$$V_S = VN(n_b) - (\exp - r(T - t))*D*N(n'_b) - (1 - \tau)\frac{C}{r}(1 - \exp - r(T - t).$$

We transform it by eliminating V

$$\mu_S = \mu_V + (\mu_V - r) * \frac{(\exp - r(T - t))*(D)*N(n'_b) + (1 - \tau)\frac{C}{r}(1 - \exp - r(T - t)}{V_S},$$

$$dV_S(t) = (rV_S + (1 - \tau)C)dt + \sigma_{\text{Call}} * \text{Call} * dW^Q.$$

That corresponds to the hypothesis 1 of financing the cash out (coupon after tax) by sale of shares.

Application 3: Calculation of the differential of the enterprise value.

$$V_E(t) = V(t) + TS(V) - BC(V),$$
$$dV_E(t) = (rV_E - C)dt + \sigma_E V_E * dW^Q,$$
$$dV_E = (\mu_E V_E - C)dt + \sigma_E V_E dW,$$
$$TS(V) = \tau\frac{C}{r}(1 - \exp - r(T - t))$$

because we suppose they will be surely paid.

$$V_E(t) = V(t) - BC(V) + \tau * G(t).$$

Using $V_E'(t)$ we will calculate the drift and the volatility of the equity. We apply the method to $C' = \tau C$, hence, $V_E' = V - BC(V) - \tau G'(t)$,

$$\mu_E' V_E' = \mu_V V - \mu_{BC} BC - r\tau G',$$

$$\sigma_E' V_E' = \sigma_V V - \sigma_{BC} BC = \sigma_V (V - y_1 BC) = \sigma_E V_E.$$

Seen AOA_V:

$$\mu_E' = r + AOA_V * \sigma_{V_E'} = r + AOA_V * \frac{\sigma_V V - \sigma_{BC} BC}{V_E'}$$

or:

$$\mu_E' = r + AOA_V * \frac{\sigma_V V - \sigma_V y_1 BC}{V_E'},$$

and

$$\mu_E = r + AOA_V * \frac{\sigma_V V - \sigma_V y_1 BC}{V_E}$$

is stochastic and depends on time

$$\mu_E = r + AOA_V * \frac{\sigma_V V - \sigma_V y_1 BC}{V_E}.$$

We transform it by eliminating V

$$V_E(t) = V(t) - BC(V) + \tau * G(t),$$

$$\mu_E = r + AOA_V * \frac{\sigma_V (V_E + BC(V) - \tau G) - \sigma_V y_1 BC}{V_E},$$

and

$$\mu_E = \mu_V + (\mu_V - r)\frac{-\tau G + (1 - y_1) BC}{V_E}$$

is stochastic with a temporal constituent

$$dV_E(t) = (rV_E - \tau * C)dt + \sigma_E V_E * dW^Q$$

and

$$dV_E = (\mu_E V_E - \tau C)dt + \sigma_E V_E dW,$$

and we find

$$dV_E = dV_S + dV_d$$

and

$$\sigma_E V_E = \sigma_S V_S + \sigma_d V_d.$$

C.2 Links Between Elasticity $\varepsilon_{F,V}$ and β

We take μ_V deterministic (non-stochastic and being able to depend on time and we also suppose the same for the market.

Therefore the elasticity to the market and the Betas ratio of the derivatives and its underlying have to be moved closer. Actually we have:

$$\beta_{F'} \equiv \operatorname{cov}\left(\frac{dF'}{F'}, \frac{dM}{M}\right) \Big/ \operatorname{cov}\left(\frac{dM}{M}, \frac{dM}{M}\right)$$

$$= \operatorname{cov}\left(\frac{dF'}{F'}, \frac{dM}{M}\right) \Big/ dt\sigma_M^2,$$

$$\beta_v \equiv \operatorname{cov}\left(\frac{dV}{V}, \frac{dM_t}{M_t}\right) \Big/ dt\sigma_M^2,$$

where

$$\rho_{V,M} dt \equiv dW_V{}^Q * dW_M^Q = \rho_{F',M} dt.$$

Hence,

$$\beta_v = \rho_{V,M} \frac{\sigma_V}{\sigma_M} = \rho_{V,M} \varepsilon_{V,M}.$$

On the other hand:

$$\beta_{F'} = \frac{IE(\sigma_{F'} dW_V^Q \sigma_M dW_M^Q)}{\sigma_M^2 dt} = IE\left(\widetilde{\varepsilon_{F',M}} \frac{dW_V^Q dW_M^Q}{dt}\right)$$

$$= IE\left(\widetilde{\varepsilon_{F',M}}\right) \rho_{V,M} = \frac{\overline{\sigma_{F'}}}{\sigma_M} \rho_{V,M} = \frac{\overline{\sigma_{F'}}}{\sigma_V} * \frac{\sigma_V}{\sigma_M} \rho_{V,M} = \frac{\overline{\sigma_{F'}}}{\sigma_V} \beta_V,$$

and thus:

$$\frac{\beta_{F'}}{\beta_V} = \frac{\overline{\sigma_{F'}}}{\sigma_V} = IE(\varepsilon_{F',V}) \frac{\beta_F}{\beta_V} = \frac{\overline{\sigma_F}}{\sigma_V}$$

$$\beta_{F'} \overline{F'} = \beta_F \overline{F}.$$

Moreover, the link between the volatilities of the capitals (weighted average) shows with this formula that the link between the Beta of the capital is not simple.

We also have by multiplying at the top and below by AOA_V:

$$\beta_{F'} = \frac{IE((\mu_{F'} - r) dW_V^Q dW_M^Q)}{AOA_V \sigma_M dt}.$$

We can also make a demonstration using Betas and CAPM.

We have:

$$\mu_F - \lambda_F = r + AOA_V * \sigma_F$$

stochastic

$$\mu_V - \lambda_V = r + AOA_V * \sigma_V$$

of which we suppose that the drift and the volatility of V are not stochastic; similarly for the market M, we have.

$$AOA_V = \frac{(\mu_{F'} - \lambda_{F'}) - r}{\sigma_{F'}} = \frac{(\mu_V - \lambda_V) - r}{\sigma_V} = \frac{(\mu_F - \lambda_F) - r}{\sigma_{F'}}.$$

Thus

$$\mu_V - r - \lambda_V \overset{CAPM}{=} \beta_V * (\mu_M - r - \lambda_M) \text{ and thus:}$$

$$\begin{aligned}\mu_F - \lambda_F - r \overset{AOA_V}{=} (\mu_V - \lambda_V - r) * \frac{\sigma_F}{\sigma_V} &= (\mu_V - \lambda_V - r) * \widetilde{\varepsilon_F} \\ &= (\mu_M - \lambda_M - r)\beta_V * \frac{\sigma_F}{\sigma_V}\end{aligned}$$

or:

$$\overline{\mu_F} \overset{CAPM}{=} r + \beta_F * (\overline{Rm} - r - \lambda_m) + \lambda_F.$$

Hence we have:

$$\beta_F = \beta_V \frac{\overline{\sigma_F}}{\sigma_V} = \beta_V IE(\tilde{\varepsilon}_F).$$

(Note: In particular when $\tilde{\varepsilon}_{F'}$ is deterministic

$$\begin{aligned}\varepsilon_{F',V} &= \frac{\beta_{F'}}{\beta_V} = \frac{\sigma_{F'}}{\sigma_V}, \\ \beta_F &= \rho_{F,M}\frac{\sigma_F}{\sigma_M} = \rho_{F,M}\varepsilon_{F,M}, \\ \frac{\mu_F - r}{\sigma_F} &= \frac{\mu_{F'} - r}{\sigma_{F'}} = \frac{\beta_{F'}(R_m - r)}{\sigma_{F'}}, \\ \mu_F &= r + \beta_{F'}(R_m - r)\frac{\sigma_F}{\sigma_{F'}} = r + \beta_{F'}(R_m - r)\frac{F'}{F}\end{aligned}$$

but it is not the case.)

Appendix D: Value of Debt and Enterprise Value in a Homogeneous DCF Model

D.1 Enterprise Valuation

As a preliminary remark it must be pointed out that for reasons of simplification, the following calculations start from a FCF approach using amortizations instead of investments, assuming that knowledgeable readers will transpose the following equations using the exact definition of FCF.

We define the risk of not going bankrupt annually as $(1-\theta_d)$.

We have two cases to add:

— if no bankruptcy:

$$(1-\theta_d)^n FCFn = (1-\theta_d)^n * (EBIT_n - \mu_{d,n}D_n) * (1-t) + (1-\theta_d)^n * \mu_{d,n}D_n;$$

— if bankruptcy:

$$(1-(1-\theta_d)^n) * \mathrm{FCF}_n = 0.$$

This therefore gives:

$$\mathrm{FCF}_n = [(1-\theta_d)^n * (EBIT_n - \mu_{d,n}D_n) * (1-t)] + [(1-\theta_d)^n * \mu_{d,n}D_n].$$

in other words,

$$\mathrm{FCF}_n = \left[(1-\theta_d)^n * EBIT_n * (1-t)\right] + \left[(1-\theta_d)^n * t * \mu_{d,n}D_n\right].$$

We must also factor in corporate risk, so let *io* be the zero-debt corporate risk. This gives:

$$\mathrm{FCF}_n * (1-i)^n = EBIT_n * (1-t) * (1-io)^n * (1-\theta_d)^n + (1-\theta_d)^n * t * \mu_{d,n}D_n,$$

where i represents corporate risk; we therefore have:

$$\mathrm{FCF}_n * (1-i)^n = (1-t) * (1-\theta_d)^n (EBIT_n * (1-io)^n - \mu_{d,n}D_n) + (1-\theta_d)^n * \mu_{d,n}D_n,$$

$$\mathrm{FCF}_n * (1-i)^n = [\mathrm{DIV}n * (1-a)^n] + [\mathrm{Fin}C * (1-\theta_d)^n],$$

where a represents the risk for the shareholder and DIV represents distributable dividends.

We can thus implement the DCF model in this way provided we determine θ_d, which we shall do at the end of the section.

To achieve a resolution, we must therefore now formulate two equations:

— the equation of the values by discounting all parts using risk-free

$$r : V_E = V_S + V_d;$$

— the equation of the expected or average flows (obtained by derivation of the previous equation;
in the case of the continuous model, if

$$V_i = V_{0,i} * \exp(\mu_i * t)$$

we get

$$\frac{dV_i}{dt} = \mu_i * V_i;$$

therefore,

$$\mu_E * V_E = \mu_S * V_S + \mu_d * V_d.$$

In the discrete model, we demonstrate the same thing by taking the annual variation from each of these values. This derivative, of course, applies to all equalities between values, the two above-mentioned axes look thus:

For the company

$$V_E = \sum \frac{\mathrm{FCF}_n * (1-i)^n}{(1+r)^n};$$

For debt:

$$V_d = \sum \frac{\mu_n * D_n * (1-\theta_d)^n}{(1+r)^n}.$$

We define α by:

$$V_d = (1-\alpha) * V_d^0 \quad \text{with } V_d^0 = \sum \frac{\mu_n * D_n}{(1+r)^n},$$

where V_d^0 is the value of the risk-free debt without future risk of bankruptcy. Similarly:

$$\mathrm{FCF}_n^0 * (1-io)^n = EBIT_n * (1-t) * (1-io)^n$$

depends only on the activities and not on the financing. We can also define:

$V' = k * V$, where V is the value of the company without debt nor risk of bankruptcy (we should have named it V^0 to have a homogeneous notation but, it is named V in the Modigliani Miller and Leland models).

$$V' = \sum \frac{\mathrm{FCF}_n^0 * (1 - i_0)^n (1 - \theta_d)^n}{(1 + r)^n},$$

$$V = \sum \frac{\mathrm{FCF}_n^0 * (1 - i_0)^n}{(1 + r)^n}.$$

This gives us tax free-value, but with the risk of bankruptcy + value of the tax savings due to the debt.

We now have:

$$V_E = V_S + V_d = V' + t * V_d$$

and

$$V_S = V' + (t - 1)V_d.$$

$$V' = V_E - tV_d = V_S + (1 - t) * V_d.$$

So we get the deleveraged and without bankruptcy WACC:

$$\mu_V = \frac{(\mu_S - \mu_d)V_S + (1 - t) * rV_d}{V_E - t * V_d}$$

is different from

$$\mu_{V'} = \frac{\mu_S V_S + (1 - t) * \mu_d V_d}{V_E - t * V_d}$$

and is different from

$$WACC \equiv \frac{\mu_S V_S + (1 - t) * \mu_d V_d}{V_E}$$

which includes tax savings effects include in V_E.

We can now describe the different equations derived from the following flows:

$$\mu_E * V_E = [(\mu_V + \theta_d) * V' - (1 - t) * (r + \theta_d) * V_d] + (r + \theta_d) * V_d$$

[a dividend portion minus the debt effect decreased by the tax effect] + a part link to the debt.

$$\mu_E * V_E = (\mu_V + \theta_d) * V' + t * (r + \theta_d) * Vd = \mu_S * V_S + (r + \theta_d) * V_d.$$

Let us now calculate μ_S:

$$\begin{aligned}
\mu_E * V_E &= \mu_S * V_S + (r + \theta_d) * Vd \\
&= (\mu_V + \theta_d) * V' + t * (r + \theta_d) * V' \\
&\quad \mu_S * V_S + (r + \theta_d) * V_d \\
&= (\mu_V + \theta_d) * (V_e - t * V_d) + t * (r + \theta_d) * V_d \\
\mu_S * V_S &= (\mu_V + \theta_d)(V_e - tV_d) \\
&\quad + (r + \theta_d) * (t - 1) * V_d.
\end{aligned}$$

Hence

$$\mu_S = \mu_V + \theta_d + (1 - t) * \frac{V_d}{V_S} * (\mu_V - r).$$

Similarly for μ_E:

$$\begin{aligned}
(\mu_E - r) * V_E &= \mu_S V_S + (r + \theta_d) * V_d - r * (V_S + V_d); \\
&= (\mu_S - r) * V_S + \theta_d * V_d; \\
\mu_E &= r + \theta_d + (\mu_V - r) * \left(1 - t * (1 - \alpha) * \frac{V_d^0}{V_E}\right).
\end{aligned}$$

We can thus see directly how α limits the beneficial impact of taxes on corporate value.

Let us express the link between β_d and β_e and V':

$$(\mu_V + \theta_d) * V' = \mu_S * V_S + (r + \theta_d) * (1 - t) * Vd.$$

Hence,

$$\mu_V - r = (\mu_S - r) * \frac{V_S}{V'} - \theta_d * \frac{V_S}{V'} = (\mu_S - r - \theta_d) * \frac{V_S}{V'}.$$

In CAPM terms, this therefore gives:

$$\beta_V = \frac{\beta_S * V_S - \theta_d * \left(\frac{V_S}{(Rm - r)}\right)}{V'} = \frac{\beta_S - \beta_d}{1 + (1 - t) * \frac{Vd}{V_S}}.$$

(Note: From the first model we deduce a variable behavior of β_S thus defined.)

Let us express the link between β_d and β_V and V_E.

We also have:

$$\mu_V - r = (\mu_S - r - \theta_d) * \frac{V_S}{V'} = (\mu_S - r - \theta_d) * \frac{V_E - V_d}{V_E - t * V_d}.$$

This leads to:

$$\beta_V = \frac{\beta_S * (V_E - V_d) - \beta_d * (V_E - V_d)}{(V_E - t * V_d)} = \frac{(\beta_S - \beta_d) * \left(1 - \frac{V_d}{V_E}\right)}{1 - t * \frac{V_d}{V_E}}.$$

D.2 Enterprise Valuation in the Case of Constant Interests of Debt and Growth

To better appreciate the proposed model, we resolve in the trivial case where interests of the debt are approximately held constant and where growth in FCF is estimated using the constant g. As usual the debt is considered constant.

V_d represents the resale value of the debt.

— thus for $\mu_{d,0} * D$ constant we have: $V_d \approx \frac{\mu_{d,0} * D}{(r+\theta_d)}$;
— if $\mu_{d,0} = (r + \theta_d)$, then $V_d = D$;
— and if the asset value grows infinitely, we obtain $V_d = V_d^0 = \frac{\mu_{d,0} * D}{r} = \frac{C}{r}$ and $\theta_d = 0$.

We also see the fact that there is no random opportunity that is creating wealth, since risk offsets profitability and, in that homogeneous (similar) way for both debt and shareholders' equity.

$$V_E = V' + t * V_d;$$

$$V_d = \sum \frac{\mu_d * D * (1 - \theta_d)^n}{(1 + r)^n} = \frac{\mu_d * D}{(r + \theta_d)} * (1 - \theta_d);$$

$$V' = \sum \frac{(EBIT(1 - t)) * (1 - io)^n (1 - \theta_d)^n * (1 + g)^n}{(1 + r)^n}$$

$$= EBIT(1 - t)\frac{(1 - io) * (1 + g) * (1 - \theta_d)}{(1 + r) - (1 - io)(1 + g)(1 - \theta_d)};$$

$$V = \sum \frac{(EBIT(1 - t)) * (1 - io)^n * (1 + g)^n}{(1 + r)^n}$$

$$= EBIT(1 - t)\frac{(1 - io) * (1 + g)}{(1 + r) - (1 - io)(1 + g)};$$

$$V \approx \frac{EBIT(1 - t)}{\mu_V - g}$$

depends only on the activity.

$$V' = V * \frac{(1+r) - (1-io)(1+g)}{(1-io)(1+g)} * \frac{(1-io)*(1+g)*(1-\theta_d)}{(1+r) - (1-io)(1+g)(1-\theta_d)}$$

$$V' = V * \frac{(1+r) - (1-io)(1+g)}{(1)}$$

$$* \frac{(1-\theta d)}{(1+r) - (1-io)(1+g)(1-\theta_d)}$$

$$\frac{V_E}{1-\theta_d} = \frac{\mu_V - g}{(\mu_V - g + \theta_d)} * V + t * \frac{\mu_d * D}{(r+\theta_d)}.$$

Note: We obtain

$$Ve \leq V + t * D$$

because the coefficients are less than 1. Let

$$a = \mu_V - g;$$

hence,

$$\frac{V_E}{1-\theta_d} = \frac{a}{(a+\theta_d)} * V + t * \frac{\mu_d * D}{(r+\theta_d)}.$$

$$V_E * (a+\theta_d) * (r+\theta_d)$$
$$= (1-\theta_d) * (a * V * (r+\theta_d) + t * \mu_d * D * (a+\theta_d)).$$

We can therefore generate a second degree equation in θ_d (which could constitute an initial approach for interpolating the risk, but it is, in a way, self-referential).

Let us look for a formula that approaches the value of shareholders' equity in the case of constant debt and growth g of FCF.

$$\frac{V_E}{1-\theta_d} = \frac{\mu_V - g}{(\mu_V - g + \theta_d)} * V + t * \frac{\mu_d * D}{(r+\theta_d)};$$

$$V_S = V' + (t-1)V_d;$$

$$V_S = (1-\theta_d) * \frac{\mu_V - g}{(\mu_V - g + \theta_d)} * V - (1-t) * \frac{\mu_d * D}{(r+\theta_d)};$$

$$V_S = (1-\theta_d) * \left(1 - \frac{\theta_d}{(\mu_V - g + \theta_d)}\right) * V - (1-t) * \frac{\mu_d * D}{(r+\theta_d)};$$

$$V_S = V - \frac{\theta_d}{(\mu_V - g + \theta_d)} * V$$

$$- \theta_d * \left(1 - \frac{\theta_d}{(\mu_V - g + \theta_d)}\right) * V - (1-t) * \frac{\mu_d * D}{(r+\theta_d)};$$

$$V_S = V - (1-t) * \frac{\mu_d * D}{(r+\theta_d)} - \theta_d * V * \left(1 + \frac{(1-\theta_d)}{(\mu_V - g + \theta_d)}\right),$$

which constitutes the formula for valuing capital in this DCF model.

This can be compared with that of the first mode, although the bankruptcy assumption used is different.

D.3 *Reintroducing the Bankruptcy Risk Derived from the First Model in the DCF Model*

We place ourselves in the classic case of pricing the assets of a company using the DCF method with constant debt but increasing growth.

We therefore start with:

$$V_d = \frac{\mu_d * D}{(r+\theta_d)} * (1-\theta_d) = \frac{C_D}{(r+\theta_d)} * (1-\theta_d).$$

Moreover, the equations of the first model gave:

$$V_d = C_D * \left(\frac{1}{r+\lambda_D} - k * \left(\frac{V}{C_D}\right)^{\overline{\Omega}}\right),$$

where

$$\overline{\Omega} = -y < 0.$$

(Note: In this case we can determine optimum debt.)

We look for θ_d by equalizing the two values. As a way of simplifying the presentation we solve the equations without factoring in information costs.

$$\frac{1}{(r+\theta_d)} * (1-\theta_d) = \frac{V_d}{C_D} = \frac{1}{r} - k * \left(\frac{V}{C_D}\right)^{-y};$$

therefore,

$$\theta_d = \frac{r}{\left(1+\frac{1}{r}\right) * \frac{\left(\frac{V}{C_D}\right)^{+y}}{k} - 1}.$$

We must now determine k and y.

One solution is to take the values at two instants (we could use a similar solution using any interpolation method if we have more than two relevant, recent values); in t_1:

$$k = \left(1 + \frac{1}{r}\right) * \frac{\theta_{d1}}{r + \theta_{d1}} * \left(\frac{V_1}{C_{D_1}}\right)^{+y};$$

hence,

$$\theta_d = \frac{r}{\frac{(r+\theta_{d1})}{\theta_{d1}} * \left(\frac{V * C_{D1}}{C_D * V_1}\right)^y - 1}. \quad (1)$$

In t_2, we will have: θ_{d2}; hence,

$$\left(\frac{C_{D1} * V_2}{C_{D2} * V_1}\right)^y = \frac{(r + \theta_{d2})}{\theta_{d2}} * \frac{\theta_{d1}}{(r + \theta_{d1})}.$$

We can therefore proceed by correlating the logarithms if we have several values, or if we only have two, we may select:

$$\overline{\Omega} = -y = \frac{\left(\ln \frac{(r+\theta_{d1})}{\theta_{d1}} - \ln \frac{(r+\theta_{d2})}{\theta_{d2}}\right)}{\ln\left(\frac{V_2}{C_{D_2}}\right) - \ln\left(\frac{V_1}{C_{D_1}}\right)}.$$

References

Bellalah, M and Jacquillat, B (1995). Option valuation with information costs: Theory and tests. *The Financial Review*, 3a(3), 617–635.

Bellalah, M and El Farissi, I (2002). Corporate debt value and optimal capital structure with shadow costs of incomplete information. *Finance India Quarterly Review*, 16(4), 1325–1356.

Black, F and Scholes, M (1973). The pricing of options and corporate liabilities. *Journal of Political Economy*, 81(3), 637–654.

Cox, J, Ross, S and Rubinstein, M (1979). Option pricing: A simplified approach. *Journal of Financial Economics*, 7(September), 229–263.

Hoogland, JK and Neumann, CDD (2001). Local scale in invariance and contingent claim pricing. *International Journal of Theoretical and Applied Finance*, 4(1), 1–21.

Leland, H (1994). Corporate debt value bond covenants, and optimal capital structure. *Journal of Finance*, 4(September), 1213–1252.

Merton, R (1973). Theory of rational option pricing. *Bell Journal of Economics and Management Science*, 4, 41–83.

Merton, R (1973). An intertemporal capital asset pricing model. *Econometrica*, 41(5), 141–183.

Merton, R (1974). On the pricing of corporate debt: The risk structure of interest rates. *Journal of Finance*, 29(May), 449–470.

Merton, R (1987). A simple model of capital market equilibrium with incomplete information. *Journal of Finance*, 42(3), 483–510.

Modigliani, F and Miller, M (1958). The cost of capital, corporation finance and the theory of investment. *American Economic Review*, 48(June), 261–297.

Modigliani, F and Miller, M (1963). Corporate income taxes and the cost of capital. *American Economic Review*, 53 433–443.

Negrea, R (2000). On the extension of Merton and Vasicek models related to the pricing of zero-coupon bonds. "*Politechnica*", University of Timisoara.

Toft, KB and Prucyk, B (1997). Options on leverage equity: Theory and Empirical tests. *Journal of Finance*, LII, 1151–1180.

Vanoverberghe, D (2006). An extension of the Merton's equations and Betas relationship between debt and asset value: Applications for valuing debt and assessing the enterprise value, *Euro Mediterranean Economics and Finance Review*, 4.

Vernimmen.net Quiry, P and Le Fur, Y (2003). Beta des capitaux propres, Beta de l'endettement et Beta de l'actif économique, La lettre Vernimmen.net No. 23, October November.

CHAPTER 16

DOES THE TUNISIAN STOCK MARKET OVERREACT?

Fatma Hammami[*,†] *and Ezzeddine Abaoub*[†,‡]

Research in experimental financial markets suggests that, most people tend to overreact to unexpected, striking, and more recent news, and underreact to ordinary or non-desirable new events. Many researchers document, as a result that, if one of these behavioral designs exist, then stock prices will follow a mean-reversion phenomenon due to investor's overreaction, and a momentum behavior due to investor's underreaction. This study investigates if such behavior affects stock prices on the Tunisian Stock Market. In other words, we tend to discover the eventual existence of return mean-reversion and/or momentum behavior on the Tunisian Stock Market over the period between January 1997 and December 2005. For this purpose, we have applied a contrarian strategy, which consists in buying the previous (12, 18, 24, and 36 months) loser portfolio and selling the past winner portfolio. Our results point out that, over periods of 18, 24, and 36 months, stock returns exhibit statistically significant mean-reversion phenomenon, while, over 12 months periods, stock returns present significant momentum behavior. This means that stock prices are predictable on the basis of their historical recordings without using any accounting data, in contrast to the weak-form efficient market hypothesis.

1 Introduction

Efficient market hypothesis (EMH) requires that security prices reflect instantaneously fully all available relevant information (Fama, 1970). Therefore, it is

[*]Doctorante en Sciences de Gestion, Faculté des Sciences Economiques et de Gestion, Université de Sfax. hammami_fatma@yahoo.fr.

[†]Laboratoire de Finance, de Comptabilité et d'Intermédiations Financière (LAFICOIF)

[‡]Professeur Agrégé en Sciences de Gestion, Faculté des Sciences Économiques et de Gestion de Tunis, Université Elmanar.
abaoub.ezzeddine@wanadoo.tn.

impossible for any investor to beat the market or to generate abnormal returns basing on the historical recording of stocks. As a result, there was widespread consensus among financial economists that stock returns were unpredictable. Unpredictability was seen as a direct consequence of the EMH (see Fig. 10 in Appendix A).

However, this consensus started to be revised after the works of DeBondt and Thaler (1985), Fama and French (1988), Poterba and Summers (1988), and Jegadeesh and Titman (1993) who document several statistical evidences that past returns are helpful to predict future returns relying on the fact that stock returns exhibit *negative autocorrelations* over long-holding-periods (DeBondt and Thaler, 1985), and *positive autocorrelations* over short-holding-periods (Jegadeesh and Titman, 1993).

The idea of *negative return autocorrelations* over time comes from the price overreaction phenomenon following the arrival of fundamental news (overestimation of news; see Fig. 11 in Appendix A).[a] Then, if prices overreact, DeBondt and Thaler (1985) advance that prices exhibit the presence of two distinct and inverse phenomenons that occur simultaneously. In a first time, stocks are pushed beyond their fundamental values. After this first over (under) evaluation, and in a second time, when the market perceives the misevaluation of stocks in relation to their fundamental values, prices will be adjusted reciprocally showing a mean-reversion of prices, from where the negative autocorrélation of returns over time. In other words, the overreaction hypothesis predicts, first, that stocks that present high abnormal returns (named winners) experience an inverse progression over time, that is to say abnormal low returns, and vice versa, secondly, the more extreme the initial price movement, the greater will be the subsequent adjustment (DeBondt and Thaler, 1985, 1987).[b]

On the other hand, the insight of *positive returns autocorrelations* over time originates from the price underreaction phenomenon at the appearance of fundamental news (underestimation of news; see Fig. 12 in Appendix A).

[a]Behavioral finance documents that the price overreaction is due to the excessive reaction of (ir)rational individuals, while the supporters of the efficient market hypothesis suppose that it is the result of apparition of additional factors of risks.

[b]This phenomenon has been discovered by several studies at long-temporal-horizons as well as at short ones. For instance, DeBondt and Thaler (1985, 1987) and Chopra *et al.* (1992), find that it is a phenomenon that characterizes the long-term stock prices behavior (from 3 to 5 years), while, Jegadeesh (1990), Lehmann (1990), Conrad *et al.* (1997) and Assoé and Sy (2004) discover a return reversion on relatively intermediate and short horizons (from 1 to 6 months).

Jegadeesh and Titman (1993, 2001) document that price does not integrate immediately the good or the bad news announced as foresee the EMH. Indeed, stocks that generate high performances in such year will continue to produce also positive returns on the following year. In the same manner, stocks that have experience bad performances on a year will not redress the situation the following year, from where the occurrence of positive returns autocorrelations over time (Jegadeesh and Titman, 1993, 2001).[c]

As a result, an extensive body of research documents show that, if these anomalies exist on stock markets, then *ex ante* stock returns are *predictable* on the basis of their *ex post* recording, in contradiction to the EMH.[d] Currently, there seems to be a wide acceptance of the idea that returns are, to some extent, predictable, see, for instance, Cochrane (2001), Lewellen (2004), Ang and Bekeart (2005), and Campbell and Yogo (2006), etc. There is also an extensive evidence that *active investment strategies* exploiting these two patterns of predictability generate significant *abnormal* returns. Then, given such time series patterns in cross-sectional stock returns, one can formulate two profitable portfolio-investment-strategies: *contrarian strategy*, based on the price reversals phenomenon, and *momentum strategy* based on the price continuation phenomenon.

Under the contrarian strategy, past loser-stocks are bought and past winners are sold. And under the momentum strategy, past winners are bought and past losers are sold. Considerable evidence proves that both contrarian and momentum investment strategies, *apparently contradictory*, produce generally statistically, and sometimes economically significant excess returns. Indeed, the degree of statistic and economic profitability of these investment strategies differs from one study to another according to the temporal horizon used (short, medium, or long-term horizons) and to the development level of the selected countries.

The purpose of this chapter is to investigate the nature of the phenomenon characterizing the behavior of the Tunisian Stock Market prices. We will concentrate on an empirical test of the over-reaction hypothesis of price behavior. We explore if stock prices follow a mean reversion or a momentum behavior

[c]Besides Jegadeesh and Titman (1993, 2001), many other researchers, among others, Rouwenhorst (1998, 1999), Chan *et al.* (1996, 2000), Grundy and Martin (2001), Lewellen (2002), Patro and Wu (2004), argue that the stock return behavior exhibit a momentum phenomenon, where, in average, past winners continue to outperform past losers, speciously, over intermediate and short term horizons (3–12 months).

[d]Our paper parts from this idea to test the stock return predictability of the Tunisian Stock Market.

or simply a random-walk phenomenon over horizons from one year to three years. For this reason, we have applied a contrarian strategy,[e] and we have tested the following two hypothesis:

(H1) If significant extreme movements in stock prices will be followed by subsequent significant extreme price movements in the *opposite* direction, then stock returns exhibit a *mean reversion phenomenon*.

(H2) If significant extreme movements in stock prices will be followed by subsequent significant price movements in the same direction, then stock returns exhibit a *momentum phenomenon*.

(H3) If neither mean-reversion nor momentum phenomenon characterizes clearly and significantly price behavior of the Tunisian Stock Market, then stock returns exhibit simply a *random-walk phenomenon*.

Briefly, the empirical validation of the first two hypotheses may imply a violation of the weak form of the EMH, in so far as, if stock prices systematically overshoot (or undershoot), then their reversal (or their momentum) should be predictable alone from past return data, with no use of any accounting data such as earnings. While under the third hypothesis, the EMH cannot be rejected.

The remainder of the paper is organized as follows. Section 2 describes the data and the methodology used to construct the winner, loser, and contrarian portfolios (called also arbitrage portfolio or zero-investment portfolios), as well as the statistical test used to measure the significance of the results. Section 3 presents the main results and their interpretation. The article ends, in a last section with a brief summary of conclusions.

2 The Over-Reaction and Under-Reaction Hypothesis: Empirical Tests

The tests involved in this study assess the extent to which systematic nonzero residual return behavior in the period after portfolio formation ($t > 0$) is associated with systematic residual returns in the pre-formation months ($t < 0$) of portfolios. We will focus on stocks that have experienced either extreme capital gains or extreme losses over different periods from 12 months up to three years.

[e]We apply the same methodology used by DeBondt and Thaler (1985).

In other words, "winner" (W) and "loser" (L) portfolios are formed conditional upon past excess returns, rather than some firm-generated informational variable such as earnings.

The EMH predicts that:

$$E(\hat{U}_{W,t}|F_{t-1}) = E(\hat{U}_{L,t}|F_{t-1}) = 0, \tag{1}$$

where F_{t-1} represents the complete set of information at time $t-1$, and $\hat{U}_{W,t}$ and $\hat{U}_{L,t}$ represent the residual returns, respectively, of the winner and loser portfolio. On the other hand, the price overreaction (or the mean-reversion) hypothesis suggests that $E(\hat{U}_{L,t}|F_{t-1}) > 0$ and $E(\hat{U}_{W,t}|F_{t-1}) < 0$, therefore:

$$E(\hat{U}_{L,t}|F_{t-1}) - E(\hat{U}_{W,t}|F_{t-1}) > 0. \tag{2}$$

Therefore, the under-reaction (or the momentum) suggests that:

$$E(\hat{U}_{L,t}|F_{t-1}) - E(\hat{U}_{W,t}|F_{t-1}) < 0. \tag{3}$$

Data as well as the basic research methodology used in the setting of this chapter are described in the following subsections.

2.1 *Data*

Monthly average of enclosure prices data[f] for 30 stocks listed on the Tunisian Stock Exchange (BVMT)[g] are used for the period between January 1997 and December 2005.[h] In fact, it is important to note that the monthly return of stock j at time t is calculated as follows:

$$R_{j,t} = \frac{P_{j,t} + \mathrm{Div}_{j,t} - P_{j,t-1}}{P_{j,t-1}}, \tag{4}$$

[f]Similar to DeBondt and Thaler (1985), the choice to use a monthly data base is in part justified by our concern to avoid certain measurement problems that have received much attention in the literature. Most of the problems arise with the use of daily data, both with respect to the risk and return variables. They include, among others, the "bid-ask" effect and the consequences of infrequent trading.

[g]The list of stocks on which we will apply the tests of mean reversion and momentum phenomenon includes the following societies: AIR LIQUIDE, ALKIMIA, AMEN BANK, AMS, ASTREE, ATB, BH, BIAT, BNA, BS, BT, BTEI, CIL, ICF, LA CARTE, MONOPRIX, PALM BEACH, PLAC DE TUNISIE, SFBT, SMPAR, SITEX, SOFI, SPDIT, STB, STS, TUNISAIR, TUNISIE LAIT, TUNISIE LEASING, UBCI, and UIB.

[h]On the list of daily closure prices of stocks traded on the BVMT, one calculated the monthly average closure prices of each of the thirty securities.

where

$P_{j,t}$ is the average closure price of stock j over month t.
$P_{j,t-1}$ is the average closure prices i over month $t-1$.
$\text{Div}_{j,t}$ is the dividend distributed by stock j for month t.

2.2 Methodology

In this section, we describe our simple strategy. Most of this section is taken from DeBondt and Thaler (1985). The empirical test methodology consists to follow the subsequent steps in order to form the winner and loser portfolios. Then, inevitably, it is necessary to measure the degree of statistical significance of the founded results.

2.2.1 Winner and Loser Portfolio Construction Procedures

This empirical study can be achieved using three types of return residuals: market-adjusted excess returns, market model residuals, and excess returns that are measured relative to the Sharp–Lintner version of the CAPM (DeBondt and Thaler, 1985). It turns out that whichever of the three types of residuals are used, the results of the empirical analysis are affirmed to be similar and that choice does not affect the main conclusion. Therefore, as maid DeBondt and Thaler (1985), we will only report the results based on market-adjusted excess returns.

Consequently, to achieve the performance test of the winner and loser portfolios formed over a period of 12 months,[i] for example, we will pass by the following steps:

(i) The first step consists to calculate — for every stock j on the tape with at least 12 months of return data, without any missing values in between — the residual return ($\hat{U}_{j,t}$). It is hence estimated by:

$$\hat{U}_{j,t} = R_{j,t} - R_{m,t}, \tag{5}$$

where

$R_{j,t}$ is the return of stock j at time t.
$R_{m,t}$ is the arithmetic average rate of return of all stocks traded in the market at time t.

[i]In order to facilitate the comprehension of the procedure used to form the winner and loser portfolios, we have chosen to present the case of formation portfolio over periods of 12 months. We apply the same procedure for the other periods of formation (18, 24, and 36 months).

We remark that there is no risk adjustment except for the movements of the market as a hole and the adjustment is identical for all stocks.

This procedure is repeated eight times[j] starting in January 1997, January 1998, etc. up to January 2004.

(ii) For every stock j, staring in December 1997 (month 12 is the portfolio formation date; $t = 0$), we compute the cumulative excess returns for the prior 12 months (the portfolio formation period is from month 1 up to month 12) as:

$$\text{Cum}\hat{U}_j = \sum_{t=-11}^{t=0} \hat{U}_{j,t}. \tag{6}$$

(iii) On each of the eight relevant portfolio formation dates (December 1997, December 1998, etc. up to December 2004), the Cum$\hat{U}_j$'s are ranked in an ascending order and portfolios are formed. The top 40% (12 securities) or 20% (6 securities) constitutes the winner portfolio (W); the bottom 40% or 20% of stocks is assigned to the loser portfolio (L).[k] Thus, the portfolios are formed conditional upon excess return behavior prior to $t = 0$, the portfolio formation date.

(iv) For each portfolios in each of the eight nonoverlapping 12-month periods ($n = 1, \ldots, N$; $N = 8$), starting in January 1998 (month 13, the "starting month") and up to December 2005, we now compute the cumulative average residual returns (CAR) of all securities in the portfolio, for the next 12 months (the "test period" begin from month 13 up to month 24), i.e. from $t = 1$ through $t = 12$. We find $\text{CAR}_{W,n,t}$ and $\text{CAR}_{L,n,t}$. If a security's return is missing in a month subsequent to portfolio formation, then, from that moment on, the stock is permanently dropped from the portfolio and the CAR will be an average of the available residual returns. Thus, whenever a stock drops out, the calculations involve an implicit rebalancing.[l]

---

[j] Eight is the number of the non-overlapping replications (noted by N) for a contrarian strategy applied for a formation period of 12 months over the period between January 1997 and December 2005. It is useful to note that the number of independent replications vary inversely with the chosen length of the formation period. Says otherwise, more the formation period is short, more one will have additional replications, and vice-versa. For instance — on the research predefined period, from January 1997 to December 2005, we have 108 months — for portfolio formed on the 12 prior months, we will obtain 8 independent replications, whereas if we take a formation period of 36 months we will have only 2 independent replications.

[k] The choice of 40% and 20% of the listed stocks is arbitrary.

[l] When a security is temporary delisted, suspended or halted, we have chosen to take the last listed price.

(v) Using the CAR's from all eight test periods, average CAR's are computed for both winner and loser portfolios and at each month between $t = 1$ and $t = 12$. These are denoted as $\text{ACAR}_{W,t}$ and $\text{ACAR}_{L,t}$, respectively. Explicitly, these are calculated as follows:

$$\text{ACAR}_{W,t} = \sum_{n=1}^{n=N} \text{CAR}_{W,n,t} \Big/ N, \tag{7}$$

$$\text{ACAR}_{L,t} = \sum_{n=1}^{n=N} \text{CAR}_{L,n,t} \Big/ N. \tag{8}$$

The overreaction hypothesis predicts that, $\text{ACAR}_{W,t} < 0$ and $\text{ACAR}_{L,t} > 0$, so that, by implication $[\text{ACAR}_{L,t} - \text{ACAR}_{W,t}] > 0$. On the other hand, the under-reaction hypothesis anticipate that $\text{ACAR}_{W,t} > 0$ and $\text{ACAR}_{L,t} < 0$, in such a way that $[\text{ACAR}_{L,t} - \text{ACAR}_{W,t}] < 0$.

Therefore, one needs to calculate, in a final step, the average cumulative abnormal return of the contrarian portfolio, noted by $\text{ACAR}_{C,t}$. It equals, for each month t into the test period, to the difference of the average cumulative abnormal return between both loser and winner portfolios, so as to:

$$\text{ACAR}_{C,t} = \text{ACAR}_{L,t} - \text{ACAR}_{W,t}. \tag{9}$$

2.2.2 Statistical Significance Level of the Results

Primarily, in order to assess whether, at any time t, there is indeed a statistically significant difference in investment performance, we need a pooled estimate of the population variance in CAR_t,

$$S_t^2 = \left[\sum_{n=1}^{N} (\text{CAR}_{W,n,t} - \text{ACAR}_{W,t})^2 + \sum_{n=1}^{N} (\text{CAR}_{L,n,t} - \text{ACAR}_{L,t})^2 \right] \Big/ 2(N-1) \tag{10}$$

with two samples of equal size N, the variance of the difference of sample means equals $2S_t^2/N$ and the t-statistic is therefore:

$$T_t = [\text{ACAR}_{L,t} - \text{ACAR}_{W,t}] \Big/ \sqrt{2S_t^2/N}\,. \tag{11}$$

Relevant t-statistics can be found for each of the 12 post-formation months but they do not represent independent evidence.

Secondly, in the goal to judge, for any month t, the average residual return makes a contribution to either $\mathrm{ACAR}_{w,t}$ or $\mathrm{ACAR}_{L,t}$, we can test whether it is significantly different from zero. The sample standard deviation of the winner portfolio is equal to

$$S_{tW} = \sqrt{\sum_{n=1}^{N} (\mathrm{AR}_{W,n,t} - \mathrm{AR}_{W,t})^2 / N - 1}. \tag{12}$$

In the same manner, the standard deviation of the loser portfolio is equal to:

$$S_{tL} = \sqrt{\sum_{n=1}^{N} (\mathrm{AR}_{L,n,t} - \mathrm{AR}_{L,t})^2 / N - 1}. \tag{13}$$

Since $s_{tW}/\sqrt{N}$ represents the sample estimate of the standard error of $\mathrm{AR}_{W,t}$, the t-statistic equals:

$$T_{tW} = \mathrm{AR}_{W,t} / (S_{tW} / \sqrt{N}). \tag{14}$$

In the same way, because $s_{tL}/\sqrt{N}$ represents the sample estimates of the standard error of $AR_{L,t}$, the t-statistic equals:

$$T_L = \mathrm{AR}_{L,t} / (S_{tL} / \sqrt{N}). \tag{15}$$

3 The Over-Reaction and Under-Reaction Hypothesis: Empirical Results

It is important to recall that, if the contrarian portfolio generates positive (negative) and significant abnormal returns over the test period, we say that the stock prices follow a mean reversion (momentum) phenomenon. Hence, the most profitable manner for such investor to generate abnormal returns consists to apply a contrarian (momentum[m]) strategy.

Finally, if the contrarian portfolio generates a weak and non-significant return values, we say simply that stock prices follow a random walk phenomenon.

[m]The momentum strategy consists, as opposed to the contrarian strategy, to buy the previous winners and to sell the past losers. Therefore, the arbitrage portfolio return will be equals to winner portfolio return minus loser portfolio return.

We have established eight different contrarian strategies on the Tunisian Stock Market in order to discover the nature of the behavior underlying the fluctuation of stock prices. These tests differ both in terms of the length of the formation/hold periods and in terms of the number of stocks in the constructed portfolios. The results of all these tests are presented in detail in Tables 1–4 in Figs. 1–8.

Throwing a general view in Tables 1–4, one can notice that all results confirm the overreaction hypothesis since the contrarian portfolios, during the period of test, generates positive abnormal returns, except the tests done on a 12 month formation/test period. These results are generally compatible to results found by DeBondt and Thaler (1985) in American Stock Markets.

We observe also that the contrarian strategies playing on the six extreme stocks generate more important and significant profits than strategies playing on the 12 extreme stocks. For this reason, the figures shown are the tendencies of winner and loser portfolios over the test periods, produced by contrarian strategies based upon the past six extreme stocks. But, in order to conceive the intensity of the abnormal return differences compared with strategies based on 12 extreme stocks, we have reported in Figs. 2, 4, 6, and 8, the evolutions of abnormal returns produced by contrarian strategies based on both 6 and 12 stocks.

In addition, from the following tables, the general remark to make is that the cumulative abnormal returns generated by both loser and winner portfolios at the end of the different periods of formation are in increasing function of the formation horizon length. Analogically, the subsequent adjustments must be also the same way, what is the case, under some reserves.[n]

In the following paragraphs, we have interpret in a detailed manner the results generated by each of the eight tests defined above. We start with the presentation and the interpretation of the test of the cumulative return evolutions (in excess of the market) of the different portfolios formed and held over a period of 36 months until lead finally to the test accomplished on a period of 12 months (Table 1).

For the test done on a period of 36 months with 20% extreme stocks (six stocks), the loser portfolio continue to generate negative excess-market-returns until the 8th month. On the other hand, the winner portfolio continues

[n]One is going to see farther than the exception touches portfolios constructed and held over 36 months since they are dominated by those formed and detained during 24 months periods.

Table 1: Evolutions of average (market adjusted) cumulative returns of the loser, winner, and contrarian portfolios at the end of a 36 months formation periods and 1, 3, 6, 9, 12, 13, 18, 20, 24, 25, and 36 months into the test periods.

No. of replications and length of the formation periods	No. of extreme stocks in the portfolio	Nature of the portfolios	ACAR (t-statistics) at the end of formation periods	*ACAR* (t-statistics) into the test periods				
				Number of months into the test periods				
				1	12	24	25	36
Two 36 months periods	12	Loser	−0.435	−0.001	0.059	0.027	0.034	0.047
		Winner	0.418	0.007	0.018	−0.033	−0.029	−0.070
		Loser–Winner	−0.854	−0.008	0.042	0.060	0.063	**0.117**
		(t-statistics)	(−4.80)	(−0.41)	(0.31)	(0.62)	(0.64)	**(0.69)**
	6	Loser	−0.627	0.005	0.181	0.173	0.185	0.258
		Winner	0.579	0.029	0.088	−0.016	−0.013	−0.139
		Loser–Winner	−1.206	−0.024	0.092	0.189	0.198	**0.397**
		(t-statistics)	(−7.73)	(−0.46)	(0.44)	(1.72)	(1.70)	**(3.00)**

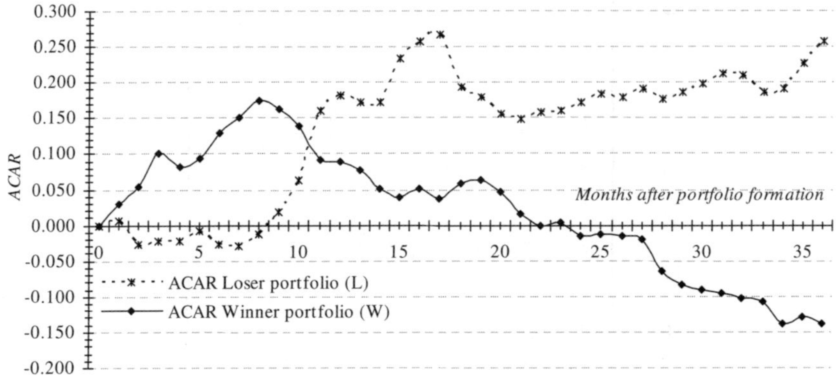

Figure 1: Evolutions of average (market-adjusted) cumulative returns of the loser and winner portfolios (six extreme stocks) during a test period of 36 months.

to produce positive excess-market-returns until the 23 month as shown in Fig. 1.

As a result, one observes that the mean-reversion phenomenon begin to appear only from the 10th month (see Fig. 2).[o] Besides, the poorest cumulative performance of the contrarian portfolio figures at the 8th month, it equals −18.8% (t-statistic: −1.98), and the highest cumulative performance is recorded at 36th month marking a return equals to 39.7% (t-statistic: 3.00).

We can also add that, while the contrarian portfolio has recorded the poorest cumulative returns of −120.6% (t-statistic: −7.73) at the end of the formation period, it come to adjust the situation over the following same length period while marking significant cumulative positive returns at a level of 39.7% at 36th month. However, with 40% extreme stocks (12 stocks), the highest cumulative return through the test period is merely about 11.7% (t-statistic: 0.69) at 36th month.

The tests achieved over a formation/hold periods of 24 months point out either the empirical validation of the overreaction hypothesis (Table 2)

Specifically, although the loser portfolio has recorded negative returns at the level of −50.8% less than the market at the end of the period of formation, it tend to adjust the situation while recording positive values statistically significant during the test period. Symmetrically, the winner portfolio, that have recorded extreme positive return of 35.6% highest than the market at

[o]This is identical for both contrarian portfolios formed upon 12 and 6 extreme stocks.

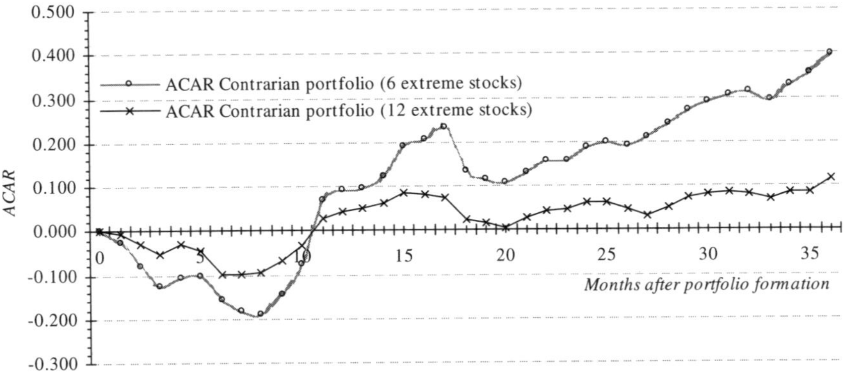

Figure 2: Evolutions of average (market-adjusted) cumulative returns of the contrarian portfolios during a test period of 36 months.

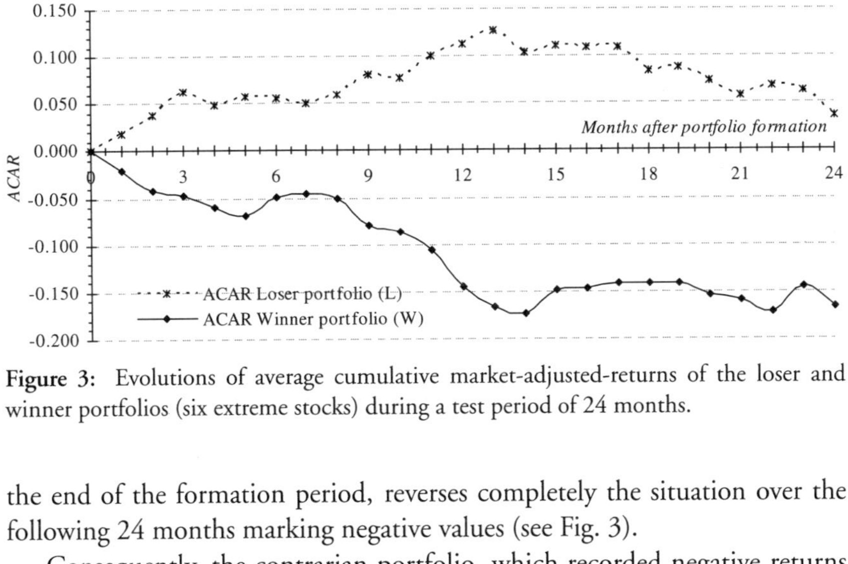

Figure 3: Evolutions of average cumulative market-adjusted-returns of the loser and winner portfolios (six extreme stocks) during a test period of 24 months.

the end of the formation period, reverses completely the situation over the following 24 months marking negative values (see Fig. 3).

Consequently, the contrarian portfolio, which recorded negative returns of 105.5% (*t*-statistic: −21.73) at the end of the formation period, recover the position while marking positive returns above the test period as capturing an extreme value of 29.3% (*t*- statistic: 2.01) at the 13th month into the test period (Fig. 4).

The next test is accomplished over a non-overlapping periods of 18 months (Table 3).

Like the tests done on a 36 and 24 month test periods, the examination of the test made on 18 months show an overreaction phenomenon insofar

Table 2: Evolutions of average (market adjusted) cumulative returns of the loser, winner, and contrarian portfolios at the end of a 24 months formation periods and 1, 12, 13, 22, and 24 months into the test periods.

No. of replications and length of the formation periods	No. of extreme stocks in the portfolio	Nature of the portfolios	ACAR (t-statistics) at the end of formation periods	*ACAR* (t-statistics) into the test periods				
				Number of months into the test periods				
				1	12	13	22	24
Three 24 months periods	12	Loser	−0.350	0.019	0.092	0.101	0.05	0.048
		Winner	0.356	−0.014	−0.089	−0.103	−0.086	−0.094
		Loser–Winner	−0.706	0.033	0.181	**0.204**	0.140	0.142
		(t-Statistics)	(−7.34)	(1.34)	(2.37)	**(2.76)**	(2.03)	(1.79)
	6	Loser	−0.508	0.018	0.113	0.127	0.068	0.036
		Winner	0.356	−0.020	−0.145	−0.166	−0.172	−0.166
		Loser–Winner	−1.055	0.038	0.258	**0.293**	0.240	0.202
		(t-Statistics)	(−21.73)	(1.16)	(1.78)	**(2.01)**	(2.10)	(1.51)

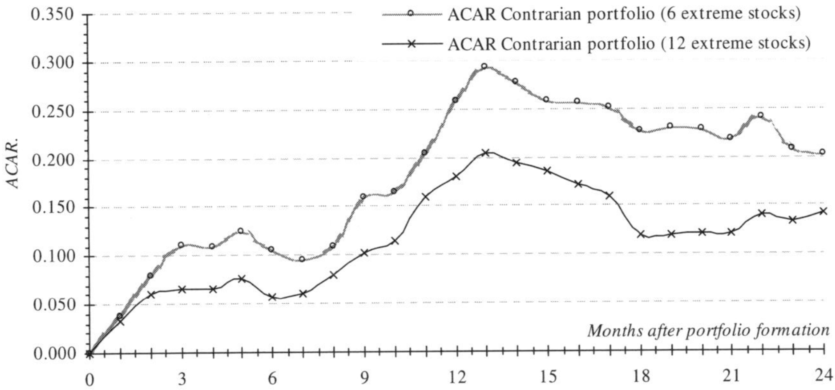

Figure 4: Evolutions of average abnormal-returns of the contrarian portfolios during a test period of 24 months.

as losers and winners oppose their past positions while marking, respectively, positive and negative significant values into the test periods (Fig. 5).

The contrarian portfolio formed in the base of the past 18-month-periods, begin to record positive returns from second month into the test period while reaching an extreme value of 27.4% (t-statistic: 2.39) at 18th month (see Fig. 6).

Nevertheless, although the positive returns recorded by the contrarian portfolio prove that prices follow an overreaction behavior, one can affirm the empirical validation of this hypothesis only for the test done with six extreme stocks, because of the non-statistical significance of values found with 12 extreme stocks.

The subsequent test studies the return behavior over a period of 12 months (Table 4).

The results of this test get the proof that, in the contrast of the previous tests, the portfolio returns does not follow a mean reversion phenomenon for a portfolios composition of 12 extreme stocks. Then, portfolios follow rather a momentum behavior insofar as, the past extreme winner portfolio keep its position over the following 12 months, and in the same way, the past extreme loser portfolio do not adjust the position so as it continue to submit negative returns. As a result, as the winner and loser portfolios record a continuity of returns in the same direction over the test period of 12 months, it is advisable for such investor to adopt a momentum strategy in order to produce abnormal positive returns. But, for the portfolios composition of 6 extreme stocks, there

Table 3: Evolutions of average (market adjusted) cumulative returns of the loser, winner, and contrarian portfolios at the end of a 18 months formation periods and 1, 6, 12, 16, and 18 months into the test periods.

No. of replications and length of the formation periods	No. of extreme stocks in the portfolio	Nature of the portfolios	ACAR (*t*-statistics) at the end of formation periods	*ACAR* (*t*-statistics) into the test periods				
				Number of months into the test periods				
				1	6	12	16	18
Five 18-months periods	12	Loser	−0.305	−0.010	−0.006	0.008	0.027	0.030
		Winner	0.321	0.000	−0.040	−0.029	−0.072	−0.066
		Loser–Winner	−0.626	−0.010	0.033	0.037	**0.099**	0.097
		(*t*-statistics)	(−10.53)	(−1.53)	(1.91)	(0.54)	**(1.26)**	(1.24)
	6	Loser	−0.450	−0.019	0.036	0.091	0.129	0.138
		Winner	0.499	0.011	−0.056	−0.057	−0.144	−0.136
		Loser–Winner	−0.950	−0.031	0.091	0.148	0.273	**0.274**
		(*t*-statistics)	(−13.05)	(−2.17)	(2.84)	(1.43)	(2.23)	**(2.39)**

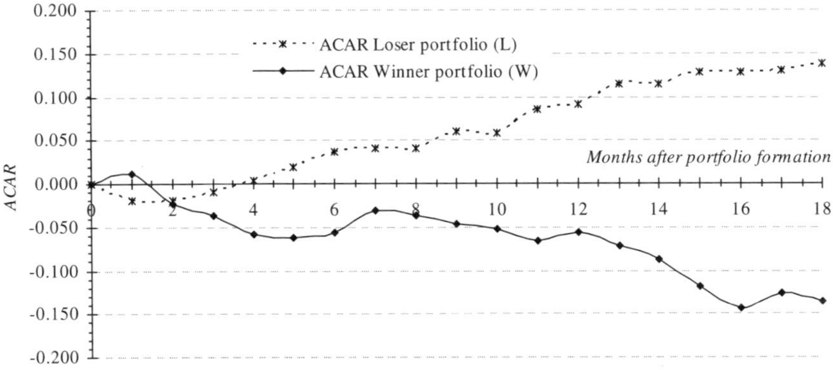

Figure 5: Evolutions of average market-adjusted returns of the loser and winner portfolios (six extreme stocks) during a test period of 18 months.

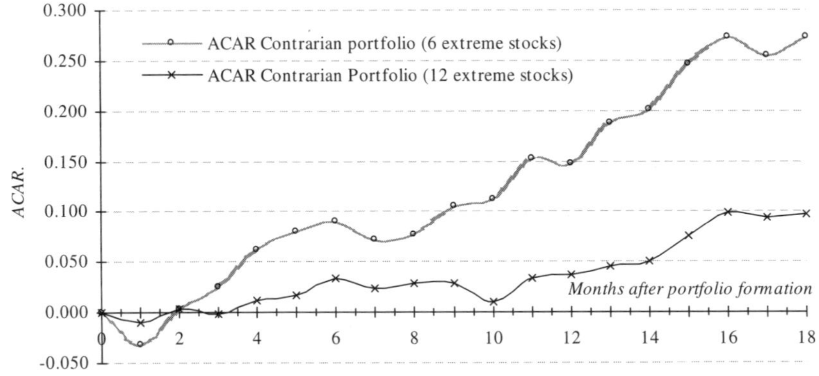

Figure 6: Evolutions of average (market-adjusted) cumulative returns of the contrarian portfolios during a test period of 18 months.

is reversion of past portfolio positions merely at the beginning of the 4th quarter of the 12 month test period. In this case, the contrarian portfolios reach merely a return level of 7.5% (t-statistic: 1.13) (Fig. 7).

Then, the momentum hypothesis cannot be rejected for the tests done on a 12 month formation/hold periods especially for a portfolio compositions of 12 stocks where contrarian portfolios generates negative values sometimes significant over the 12 month test period. However, according to the results generated by the strategies made on the basis of six extreme stocks, neither the mean reversion nor the momentum phenomenon is statistically significant, so, the random walk return hypothesis cannot be rejected in this case (Fig. 8).

Table 4: Evolutions of average (market adjusted) cumulative returns of the loser, winner, and contrarian portfolios at the end of a 12 months formation periods and 1, 3, 7, 9, and 12 months into the test periods.

No. of replications and length of the formation periods	No. of extreme stocks in the portfolio	Nature of the portfolios	ACAR (t-statistics) at the end of formation periods	*ACAR* (t-statistics) into the test periods				
				Number of months into the test periods				
				1	3	7	9	12
Eight 12 months periods	12	Loser	−0.246	−0.007	−0.016	−0.040	−0.033	−0.001
		Winner	0.238	0.007	0.024	0.027	0.014	−0.013
		Loser–Winner	−0.485	−0.014	−0.040	−0.067	−0.047	0.012
		(t-statistics)	(−10.82)	(−1.42)	(−2.10)	(−2.25)	(−1.17)	(0.24)
	6	Loser	−0.280	−0.006	0.002	−0.015	−0.003	0.049
		Winner	0.384	0.024	0.034	0.043	0.021	−0.025
		Loser–Winner	−0.664	−0.030	−0.032	−0.059	−0.024	0.075
		(t-statistics)	(−13.72)	−1.59	−1.16	(− 1.54)	(− 0.50)	(1.13)

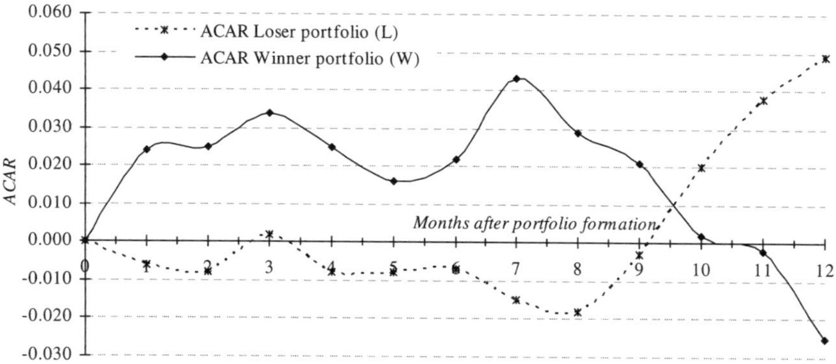

Figure 7: Evolutions of average excess-market-returns of the loser and winner portfolios (six extreme stocks) during a test period of 12 months.

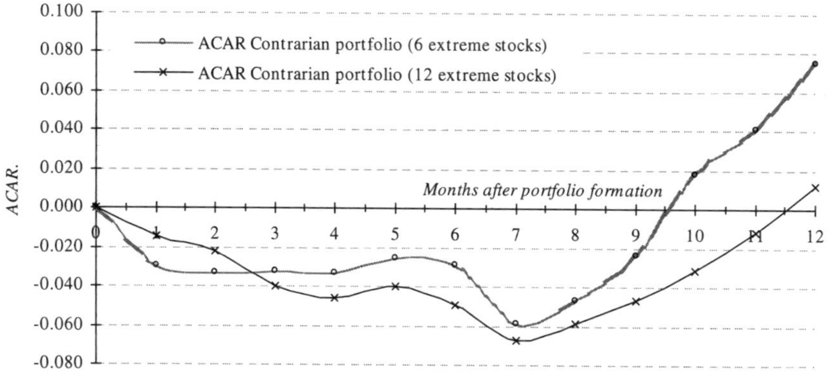

Figure 8: Evolutions of average (market adjusted) cumulative returns of the contrarain portfolios during a test period of 12 months.

In order to conceive the length of the period in which appears the most intensive overreaction phenomenon, we have reported in Fig. 9 the tendencies of the average cumulative returns owned by each of the four constructed contrarian portfolios, which contain six extreme stocks.

It is clear that up to the first 15 months, the 24 months contrarian strategies dominate all other strategies insofar as, the contrarian portfolios records the most important cumulative returns. For the temporal intervals between 16 and 18 months into the test periods, it is the 18 months contrarian strategies which receive the most superior cumulative returns. Then, from 19th month to 24th month, the 24 month contrarian portfolio rejoins the dominance situation.

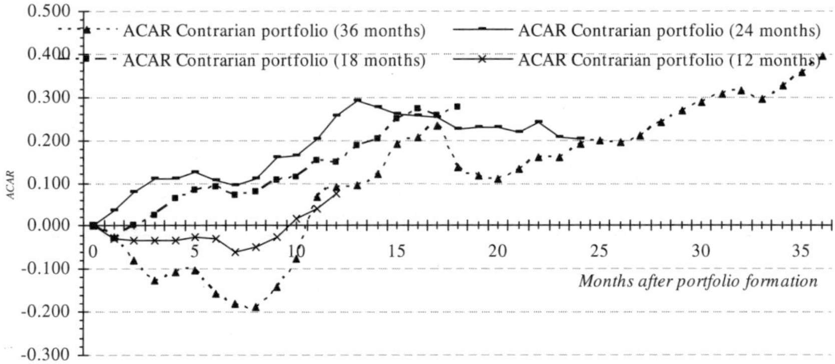

Figure 9: Evolutions of average (market-adjusted) cumulative returns of the contrarain portfolios during the different length test periods.

Nevertheless, among all these four contrarian strategies, the most important cumulative return is reached by the contrarian portfolio constructed over 36 month periods at the final month (39.7%).

In summarizing, we found that the overreaction phenomenon characterizes the behavior of prices on the Tunisian stock market over long terms (from 18 months to 36 months). For the 12 month period, we observe a momentum phenomenon for the portfolios compositions of 40% extreme stocks, while we found that the efficient market hypothesis of price random walk cannot be rejected for the portfolios compositions of 20% extreme stocks. In general, all these results confirm the results found by DeBondt and Thaler (1985). Reste à savoir, quelle est, le ou les origines derrière ces phénomènes de sur et de sous réaction des rendements.[p]

4 Implications for Other Empirical Research

The principle goal of this study was to discover the nature of the phenomenon characterizing the behavior of return fluctuation of stocks over time on the Tunisian stock market in order to discover the possibility of their predictability. Nevertheless, we did not study the reasons of generated phenomenon. The possible reasons evoked in the literature are of two types: the behavioral (non-rational) explanations and fundamental (or rational) explanations.

[p]This point is the object of an ulterior research on sources underlying the apparition of the over and underreaction phenomenon.

The behavioral explanations are specifically linked to the irrational behaviors among investors due to the appearance of psychological bias when they process new information. In fact, DeBondt and Thaler (1985) assign the long-term overreaction phenomenon to the overreaction of investors to recent information. They leave from this idea to discover the anomaly of prices overreaction. They explain also that investors overvalue in a first stage the recent information to the detriment of the past one, therefore, they are going to buy attractive securities more and to sell more non-promising stocks. Following this first reaction of investors, prices move away from their fundamental values. At this level appear portfolios, so-called losers, those that the unfavorable news has been overvalued; and portfolios called winners, whose initial news was favorable, but also overestimated. Considering a long term period, investors, conscious of the initial overestimation of prices, are going to adopt arbitrage strategies permitting to conduct prices toward their fundamental values. Selling the overvalued winners, they are going to induce a downfall of prices, and buying the undervalued losers, they tend to generate a rise of prices, until leading the two mispriced stocks toward their intrinsic value. From this fact appear the price mean-reversion phenomenons. DeBondt and Thaler (1985) attributes as a result the price overreaction phenomenon to the excessive reaction of "irrational" investors at recent news.

The second approach is found mainly on factors bound to changes of the stock risk level or other factors conform to the efficient market hypothesis. This approach argue that, if the loser portfolios assemble the most risky securities, it is typical that they generate the most important returns, considering the positive correlation between risk and return of such security.

Testing if the market risk (measured by "β") can be the main source of the abnormal returns generated by the contrarian strategies, DeBondt and Thaler (1985) discovered the results that are likely to bias the research design against the overreaction hypothesis. Explicitly, they found that the average betas of the securities in the winner are significantly larger than the betas of the loser portfolios over the test periods. This means that the risk associated to the loser portfolios is least than the risk of the winner portfolios. Considering the existing link between return risk, losers portfolios are, therefore, supposed to generate least return than winners. Observing an inverse effect on markets, DeBondts and Thalers (1985) reject the factor "risks" as the explanation of the price overreaction hypothesis. They even consider that differences of risk observed between portfolios underestimate the real effect of individuals' excessive reactions. They add also that, so that an extreme past loser portfolio has a weak risk generates a return, in absolute value, more important than past winner portfolio (more riskier), it is necessary that investors have advantage invest in the loser securities.

Using a time-varying three-factor pricing model, Assoé and Sy (2004) examines the profitability of the short-term contrarian strategy in Canadian stock markets from January 1964 to December 1998. They found that this strategy generates statistically significant excess unrestricted returns. However, they show that this result is mainly driven by small firms, especially in January. Moreover, the short-term contrarian investing is not economically profitable when they account for transaction costs.

Antoniou *et al.* (2005) investigate also the existence of contrarian profits and their sources for the Athens Stock Exchange. Their empirical analysis decomposes contrarian profits to sources due to common factor reactions, overreaction to firm-specific information, and profits not related to the previous two terms. Furthermore, in view of recent evidence that common stock returns are related to firm characteristics such as size and book-to-market equity, they decomposes contrarian profits to sources due to factors derived from the Fama and French (1993, 1996) three-factor model. The results of their study indicate that serial correlation is present in equity returns and that it leads to significant short-run contrarian profits that persist even after they adjust for market frictions.

While studying the sources of an overreaction effect on the Japanese stock market, Chiao and Hueng (2005) show that the firm size (SZ) and the book-to-market ratio (BM) cannot fully explain stock returns on prior-return-based portfolios in Japan. They found that, after controlling for SZ and BM effects, the overreaction effect persists significant and plays an important role in explaining the zero-investment returns constructed by a contrarian strategy.

5 Conclusion

The results of this study violate the weak version of the efficient market hypotheses that predicts that the stock past recording of price has no predictive power future prices (Fama, 1970). The tests that we have realized on the Tunisian stock market confirms the possibility of the return predictability only from *ex post* series and the possibility to generate abnormal returns, without using any accounting news.

However, the limit that we can address to our study is the non-investigation of the sources that derives the overreaction phenomenon, and hence, the apparent important profitability generated by the contrarian portfolios. It is, hence, important to signal that these apparent significant returns produced by contrarian portfolios may represent simply the compensation of additional risk factor, such as, the market-risk, the bid-ask-spreads, transaction costs, firm-size effect, seasonal-effect, etc. This problematic leads us to further examine the possible sources of overreaction phenomenon discovered by the current study on the Tunisian Stock Market.

Appendix A

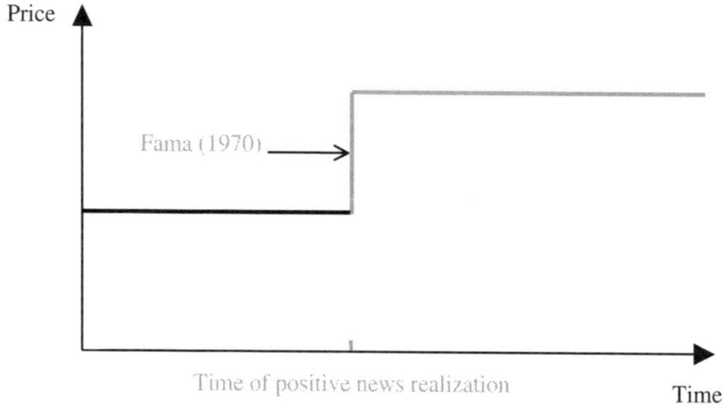

Figure 10: Instantaneous and accurate adjustment of information.

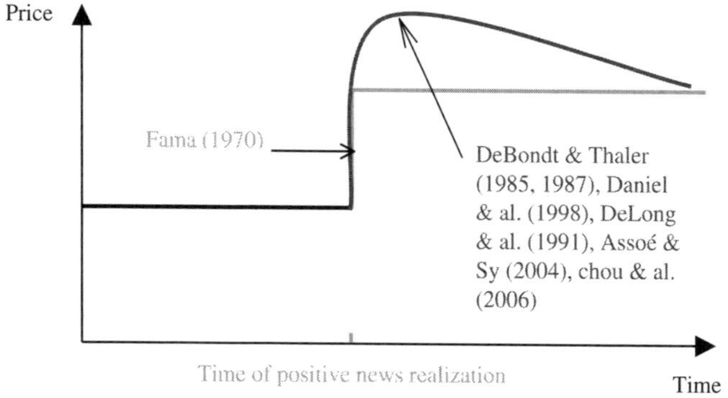

Figure 11: Instantaneous but excessive adjustment of information.

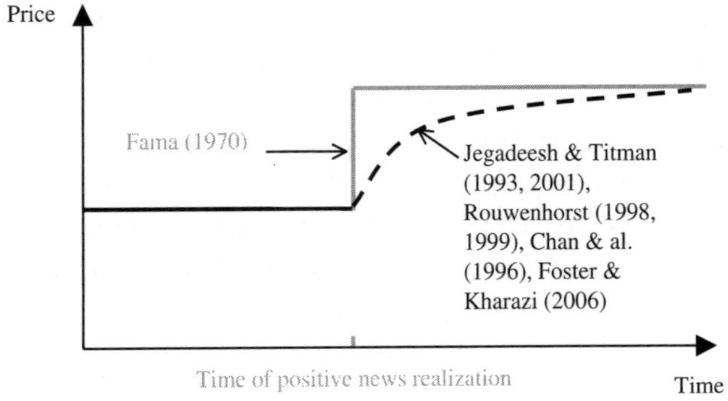

Figure 12: Gradual adjustment of information.

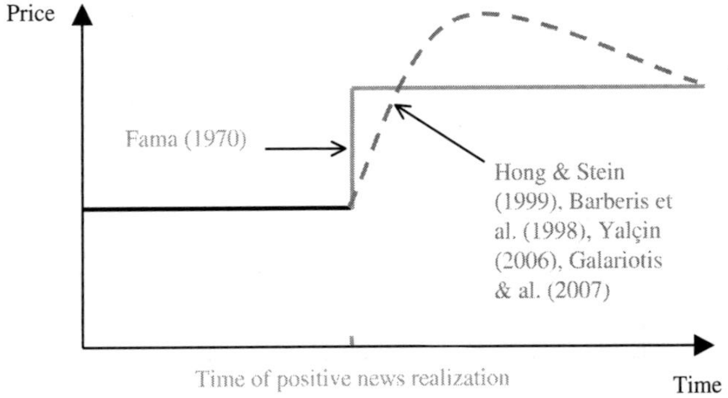

Figure 13: Short-term gradual and long-term excessive adjustment of information.

References

Ang, A and Bekaert, G (2005). Stock return predictability: Is it there? Working Paper, Columbia Business School.

Antoniou, A, Galariotis, EC and Spirou, SI (2005). Contrarian profits and the overreaction hypothesis: The case of the Athens Stock Exchange. *European Financial Management*, 11, 71–98.

Assoé, K and Sy, O (2004). Profitability of the short-run contrarian strategy in Canadian stock markets. Les cahiers du CREF 04-12, ISSN: 1707-410X.

Barberis, N, Shleifer, A and Vishny, R (1998). A model of investor sentiment. *Journal of Financial Economics*, 49, 307–343.

Campbell, JY and Yogo, M (2006). Efficient tests of stock return predictability. *Journal of Financial Economics*, 81, 27–60.

Chan, HA, Hameed, A and Tong, W (2000). Profitability of momentum strategies in the international equity markets. *Journal of Financial and Quantitative Analysis*, 35, 153–172.

Chan, LK, Jeageeesh, N and Lakonishok, J (1996). Momentum strategies. *Journal of Finance*, 51, 1681–1713.

Chiao, C, and Hueng, JC (2005). Overreaction effects independent of risk and characteristics: Evidence from the Japanese stock market. *Japan and the World Economy*, 17, 431–455.

Cochrane, J (2001). *Asset Pricing*. Princeton University Press.

Conrad, J, Gulktekin, MN and Kaul, G (1997). Profitability of short-term contrarian strategies: Implications for market efficiency. *Journal of Business and Economic Statistics*, 15, 379–386.

DeBondt, W and Thaler, R (1985). Does the stock market overreact? *Journal of Finance*, 40, 793–805.

DeBondt, W and Thaler, R (1987). Further evidence on investor overreaction and stock market seasonality. *Journal of Finance*, 42, 557–581.

Fama, EF (1970). Efficient capital markets: A review of theory and empirical work. *Journal of Finance*, 25, 383–417.

Fama, EF and French, KR (1988). Permanent and temporary components of stock prices. *Journal of Political Economy*, 96, 246–273.

Fama, E and French, KR (1993). Common risk factors in the returns of stocks and bonds. *Journal of Financial Economics*, 33, 3–56.

Fama, E and French, KR (1996). Multifactor explanations of asset pricing anomalies. *Journal of Finance*, 51, 55–84.

Foster, KR and Kharazy, A (2006). Contrarian and momentum returns on Iran's Tehran Stock Exchange. *Journal of International Financial Markets, Institutions & Money*, doi:10.1016/j.intfin.2006.05.003.

Galariotis, EC, Holmes, P and Ma, XS (2007). Contrarian and momentum profitability revisited: Evidence from the London Stock Exchange 1964–2005. *Journal of Multinational Financial Management*. doi:10.1016/j.mulfin.2007.01.003.

Grundy, BD and Martin, JSS (2001). Understanding the nature of the risks and the source of the rewards to momentum investing. *Review of Financial Studies*, 14, 29–78.

Hong, H and Jeremy, CS (1999). A unified theory of underreaction, momentum trading and overreaction in asset markets. *Journal of Finance*, forthcoming.

Jegadeesh, N (1990). Evidence of predictable behavior of security returns. *Journal of Finance*, 45, 881–898.

Jegadeesh, N and Titman, S (1993). Returns to buying winners and selling losers: Implications for stock market efficiency. *Journal of Finance*, 48, 65–91.

Jegadeesh, N and Titman, S (2001). Profitability of momentum strategies: An evaluation of alternative explanations. *Journal of Finance*, 56, 699–720.

Lehmann, BN (1990). Fads, martingales, and market efficiency. *Quarterly Journal of Economics*, 105, 1–28.

Lewellen, J (2002). Momentum and autocorrelation in stock returns. *Review of Financial Studies*, 15, 533–563.

Lewellen, J (2004). Predicting returns with financial ratios. *Journal of Financial Economics*, 74, 209–235.

Patro, DK and Wu, Y (2004). Predictability of short-horizon equity returns in international equity markets. *Journal of Empirical Finance*, 11, 553–584.

Poterba, J and Summers, L (1988). Mean reversion in stock returns: Evidence and implications. *Journal of Financial Economics*, 22, 27–60.

Rouwenhorst, KG (1999). Local return factors and turnover in emerging stock markets. *Journal of Finance*, 54, 1439–1464.

Rowenhorst, GK (1998). International momentum strategies. *Journal of Financial and Quantitative Analysis*, 25, 113–125.

Yalcin, A (2006). Gradual information diffusion and contrarian strategies. *The Quarterly Review of Economics and Finance*, doi:10.1016/j.qref.2006.06.002.

CHAPTER 17

INVESTOR–VENTURE CAPITALIST RELATIONSHIP: ASYMMETRIC INFORMATION, UNCERTAINTY, AND MONITORING

Mondher Cherif[*,†] *and Skander Sraieb*[*]

In an environment characterized by uncertainty and moral hazard, the chapter studies the role and impact of monitoring on the performance of an investor–venture capitalist relationship. Monitoring (ensured by funds of funds in our model) allows minimization of uncertainty concerning the GP behavior and reduces the risk. The impact of monitoring on both the level of effort provided by the GP and the expected return of LP is determined by mean of modeling the expected return of LP and GP. Our main finding concerns the role of monitoring as a mechanism that allows maximization of the investor's return and limits the opportunistic behavior of the venture capitalist by providing him with incentives to raise his effort level.

1 Introduction

Wright and Robbie (1998) considered that the main feature characterizing the venture capital firm is to be in the core of a dual contractual relationship: the venture capitalist–entrepreneur relationship that mainly attracted the attention of researchers on the one hand, and the investor (limited partner)–venture capitalist (general partner) relationship whose understanding is crucial for explaining the participation policy of venture capitalist on the other hand. Gompers and Lerner (1999) admit that venture capitalist–entrepreneur relationship is affected by the investor–venture capitalist relationship. The analysis

*Université de Reims – LAME, France.
†cherifmondher@yahoo.fr

of this relationship was mainly developed in the theoretical context of agency theory. The limited partner (LP: principal) delegates the right to manage the resources to general partners (GP: agent). The delegation task conveys the idea of separation between ownership and control.

Due to uncertainty and asymmetric information, this relationship can be characterized by conflicts that reduce the value generated by the venture. This implies two attitudes relative to risk: adverse selection and moral hazard. Indeed, LP has to manage the moral hazard situations that appear during the evaluation and selection process of a GP. Reputation, realized performance, quality of her team, and her sectoral specialization are the factors the limited partner may include in her different arbitrages.

The LP faces also a post-contractual hazard translating situations where GP actions are not observable by the LP. Recall that the well-being of the later depends on the behavior of the former. Conflicts have several sources among which we find the venture capital investment duration, its low liquidity degree, funds that are usually tied up for many years (in return for this risk, LPs require a higher return rate), the under-optimal participation policy pursued by GP, and possible opportunistic behavior of GPs concerning the evaluation of stakes portfolio (Fried and Hisrich, 1994). Several mechanisms can be used to minimize these agency problems: (i) the mutual gains incentives, (ii) the limitation of GP actions that are proven to be sources of conflicts of interests, (iii) the limited life span of the fund, (iv) the mechanisms guaranteeing that profits will be distributed to the LP, (v) monitoring of activities of GP, and (vi) to keep regularly the LP informed (Sahlman, 1990). All these strategies are supposed to put in line the interests of LPs and GPs.

The LP set-up control procedures that generate agency costs. The most used mechanism is related to the different incentives systems created by the LP in order to conform her targets to those of GPs. Our main objective is to investigate the characteristics of the investor–venture capitalist relationship using a theoretical model. We put in evidence the financing mode of this relationship using a formulation of the expected profit of the LP and GP in the context of uncertainty and moral hazard. We also evaluate the impact of monitoring on the effort level of GP and the expected profit of LP.

This chapter is organized as follows. In Sec. 2, we define the model analyzing the investor–venture capitalist relationship under uncertainty and moral hazard. In Sec. 3, we solve for equilibria without monitoring of the financing scheme. In Sec. 4, we introduce a monitoring mechanism ensured by funds of funds, and we solve for the equilibria. Section 5, is devoted to discussion and analysis of the main results. Finally, Sec. 6 presents the conclusion of the chapter.

2 The Model

We describe, here, a model used to analyze limited partner–general partner relationship. We consider a one period model, in which the fund starts and the long term investment opportunities arise at the same time, $t = 0$. Our analysis is carried out on an individual project basis. We ignore interaction effects between different project in the fund portfolio and issues related to optimal portfolio size.[a]

2.1 *The Project*

We have a venture capital fund which has a one period time horizon from $t = 0$ to $t = 1$. That is, it is created at $t = 0$ and must be dissolved at $t = 1$. Venture capital fund has two types of partners: one General Partner, GP, who manages the fund and Limited Partners, LPs, who are passive investors. LPs commit to provide the total amount of capital, I, for investment. GP provides managerial assistance throughout fund life time, and which requires effort e. The cost of effort for the GP is $c(e)$. Repullo and Suarez (1998) suppose that advises given by the GP are essentials to success of project. Without this effort the payoff will be zero.[b]

$$c(e) = \beta\frac{e^2}{2} \quad \text{with } c'(e) \succ 0 \quad \text{and} \quad c''(e) \succ 0.$$

With effort input, e, from the GP and with total capital input, I, from the LP, the expected output is $R(e, I)$. As in Wang and Zhou (2004), we suppose that this output faces a random shock, ξ, such that the realized output is $V = \xi R(e, I)$. The GP knows the distribution function of ξ at the beginning of the investment process, and this information will be revealed to LP only at the end of fund life time. This uncertainty characterizes the relationship between LP

[a]Optimal portfolio size is studied in Kanniainen and Keushnigg (2000), while for effects of interaction between portfolio projects see, for example, Leshchinskii (2002).

[b]Although this assumption appears to impose "non-credible" restriction, it is largely accepted by both practitioners and academics, like in Gompers (1995).

and GP. In fact, due to the limited liability, the legal structure of limited partnership forbids LP to manage the day-to-day ordinary activities of the fund.

To resolve this uncertainty problem concerning the activities of the GP, the LP will use the intermediation of funds of funds. Due to their diversification power and expertise, the funds of funds are able to reduce the risk and more controlling the GPs. Suppose, here, that the LP finances the GPs through funds of funds. The funds of funds exert a monitoring m generating a cost supported by the LP. The monitoring cost is supposed fixed. It represents the intermediary charges of funds of funds.

$$c(m) = \theta.$$

2.2 *The Contract*

At the first stage, the venture capital fund is created and the investors commit to provide the total amount of capital I. The GP's compensation is determined by the contract. It is a function of the realized output (V) minus the investment (I). The GP receives his compensation in two forms: a pre-agreed management fee, which is in general a percentage (1.5%–2.5%) of the fund size (ϕI), and the carried interest, which is a significant part (20%) of the fund net capital gains ($\alpha\,(V - I)$). In our model, the GP invest the total fund collected in the initial period.

Assumption: *We suppose that GP's compensation is linear and equal to* $\alpha\,(V - I) + \phi I$, *where* V *is the output realized by the venture capital fund and* I *is the total amount invested by LP in the project.* At the end of the fund life (i.e. $t = 1$), the LP will be reimbursed for his investment, I, and will receive almost 80% of the fund net capital gains.

At the first stage, the investor (LP) offers a sharing contract $(\alpha, 1 - \alpha)$ to the venture capitalist (GP). In our model, the value of α received by GP is exogenous. If the contract is accepted, the LP invests the amount I requested to the project realization and the GP applies effort e and sustains cost $c(e)$. At the start of the project, the LP carries out a monitoring procedure of GP activities throughout a fund of funds m that costs $c(m)$.

At this first stage, a moral hazard problem might arise. Indeed, the GP can obtain information on the project quality and on its expected time to exit, she decides what projects will be continued. The limited time horizon of the venture capital fund forces the GP to dispose of all the unfinished projects at the end of the contract period. According to Kandel *et al.* (2004), the limitation of time horizon of the fund combined with the informational asymmetry lead to inefficient decisions by the GP during the intermediate investment stage.[c] At the second stage, the project is finished and the venture capital fund is dissolved. The uncertainty is resolved, the LP first receives his investment back, and the remaining part of fund's claim is divided between LP and GP according to the terms of the existing contract.

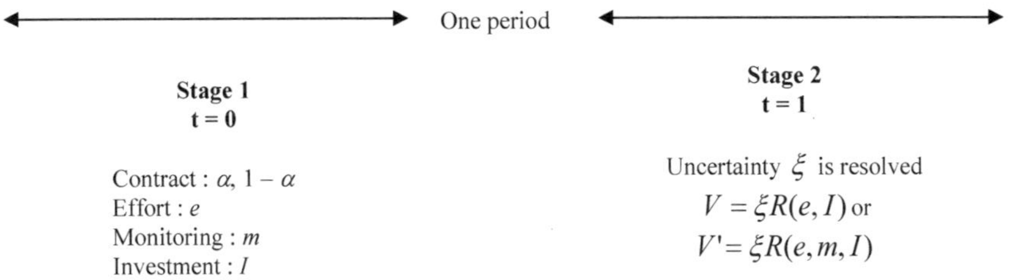

1. Time Structure of Venture Capital Fund

2.3 *Hypothesis*

A few assumptions are needed for the realization of our model.

- At the end of the fund, we obtain: $V = \xi R(e, I)$. Since I is fixed, we can write: $V = \xi r_I(e)$.

$r_I(e) = \gamma e$ is a linear production function, and γ is the inherent quality of the project and is exogenous.

- $\xi \sim U\ [0, 2]$. This hypothesis stipulates that ξ is uniformly distributed on interval [0, 2]. This hypothesis allows the realization of explicit solutions.

If $\xi > 1$, then we obtain an expansion of output V; and if $\xi < 1$, we have a contraction of output V.

- $c(e) = \beta \frac{e^2}{2}$, with $e \geq 0$. The effort cost of the GP is an increasing function of β, with $\beta \geq 1$.
- $c(m) = \theta$, with $m \succ 1$. The monitoring cost of the LP is fixed and represents expenses of intermediation of funds of funds.
- Since in our model the GP would invest the total amount collected in the initial stage, we suppose that management fee of GP (ϕI) are equal to zero. Therefore, her compensation is equal to $\alpha\,(V - I)$.

[c]According to these authors, suboptimal decisions include continuations of bad projects as well as write-off of good projects.

3 Financing Without Monitoring

In this section, we investigate the case where LP decides to attribute funds directly without the intermediation of funds of funds. With this financing scheme without monitoring, the LP cannot control for the venture capitalist actions and she does not exert monitoring. The sharing contract is the only instrumental variable that can be used to control for moral hazard. Note that the LP is also unable to check the final value of the project. The effort e of the GP is unverifiable in this case.

The expected compensation of the GP is

$$\pi^{\mathrm{GP}} = \alpha\left[\int_0^{\infty} Vf(\xi)d\xi - I\right] - c(e).$$

The expected compensation (profit) of the LP is

$$\pi^{\mathrm{LP}} = (1-\alpha)\left[\int_0^{\infty} Vf(\xi)d\xi - I\right].$$

The individual rationality (IR) condition of GP is

$$\alpha\left[\int_0^{\infty} Vf(\xi)d\xi - I\right] \geq c(e).$$

The incentive compatibility (IC) condition of GP is

$$\frac{\partial}{\partial e}\alpha\left[\int_0^{\infty} Vf(\xi)d\xi - I\right] = c'(e).$$

Our optimal contract problem is solved by maximizing the expected profit of LP under the GP's individual rationality and incentive compatibility constraints. Let E be the GP's effort space and suppose that $I \in \Re_+$. The LP's maximization problem writes

$$\begin{aligned}
\pi^{\mathrm{LP}} &= \max_{e\in E}\ (1-\alpha)\left[\int_0^{\infty} Vf(\xi)d\xi - I\right],\\
&\quad \text{st } \alpha\left[\int_0^{\infty} Vf(\xi)d\xi - I\right] \geq c(e),\\
&\quad \frac{\partial}{\partial e}\alpha\left[\int_0^{\infty} Vf(\xi)d\xi - I\right] = c'(e).
\end{aligned}$$

This maximization problem implies the following solution 1:

$$e^* = \frac{\beta\gamma}{2},$$

$$\pi^{*\text{LP}} = (1-\alpha)\left(\frac{\beta\gamma^2}{2} - I\right).$$

4 Financing with Monitoring

In this section, the LP exerts a control on the actions of the GP. This control activity is realized via intervention of funds of funds. The fund of funds will exert a monitoring m allowing a decrease in uncertainty concerning the expected value of the project.

This service will cost $c(m) = \theta$, and will influence, therefore, the expected output of the project which will be equal to:

$$V' = \xi R\,(e, m, I)\,.$$

However, I is fixed, thus: $V' = \xi\, r_I\,(e, m)$ where $r_I\,(e, m) = \gamma em$.

The final value of the project is a function of effort e of GP and monitoring m.

The expected compensation of the GP is

$$\pi^{\text{GP}} = \alpha\left[\int_0^{\infty} V' f\,(\xi)\, d\xi - I\right] - c(e).$$

The expected compensation (profit) of the LP is

$$\pi^{\text{LP}} = (1-\alpha)\left[\int_0^{\infty} V' f(\xi) d\xi - I\right] - c(m).$$

The maximization profit program of LP is the following:

$$\pi^{\text{LP}} = \max_{e\in E}\,(1-\alpha)\left[\int_0^{\infty} V' f(\xi) d\xi - I\right] - c(m),$$

$$\text{st}\;\alpha\left[\int_0^{\infty} V' f(\xi) d\xi - I\right] \geq c(e),$$

$$\frac{\partial}{\partial e}\alpha\left[\int_0^{\infty} V' f(\xi) d\xi - I\right] = c'(e).$$

The solution 2 to this maximization problem is given by the following values:

$$e^{**} = \frac{\alpha\gamma m}{\beta},$$

$$\pi^{**\mathrm{LP}} = (1-\alpha)\left(\frac{\gamma^2 m^2 \alpha}{\beta} - I\right) - \theta.$$

5 Results Analysis

In this section, we study the impact of monitoring on the profit of the LP and will check if this procedure allows to reduce the moral hazard problem and uncertainty concerning the final value of the project. It is also interesting to check whether the monitoring induces a higher effort on the GP side and whether it creates incentives to increase the value of the firm.[d]

The following table summarizes the equilibrium solutions:

Financing without monitoring	Financing with monitoring
$e^* = \frac{\alpha\gamma}{\beta}$	$e^{**} = \frac{\alpha\gamma m}{\beta}$
$\pi^{*\mathrm{LP}} = (1-\alpha)\left(\frac{\alpha\gamma^2}{\beta} - I\right)$	$\pi^{**\mathrm{LP}} = (1-\alpha)\left(\frac{\gamma^2 m^2\alpha}{\beta} - I\right) - \theta$

Figure 1 illustrates LP profits with and without monitoring as a function of β. Indeed, the β coefficient measures the strength of the moral hazard problem faced by the LP. In our model, higher values of β means that the LP faces a strong degree of moral hazard.

We observe that the LP profits are a decreasing function of moral hazard degree. To get more important profits, the LP has to minimize the strength of moral hazard by monitoring and controlling efficiently for the actions of the GP. We note that the profit of the LP is more important when she contracts for monitoring.

However, when the moral hazard is very serious, the LP must increase her monitoring level to obtain more important expected profits.

Figure 2 puts in relationship the GP effort level and the strength of moral hazard. We observe that with higher moral hazard, the GP tends to minimize

[d]In our study, the parameters α, γ, θ, — being fixed —, and I are irrelevant in the comparisons.

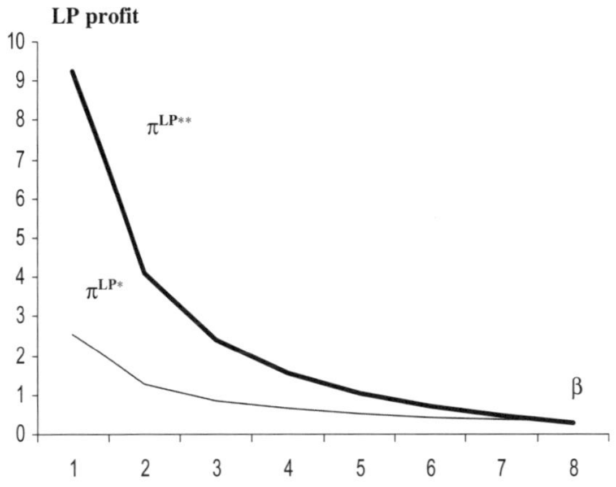

Figure 1: Comparison of LP profits with and without monitoring.

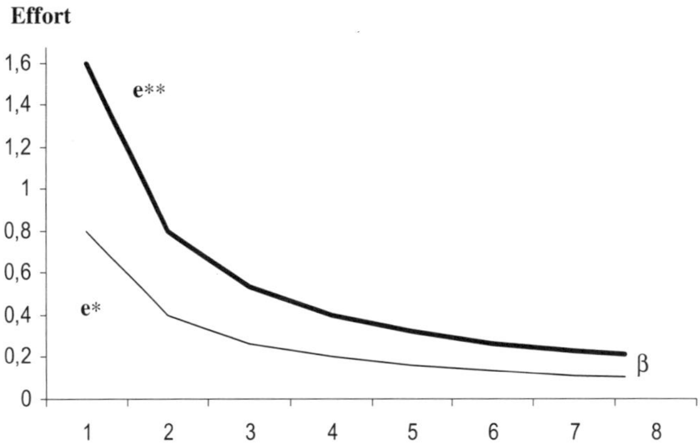

Figure 2: Effort comparison.

her effort and, therefore, to reduce the final value of the firm, which is prejudicial to LP. The monitoring of GP activities induces a higher effort level. In fact, the monitoring has a disciplinary function and the use of funds of funds services implies a decrease of risks associated to financing as well as a better control of GPs activities. This result also confirms the expertise capacity and the diversification power of funds of funds.

Two main findings arise from the analysis in the paper. In an environment characterized by uncertainty and moral hazard, the monitoring of GPs activities by the LP allows the realization of a higher profit and encourages GPs to exert a higher effort level and to get involved in increasing the final value of the firm. Indeed, the monitoring allows to minimize the performance losses related to the lack of perfect control on the managers' strategies and their opportunistic behavior.

6 Conclusion

Long term contracts governing relationships between LPs and GPs determine the rights and obligations of contractual partners during an investment period. Sophisticated contractual forms can reduce the principal–agent costs in this relationship. Agency problems in the venture capital market were treated mainly in the context of entrepreneur–venture capitalist relationship. The venture capitalist has a multitude of tools to alleviate these problems. These control mechanisms (management support, control rights, syndication, staging of the investment, management replacement, exit...) have been widely developed in the literature. However, the theoretical and empirical literature pays much less attention to the investor–venture capitalist relationship.[e] Although Gompers and Lerner (1999) and Kandel *et al.* (2004) study the relationship between the LP and GP, there is still not enough research regarding the impact of monitoring on LP profit. With this in mind, we modeled the investor–venture capitalist relationship using a simple model principal–agent. This relationship is characterized by the uncertainty and higher moral hazard. Moral hazard arises when the investor fails to identify the appropriate criteria to select the venture capital (her reputation, the realized performance, the quality of her team and stakes portfolio, sectoral specification, etc.). We analyze the way monitoring (ensured by funds of funds in our model) is used to mitigate moral hazard problems, and his impact on the profit and the effort level exerted by the venture capitalist. We find that monitoring allows maximization of the profit of the investor and limits the opportunistic behavior of the venture capitalist. In particular, monitoring induces a higher effort level from the venture capitalist. In this paper, we supposed the existence of a monitoring ensured by funds of funds. In reality, funds of funds are exposed to multiple agency problems. Consequently, they will try to alleviate these agency problems and maximize their profits. An extension of our research would be to realize a dynamic analysis of profits of the three agents (LP, GP, and funds of funds) simultaneously. Also, additional

[e]However, few papers have explored this issue among. See Gompers and Lerner (1999), Schmidt and Wahrenburg (2003) and Kandel *et al.* (2004).

theoretical work is needed to check the possibility of the simultaneous use of the monitoring and contracting hypothesis (preferred returns and compensation structure[f]).

Appendix A. Proof of Solution 1

The compensation of the GP is

$$\pi^{\mathrm{GP}} = \alpha\left[\int_0^{\infty} Vf(\xi)d\xi - I\right] - c(e),$$

$$\pi^{\mathrm{GP}} = \alpha\left[\int_0^{\infty} (\xi\gamma e)f(\xi)d\xi - I\right] - c(e).$$

Let $f(\xi) = \frac{1}{2}$ for $\xi \in [0, 2]$, we have then:

$$\pi^{\mathrm{GP}} = \alpha\left[\left[\frac{1}{2}\frac{\xi^2}{2}\gamma e\right]_0^2 - I\right] - c(e),$$

$$\pi^{\mathrm{GP}} = \alpha\,(\gamma e - I) - c(e).$$

The expected profit of the LP is

$$\pi^{\mathrm{LP}} = (1-\alpha)\left[\int_0^{\infty} Vf(\xi)d\xi - I\right],$$

$$\pi^{\mathrm{LP}} = (1-\alpha)\left[\int_0^{\infty} (\xi\gamma e)f(\xi)d\xi - I\right],$$

$$\pi^{\mathrm{LP}} = (1-\alpha)\left[\left[\frac{1}{2}\frac{\xi^2}{2}\gamma e\right]_0^2 - I\right],$$

$$\pi^{\mathrm{LP}} = (1-\alpha)(\gamma e - I).$$

Then, the maximization program writes:

$$\pi^{\mathrm{LP}} = \max_{\alpha\in[0,1],e\in E} (1-\alpha)(\gamma e - I), \tag{1}$$

$$\text{st } \alpha\,(\gamma e - I) \geq c(e), \tag{1a}$$

$$\alpha\gamma = c'(e), \tag{1b}$$

[f]For more explanations, see Covitz and Liang (2002).

$$\alpha\,(\gamma e - 2I) \geq \beta\frac{e^2}{2},$$

$$\alpha\gamma = e\beta.$$

(1b) implies: $e^* = \frac{\alpha\gamma}{\beta}$. (1c)

The value of e^* allow us to obtain the optimal value of profit of the LP:

$$\pi^{\mathrm{LP}} = (1-\alpha)\,(\gamma e - I)\,,$$

$$\pi^{*\mathrm{LP}} = (1-\alpha)\left(\frac{\alpha\gamma^2}{\beta} - I\right).$$

Appendix B. Proof of Solution 2

The compensation of the GP is

$$\pi^{\mathrm{GP}} = \alpha\left[\int_0^{\infty} V'f\,(\xi)\,d\xi - I\right] - c(e),$$

$$\pi^{\mathrm{GP}} = \alpha\left[\int_0^{\infty} (\xi\gamma em) f(\xi) d\xi - I\right] - c(e).$$

Let $f(\xi) = \frac{1}{2}$ for $\xi \in [0, 2]$, then, we have:

$$\pi^{\mathrm{GP}} = \alpha\left[\left[\frac{1}{2}\frac{\xi^2}{2}\gamma em\right]_0^2 - I\right] - c(e),$$

$$\pi^{\mathrm{GP}} = \alpha\,(\gamma em - I) - c(e).$$

The expected profit of the LP is

$$\pi^{\mathrm{LP}} = (1-\alpha)\left[\int_0^{\infty} V'f(\xi)d\xi - I\right] - c(m),$$

$$\pi^{\mathrm{LP}} = (1-\alpha)\left[\int_0^{\infty} (\xi\gamma em) f(\xi) d\xi - I\right] - c(m),$$

$$\pi^{\mathrm{LP}} = (1-\alpha)\left[\left[\frac{1}{2}\frac{\xi^2}{2}\gamma em\right]_0^2 - I\right] - c(m),$$

$$\pi^{\mathrm{LP}} = (1-\alpha)(\gamma em - I) - c(m).$$

Then, the maximization program writes:

$$\pi^{\mathrm{LP}} = \max_{\alpha\in[0,1],e\in E}(1-\alpha)(\gamma em - I) - c(m), \tag{2}$$

$$\text{st } \alpha\,(\gamma\, em - I) \geq c(e), \tag{2a}$$

$$\alpha\gamma m = c'(e), \tag{2b}$$

$$\pi^{\mathrm{LP}} = \max_{\alpha\in[0,1],e\in E}(1-\alpha)(\gamma\, em - I) - \theta, \tag{3}$$

$$\alpha\,(\gamma em - I) \geq \beta\frac{e^2}{2}, \tag{3a}$$

$$\alpha\gamma m = e\beta. \tag{3b}$$

$$\text{(2b) implies: } e^{**} = \frac{\alpha\gamma m}{\beta}. \tag{3c}$$

The value of e^{**} allows us to obtain the optimal value of the profit of the LP:

$$\pi^{\mathrm{LP}} = (1-\alpha)\,(\gamma me - I) \Leftrightarrow \pi^{\mathrm{LP}} = (1-\alpha)\left(\gamma m\left(\frac{\alpha\gamma m}{\beta}\right) - I\right) - \theta,$$

$$\pi^{**^{\mathrm{LP}}} = (1-\alpha)\left(\frac{\gamma^2 m^2\alpha}{\beta} - I\right) - \theta.$$

References

Covitz, D and Liang, N (2002). Recent developments in the private equity market and the role of preferred returns. *Division of Research and Stastics*, Board of Governors of the Federal Reserve System, Washington, DC.

Fried, VH and Hisrich, RD (1994). Toward a model of venture capital investment decision making. *Financial Management*, 23(3), 28–37.

Gompers, PA (1995). Optimal investment, monitoring and the staging of venture capital. *Journal of Finance*, 50(5), 1461–1489.

Gompers, PA and Lerner, J (1999). *The Venture Capital Cycle*. Cambridge: The MIT Press.

Kandel, E, Leshchinskii, D and Yuklea, H (2004). VC fund's limited horizon as a source of inefficiency. RICAFE, Working Paper No. 17.

Kanniainen, V and Keusching, C (2003). The optimal portfolio of start-up firms in venture capital finance. *Journal of Corporate Finance*, 9, 521–534.

Leshchinskii, D (2000). Project externalities and moral hazard. Working Paper.

Repullo, R and Suarez, J (2000). Venture capital finance: A security design approach. CEPR Discussion Paper No. 2097.
Sahlman, W (1990). The structure and governance of venture capital organisations. *Journal of Financial Economic*, 27(2), 473–521.
Wang, S and Zhou, H (2004). Staged financing in venture capital: Moral hazard and risks. *Journal of Corporate Finance*, 10(1), 131–155.
Wright, M and Robbie, K (1998). Venture capital and private equity: A review and synthesis. *Journal of Business Finance and Accounting*, 25, 521–570.

CHAPTER 18

THRESHOLD MEAN REVERSION IN STOCK PRICES

*Fredj Jawadi**

This chapter studies efficient capital market hypothesis and checks whether adjustment stock prices dynamics is instantaneous, continuous, or linear. In particular, we propose to analyze stock prices evolution while taking into account the presence of transaction costs, the coexistence of heterogeneous investors and the interdependence between stock markets. Thus, we show, on the one hand, that efficiency hypothesis is rejected. On the other hand, we prove that stock indexes adjustment is rather discontinuous, asymmetrical, and nonlinear. While using threshold cointegration techniques, we propose a new nonlinear representation to reproduce CAC40 adjustment dynamics that not only replicates French market adjustment dynamics in presence of market frictions, but also it captures interdependence between French and American stock markets and reaction of French shareholders in relation to American speculators behavior change.

1 Introduction

Stock prices adjustment dynamics are subject to several studies. The number of these studies increased considerably particularly because of important financial markets development, increase of investors and transactions volumes and interaction between different stock markets. Indeed, financial globalization and integration implied more interdependence between financial markets and generate a mimetic behavior in the investors logic notably in periods of crises, scandals, and stock crashes.

*Amiens School of Management and University of Paris 10-Nanterre EconomiX-UMR 7166. ESC Amiens, 18 place Saint Michel 80000 Cedex, France.
fredj.jawadi@supco-amiens.fr

For example, French stock market seems to be correlated to American stock market. Indeed, after a prosperous period (i.e.+51.12%) in 1999, CAC40 lost 15% in about four months in September 2000 because of the first signs of a slowing of American growth. In 2001 and 2002, CAC40 lost, respectively, 21.97% and 33.75% in reason of American attempts, the fall of new technology markets and the fear of an American recession. Otherwise, Internet Bubble showed also that stock markets are strongly correlated and that investors are imitating each others. Indeed, while NASDAQ recorded a fall of 75% in October 2002, IT CAC40 fell of 90% between 20 March 2000 and 8 October 2002.

Thus, resurgence of crises since 2000 revived researches around stock prices adjustment dynamics and efficient capital market (i.e. Manzan (2003), Boswijk *et al.* (2005), Jawadi (2006), Jawadi and Koubba (2006)). Consequently, the survey of stock indexes adjustment dynamics renewed the debate on informational efficiency and investors rationality. Indeed, for some studies, these crises showed that markets are not efficient, whereas on the contrary for other authors, these crises played the role of recall strengths bringing back prices toward their equilibrium (i.e. Jawadi (2006)).

Then, several questions can be considered: How to explain absence of unanimous conclusions on stock markets evolution? How can we explain stock indexes variations in presence of market frictions? Is it possible to specify stock prices adjustment dynamics? How to replicate interdependence between different financial markets and to reproduce mimetic behaviors, contagion phenomenon and these likeness between investors in financial markets that are more and more integrated and interdependent.

The aim of this chapter is to answer these questions. Therefore, we propose to study French stock market adjustment dynamics in the presence of transaction costs and heterogeneous shareholders, while taking into account interdependence between French and American stock markets. Indeed, we focalize our study on CAC40 evolution, whereas we check whether French investors base their calculations and reasonings as well as on the fundamental of local market that on variations of New York stock market.

Formally, we propose a new nonlinear modeling that captures stock price adjustment in presence of market frictions: Threshold Adjustment Techniques. These techniques are an extension of STECM developed by Van Dijk *et al.* (2002). We highlight that this type of modeling provides an innovative and an adequate approach to fear efficient hypothesis and reproduce stock prices adjustment dynamics.

In particular, we propose to study the CAC40 adjustment dynamics in a nonlinear framework at short- and long-term and to examine the impact of S&P500 on its evolution in order to reproduce this dependence relation. We show that in presence of market frictions and strong interdependence between financial markets, Linear Error Correction Model (LECM) can no more constitute an adequate alternative to describe and reproduce stock prices adjustment. Thus, using nonlinear adjustment and threshold cointegration techniques is henceforth an indispensable, interesting and promising alternative to study stock indexes adjustment and to test efficiency hypothesis.

This chapter is organized as follows. The next section will briefly present efficiency and stock prices adjustment hypothesis. Section 3 will explain and justify the nonlinearity inherent to prices adjustment. In Sec. 4, we will describe nonlinear adjustment techniques. We report our empirical results in Sec. 5. A final section will conclude and offer a summary.

2 Efficiency and Stock Prices Adjustment

Efficiency hypothesis has been analyzed in several studies (Fama, 1965; Fama, 1970; Campbell and Shiller, 1987; Fama, 1990; ...). According to Fama (1965), in an efficient market, all available information is instantaneously and completely reflected in stock prices. Thus, it is not possible to forecast future price evolution on the basis of previous stock prices variations because this information is already integrated in the present price. Therefore, stock prices adjustment dynamics is to be currently reproduced while using a random walk relation, meaning that the expectation of future price is today's price. Therefore, returns cannot be forecasted and they are often assimilated to a white noise.[a]

In such context, it was fluent to test the weak-form efficiency hypothesis while checking if it is possible to forecast future returns from past returns. In practice, authors have tested the existence of a serial interrelationship in returns series. The rejection of this hypothesis makes it possible to retain efficiency in the weak sense. Nevertheless, Fama (1970) showed more lately that even though autocorrelations are statistically significant in the short-term, they are not economically significant. Moreover, Fama noted that, in spite of their statistical significativity, these autocorrelations remain close to zero. Thus, Summer

---

[a]Stock indexes returns are given by the following relation: $R_t = \frac{P_t - P_{t-1} + D_t}{P_{t-1}}$, where P_t and D_t are, respectively, the stock price and the dividend at t. But, returns can also be gotten while considering the relative variations of prices and using the following logarithmic approximation: $R_t = \log(P_t) - \log(P_{t-1})$.

(1986) and Fama and French (1988) proposed to test efficiency hypothesis in the weak sense at long horizons while using linear cointegration techniques.

Cointegration theory, which has been introduced by Granger (1981) and developed by Granger (1986), Engle and Granger (1987) and Johansen (1988), stipulates that some variables undergo some short-term disruptions, but while possessing the long-term same properties, they can tie between them stable relations which converge toward an equilibrium of long-term. Formally, let X_t and Y_t be two variables that are not stationary in level but stationary while differentiating them d times. In the long-term, if it is possible to find a linear combination z_t between these two variables which is stationary, then X_t and Y_t are cointegrated.

$$z_t = X_t - a_0 - a_1 Y_t \tag{1}$$

z_t is defined as the error term or the residual of the cointegration relationship (Eq. (1)). It measures the variation between X_t and Y_t. In a such context, X_t and Y_t can be, respectively, either stock price of a financial asset and its fundamental value (or dividends) or a two stock prices indexes. Thus, stationarity of z_t indicates existence of stable economic relationship between these two variables. It implies also that it is possible to anticipate the evolution of X_t while knowing that of Y_t. Therefore, it is possible to forecast X_t future dynamics while knowing that of Y_t and efficiency hypothesis is then rejected.

In practice, linear cointegration techniques were used in order to check efficiency hypothesis and study stock prices adjustment dynamics, but results of previous studies are divergent and sometimes contradictory. For example, Campbell and Shiller (1987) tested cointegration hypothesis between dividends and prices. They showed that these two variables are cointegrated and accepted this hypothesis because of the existence of a long-term stable relation between the price and its fundamental value. On the other hand, Fontaine (1990) showed that stock price evolutions are divergent and concluded to efficiency of financial market. Lilti (1994) studied the causality sense between dividends and prices in order to determine if it is possible to forecast dividends from prices and the past dividends. He concluded to the absence of cointegration between prices and dividends but his interpretation is different from that of Fontaine as he considered that absence of cointegration relationship leads to rejection of efficiency.

Nevertheless, studying stock prices and efficiency while using linear cointegration techniques supposes that stock prices adjustment dynamics is symmetrical, linear, and continuous. Efficiency hypothesis admits that transaction costs are hopeless, information is free and not asymmetric. It stipulates that investors are rational, have the same degree of perception and understanding of information and that they react instantaneously and simultaneously to the arrival of a new information. However, these hypotheses seem to be very restraining because of presence of market frictions such that transaction costs, noise traders, and mimetic behavior. Otherwise, using linear cointegration can reject wrongly efficiency hypothesis and can lead to an unavailable conclusion. To face limits, few studies extend linear modeling to the nonlinear one in order to test efficiency hypothesis at long-term not only against linear dependence, but also against an alternative of nonlinear type. In such a context, we propose to examine the dynamics of long-term adjustment of the price toward equilibrium by testing the efficiency hypothesis against a nonlinear model of STECM type. Justifications of this choice are given in next section.

3 Transaction Costs and Nonlinearities in Stock Indexes Dynamics

Stock prices adjustment cannot be neither immediate nor continuous since a delay is sometimes necessary to integrate correctly the new information in the course. In addition, market time reaction can depend on the degree of competition, transaction costs level and the type of investors (ordinary or professional investors). Thus, investors can take time to decode information that is transmitted to them inducing a slowness and inertias effects which can mislead delays of adjustment in stock prices dynamics.

Therefore, transaction costs appear as a limit to arbitration and efficiency and can have many considerable repercussions. Indeed, these expenses cannot incite investors to exchange financial assets particularly when the anticipated potential gain is lower than the assumed costs. Thus, transaction costs imply discontinuous prices adjustment and persistent deviations of stock prices from fundamentals. Stock prices deviations from equilibrium last for a very long time. They could be persistent and may be governed by nonlinear adjustment process that is mean-reverting with a slow adjustment speed.

Transaction costs create two zones (Dumas (1992)). Within the first zone of no trade called also "transaction band", no trade or adjustment takes place. Prices spend most of the time away from their fundamental values. This implies that prices deviations from equilibrium last for a very long time, are divergent and admit often an unit root, although they do not follow necessarily a random walk. In the second zone, exchange and adjustment are rather active and stock prices adjustment speed depends on price disequilibrium size. Thus, prices deviations seem to follow a nonlinear process that is mean-reverting with a convergence speed varying directly with the extend of the deviation from equilibrium.

In addition, according to Anderson (1997), transaction costs are often heterogeneous. This implies that adjustment can be active for some assets or some shareholders but not necessarily for all investors and assets. So, some delays can be introduced in investors reactions and reproduced in prices adjustment process making it more smooth (i.e. Jawadi (2006), Jawadi and Chaouachi (2006)). Indeed, such delays in reaction or adjustment can mislead effects of inertia and persistence in the course, rejecting efficiency and instantaneous adjustment hypotheses.

Otherwise, investors have often different degrees of information understanding and heterogeneous anticipations (i.e. noise traders, chartists, fundamentalists, aware investors, professional investors, . . .). Interaction between these different categories of agents can also imply delays in courses adjustment when they tempt to rejoin their fundamental values and introduce a succession of ephemeral rises and violent recession periods in prices dynamics (i.e. De Grauwe and Grimaldi (2003)). In such a context and because of information costs, some investors can have interest to follow other operators decisions and copy the market middle opinion and the psychology of mass, whereas these are baffled in time and sometimes divergent (i.e. Orléan (1990)). However, following some gregarious behaviors risks sometimes to generate an asymmetric stock courses deviations toward their fundamental.

Indeed, according to fundamentalists, every asset has a fundamental value around which it fluctuates. Prices can deviate at short-term, but they often return toward their equilibrium values under the market strengths influence. Chartists believe rather to the existence of a strong interrelationship between future course and its past tendencies.

Consequently, interaction between these different kinds of investors can imply a price that its dynamics is sometimes complicated, discontinuous, asymmetrical, and nonlinear. Linear models are not often able to reproduce such adjustment dynamics. In order to understand and explain stock prices evolution in presence of transaction costs and heterogeneous shareholders, we propose to center our study on the French stock market adjustment relating to American market deviations in a nonlinear framework. We check whether

CAC40 adjustment dynamics is linear or nonlinear. We test efficiency hypothesis and we study the impact of transaction costs on speculation. We study reaction of French investors toward American stock market variations and we test whether the operators copy American opinion market.

4 Modeling Nonlinear Adjustment in Stock Prices

Threshold cointegration models were introduced by Balke and Fomby (1997). Anderson (1997) proposed an extension of these models that takes into account gradual transition rather than abrupt one, giving thus a new class of models: Switching Transition Error Correction Models (STECMS). Statistical properties and specification and estimate steps of these processes were developed by Van Dijk *et al.* (2002). STECM and nonlinear adjustment techniques are often used to reproduce financial assets adjustment dynamics toward equilibrium (i.e. Anderson (1997), Michael *et al.* (1997a), Michael *et al.* (1997b), Van Dijk *et al.* (2002), Jawadi (2006), Jawadi and Koubbaa (2006)).

This type of modeling is able to reproduce asymmetrical and discontinuous adjustment in presence of market frictions such as transaction costs. STEC models define different regimes and specify differently adjustment in each regime according to transaction costs impact and strengths exercised by investors reactions. In such a context, we develop a new nonlinear adjustment dynamics that characterized the French market adjustment dynamics by two regimes and for which adjustment takes place in every period, but the speed of adjustment varies with the extend of CAC40 deviation from equilibrium.[b] In the first regime, CAC40 can diverge from S&P500 dynamics and can be determined by fundamental of local market or chartists action, and adjustment or error correction mechanism cannot be active. But, while CAC40 deviations toward S&P500 (z_t) exceed some threshold given often by transaction costs, adjustment will be active and CAC40 will be mean-reverting toward its equilibrium level (Eq. (1)).

According to Orléan (1990), it is possible to identify two kinds of dynamics. In the first one, fundamentalists dominated the market and stock price is mean-reverting, while in second regime, trust fundamental is weak and

[b]In this study, we center analysis on CAC40 adjustment toward S&P500 level and not toward its fundamental value. This can help to reproduce CAC40 adjustment, while tacking into account interdependence between American and French stock markets, and reproduce contagion and mimetic phenomena between these two stock markets. American stock market is considered since many years as a reference market.

investors could believe on non-fundamental information and have tendency to copy the middle market opinion.

Formally, nonlinear adjustment representation is defined as follows:

$$\Delta Y_t = \alpha_0 + \lambda_1 z_{t-1} + \sum_{i=1}^{p} \alpha_i Y_{t-i} + \sum_{j=1}^{p} \beta_j X_{t-j} + \lambda_2 z_{t-1} \times F\left(\gamma, c, z_{t-d}\right) + \varepsilon_t, \tag{2}$$

where $F(\gamma, c, z_{t-d}) = 1 - \exp[-\gamma(z_{t-d} - c)^2], \gamma > 0$, and c are, respectively, transition speed and threshold parameter, $\varepsilon_t \rightarrow N(0, \sigma^2)$ and z_t is error correction term of linear cointegration relationship (Eq. (1)).

This specification describes two regimes corresponding to the extreme values of F and an intermediate states continuum. Central regime is defined when CAC40 adjustment dynamics is close to equilibrium and it is described by the following linear representation:

$$\Delta Y_t = \alpha_0 + \lambda_1 z_{t-1} + \sum_{i=1}^{p} \alpha_i Y_{t-i} + \sum_{j=1}^{p} \beta_j X_{t-j} + \varepsilon_t. \tag{3}$$

Extreme regimes are defined as follows:

$$\Delta Y_t = \alpha_0 + (\lambda_1 + \lambda_2)\ z_{t-1} + \sum_{i=1}^{p} \alpha_i Y_{t-i} + \sum_{j=1}^{p} \beta_j X_{t-j} + \varepsilon_t. \tag{4}$$

In our specification, λ_1 and λ_2 are the more important parameters as their values and signs specify stock prices adjustment dynamics and determine their convergence speed toward equilibrium. Indeed, even if λ_1 is positive, λ_2 and $(\lambda_1 + \lambda_2)$ have to be negative and meaningful in order to validate and confirm a nonlinear mean-reverting process of stock prices toward equilibrium. This implies that for small deviations, CAC40 deviations would diverge from equilibrium and would be characterized by an unit root or an explosive behavior, while for an important deviations, adjustment process would mean-reverting.

In practice, according to Van Dijk *et al.* (2002), STECM methodology is similar to that of Smooth Transition Autoregressive Models (STAR) of Granger and Teräsvirta (1993) and Teräsvirta (1994) and it is defined in many steps. We test, first, presence of linear cointegration. Secondly, we apply specification and linearity tests in order to check whether the stock prices adjustment is linear or nonlinear. Finally, we estimate STECM while using Nonlinear Least Squares (Gallant (1987), Gallant and White (1988)).

5 Empirical Analysis

5.1 Data

Daily data for France and United States for the period 1 January 1988–4 February 2006 were obtained from DATASTREAM. The series are closing prices of CAC40 and S&P500. The choice of CAC40 and S&P500 is justified by the fact that these two indexes would reproduce French and American stock markets activities and dynamics. All data were converted to natural logarithms in order to reduce stock prices variance. Stock returns are defined as a stock prices logarithmic difference.[c]

5.2 Linear Cointegration Tests

As in Engle and Granger (1987), we need to establish the stationarity of z_t in order to test linear cointegration hypothesis between CAC40 and S&P500. Stationarity of z_t implies that CAC40 and S&P500 are linear cointegrated and that French and American stock markets are interdependent and integrated. But, it does not necessarily mean that CAC40 adjustment toward equilibrium is linear, continuous and of a constant speed.

In practice, we follow the two-stage procedure of Engle and Granger (1987). On the one hand, we test stationarity hypothesis for these two indexes. Thus, we apply Augmented Dickey–Fuller tests, noted ADF, of Dickey and Fuller (1981) and the semiparametric test Phillips–Perron test (Phillips and Perron (1988)). We find that both series are not stationary in level but stationary in the first difference. CAC40 and S&P500 are then I(1). This implies that these two variables can be linearly cointegrated if z_t would be stationary. On the other hand, we test the null hypothesis of noncointegration and we find that there is strong evidence to reject the null hypothesis meaning that z_t is stationary. This implies also that French stock market is not efficient and suggests that z_t may be white noise.

However, we have to be careful in analyzing these results as linear cointegration tests could have a lower power in presence of market frictions. Simulations

[c]All empircal results are presented in appendices.

of Taylor and Sarno (2001) showed that ADF tests can be affected by non-linearity that is due to transaction costs. So, while using linear cointegration tests in presence of transaction costs, we would conclude wrongly in market inefficiency. According to Van Dijk *et al.* (2002), we propose to extend our study to nonlinear framework. Thus, we test nonlinear adjustment hypothesis in order to check efficiency hypothesis while applying linearity tests that are robust to market frictions such as transaction costs.[d]

5.3 Nonlinear Adjustment Tests

According to Teräsvirta (1994), we specify in a first step linear models that form the basis of linearity tests and we determine the linear model (LECM) of order p. Specification of linear model is important since underspecification or overspecification may affect linearity tests. Therefore, we define lags number of linear model so that its residuals would be a white noise. Thus, we use not only Information Criteria (AIC, Shwarz) and tests of Ljung–Box (1978), but also the partial autocorrelation function. These specification tests showed that residuals of estimated linear model on French returns have the good statistical properties for $p = 3$.

In a second step, we check nonlinear stock prices adjustment hypothesis while testing linear adjustment hypothesis against its alternative of nonlinear adjustment. Given the daily frequency of the data employed, we consider $d \in [1, 2, 3, 4, 5]$ as plausible values of the delay parameter.

Formally, as in (2), $F = 0$ when $\gamma = 0$. So linearity hypothesis can be expressed as H_0: $\gamma = 0$ and linearity test is defined by testing H_0 against H_1: $\gamma > 0$. In order to apply this test, we use Luukkonen *et al.* (1988) Lagrange Multiplier-type test Statistics that follow a standard χ^2 under H_0.

However, these tests are at the basis of some problems, in particular, the existence of several definitions of the null hypothesis (i.e. $\gamma = 0$ or $\delta_1 = \delta_2 = 0$). This can generate several problems of nuisance of parameters. In order to avoid these problems, Luukkonen and Saïkkonen (1988) proposed to replace exponential transition function by its Taylor approximation. The first-order Taylor approximation of exponential function is given by the following auxiliary regression:

$$y_t = \delta_0 z_t + \delta_1 z_t s_t + \delta_2 z_t s_t^2 + \mu_t, \quad O\grave{u}: \quad \mu_t = \varepsilon_t + \alpha_2 z_t e_{2t}. \qquad (5)$$

[d]Nonlinear modeling will concern stock returns as prices are I(1).

Linearity test statistic[e] for this regression is given by the following statistic: $LM_2 = T(SCR_0 - SCR_2)/SCR_0$, where SCR_2 is the residual squared sum of nonlinear model (Eq. (2)). LM_2 statistic is distributed asymptotically as a $\chi^2(2(p+1))$.

Nevertheless, Escribano and Jorda (1999) showed more recently that the first-order of exponential function Taylor approximation is not sufficient to reproduce the two inflection points characterizing exponential function. Thus, authors suggested to use Taylor approximation of second-order that is given as follows:

$$y_t = \delta_0' z_t + \delta_1' z_t s_t + \delta_2' z_t s_t^2 + \delta_3' z_t s_t^3 + \delta_4' z_t s_t^4 + \nu_t. \tag{6}$$

In such a case, the null hypothesis of linearity test is defined as follows: $H_0 : \delta_1 = \delta_2 = \delta_3 = \delta_4 = 0$. The linearity test statistic is noted LM_4 and is also distributed as $\chi^2(4(p+1))$.

We apply in what follows these two test for plausible values for d. From Table A.1, it can been seen that linear adjustment hypothesis is strongly rejected at 5% for many values of d, but linearity is more rejected for $d = 2$ and we retain then z_{t-2} as a transition variable. Thus, CAC40 adjustment dynamics toward S&P500 is nonlinear. We focus in the last step on estimation of this adjustment dynamics while using ESTECM.

5.4 *Nonlinear Estimation Results*

We refer to Michael *et al.* (1997), Michael *et al.* (1997a), and Van Dijk *et al.* (2002) to estimate STECM. Indeed, we estimate on the one hand LECM by OLS (see Table A.2) in order to define initial values for nonlinear model parameters. On the other hand, we estimate nonlinear model by NLS. In practice, as STECM estimate depends on initial values of γ and c, we experimented with various starting values and we got identical results indicating the location of a global minimum of criterion function.

Results presented in Table A.3 indicated, on the basis of "t-ratio", that estimators are strongly significant and that nonlinear model has the good statistical properties. Indeed, transition and threshold parameters are strongly meaningful. The standardized transition parameter $\hat{\gamma}$ showed that

[e] s_t is transition variable.

the speed of transition is slow between regimes and confirmed our choice of STECM. Adjustment terms λ_1 and λ_2 are strongly and statistically meaningful indicating that adjustment process is nonlinear. In addition, λ_2 and $(\lambda_1 + \lambda_2)$ are negative implying that CAC40 deviations toward equilibrium are mean-reverting with a slow transition speed.

Thus, ESTECM presents good statistical properties and implies a strongly nonlinear adjustment of French market toward the American one. In other words, CAC40 and S&P500 can undergo some short-term disruptions, but while having the same properties at long-term, they can tie between them steady relations which converge toward an equilibrium for which adjustment dynamics is nonlinear. Indeed, adjustment term in the first regime λ_1 is positive. It is significant and superior to unity indicating that the dynamics of CAC40 in the first regime diverges from S&P500 one. CAC40 seems having an exploding behavior in the first regime. But, as soon as one passes a certain threshold, CAC40 variation in relation to American index tends toward a stationary state.

ESTECM conditions validity are verified as adjustment term in the second regime λ_2 is negative and significant and the sum of the two strengths of recall $(\lambda_1 + \lambda_2)$ is also negative and significant. Moreover, linear adjustment term belongs to the interval $[\lambda_1 + \lambda_2, \lambda_1]$. Consequently, threshold cointegration model is appropriate to reproduce nonlinearities and cyclic movements characterizing stock prices adjustment process. However, this result is not compatible with the weak-form of efficiency hypothesis. Indeed, an STEC representation between CAC40 and S&P500 shows that it would be possible to anticipate CAC40 evolution while knowing American stock market variations. It implies that both stock markets are nonlinearly correlated, integrated, and interdependent.

These nonlinearities are often due to mimetic behavior, information asymmetry, and transaction costs. Indeed, investors who are better informed, can get information more quickly and pay less transaction costs as those who placed on the international market. Moreover, operator's behavior can be determined according to other variables such as the relative degree of confidence, the country level of development, the degree of risk aversion and non-anticipated information and the role of surprise effects.

Otherwise, other interpretation of nonlinearity presented in investor behavior and adjustment prices dynamics fits portfolio choice theory. Indeed, investors optimal choice is made on the basis of a comparison between expected gains and assumed costs. Investors can have tendency to choose investment in national market so much that profit is optimal. But as soon as they anticipate a more important gain while buying international assets, they can reach to the international market.

6 Conclusion

In this paper, efficiency hypothesis has been tested using nonlinear techniques and fearing independence hypothesis against nonlinear dependence defined by STECMs. We showed that stock prices adjustment is nonlinear. We found statistically significant evidence of nonlinearity in the French stock adjustment dynamics which was well approximated by an ESTECM. Estimation results rejected efficiency and stock prices linear adjustment hypotheses. An important empirical finding is about presence of high persistence in CAC40 deviations from S&P500. These results showed that French and American stock market are nonlinearly interdependent, integrated, and correlated. They imply a mean-reverting nonlinear adjustment process with a slow transition speed between regimes. In particular, the larger the CAC40 deviations from S&P500, the stronger the tendency to move back to equilibrium. Stock prices deviations are near-unit root for small disequilibrium but white noise for large deviations from equilibrium.

This slowness in adjustment is explained by market frictions and transaction costs. Indeed, with the transaction band, the process is divergent so that CAC40 spends most of the time away from equilibrium implying highly persistent deviations that are mean-reverting in particular when courses become strongly disaligned or away from equilibrium. These results may help to explain alternation of stock crises and "comovements" of stock indexes. A possible extension of this work is the study of forecasting performance of such nonlinear models against linear process.

Acknowledgments

The author is very grateful to Georges Prat for his constructive comments and suggestions. Helpful comments were also received from Professors Timo Teräsvirta, Dick Van Dijk, and Philip Hans Franses. The author is also thankful for Mrs Nabila Jawadi for her reading and correction of English and for financial support from Amiens School of Management.

Appendix A

Table A.1: p-values for the linearity tests.

d	LM statistics	p-values
$d = 1$	LM_2	0.05
	LM_4	0.10
$d^* = 2$	LM_2	0.004
	LM_4	0.009
$d = 3$	LM_2	0.04
	LM_4	0.07
$d = 4$	LM_2	0.04
	LM_4	0.11
$d = 5$	LM_2	0.12
	LM_4	0.13

Note: (*): Linearity is strongly rejected for $d = 2$.

Table A.2: Linear error correction model estimation results.

Variables	LECM	
	Coefficients	t-ratio
Constant	0.002	1.24
ΔY_{t-1}	0.027	1.85**
ΔY_{t-2}	0.013	1.45
ΔY_{t-3}	0.026	1.64**
ΔX_{t-1}	0.123	1.65**
ΔX_{t-2}	0.051	2.58*
ΔX_{t-3}	0.175	7.54*
ΔX_{t-3}	0.102	2.58*
z_{t-1}	−0.023	−2.71*
$\bar{R}^2$	0.36	

Note: (*) and (**) indicate estimators significativity, respectively, at the 5% and 10% level.

Table A.3: Estimates results of ESTECM.

	ESTECM (3,2)	
	Coefficients	t-ratio
α_0	0.017	1.08
λ_1	1.081	1.82**
α_1	−0.286	−1.51
α_2	0.084	1.86**
α_3	0.678	1.97*
β_1	0.931	2.52*
β_2	0.435	7.26*
β_3	0.076	4.59*
λ_2	−1.124	5.18*
γ	2.79	3.02*
c	0.13	12.1*
$\frac{\sigma_{NL}}{\sigma_L}$	0.71	
$\bar{R}^2$	0.68	

Note: σ_{NL} and σ_L are, respectively, standard deviation of nonlinear and linear models.
(*) and (**) indicate estimators significantly, respectively, at the 5% and 10% level.

References

Anderson, HM (1997). Transaction costs and nonlinear adjustment towards equilibrium in the US treasury bill markets. *Oxford Bulletin of Economics and Statistics*, 59, 465–484.

Balke, NS and et Fomby, TB (1997). Threshold cointegration. *International Economic Review*, 38, 627–646.

Boswijk, HP, Hommes, CH and et Manzan, S (2005). Behavioural heterogeneity in stock prices. Working Paper, CeNDEF, University of Amsterdam, Netherlands.

Campbell, JY and et Shiller, RJ (1987). Cointegration and tests for present value models. *Journal of Political Economy*, 95(5), 1062–1088.

De Grauwe, P and et Grimaldi, M (2003). Heterogeneity of agents, transaction costs and the exchange rate. *Actes de la Conférence Internationale de l'Association d'Econométrie Appliquée (AEA)*, 6 et 7 mars, Marseille, France.

Dickey, DA and Fuller, WA (1981). Likelihood ratio statistics for autoregressive time series with a unit root. *Econometrica*, 49, 1057–1072.

Dumas, B (1992). Dynamic equilibrium and the real exchange rates in a spatially separated world. *Review of Financial Studies*, 2, 153–180.

Engle, RF and Granger, CWJ (1987). Cointegration and error correction: Representation, estimation and testing. *Econometrica*, 55(2), 251–276.

Escribano, A and Jordă (1999). Improving testing and specification of smooth transition regression models. In *Nonlinear Times Series Analysis of Economic and Financial Data*, Rothman P. (ed), pp. 298–319 Boston: Kluwer.

Fama, EF (1965). The behaviour of stock market prices. *Journal of Business*, 38(1), 31–105.

Fama, EF (1970). Efficient capital markets: A review of theory and empirical work. *Journal of Finance*, 25(2), 383–417.

Fama, EF (1990). Efficient capital markets: II. *Journal of Finance*, XLVI(5), 1575–1617.

Fama, EF and French, K (1988). Dividend yields and expected stock returns. *Journal of Financial Economics*, 22, 3–25.

Fontaine, P (1990). Peut-on prédire l'évolution des marchés d'actions à partir des cours et des dividendes passés? *Journal de la Société Statistique de Paris,* 131(1), 16–36.

Gallant, AR (1987). *Nonlinear Statistical Models.* New York: Wiley.

Gallant, AR and White, H (1988). *A Unified Theory of Estimation and Inference for Nonlinear Dynamic Models.* Oxford: Oxford University Press.

Granger, CWJ and Teräsvirta, T (1993). *Modelling Nonlinear Economic Relationships*, Oxford University Press.

Granger, CWJ (1981a). Some properties of time series data and their use in econometric model specification. *Journal of Econometrics*, 121–130.

Granger, CWJ (1981b). Cointegrating variables and error correcting models. UCSD Discussion Paper No. 83–13a.

Jawadi, F (2006). Ajustements Non-linéaires des cours boursiers dans les pays du G7: Essai de modélisation, Thèse de Doctorat, Université de Paris 10-Nanterre.

Jawadi, F and Chaouachi, S (2006). Coûts de transaction et dynamique non-linéaire des prix des actifs financiers: Une note théorique. *Euro Mediterranean Economics and Finance Review*, 1(5), 161–177.

Jawadi, F and et Koubbaa, Y (2006). Dynamique d'ajustement à seuil des rentabilités boursières des pays G7: Application des modèles STECM. *Euro Mediterranean Economics and Finance Review*, 1(2), 151–163.

Johansen, S (1988). Statistical analysis of cointegration vectors. *Journal of Economic Dynamics and Control*, 12, 231–254.

Lilti, JJ (1994). Les apports de la cointégration aux tests d'efficience. *Journal de la Société Statistique de Paris,* 135(4), 47–63.

Ljung, G and Box, GE (1978). On a measure of lack of fit in time series models. *Biometrika*, 65, 297–303.

Luukkonen, R and Saïkkonen, P (1988). Lagrange multiplier tests for testing nonlinearity in time series models. *Scandinavian Journal of Statistic*, 15, 65–68.

Luukkonen, R, Saïkkonen, P and Teräsvirta, T (1988). Testing linearity against smooth transition autoregressive models. *Biometrika*, 75(3), 491–499.

Manzan, S (2003). Essays on Nonlinear Economic Dynamics, PhD thesis, University of Amsterdam.

Michael, P, Nobay, AR and Peel, DA (1997a). Transactions costs and nonlinear adjustment in the real exchange rates: An empirical investigation. *Journal of Political Economy*, 105, 862–879.

Michael, P, Peel, DA and Taylor, MP (1997b). Ajustement non linéaire vers le taux de change d'équilibre à long terme: le modèle monétaire revisité. *Revue Economique*, 48(3), 653–659.

Orléan, A (1990). Le rôle des influences interpersonnelles dans la détermination des cours boursiers. *Revue économique*, 41(5), 839–868.

Phillips, PCB and Perron, P (1988). Testing for unit root in a time series regression. *Biometrika*, 75, 335–346.

Summers, LM (1986). Does the stock market rationally reflect fundamental values? *The Journal of Finance*, XLI(3), 591–601.

Teräsvirta, T (1994). Specification, estimation and evaluation of smooth transition autoregressive models. *Journal of the American Statistical Association*, 89, 208–218.

Van Dijk, D, Teräsvirta, T and et Franses, PH (2002). Smooth transition autoregressive models — A survey of recent developments. *Econometric Reviews*, 21, 1–47.

CHAPTER 19

HOUSEHOLDS' EXPECTATIONS OF UNEMPLOYMENT: NEW EVIDENCE FROM FRENCH MICRODATA

*Salah Ghabri**

This chapter studies the short-term expectations of unemployment. A simple bounded rationality model (augmented adaptive–extrapolative process) of households' expectations of unemployment was proposed to analyze the microdata of French Household Surveys (ECAM). The households' perceptions of the French labor market was characterized by a pessimistic attitude which came on gradually.

1 Introduction

Katona (1960, p. 20) defined economic expectations as "*subjective notions of things to come, and attitudes about the future rather than reports on information or reflections of deep-seated attitudes, which tend to endure in spite of changing circumstances*". Expectations allow us to study the interaction between economic behavior and individual attitudes. The availability of direct observations on expectations allows us to test empirically the process of expectation formation. For instance, Pesaran (1987, p. 207) justified this idea by showing that "only when direct observations on expectations are available it is possible to satisfactorily compare and contrast alternative models of expectations formation". Several studies on the formation of expectations have been undertaken making use of available survey data. Considerable attention has been devoted to survey data in which only the average response was reported and some results based on this kind of data have suffered from aggregation bias and the restrictive hypothesis of stability of the expectations parameters. In spite

*CEEE — Centres d'études de l'emploi, Polytechnicum-Marne-La-vallée.
ghabri@univ-paris1.fr

of the advantages, the use of individual level data (for example, household surveys) is rare and few micro-studies have been undertaken.

This study concerned short-term economic expectations. The main purpose of this chapter is to show that subjective data tend to conflict with the usual assumptions made about rational expectations and macroeconomic shocks. Expectations formation models may have time-varying parameters, consistent with the pervasive evidence of model instability in empirical economics (Pesaran, 2000).

We propose a realistic, simple, and individual model of households' expectations of unemployment. Using French microdata on expectations with respect to unemployment, Gardes *et al.* (1997) showed that the adaptive model is the most plausible mechanism in the formation of household expectations. However, they excluded other expectation-forming mechanisms such as extrapolative and regressive models. Section 2 presents the model. Section 3 describes the data. Since the estimation of the proposed model requires numeric data, we have presented in Sec. 4 two methods to enable us to quantify qualitative data. The specifications of the estimated model and the results are given in Sec. 5. Conclusions are given in Sec. 6.

2 The Model

Both the classic criteria of Muth (1961) rationality (properties of bias and orthogonality) and the simple expectations process are not able to explain realistically the formation of unemployment expectations. The literature on tests of rationality is enormous and the main conclusion is that survey expectations were not rational. A few studies like that of Keane and Runkel (1990, 1998) did not reject the rational expectations hypothesis. When we test Muth rationality, theoretical and empirical problems arise in the definition of the households' information set (Maddala, 1992). For example, aggregation bias may lead to the false rejection or acceptance of rational expectations. In addition, the power of weak tests (hypotheses of bias and efficiency) usually made to test rationality seems to be weak since we consider only a subset of information. The question is what variables (apart from the past observations of the expectations) should be included in the information set.

Adaptive process is also not satisfactory to describe households forecasts. The error forecast of the variable of interest was insufficient to explain the expectations formation due to the possible omission of relevant variables rather than the time lags of the expectations (Holden *et al.*, 1986). For example, in the formation of unemployment expectations, it may be more plausible to suppose that households' unemployment expectations can be formed by adjusting the unemployment forecast error and by using additional information like the change of the inflation rate.

In this chapter, we suggest a simple linear model of bounded rationality such as an augmented linear adaptive–extrapolative process. The model is based on the available individual household information set including the previous perceptions and expectations of both price (π) and unemployment. The general form of the model is:

$$u_i^e = f(X_i', Z_i) = \alpha' X_I + \eta' Z_i + e_i, \qquad (1)$$

where
α and η are vectors of parameters to be estimated;
u_i^e is the unemployment expectation made by a household i at time t;
X_i' is a set of five variables including:

— the unemployment expectation made at time $(t - 1)$;
— the current and previous perceptions of unemployment made at time t and $t - 1$;
— the current and the previous price expectation made at time $(t - 1)$ and $t - 1$.

Z_i' is a set of the principal household characteristics (sex, age, province, level of education...); and e_i is the individual error term.

3 The French INSEE Household Surveys

We used the French INSEE household surveys "les Enquêtes de Conjoncture de l'INSEE auprès des Ménages" (ECAM).

From the late 1950s to 1994, the French National Institute of Statistics and Economic Studies (INSEE) has conducted a situation survey three times a year, interviewing some 6000–8000 households. From 1994, this survey was replaced by a monthly European phone survey. In the earlier survey, the same household was interviewed in two consecutive years during October–November. This allowed us to compare expectations at the time of the first interview with perceptions of the changes occurring between the two interviews. By matching this information for the period 1977–1994, we built 17 two-year panels, each one containing approximately 2500 households. Expectations and perception questions concerned the general standard of living, the situation in the labor market, inflation, and the household financial situation and saving intentions. Responses were qualitative and pre-coded. Except for income, it consisted of five ranked items: from "much worse" to "much better" (see Appendix A).

On average, non-response rates for expectations and perceptions were 15.4% for inflation, 16.9% for unemployment, and 17.2% for the general standard of living in France. The empirical study of the rationality of households' behavior was (generally) conducted by comparing the expectations and realizations of an economic variable at different points in time. With these INSEE surveys containing perceptions and expectations questions, we were able to estimate household expectations processes much more precisely than in the aggregate case where expectations are compared with realizations (like the study of inflation expectations in almost all previous studies).

4 Quantification

Three methods have been used to analyze qualitative surveys. The first is to study them as they are, usually using contingency tables (Nerlove, 1983; Gourriéroux and Pradel, 1986; Nerlove, 1997). The studies of Gardes *et al.* (2000) and Nerlove and Schurman (1997) are recent examples of the direct use of qualitative data. The second is the famous Carlson–Parkin method frequently used to convert qualitative data into quantitative measures. The third is the Pesaran or the regressive approach (1987).

Because the French survey results are presented as qualitative items and the estimation of model (1) requires quantitative data, we need to quantify the categorical answers. As opposed to the macroeconomic level, few types of individual quantification have been performed (Gardes and Madre, 1990; Ghabri, 1998). We used the probability approach because it allowed us to generate perceived and expected individual measures of unemployment. This approach converts qualitative expectations responses into quantitative expectations. The quantification is based on the hypothesis of normal or logistic (or uniform) distributions of the answers (both the distributions giving similar results). This method has often been used for aggregate data (Carlson and Parkin, 1975; Batchelor, 1986; Pesaran, 1990; Smith and McAleer, 1995) and was adapted here to individual data, as in Gardes and Madre (1991) and Ghabri (1998).

4.1 Aggregate Quantification

The main assumption of this technique is based on the existence of an "indifferent" interval around zero for which individuals do not experience a change in a particular variable they observe (they report the expected change in a variable as being zero), whereas outside this interval they report a variation of this variable (for further details, see Pesaran, 1990). Let us define the following variables.

${}_t u^p_{i,t-1}$ is the perceived percentage change in the unemployment variable u for a household i conditional on household i's own information set.

${}_{t-1}u^a_{i,t}$ is the household's expected change in the variable between the first and the second survey, with expectation generated in period $t-1$. The indifference interval is $[-l_1, l_2]$ such that a household i reports an expected increase if ${}_{t-1}u^a_{i,t} \geq l_2$ and an expected decrease if ${}_{t-1}u^a_{i,t} \leq -l_1$. We assume that the thresholds l_1 and l_2 are the same for both expectations and perceptions. In addition, we assume that they are constant across both households and time. Hence, it follows that:

$$\Pr\{u^e_t \leq -l_1 | \Psi_t\} = H_t(-l_1) = {}_{t-1}F^e_t, \tag{2a}$$

$$\Pr\{u^e_t \geq -l_2 | \Psi_t\} = H_t(l_2) = {}_{t-1}R^e_t, \tag{2b}$$

$$\Pr\{u^p_t \leq -l_1 | \Psi_t\} = H_t(-l_1) = {}_tF^p_{t-1}, \tag{3a}$$

$$\Pr\{u^p_t \geq -l_2 | \Psi_t\} = H_t(l_2) = {}_tR^p_{t-1}, \tag{3b}$$

where u_t is the weighted sum of $u_{i,t}$, Ψ_t is the aggregate information set, and H is the cumulative density function of u_t; ${}_{t-1}F^e_t({}_tF^p_{t-1})$ is respectively the proportion of households, appropriately weighted to account for their size in a sample size N, that expect (perceive) increase of the unemployment rate over the period $t-1$ to t; ${}_{t-1}R^e_t({}_tR^p_{t-1})$ is the proportion of households that at time t expect (perceive) a decrease of the unemployment rate over the period $t-1$ to t.

The solution of systems (2a), (2b) and (3a), (3b) are respectively the aggregate estimates $(\bar{u}^p_t, \bar{\sigma}^p_{u^a})$ and $(\bar{u}^e_t, \bar{\sigma}^e_{u^e})$, where $\bar{u}^p_t$ and $\bar{u}^e_t$ are respectively the average of the aggregate distribution of unemployment perceptions and expectations; $\bar{\sigma}^p_{u_t}$ and $\bar{\sigma}^e_t$ are respectively the standard errors of the aggregate distribution of unemployment perceptions and expectations.

Using annual aggregate data, we, first, estimated the thresholds of perception and expectation by applying the equations to standard normal distribution, logistic and uniform distributions. Secondly, we computed the aggregate time series.

4.2 Microquantification

The quantification of individual expectations and perceptions for the unemployment variable are based, respectively, on the formerly obtained average values of unemployment:

$$ {}_t u^p_{i,t-1} = {}_t \bar{u}^p_{t-1} + s_{it} \cdot \bar{\sigma}^t_{u^p}, \tag{4a} $$

$$ {}_{t-1} u^e_{i,t} = {}_{t-1} \bar{u}^e_t + s_{it} \cdot \bar{\sigma}^t_{u^e}, \tag{4b} $$

where s_{it} is the median threshold of the normal, logistic, or uniform distribution corresponding to the item i chosen by the household: for example, for the first item, the threshold s_{1t} corresponds to the proportion of households $a(t)/2$, where $a(t)$ is the proportion of answers corresponding to the first item of the question dealing with expectations of unemployment; t indicates the index of the survey (the first or the second interview).

For the inflation variable, individual perceptions are given similarly by the equation:

$$ {}_t \pi^p_{i,t-1} = {}_{t-1} \bar{\pi}^p_t + s_{it} \cdot \bar{\sigma}^t_{\pi^p}. \tag{5a} $$

However, special attention was given to the structure of households' inflation expectations. Since the expectation question is about the future change of the inflation rate and the perception question concerns the price level, expectations had to be transformed in terms of price level in order to compute the expectation error. As suggested by Gardes *et al.* (1997), two neighboring quantifications can be used: either, the quantified expectations are added to the individual perceptions of each household (quantification (5b)), or added to the mean perception of the whole population (quantification (5c)). We chose the latter method because it was more closely related to the perception question and gave better empirical results. The formulas of quantification are:

$$ {}_{t-1} \pi^e_{i,t} = {}_{t-1} \bar{\pi}^e_t + s_{it} \cdot \bar{\sigma}^t_{\pi^e}, \tag{5b} $$

$$ {}_{t-1} \pi^e_{i,t} = {}_t \bar{\pi}^p_{t-1} + s_{it} \cdot \bar{\sigma}^t_{\pi^e}. \tag{5c} $$

Seventeen short panels of two years were used: (1977–1978), (1978–1979) ··· (1993–1994). The average size of each panel was 2500 households. Both the individual unemployment and inflation expectations and perceptions series were treated as given data. However, we have to recognize that they may be subject to measurement errors which may be due to incorrect scaling of the qualitative data or due to the choice of the functional form of expectations and perceptions distributions.

5 Specification of the Model and Empirical Results

5.1 *Model Specification*

The structure of the French panel data allows us to obtain eight individual variables which are necessary to take into account the first part of the explanatory variables X_i of model (1): four for perceived unemployment and inflation (${}_{t-1}u^p_{i,t-2}; {}_t u^p_{i,t-1}; {}_{t-1}\pi^p_{i,t-2}; {}_t\pi^p_{i,t-1}$) and four others for anticipated unemployment and inflation (${}_{t-2}u^e_{i,t-1}; {}_{t-1}u^e_{i,t}; {}_{t-2}\pi^e_{i,t-1}; {}_{t-1}\pi^e_{i,t}$).

We used the robust ordinary least squares method to estimate the reduced form of model (1) in terms of first differences[a] because it takes into account all the specific individual effects (including the influence of those control variables which are constant through time) and because it is equivalent for two-year panel within the estimation, which is unbiased under usual assumptions (Baltagi, 1995).

To include the greatest possible part of the fixed individual effects (on the first differences data), we retained the major socio-demographic variables (Z_i): age (eight categories), education (three levels), region (Paris versus the other regions of France), and sex. Equation (6) which we estimated had the following linear form:

$$du^e_i = \beta_u \cdot eu^e_i + \alpha \cdot du^p_i + \beta_\pi . \pi^e_i + \sum_{k=1}^{8} \lambda_k(\text{age}_k) + \sum_{j=1}^{3} \gamma_j(\text{education}_j) + s(\text{sex}) + l(\text{region}) + w_i,$$

where $eu^e_i = u^p_{i,t} - u^e_{i,t-1}$; $e\pi^e_i = \pi^p_{i,t} - \pi^e_{i,t-1}$; $0 \leq \beta_u \leq 1$; $du^e_i = u^e_{i,t} - u^e_{i,t-1} du^p_i = u^p_{i,t} - u^p_{i,t-1}$; α is the coefficient of the perception (calculated in first difference); α may be positive or negative; β_u is the coefficient of unemployment adaptation: $0 \leq \beta_u \leq 1$; β_π is the coefficient of inflation adaptation (the augmented variable): $0 \leq \beta_\pi \leq 1$.

Estimations were performed using SAS ®software (version 8).

---

[a] In this case, estimation in the first differences allows us to eliminate also the correlation occurring when we estimate adaptive and extrapolative processes in level; so the dependent variable and the variable reflecting the extrapolative component are calculated in first differences.

5.2 *Empirical Results*

5.2.1 A Simple Augmented Adaptive–Extrapolative Process to Describe the Formation of Expectations

Tables B.1–B.4 (Appendix B) showed the results from ordinary least squares estimation of Eq. (6). The coefficients related to the expectation errors of unemployment and inflation were positive and significant (at the level of $\alpha = 5\%$) while the effect of the unemployment perception was negative and significant (at the level of $\alpha = 5\%$).

The simple adaptive model was not sufficient for the understanding of the formation of household expectations: in fact, apart from the correction of their expectation error, households not only extrapolated from the previous situation of the labor market, but also took into account information from price changes.

Contrary to the findings of macro-studies based on aggregate time-series data, expectations coefficients changed over time.

Available control variables (socio-demographic variables) contributed weakly to the explanation of the expectations. The province of residence was only significant for the period of high inflation and high unemployment. The effect of the age variable was not regular over time. The effect of education was ambiguous and when it was significant it showed that less-educated households expected an amelioration of the labor market.

5.2.2 Pessimistic Perception of an Improvement in the Labor Market

The weak influence of control variables on perceptions might be explained by a systematic common household attitude such as pessimism about the improvement of the labor market.

To confirm this hypothesis, we attempted to analyze the pessimistic perception of the labor market situation by identifying three groups of households: pessimistic, optimistic, and indifferent households (Table 1). We supposed that a household was pessimistic if the item j of its perception of economic conditions declared in the first and the second interview ($t = 1, 2$) was superior to its expectation. ($u^P_{j,t} < u^a_{j,t}$ and $u^p_{j,t-1} < u^a_{j,t-1}$).

For example, an individual i was pessimistic (first and second interview) if he perceived that the situation in the labor market had improved slightly during the previous months (item 2, question 1), and if he expected that, for the months to come, the number of unemployed would substantially increase

Table 1: Households categorization.

Definition of households categorization
Optimists (comparing first and second interview)
$u^P_{j,t} < u^a_{j,t}$ and $u^P_{j,t-1} < u^a_{j,t-1}$, $j = 1, 2, 3, 4, 5, t = 1, 2$
Pessimists (comparing first and second interview)
$u^P_{j,t} > u^a_{j,t}$ and $u^P_{j,t-1} > u^a_{j,t-1}$
Indifferent (comparing first and second interview)
$u^P_{j,t} = u^a_{j,t} = 3$ and $u^P_{j,t-1} = u^a_{j,t-1} = 3$

(item 1, question 2). Indifferent households were those who chose the third item.

Figure B.1 (see Appendix B) indicated that, over time, a pessimistic phenomenon seemed to characterize the attitudes of the different groups of households defined by their level of education. Over time, educated households become more pessimistic and the difference between the four categories of households tends to decrease. Two explanations are possible:

— Heterogeneity of the expectations has tended to disappear since the nineties because of the persistence and low variability of the unemployment rate (the unemployment rate did not decrease but it was characterized by low variability).
— The increase of the unemployment rate for educated French citizens especially during the period 1991–1995.

5.2.3 Limitations of the Study

The limitations of the results include:

(1) the loss of information which may be induced by the procedure of quantification. Being purely statistical methods, the mentioned quantification schemes
  — did not attempt to include any prior information about the underlying process driving the variable of interest (Dahl and Xia, 2003).
  — contributed to reduce the heterogeneity of households' opinions and a quantification bias can lead to a misestimation of the dispersion.
(2) the influence of other "intrinsic" psychological variables on the behavior of households which are not described in the surveys.

(3) the possible influence of such uncertainty measures of unemployment expectations like the variance of the actual unemployment rate. Unfortunately, we could not introduce a measure of uncertainty into the model because we had only short panels (two years).

6 Conclusion

In this chapter we have studied the process of the formation of unemployment expectations of French households. The estimation of the model confirmed that the simple learning process (adaptive model) was not sufficient to interpret the formation of households'expectations. This result allowed us to conclude that a bounded rationality model (augmented adaptive–extrapolative process) seemed to be the main process in the formation of unemployment perceptions or expectations of French households. The weak effect of control variables (i.e. level of education) can be interpreted by households pessimistic attitudes with respect to the improvement of the labor market situation.

Acknowledgment

The author is grateful to François Gardes, Jean Loup Madre, Mary Claude Pichery, Claude Montmarquette, Andrew Clark, Ashly Elizabeth, Georges Prat, Roy Batchelor and Thierry Chauveau of the 25th IAREP-SABE Congress (Vienna), 39th Congress of the "société canadienne de sciences économiques" (Hull) for their comments. The author is especially grateful to the INSEE for providing the individual data of the "Enquetes de conjoncture INSEE auprès des ménages". The original collector bears any responsibility for the analyses or interpretations presented here.

Appendix A

Reference List Variables

— *Unemployment perception* (u^p)
Answer to the question: According to what you see around you, do you think that the situation of the labor market during recent months has:
1. Substantially worsened; 2. Worsened slightly; 3. Stayed the same; 4. Improved slightly; 5. Substantially improved; 6. Do not know.

— *Unemployment expectation* (u^e)
Answer to the question:
Do you think that, in the next few months, the number of unemployed will:
1. Substantially increase; 2. Increase slightly; 3. Stay the same; 4. Decrease slightly; 5. Substantially decrease; 6. Do not know.

— *Price perception* (π^p)
Answer to the question: Do you feel that, in the last few months, prices have: 1. Clearly improved; 2. Improved a little; 3. Remained stationary; 4. Decreased a little; 5. Clearly decreased; 6. Do not know.

— *Price expectation* (u^e)
Answer to the question: Compared to the present situation, do you think that over the next few months: 1. There will be a greater price increase; 2. An equivalent price increase; 3. A smaller price increase; 4. Prices will remain stationary; 5. Prices will decrease slightly; 6. Do not know.

Age

Eight categories: Age 1 = (18–24 years); Age 2 = (25–29 years); Age 3 = (30–39 years); Age 4 = (40–49 years); Age 5 = (50–54 years); Age 6 = (55–59 years); Age 7 = (60–64 years); Age 8 = (65–70 years).

Education

Three levels: primary school (education 1), secondary (education 2: 2a — colleague; 2b — secondary) and university (education 3).

Region

Region of "ile de France" versus the other regions of France.

Gender

(reference = men)

Rate of inflation

(1978–1994).

Rate of unemployment

(1978–1994).

Appendix B

Empirical Results

Table B.1: First differences estimation of model (6).

Panel	Sample size	R^2	β_u	α_U	β_π	Region
1977–78	1932	0.293	0.363 (0.015)	−0.319 (0.018)	0.258 (0.042)	0.719 (0.374)
1978–79	2059	0.193	0.292 (0.016)	−0.380 (0.022)	0.260 (0.042)	0.960 (0.368)
1979–80	2227	0.304	0.382 (0.014)	−0.318 (0.019)	0.250 (0.041)	ns
1980–81	2295	0.300	0.486 (0.019)	−0.580 (0.025)	0.324 (0.047)	ns
1981–82	2322	0.219	0.335 (0.015)	−0.298 (0.018)	0.094 (0.033)	ns
1982–83	2500	0.215	0.307 (0.014)	−0.212 (0.015)	0.192 (0.035)	ns
1983–84	2024	0.404	0.519 (0.015)	−0.419 (0.024)	0.278 (0.042)	ns
1984–85	2012	0.212	0.395 (0.020)	−0.465 (0.031)	0.315 (0.047)	ns
1985–86	1993	0.300	0.363 (0.017)	−0.457 (0.021)	0.301 (0.039)	−1.023 (0.389)
1986–87	1977	0.229	0.268 (0.013)	−0.365 (0.015)	0.181 (0.041)	ns
1987–88	1833	0.247	0.310 (0.018)	−0.421 (0.022)	0.224 (0.038)	ns
1988–89	1784	0.197	0.248 (0.017)	−0.314 (0.019)	0.221 (0.032)	ns
1989–90	1792	0.221	0.286 (0.016)	−0.341 (0.019)	0.071 (0.032)	ns
1990–91	1885	0.436	0.491 (0.014)	−0.458 (0.019)	0.140 (0.032)	ns
1991–92	1814	0.324	0.465 (0.017)	−0.509 (0.025)	0.175 (0.045)	ns
1992–93	2151	0.443	0.642 (0.017)	−0.391 (0.030)	0.195 (0.045)	1.362 (0.515)
1993–94	2073	0.106	0.230 (0.028)	−0.515 (0.037)	0.231 (0.049)	ns

(Standard errors are in parentheses, ns: not significant).

Table B.2: First differences estimation of model (6).

Panel	Sex	Age 1	Age 2	Age 3	Age 4
1977–78	ns	ns	1.975 (0.635)	1.516 (0.577)	1.898 (0.565)
1978–79	ns	ns	ns	ns	0.802 (0.571)
1979–80	0.449 (0.269)	ns	ns	ns	ns
1980–81	ns	ns	1.625 (0.723)	1.998 (0.627)	2.831 (0.628)
1981–82	ns	ns	ns	ns	1.262 (0.600)
1982–83	ns	ns	ns	ns	1.263 (0.543)
1983–84	ns	ns	ns	1.196 (0.562)	1.856 (0.583)
1984–85	ns	ns	ns	ns	ns
1985–86	ns	ns	2.617 (0.671)	2.054 (0.550)	1.233 (0.581)
1986–87	ns	ns	ns	ns	ns
1987–88	ns	ns	ns	1.439 (0.581)	1.009 (0.591)
1988–89	ns	ns	ns	ns	ns
1989–90	ns	−1.248 (0.673)	ns	ns	ns
1990–91	ns	ns	−1.346 (0.631)	ns	ns
1991–92	ns	−2.898 (0.970)	ns	ns	ns
1992–93	ns	ns	ns	ns	2.491 (0.711)
1993–94	ns	0.431 (1.260)	ns	ns	ns

(Standard errors are in parentheses; ns: not significant).

Table B.3: First differences estimation of model (6).

Panel	Age 5	Age 6
1977–78	1.674 (0.665)	2.019 (0.668)
1978–79	ns	0.155 (0.688)
1979–80	ns	1.045 (0.584)
1980–81	ns	1.420 (0.721)
1981–82	ns	ns
1982–83	ns	0.942 (0.655)
1983–84	2.517 (0.671)	1.255 (0.683)
1984–85	ns	1.250 (0.775)
1985–86	1.281 (0.673)	ns
1986–87	ns	ns
1987–88	1.291 (0.688)	ns
1988–89	ns	ns
1989–90	ns	ns
1990–91	ns	ns
1991–92	ns	ns
1992–93	2.777 (0.921)	2.317 (0.879)
1993–94	ns	ns

(Standard errors are in parentheses; ns: not significant).

Table B.4: First differences estimation of model (6).

Panel	Education 1	Education 2
1977–78	−0.809 (0.445)	ns
1978–79	ns	ns
1979–80	ns	ns
1980–81	ns	ns
1981–82	ns	ns
1982–83	ns	ns
1983–84	ns	−0.986 (0.478)
1984–85	ns	ns
1985–86	ns	−0.997 (0.458)
1986–87	ns	ns
1987–88	ns	ns
1988–89	ns	ns
1989–90	ns	−1.068 (0.367)
1990–91	ns	ns
1991–92	ns	ns
1992–93	ns	−1.543 (0.559)
1993–94	ns	ns

(Standard errors are in parentheses; ns: not significant).

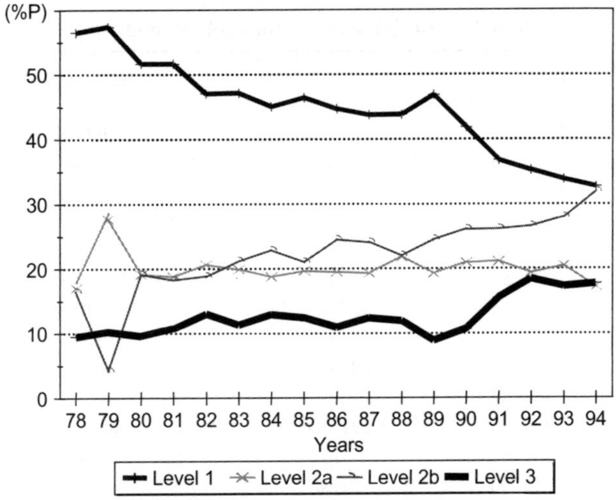

Figure B.1: Convergence of pessimistic attitudes of French households'expectations of unemployment (according to levels of education).
Legend: % P: percentage of pessimstic households.
The level of education: *level 1*: Primary school; *level 2a*: Colleague; *level 2b*: Secondary school; *level 3:* University.

References

Baltagi, B (1995). *Econometric Analysis of Panel Data.* New York: John Wiley and Sons.

Batchelor, RA (1986). Quantitative and qualitative measures of inflation expectations. *Oxford Bulletin of Economics and Statistics*, 48, 99–120.

Carlson, JA and Parkin, M (1975). Inflation Expectations. *Economica*, 42, 123–138.

Dahl, CM and Xia, L (2003). Quantification of qualitative survey data and tests of consistent expectations: A new likelihood approach. Working Paper, Krannert School of Management.

Darity, WJR and Goldsmith, AH (1996). Social psychology, unemployment and macroeconomics. *Journal of Economic Perspectives*, 10(1), 121–140.

Farber, HS (1995). Are lifetime jobs disappearing?: Job duration in the United States: 1973–1993, *National Bureau of Economic Research*, Working Paper 5014.

Gardes, F, Ghabri, S, Madre, JL and Pichery, MC (2000). Rationality of household expectations: Qualitative tests on French individual data. In *Price Expectations in Good and Financial Markets: New Developments in Theory and Empirical Research*, Gardes, F and Prat, G (eds). Edward Elgar.

Gardes, F, Ghabri, S, Madre, JL and Pichery, MC (1997). Rationalité des anticipations des ménages: Tests qualitatifs sur données individuelles françaises. *Revue Economique*, 48(3), 639–652.

Gardes, F and Madre, JL (1990). Comment se forment les anticipations d'inflation? *Economie et prévision* (99), 13–29.

Ghabri, S (1998). Les processus de formation des anticipations des ménages: une analyse à partir des enquêtes de conjoncture de l'INSEE. Unpublished PhD, Université of Paris I Panthéon-Sorbonne.

Ghabri, S (1999). Household expectations and pessimism: Evidence from French micro data. Paper presented at the *XV Congress of International Association of Research in Economic Psychology*, 1–3 July, Belgirate, Italy.

Gourieroux, C and Pradel, J (1986). Direct test of the rational expectation hypothesis. *European Economic Review*, 30(2), 265–284.

Holden, K, Peel, DA and Thompson, JL (1985). *Expectations: Theory and Evidence.* London MacMillan.

Katona, G (1960). The quality and economic significance of anticipation data. *A Conference of the Universities-national Bureau Committee for Economic Research*, A report of the National Bureau of Economic Research. New York: Princeton University Press.

Katona, G (1968). Behavioural and ecological economics: Consumer behavior: Theory and findings on expectations and aspirations. *American Economic Review*, 58, 19–30.

Keane, MP and Runkle, DE (1990). Testing the rationality of price forecasts: New evidence from panel data. *American Economic Review,* 80(4), 714–735.

Keane, MP and Runkle, DE (1995). Testing the rationality of price forecasts: Reply. *American Economic Review*, 85(1) 290.

Keane, MP and Runkle, DE (1998). Are financial analysts' forecasts of corporate profits rational? *Journal of Political Economy*, 106(4), 768–805.

Lolivier, S (1999). Anticipations des ménages et environnement économique. *Economie et Statistique*, 324–325.

Maddala, GS (1992). Survey data on expectations: What have we learnt?. *Econometric Methods and Applications*, 1, 469–491.

Muth, J (1961). Rational expectations and the theory of price movements. *Econometrica*, 24, 315–335.

Nerlove, M (1983). Expectations, plans, and realisations in theory and practice. *Econometrica*, 51, 1251–1279.

Nerlove, M and Schurmann, T (1997). Expectations are neither rational or adaptive. Discussion Paper No. 97-01, Publikatationen Industrieokonmik und Internationale Unternehmensfuhrung.

Pesaran, MH (1987). *The Limits to Rational Expectations*. New York: Basil Blackwell, Inc.

Pesaran, MH (1990). Measurement of expectations and direct tests of the REH. In *Advanced Lectures in Quantitative Economics*, Van Der Ploag, F (ed.), Chap. 12, London: Academic Press.

Pesaran, MH (2000). Foreword. In *Price Expectations in Good and Financial Markets: New Developments in Theory and Empirical Research*, Gardes, F and Prat, G (eds). London: Edward Elgar.

Sheffrin, SM (1996). *Rational Expectations*, 2nd Ed. Cambridge: Cambridge University Press.

Smith, J and Mc Aleer, M (1995). Alternative procedures for converting qualitative response data to quantitative expectations: An application to Australian manufacturing. *Journal of Applied Econometrics*, 10, 165–185.

CHAPTER 20

CORPORATE GOVERNANCE AND MANAGERIAL RISK TAKING: EMPIRICAL STUDY IN THE TUNISIAN CONTEXT

Amel Belanes Aroui [*,†] *and Fatma Wyème Ben Mrad Douagi* [†,‡]

This research aims at pointing out the impact of some governance mechanisms susceptible to influence the managerial risk taking within the Tunisian firms. Therefore, we ought to highlight the specificities of these firms. On the basis of a 46-quoted firm sample observed over a one nine-year period spreading from 1996 to 2004, we draw out some interesting findings. First of all, the firm belonging to a financial industry, the State shareholding, the institutional shareholding, the concentration of the property as well as the accumulation of the functions of manager and chairman of board slow down the managerial risk taking within the Tunisian enterprises. However, the industry-based rules and the participation of supervisors into the capital incite the risk taking of Tunisian managers. Furthermore, our results reveal that the latter is positively influenced by both the size and the growth potential of Tunisian firms.

1 Introduction

Risk taking has been widely debated in the financial literature since the eighties. Several theoreticians mainly Bowman (1980), Tversky and Kahneman (1981), MacCrimmon and Wehrung (1986), March and Shapira (1987), and Bromiley (1991) shed some light into this problematic. Nowadays, further to the

*Corresponding author. 20 bis 1er Etage Rue 8204 Cité Elkhadra 1003 Tunis.
amel_bns@yahoo.fr
†University of FSEGT.
w.benmrad@voila.fr
‡Research Unit, Finance et Stratégie des Affaires — FIESTA — Institut Supérieur de Gestion de Tunis

scandals of Enron, Worldcom, Global Crossing and other well-known companies, that is managerial risk taking that has been specifically emphasized. Indeed, it becomes worth pointing out the determinants of managerial risk taking. The downfall of these big enterprises has been largely explained by the weakness of the systems of governance. In this vein, Healy and Palepu (2003) asserted that the main reason behind these bankruptcies is the dangerous and even deceitful strategies of management for the benefit of leaders and hence the renewal of public interest for governance problems whose background is so classic.

The agency theory, according to Barney and Hesterley (1996), already put in relief the risk taking of both agents (managers) and principals (shareholders). While the principals are indifferent toward risk as they can diversify their wallets through several firms, the agents are mainly risk averse. Donaldson (1961) and Williamson (1963) noted that managers' careers and remunerations are tied to the firms' welfare. Indeed, they considered the big link of the stability of the job and the payment of the manager with the situation of the firm. The latter often manifests an aversion of risk and is tempted to restrict his risk taking. Such attitude may create opportunity costs for the investor who prefers that the agent maximizes the enterprise value by intaking more risks. This hypothesis was approved by several theoreticians mainly Morck *et al.* (1988), Hoskisson *et al.* (1991), and Garen (1994). This gap between attitudes toward risk, according to Coffee (1988), Beatty and Zajac (1994), Tufano (1996), Dionne and Triki (2004) and Roger (2005), may feed interests conflicts between the two sides and hence agency problems.

Tosi and Gomez-Mejia (1989), Beatty and Zajac (1994) and Gomez-Mejia (1994) outlined in this frame that the challenge is to institute a reliable governance system that is susceptible to align the interests of managers and shareholders notably concerning risk taking. However, Tosi and Gomez-Mejia (1989) and Westphal and Zajac (1995) stipulated that in spite of the fundamental role of risk in agency theory, its formulation was very naive and restricted. Besides, behavioral theory bloomed and developed regardless of agency theory although they are complementary. In this vein, Wiseman and Gomez-Mejia (1998) proposed a behavioral agency model emphasizing managerial risk taking. This model on one hand underlines the efficiency of governance mechanisms dedicated to improve the agent's control by the principal and on the other hand points out the influence of these mechanisms on managerial risk taking. In the same way, Kose *et al.* (2005) appreciated the quality of investors' protection by the capacity to influence the investments choices of the manager and rationalize his risk taking. Thus, our main incentive is to contribute into the development of this twinning framework "agency theory — behavioral theory" that is ever relevant.

Our survey, elaborated in the Tunisian context, is certainly based upon researches concerning with both prospective theory and agency theory but especially suggests to explore the specificities of firms operating in developing countries. Therefore, we propose to highlight not only the governance mechanisms that are operating in emerging countries but above all the attitudes and behaviors of leaders in these countries. In fact, despite the multitude studies within industrialized countries, emergent countries and notably Tunisia is still a not thoroughly — explored field that is worth investigating. Our survey wishes to be the first study focusing on this frame in Tunisia. It tries to find out the impact of some governance mechanisms on the Tunisian managerial risk taking.

Indeed, most Tunisian managers seem to be risk averse and scarcely undertake risky projects. According to a recent survey led by the BVMT, Tunisian managers would rather opt for secure and certain investments such as accounts savings, Treasury bills, and cash vouchers than receipts in risky reinvestments such as the SICAR, the mutual funds, and stocks despite the various measures granted by authorities namely fiscal ones so as to promote such financial products.

Concerning the governance mechanisms, it should be pointed that the State is no longer a predominant shareholder in most Tunisian companies thanks to the State disengagement strategy and the privatization program that dated back to three decades. Nevertheless, the public authorities still constitute the ruling foundation and define a set of preventive and repressive measures so as to discipline the managers. These measures will certainly have a non-deniable impact on the Tunisian managerial risk taking.

Besides, most Tunisian firms are still family firms and managers have tendency to preserve the maximum of opacity on the family's business. More above, the code of the commercial societies stipulates that social decisions can only be taken by the shareholders gathered in a general assembly. This assembly is also held to control the manager's acts and approve the management accounts. In the same vein, shareholders can resort to the referee judge to notice the nullity of an action or even condemn some managerial decisions. The shareholders seem to be then the direct supervisors of managerial risk taking.

Furthermore, it is the board of supervisors that embodies the second organism of inspection. This board, whose members are already nominated by the shareholders, is invested with the most extended powers to act in all circumstances within the limits of business without encroaching on the powers reserved to the shareholders. The manager can neither act nor contract some agreements unless he got the authorization of the board and the approval of the general assembly. Thus, the board of supervisors controls the Tunisian manager and can extensively influence his risk taking.

As for the Stock Exchange market, its role in financing the economy remained pretty limited although its creation dated back to 1969, and this is due to the predominance of the State and banks. The latter remain the main financing sources of the economy despite the multitude efforts engaged in order to merchandize debt and capital and revive the stock market. Moreover, the Tunisian manager often escapes the financial market for fear to reveal to the public financial states or information concerning the capital repartition or the powers hierarchy. The role of the stock market proved then to be limited in controlling the Tunisian managerial risk.

This brief description of the Tunisian context reveals that the State is no longer the only guardian of shareholders' rights as it is in other emergent countries, through either its presence in the capital or the regulations that it puts in force as attested by La Porta *et al.* (2002). Shareholders can henceforth protect themselves and the board of supervisors also aims at controlling the manager. Our problematic sets then likewise: "what is the impact of the law, the shareholders and the board of supervisors on the risk taking of the Tunisian managers?"

The chapter is organized as follows. We first describe the conceptual framework about the impact of the governance mechanisms mentioned above on managerial risk taking. We then develop our research methodology as well as the econometrical modeling which resorts to the canonical analysis, what constitutes afterwards our third contribution. Indeed, most previous studies often opt for a simple and linear-modeling sample. Finally, we expose the empirical evidence observed within the Tunisian firms and conclude by the limits and perspectives of our research.

2 Literature Review

Several theoreticians namely Shavell (1979), Coffee (1988), Tosi and Gomez-Mejia (1989), Hoskisson *et al.* (1991), Beatty and Zajac (1994), Gomez-Mejia

(1994), and Westphal and Zajac (1995) proved the tied link between the governance mechanisms and managerial risk taking. Besides, Wiseman and Gomez-Mejia (1998) highlighted the explanatory and forecasting power of the models generated by the agency theory in explaining managerial risk taking. Nevertheless, the sense of this relation is still ambiguous.

The law, the shareholders, and the board of supervisors are some governance mechanisms that are effective in Tunisia and are susceptible to align the interests of shareholders and managers and to influence therefore managerial risk taking.

2.1 The Legal Setting

The role of law in protecting investors' interests was initially put in evidence in Jensen and Meckling's (1976) works. So, the legislation can play an important role to align the attitudes of managers toward the risk with those of shareholders.

La Porta *et al.* (2002) asserted that public authorities often impose strict enough rules so as to supervise managerial decisions and restrict their discretionary behaviors. They added that the role of public authorities proved to be more prevailing and eminent in developing countries, which are characterized by a weak protection of shareholders rights. They noted that the State shareholding in such countries becomes more significant and is usually conjugated in an intensive intervention of government, as an attempt to protect these shareholders. Besides, La Porta *et al.* (2002) proposed to allocate the task of protecting and developing the shareholders rights to benevolent delegates. More above, Walker *et al.* (2002) attested that several legal and judicial reforms have been taken in public corporations further to different financial scandals. Shareholders including the State require henceforth more mastery and control of any risk that the firm may face so as to preserve the firm value and improve it perpetually.

Maguire and Albright (2005) also assigned to the law a relevant and effective role in controlling managerial risk taking. The manager fears to be criticized or convicted by the court in full public and even to lose his job in case of serious mistakes resulting from his audacious and adventurous behavior. Such a measure is supposed to restrict managerial latitude and force managers to follow rational strategies presenting an attractive report in terms of return-risk. Furthermore, Maguire and Albright (2005) outlined the role of media in cultivating this culture of risk aversion and thus dissuade managers to undertake risky opportunities, and this through the various reports and enquiries condemning the adverse events and the abusive behaviors of managers.

In the same vein, Gebauer and Fleisch (2007) put in evidence the role of law and legislation in turning out the managers from risky projects. Although managers are convinced of the advantages of risk taking, they often estimate that political and social costs that may rise are much more noteworthy than latent gains. They are thus dissuaded from incurring risky projects. The managers are also afraid of losing their power and their authority and show then their reticence toward all new strategy susceptible to increase the potential of risk.

However, Kose *et al.* (2005) showed that systems privileging shareholders protection incite managers to invest in risky and profitable projects so as to accelerate the economic growth. Kose *et al.* (2005) appreciated the vigor of laws by the level of shareholders protection. It is according to this vigor that the manager will either give up risky projects capable to increase the firm value and drain deferred and enormous incomes or avoid such projects to protect his immediate and small profits. In fact, the consumption cost of small profits increases while the optimal satisfaction level of manager decreases. Kose *et al.* (2005) also proposed to design benevolent agents to protect and develop shareholders rights and showed the incontestable weight of social groups on managerial risk taking.

Finally, the impact of legislation upon managerial risk taking is not restricted to some domains but concerns all of them. Therefore, Whitfield (2004) announced that the educational institutions in addition to financial institutions began to institute this new tendency. Likewise, insurance companies recognized the contributions of managerial risk taking in value creation and resources allocation. However, Beasley *et al.* (2005) clarified that managerial risk taking must not be led in the same way as the legal setting varies through activities. According to them, bankers are the pioneers in managerial risk taking thanks to the last international reforms introduced by "Basel II, 2004". It seems that legislation wholly discourages managers from incurring risks but also punishes them when they do not maximize the firm value. Its impact on managerial risk taking is then confused and it depends on the specificity of the business itself.

2.2 The Shareholders

The shareholders embody the second mechanism of governance that is susceptible to align the managers' interests with theirs notably concerning risk taking. Their impact depends on both their concentration and their category.

Jensen and Meckling (1976) advanced that the property dispersal dissuades shareholders from exercising an active control upon the manager which lets the latter behave against the shareholders interests mainly when he differently perceives risk taking. In the same way, Shavell (1979) presumed that firms whose capital is detained by majority shareholders often undertake risky projects and that is this category of shareholders who incite the manager to adopt such a strategy. The main reason is to improve the firm profitability and hence shareholders wealth. Besides, Shleifer and Vishny (1986) and Holderness and Sheehan (1988) showed that property concentration allows the shareholders to control more efficiently the managerial decisions and compel them to work in their favor. Indeed, a scattered-property structure increases costs and necessary efforts to influence managerial decisions. The pressure of shareholders on managers is then less efficient. Thus, Gadhoum (1999) confirmed that the property concentration has a significant impact on managerial entrenchment and manager is therefore obligated to maximize his risk taking in order to enhance the value of the firm; otherwise he will be fired and replaced. Similarly, Beck and Levine (2002), Beck *et al.* (2003) attributed to this type of property an eminent role in the protection of outside shareholders rights against the abuses of managers particularly when they adopt too risky businesses without worrying about the threatening effects that can occur. Pritsker (2005) suggested in this respect that the presence of majority shareholders modulates the strategic choices of management in favor of firm value maximization and reduced therefore the conflicts inherent to managerial risk taking that may arise. Similarly, Charléty (2006) showed that "small" shareholders, individually, are not incited to play an active role, which seems too expensive compared with potential profits which are proportional to their participations in the capital. On the other hand, a "big" shareholder (or an association) may be interested in looking for any worthwhile information that might improve the value of his stocks. The managerial risk taking proves then to be stimulated by a concentrated-structure capital.

Also, the shareholding category may influence the managerial behavior. Smith and Stulz (1985) and Pearce and Zahra (1992) sustained that institutional investors are better aware and more competent than other shareholders. Besides, this category of shareholders can afford more efficient tools and professional means to actively control the management. They can even rent financial expertize services in order to appreciate the investments value and judge their opportunity in terms of risk-return. Likewise, Knopf and Teall (1996) advanced that institutional shareholders, thanks to their expertizes and their outside diversified portfolios, usually incite the manager to undertake riskier projects so as to maximize firm value and hence shareholders wealth. Wright *et al.* (1996) also showed that institutional shareholders deeply influence managerial risk taking and positively stimulate it. Dionne and Triki (2004) approved of this hypothesis but specified that only institutional shareholders detaining more than 5% of the capital are powerful to decrease the costs of information asymmetry and oblige the manager to adopt a measured-risk strategy to optimize the firm value. Nevertheless, Davis *et al.* (2005) showed a negative impact of block shareholders who would rather align their interests with those of managers in order not to gamble their welfare. Besides, Davis *et al.* (2005) advanced that such shareholders consider that is strategically more appropriate to cooperate with manager. We therefore expect that the presence of institutional shareholders wholly induce managerial risk taking.

More above, Rosenstein and Wyatt (1997) put in evidence the property concentration within the supervisors which may incite to efficiently control the management. The alignment of interests of both supervisors and shareholders should provide a better control of managerial decisions and behaviors and therefore contribute to the maximization of the firm value. Furthermore, Paquerot (1996) attested that the more the part of capital detained by the supervisors is important; the less a fraudulent and dishonest management is tolerated. The influence of the supervisors-shareholders on managerial risk taking is hence supposed to stimulate managerial risk taking.

2.3 *The Board of Supervisors*

The Board of supervisors constitutes the backbone of the governance. According to Jensen and Meckling (1976), the shareholders elect the supervisors to control the management and drive the firm strategy; what would incite managers to incur more risks and undertake riskier projects in order to enhance the value of the company.

In the same vein, Wiseman and Gomez-Mejia (1998) attested that a strong custody from the supervisors' board leads to hard-reached objectives; which stimulates managerial risk taking. Morellec and Smith (2005) already sustained the hypothesis that the board of supervisors can influence managerial risk taking. According to them, the board of supervisors cannot dictate the investment policy as the relative decisions are neither verifiable nor contractual although they are observable. Nevertheless, both financial strategy and managerial risk taking are observable and contractual. The board of supervisors can therefore influence such decisions and even threaten the manager when he shows his lack of either diligence or responsibility. However, Charléty (2006) considered that the board efficiency is often controversial since the supervisors are not always chosen for their expertize and competence nor remunerated according to the achieved performance. Similarly, Healy and Palepu (2003) signaled that some supervisors of Enron were conscious of the too risky and abusive behavior of some managers and even reached the true information not released in reports, but did not pronounce. It seems then relevant to discern the impact of the supervisors' board on managerial risk taking according to its composition, its size, and its chairmanship.

First of all, Fama and Jensen (1983) considered that the existence of external supervisors, which are outside the firm, increases the viability of the board and reduces the probability of collision for the expropriation of shareholders wealth by the manager. Short *et al.* (1999) noted that independent supervisors assure the mission of strategic consultant and controllers for the manager and approach with objectivity the managerial decisions. Therefore, the manager must be careful to take prudent and rational measures in terms of risk-return. Besides, Borokhovich *et al.* (2004) showed that firms whose boards essentially consist of external supervisors usually undertake risky projects but above all afford the most sophisticated instruments to manage and control risks. Beasley *et al.* (2005) also put in evidence that the supervisors' independence increases the efficiency and the perspicacity of the board. That is why they asserted that such a board positively influences managerial risk taking and guarantees its conditions of success. Likewise, Hossain *et al.* (2000) advanced that the presence of internal administrators, employees of the enterprise, provides the manager with a more important discretion and lets him have an opportunist behavior through either underinvesting or undertaking too risky projects. They are often incited to enhance the manager's career without worrying about the firm performance as their careers are also tied to the manager's one. However, Buckley and Van Der Nat (2003) and Dionne and Triki (2004) found that the presence of external supervisors is meaningless. According to them, such supervisors do not stimulate managerial risk taking because either they do not have the required profile and necessary formation or they do not know how to manage risk or even do not arrange worthwhile information. Healy and Palepu (2003) also attested that although most members of Enron board were independent, they were inefficient in their mission. Thus, it seems that external supervisors are supposed to stimulate managerial risk taking but this is not always true.

The size of the board of supervisors can also have an impact on managerial risk taking. Adams and Mehran (2003) revealed that large-board firms usually recorded higher performances associated with higher managerial risk taking. They also found that small-board firms can be easily manipulated and influenced by managers. In the same vein, Blanchard and Dionne (2004) suggested that the more the number of supervisors increases, the more developed and sophisticated are the instruments used to hedge, which justifies a more intensive managerial risk taking. However, Lipton and Lorsh (1992) noted that even though the board capacities increase with its size, this advantage will be counterbalanced by inherent additional costs due to the lack of coordination and synchronization of efforts. The process of exchange of information and decision making becomes more difficult and slow. Besides, Wiseman and Gomez-Mejia (1998) stipulated that by increasing the number of supervisors, criteria proposed to appreciate managerial behavior diversify and become more ambiguous. The manager becomes then indecisive and confused and hence risk averse and prudent. Thus, managerial risk taking seems to be reduced by the enlargement of board size.

Finally, the board of supervisors' chairmanship can also influence managerial risk taking. Whenever, the manager heads the board of supervisors, he becomes more powerful and abuses that. He would rather minimize his risk taking in order to secure himself without worrying about the firm value. His primordial objective is to maximize his wealth even at the expense of the firm value. Therefore, several theoreticians denounce the duality because of the abuse of power by the manager. Indeed, neither the impartiality of the manager's surveillance nor the determination of the respective responsibilities will be clear in case of duality. Boyd (1995) affirmed that firms that are separating these two functions are the most effective. Not only they enjoy better vision of strategies but also better leadership with regard to an independent president of the board. Lorsch and Maclever (1989) concluded in this regard that the separation of these two functions can help the board of supervisors to control the agency problems. Gary and Gleason (1999) added that the conflicts of interests and hence the agency costs become more pronounced when the manager is at the same time the chairman of the board. On one hand, the manger exercises more power concerning the board decisions. On the other hand, he controls the required information for the other supervisors' functions. Thus, it seems that the separation of the post of manager and chairman of board allows maximizing the firm value and incites by the same way managerial risk taking. However, Dionne and Triki (2004) found that the fact that the manager presides or not the board of supervisors does have no significant effect on managerial risk taking.

To summarize, we have just presented an overview about theoretical and empirical framework dealing with the potential influence of some governance mechanisms on managerial risk taking. We continue to explore this axis of research by concentrating on the specificities of Tunisian enterprises.

3 Impact of the Governance Mechanisms on Managerial Risk Taking in the Tunisian Enterprises

We are going to describe at first the sample of the considered companies. Then, we shall present the variables held in the analysis as well as the econometric model to be estimated. Finally, we shall expose the found empirical results.

3.1 Presentation of the Sample

The research deals with the impact of some governance mechanisms on the Tunisian managerial risk taking. Major difficulty concerns the availability of information collected from the annual reports of the Council of Capital Market and the official bulletins of the Tunisian Stock Exchange. Indeed, some information related to some explanatory variables is not available on the totality of the survey period. Also, Tunisian firms that are non-quoted have not to reveal the needed information. For such reasons, we cannot spread the survey for all Tunisian companies. The sample is only made up of the 46 quoted firms. Furthermore, in a purpose of robustness and efficiency of estimations, we intend to consider them on a temporal horizon of nine years going from 1996 to 2004. Combining cross-section and time series data is worthwhile as it provides a wealth of information. Besides, the use of panel data allows increasing the sample size and hence the gain in degrees of freedom which is particularly relevant when a relatively large number of regressors and a small number of firms are used which is our case here. Indeed, the number of observations increases from 46 to 369. However, some firms are not observed on the totality of the period of study. We have then a non-completed panel.

3.2 Variables Measures

In what follows, we are going to present the various variables, both endogenous and exogenous, that will be used throughout our empirical research.

3.2.1 Endogenous Variables

Our research focuses on managerial risk taking and tries to find out which mechanism of governance is susceptible to influence it in the Tunisian context. Our endogenous variables deal so with the managerial risk taking. On one hand, some researchers namely Dionne and Triki (2004), Beatty *et al.* (2005), Davis *et al.* (2005), and Coles *et al.* (2006) appreciated the risk taking of the manager through his payment in stock options. These researchers approve of the arguments of Coffee (1988), Hoskisson *et al.* (1991), and Mehran (1995) that a manager rewarded accordingly to the firm performance, his risk aversion decreases and would prefer risky projects with increasing variance. However, this argument did not enjoy the unanimity according to Beatty and Zajac (1994). Some researchers of whom Shavell (1979) and Lewellen (2004) suggested that when the manager supports too much risk, he becomes excessively risk averse in spite of stock options. Besides, it seems that the manager payment is rather a determinant than a measure of managerial risk taking.

On the other hand, some researchers namely Zahra (2005) linked the risk taking of manager to the risk of the company given that the manager is the decision maker. Therefore, Chen and Steiner (1999), Yoshikawa *et al.* (2004), Beatty *et al.* (2005), Kose *et al.* (2005), and Coles *et al.* (2006) attested that business diversification was abundantly used in financial literature as indication of a moderate and careful risk taking. Other researchers of whom Crutchley and Hansen (1989), Jensen *et al.* (1992), Davis *et al.* (2005), and Coles *et al.* (2006) estimated the risk taking of manager by expenses in research and development and capital expenditures. As for Zahra (2005), he evaluated it through the strategies of alliances adopted on the local market or abroad, the conquest of new local or foreign markets and the investments in new technologies. We cannot exploit such measures for lack of data. We are going on the other hand to consider the volatility of both stock-exchange returns and accounting performance as well as the indebtedness ratio so as to appreciate Tunisian managerial risk taking.

The first endogenous variable, RISK1, represents the volatility of the stock-exchange profitability. It is defined by the standard deviation of the registered stock-exchange returns. This variable according to Chen and Steiners (1999),

Guay (1999), and Coles *et al.* (2006) translates the risk taking of the manager as estimated and felt by the financial market through the fluctuations of the values of companies. It is estimated that the more managerial risk taking increases, the more this volatility increases. Besides, managerial risk taking can be appreciated through the financial situation of the firm and specifically through the volatility of accounting performance and the financial leverage. One distinguishes then two other endogenous variables RISK2 and RISK3.

The second endogenous variable, RISK2, measures the volatility of the accounting performance. It is defined by the standard deviation of net incomes reported to total assets. It is an approximation of the risk of operations linked to the exploitation and reveals the manager's strategy according to which he behaves, risky or moderate. This was held by Leuz *et al.* (2003), Cebenoyan and Strahan (2004), Kose *et al.* (2005) who suggested in this respect that the management of results allows the leaders to hide the real profitability of the company. They added that a strong protection of investors limits the deprived profits of the manager and restricts his discretion. One foresees that the higher is managerial risk taking, the higher is this volatility.

The third endogenous variable, RISK3, is measured by the report between total debts and stockholders equities. It is the third appreciation of managerial risk taking and reveals itself through the rate of debts which presses enormously on the potential of growth of the firm. This measure was used by Myers (1977), Chen and Steiner (1999) and Coles *et al.* (2006) who asserted that managerial risk taking can be appreciated through an aggressive indebtedness policy. Chen and Steiner (1999) noted in this regard that excessive debts increase the risk of bankruptcy. It is the financial leverage that leads to a non-diversifiable managerial risk. Besides, we appreciated the rate of debts by total debts reported to total assets, total debts reported to total market value, and total debts reported to market value of stocks. It is the last ratio that provided the most robust estimations. We expect that the more aggressive is managerial risk taking, the higher is this ratio.

3.2.2 Exogenous Variables

The exogenous variables are relative to the mechanisms of governance that might influence managerial risk taking. This problem was abundantly approached by the financial literature and several variables were proposed. In our study, we hold the legal context, the property structure and the board of supervisors as governance mechanisms susceptible to influence Tunisian managerial risk taking. These mechanisms seem to be *a priori* the most significant mechanisms of governance in the Tunisian context. As variable of control, we hold the size of the firm and its potential of growth.

3.2.2.1 The legal context

To estimate the impact of rules on managerial risk taking, we resort to three explanatory variables corresponding to sector-based ruling, the membership of the firm to the financial industry and the State shareholding.

La Porta *et al.* (2002) introduced the quality of accounting norms to appreciate the power of the rule. Kose *et al.* (2005) resorted to an anti-manager index allowing evaluating the degree of protection of shareholders rights. In the Tunisian context, one can classify the quoted firms in two classes according to the degree of rule governing the sector where evolves the firm. We introduce a dummy variable REG to account for this difference between regulated and non-regulated firms. REG is worth 1 if the firm is regulated and 0 otherwise. The regulation is more stuff in financial industry, aerial transport, telecommunications, bio-pharmacy, and dairy farming. We expect that such regulation will have a negative impact on managerial risk taking like Maguire and Albright (2005) and Gebauer and Fleich (2007). However, we are anxious to discern among the regulated companies those that are financial having seen the specificities. Prior work implicitly recognizes differences in determinants in financial decisions between financial and non-financial firms by excluding financial firms from the analysis. In this work, we explicitly recognize the potential difference in managerial risk taking between them by adding a dummy variable FIN to account for this difference and one expects that it would have a positive impact on the risk-taking following the example of Beasley *et al.* (2005).

The third variable, ETCP, measures the shareholding of the State. According to La Porta *et al.* (2002), the shareholding of the State increases in emerging countries and conjugates in an intervention stressed by the government. Such involvement is considered as an attempt to protect shareholders rights and discipline non-competent managers. Therefore, we estimate that the more this percentage increases, the more managerial risk taking decreases.

3.2.2.2 The shareholding structure

We are interested in three aspects of shareholding structure: the concentration of the property, the institutional property, and the property of supervisors.

Property concentration. The concentration of the property, CONCP, is measured by the percentage of the actions possessed by majority shareholders detaining more than 5% of the capital. This percentage is justified by several authors mainly Dionne and Triki (2004) and constitutes a significant threshold to exercise control on behalf of shareholders. According to Shavell (1979), Shleifer and Vishny (1986), and Pritsker (2005), majority shareholders incite the manager to adopt risky projects in order to maximize the firm value. We estimate a positive relationship between managerial risk taking and the part owned by majority shareholders in the capital.

Institutional property. Institutional property, INSCP, is measured by the proportion of capital detained by institutional investors. Pearce and Zahra (1992), Wright *et al.* (1996), and Dionne and Triki (2004) confirmed the relevant role of these investors in controlling the manager and inciting his risk taking so as to improve the performance. We guess that institutional property positively influences managerial risk taking.

Supervisors' property. The property of the supervisors, ADMCP, is measured by the percentage of the actions owned by the members of board of supervisors. According to Paquerot (1996) and Rosenstein and Wyatt (1997), the board of supervisors constitutes one of the most effective mechanisms of control notably for the control and the discipline of managers notably as regards their management of risk. One expects that the more percentage possessed by the supervisors increases, the more they are implied and the more managerial behavior becomes risky in order to enhance the value of the firm.

3.2.2.3 The board of supervisors

The variables used to put in evidence the impact of the board on managerial risk taking concerns its composition, its size, and its chairmanship.

Composition of the board. The composition of the board of supervisors is estimated by the variable ADMEX representing the percentage of external supervisors. It is calculated by their number brought back to the total number of supervisors within the board. According to Borokhovich *et al.* (2004) and Beasley *et al.* (2005), the more this percentage increases, the more the instruments used to hedge are sophisticated, which justifies an intensive managerial risk taking. One foresees then a positive coefficient associated with this variable.

The size of the board. The size of the board, TAILCA, is simply measured with the total number of supervisors. Adams and Mehran (2003) and Blanchard and Dionne (2004) revealed that the large-board firms recorded the highest performances thanks to a more thorough risk taking. Thus, we expect that the more the number of supervisors increases, the more managerial risk taking increases.

The duality: Chairman of the board and manager. The duality, DUAL, is a dummy variable. It equals 1 if the chairman of the board is at the same time the manager and 0 otherwise. According to Boyd (1995) and Gary and Gleason (1999), the president of the board plays an eminent role in the management control whenever he does not fill himself the function of manager. In such case, it is more allowed to control the behavior of the manager and incite him to adopt risky projects in order to enhance the value of the firm. Therefore, the coefficient associated with this variable is estimated to be negative.

3.2.2.4 The firm size

It is the first variable of control and it measures the size of the firm, SIZE. It is approximated by the logarithm naperian of total assets. We also measured it by the logarithm naperian of total market value. But, it is the first measure that has provided the most robust results. Smith and Stulz (1985) suggested that the costs of managerial risk taking are proportional to the firm size. The managers of small firms will be then more risk averse. Besides, Howard (1988) noted that as the firm grows, its wealth increases and so does its ability to manage bigger and riskier projects. Dionne and Triki (2004), Beatty *et al.* (2005) and Walls (2005) approved of such results and concluded that managerial risk taking is a heavy burden for small firms. In our study, we expect similar result, which is a positive relationship.

3.2.2.5 The firm growth potential

The second variable of control is the growth potential of the firm, MBVA. It is measured by the ratio market-to-book value of assets. Gay and Nam (1999), Knopf *et al.* (2002), Dionne and Triki (2004), Davis *et al.* (2005) and Coles *et al.* (2006) gave evidence that external financing is much more expensive than internal one. The managers would rather select riskier projects so as to generate more internal funds to finance the new opportunities of investments. Managerial risk taking is then justified as a means to avoid the underinvestment problem. One foresees a positive relationship between managerial risk taking and this growth potential.

3.3 Econometrical Modeling

To appreciate managerial risk taking, we appeal to three endogenous variables namely RISK1, RISK2, and RISK3. As for governance mechanisms, they are put in evidence through nine other variables namely REG, FIN, ETCP, CONCP, INSCP, ADMCP, ADMEX, TAILCA, and DUAL. The two variables SIZE and MBVA are variables of control. Actually, all of these variables interact and it is worthwhile highlighting such inter-relations. Thus, we resort to canonical analysis, like Zahra (2005), which seems according to him the most suitable specification for our test although it is little exploited in the finance literature.

The canonical analysis consists in understanding the linear combinations which exist between a group of variables to explain and an other group of explanatory variables. It consists then at determining the canonical interrelationships between these two sets of variables. Indeed, when n firms are described by two sets of variables, one tries to analyze the probable relationships existing between these two sets in order to know whether they describe or not the same properties. If these two sets are confounded, only one is sufficient for the statistical description. Likewise, if these two spaces are orthogonal in R_n; that is the two sets of variables reveal different phenomena. Between these two extreme cases, one is interested in the relative positions of these two spaces of data while looking for the most closed elements. The aim of canonical analysis consists in looking for couples of variables in maximal correlation. Such aim is fundamental as it is met in other methods notably in correspondences analysis and discriminative analysis. This method of evaluation was initiated by Hotelling (1936) and extended afterwards to several sets of variables by Horst (1961). This aspect of analysis had remained unfamiliar and even ignored for a long time, considered without convenient or practical utility. Pontier *et al.* (1987) revived this topic and outlined how it is meaningful to determine pertinent linear functions of a set of variables without any potential correlation with the other set. These authors suggested calling complete canonical analysis whenever the latter is thoroughly developed and pushed until the end.

4 Empirical Results

Two sets of results will be displayed and discussed in this section: those corresponding to the descriptive features of the retained variables and those dealing with the impact of governance mechanisms on Tunisian managerial risk taking.

Table 1: Descriptive statistics of endogenous variables.

Variables	Mean	St-deviation	Minimum	Maximum
RISK1	0.344	0.230	0.054	1.248
RISK2	0.026	0.027	0.002	0.107
RISK3	7.794	9.422	0.000	39.828

Table 1 summarizes some descriptive statistics of endogenous variables that are used in our modeling.

According to the above table, Tunisian companies are characterized by an average volatility of 0.344 of the accounting profitability (net incomes reported to total assets) whereas stock returns volatility is much less and is worth 0.026. The third measure of risk reveals that Tunisian firms are highly indebted. The rate of raised debts exceeds on average 7.7 due to the frequent and perpetual appeal to banking loans. These three measures enormously fluctuate through the 46 enterprises all over the considered period.

Table 2 puts in evidence the high correlation between the three endogenous variables, which justifies the resort to the canonical analysis.

Besides, we are interested in the pertaining descriptive statistics of exogenous variables held in our analysis. Table 3 sums up some statistical indicators of these data.

The table below shows that 63.4% of the Tunisian enterprises are regulated, that means they are either financial firms operating in aerial transport, telecommunications, bio-pharmacy, and dairy farming. It is worth noting that the volatility of both accounting profitability and stock returns are globally higher in non-regulated firms than regulated ones while the indebtedness ratio is more raised in regulated firms thanks to their tied relationship with banks. These results are recapitulated in Table 4.

Nevertheless, it should be noted here that regulated firms include financial institutions which are usually especially indebted. That is why the ratio

Table 2: Correlation matrix of endogenous variables.

Variables	RISK1	RISK2	RISK3
RISK1	1.000		
RISK2	0.291	1.000	
RISK3	−0.215	−0.480	1.000

Table 3: Descriptive statistics of exogenous variables.

Variables	Mean	St-deviation	Minimum	Maximum
REG	0.634	0.482	0.000	1.000
FIN	0.415	0.493	0.000	1.000
ETCP	0.098	0.191	0.000	0.678
CONCP	0.640	0.172	0.312	0.983
INSCP	0.622	0.202	0.026	0.939
ADMCP	0.569	0.204	0.053	0.983
ADMEX	0.497	0.230	0.000	0.900
TAILCA	9.881	1.867	5.000	12.000
DUAL	0.762	0.427	0.000	1.000
TAILLE	18.725	1.683	16.055	22.179
MBVA	1.337	0.624	0.574	7.099

Table 4: Evolution of managerial risk taking through regulated versus non regulated firms.

Variables	Number	Mean	St-deviation	Minimum	Maximum
Non regulated firms					
RISK1	135	0.364	0.282	0.054	1.248
RISK2	135	0.036	0.025	0.004	0.084
RISK3	135	1.428	2.101	0.000	15.071
Regulated firms					
RISK1	234	0.333	0.194	0.101	0.985
RISK2	234	0.021	0.027	0.002	0.107
RISK3	234	11.467	10.032	0.000	39.828

of indebtedness is on average more raised in regulated firms. Thus, we introduce another dummy variable FIN which separate out financial firms of which banks, insurance companies, societies of investments, and leasing. The latter constitute 65.4% of the regulated firms. One notices that the volatility of accounting profitability as well as stock returns is raised, whereas the indebtedness ratio is reduced in non-financial firms. Indeed, financial institutions often present an extremely heavy financial structure of debts, part of which is at sight monetary. These results are summarized in Table 5.

Besides, we notice that the Tunisian State possesses an average percentage of 9.8% in the capital of quoted societies and it varies from 0% to 67.8%. This percentage is reduced enough and it is already online with the objectives

Table 5: Evolution of managerial risk taking through financial versus non-financial firms.

Variables	Number	Mean	St-deviation	Minimum	Maximum
Non-financial firms					
RISK1	216	0.415	0.263	0.054	1.248
RISK2	216	0.035	0.027	0.004	0.107
RISK3	216	3.601	4.342	0.000	18.159
Financial firms					
RISK1	153	0.244	0.114	0.101	0.592
RISK2	153	0.015	0.022	0.002	0.097
RISK3	153	13.713	11.314	0.001	39.828

of the State disengagement and the wave of privatizations of public companies that have occurred within the structural adjustment plan. Such disengagement allows the development of other disciplinary mechanisms substituting for the State such as the majority shareholders, the institutional shareholders and the board of supervisors. Indeed, the State is no more the only protector of minority shareholders rights.

Furthermore, according to descriptive statistics, the structure of property of Tunisian enterprises is concentrated among the majority shareholders, for an average of 64% of the capital; and hence the irrefutable impact of majority shareholders on managerial risk taking. Similarly, the institutional shareholders and the supervisors–shareholders detain on average and, respectively, 62% and 57% of the capital of Tunisian firms. That is why we could not deny any more the eminent weight of the institutional shareholders and the supervisors–shareholders on Tunisian managers' decision makings.

More above, the external supervisors represent on average 50% of the board and can even reach 90%. Therefore, we stipulate that external supervisors can influence managerial risk taking thanks to their potential power within the board. We also notice that the average size of the board is of 10 members and it varies from 5 to 12; what puts again in evidence the incontestable role of the board of supervisors. However, this board is run for 76% of the enterprises by the general manager, what makes contestable the influence of the board of supervisors on managerial risk taking.

As variables of control, we retain two measures corresponding to the size of the firm as well as its potential of growth. The above descriptive statistics show a considerable variability inter- and intra-firms and hence their worth considering.

Also, we test the degree of possible correlation among the exogenous variables in order to verify the robustness of our estimations. We construct the matrix of correlation of exogenous variables which appears as follows in Table 6.

This matrix shows a globally weak interrelationship between various independent variables, what supposes the absence of the problem of multi-colinearity among the different variables and hence the validity of our modeling and the robustness of our estimations.

At this stage, we attempt to understand the various determinants inherent to governance and that might influence Tunisian managerial risk taking. To be able to identify the impact of the various mechanisms of governance, we expose in Table 7 the estimation results of canonical analysis. The canonical ratio rises to 0.9479 which approves of the robustness of the model.

Our analysis is made up of three axes of research corresponding to the governance mechanisms that may influence Tunisian managerial risk taking namely the legal context, the structure of property and the board of supervisors. We present for each mechanism the econometrical signification associated with the relative variables as well as the financial implications.

Concerning the industry-based rules, the results of regression reveal a meaningful and negative relation between the State shareholding and Tunisian managerial risk taking. This result corresponds to the suggestions of La Porta *et al.* (2002). Indeed, in public companies, contracts programs impose the control of the State over the manager and consequently limit the area of his risk taking. Nevertheless, this vertical control approved to be inefficient and a movement of privatization was observed. The governance structure is no longer vertical but horizontal. The latter consists on sector-based rules and pretends a better monitoring. This measure is highlightened through the variable REG. The significant and positive coefficient of this variable foretells that operational efficiency is only obtained by inciting managerial risk taking what confirms the results of Kose *et al.* (2005). However, we disapprove the comments of Beasley *et al.* (2005) as we find that managerial risk taking is restricted and slowed down in financial institutions. Perhaps, this is due to the fragility of this sector and its eminent role in financing the Tunisian economy.

Involving the structure of property, we notice that the concentration of shareholding has a negative impact on managerial risk taking. Thus, we deduce that majority shareholders check and discourage the risk taking of Tunisian manager, what contradicts the hypotheses of Shavell (1979), Ghadoum (1999), and Charléty (2006). This phenomenon may be owed

Table 6: Correlation matrix of exogenous variables.

Variables	REG	FIN	ETCAP	ADMEX	TAILCA	DUAL	CONCP	INSCP	ADMCP	TAILLE	MBVA
REG	1.000										
FIN	0.639	1.000									
ETCAP	0.224	0.100	1.000								
ADMEX	0.101	0.180	−0.436	1.000							
TAILCA	0.428	0.373	0.160	−0.020	1.000						
DUAL	0.050	−0.110	0.007	−0.128	−0.172	1.000					
CONCP	−0.188	−0.228	−0.063	−0.061	−0.278	0.179	1.000				
INSCP	0.090	−0.103	0.018	−0.030	−0.067	0.206	0.616	1.000			
ADMCP	0.004	−0.165	−0.039	−0.350	−0.058	0.289	0.633	0.464	1.000		
TAILLE	0.536	0.582	0.254	0.020	0.560	0.003	−0.334	−0.187	−0.267	1.000	
MBVA	−0.362	−0.236	−0.103	0.082	−0.028	−0.025	0.054	0.133	−0.040	−0.271	1.000

Table 7: Estimation results of canonical analysis.

		Coefficients	*t* student
Endogenous variables			
Market profitability volatility	RISK1	1.208	18.31***
Accounting profitability volatility	RISK2	6.155	9.37***
Indebtedness ratio	RISK3	0.042	25.67***
Exogenous variables			
	REG	0.464	7.87***
Legal context	FIN	−0.350	−6.97***
	ETCAP	−0.517	−4.50***
	CONCP	−0.610	−3.58***
Property structure	INSTCP	−0.438	−3.59***
	ADMCP	0.266	1.96*
	ADMEX	−0.045	−0.44
Board of supervisors	TAILCA	0.012	0.94
	DUAL	−0.110	−2.38**
Size	TAILLE	0.064	7.57***
Growth potential	MBVA	0.117	3.65***

Notes: Canonical: 0.9479 Correlations: 0.7809 0.3448
(*), (**), (***), signification at 10%, 5%, and 1% levels.

to the increase of the risk incurred by the majority shareholders further to the increase of managerial risk taking. In the same vein, our survey puts in evidence that institutional shareholders have a significant and negative effect on Tunisian managerial risk taking. This result contours those of Pearce and Zahras (1992) and Dionne and Triki (2004) but confirms those of Davies *et al.* (2005) who showed that within a strategic perspective, institutional shareholders often consider more convenient to cooperate with the manager. As for the shareholders–supervisors, they stimulate managerial risk taking. This result joins the suggestions of Paquerot (1996) and Rosenstein and Wyatt (1997) who stipulated that more important is the part of capital detained by supervisors, the less flawed and failing management is tolerated.

As for the third mechanism of governance which is the board of supervisors, the regression results confirm that neither the size nor the presence of external supervisors have a statistically significant impact. These results were approved of by Buckley and Van Der Nat (2003) and Dionne and Triki (2004). However, we notice that duality manager–president of the board has a statistically significant and negative impact on managerial risk taking within the

Tunisian context. Dionne and Triki (2004) explained that the accumulation of the functions of president of the board and general manager allows the leader to accumulate more power. He would rather minimize his risk taking to secure himself without worrying about the value of the firm. His primordial objective is to maximize his wealth even at the expense of the firm's one.

Finally, we notice that both the size of the firm and its potential of growth do have a significant and positive impact on managerial risk taking. On one hand, our results approve of the hypotheses advanced by Smith and Stulz (1985), Howard (1988), Beatty *et al.* (2005), and Walls (2005) that the costs of risk taking are proportional to firm size. On the other hand, our results re-close those of Froot *et al.* (1993), Knopf *et al.* (2002) and Dionne and Triki (2005) stipulating that managers can take advantage of new opportunities of investment and commit in risky projects in order to increase the firm wealth.

5 Conclusion

The aim of this study is to identify, at first, the governance mechanisms that might influence the risk taking of the manager within the Tunisian companies and to, secondly, highlight their corresponding impact. But above all, we take care to accentuate the specificities of Tunisian firms. On the basis of a 46-quoted firm sample observed on a nine-year period spreading from 1996 to 2004, we put in evidence three meaningful mechanisms of governance namely the rules, the structure of property, and the board of supervisors.

The empirical validation of our study uncovers a considerable shareholding of the State, what already constitutes a specificity of emergent countries. This dimension seems to be a double-edged weapon. In fact, it is, on one hand, an attempt to protect shareholders interests against managers' abuses. On other hand, it drives a degradation of the performance of firms. Therefore, the sector-based ruling appears more powerful and stiff. Such a measure stimulates Tunisian managerial risk taking in order to increase the value of firms and improve their competitiveness. Besides, managerial risk taking seems to be more intensive in non-financial firms. Our results also reveal that most Tunisian enterprises present a concentrated property with a considerable dominance of institutional shareholders. However, not only the majority shareholders but also the institutional shareholders do not incite the manager to adopt risky strategies, whereas the shareholders–supervisors do stimulate Tunisian managerial risk taking. In addition to this, we notice that most Tunisian managers are meanwhile chairman of the boards of their corresponding firms.

Nevertheless, this duality has a negative impact on risk taking. Actually, the leader becomes more averse toward risk and his concern of his self safety dominates his anxiety about the firm value improvement. Finally, our survey attests that the risk taking of the Tunisian manager is positively influenced by the size of the firm and the potential of growth as well.

To conclude, it is worth noting that the impact of governance mechanisms on managerial risk taking within the Tunisian firms presents some divergent results with regard to the financial literature, and hence the reason why the firms features and the context specificities should be outlined. The adopted models of governance depend essentially on characteristics of the context in which evolve the considered firms. Therefore, our survey could offer a modest trial to shed some light on the impact of some governance mechanisms on managerial risk taking in the Tunisian context as a sample of an emergent market.

Last but not least, Lewellen (2004) suggested that no instrument could claim to stimulate or to slow down the risk aversion of the manager unless some necessary and sufficient conditions are required. Thus, we ought to add other pertinent factors. It would be interesting to duplicate this type of investigation on the totality of Tunisian firms to point out further sectorial differences characterized by very divergent levels of risk taking. Also, the survey can be enhanced by considering the manager's individual characteristics such as his risk aversion, his self confidence, his age, his experience. Indeed, this research belongs to a very appealing frame joining the prospective theory and the agency theory and hence the relevance of psychological and behavioral characteristics of the manager. Moreover, although the resort to canonical analysis has resolved the problem of endogeneity of the managerial risk taking components, another econometrical technique consists in synthesizing all these variables into one global risk index. Several authors proceeded to the construction of such an index especially in the governance field. These are in fact some promising ways for future research.

References

Adams, R and Mehran, H (2003). Board structure, banking firm performance and the bank holding company organizational form. *Federal Reserve Bank of Chicago Proceedings*, 408–422.

Barney, JB and Hesterley, W (1996). *Organizational Economics: Understanding the Relationship between Organizations and Economic Analysis*. In *Handbook of Organization Studies*, Cleg, SR, Hardy, C and Nord, WR (eds.), pp. 115–147. London: Sage.

Beasley, MS, Clune, R and Hermanson, DR (2005). Enterprise risk management: An empirical analysis of factors associated with the extent of implementation. *Journal of Accounting and Public Policy*, 24, 521–531.

Beatty, A, Gron, A and Jorgensen, B (2005). Corporate risk management: Evidence from product liability. *Journal of Financial Intermediation*, 14, 152–178.

Beatty, RP and Zajac, EJ (1994). Managerial incentives, monitoring and risk bearing: A study of executive compensation, ownership and board structure in initial public offerings. *Administrative Science Quarterly*, 39, 313–335.

Beck, T and Levine, R (2002). Industry growth and capital allocation: Does having a market- or bankbased system matter? *Journal of Financial Economics*, 64, 147–180.

Beck, T, Demirguç-Kunt, A and Levine, R (2003). Law, endowments, and finance. *Journal of Financial Economics*, 70, 137–181.

Blanchard, D and Dionne, G (2004). The case for independent risk management committees. *Risk*, 17(5), S19–S21.

Borokhovich, KA, Brunarski, KR, Crutchley, CE and Simkins, BJ (2004). Board composition and corporate investment in interest rate derivatives. *Journal of Financial Research*, 27, 199–216.

Bowman, EH (1980). A risk/return paradox for strategic management. *Sloan Management Review*, 21, 17–31.

Boyd, BK (1995). CEO duality and firm performance: A contingency model. *Strategic Management Journal*, 16, 301–312.

Bromiley, P (1991). Testing a causal model of corporate risk taking and performance. *Academy of Management Journal*, 34, 37–59.

Buckley, A and Van der Nat, M (2003). Derivatives and the non-executive director. *European Management Journal*, 21, 389–397.

Cebenoyan, AS and Strahan, PE (2004). Risk management, capital structure and lending at bank. *Journal of Banking and Finance*, 28, 19–43.

Charléty, P (2006). Les Stock-options: un mode de rémunération controversé. *Les Echos*.

Chen, CR and Steiner, TL (1999). Managerial ownership and agency conflicts: A nonlinear simultaneous equation analysis of managerial ownership, risk taking, debt policy and dividend policy. *The Financial Review*, 34, 119–136.

Coffee, JC (1988). Shareholders versus managers: The strain in the corporate web. In *Knights, Raiders and Targets: The Impact of the Hostile Takeovers*, Coffee, JC, Lowenstein, L and Rose-Ackerman, S (eds.), pp. 77–134. New York: Oxford University Press.

Coles, JL, Daniel, ND and Naveen, L (2006). Managerial incentives and risk-taking. *Journal of Financial Economics,* 79, 431–468.

Crutchley, C and Hansen, RS (1989). A test of the agency theory of managerial ownership, corporate leverage and corporate dividends. *Financial Management*, 18, 36–46.

Davis, JR, Hillier, D and McColgan, P (2005). Ownership structure, managerial behavior and corporate value. *Journal of Corporate Finance*, 11, 645–660.

Dionne, G and Triki, T (2004). On risk management determinants: What really matters? Working Paper, CIRPEE, 0417.

Donaldson, G (1961). *Corporate Debt Capacity: A Study of Corporate Debt Policy and the Determinants of Corporate Debt Capacity*. Boston: Harverd University Press.

Fama, EF and Jensen, MC (1983). Agency problems and residual claims. *Journal of Law and Economics*, 26, 301–325.

Froot, K, Scharfstein, D and Stein, J (1993). Risk management: Coordinating corporate investment and financing decisions. *Journal of Finance*, 48, 1629–1658.

Gadhoum, Y (1999). Potential effects on the manager's entrenchment and shareholdings on competitiveness. *European Journal of Operational Research*, 118, 332–349.

Garen, JE (1994). Executive compensation and principal agent theory. *Journal of Political Economy*, 102, 1175–1199.

Gary, S and Gleason, E (1999). Board structure, ownership and financial distress in banking firms. *International Review of Economics and Finance*, 8, 281–292.

Gay, G and Nam, J (1999). The underinvestment problem and corporate derivatives use. *Financial Management* 27, 53–69.

Gebauer, H and Fleisch, E (2007). An investigation of the relationship between behavioral processes, motivation, investments in the service business and service revenue. *Industrial Marketing Management*, forthcoming.

Gomez-Mejia, L (1994). Executive compensation: A reassessment and a future research agenda. In *Research in Personal and Human Resources Management*, Vol. 12, pp. 161–222, Greenwich, CT: JAI Press.

Guay, W (1999). The sensitivity of CEO wealth to equity risk: An analysis of the magnitude and the determinants. *Journal of Financial Economics*, 53, 43–71.

Healy, PM and Palepu, KG (2003). The fall of Enron. *Journal of Economic Perspectives*, 17, 27–50.

Hoskisson, RE, Hitt, MA and Hill, CWL (1991). Managerial risk taking in diversified firms: An evolutionary perspective. *Organization Science*, 2, 296–314.

Holderness, CG and Sheehan, DP (1988). The role of majority shareholders in publicly held corporations: An explanatory analysis. *Journal of Financial Economics*, 20, 317–346.

Horst, P (1961). Relations among *m* sets of variables. *Psychometrika*, 26, 126–149.

Hossain, M, Cahan, SF and Adams, MB (2000). The investment opportunity set and the voluntary use of outside directors: New Zealand evidence. *Accounting and Business Research*, 30, 263–273.

Hotelling, H (1936). Relations between two sets of variables. *Biometrika*, 28, 321–377.

Howard, RA (1988). Decision analysis: Practice and promise. *Management Science*, 34(6), 679–695.

Jensen, MC and Meckling, WH (1976). Theory of the firm: Managerial behaviour, agency costs and ownership structure. *Journal of Financial Economics*, 3, 305–360.

Jensen, GR, Solberg, DP and Zorn, TS (1992). Simultaneous determination of insider ownership, debt and dividend. *Journal of Financial and Quantitive Analysis*, 27, 247–263.

Knopf, J, Nam, J and Thornton, J (2002). The volatility and price sensitivities of managerial stock option portfolios and corporate hedging. *Journal of Finance* 57, 801–813.

Knopf, JD and Teall, JL (1996). Risk taking behavior in the US thrift industry: Ownership structure and regulatory changes. *Journal of Banking and Finance*, 20, 1329–1350.

Kose, J, Litov, L and Yeung, B (2005). Corporate governance and managerial risk taking: Theory and evidence. Working Paper, New York University.

La Porta, R, Lopez-De-silanes, F, Shleifer, A and Vishny, R (2002). Investor protection and corporate valuation. *Journal of Finance*, 57, 265–301.

Leuz, C, Nanda, D and Wysocki, P (2003). Earnings management and investor protection: An international comparison. *Journal of Financial Economics,* 69, 506–527.

Lewellen, K (2004). Financing decisions when managers are risk averse. Working Paper, MIT Sloan School of Management, 4438–03.

Lipton, M and Lorsh, J (1992). A modest proposal for improved corporate governance. *Business Lawyer*, 48, 59–77.

Lorsch, JW and Maclever, E (1989). *Pawns or Potentates: The Reality of American's Corporate Boards*. MA: Havard Business School Press.

Maguire, LA and Albright, EA (2005). Can behavioral decision theory explain risk-averse fire management decisions? *Forest Ecology and Management*, 211, 47–58.

March, J and Shapira, Z (1987). Managerial perspective on risk and risk-taking. *Management Science*, 33, 1404–1418.

Mehran, H (1995). Executive compensation structure, ownership and firm performance. *Journal of Financial Economics*, 38, 163–184.

Morck, R, Shleifer, A and Vishny, RW (1988). Management ownership and market valuation: An empirical analysis. *Journal of Financial Economics*, 20, 293–315.

Morellec, E and Smith, CW (2005). Agency conflicts and risk management. Working Paper, University of Lausanne, University of Rochester.

Myers, SC (1977). Determinants of corporate borrowing. *Journal of Financial Economics*, 5, 147–175.

Paquerot, M (1996). L'Enracinement des dirigeants et ses effets. *Revue française de gestion*, 111, 212–225.

Pearce, JA and Zahra, SA (1992). Board composition from a strategic contingency perspective. *Journal of Management Studies*, 29, 411–438.

Pontier, J, Jolicoeur, P and et Pernin, MO (1987). Analyse canonique complète. *Statistique et analyse des Données*, 12(1–2), 124–148.

Pritsker, M (2005). Large investors: Implications for equilibrium asset, returns, shock, absorption and liquidity. *Finance and Economics Discussion Series 2005-36*, Board of Governors of the Federal Reserve System US.

Rogers, DA (2005). Management risk-taking incentives and executive stock option repricing: A study of US casino executives. *Financial Management*, 34(1), 95–121.

Rosenstein, S and Wyatt, JG (1997). Inside directors, board effectiveness and shareholder wealth. *Journal of Financial Economics*, 44, 229–250.

Shavell, S (1979). Risk sharing and incentives in the principal and agent relationship. *Bell Journal of Economics*, 10, 55–73.

Shleifer, A and Vishny, RW (1986). Large shareholders and corporate control. *Journal of Political Economy*, 95, 461–488.

Short, H, Wright, K and Hull, M (1999). Corporate governance from accountability to entreprise. *Accounting and Business Research*, 29(4), 337–353.

Smith, C and Stulz, R (1985). The determinants of firms' hedging policies. *Journal of Financial and Quantitative Analysis*, 20, 391–405.

Tosi, HL and Gomez-Mejia, L (1989). The decoupling of CEO pay and performance: An agency theory perspective. *Administrative Science Quarterly*, 34, 169–190.

Tufano, P (1996). Who manages risk? An empirical examination of risk management practices in the gold mining industry. *Journal of Finance*, 51, 1097–1137.

Tversky, A and Kahneman, D (1981). The framing of decisions and the psychology of choices. *Science*, 211, 453–458.

Walker, PL, Shenkir, WG and Barton, TL (2002). Enterprise risk management: Putting it all together. *Institute of Internal Auditors Research Foundation*, FL: Altamonte Springs.

Walls, MR (2005). Corporate risk taking and performance: A 20 year look at the petroleum industry. *Journal of Petroleum Science and Engineering*, 48, 127–140.

Westphal, J and Zajac, EJ (1995). Who shall govern? CEO board power, demographic similarity and new director selection. *Administrative Science Quarterly*, 40, 60–83.

Whitfield, R (2004). Creating a risk-conscious climate. *NACUBO Business Officers*, 27–32.

Williamson, OE (1963). Managerial discretion and business behavior. *American Economic Review*, 53, 1032–1051.

Wiseman, RM and Gomez-Mejia, LR (1998). A behavioral agency model of managerial risk taking. *Academy of Management Review*, 23(1), 133–153.

Wright, P, Ferris, SP, Sarin, A and Awasthi, V (1996). Impact of corporate insider, blockholder, and institutional equity ownership on firm risk taking. *Academy of Management Journal*, 39(2), 441–463.

Yoshikawa, T, Phan, PH and Linton, J (2004). The relation ship between governance structure and risk management approaches in Japanese venture capital firms. *Journal of Business Venturing*, 19, 831–849.

Zahra, SA (2005). Entrepreneurial risk taking in family firms. *Family Business Review*, XVIII(1), 23–40.

CHAPTER 21

NONLINEARITY AND GENETIC ALGORITHMS IN THE DECISION-MAKING PROCESS

Nizar Hachicha and Abdelfettah Bouri†*

The irruption of the nonlinearity leads to an in-depth transformation of a number of financial fields such as stock exchange decision-making. Nonlinearity leads to a source of infinity of behaviors making, which allows to better understand the phenomena considered complex. Nevertheless, the nonlinear models consider the stocks only by their consequences. Thus, it is proved to be difficult to explain the emergent phenomena due to the interaction of these individual behaviors.

For the last two decades, thanks to the advent of the data-processing techniques, many works have followed one another in shedding light on the behaviors of the markets. The sophisticated tools borrowed from biology, such as the genetic algorithms, have been introduced in the field of finance and stock exchange decision-making.

In this chapter, we have compared the decision-making based on the nonlinear models and the genetic algorithms on the BVMT. It is true that the nonlinear models had a good capacity of estimation, but they lose their quality in term of stock exchange's decision. However, the genetic algorithms had a better capacity (94%) compared to the nonlinear models in the total of the decisions taken.

1 Introduction

When we are interested in the stock exchange phenomena, we try to understand and reproduce the subjacent mechanisms with the protocols of decisions

*Faculty of Management of Sfax Rte aéreport km 4, Tunisia. hachicha_nizar@yahoo.fr
†Faculty of Management of Sfax Rte aéreport km 4, Tunisia. abdelfettah.bouri@fsegs.rnu.tn

and actions which generate the investors to optimize their portfolios. The irruption of the nonlinearity leads to an in-depth transformation of a number of financial fields such as stock exchange decision-making. Taking nonlinearity into account leads to a source of infinity of behaviors making, which allows to better understanding the complex phenomena.

Nevertheless, the nonlinear models consider the stocks only by its consequences. Thus, it is proved to be difficult to explain the emergent phenomena due to the interaction of these individual behaviors. For the last two decades, thanks to the advent of the data-processing techniques, many works have followed one another in shedding light on the behaviors of the markets. The sophisticated tools borrowed from biology, such as the genetic algorithms, have been introduced in the field of finance and stock exchange decision-making.

In this chapter we compared the decision-making based on the nonlinear models and the genetic algorithms on the BVMT. It is true that the nonlinear models had a good capacity of estimation, but they lose their quality in term of stock exchange's decision. However, the genetic algorithms had a better capacity (94%) compared to the nonlinear models in the total of the decisions taken.

2 Database

Our database is composed of the day laborer observations of the Tunindex from 03/01/1998 to 31/12/2005 (Fig. 1).

This series shows the following characteristics (Table 1).

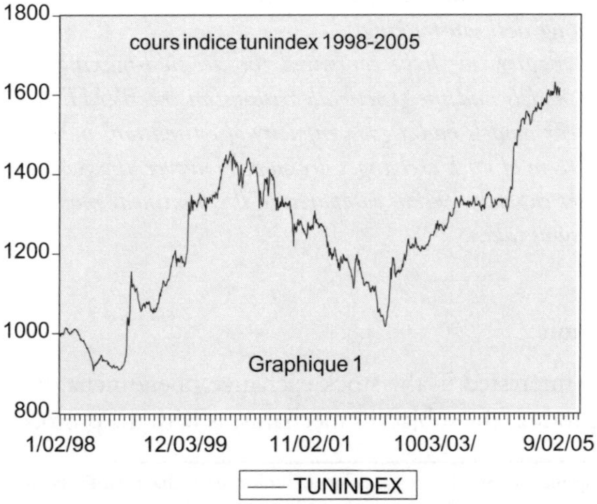

Figure 1: Tunindex course.

Table 1: Descriptive statistics of series BVMT.

Average	Median	Min	Max	S	K	JB
1241.458	1261.670	905.7400	1630.770	−0.016801	2.525605	18.87660

This series will be divided into two periods

- *First period* (period of estimation or training): A period of 4 years from 02/01/1998 to 31/12/2001 (i.e. 50% of the observations). In this period, we study the stochastic characteristics of our index, we estimate the parameters of the econometric models, and we choose the best models to do the training for our genetic algorithm.
- *Second period*: A period of test and comparison of the models according to the nonlinear econometric models and the genetic approach.

The market return is a relative variation of the general index of the price of the constituting this index. Formally, the course of a credit at time T is P_t; profitability can be written as follows:

$$R_t = \frac{P_t - P_{t-1}}{P_{t-1}}. \tag{1}$$

The "dividend/course" ratio is generally considered as negligible compared to the relative variations of the prices. That is why the relative variations of the prices of the stocks are frequently assimilated to returns

$$\frac{P_t - P_{t-1}}{P_{t-1}} \approx L_n\left(\frac{P_t}{P_{t-1}}\right). \tag{2}$$

The use of the logarithm of the prices rather than the prices themselves is due to the fact that the financial variables generally have non-stationary variances in the course of time. To convert them into stationary variances, we transform the data into logarithmic values (Fig. 2).

3 The Nonlinearity in the Foreseeability of the Courses Dynamics

For a long time, the economic models were elaborated from algebraic constructions with a linear nature. The discovery that a nonlinear simple equation offers various types of behaviors opened considerable possibilities in the formalization of the economic and financial phenomena. Since more than 30 years, the irruption of nonlinear led to a large number of empirical and financial fields.

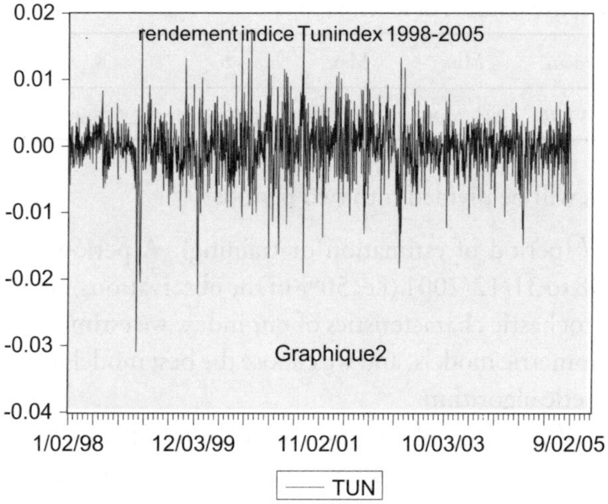

Figure 2: Tunindex return.

Taking nonlinearity into account leads to a source of diversity of behaviors, making it possible to better understand the natural and complex phenomena which were refractory with all modeling before.

Before all, we check some statistical properties such as stationarity and normality.

3.1 Study of Stationarity

A chronological series is stationary if its stochastic characteristics (hope, variance, and covariance) are invariant (not modified along with time). The study of stationarity is carried out with the application of the unit root tests. The more used test is the one of augmented Dickey and Fuller (1981). The application of tests ADF to the series of day labourers returns of the Tunindex leads to the results represented in Table 2:

Table 2 details the stationarity of the series, and it is seen that the ADF statistics are lower than the critical values.

3.2 Descriptive Statistics (Test of Normality)

The series of day laborers returns of the Tunindex has the following statistical characteristics (Table 3).

Table 2: ADF test.

Model 1 (None)	Statistic ADF	Critical value
Parameter:		For a level of risk 1%: −2.5668
$Y(-1) = -0.577406\ (-23.70653)$	−23.70653	For a level of risk 5%: −1.9395
		For a level of risk 10%: −1.6157
Model 1: (Intercept)		
Parameters :		For a level of risk 1%: −3.4366
$Y(-1) = -0.580114\ (-23.77474)$	−23.77474	For a level of risk 5%: −2.8635
$C = -0.000148\ (-1.658562)$		For a level of risk 10%: −2.5678
Model 1: (Intercept and trend)		
Parameters		For a level of risk 1%: −3.9680
$Y(-1) = -0.580224\ (-23.77209)$	−23.77209	For a level of risk 5%: −3.4146
$C = -9.39E - 05\ (-0.524570)$		For a level of risk 10%: −3.1291
@ trend $= -5.46E - 08\ (-0.352574)$		

Table 3: Descriptive statistics of series BVMT.

Average	Median	Min	Max	S	K	JB
−0.000249	−3.2*E*−05	−0.030872	0.017687	−0.628936	6.953227	1435.621

To check the normality of the series, we depend on these coefficients:

(1) *Skewness* = −0.628936: Coefficient of asymmetry of the series compared to the average (in the case of a normal distribution, skewness = 0).

$$v1 = \left| \frac{-0.628936 - 0}{\sqrt{6/2002}} \right| = 11.48 > 1.96.$$

(2) *Kentosis:* It is a coefficient of flatness, that is to say weak probability of the extreme points. In the case of a normal distribution, $K = 3$.

$$v2 = \left| \frac{6.953 - 3}{\sqrt{24/2002}} \right| = 36.103 > 1.96.$$

Statistics of Jarque Bera = 1435.621 > 5.99.

We note, for this series, that the hypothesis of normality is rejected.

The negative coefficient of skewness indicates that the distribution of the set is dispersed toward the left. This asymmetry can be the sign of the nonlinearity present in the process of return evolution. This possible nonlinearity can testify the presence to an effect ARCH frequently met in the financial series.

Therefore, starting from the statistical properties studied in this part, we can state initially that the diagram of random movement is not respected by the series of returns of the Tunindex index.

3.3 The ARMA Modeling

After having checked the stationarity of the series of profitability, one will proceed to modeling ARMED according to the method of Box and Jenkins which is summarized in three stages:

- Specification of the model (or identification).
- Adjustment of the model (or estimation).
- Validation of the model (or adequacy).

3.3.1 Identification and Estimation of the ARMA Model

We based the stage of the identification on the series of the total and partial auto-correlations of the series. Let us estimate this identification by the following model:

$$RTun_t = \underset{(19.988)}{0.408300}\, RTun_{t-1} + \varepsilon_t \quad \varepsilon_t \to N(0,1).$$

3.3.2 Validation of the Model

This model was selected and validated according to the following methodology: we checked the significativity of the parameters estimated while basing ourselves on the statistics t^* of Student whose absolute value exceeds 1.96. In the same way the statistics of Fisher higher than the breaking value (3.84).

In the end, we note that the selected model is compared with the model candidates on the level of its predictive capacity on the one hand (since it is characterized by a minimal residual variance and a higher coefficient of determination) and on these information's criteria (AIC, SIC) which are minimal, on the other hand. We can also, note that the other tests are necessary for the validation of this model like:

- The residue's normality and Jarque Bera.
- Test of homoscedasticity.

Table 4: Normality of the residues.

Average	Median	Max	Min	S	K	JB
−0.000151	−4.4*E*−05	0.017167	−0.022780	−0.237618	4.79998	288.962

(a) Test of the residue's normality

To test the residue's normality of the series resulting from modeling carried out, we will examine the values of Skewness and Kurtosis and the statistics of Jarque and Bera (Table 4).

We note that Skewness and Kurtosis's values are, −0.237618 and 4.79998 respectively, then the distribution of the residues seem to be asymmetrical and appears leptokurtic. Moreover, the Jarque–Bera value (288.962) is larger than the critical value (χ^2).

$$V_1 = \left| \frac{-0.237618 - 0}{\sqrt{\frac{6}{2001}}} \right| = 4.34 > 1.96$$

$$V_2 = \left| \frac{4.79998 - 3}{\sqrt{\frac{24}{2495}}} \right| = 16.435 > 1.96.$$

So, we conclude the rejection of the hypothesis of the residue's normality.

(b) The homoscedasticity

To test the homoscedasticity, we will be dependent on the tests of multiplier of Lagrange. Under the null hypothesis, statistics TR^2 calculated for the regression of e_t^2 (represents the residues of the model previously elaborate) follow a law of χ^2. The freedom of degree is given by the total number of regressors. The results of this test, applied on the stock exchange series in Table 5, show clearly the rejection of the null hypothesis: $TR^2 > \chi^2_{0.05p}$ (p: from 1 to 5).

Table 5: Test of ARCH effect (statistical LM).

	1	2	3	4	5
$\chi^2_{0.05\mathrm{p}}$	3.84	5.99	7.82	9.49	11.07
TR^2	345.4302	182.6049	123.5611	92.64090	75.13516

We can conclude that the series is heteroscedastic, which is due to the presence of an ARCH effect. The ARCH processes supplanted the ARMA processes. The later processes are unsuited for the financial series, which have asymmetrical structures and strong volatility of variance. Processes ARCH integrate, in an endogenous way, the parameters of conditional variance and are very used in optimization of the choices of the financial portfolios.

Thus, to model the process of the Tunindex return, it is necessary to take nonlinearity into account. In this connection, the advantage of the conditional heteroscedastic models is that the conditional variance is expressed in the form of a linear combination of the last forecasts error and last conditional variances. In this work, we limit ourselves to the presentation of the models: GARCH (*p, q*), ARMA-EGARCH, and GARCH-M.

3.4 The GARCH (p, q) Model

To take variability into account, we use GARCH (*p, q*) model. This model was formulated by Bollerslev (1986) as follows:

$$E(\varepsilon_t/I_t) = 0,$$

$$E(\varepsilon_t^2/I_t) = h_t = \alpha_0 + \sum_{i=1}^{q} \alpha_i \varepsilon_{t-i}^2 + \sum_{j=1}^{p} B_j h_{t-j}$$

where I_t is the information available.

According to Bollerslev and Kroner's research carried out on the return modeling by GARCH (p, q) model, we will be interested only on the following models: GARCH (1, 1), GARCH (2, 1), and GARCH (1, 2). GARCH (1, 1) model is selected and estimated as

$$RTun_t = \underset{(11.279)}{0.408}\ RTun_{t-1} + \varepsilon_t \quad \varepsilon_t \to N(0, ht),$$

$$h_t = \underset{(0.333)}{1.42E} - 06 + \underset{(3.014)}{0.1499\varepsilon_{t-1}^2} + \underset{(4.250)}{0.599h_{t-1}}.$$

We notice that all the coefficients are significantly different from 0. This checks the existence of an ARCH effect. In the same way, the coefficients of α_1 and β_1 are positive, and $\alpha_1 + \beta_1 < 1$, which imply that the return process is slightly stationary.

3.5 The ARMA–E GARCH Model

The interest of this model is to take into account the asymmetrical effect of volatility. It comes that, on the one hand, a linear specification of the conditional average found previously to represent the return process; and on the other hand, a specification of the conditional variance to measure its volatility which represents the risk of any financial asset. So the nonlinearity process of returns is introduced in the level of the second order moments. The first order moments are incorporated in a more general model of type ARMA-GARCH (Weiss, 1984) which arises as follows:

$$\Phi(L) = \theta(L)\varepsilon_t; \quad \varepsilon_t \text{ satisfies the GARCH model.}$$

The estimation of the model gives the following results:

$$RTun_t = \underset{(11.134)}{0.256} RTun_{t-1} + \varepsilon_t \quad \varepsilon_t \to N(0, ht),$$

$$h_t = \underset{(-7.414)}{-1.355} + \underset{(59.107)}{0.904} \log(h_{t-1}) + \underset{(12.578)}{0.361} \frac{\varepsilon_{t-1}}{\sigma_{t-1}} - \underset{(-2.207)}{0.003} \left| \frac{\varepsilon_{t-1}}{\sigma_{t-1}} \right| .$$

We note that the coefficient λ_2 is negative and statistically different to zero. This indicates the existence of an asymmetrical effect.

3.6 The GARCH-M Model

For several years, the volatility of the financial assets has increased and would have even become one of its permanent characteristics. The volatility is proved to be one of the principal explanatory variables of the return. The modeling of this volatility for the determination of return has interested several authors. Known under the name ARCH-M, the model of Engle *et al.* (1987) was proposed to let the risk premium be a linear function of the conditional variance supposed to be variable. The model can be written as follows:

$$Y_t = x_t b + \delta h_t + \varepsilon_t \quad \varepsilon_t \text{ satisfies a model GARCH.}$$

The interest of this model is to take into account the influence of the volatility on returns. It results from volatility that a GARCH-M modelling, in which the conditional variance is an explanatory variable in the conditional average, can be adapted for the description of this influence. The estimated model is as follows:

$$RTun_t = \underset{(11.134)}{0.258} RTun_{t-1} - \underset{(-2.152)}{6.302} h_t + \varepsilon_t \quad \varepsilon_t \to N(0, ht),$$

$$h_t = \underset{(-7.414)}{-1.355} + \underset{(58.590)}{0.904} \log(h_{t-1}) + \underset{(12.512)}{0.361} \frac{\varepsilon_{t-1}}{\sigma_{t-1}} - \underset{(-2.544)}{0.008} \left| \frac{\varepsilon_{t-1}}{\sigma_{t-1}} \right|.$$

3.7 *The Choice of the Model*

For the choice of the more adapted model, we will be dependent on the following four criteria:

3.7.1 Root Mean Square Error (RMSE)

$$\text{RMSE} = \sqrt{\frac{\sum_{i=1}^{n} (\hat{y}_i - y_i)^2}{n}}.$$

This criteria informs us about the distance separating the predicted series $\{\hat{y}_i,\ i = 1, 2, \ldots, n\}$ and the observed series $\{y_i,\ i = 1, 2, \ldots, n\}$, where n represents the observation of the sample test and y_i represents the day laborer return of the Tunindex index.

3.7.2 Mean Absolute Error "MAE" and Mean Absolute Percentage Error "MAPE"

$$\text{MAE} = \frac{\sum_{i=1}^{n} \left| (\hat{y}_i - y_i)^2 \right|}{n} \qquad \text{MAPE} = \frac{\sum_{i=1}^{n} \frac{|\hat{y}_i - y_i|}{y_i}}{n}.$$

These measurements penalize less heavily the great errors made by the model tested than RMSE.

3.7.3 MSE

$$\text{MSE} = \frac{1}{n} \sum (y_t - \hat{y}_t)^2.$$

3.7.4 MAD

$$\text{MAD} = \frac{1}{n} \sum \left| (y_t - \hat{y}_t) - \frac{1}{n} \sum (y_t - \hat{y}_t) \right|.$$

Table 6: The best model.

	MAE	MSE	RMSE	MAD
ARMA	0.00281216	1.88343$E-05$	0.004339847	0.00276396
GARCH	0.00280181	1.90429$E-05$	0.004363812	0.00279435
E-GARCH	0.002802	1.89379$E-05$	0.004351775	0.00279572
GARCH-M	0.00275895	1.85647$E-05$	0.004308681	0.00276396

The best model is the one which has the low values of these criteria.

According to Table 6, we can conclude that the model GARCH-M provides us the best result of estimation compared to the other models.

4 Genetic Algorithms in the Stock Exchange Decision-Making

The general idea of the genetic algorithm is to promote the best individuals and to make them evaluate to improve their adaptation or quality (Holland, 1975). So, the genetic algorithm is a method of optimization in which a set of potential solutions (the rules of investments decision), called invidious (market model), are gradually updated by a mechanism of selection and genetic operations: the crossing and the mutation.

In practice, the genetic algorithms are very diversified according to the applicability of the algorithm (finance, engineering, industry, etc.), the objective of the genetic algorithm (maximization of a function, classification of data, etc.), and genetic operations choosen. The genetic algorithms are the subject of several applications in several fields. In finance particularly, research related to forecast (time series, econometrics, etc.), optimization, and the financial decision-making in general.

Pan *et al.* (1995) used the genetic algorithms in order to find the optimal parameters of the nonlinear regression. Compared to the other numerical resolution methods, the genetic algorithms are perform and require less analytical information.

Boné *et al.* (1998) used the genetic algorithms to find the most adapted theoretical econometric form to temporal series modeling. On their premises, the population of chromosomes defines the type of modeling (AR, MA or ARMED) and the value of the associated coefficients.

Julia and Sutcliffe (2004) compare the performance of the BLACK–SCHOLES model to the genetic algorithm in the European evaluation of the options on the FTSE 100 INDICES. They showed that, generally, the genetic algorithms have a higher performance than the BLACK–SCHOLES model in the evaluation of the options.

Weiss (1999) and Weiss and Hirsh (1998, 2000) applied the genetic algorithms, from a study similar to data mining, in order to envisage rare events. To realize such prevision, the authors developed a system of training based on the genetic algorithms called Time weaver. From a historical series of data, the algorithm seeks and builds rules of forecast making it possible to know if a rare event is likely to appear in an immediate future.

Szpiro (1997a, 1997b) and Beenstock and Szpiro (1999) applied the genetic algorithms in order to seek the nonlinear functional forms reproducing as well as possible a set of data. Szpiro (1997b) shows that even if the genetic algorithms are able to find functional forms "solutions" giving of good results, they have not a high economic pertinence.

Eddelbüttel (1996) used the genetic algorithms, in the framework of passive management; in order to find portfolios which reproduce index DAX (defines as the optimal solution to reach).

For our study, the genetic algorithm is interested in the field of the finance (stock exchange decisions). It will make possible to our investor to take the best decisions following the evolutions of the financial market model (BVMT), throughout the two periods quoted before (training period, test period, investment period).

We will base our study on the genetic algorithm used by Korajczyk and Sadka (2004) which is presented in Fig. 3.

4.1 Fitness Function

The aim of the evolutionary approach of the genetic algorithm is to discover an artificial expert who is able to make the optimal decisions starting from stock exchange data. To guess the optimal decision, it is necessary to evaluate the expert performances by using a function of evaluation or, genetically speaking, a fitness function.

In the field of forecast and stock exchange investments, several functions of evaluation of the expert quality can be used according to the selected criterion of evaluation. In this work, we chose a function of evaluation which tends to maximize the optimal decisions and, consequently, the quality of expert forecast

$$\text{Function Fitness} = F(m) = 1 - \left[\sum_{i=1}^{n} (d_{0i} - d_{Fi}) \Big/ n \right],$$

1- To choose the parameters of evolution:

- criterion of stop;
- Operator of selection;
- Operator of mutation;
- Operator of crossing;
- Decision rule.

2- Initialization of the first generation (this initialization is arbitrary according to the investor experiment). The size of the population, K model, is:

$$M_0 = \{m_{01}, m_{02}, \ldots, m_{0K}\}$$

3- Evaluation of the models M_0.

4- As long as the criterion of nonsatisfied stop To make, I = I + 1

To make m_{ij} = better model $\{M\}$

Easticity strategy, p better pass to the following population without modification.

For J = p + 1… K; To make Selection of the parents

M_{j-1} = Selet M_{j-1}

Crossing ((K-p) model M_J)

$m_{j,1}$ = Cross-country race over M_{j-1}

Change

$m_{j,1}$ = mutate $m_{j,k}$

End for evaluation of the models M

End To make

End As long as.

Figure 3: Genetic algorithm.

where d_{0i} is the optimal decision which must be made by the investor at the date i; d_{Fi} is the final decision or decision taken by the expert at the date t this decision is made at the date $t - 1$; and n is the number of days of training or test

$$\begin{cases} \text{If } d_{0i} = d_{Fi} & \text{then } d_{0i} - d_{Fi} = 0, \\ \text{If } d_{0i} \neq d_{Fi} & \text{then } d_{0i} - d_{Fi} = 1. \end{cases}$$

By applying the financial rules, each expert must undertake one of the three positions: "To buy", "To sell" or "Anything to make". The decisions are made each day (d_F). Every decision (d_{Ft}) is known as being good or bad the following day, by comparing this decision with the optimal one (d_{0t} is the optimal decision which must be made if we know, at date $t-1$, of the stocks courses of the date t).

From this function, we can conclude that the model which will have a fitness function equal to 1 is the optimal model. In practice, this value cannot be reached; but we can consider that the best model is the one which has a fitness function nearest to 1.

4.2 The Genetic Operators

The genetic operators define the way in which the market models combine and are arranged during the phase of reproduction. Thus, new chains are created. The most significant operators are: the crossing and the mutation.

4.2.1 The Selection

The operator of selection allow the individuals of a population to survive, reproduce or to die. The probability of an individual survive will be directly related to this relative efficacy within the population.

In the framework of this study, we will use the proportional selection: the wheel of the caster also called the wheel of the lottery. This basic method allot to each models of market M_i, a probability of survive p_i proportionally to its adaptation in the population. At the phase of selection, the individuals are selected by chance, by respecting the associated probability p_i, form a new generation's population. This is carried out by the calculation of a probability of selection such as $q_i = \sum p_j$, $J = 1, \ldots, i$. Then, we generate, by chance, a real R on the interval [0, 1] n successive times (n is the size of the new population individual, v_i is selected when $q_{i-1} < r < q_i$).

4.2.2 The Crossing

The crossing is defined as follows: we suppose that two individuals 1 and 2, the crossing cut them in one or more points chosen by chance and with a probability P_c. There are three types of crossings:

- crossing at a point;
- crossing at two points;
- uniform crossing.

We have to use the crossing at a point. This operator is defined as: we suppose two juxtaposed models M_1 and M_2, the crossing cuts them in a point chosen by chance and produces two new models Me_1 and Me_2 after having exchanged the cut parts. In this operation, the two participant models M_1 and M_2 are compared to the parents and the two resulting chains to the descendants. Each individuals see itself allotted the same probability $p_i = 0.9$ to take part in the crossing and it is a pulling random which determines its effective participation in this operation. This probability p_i of crossing is strong but steals lower than 1 which means that certain models pass to the following population without modification: it is the principle of an elitist strategy which tends to maintain the best models for the following population.

4.2.3 The Mutation

A mutation is a random change of one or more bits of the coding chains of the individual. We proceed to the simplest operator of the change which tends to insert or remove a rule. Thus, the mutation is a random change of one or several rules of the chain coding the model. Each rule of the whole of the chains of the population has a probability p_m of undergoing a change with each generation. The probability $p_m = 0.05$ that a rule undergoes a change is weak but necessary because the crossing operator becomes less effective with time, seen that the models become similar. It is at this time that the phenomenon of change takes all its importance: generally, these changes do not create the best models, but they avoid the establishment of populations of uniform models which cannot evolutes. That is why it is called troublemaker operator.

5 Method of Coding of the Models and the Evolution Process

The problem of this study is to find the model (expert) which adapts the best with the data of the BVMT. Thus, each linear chain constitutes an "expert" model. The first problem which we met is to determine the length of the linear chain constituting the models. In practice, there is no rule or method to determine the length of the linear chain which constitutes an expert. This length is fixed arbitrarily. For that, we will refer ourselves on the study of Korzak and we will proceed to models made up of 60 bits or chromosomes. Each chromosome represents a rule of financial decision, the coding of these rules is a linear coding (0, 1), whose significance is represented in Table 7.

So, each model or expert can represented in the following way:

$$\begin{array}{ccccccccccc} M_1 & 0 & 0 & 1 & 1 & 1 & 0 & 1 & 0 & 1 & 1 \\ & R_1 & R_2 & R_3 & R_4 & R_5 & R_6 & R_7 & R_8 & R_9 & R_{10} \end{array}.$$

Table 7: The codification rules.

Chromosome code	Signifiance
$Ri = 0$	Rule Ri does not take part in the final decision of the model
1	Rule Ri takes part in the final decision of the model

Table 8: Coding of the decision.

To buy	1
To sell	0
Nothing to make	0.5

The representation of the model M_1 means that it is composed of 10 rules of decision $(R_1, \ldots, R_{10})$ of which only R_3, R_4, R_5, R_6, R_7, R_8, R_9, and R_{10} participate in the decision of the model M_1. The others are inactive in this generation, but they can be active in another generation, as it can disappear by the genetic operators (crossing and change).

The second problem is the coding of the decision of the expert. For that we carry out the following method: each decision rule, which composes the expert, calculates its forecast for the next day. If this rule envisages a rise of the course, the decision will be "to buy", if it envisages a fall of the courses, the decision will be "to sell", if it envisages the stability of the course, the decision will be "nothing to make". The decisions of each rule are coded is represented in Table 8.

The answers to the rules of an expert are not necessarily identical. In this case, the model calculates the average, used to generate the final answer of the expert, with taking into account the threshold of decision of 0.75, for the buying, and 0.25 for the sale.

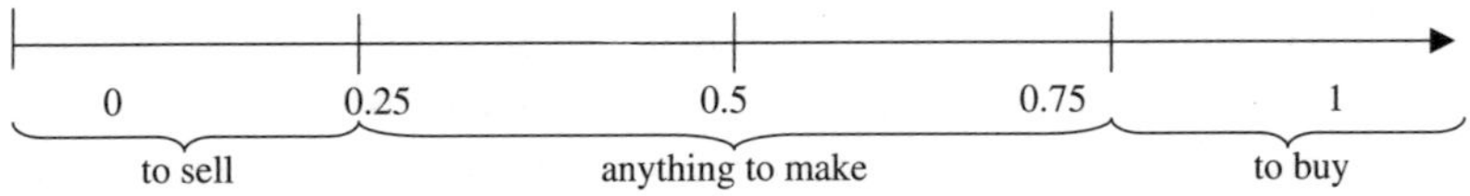

6 The Financial Decision Rules

The stage of the specification of the decision rules very interesting: these rules are the principal components of the expert. They are very varied, they can be:

- Simple: For example, course of closing > opening price.
- Econometric: With using an econometric model to envisage the fall or the rise of the courses.

- Complex: As the models which evaluate the quality of information and the degree of rationality of the investors and their risk aversion.
- Irrational: Rain days, cyclic effect (end week, end of the year).

Within the framework of this study, the decision rules are presented in the following form: *If the conditions are reached, then decision taken.* The left part of the rule is a formal expression describing a mathematical formula or a financial indicator (60 financial rules and indicators).

7 Result

The objective of this step was to analyze and compare the performance of the methods of forecast as regard, to financial decision by using the same financial series (the Tunindex index) for the same period and observing the same conditions. This series represent day laborer quotation of the Tunindex index throughout the period separating the 02/01/1999 until the 31/12/2005. We arbitrarily divide the series into two parts:

- First part: 50% of the observations which represent the daily course of the Tunindex during the period 02/01/1998 until the 31/12/2001 for the training of genetic algorithm.
- Second part: 50% of the observations which represent the daily course of the Tunindex during the period 02/01/2002 up to 31/12/2005. This part will be useful like period test of the genetic algorithm.

This approach is illustrated by using the computerized decision-making (used by Korajczyk and Sadka (2004) in its study carried on the modelling of index CAC 40).This system has sudden changes which touched mainly the financial rules of decision and with the level of its function fitness. To obtain the satisfying models for each period, the execution time (each generation) was approximately 3–5 min. This interval of time, necessary to obtain a new generation, does not pose a problem in our problematic (day labourer stock exchange decision-making); but it poses a major limit if our objective is the intra-day labourer stock exchange decision-making.

This system provides us three types of information: the stock exchange decisions, lists of the best experts as well as the value of their fitness functions and their compositions as regards of decisions rules; and a general representation of the presence probability of each rule of decision in the experts for each generation.

7.1 Degree of Participation of the Decision Rules

The decision rules can stay alive (to exist in the experts) during several generations (investment days); they can disappear from the first generations too. This appearance or disappearance is a performance function of decision rules in the forecast of the courses movements on the BVMT. Our system provides us a representation of the participation of the decision rules by a graph (see Fig. 4) whose *x*-axis represents the number of the generation and *y*-axis represents the percentage of appearance of the decision rules. We note, from Fig. 1 (which represents only the 20 first and last generations), that at the beginning of the training process, all the rules have a probability of appearance almost identical; but, at the end of the training process, we note that:

- Certain rules are already eliminated or existing in few models (their percentage of appearance is close to 0).
- Certain rules, which we can say that they are relevant and effective, are more and more present in the market models.
- Certain rules always "are not decided" and move in the top, below or in the medium of the diagram. This instability is caused by the participation of the rules in the very advantageous and non-advantageous models.

We also notice that the majority of the rules, which have a great percentage of appearance, are rules of weak memory.

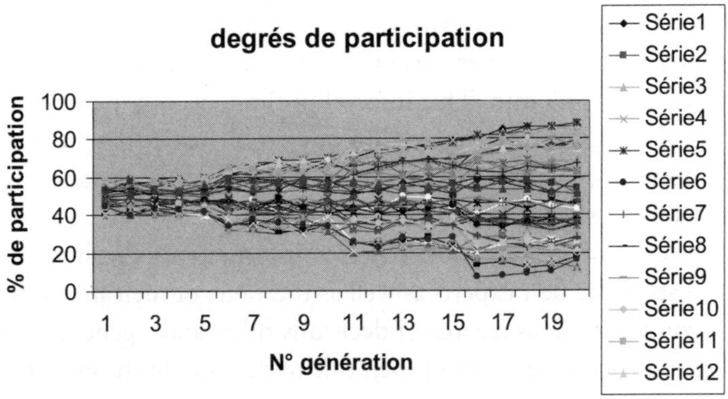

Figure 4: Participation of the rules.

7.2 *The Experts (Market Models): Compositions, Fitness Function Values, and Decisions*

The system provides us at each day end (for each generation) the rules used for each expert, like their fitness values in a table of Excel (see Fig. 5). The first column represents the row of the model (no. 1 represents the best expert). The second column represents the value of the fitness function of each expert. We notice that the best expert (no. 1) has a value of fitness equalizes to 0.78, that is to say that this model made 78 good decisions on 100 decisions. This percentage of efficacy is considered to be significant, while referring to studies made by other methods of investment. The other columns which are numbered from 1 up to 60, represent the numbers of the decision rules. These numbers are given arbitrarily.

The rules used in each model are marked by symbol X; then the analysis of the rules of the best model shows that the majority of the rules carries on the weak memory indicators. That explains the behavior of the BVMT and its strong sensitivity to the short-term changes of the prices. This result confirms the result of the inefficiency of the BVMT, since, according to the genetic approach, we can draw the future decisions while basing ourselves on the

Row	fitness	1	2	3	4	5	6	7	8	9	10	11	12	13	14	15	16	17	18	19	20	21	22
1	0.7852	X				X				X													
2	0.7812		X			X															X	X	
3	0.7562	X				X				X			X					X					
4	0.7437		X							X	X										X	X	
5	0.7421																	X	X		X	X	
6	0.7385		X												X						X	X	
7	0.7310	X				X	X			X								X					
8	0.7293																						
9	0.7242	X									X							X	X				
10	0.7150		X			X					X					X							
11	0.698						X				X							X	X			X	
12	0.6754						X			X					X			X	X				
13	0.6462													X		X			X	X			X
14	0.6421																X						
15	0.6213													X								X	X
16	0.6121													X	X	X				X			X

Figure 5: Composition of experts.

historical data. This result is not contradictory with that of the econometric models (all the econometric models considered and validated used to the maximum two delays).

7.3 The Expert Decisions

To make a decision, each model uses its single whole of rules. The signals sent by the rules are combined by a voting system; that is, the final decision is calculated by a simple average of the answers generated by the individual rules. The threshold of decision is taken into account for the final decision of the model. For our investor, the decision taken into account is that of the best expert. The decisions of the other models will be used to revalue the experts to determine the new best expert. This last is taken into account for the decision of our expert the following day.

8 Conclusion: Comparison of the Results of Stock Exchange Decision-Making of the Genetic Approach to the Econometric Models

To compare the genetic results with the econometric model, we base ourselves on a method which consists in calculating the percentage of the good decisions in term of rise, stability, and low. This method made us possible to draw Table 9

We notice that:

- The percentage of the good decisions of the econometric model does not exceed 59% ; and it decreased for the period of test compared to the period of modeling. On the other hand, for the genetic algorithm, we note, throughout the period of training and the period of the test, that the percentage of the good decisions improves one period to another. This result justifies the use of the evolutionary systems which adapt better with the stock exchange market trends.
- Although the percentage of the good decisions of the genetic approach is better than that of the econometric models, one cannot be satisfied with this result for two reasons:
  — The first reason is that 78% of success, mean 22% of failure: this percentage of failure is not negligible; that means that our genetic algorithm cannot explain the exact dynamics of the BVMT. This can be due to the basic elements, which determine the dynamics of the market, and

Table 9: Comparison of the results of stock exchange decision-making of the genetic approach to the econometric models.

Results of the econometric model observed over the period of modelling		
	Raise	Drop
Raise	59%	17%
Stability	22%	28%
Drop	19%	53%
Results of the econometric model observed over the period "test"		
Raise	48%	27%
Stability	34%	32%
Drop	18%	41%
Results of the genetic algorithm observed over the period of training		
Raise	70%	27%
Stability	34%	32%
Drop	12%	41%
Results of the genetic algorithm observed over the period of test		
Raise	78%	10%
Stability	13%	17%
Drop	9%	73%

which were not taken into account by our algorithm. Among these elements we can quote: aversion to the risk degree, function of utility of the investors, degree of rationality of the investors, quality of information.

— The second reason is that this system cannot be used in the intra-laborer day stock exchange decisions, seen her proportional heaviness of decision-making.

References

Beenstock, M and Szpiro, G (1999). Specification search in non-linear time series models using the genetic algorithm. Working Paper.

Bennel, JA and Sutcliffe, C (2004). UK Black–Scholes versus artificial neural networks in pricing FTSE 100 options. *Intelligent Systems in Accounting, Finance and Management*, 12, 243–260.

Boné, R, Thillier, R, Yvon, F and Asselin, J (1998). Optimisation by genetic algorithm of stochastic linear models of time series. In *Bio-Mimetic Approaches in Management Science*, Aurifeille, J-M and Deissenberg, C (eds.), pp. 153–162.

Eddelbüttel, D (1996). A hybrid genetic algorithm for passive management. Working Paper presented at the *Second International Conference on Computing in Economics and Finance, Society of Computational Economics*, Geneva, Switzerland.

Engle, RF, Lilien, DM and Robins, RP (1987). Estimating time-varying premia in the term structure: The ARCH-M model. *Econometrica*, 55, 391–407.

Korajczyk, RA and Sadka, R (2004). Are momentum profits robust to trading costs? *Journal of Finance*, 59, 1039–1082.

Pan, Z, Chen, Y, Khang, L and Zhang, Y (1995). Parameter estimation by genetic algorithms for nonlinear regression. In *Proceeding of International Conference on Optimization Techniques and Applications*, pp. 946–953.

Szpiro, G (1997a), Forecasting chaotic time series with genetic algorithms. *Physical Review E*, 55, 2557–2568.

Szpiro, G (1997b), A search for hidden relationships. Data mining with genetic algorithms. *Computational Economics*, 10, 267–277.

Weiss, G (1999). Timeweaver: A genetic algorithm for identifying predictive patterns in sequences of events. In *Proceedings of the Genetic and Evolutionary Computation Conference* (GECCO-99), Morgan Kaufmann, pp. 718–725.

Weiss, G and Hirsh, H (1998). Learning to predict rare events in event sequences. In *Proceedings of the Fourth International Conference on Knowledge Discovery and Data Mining* (KDD-98), AAAI Press, pp. 359–363.

Weiss, GM and Hirsh, H (1998). Learning to predict extremely rare events. In *Proceedings of Learning from Im-balanced Data Sets*, AAAI Workshop. Technical Report WS-00-05, pp. 64–68.

CHAPTER 22

ICT AND PERFORMANCE OF THE COMPANIES: THE CASE OF THE TUNISIAN COMPANIES

*Jameleddine Ziadi**

This chapter aims to identify the determinist relationship between companies, performance and their ICT use. Based on the literature review which seems to support the hypothesis of our research positing that the use of ICT by firms is meant to improve their performance, we developed a stochastic of formulation relationship in which different aspects of the ICT use were retained having explanatory constructs of performance improvement. This relationship was empirically tested based on the data collected from the sample of Tunisian companies.

The obtained results suggest that ICT use by companies contributes to increasing their performance, especially the exporting ones. This study draws attention to the dependence of the performance improvement on the existence of required competences, the Net culture, the horizontal organizational structure, and the use of ICT by partners of the firm.

Post-industrial company, company of knowledge, economy of information, economy of immaterial are the concepts that are of much interest today and represent relevant fields of investigation for much of researchers and statisticians. These various concepts characterize the dynamic news related to the technological processes of change in progress. Indeed, the relevant growth and the increase in the productivity in the United States, as well as the developments around the information and communication technology (ICT) in the

*Professor in Faculty of Laws, Economics and Management Sciences, Jendouba University, Tunisia, President of World E-management Consortium.
j.ziedi@yahoo.fr.

second half of the eighties to the 20th century after one period of crisis of productivity (1970–1995), are explained by many economists and historians by the emergence of a new technical system.

This new system is founded on ICT, information and knowledge being the key factors of production and competitiveness at the macroeconomic level like microeconomic. This new technical system was used by several economists, Freeman (1992), the cause of the deceleration of the profits of productivity in the seventies and eighties compared to the former period.

In the same way, David (1991), while trying to explain the paradox of Solow, by comparing the "data-processing revolution" with a major innovation, electricity, shows that it was necessary more than 30 years so that the inventions first result in significant profits of productivity at the macroeconomic level. The same phenomenon is thus reproduced for the ICT after one period of technical and social training; the idea of the emergence of a new technical system is reinforced by the major changes in the organization of the companies, in the production process, is the organization of work, and is the relationship between individuals and company. However, the stagnation and the return of economic situation since the entry in the new century made a doubt concerning the impact of the ICT on the economic growth and stimulate research on these problems.

"Although extremely different, the wait-and-see policy of the eighties of the 20th century and the lull of the economic situation of the end of the 20th century had both the merit to stimulate research as well theoretical as empirical trying to explain the mechanisms by which the ICT are likely to influence the performances of the companies and the economic growth" (Mairesse, 2003).[a]

The problems of this chapter consist in seeing: Which is the incidence of the ICT on the performance of the company? And which are the mechanisms through which the ICT influence the economic performance of these companies?

Our principal contribution is to tackle a question which almost always was studied only in the developed countries which profited from a significant diffusion of ICT compared to the rest of the world. And, in this direction ICT could be at the origin of a modification in the rate and the rhythm of growth and development of the firms in the countries in the process of development.

The irruption of new technologies can indeed allow the opening of "window" of Re-specialization for the *developing countries* (Ben Youssef and

[a]Mairess, J (2003). Y' still has it a paradox of productivity. *Mimeo Seminar of Research TIC Social Productivity and Conditions*. CKEST, INSEE, Paris.

Mhenni, 2004)[b] and to catch up with the industrialized countries as it is the case for China in the industry of the computers and India for the software.

It seems very interesting to know: What are the repercussions of its technology of information and communication over the Tunisian companies? How did their structures, their management, and operating mode in order to fully exploit, evolve/move the opportunities offered by these technologies? What are the challenges which Tunisia and its companies will have to overcome to enter what we call: new economy?

The review of a theoretical and empirical literature which studies the incidences of technologies of information and communication on the performance of the company in particular enabled us to draw the three assumptions below:

(1) The ICT influence positively the global performance of the company. The global performance of the company is a construct which integrates several under-constructs: the physical performance, the commercial performance, the financial performance, and the society performance. Each of these under-constructs results itself from several directly observable variables. To test this assumption, we will have to test the assumptions below:
    (i) the ICT influence the physical performance positively (the indicator selected is Labour productivity),
    (ii) the ICT influence the commercial performance positively (the indicators selected are the innovations of products and those of processes),
    (iii) the ICT influence the financial performance positively (the indicators selected are the sales turnover and the benefit),
    (iv) the ICT influence the society performance positively (the indicator returned is manpower).
(2) The organizational ICT and changes are complementary in the assignment of the performance of the company.
(3) The ICT and the human capital are complementary in the assignment of the performance of the company.

To answer our problems and to check these assumptions, we articulated the development of the chapter around three parts as follows.

In the first, we started with the different theoretical approaches to study the technological changes which we face today as well as the opportunities that these changes for the economy constitute. The analyses were adopted starting

[b]Ben Youssef, A and Mhenni, H (2004): Effects of communication and information technologies on the economic growth: the case of Tunisia, Review *Area and Development*, No. 19, p. 133.

from the approach of the industrial economy and the economy of immaterial to understand the impact of these technologies on the microeconomic level.

In this work we are interested especially in the company since the most convincing elements with the incidence of the use of the ICT come from the data on the level of this company. Thus, we were interested in studying the mechanisms through which the ICT influence the performance of the companies as well as the conditions of a better use of these technologies. Four mechanisms are studied. The first mechanism is the strategic role played by these technologies. While basing itself on the model by To carry (1985), we show how these technologies can be a strategic weapon, able to direct the strategy of the company, in order to acquire a competing advantage of the reduction type of the costs or differentiation; How these technologies can make play the competitive strengths with the advantage of the company? We also show the role which the ICT can play in the establishment of the partnerships between the competitors or supplier–customers types in order to obtain a co-operative advantage. The second mechanism is the role of support which the ICT can play in the organizational new fashions in order to improve the performance of the company on all its levels. These new fashions are, especially: orientation toward the team work, the externalization, the over measure production, and the virtual company. A third mechanism is relative in role which can play the ICT in the effective way and decision-making in order to act as real time which results in an improvement of the performance. Finally, a fourth mechanism relates to the management of human resources in which the ICT can play a significant role.

However, the positive effects of the ICT on the performance of the company are not automatic. It is enough to explain the paradox of Solow to understand the conditions necessary so that a company makes a success by introducing the ICT.

Lastly, we chose to check the positive impacts of the ICT on companies working within the mechanical and electric sector. This choice is justified by the increased importance of these activities in the Tunisian economy as regards employment, creation of added value, and export. With this intention we adopted the technique of the investigation based on a survey near a sample of companies. It will be related to the level of use of the ICT by the companies forming our sample for the year 2006, level of the organizational changes (2003–2006), the level of the human capital, the level of performance for the year 2006 reasons for the ICT, their utility, and the obstacles to use these technologies.

1 The ICT and Firm's Performance

1.1 Definition of the ICT

Technology was at the beginning comparable to the component material (hardware) or with information easily transferable and usable (Arrow, 1962).[c] It is comparable thereafter with a combination of the material components and the other immaterial ones (Rosenberg, 1982[d]; Zimmermann, 1989[e]). The immaterial part of technology i.e. knowledge, the relations between individuals who take part in this production, form a part of this technology completely. They constitute in this fact the significant obstacles to transferability like in the conditions of its appropriation such as the knowledge held by the users and their capacity to improve and integrate these new techniques in new configurations of products or processes. Bell (1979),[f] defines technology as "the use of scientific knowledge to determine the ways of making the things in a reproducible way". By marrying these definitions, Castells (1996),[g] defines communication and information technology adding to the preceding definition: "the converging whole of technologies of micro-electronics, data processing (machine and software), of the telecommunications/diffusion and optoelectronics". It will add thereafter, the engineering and its growth series of development and application and "by what in the years 1990 biology, electronics and data processing seem to converge and interact in their applications, their materials and more basically, their conceptual approach".

1.2 Evolution of the ICT and Firm Performance

The development of communication and information technologies knew three successive phases: technologies of automation in the seventies, technologies of computerization in the eighties, and technologies of communication in the nineties. These technologies overlap in the industrial applications and follow one another by crossing two axes of evolution. First is that each generation of technologies is carrying a structural change which is specific. Technologies

[c]Arrow, K (1962). Economic welfare and the allowance of resources to invention. In *"Current Dimensions of the Technological Phenomenon"*, Guilhom B (ed.) (1993), Paris: Harmattan.

[d]Rosenberg, N (1989). Inside the black box: Technology and economics. In Guihon, B (ed.) (1993).

[e]Zimmermann, JB (1989). Industrial groups and technological bunches. *Review of Industrial Economy* (47), 89–102.

[f]Bell, D (1979). *"Cultural Constructions of Capitalism PUF*, Paris.

[g]Castells, M (1996). *"The Company in Network"*. Paris: Beech, p. 52.

of automation aim especially the profits of productivity; technologies of computerization aim primarily the profits of reactivity and reduction of the costs of transaction; technologies of communication aim in first order at improving quality of the exchanges and the processes of training. The second axis of evolution corresponds to the degree of centralization and the data-processing type of architecture to work. Indeed technologies successively passed from hierarchical centralized technologies (1970–1980), with the architectures customer waiter distributed with the arrival of the microcomputers (data-processing by department, workstation) (1980–1990), then with the data-processing distributed of network (1995–2000).

From a strategic point of view, the ICT were until the mid-1990, considered as utility function of support aiming the improvement of the informational processes. The traditional information systems were not able to take into account "the major part of the information which the company produced and manages: that which does not obey naked a rationality predetermined nor with standard treatments" (Prax, 1997).[h] In fact rather the new technological developments gave a strategic character to the investments in this field.

These technological developments introduced significant ruptures into the manner of designing and of making the spots based on the communication. They supported the access on-line to databases, the message and exchanges of information in groups of decision sets of themes or firms, the supply and the consultation of various services of information, as well as new commercial applications. The expansion of mobile telecommunications is another significant modification of the technological landscape. It does not relate to only the telephone vocal, of the same syntheses that can transmit faxes or data, professional applications relating to all the directly interested parties.

Of very different field which is that of the "immaterial" part in communication and information technologies, the significant innovations took place.

2 Impact of the ICT on the Firm's Performance: Empirical Validation in Electric and Mechanical Tunisian Manufacturing Sector

Tunisia made, for a long time and more particularly since the last decade, information technologies and communication, one of the principal axes of its

[h] Prax, JY (1997). *To Manage Knowledge in the Company: New Technologies with the Service of the Engineering of Knowledge*. Paris: INSEP, p. 107.

strategy of development. However, the situation of our country is still very far from the developed countries. The question of studying the diffusion of these technologies near a sample of Tunisian companies, the complementary investments, like checking the positive incidences of these technologies which, almost always, was made only in the developed countries, seems very interesting to us. The absence of the statistics on the levels of the use of the ICT in the Tunisian companies, and the specificity of the indicators measuring the performance, pushes us to resort to a survey which is put near a sample of manufacturing companies working within the mechanical and electric sector.

We will present initially the methodology adopted as well as specificities of the companies questioned as regards investment in ICT, organizational investment, and investment in human capital (Sec. 2.1). This section will be then supplemented by a second which aims at studying the bonds between these investments and the performance of the company as well as the complementarities which can exist between these various investments in order to reinforce these bonds.

2.1 Methodology of Work and Characteristics of the Sample

2.1.1 Technological Characteristics

2.1.1.1 Level of use of the ICT

Our sample includes/understands 40 companies (Table 1). We considered the companies of big size, those which have a total staff complement higher than hundred; the others are regarded as small and medium-sized undertakings. Since the latter represents more than 70% of the totality of the Tunisian companies, we tried to respect this rate in the choice of the questioned companies.

Table 1: Presentation of the sample.

Variables	Numbers	Percentage
Cut		
Large companies	15	37.5
Small and medium-sized undertakings	25	72.5
Total	40	100
Target market		
Exporting companies	28	70
None exporting companies	12	30
Total	40	100

Thus, as shown in the table, meadows of three quarters of the companies forming our sample are small and medium-sized undertakings. Moreover, the majority of the companies are exporting (70%).

In order to define that they are the information and communication technologies used by the surveyed companies, we resorted to a study made by Baldwin *et al.* (2001)[i] on the manufacturing sector of Canada. This study gathers these technologies in three groups based on the technology of the electronic microcomputer. Indeed, the computer and the software now form integral part of apparatuses such as the robots and the flexible systems of manufacture. Twenty-three technologies are thus defined. That went from the computer-assisted technologies applied to the design and the assembly to the robots used in manufacture and the assembly while passing by the data-processing networks used to communicate and control. These communication and information technologies are divided into three groups which are: software, communications in network, and the hardware (Table 2).

Table 2 provides the proportion of the companies which adopt various technologies. It shows that the companies of our sample adopt the three groups of ICT in an almost similar way 75% of the factories use at least a technology each of these variables and the performance of the company. Then, in a multivariate study we will try using an econometric model (logit) to explain the performance of the companies by taking into account various variables in the same equation. In addition, we will try to estimate the complementarities which can exist between these various technological investments, organizational and human in the assignment of the performance of the company.

However, without being delayed on the univaried and bivaried analysis, we will present the section relating to the multivariate analysis which seems to be of a significant contribution for our research.

3 Incidences of the ICT on the Performance of the Surveyed Companies

3.1 Multivariate Analysis

3.1.1 Presentation of the Econometric Model

In this part, we will use a multivariate framework which examines the bond between the use of the ICT and the six binary measures of performance relating to year 2004 previously advanced: labor productivity, benefit, sales turnover,

[i]Baldwin, JR and Sabourin, D (2001).

Table 2: Proportion of the companies' users of technologies ICT.

Technologies' groups	Technology used	Proportion of companies' users (%)
Software	Do not matter	75
	Design and engineering computer-assisted (CAO/IAO)	40
	CAD applied to the control of the machines used in manufacture (PRF)	32
	Technologies of modeling and simulation	23
	Resource requirements planning of manufacture (PRF)	40
	Production computer-assisted (CAM)	35
	Systems of acquisition and control of data (SACD)	18
	Use of the data of inspection for control of the production	20
	Software containing knowledge.	43
Tools of communication	Do not matter	73
	Exchange of files CAD	38
	Local area network for the needs of engineering or the production	73
	Widened data-processing networks	13
	Data-processing networks between firms	40
	Control numerical remotely of processes of the factory	7.5 E-02
Material	Do not matter	68
	Flexible systems of manufacture	18
	Programmable control devices	40
	Robots provided with sensors	28
	Robots deprived of sensors	12
	Systems of rapid prototyping	13
	Identification of the parts for automatic machining	10
	Automated system of storage	30
	Systems of artificial vision being used for the inspection or the setting with the test	20
	Other automated systems provided with sensors being used for the inspection or the setting with the test	25
	Computers exert a control on the activities of the factory	22

innovations of products, innovations of processes, and manpower. A particular importance is also attached to the relation between these measurements of performance and the innovations organizational and the human capital. Two other binary variables of control, which are the size of the company and its market targets, were taken into account. Indeed, much of studies show a positive bond between the size of the company and its target market, and the performance of the company (Baldwin and Sabourin, 2001)[j]; Gu and Gera, 2004).[k] The exporting companies and/or of big size are more likely to use technologies (like one showed higher) of information and communication and thus improve their performance. Due to the fact that our dependent variables are qualitative, we chose a logic model which establishes a bond between the performance of the company, the ICT, the organizational innovations, and the human capital. This model is built on the basis of two Canadian operation facts by Baldwin and Sabourin (2001),[l] and Gu and Géra (2004)[m]:

$$y_{\mathrm{I}}^{*}= C + \alpha_1 \mathrm{TIC} + \alpha_2 \mathrm{CO} + \alpha_3 \mathrm{KHM} + \beta_1 \mathrm{TAL} + \beta_2 \mathrm{MCB} + E_I,$$

where E_I indicates the measurement of unobserved performance of company, I the equivalent there observed $_{\mathrm{I}}$ of the measurement of unobserved performance of the company it represents change concerning the productivity, the benefit, the sales turnover, the innovations of products, innovations of the processes, and employment. The variable y; a value of if has the company indicates an increase in its productivity, its benefit, its sales turnover, its manpower, adoption of the innovations concerning the products and the innovations concerning processes. Otherwise, it is equal to zero.

$$\mathbf{yi = 1, \quad so\ there_{I}^{*} > 0, \quad and \quad yi = 0, \quad so\ there_{I}^{*} <= 0.}$$

For the use of the ICT we will carry out the following three measurements:

— LT: The proportion of the workers who use computers compared to the total staff complement, on the day of the investigation.
— INVT: The proportion of investment in ICT (ratio) with the total investment out of equipment relating to 2004; this measurement takes:
  - value 1, if the company had invested in ICT less than 25%,
  - value 2, if the company had invested in ICT between 25% and 50%,
  - value 3, if the company had invested in ICT between 50% and 75%,
  - value 4, if the company had invested in ICT between 75% and 100%,
— tce: The number of technologies (pertaining to the three groups: software communication and hardware), used by the company on the day of the investigation.

[j] Baldwin, JR and Sabourin, D (2001).
[k] Gu, W and Gera, S (2004).
[l] Baldwin, JR and Sabourin, D (2001).
[m] Gu, W and Géra, S (2004).

The workers using the computers and the number of technologies hold account the last and the present investments in ICT, whereas, the proportion of investment relates only to the investment in 2004. This last measurement is thus less exhaustive than the first two, or the measurement of the organizational innovations (CO) relating to the years 2003 and 2004, one used the three measurements advanced in the first section, namely,

— EPP: Numbers of innovations relating to the practices related to the production and efficiency.
— GRH: Numbers of innovations relating to the practices related to the human stock management.
— PQT: Numbers of innovations relating to the practices related to total quality.
— KHM: Proportion of the workers of knowledge defined in top.
— TAL: Cut company; it measures itself by a binary variable taking a value if the size is large (total staff complement higher than 100), otherwise it is equal to zero.
— MCB: Target market; it is measured by a binary variable taking a value if the company is exporting, otherwise it takes zero value.
  *E_I: Term of error.

4 Interpretation of the Results

4.1 The Contribution of the ICT to Improve the Performance of the Companies of Our Sample

Table 3 shows us that the independent variables explain clearly the dependent variables. Thus, the independent variables explain the labor productivity, the increase in the benefit, the increase in the sales turnover, innovations concerning the products, innovation concerning the processes, and the increase in the manpower, respectively of 60%, 44%, 35%, 42%, 52%, and 25%.

This same table shows that the coefficient attached to the proportion of the computers' users is negative for all the measurements of performance selected. However, it is significant only for the case of the innovations concerning the products, the innovations concerning the processes, and employment. The proportion of workers using the computer has a negative effect to these measures of performance. This effect is of great width especially on the innovations

Table 3: Factors influencing the performance of the surveyed companies.

Variables	Labor productivity	Benefit	Sales turnover	Innovation of products	Innovation of process	Manpower
LT	−0.0414	−0.0028	−0.0214	−0.1289	−0.2006	−0.0849
	(−0.7276)	(−0.0657)	(−0.5346)	(−1.9364)	(−2.0102)	(−1.8833)
INVT	3.6152	1.8461	0.7914	0.9576	0.4394	1.0830
	(1.9541)	(1.6997)	(1.5921)	(1.2864)	(0.5613)	(2.0255)
Tce	1.1608	0.6532	0.3890	0.3750	0.4665	0.0635
	(1.8006)	(2.3574)	(2.6065)	(2.1465)	(1.8971)	(0.6062)
EPP	−1.8795	−0.4708	−0.4198	−0.1521	0.0151	−0.1435
	(−1.6978)	(−1.0472)	(−1.0922)	(−0.4120)	(−0.0428)	(−0.4821)
GRH	0.8999	0.1848	−0.1973	−0.0245	0.2809	0.0664
	(1.9073)	(1.0571)	(−1.3168)	(−0.1632)	(1.7978)	(−0.6040)
GQT	2.0000	−0.3831	0.3347	2.4838	−0.3987	0.5370
	(0.8657)	(−0.2784)	(0.2888)	(1.4618)	(−0.2872)	(0.4959)
KHM	0.0264	−0.0210	−0.0079	0.1045	0.2043	0.0527
	(0.5504)	(−0.5880)	(−0.2415)	(1.6447)	(1.7228)	(1.5136)
TAL	−9.4929)	−4.8649	−3.3366	−4.0733	−0.1316	0.5632
	(−1.7931)	(−2.1859)	(−1.9324)	(−1.9402)	(−0.0834)	(−0.4756)
MCB	−0.8088	−0.6262	2.2185	2.3082	3.2010	1.0051
	(−0.3230)	(−0.3764)	(1.4801)	(1.2471)	(1.0323)	(0.7663)
McFadden R^2	60	44	35	42	52	25

Note: The statistics T appear between brackets, they are corrected to take account of the heteroscedasticity by means of the Huber–White method.

concerning the processes; an increase of 10 points of the proportion of the workers using a computer is likely to decrease by 2 points, the probability that the company makes innovations concerning the processes, 1.2 points which it adopts of the innovations concerning the products, and 0.8 points that it increases its manpower.

For the first two measurements we can explain that by the insufficiency of the complementary investments in the organizational changes, the human capital, the other types of technologies information, and of the communication (especially communication software and networks), which support some work groups as well as the need for a time of training for handling these technologies well. With regard to the negative effect on the growth of the manpower which represents a significant vector of the society performance company, beside the higher advanced arguments one adds the possibility that the companies use the computers in simple applications carried out ahead by not-qualified employees or which do not require a high qualification. Therefore, some of them will have a formation and the others will be laid off.

The situation is more ambiguous with regard to the using effect of the workers of the computers on labor productivity, the benefit, and the sales turnover. The coefficient attached to this category of workers is negative and statistically not significant. That let us think that the effect of the use of the computers is negligible as against the effects of the other technological and organizational variables.

The positive effect of communication and information technologies appears with the proportion of investment in ICT compared to the total investment out of the equipment carried out by the company as well as the number of technologies which it adopts.

Thus, these two measurements relating to the ICT have a positive influence statistically significant on the productivity and the benefit of the company. This effect is very significant, the fact of increasing the proportion of investment in ICT of 1 point, the probability of improving the productivity and the benefit increase by 3.6 points and 1.8 points, respectively. In the same way, the use of an additional technology can make the probability of increasing the productivity and the benefit of the company, respectively by 1.16 points and 0.65 points.

Moreover, the proportion of investment in ICT more intensively influences these two measurements of performance than the number of technologies ICT used.

That can be explained by the fact that a significant proportion of these investments is made to replace other technologies ICT or with the maintenance of existing technologies which are deadened and become none profitable.

Indeed, of the two companies which have the same number of technologies, it is that which invests in the renewal of this equipment and their maintenance which has more chance to increase its productivity and its benefit.

Moreover, the analysis of correlation shows a positive relation between the proportion of investment in ICT and the use of software and not of the intensity. The bivaried analysis differentiates the companies more on the level of productivity and improvement from the benefit; it is from one technology — software or hardware. Therefore, it appears that the investments are made more in the renewal of certain exceeded software and deadened hardware.

This reasoning is compatible with the positive and non-significant effect of these investments on the sales turnover, the innovations concerning the products, and the innovations concerning the processes which take time so that the workers learn how to use these recently acquired technologies in a reliable way.

It is the number of technologies which takes into accounts the level of training of the workers and which influences the performance in term of sales turnover and the innovations of products and processes. Thus, our results show that the number of technologies adopted by the company influence positively and in a significant way these three measurements of performance. Two additional technologies can make it possible for a company to increase the probability of improving its sales turnover, to adopt innovations concerning the products, of the innovations concerning the processes of meadows of a point.

In what milked with the increase in the manpower of the company, we note a positive and statistically significant relation between this one and the proportion of the investment in ICT made by the company. This effect is significant; the increase in a point of the proportion of investment increases the probability that the company increases its manpower, of a point. That is coherent with what we have advanced; if the investments in ICT are made primarily on new software and hardware which are not very complex, it will be very early to reduce the number of workers not qualified and on the contrary require the recruitment of a personnel qualified in ICT.

However, the number of technologies has positive effect on employment but non-significant. That can be explained by the fact that the number of technologies does not have a significant influence if one takes into account the proportion of investment.

The conclusions which we can retain concerning the impact of the ICT on the performance of the company are as follows:

- The investment in ICT influences positively and in a significant way the physical performance (labor productivity), financial (benefit), and societal (manpower). This is not in agreement with the conclusions drawn by a Canadian study which shows a non-significant effect of the proportion of investment in ICT (Gu *et al.*, 2004)[n] on the increase in the benefit and the productivity of work. On the other hand, we found the same results with regard to the absence of effect on the sales turnover and the innovations concerning the products and the processes.
- Technologies ICT, in addition to that of the autonomous computer, influence positively and in a significant way the physical performance (labor productivity), the commercial performance (innovations of products and innovations of processes), and the financial performance (benefit and sales

[n]Gu, W and Géra, S (2004).

turnover). This is in conformity with the results found by Baldwin *et al.* (2001)[o] in a study made on the Canadian manufacturing sector.

- The proportion of the users of the computers has negative effects on the four levels of the total performance as already shown by Brynjolfsson and Hitt (1996)[p] concerning the non-significant effect of the computers on the labor productivity and by the work of Gu *et al.* (2004)[q] concerning the absence of a significant bond between the proportion of the workers using the computers and the sales turnover, as well as the benefit and the existence of a negative bond between this proportion and the innovations concerning the products and the processes in a study made on the Canadian companies. However, the effects noted in our study are statistically significant only on the levels of the commercial performance (innovations of products and those of processes) and the society performance (effective). This is explained, partly, by the under-utilization of the computers which can be due to an insufficiency of the investments complementary inside the companies and/or the insufficiency of the informational and communication infrastructure and Tunisian legislation as is the state for the majority of the developing countries.

On the whole, our under-assumptions are checked and consequently, we can affirm that our assumption which aims at putting a positive relation between the ICT and the total performance of the company is true in the case of our sample. This assertion has just confirmed other studies (Baldwin *et al.*, 2001[r]; Gu *et al.*, 2004[s]) which showed a positive relation between the ICT and the performance of the company. However, we cannot generalize this result for all the sector or all the Tunisian companies, but that encourages us to widen the sample in order to be a representative of the sector or the Tunisian economy as a whole.

5 Conclusion

Through this chapter we could highlight the various technologies used by some of the Tunisian companies which form our sample. We noted that 23 technologies of information and communication are diffused in Tunisia. This

[o] Baldwin, JR and Sabourin, D (2001).
[p] Brynjolfsson, E and Hitt, L (1996).
[q] Gu, W and Géra, S (2004).
[r] Brynjolfsson, E and Hitt, L (1996).
[s] Gu, W and Géra, S (2004).

diffusion is accompanied by the phenomena of reorganization and managerial innovations. Thus, the current tendency is toward decentralization, the rationalization of production, the adoption of the more flexible methods of work, under-treatment, the resolution of the problems in team, remuneration with the merit and competences, the design-flexible devices of the spots, the training structure related to employment, the rotation of the stations, the division of information with the employees, the increase in the participation of the employees, the improvement of the satisfaction of the customers, the improvement of coordination with the clients/suppliers, and the management of total quality.

This study confirms the positive relation between the size of the company and its level of equipment in ICT shown by other studies. The same relation is noted between the target market and the level of adoption of these technologies. In fact the exporting companies adopt the ICT more than the non-exported ones.

The companies of big size and exporters are also more likely to make organizational innovations.

We also showed that the performance of these companies is explained by the adoption of communication and information technologies by the adopted organizational innovations or the equipment in personal element. However, these organizational innovations and the human capital are the spirit to establish a bond of complementarities with the ICT, in the improvement of the performance of the surveyed companies.

Finally, these conclusions are relevant and encouraging to make more advanced research by widening the sample and by differentiating the sectors from the study or by looking further into certain problems like the relation between the introduction of the ICT and the organizational change or the human capital, the conditions of success of setting the three investments open mutually at the companies in order to improve their performance in the context of the Third World.

References

Amabile, S and Gadille, M (2002). Internet, factor of profits of productivity and diversification in SME: Characterization of the contexts of use. *Review International SME*, 15(3–4), 15–138.

Amabile, S and Gadille, M (2003). NTIC in SME: Organisational strategies, capacities and competing advantages. *French Review of Management*, 29(144), 43–63.

Baily, MN (2002). The new economy: Postmortem gold second wind. *Newspaper of Economic Prospects*, 16(2), 3–22.

Baldwin, JR and Sabourin, D (2001). Impact of the adoption of technologies of information and the communications of point on the performance of the companies of the sector of manufacture in Canada. Division of the Microeconomic Analysis Statistical Canada.

Bitouzet, C (1999). *Electronic Trade: Creation of Value for the Company.* Paris: Hermès Science Publications.

Buck, J (2000). The management of knowledge and competences in practice. Editions of Organization

Bussler, L and Davis, E (2002). Systems information: The calm revolution in human resource management. *Newspaper of Computer Systems Information* (Winter), 17–20.

Caccomo, Jl (1996). Economic challenges of information, digitalization. Editions: Harmattan.

Castells, M (1996). *The Company in Network.* Paris: Beech.

Cowherd, B (2002). Up to what point the TIC plays a strategic role for SME. *International Revue SME,* 15(364), 37–61.

Desreumaux, A (1996). New forms of organization and evolution of the company. *French Review of Management,* (107), 86–108.

Detchessahar, M, Journé, B and Kessous, E (2003). Logistic and models of businesses: The example of the electronic trade. *French Review of Management,* 29(143), 13–26.

DeTournemine, L (1991). Technological strategies and process of innovation. Editions of Organization.

Dubé, L and Avoided, G (1999). Information technologies and the organization at the era of virtual. *International Review of Management,* 24(2) 14–22.

Eccles, RG (1999). The proclamation of the performance evaluation. In *Harvard Business Review Systems of Measurement of the Performance.* Editions of Organization.

Greenan, N (2003). Communication and information technologies, productivity and employment two paradox. Oxford.

Guilhon, B (1998). Total firms. *Economica.*

Guillon, B, Huard, P, Orillard, M and Zimmermann, J-B (1997). Economy of knowledge and organizations: Companies, territories, networks. *Conference pplô- 38,* Editions: Harmattan.

Howells, JR (1995). Total going: The uses of HERE networks in research and development. *Research policy* (24).

Kalika, M (2000). Management is sharp death E-management! *Re-examined French of Management,* (129), 68–74.

Mayere, W (1995). The management of the savoirs vis-a-vis the new industrial model. *French Review of Management,* (105), 8–16.

Morris, L (1999). The chain of knowledge: Strategies of company for the Internet. World Village.

Morvan, Y (1992). Base of industrial economy. *Economica,* 2nd edition.

Neighbor, C, Ben Mahmoud-Jouini, S and Edourd, S (2004). Networks: Strategic and organisational dimensions. *Economica.*

Niederman, F (1999). Total information system and HRM: Has research diary. *Journal of Global Information Management,* 7(2), 33–39.

Nonaka, I and Takeuchi, H (1997). Creative knowledge. The dynamics of the learning company. Translation of Ingham M, DeDoeck University, Brussels.

Peretti, JM (2001). E-Rh and renewal of the practices managériales. *Human Resources and Management* (2), 16–17.

Pine, BJ and Victor, B and Boynton, AC (1993). Making mass customization work. *Harvard Business Review*, 71(5), 108–119.

Study GMV CONSUL (2000). Impact of the NICT on the competitiveness of the industrial companies.

To carry, ME and Millar, VE (1985). How information gives you competitive advantage. *Harvard Review Business*, 149–160.

To carry, ME (2001). Strategy and the internet. *Harvard Review Business*, 79(3), 63–78.

Tardieu, H and Guthmann, B (1991). The strategic triangle. Editions the Organization.

Tripllett, JE (1999). The slow fox trot productivity paradox: What C computers C to productivity. *Re-examined Canadian of Economic*, 32(2), 309–334.

Ulrich, D (2001). From business to e-HR. *Human Resources Planning*, 86–98.

Villarmois, O (1998). The concept of the performance and its measurement. *Acts of XIVth Days of the I.A.E, Nantes, t2*, 2, 199–216.

Zimmermann, JB (1989). Industrial groups and technological bunches. *Review of Industrial Economy*, (47), 89–102.

CHAPTER 23

OPTION MARKET MICROSTRUCTURE

*Jean-Michel Sahut**

In this chapter, we study the problem of the bid–ask spread formation on option markets. The market microstructure literature tried to study the behavior of market makers, and the elements they take into account when they calculate the size and the quantities of their spread using three complementary theoretical approaches — transaction costs, inventory costs, and asymmetry information costs. In order to overlap the limits of existing models which are not able to integrate these three types of costs, we developed an empirical approach.

Our research of the French market shows that modeling an option bid–ask spread is first and foremost a question of evaluating this option, and, second, a problem of microstructure. Moreover, the existence of moderate asymmetry information costs shows that this market is not dominated by informed operators, contrary to the generally accepted ideas concerning this type of derivatives market. In addition, we have demonstrated that the stock market liquidity characteristics are transmitted to their option. So, the interactions between the stock and the option spread are strong and the liquidity of the stock market determines the efficiency of the option market.

1 Introduction

The intense competition between financial markets leads brokers, dealers, and regulation authorities to ask about market organizational efficiency and in particular for derivative markets. Option markets are by nature strongly atomized markets where supply and demand are split between a great number of quotation lines, called series, which are characterized by a different option

*Groupe Sup de Co Amiens — University of Poitiers CEREGE

type (call or put), maturity date and strike price. These markets, therefore, can work in continuous mode only if market makers provide them with a liquidity guarantee. Market makers thus take part directly in the option prices determination, by quoting bid–ask spreads which they are ready to negotiate.

Their role consists in smoothing discontinuities of demand or supply, and solving "the predictable instantaneity" problem (i.e. the fact that an investor can constantly know the price for which an asset can be exchanged). Their bid–ask spread is interpreted by investors as the price to pay for having the right to immediate liquidity, and by market makers as the remuneration received for the risks that they take. Indeed, market makers use their own inventory in order to provide this service, and consequently they accept to undergo the risk of the options price variation while waiting for new orders to arrive on the market.

The observation of market makers uses shows that the elaboration of their bid–ask spread is based generally on a complex and arbitrary "alchemy". However, if we wish to improve the liquidity, the transparency and the depth of option markets, it is necessary to draw up an analysis framework making it possible for these operators to rationalize their decision-making and offer much more competitive spread, while preserving a margin likely to remunerate their risks.

The analysis of the option bid–ask spread determinants on the French market which we propose in this article aims on the one hand to provide an alternative to the functional evaluation models, and on the other hand to advise the market authorities on the reforms to make in order to minimize the transaction costs, and increase the liquidity of this market.

After a presentation of the Paris Options Market (MONEP), which is characterized by a mixed structure (an order book and the presence of market makers), and the rule of market makers on its efficiency, we try to identify the determinants of market makers bid–ask spread, and consequently the costs of market making activity on this option market.

2 Organization and Rule of Market Makers on the MONEP Efficiency

The Paris Options Market (MONEP), open since 10 September 1987, aims to develop investments in shares. It appears today among the most active options markets in the world. It is managed by Euronext Paris SA, which ensures its organization and regulation.

Following the purchase of the LIFFE by Euronext, the activities on derivatives contracts of Euronext and the LIFFE were merged under the name of Euronext.LIFFE in 2002. Thus, in addition to stocks options contracts of very large French companies and CAC 40 index, new options contracts were launched in January 2003 on trackers, and in particular on two most liquid of Euronext: CAC 40 Master Unit and the Dow–Jones Euro STOXX 50 Master Unit.

Since its creation, the MONEP has undergone deep changes in its organization and trading rules, in particular in the liquidity services provided by market makers. The development of this market aims at improving its general efficiency, adapting its structures to the investor's requirements, and making it more attractive in comparison with the other option markets, especially Eurex and CBOE.

Market makers play an important role in terms of liquidity, transparency, and depth on the MONEP. They offer a real service to this market. Without these intermediaries, the MONEP could not exist, because it is improbable, given the great number of series, that each order from a customer finds an opposite order, on the same option, at the same time, and price.

On the MONEP, there are two kinds of market makers: Permanent Market Makers (PMMs), and Responding Market Makers (RMMs).[a]

The functions, legal constraints and advantages which are attached to the first category of market makers are stronger than for the second category. To compensate for obligations regarding the supply of liquidity, market makers benefit from a reduction in expenses, and provide a reduced insurance to cover their open position. More precisely, the reductions concern:

- The transaction costs for their trading on the MONEP (according to a sliding scale tariff).
- The overheads on their internal accounts open in the clearing system.
- The transaction costs for their trading on the underlying asset in order to cover their positions.

This paragraph intends to show how the market makers calculate their spread, their role, and their impact on the MONEP.

2.1 *The Market Makers Bid–Ask Spread*

By their action, market makers smooth discontinuities of the demand or the supply in order to be ready to sell or buy at quoted prices. As they intervene with the aim of making profits, their spread must at least cover the cost of this instantaneity service provided to the market. For Stoll (1989), the cost of

[a]http://www.monep.fr/pub/schemamarket.pdf.

this service comprises three types of costs: transaction costs, inventory holding costs, and those due to unfavorable information.

2.1.1 The Transaction Costs

These costs, named also the order processing costs, come from the obligation to remain present on the market (information costs and access to the market) and the costs of processing and executing orders. As the market makers benefit from significant reductions in the negotiation and management expenses of their accounts in the compensation system, these are the costs related to the obligation to remain present on the market that they must recover. In fact, the companies operating as market makers must specifically assign significant human, material (especially data-processing) and financial means to this operation.

The order processing cost remunerates the liquidity and immediacy service (Demsetz, 1968) which ensures the market maker. Whereas on the markets dominated by the orders, part of these costs appears in explicit form through the commissions and brokerage fees regulated to the intermediaries, it does not remain one implicit share represented by a spread fraction. In fact, the agents who make the orders with limited prices are suppliers of liquidity and play the role which the market maker ensures on the counterpart markets.

The purchaser with limited price is a seller of an option to sell; the seller with limited price is the seller of an option to buy (Copeland and Galai, 1983). When an agent fixes his limiting price, he needs to be remunerated for the option he is offering and that increases the asking price if he sells or decreases the bid price if he buys, which leads to the widening of the spread in the order book.

2.1.2 The Inventory Holding Costs

These costs are related to the stocks fluctuation risk on which market makers take a position and at the opportunity cost of holding on to these stocks.

To respond to public liquidity needs, a market maker can be made to take a position that does not correspond, in terms of risk and diversification, with his preferences. Consequently, he undergoes a utility loss. He can then either continue to hold this portfolio, or to implement an attractive pricing policy in order to reconstruct his portfolio according to his preferences.

In the second case, he will change the position of his spread in relation to the equilibrium prices in order to induce public transactions which would equalize his position: he will lower his selling price after a purchase, and will increase his purchase price after a sale. Thus, to compensate for his utility loss or to prevent this policy reducing its expected profits, he will systematically increase his initial spread, and he will pass on his anticipated costs to all the investors. In fact, the choice between one or the other of the two strategies will depend on their respective expected costs.

The inventory holding costs were modeled by Ho and Stoll (1981). They were also studied by Amihud and Mendelson (1980), Demsetz (1968), Ho and Stoll (1983), and Stoll (1978). On the markets dominated by prices, a market maker must execute the orders which are delivered to him. That leaves him holding a non-optimal and badly diversified portfolio. To limit this problem, the market maker practices an attractive pricing policy in order to reabsorb his open positions and to regain his equilibrium position.

When the market maker executes a sale order, he buys securities and increases his stock. In order to justify transactions to the purchaser which would enable him to decrease this stock, he also lowers his asking price, and in parallel, he decreases his bid price in order to discourage the sale orders. In the same way after having executed a sale order, the market maker increases his bid price and his asking price in order to justify the buying orders and to slow down the sale orders.

On the markets with orders book, this phenomenon persists if we suppose the presence of agents making orders with limited price. These agents play the role of market makers and can practice an attractive inciting pricing policy in order to accelerate the lifting of the option which they propose.

2.1.3 The Adverse Selection Costs

These costs are related to the presence on the market of investors having privileged information. When market makers negotiate with these operators, they lose money because the publication of this information involves a modification of the stock equilibrium price that this market maker had not anticipated.

Consequently, if the market makers are unable to identify the informed investors on a market, they will systematically increase their spread in order to reduce the load of the potential losses (caused by any change of the stock equilibrium price) on all the operators. However, if their spread is too broad, they lose the expected incomes coming from the exchanges with the agents motivated by liquidity. The optimal spread is thus the result of a compromise between the expected profits on the liquidity transactions, and the expected losses of the exchanges revealing privileged information.

The adverse selection component was modeled by Copeland and Galai (1983), Glosten and Milgrom (1985), and Easley and O'Hara (1987). The market maker constantly risks making exchanges with investors likely to be better informed than him. He fixes his prices at the purchase and at the sale in order to maximize his profit which is none other than the difference between the profits realized with the non-informed agents and the losses recorded in his transactions with the informed ones. The response of the market maker unable to discriminate between the informed agents and the non-informed is to systematically widen the spread.

These costs involve the same evolution of the spread as the position costs, but for different reasons. After the execution of a sale order, the market maker decreases his bid price and his asking price because a sale realized on the lower limit, i.e. with the bid, means that the expectation of the true value of the security is lower than the market maker had anticipated.

On the markets with order books, this component persists. An agent making orders with limited price is constantly exposed to be outdone by better informed agents and he therefore fixes his limiting price by taking into account this risk of adverse selection, thus, widening the order book spread.

In practice, the options market makers on the MONEP determine their bid–ask spread in two stages.

First of all, using models derived from the Cox, Ross and Rubinstein model, or that of Black and Scholes (their models integrate the American character of the stock options and the short term index options, and the dividend payments), they calculate the option theoretical price for various assumptions of the underlying asset volatility and price, and they obtain a "sheet of price".

Then, they determine their spread starting from the theoretical price corresponding to the volatility observed on the market, or to the historical volatility which they estimate for the day (if need be, by updating it if significant information arrives during the session). For their purchase price they generally cut off a margin of one point of volatility from the theoretical price. While, for their selling price, they generally add a margin of one volatility point to the theoretical price.

However, sometimes, when competition is intense and when they wish to reverse their position on certain classes, they agree to take a weaker margin, of approximately a half point of volatility. The result is that they have a spread of generally two points of volatility. For this value, all the expense are covered. But when is one point of volatility determined? In fact, these observations show that the market makers take an arbitrary margin and that they do not know their reserve spread with precision (spread which equalizes their costs).

The spread actually realized on an outward and a return journey (a purchase followed by a sale or conversely) does not correspond inevitably to that initially quoted. In an efficient market, following a great number of operations, the quoted spread is equal on average to that realized in the condition of an absence of systematic displacement of the spread after a transaction. This is why it is noted in general that the realized spread is on average lower than that quoted.

The literature finds two reasons for the systematic variations of the spread after an exchange. On the one hand, a market maker is likely to move his spread in order to facilitate his end position. He thereby decreases the length of time he is holding the stocks on which he has declared, and consequently the risk of price fluctuation. After having bought a significant quantity of stocks, he lowers his selling price, and symmetrically, increases his purchase price after a sale.

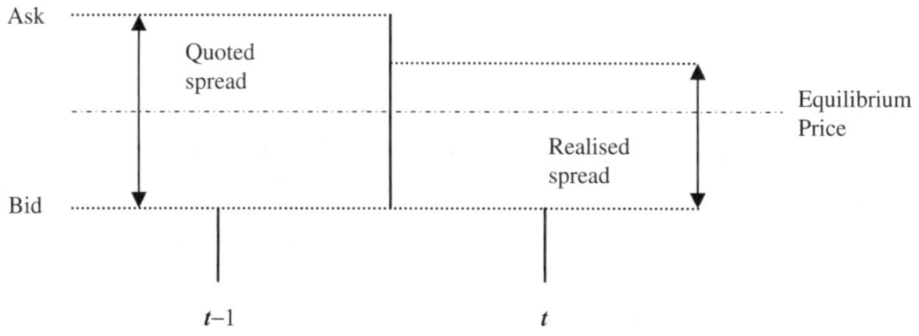

In addition, the presence of investors having private information and going counterpart the market makers is a factor in the reduction of the realized spread compared to the initial spread because the equilibrium price varies. Indeed, after a sale carried out with one of these operators (it is a purchase for the market maker), the equilibrium price will drop because privileged information becomes public.

The market makers will shift their spread so that it encompasses this new equilibrium price. Then, they will resell the stocks at a demand price in T lower than that in $T-1$. Then the realized spread in T will be lower than that quoted in $T-1$.

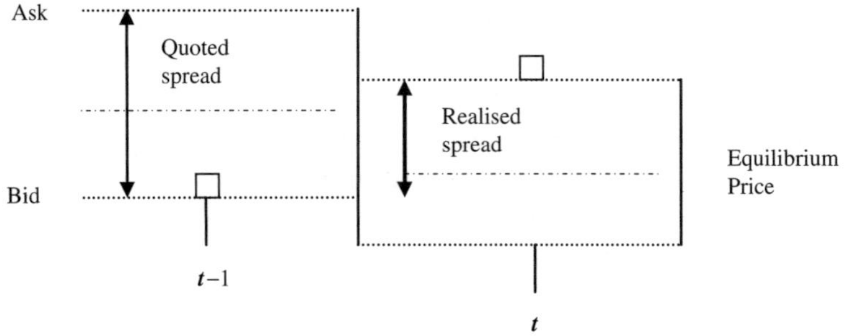

Consequently, following systematic displacements of the spread, the realized spread is lower than the announced spread.

2.2 Impact of Market Makers on the MONEP Efficiency

The market makers are the second most significant player on the MONEP[b] (more than 35% of the options negotiated in the 2001 second semester), after the investment companies and ahead of the credit institutions. Their share in this market activity decreased overall since 1991 (they were then responsible for 55.44% of the transactions), because now a lot of transactions are realized between "final customers".

In fact, several markets makers intervene only on some very active option classes (such as, for example, the two classes of stock index options) and because they have a weak market share of the total activity. With regard to competition created by the market makers, it differs according to the particular segment: the stock options or the stock index options market.

On the stock options market, the market makers take only small positions because the low volume of operations does not enable them to make a sufficient profit to cover the risks related to the evaluation errors, the existence of investors having privileged information, and the difficulty of covering themselves for the underlying asset with the monthly payment. In fact, the low volume of the underlying asset transaction does not allow them most of the time to intervene without influencing the underlying asset prices.

However, this price shift is not taken into account in the initial evaluation of the option. Moreover, as these market makers make weak profits (the margins are significant but treated volumes are low) on each options class, this activity

[b] http://www.euronext.com/tools/statisticscenter.

is profitable for a company only in the circumstances where it affects market makers on several classes.

On the other hand, on the stock index options market, there are many operations, and the market makers can be covered easily at lower cost on the stock index futures. This means that the market makers are subjected to strong competition, and they take a small margin which is compensated by significant negotiated volumes. In addition, we note, since the opening of MONEP, a contracting of the spreads which is explained by: greater competition, increase in the transaction volume, growth of the orders number with limited price, and the pressure of the market authorities.

2.3 *Advantages of this Counterpart System*

The market makers or specialists take part directly in the price determination, by listing a spread to which they are ready to negotiate. The width of this spread depends on their legal obligations, the competition they deliver, the information they hold, and the arrival of orders from the public.

The compensation guaranteed by the market makers compared to that observed on the specialists traditional markets (such as, for example, the NYSE, and the AMEX), has the following advantages:

- By narrowing the spreads it makes it much easier to approach the equilibrium price. In fact, Ho and Stoll show that the greater the number of markets makers, the narrower the spread is, and the lower the profit per transaction. At the equilibrium point, the number of market makers is such that their profit is equal to the marginal cost associated with the stock detention to which they are entitled. In this context, this cost depends only on the characteristics of this stock, and no longer on the preferences of the counterparts (as it is the case when it is in a monopoly situation).
- Such a system increases the instantaneity of the execution of orders because the market makers must always post a spread, in order to maintain the authorized maximum variation, and to offer a minimal quantity at the posted prices.
- Finally, it improves the market elasticity: it makes it possible to absorb significant volumes of transaction without causing strong fluctuation of the prices. It thus decreases the volatility of prices and avoids resorting to the suspension of quotations. For example, at the time of the October 1987, October 1989, and August 1990 crashes, many stocks on the NYSE could not be listed because the specialists system did not ensure the

immediate compensation for the massive sale orders, while the derivatives markets (where markets makers are present), like the MONEP, were very active.

However, these assertions must be moderated if we refer to the Reiganum study.[c] This author studied the influence of the market microstructure on the instantaneity supply, by comparing the NASDAQ liquidity premiums (market of markets makers competition), with those of the NYSE (market of the specialists in monopoly situation). He observes that neither of the two markets dominates the other in this function. He explains this as being the result of the economy of scale carried out on the NYSE, which centralizes the Stock Exchange orders, thus lowering the transaction costs. This measure makes it possible to compensate for the disadvantage caused by the lack of competition.

In conclusion, we can say that the assessment of the market makers on the MONEP is generally speaking positive. They bring liquidity to a cost which tends to decrease as the clear improvement of the market indicators has shown for several years (a reduction of the spreads, a better liquidity ...). But, that organizational and liquidity problems remain on this market, in particular for the stock options.

3 The Bid–Ask Spread Components

In this section, we seek to estimate the factors explaining the formation of the stock options spread on the MONEP and to test if they confirm to the "*bid–ask spread*" theory.

3.1 Methodology

The literature typically distinguishes dealer markets and auction markets. Market makers are the only providers of liquidity in dealer markets. Due to the unpredictability of the order the demand and supply is not always balanced. If the order must be submitted immediately it requires that costs be made by market makers who stand ready and wait to trade the incoming orders. These costs are compensated by the bid–ask spread.

The spread of a stock is the difference, at a given date, between its purchase price and its selling price. In dealer markets, the spread is obtained by

[c]Reiganum MR., Market microstructure and asset pricing: Year empirical investigation of NYSE and NASDAQ stocks. *Newspaper of Financial Economics*, 28, 127–147.

incorporating the various proposals of the market makers, while in auction markets, it corresponds to the difference between the two best limits of the limit order book.

The market microstructure literature tried to study the behavior of market makers, and the elements which they take into account at the time to calculate the size and the quantities of their spread. It was mainly based on the following three theoretical approaches:

- Models that include transaction costs — The spread compensates market makers' transaction costs: Roll (1984), and Cohen *et al.* (1981, and 1986).
- Inventory models: In these models, the spread is the remuneration of market makers for the stock storage costs, for which they agree to offer instantaneity: Ho and Stoll (1980, 1981, and 1983), O' Hara and Oldfield (1986), Grossman & Miller (1988), and Stoll (1978, and 1989).
- Models of asymmetry information. Glosten and Milgrom (1985), Kyle (1985), and Admati and Pleiderer (1988) show that market makers face a risk of asymmetry information, because the activity of market making obliges them to negotiate with investors who have more information. Market makers try to compensate for their losses due to trading with informed investors, by requesting a higher spread for the trade with the non informed investors.

The study of the different models of the spread on stock and option markets shows that these three explanatory approaches are complementary. Indeed, when a market marker posts a spread, and takes a position to go counterpart, it supports the transaction, inventory, and asymmetry information costs:

- The transaction costs are related to the obligation of presence on the market, and include, the costs of information, access to the market, treatment, and execution of the orders.
- Moreover, as liquidity suppliers, the market makers are frequently obliged to take on a stock of securities, and the inventory costs reflect the diversification loss which results from holding these securities.
- The costs of asymmetrical information result from the presence of informed operators. Each market maker fixes its spread therefore by maximizing the resulting expected profits from the transactions with the investors of liquidity, and by minimizing the expected losses, coming from the exchanges with the informed agents.

So, it is necessary to develop a general approach integrating all these costs. But existing theoretical models fail to break up the spread into all its components. This is the reason why we choose to develop an empirical approach.

According to the inventory theory, the spread is the remuneration that the market makers received to compensate for the costs of holding the stocks on which they offered instantaneity. The price (noted "P_o" in our model) of the option represents the immobilized capital to ensure the service of liquidity on the options market, while the share price (P) corresponds to the cover cost on the market of the underlying asset. The higher the share price (option), the higher the inventory cost will be, and the same for the spread. Consequently, the predictions for the relation between the spread and these variables are positive.

In addition, the more a stock is liquid, the more the market makers can hope to turn over their positions quickly and find a portfolio corresponding to their preferences, and the lower the inventory cost will be. To measure the level of market activity, we chose the following variables: the transaction volume of the option (V_o) and the stock (V), the transaction number of the option (T_o), and the stock (T). We wait therefore until the relationship between the spread and these variables is negative.

However, the effect of volume on the spread is ambivalent. Indeed, the literature indicates that according to the asymmetrical information costs approach, the volume transmitted information ignored by the market makers. Thus, the more the volume the market makers declare is raised, the more it increases the spread.

But, under pressure of competition, the market maker can be forced to reduce his spread and to exploit volume. Consequently, the effect of the volume of the (V_o) option on the spread is *a priori* unspecified. In addition, the more remote the maturity (E), the more likely it is that the option becomes "in the money", and the price is higher. This results in more significant inventory costs than if the option maturity were shorter (a positive sign is expected for this relation).

According to the approach based on information asymmetry, the compensation activity obliges the market makers to negotiate with investors who have more information than them. The volatility of the option price (stock) reflects the risk of an unfavorable change[d] of price to which the market makers is

[d]This variation of course not anticipated by the contents of market is caused by the transactions carried out with the informed operators.

exposed. In theory, by taking a position on the support market, the market makers can be covered perfectly. But in practice that is not always possible because of the transaction costs (the higher the recombining number, the greater the cover cost) and an insufficient counterpart on the First Market. The result is, that the systematic risk remains and the market makers seek to compensate for their loss by a broader spread (positive sign hoped for the two variables).

Finally, we defined a variable, called Bloc (the ratio of the number of block transactions to the total transaction numbers of the stock on the day), in order to estimate the impact of the block stock transactions on the options market.

This impact is double, and is explained both by the inventory costs theory, and by the asymmetrical information costs theory. In fact, the more the number of blocks exchanged on the stock market grows, the more the liquidity cost increases on this market, thus the cover cost in stocks rises, and the market makers reflect this cost with the final customers by widening their spread. But this variable can be also interpreted like a measurement of unfavorable information. Accordingly, the more the ratio grows, the more the market makers require a high spread in order to compensate for their losses due to the informed operations. In both cases, a positive relationship is expected between the variable "Block" and the options spread.

The formal model, defined by the three explanatory theories of the spread, is written as follows:

$$\begin{aligned}\text{Relative Spread} = B_0 + B_1\ P + B_2\ V + B_3\ E_p + B_4\ T + B_5\ B + B_6\ P_0 \\ + B_7\ V_0 + B_8\ E_{p0} + B_9\ T_0 + B_{10}\ E + \mu,\end{aligned}$$

where

$P(P_0)$: the daily average price of stock (of option)
$V(V_0)$: the daily transaction average volume on stock (on option)
$Ep(E_{p0})$: the average standard deviation price of stock (of option)
$T(T_0)$: the average transaction number, by day, on stock (on option)
B: the transaction number ratio in block by the daily transaction number on stock
E: the number of days before the option maturity
μ: a white noise.

The average relative spread is calculated for each series (maturity, strike) based on the difference between the best bid–ask price divided by the medium of this variation. In fact, a small number of research reports relate to the analysis of the bid–ask spread determinants on the options markets. This state of affairs results at the same time from the complexity of this type of financial product, the relative youth of the options markets compared to the stock markets, and more prosaically from the difficulty of obtaining, and of treating data on these markets.

This last difficulty comes mainly from the organization of quotations and from the market authority policy with respect to the diffusion of information. Before October 1995, all the MONEP options were negotiated by auction and the spreads announced on the floor were not recorded in the quotation system. The data-gathering is carried out not only under the theoretical condition of data availability, but also under that of their accessibility.

With respect to the intra-daily stock data (transaction price and volume of stocks), the extraction was carried out directly from the data base of the Euronext market, as was the case for the daily data on volatilities. While for the options intra-daily data, we had to recover them and make auto-savings from the "Reuters" quotations screens. Our data relates to the stock option over a six weeks period from 4 February to 18 March, 2002.

3.2 *Results Analysis*

First, we built a regression model which we calculated according the least squares ordinary method. However, according to the literature, the form of this model is generally log-linear in order to reduce heteroscedasticity problems, and to obtain a better adjustment. But in our case, the use of this form does not make it possible to increase the explanatory capacity of our regression model.[e] The results of this regression are presented in Table 1.

The results obtained show that all the variables are significant and have the expected signs, except for three variables (P_o, T, B). With respect to these variables, two have non-significant T for a 5% risk: the transaction number of stock (T), and the transaction type (B). On the other hand, the third variable, the option price (P_o), does not have the expected sign. These results call for the following observations.

First, the two non-significant variables (T and B) do not seem to have an effect on the market makers spread formation. The result concerning the stock transaction number contradicts the assumptions partially formulated above. However, the absence of variable T significance is probably due to the strong

[e]Indeed, R^2 of the model log-linear is lower than that of the model of linear regression.

Table 1: Results of the linear regression model.

Variable	Estimated coefficients of the parameters
(Constant)	0.0878*
P	0.0094*
P_o	−0.0197*
V	−0.0003*
V_o	−0.0004*
T	−0.0001
T_o	−0.0135*
Block	−0.0087
Expiry	0.0019*
Ep	0.0652*
Epo	0.0941*

Notes:
R^2 adjusted = 0.621
The Fisher statistics significance degree = 0.00
Durbin–Watson statistics = 2.53
The sign ($*$) means that the T student test is significant at the 95% threshold.

correlation that exists with the variable indicating the transaction volume on the stock market (V).

The absence of statistical significance of the variable BLOCK can be related to the taking into account of the blocks only exchanged on SUPERCAC system. With an aim of checking if the totality of block operations, including those carried out outside market, had an impact on the spread, we defined a new variable called BLOC_HM which is similar to the variable BLOCK, but whose reference is the totality of the transactions carried out on and outside the market. More precisely, it is the ratio of the number of block transactions (on the NSC and beyond) to the total number of daily stock transactions (on and outside market).

Then, we estimated the model of regression again. This new variable is not statistically significant. This result was foreseeable given the strong correlation between the two variables (0.9814). These results tend to show that the decisions of the institutional investors are independent and that the rate of concentration of these investors on the same stock is weak. Thus, a first result is that the variables T and B do not have an effect on the market makers spread formation, and thus on the liquidity cost.

Secondly, however, the option price (P_0) is significant, but does not have the expected sign. This result can be explained by taking into account the specificities of the MONEP. Let us recall that, according to the inventory paradigm, P_0 represents the amount invested in options to offer instantaneity.

However, the market makers on the MONEP generally have a clear sales position on their options portfolio. In fact, they more often go counterpart to options purchasers than they do to sellers, because of the existence of asymmetrical risk between a purchaser and a seller of options. The purchaser of an option pays a premium to the seller and can lose at maximum the amount of his premium (limited risk), while the seller receives this premium, but in a situation of unlimited risk. As the market makers of the MONEP have in general a seller net position, that means that they receive more premiums than they pay, this is why the sign of P_0 is reversed with respect to our starting assumption.

We can now look at the adjustment quality. It can be noted that with the degree of significance of the Fisher statistics of the regression near to zero, and an R^2 correction of 62.1%, this model has a fairly good capacity to explain the evolution of the options spread. Moreover, the Durbin–Watson statistics show that the residues are not auto-correlated. The estimation of the model by the method "of Ordinary Least Squares" thus seems validated.

The option price, that of the stock and the option transactions number are the most significant explanatory factors of our model, since the three of them account for 68% of total R^2. These results are consistent with our assumptions and show that:

- On the one hand, the modeling of the option spread is first a problem of the option price evaluation (the option price only accounts for 24% of the spread), and on the other, a problem of microstructure, or more precisely of liquidity services cost. This cost has a great influence since it relies on the funded capital to cover itself on the stock market (the stock price, P, accounts for 13% of the spread), on the option market liquidity (the option transactions number, T_0, accounts for 11% of the spread), and on the degree of transmission of the liquidity characteristics of the underlying asset (the transaction volume, V, and it transaction numbers, T, of stock accounts for 3% of the option spread).

  The biggest cost in the liquidity supply is thus due to the cover cost on the stock market, because if the market makers do not hold the portfolio shares, they must acquire them. To do this they must:
  - — immobilize funds which they have. This cost is therefore allied to an opportunity cost,

— borrow the corresponding sum. The cost is equal to the interest rate paid to have the funds.

- In addition, the asymmetrical information cost is relatively weak in comparison to the significant increase in volatility (more than 35% over the studied period). The standard deviation of the stock price and that of the option account for 14% of the spread, while the variable "BLOCK" is non-significant. However, these standard deviations reflect the risk of an unfavorable change of price to which the market makers is exposed when it takes a position "in option". However, since the explanatory capacity of these variables is equal to only 14%, one can conclude from it that the MONEP is not dominated by informed operators.

Last, the impact of the liquidity variables (volume and a number of transactions in particular) shows that the liquidity characteristics of the support market are transmitted to the option.

The principal results show that:

- The modeling of the option spread is a problem of option price evaluation and microstructure, or more precisely of liquidity services cost.
- The strongest cost in the supply of liquidity corresponds to the amount invested to cover itself on the stock market.
- The asymmetrical information cost is "relatively" weak taking into account strong volatility observed.
- The liquidity characteristics of the stock market transmit to the market options.

These results are comparable with those obtained by Khoury *et al.* (1991) on the Canadian options market, and contributed to identify other factors influencing the spread than those highlighted by Ho and Stoll (1983). Last, the existence of moderate asymmetry information costs confirms the results of Mannaï (1995), and leads us to conclude that the MONEP is not dominated by informed operators, contrary to the generally accepted ideas concerning this type of derivatives market.

4 Conclusion

In conclusion, this study made it possible to understand better the formation of the spread on the French option market. It shows that the modeling of an option spread is first a problem of the option price evaluation, and second a microstructure problem.

However, the principal adjustment variable of the evaluation models used by the market makers is the volatility, which remains largely unforeseeable. In order to allow the market makers to manage the risk of volatility better, one could advise the market authorities to create, like the CBOE, a future contract on volatility. That would encourage the market makers to decrease their spreads, because they could evaluate their reserve spread more precisely (which equalizes all their costs), and thus would contribute to improving the MONEP liquidity.

In this perspective, MONEP SA developed two indices of volatility on the CAC 40 index, released since 8 October, 1997. Nevertheless, no long term contract on these supports yet currently exists, and the MONEP does not propose anything for stock options.

With regard to the market making activity costs, the highest cost is the inventory cost and corresponds to the cover cost on the underlying asset, while the asymmetrical information cost is weak. This last result corroborates the conclusion that this market is not dominated by informed operators. But the two types of models, inventory and asymmetrical information costs, are strongly independent. In order to analyze their individual effects more precisely, it will be interesting to develop two alternative extensions. The first extension relies on the fact that inventory effects induce negative serial correlation in orders and in quotes, in addition to the serial correlation from the bid–ask bounce of prices (Huang and Stoll, 1997). Whereas, the second extension takes a cross-section approach and uses information on trading pressures in other stocks to infer the inventory component of the spread in a particular stock.

Moreover, we showed that the liquidity characteristics of the stock market are transmitted to their option. Thus, the two principal explanations of the MONEP growth are, on the one hand the reforms carried out to improve its general efficiency, to adapt its structures to the investors requirements, and to make it more attractive compared to the other options markets, and, on the other hand, the development of the stock market.

References

Admati, AR and Pfleiderer, P (1988). A theory of intraday trading patterns. *The Review of Financial Studies*, 1, 3–40

Copeland, TE and Galai, D (1983). Information effects on the bid-ask spread. *Journal of Finance*, 1457–1469.

Easley, D and O'Hara, M (1987). Price, trade size, and information in security markets. *Journal of Financial Economics,* 19, 69–90.

George, T and Longstaff, F (1993). Bid-ask spreads and trading activity in the S& P100 index options market. *Journal of Financial and Quantitative Analysis,* 28, 381–397.

Glosten, LR and Harris, L (1988). Estimating the components of the bid-ask spread. *Journal of Financial Economics,* 21, 123–142.

Glosten, LR and Milgrom, PR (1985). Bid, ask and transaction prices in a specialist market with heterogeneously informed traders. *Journal of Financial Economics,* 14, 71–100.

Grossman, SJ and Miller, M (1988). Liquidity and market structure. *Journal of Finance,* 43, 617–637.

Ho, T and Stoll, H (1983). The dynamics of dealer markets under competition. *Journal of Finance,* 38, 1053–1074.

Huang, RD and Stoll, HR (1997). The components of the bid-ask spread: A general approach. *The Review of Financial Studies,* 10(4), 995–1034.

Jameson, M and Wilhem, W (1992). Market making in the options markets and the costs of discrete hedge rebalancing. *Journal of Finance,* 47(2), 765–779.

John, K, Kochita, A and Subrahmanyam, MG (1993). The microstructure of options market: Informed trading, liquidity, volatility and efficiency. Working Paper, New York University.

Khoury, N, Yourougou, P and Vigneau, G (1991). Les déterminants du coût de la liquidité sur le marché canadien des options. *Revue d'analyse économique,* 67, 499–516.

Kyle, SA (1985). Continous auction and insider trading. *Econometrica,* 53, 1315–1335.

Mannai, S (1995). De la microstructure en général et de la liquidité en particulier: Théories et études empiriques sur le MONEP, *Economica,* Col. Recherche en Gestion.

Mayhew, S (2002). Competition, market structure, and bid-ask spreads in stock option markets. *Journal of Finance* 57, 931–958.

Mayhew, S, Sarin, A and Shastri, K (1998). The relationship between option trading intensity and the market microstructure of the underlying security. http://papers.ssrn.com/sol3/papers.cfm?abstract_id=6233.

Petrella, G (2001). Option market making: Theory and evidence. Working Paper, Università Cattolica del Sacro Cuore.

Roll, R (1984). A simple implicit measure of the effective bid-ask spread in an efficient market. *Journal of Finance,* 1127–1139.

Steigerwald, D and Vagnoni, RJ (2001). Option market microstructure and stochastic volatility. Department of Economics, UCSB. Departmental Working Papers, Paper 17–01, http://repositories.cdlib.org/ucsbecon/dwp/17-01.

Stephan, JA and Whaley, RE (1990). Intraday price change and trading volume relations in the stock and stock option markets. *Journal of Finance,* 45, 191–220.

Stoll, HR (1989). Inferring the components of the bid-ask spread: Theory and empirical tests. *Journal of Finance,* 115–134.

Vijh, AM (1990). Liquidity of CBOE equity options. *Journal of Finance,* 45(4), 1157–1179.

Wang, E (2000). Competition among exchanges: Does multiple listing affect trading costs on option markets? Working Paper, University of Chicago.

CHAPTER 24

DOES THE STANDARDIZATION OF BUSINESS PROCESSES IMPROVE MANAGEMENT? THE CASE OF ENTERPRISE RESOURCE PLANNING SYSTEMS

*Tawhid Chtioui**

Enterprise Resource Planning (ERP) systems have currently become tools that enable organizations to standardize business processes. They offer rich functionalities based on best practices. The purpose of this chapter is to study the impact of this standardization on organizations with reference to the different theoretical hypotheses linked to the relation Information Technology / organizational change and according to four firm's cases (Airports of Paris, Pechiney, France Telecom and L'oréal).

1 Introduction

Enterprise Resource Planning (ERP) is currently a great success with companies and its implementation has entailed remodelling management information systems (MIS), and above all, reconsidering management procedures within the organization. Henceforth, ERP systems are now tools that enable companies and multinationals to standardize their management processes. They offer rich and proven functionalities, based on best practices.

*Reims Management School and DRM-CREFIGE, Université Paris Dauphine 59, rue Pierre Taittinger — BP 302- 51061 Reims Cedex — France.
tawhid.chtioui@reims-ms.fr

Thus, most global companies are already equipped with ERP systems,[a] and more and more medium-sized companies are trying to build up unified information system based on this software package. "ERP meet the requirements of universality: that everyone should work in his own language and understand each other." (Mourlon & Neyer, 2002).

The introduction of ERP systems in organizations then induces a standardization of management processes that has been called for by organizations to help them lay the foundations of an international system and assist them with their globalization strategy.

However, this standardization of organizational cultures can fail to produce the expected results. "The implementation of ERP aims to change the organization but this process can prove risky." (Besson, 1999). So, then what are the effects of this standardization induced by ERP-Systems on organizations?

To answer this question, we conduct an empirical study in four firm's cases (Airports of Paris, Pechiney, France Telecom and Loréal).

After attempting to illustrate and define the ERP concept, this chapter shows the standardization potential of this tool. It then presents the effects of this standardization in accordance with the different theoretical approaches to the relation information and communication technologies versus organizational change.

2 The ERP Concept

Nowadays, ERP systems appear to have made their mark and become the standard for company information systems. Historically, company functional systems were developed on different equipment with different methodologies: realizations were thus generally heterogeneous both in terms of data representation and processing modes. This entailed many communication problems and some difficulties to control processing operations. Thus, the concept of ERP appeared in the form of integrated software packages whose purpose was to improve global coherence while contriving some form of modularity. It is thus an information system composed of standard functional modules directly linked to a single data base and that covers all the company's processes. Moreover, an ERP system is more often than not a solution with an international dimension, capable of managing multilegislation, multilingual,

---

[a]Seven in 10 of the highest profit-making companies and nine of the top 10 in terms of stock market capitalization are equipped with SAP (the undisputable market leader of ERP-systems) (Source: Curran *et al.*, 1998 and R. Scapens *et al.*, 1998).

and multicurrency contexts. Information feedback from the subsidiaries of a group, which are in different countries, has become possible. This is a major advantage in a globalization context since legal and linguistic environments are structuring levers for companies.

In parallel, other software packages have been developed to complement ERP to improve certain low performance functions or to add new ones. Most of these applications concern decision support: the whole system is then called SO-ERP or System Organized around an ERP.

In spite of the diversity of ERP systems offered on the market, the architecture and the functioning of these software packages are similar. They are organized in modules, each module covering one of the major functions of the company, including the data processing for the different management processes involved.[b] The accountancy or the financial modules often form the core around which the other modules are organized.

3 ERP and Standardization

The characteristics described below, have led corporations and multinational groups to consider ERP as tool that standardize processes within their organizations. Indeed these tools meet the requirements of local regulations (accounting plan, legal statements and multilingual management). ERP systems have thus enabled multinationals to lay the foundations of an international system, and support their globalization strategy.

3.1 The Evolution of Standardization in Organizations

The basic purpose of standardization is to achieve the most efficient use of resources. The most important resources being the employees, standardization has always focused on the best use of human resources. Adam Smith mentions work standardization in his book "A guide to the wealth of nations". The next great step came with Taylor's research, in which he talked about standardizing all types of work. Eventually, as work became more and more complicated, people were trained to perform specific tasks. This was the beginning of the era of professionalism: it meant standardizing people. Nowadays, with the development of economic activity, increasingly large companies and the modernization of management methods, we are witnessing the standardization of organizations.

---

[b]In the case of SAP R/3 (the most current ERP in the world), a process is a set of activities using and producing data.

Until recently, information technology did not play a significant role in standardization. As organizations developed and competition increased, companies were led to improve performance. As work became more and more mechanized, Production, Finance and Human Resources were the first departments to be computerized. Financial accounting Software (FAS), the Payroll Package had a great impact on these three departments. This was the great step towards the organized entry of information technology into companies: the standardization of departments within organizations. The next logical step for any company was then to extend the standardization concept across all departments within the organization. And since each department is necessarily linked to another, a comprehensive suite called Enterprise Resource Planning (ERP) led to the standardization of work practices.

3.2 The Standardization of Business Processes

Beyond its tool aspect, ERP is above all a management concept. Its implementation has externalities on the overall functioning of the company. It affects two major elements: the information system and the organizational processes. Indeed, the systems organized around an ERP are presented as a solution to the dispersion and fragmentation of information problem in companies. They use integrated client-server technology and set up large data bases which considerably improve the availability and the circulation of information in the organization: all the information is captured once, is accessible at every level of the organization and is available in real time. The implementation of ERP is coupled with a standardization of the processes based on the benchmarking offered by the software chosen. Thus, the implementation of an integrated management software package induces two sorts of standardization: inside the organization and outside it.

3.2.1 Standardization Inside the Organization

An ERP is based on a single referential: all the data and the objects used by the different modules are defined in a single standardized format and managed by only one type of software (very often a management system of relational data bases). In the same way, user interfaces are defined identically, whatever the modules. Thus, capture screens and financial statements can appear in the same form whatever the language of the user.

ERP systems offer technological evolution that corresponds to the introduction of intranet transactional architectures and technologies linked to the Internet. Thanks to its standardized communication protocol, the Internet has contributed to the improvement of the system of data exchange. Data exchange is easier and access to applications has extended to a larger number of users. This is standardization of communication within the organization induced by ERP. In addition, this expansion of data sharing technologies has led to job sharing without geographical constraints. This development has extended to a new concept "knowledge management", which involves the standardization of knowledge throughout the organization.

3.2.2 Standardization Outside the Organization

The first ERP systems were custom-built. But very soon, new ERP systems appeared that offered a major advantage, that is to say, not only were they better than their predecessors, but they also aimed to optimize management processes. Thus, the engineer who designed the integrated software package

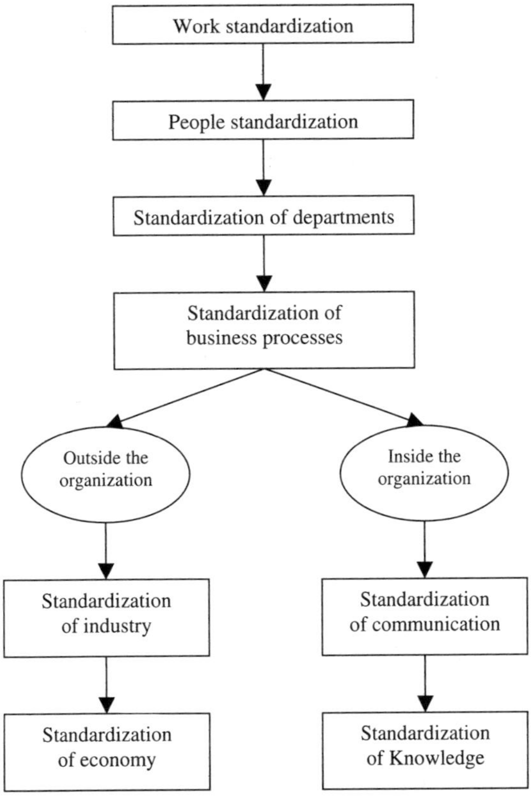

Figure 1: The evolution of standardization in organizations

based it on process models stemming from best practices in the sector (the know-how of the best companies in a given sector is capitalized on). Lee and Lee (2000) describe ERP systems as a basis for the best practices and best management processes, offering methods that are recognized as the most advanced in the business world or in a given industry. The analysis of best practices enables the publisher of software packages to define a set of management rules which constitute a standard for a given sector. This then brings about the standardization of business processes not only on the scale of the organization, but also on that of the entire industry. We even believe that with the continuous development of the new information and communication technology industry, the next step will lead to a standardization of the economy.

4 Research Method

This chapter describes the main results of a research study that aimed to propose a set of guidelines for the impact of business process standardization on management, when implementating an ERP. Four case studies involving big companies were retained. The first case study was undertaken at L'Oreal Group International, a leader in cosmetics and beauty. The second case study was carried out at Pechiney Group, the world's fourth largest producer and transformer of primary aluminum. The third case study was conducted in "Aéroport de Paris" Group (ADP), the leading airport group in Europe. The fourth case is that of France Telecom (FT), first French telecommunication company. The first three groups use the same ERP: the last generation of SAP: SAP R/3 while France Telecom uses Oracle Applications.

We select for this work a hybrid exploration of empirical observations and theoretical knowledge. Indeed, we initially mobilized concepts and integrated the literature concerning our research object. And then we lean on this knowledge to give sense to our empirical observations. The explorative character of this research drove us to choose a qualitative approach. The empirical research was conducted using a semi-structured interview method. Altogether 20 management controllers and managers from different levels were interviewed in the four companies in our sample.

For the data analysis, we chose to use the method of matrix analysis proposed by Miles and Huberman (1984). This mainly for two reasons: first, it is simple, rigorous and asks less time than the other methods of content analysis; second, it corresponds perfectly to the data collected through interviews. This method consists in analyzing the results by drawing a matrix where all the questions appear in the top of page (columns) while the referees are identified on the side of page (lines). Visually the subjects emerge clearly from such a shaping, made by direct reference to the transcriptions of interviews.

5 ERP: Effects of Standardization and Organizational Change

The standardization of management procedures induced by ERP can have very varied effects on organizations. It appeared essential to position the different case studies in relation to the different theoretical theses on the relation of ICT[c] versus organizational change. In the literature on the subject, three competing approaches are generally used to describe this ICT vs organizational change relation: the contingent approach to technological determinism, the intentional approach and the emerging approach.

5.1 The Effects of Standardization According to the Technological Determinist Hypothesis

5.1.1 The Contingent Approach to Technological Determinism

According to this hypothesis, ICTs of exogenous origin strongly determine and restrict the structure and the practices of organization management. The use of the same technology automatically or almost automatically entails the same effects in all organizations. Leavitt and Whisler (1958), as well as Simon (1977),[d] estimate that ICTs can cause lasting changes to organizations and to the nature of managerial work. Leavitt and Whisler (1958) estimate that the development of ICTs could generate centralization and a reduction in hierarchical levels. Simon (1977) claims that middle managers should stay on and that structures could become more complex with the development of transversal links. Leavitt and Whisler's vision comes within the scope of the theory of contingence, which was to develop subsequently and which considers technology as one of the main determinants in the structure of organizations.

In 1977, Chandler, a company historian asserted that the invisible hand of managers has replaced the invisible hand of the market where new techniques and market expansion have enabled an unprecedented volume of products to pass through the different stages of production and distribution at an unprecedented pace. He illustrated the case of the big railway companies which could

---

[c]Information and communication technology.

[d]In Markus and Robey, 1988.

not have developed without the telegraph, which enabled people geographically scattered to communicate. Technologies and more particularly ICTs could thus be decisive in explaining the development of large companies and their structures.

According to Berry (1983), management instruments (e.g. ratios, matrixes, computerized management systems) determine behavior and thus act like invisible technology. In his view, these instruments (conceptual or material) simplify reality, structure the behavior of agents, generate local logics often opposed to reform, regulate the balance of power and condition the coherence of an organization.

Rowe (1999) explains the considerable development of the market for ERP software in the last few years (though these systems are very costly for companies) by the fact that the marketing of ERP is based on a determinist explanation of standardization and on the transferability of some of the knowledge linked to experience.

5.1.2 Pechiney: Optimizing Management Processes

Strong data and language standardization simplifies communication and reduces the difficulties of training users. It obliges all the entities in a same company to work in the same way, which facilitates comparisons between the different units; the consolidation of data and the exchange of information. The standardization induced by ERP has thus enabled Pechiney to lay the foundations for an international system and thus accompanies them in their globalization strategy. When SAP R/3 was implemented, operational processes such as the follow-up of customer orders, manufacturing management, accountancy were studied, modeled, and optimized since ERP is designed around best practices. The customer company thus benefits from these best practices when it harmonizes the organization around its information system.

So, groups resulting from multiple mergers or companies disorganized by fast growth can thus find a rational framework to structure themselves. Bancroft *et al.* (1998), Davenport (1998), Bingi *et al.* (1999), Adam and O'Doherty (2000), Parr and Shanks (2000), and Summer (2000) specify that ERP is associated with a set of management processes based on best practices and composed of knowledge which ideally should be transferred to organizations. This knowledge is produced outside the organization, by a group of experts and is introduced in the organization in addition to existing knowledge. Implicitly or explicitly, this supposes a "transfer of knowledge" between two separate entities — the expert who develops the information system and the organization. On one hand, this transfer results in a better functioning organization. On the other, it results in the benchmarking of work procedures, methods and rules.

5.2 The Effects of Standardization According to an Intentionalist Hypothesis

5.2.1 The Intentionalist Hypothesis

According to this approach, the structure of an organization is the result of a deliberate strategy freely decided by the managers. Managerial perception and will are the main explanatory elements in the conception of organizations. From this perspective, ITCs are mere tools that managers adopt and use according to their needs. As early as 1977, Galbraith presented the different alternatives available to managers to adapt to the incertitude of the environment. They can either reduce incertitude (e.g. by changing the environment) or increase the organization's information processing capacity (by developing transversal links or by designing higher performance information systems).

Following the example of Galbraith; Tushman and Nadler (1978), estimate that to answer the needs for information, managers are not forced to develop their information system. They can adapt the structure of their companies or choose among other optimal solutions according to the context.

For Daft and Lengel (1986), companies need information systems, not only to deal with incertitude, but also to face up to the ambiguity of any situation. The richer a system is in terms of quantity of information, the more it helps in dealing with incertitude, but it also generates more ambiguity. Managers have to try and determine the information system that is best adapted to their needs.

This research work falls within the scope of a normative and contingent approach to the conception of organizations, namely that there are several optimal solutions according to the context. It is the manager's duty to look for them. ICTs are the means available to managers who have to be adapted to the strategy of the organization.

Thus, to avoid the unforeseen effects of a strong standardization of management processes induced by the use of ERP, organizations have adopted alternative solutions.

5.2.2 L'Oréal: Personalizing ERP to Adapt it to the Organization

The managers in L'Oréal consider that one of the key factors of the success of their company partakes of its capacity to differentiate units and to personalize the processes. So, standardization can weaken essential sources of competitive advantage. So, L'Oréal opted for more personalization by reconfiguring some modules.

However, configuration does not authorize all company fantasies. It is often up to the company to adapt its procedures to those of the tool. The operating process of an ERP system is invariable from one company to another. "Configuration only acts at the margin, through the choice of the fields available on a screen or a document, for example." (Coat and Favier, 1999).

The final system will then depend, on one hand, on the limited possibilities and high additional costs of the adaptation of ERP, and on the other hand, on the often divergent needs of different users.

5.2.3 France Telecom: Limiting the use of ERP to the Internal Information System

In France Telecom (FT), managers choose to limit the use of ERP system to the back office (accountancy and human resource). For the front office (account management, customer service), they continue to use their in-house information system.

In fact, they consider that one of the key factors of their success partakes of their capacity to differentiate units and to personalize the processes. However, an ERP can weaken essential sources of competitive advantage. Indeed, for some sectors of activity (mainly banks and insurance companies), the essential element of competitiveness is their information system. These companies devote huge investments, both technical and human to master the systems of information they have developed, implemented and used. For FT managers, adopting an ERP for the front office would be "an unacceptable regression". In fact, the pooling of software packages between user companies and the resorting to best practices foreseen as standard in ERP, constitute the main danger when it concerns the core business. This revolutionary tool, which should provide decisive competitive advantage, is likely to be immediately available to the competition. That is why in FT, they use ERP for the back office, but retain in-house software for everything that concerns price fixing and customer relations, their "*core business*".

5.3 The Effects of Standardization According to an Emerging Hypothesis

5.3.1 The Emerging Hypothesis

The emerging hypothesis attempts to make a dialectic synthesis of the two antagonistic approches presented previously. According to this approach, the use and the consequences of ICTs emerge unexpectedly from social interactions. Managers choose a new ICT and define objectives once it is adopted, but its implementation takes place in an already existing organization and its use is therefore not wholly predetermined. ICTs only have potential effects on the organization.

According to David (1998), when a management tool is introduced within an organization, its members adapt the tool to their needs, but at the same time, the tool has an influence on the behavior of the players. Indeed, the contribution to knowledge generated by the tool alters both the cognitive schemes of each of the members of the organization and social relations.

Reix (1999), Marciniak and Rowe (1997) and De Ronge (1998) consider that the emerging hypothesis is the most realistic of the three, but that it still needs to be confirmed empirically.

Finally, the effects of standardization induced by the introduction of an ERP on the functioning of an organization are somewhat unforeseeable. As Besson (1999) says: "*an ERP project is like a laboratory in which organizational coherence is being reconstructed*". Reix (1999), when talking about ERP, adds that "*the results of this reconstruction are uncertain: it is an emerging process and not an action that can be rigorously planned*".

5.3.2 Effects Tempered by the Organizational Context

Man has the ability to constantly examine and revise practices in accordance with the new information he receives (Giddens, 1991). Company leaders are currently aware of the standardization effects of ERP. They can actually choose these with a view to introducing structural change and modifying the behavior of the other members of the organization. The intentionality hypothesis then appears to be fully justified. But if we push this reasoning further, everything becomes more complicated. The other members are also aware of the mameuvering of the decision makers. In the end, the reflexivity of man, makes the consequences of this standardization of management procedures unpredictable, and thus supports the emerging hypothesis. The integrated software package whatever its degree of standardization will be influenced by the organizational context in which it is implemented.

The ERP system is confronted with the organization, characterized by some of the relations between the individuals who are part of it and by values and rules which are not necessarily consistent with the rules imposed by the system. Thus, the relation established between the ERP system and the organization is characterized by circularity and complexity. What kind of effects of business processes standardization induced by ERP in a given organization is a question with no preliminary answer (except in a determinist perspective)?

5.3.3 ADP: The Flip Side of the Coin

As demonstrated by Merton (1940), any action undertaken to produce efficiency generates a certain amount of inefficiency. Thus, the adoption of a ICTs generates efficiency and also some dysfunctioning, that is to say, unpredictable consequences. This is how, in ADP, standardization due to ERP, in the first stage, facilitated coherence within the organization, but in the second stage, reduced the organization's ability to innovate by limiting variety.

It improves short term efficiency, but also limits the local experimentation that favors apprenticeship. Moreover, this standardization restricts the scope of choice and the possibility to follow the reactivity of the company in different sectors of activity. It is simpler and faster to revise processes and find the right configuration when dealing with one country or one company. It becomes very complex to implement an ERP system when having to consolidate management rules and data in several companies or countries. It can actually become a utopian challenge.

On the other hand, the intervention of an outside integrator for the implementation of ERP is founded on an implantation methodology based on the use of standardized processes resulting from best practices. This constitutes a major change in the organization of companies. Davenport (1998, p. 122) stresses the dangers of such a practice: "An ERP system, due to its intrinsic nature, imposes its own logic to the strategy, organization and culture of the company." Integrators and editors of ERP systems structure the processes so that they reflect best practices, but this corresponds to their vision of best practice which is not necessarily the same as the client's. "In some cases, the system will lead to the better functioning of the company, however, in some cases the bias of the system is likely to clash with the interests of the company." (Davenport 1998, p. 125) Indeed, in the past, companies chose systems which adapted their own processes, which in turn required rewriting some of the software's data processing lines so that it best complied with the conditions of the organization. However, in ADP, managers think that with SAP, it is their company which chose to adapt its processes, which triggered an upheaval in internal culture and posed threats to the entire organization.

6 Conclusion

The different theoretical approaches to the relation of Information and Communication Technologies versus Organizational Change can give a first answer to the effects on management of business processes standardization induced by ERP systems.

In a determinist approach, standardization results in the optimization of business processes and helps companies develop their globalization strategy.

In an intentionalist approach, managers have to look for and find a subtle balance between an over costly adaptation of the software package to the characteristics of the organization (which reduces the benefits of standardization) and imposing too brutal change to the organization (which can result in undesirable effects).

Finally, the emerging approach brings to the fore the great incertitude concerning the expected effects of standardization which can generate inefficiency and subsequently constitute a non-negligible risk for the entire organization.

In our opinion, it is very important to carry out an in-depth study of this question with a wider field research, so as to observe the real effects of the uniformization of the organizational sub-cultures generated by ERP systems. The results of this research work could constitute, in our opinion, hypotheses for future research.

References

Adam, F and O'Doherty, P (2000). Lessons from enterprise resource planning implementations in Ireland — Towards smaller and shorter ERP projects. *Journal of Information Technology*, 15, 305–316.

Bancroft, NH, Seip, H and Sprengel, A (1998). *Implementing SAP R/3*, 2nd Ed., Greenwich: Manning Publications Co.

Berry, M (1983). *Une technologie invisible ? L'impact des instruments de gestion sur l'évolution des systèmes humains*. France: Centre de Recherche en Gestion, Ecole Polytechnique.

Besson, P (1999). Les ERP à l'épreuve de l'Organisation. *Systèmes d'Information et Management*, 4(4), 21–51.

Bingi, P, Sharma, MK and Jayanth, K (1999). Critical issues affecting an ERP implementation. *Information Systems Management*, 16(3), 7–14.

Chandler, AD (1977). *The Visible Hand: The Managerial Revolution in American Business* (trad.). Langer, F (1989). *La main visible des managers: une analyse historique*. Paris: Economica.

Coat, F and Favier, M (1999). Passage à l'ERP et refonte du système d'information: le cas des ASF. *Systèmes d'Information et Management*, 4(4), 107–128.

Curran, Keller and Ladd (1998). *SAP R/3 Business Blueprint understanding the business reference model*. Englewood Cliffs, NJ: Prentice-Hall.

Daft, RL and Lengel, RH (1986). Organizational information requirements, media richness and structural design. *Management Science*, 32(5), 554–571.

Davenport, TH (1998). Putting the enterprise into the enterprise system. *Harvard Business Review*, 76(4), 121–131.

David, A (1998). Outil de gestion et dynamique du changement. *Revue française de gestion*, 120, 44–59.

De Ronge, Y (1998). The impact of new information and communication technologies on management control system. *Working Paper at the 21st Congress of the EAA*, 15p.

Galbraith, JR (1977). *Organizational Design*. Reading, MA: Addison–Wesley.

Giddens, A (1991). *The Consequences of Modernity*, Paris: l'Harmattan.

Leavitt, H and Whisler, T (1958). Management in the 1980s. *Harvard Business Review*, November–December, 41–48.

Lee, Z and Lee, J (2000). An ERP implementation case study from a knowledge transfer perspective. *Journal of information technology*, 15, 281–288.

Marciniak, R and Rowe, F (1997). *Systèmes d'information, dynamique et organisation*, Paris: Economica.

Markus, ML and Robey, D (1988). Information technology and organizational change: Causal structure in theory and research. *Management Science*, 34(5), 583–598.

Merton, RK (1940). *Eléments de théorie et de méthode sociologique*. Paris: Plon.

Miles, MB and Huberman, AM (1984). *Qualitative Data Analysis: A Sourcebook of New Methods*, London: Sage.

Mourlon, S and Neyer, L (2002). *Tout ce que nous avons voulu savoir sur les ERP*, Paris : Les Annales des Mines.

Parr, A and Shanks, G (2000). A model for ERP project implementation. *Journal of Information Technology*, 15, 289–303.

Reix, R (1999). *Système d'Information et Management des Organisations*, 3rd Ed., Paris: Vuibert.

Rowe, F (1999). Cohérence, intégration informationnelle et changement: Esquisse d'un programme de recherche à partir des Progiciels Intégrés de Gestion. *Systèmes d'Information et Management*, 4(4), 3–20.

Scapens, R, Jazayeri, M and Scapens, J (1998). SAP: Integrated information systems and the implications for management accountants. *Management Accounting*, September, 46–48.

Simon, HA (1977). *The New Science of Management Decision* (3rd ed). Englewood Cliffs, NJ: Prentice-Hall.

Summer, M (2000). Risk factors in enterprise-wide/ERP projects. *Journal of Information Technology*, 15, 317–327.

Tushman, ML and Nadler, DA (1978). Information processing as an integrating concept in organizational design. *Academy of Management Review*, 3, 613–624.

CHAPTER 25

DOES MACROECONOMIC TRANSPARENCY HELP GOVERNMENTS BE SOLVENT? EVIDENCE FROM RECENT DATA

Ramzi Mallat and Duc Khuong Nguyen†*

This chapter investigates whether macroeconomic and data transparency standards lead to lower borrowing costs in sovereign bond markets. We essentially show that emerging market countries which subscribed to the Special Data Dissemination Standard (SDDS) experienced a significant decline in borrowing cost proxied by sovereign yield spreads on secondary markets. However, the adherence of these markets to the Code of Good Practices on Transparency in Monetary and Financial Policies caused a significant increase in the yield spreads. There is no impact of the adherence to the Code of Good Practices in Fiscal Transparency on the changes of sovereign spreads. In addition, the results suggest that a debtor country's internal liquidity factor (measured by the total reserves to total external debt service ratio) and external liquidity conditions (measured by the yield on US long-term bond) are the most important determinants of emerging market spreads.

1 Introduction

The debt market in emerging market countries consists of sovereign debt and corporate debt, of which sovereign debt segment has become, in recent years,

*EM Lyon Business School & University of Lyon 2, 88 Rue Pasteur, 69007 Lyon, France.
mallat@em-lyon.com
†Corresponding author. ISC Paris School of Management, 22 Boulevard du Fort de Vaux, 75848 Paris cedex 17, France.
dnguyen@groupeisc.com

an integral part of the global fixed income investment landscape given their size and rapid growth. Therefore, understanding emerging market debt and its return-risk profile is of great interest.

One of the stylized facts of sovereign debt markets in emerging countries is the Mexican financial crisis from 1994–1995 because its occurrence revealed the need for better information available to the public and financial market players. More generally, the emerging market crises during the 1990s have generated considerable debate among officials, researchers, institutional investors and the international community about the role of transparency as an explanation of the triggering of crises and further on its role in international financial stability. The adoption of internationally recognized standards and codes of best practices came to be seen as a way to strengthen the international financial system. This was thought to be necessary for markets to make prudent lending and investment decisions. While many agree that greater availability of information would not by itself be sufficient to prevent financial crises, it was nevertheless generally accepted that disclosure and transparency are necessary to improve the International Financial Architecture.

The international community has started actions on setting standards for improving, on the one hand, the timeliness and quality of information contained in key macroeconomic variables, and on the other hand, the transparency of public sector activities including fiscal, monetary and financial policies. In particular, the International Monetary Fund has devoted efforts to the establishment of the data and macroeconomic policy transparency standards which aim to improve the timely release of economic and financial data to the public as well as information on their compilation procedures. Most importantly, IMF member countries have been engaged to adopt, on a voluntary basis, those international standards and codes of good practices to help their economies and financial systems function properly at the national and international levels, and to share with the public timely and accurate data.

So far, several studies have examined the impact of standards and codes on emerging market economies' borrowing costs and access to international capital markets by measuring their effect on sovereign bond spreads, which are generally considered to be a measure of the market's perception of the probability of future crises. The empirical evidence according to which the borrowing costs are reduced for emerging markets adhering to internationally recognized standards has been presented (Gelos and Wei, 2002; Christofides, Mulder and Tiffin, 2003; Glennerster and Shin, 2003; Cady, 2005). Despite their great contribution in understanding the effect of macroeconomic and data transparency, these studies mainly concentrated, on the impact of the international standards and codes on the spreads of the primary debt market. There is still a need for empirical findings in the secondary markets.

This chapter attempts to fill this gap by evaluating the impact of data and macroeconomic transparency standards on sovereign bond spreads of emerging markets as a measure of the borrowing costs. We focus on the following standards and codes: the Special Data Dissemination Standards, the Code of Good Practices on Transparency in Monetary and Financial Policies, and the Code of Good Practices on Fiscal Policy Transparency. Using data on Emerging Market Bond Index spread, we show that the SDDS subscription significantly reduces the borrowing costs of emerging markets' issuers. The adherence to monetary and financial policy transparency codes generates a significant impact on the sovereign spreads but the sign of the effect remains difficult to interpret. The fiscal policy transparency codes have an insignificant effect on the spreads.

The remainder of this chapter is organized as follows. Section 2 presents the economic background of the studied problem and a brief review of literature. Section 3 discusses the empirical approach. Section 4 describes the data used in the paper. Section 5 reports and interprets the obtained results. Summary remarks and policy implications are provided in Sec. 6.

2 Economic Motivations and Literature Review

In the aftermath of the 1994 Mexican financial crisis and the 1997 East Asian crisis, the international community has been engaged to reform the so-called International Financial Architecture. Of the possible explanations for the advent of these crises, the lack of transparency has received great attention and has been widely discussed. International financial institutions and governments of creditor countries claimed that lack of relevant information may have produced, triggered or exacerbated the crises, leading to contagion and herding behaviour. Aware of the essential role of data transparency in reducing the likelihood of financial crises (thus strengthening the international financial stability), the international community called for the release of timely dissemination of macroeconomic and financial data to market participants.

Given its role in promoting greater financial stability in global context, the IMF engaged in the establishment of different standards and codes concerning the timing and availability of macroeconomic data. Its work on data dissemination standards began in October 1995 just after the Mexican crisis. The aim of these standards is to provide a conceptual framework for countries that might seek access to international capital markets to render public their economic and financial data through the availability of timely and comprehensive statistics. This clearly contributes to the pursuit of sound macroeconomic policies and to get better functioning of financial markets. These standards are named Special Data Dissemination Standards (SDDS) which were approved by the IMF Executive Board in March 1996. On 26 September 1999, the Interim Committee (currently called the International Monetary and Financial Committee) adopted the Code of Good Practices on Transparency in Monetary and Financial Policies, designated to guide member countries to increase transparency in the conduct of these policies. Two year later, the Executive Board of Directors of the IMF approved the Code of Good Practices on Fiscal Transparency on 23 March 2001. The objective of this code is to help member countries increase their transparency through better informing the public about the design and results of fiscal policy, making governments more accountable for the implementation of fiscal policy, and thereby strengthening credibility and public understanding of macroeconomic policies.

It is also important to mention that the establishment of the Financial Stability Forum in February 1999 by the G7 finance ministers and central bank governors was a response to the willingness of the international community to promote the adoption and implementation of these standards both domestically and globally. To date, each country has at its disposal the list of the various economic and financial standards that are considered as important for sound, stable and well functioning financial systems as indicated in the appendix.

The apparition of internationally recognized standards and codes raises some intriguing questions. Among other things, one may well ask what the relationship between standards and codes on the one hand and their economic outcomes on the other hand is. Several studies have empirically examined the effect of international standards and codes on emerging market economies' sovereign bond spreads, ratings and other relevant issues. For instance, Chortareas *et al.* (2001) found that countries which release more macroeconomic data have lower inflation rate. Gelos and Wei (2002) proved, in addition to the conclusion of Chortareas *et al.* (2001), that these countries attract more foreign direct investment inflows. In a recent study, Christofides, Mulder and Tiffin (2003) showed that the subscription to international standards contributed significantly to explain changes in sovereign credit spreads and ratings. The Institute of International Finance (2002) and Glennerster and Shin (2003) provided evidence that the sovereign risk premium in emerging markets is significantly reduced after the subscription to international standards. Cady (2005) used data on launch credit spreads and reached similar conclusion as in Glennerster and Shin (2003). Finally, in a related study, Andritzky *et al.* (2007) found that macroeconomic and data announcement effects in emerging market bonds reduce uncertainty and contribute to stabilize spreads. This result particularly leads to think about an eventual diminution of spread levels.

This chapter is part of the above literature, but also different in two crucial points. First, we focus on the secondary markets and not on the primary markets as in the majority of previous studies. The rationale behind this proving ground is based on the fact that secondary markets better reflect the changes in investors' sentiment about the engagement of one country to improve the accuracy and frequency of macroeconomic information released to the public. Second, we only relate the evolution of emerging market bond spreads to three most important international standards and codes: the SDDS, the monetary and financial policy transparency, and the fiscal policy transparency. Meanwhile, by adopting this choice, our study is not general like that of Christofides, Mulder and Tiffin (2003) in the sense that these authors investigated a greater number of standards and codes, and thus were broadly interested in the impact of institutional aspects on economic outcomes.

3 Model and Estimation Issues

We assess the impact of macroeconomic and data transparency standards and codes represented by the Monetary and Financial Transparency, the Fiscal Transparency and the SDDS on the changes in emerging market countries' mean sovereign credit spreads using a pooled time-series cross-sectional model with fixed effects of the following form (see Edwards, 1984)[a]:

$$\log(SP_i) = \alpha_i + \sum_{j=1}^{J} \beta_j X_{jit} + \varepsilon_i \quad (i = 1, 2, \ldots N; t = 1, 2, \ldots T) \quad (1)$$

In this specification, $\log(SP_i)$ refers to a continuous dependent variable which is measured by the logarithm of the EMBIG spread for the emerging country i. X_{jit} refers to the explanatory variable j for the country i at time t. The intercept coefficient α_i reflects the country i's characteristics that are assumed to be unchanged over the estimation period. β_j refers to slope parameters of a specific

[a]The log-linear relationship of the sovereign spread determinants is derived from assuming the risk neutral lenders and the competitive financial market. In the more complex context, Feder and Just (1977), Eaton and Gersovitz (1980), and Sachs (1981) obtained the similar relationship.

explanatory variable j that captures the common effect of that variable on the sovereign credit spread movements. ε_t is a random error term. N is the total number of cross-sections included in the empirical model. T stands for the total number of observations of the panel data set.

Here, the set of explanatory variables includes a dummy variable which represents the subscription date of each country to newly introduced international codes and standards, and ten macroeconomic fundamentals. Since our study focuses on the FPT, the MFPT and the SDDS, three alternative models will be estimated. To be more precise, dummy variables are of our preliminary interest because they controls for the changes in the sovereign spreads before and after an emerging country decided to become more transparent via a publication of the related standards. They take the value of one from the subscription date to the end of the study period and zero otherwise. If the enhanced macroeconomic and data transparency reduce the country's default risk, all dummy variables are expected to exercise a negative and significant influence on the EMBIG spread fluctuations. Macroeconomic fundamentals are introduced in the empirical model for two main reasons. First, their presence offers an easy framework to isolate the specific effects of the transparency factor because sovereign spreads' movements also depend on the changing macroeconomic conditions. Second, by doing so, we are able to, like previous studies, identify the determinants of the sovereign spreads whose level is informative of the quality of emerging market debt issuers. Effectively, we construct the following macroeconomic variables[b]: the inflation rate or the growth rate of changes in the consumer price index (CPI), the budget deficit as a share of GDP (BUD/GDP), the ratio of total external debt to GDP (DEBT/GDP), the ratio of total imports plus exports to GDP (TRA/GDP), the ratio of total current account to GDP (CUR/GDP), the ratio of total interest amount to GDP (INT/GDP), the liquidity ratio measured as the total of reserves in proportion of the total external debt service (RES/DEBT), the growth rate of GDP denominated in local currency (GROWTH), the logarithm of the US federal funds interest rate (USFED) and the logarithm of the yield on the 10-year US Treasury bond (USLONG). By default, these variables mirror the general monetary and liquidity conditions in sample emerging markets.

[b]Most of these variables have been used in the previous literature and have been found to have a significant impact on sovereign credit spreads (see Eichengreen and Mody, 2000; Min *et al.*, 2003; Jüttner *et al.*, 2006).

The estimation of the time-series cross-sectional model is often carried out by using Ordinary Least Squares (OLS) procedure. As widely discussed in econometric literature, this model solves many problems of the traditional methods of comparative research which employs either time series analysis or cross-sectional analysis. For instance, the limited number of spatial units in cross-sectional analysis and the limited number of available data over time (i.e. small "N" and "T") often result in these two individual techniques violating basic assumptions of standard OLS analysis. Most obviously, estimated results are largely biased if the model contains many explanatory variables comparatively to very few observations. In this schema of things, the pooled time-series cross-sectional design allows the removal of this restriction because the number of observations is now the product between N and T. This feature is also useful in that one can easily set a framework allowing for a multivariate analysis (i.e. large number of independent variables). Next, pooled time-series cross-sectional models offer the possibility to investigate not only the variation of what emerges through time or space, but also the variation of these two dimensions simultaneously. The reason is that, instead of testing a cross-section model for all countries at one point in time or testing a time-series model for one country using its time-series data, a pooled model is tested for all countries through time. Accordingly, the pooled time-series model with fixed effects developed above is highly suitable for assessing the effects of sample countries' increased transparency because it captures both cross-sectional effect of explanatory variables on credit spreads as well as the time-series effect within markets.

It is, however, important to note that the pooled model encounters some methodological problems despite its advantages in dealing with both time and space, of which the most important include the serial correlation between a country i's errors, the contemporaneous cross-sectional correlation of the errors, the cross-sectional heteroscedasticity of the errors and the possibly causal heterogeneity of parameters across cross-section units[c] (Hicks, 1994; Beck and Katz, 1996). So, in this paper we employ the seemingly unrelated regression (SUR) method, also referred to as the Parks estimators, to correct these estimation problems. In fact, the seemingly unrelated regression procedure treats each cross-section (or market) and the time series within that cross-section as a separate equation unrelated to any other cross-section and its time series in the pooled data set. Most specifically, this estimation procedure

[c]In some cases, the slope coefficients of the pooled model are heterogeneous across cross-section units because the errors tend to be non-random. Then, the assumed homogeneity of slope coefficients might be not reasonable.

is interpretable as a series of a country specific regression analysis that utilizes contemporaneous cross-equation error correlations among the error of a system of equation to improve the efficiency of the estimates of an equation system (Hicks, 1994).

4 Data

In this section the question of whether the improving macroeconomic and data transparency leads to lower yield spreads (or country risk reduction) in sovereign bond markets is investigated. Sample emerging markets include Argentina, Brazil, Croatia, Ecuador, Mexico, Turkey and South Africa. Quarterly data on yield spreads of the JP Morgan Emerging Market Index Global (EMBIG) are used over the period from January 1994 to December 2002.[d] The choice of EMBIG to the detriment of EMBI is explained by the wider range of debt instruments that the EMBIG covers. Yield spread, often measured by the number of basis points, is the difference between the yield on emerging market bond index and the yield on a bond of similar characteristics, but considered as free of default risk (typically a US Treasury security). One basis point is equal to a hundredth of a percentage point. More detailed description of emerging market debt indices is provided in Cunningham (1999).

Table 1 gives the summarized characteristics of our sample data. At the first sight, we observe that the sovereign spread is around 801 basis points on average with a highest value of 6475 which is equivalent to 67.75%. Besides, it should be noted that the average deficit or surplus budget and the current deficit over GDP stand both at -1% ; the inflation rate is somewhat high for sample markets because it comes to 74% ; the total external debt is near to 50% of the GDP; and finally, the total reserves represent only 22% of the total external debt.

Table 2 offers a close look on the dates of subscription of sample markets to different transparency policies. Our selected markets have mainly subscribed to the SDDS in 1996, except for Brazil and Ecuador. With regards to the

[d]To measure the historical performance of emerging market debt, JP Morgan publishes two main variants of sovereign bond indices. The first measure, called Emerging Market Bond Index, tracks returns and spreads on Brady bonds and some other restructured sovereign instruments in emerging market countries. The second measure is the Emerging Market Bond Index Global (EMBIG), which is designated to track the total returns for dollar-denominated Brady bonds, Eurobonds, traded loans and local market debt instruments issued by sovereign and quasi-sovereign entities of emerging markets countries. Currently, the EMBI Global covers 188 instruments across 33 emerging countries. For being selected in these indices, sovereign debt instruments must have a face value of over US$ 500 million and at least 2.5 years to maturity, and they must also pass a liquidity test.

Table 1: Basic statistics of the cross-sectional data.

	Mean	Std. Dev.	Maximum	Minimum	Jarque–Bera	Probability
SP (Spread)	801.00 0	938.95	6475.00	80.00	3109.21	0.00
BUD/GDP	−0.01	0.01	0.01	−0.05	138.84	0.00
CPI	0.74	4.05	44.53	−0.02	64053.32	0.00
CUR/GDP	−0.01	0.01	0.06	−0.07	277.28	0.00
DEBT/GDP	0.47	0.24	1.38	0.14	86.88	0.00
GROWTH	0.06	0.08	0.37	−0.11	139.00	0.00
INT/GDP	0.03	0.01	0.07	0.01	21.61	0.00
RES/DEBT	0.22	0.11	0.68	0.05	177.99	0.00
TRA/GDP	−0.01	0.02	0.04	−0.09	102.14	0.00
USFED	0.05	0.01	0.07	0.01	62.32	0.00
USLONG	0.06	0.01	0.08	0.04	1.45	0.48

Notes: This table provides basic statistics of the cross-section data used in our study. The dependent variable is none other than the logarithm of the Emerging Market Bond Index Global spreads. BUD/GDP, CPI, CUR/GDP, DEBT/GDP, DEBT/GDP, GROWTH, INT/GDP, RES/DEBT, TRA/GDP, USFED and USLONG refer respectively to the ratio of budget deficit to GDP, the inflation rate, the ratio of total current account to GDP, the ratio of total external debt to GDP, the growth rate of GDP denominated in local currency, the ratio of total interest amount to GDP, the liquidity ratio measured as the total of reserves in proportion of the total external debt service, the ratio of total imports plus exports to GDP (TRA/GDP), the logarithm of the US federal funds interest rate and the logarithm of the yield on the 10-year US Treasury bond. These macroeconomic fundamentals are used in order to control for the general macroeconomic conditions of sample countries.

Table 2: Subscription dates of sample markets to the Special Data Dissemination Standards (SDDS), Fiscal Policy Transparency (FPT) and Monetary and Financial Policy Transparency (MFPT).

Country	Date of SDDS subscription	Date of FPT subscription	Date of MFPT subscription
Argentina	August 16, 1996	April 15, 1999	April 15, 1999
Brazil	March 14, 2001	December 6, 2001	Nonsubscriber
Croatia	May 20, 1996	November 24, 2004	August 12, 2002
Ecuador	March 27, 1998	Nonsubscriber	Nonsubscriber
Mexico	August 13, 1996	September 16, 2002	October 11, 2001
South Africa	August 2, 1996	Nonsubscriber	Nonsubscriber
Turkey	August 8, 1996	June 27, 2000	Nonsubscriber

Source: The information about subscription dates of sample markets is taken from various publications of the International Monetary Fund.

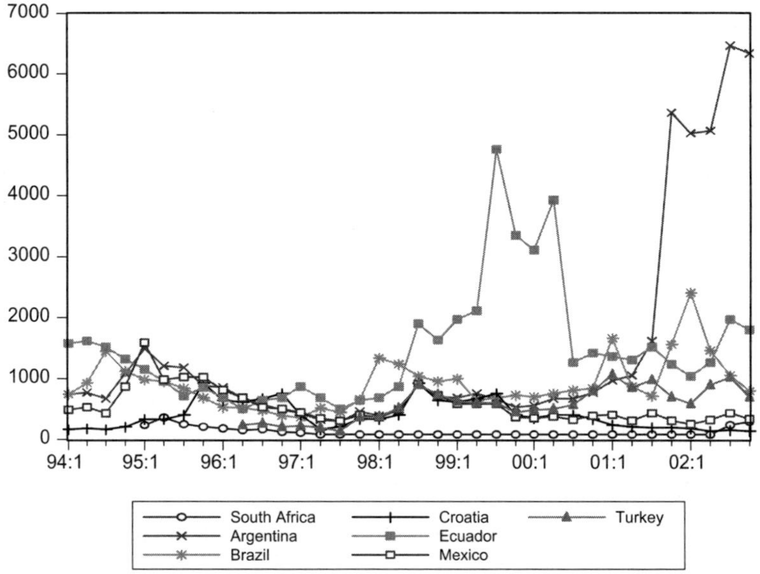

Figure 1: The evolution of EMBIG spreads over the period 1994–2002.

FPT and MFPT, the newest subscription dates started in 1999, which clearly restrict the possibility to include a large number of countries in our sample. This also limits our interpretations of the empirical results in the later section.

Figure 1 depicts the evolution of the emerging market sovereign spreads from the first quarter of 1994 to the fourth quarter of 2002. As we can observe, sovereign debt markets in Argentina and Ecuador pay the highest spread level which indicates the particular importance of default risk in these markets. If we look at the dates of subscription to the SDDS of sample markets, we are able to notify that credit spreads globally went down in the aftermath of the 1994 debt crisis in the Latin American region. The time-paths also testified to an upward trend of credit spreads since the beginning of 1998, and that continued until the end of our study period.

To close this section, it is important to mention that data for the EMBIG spreads are drawn from JP Morgan and macroeconomic fundamentals and external debt variables are obtained from the IMF's International Financial Statistics and the World Bank's Global Development Finance. To preserve the country-specific factors, we construct all our variables based on local currency basis.

5 Empirical Results

This section presents the empirical results from the estimation of our pooled model described in Sec. 3. Particularly, the results are divided into three groups depending on the types of subscription events (the SDDS, the FPT or the MFPT). First, we study the impact of the SDDS subscription on the time-varying level of the EMBIG spreads by adding the dummy variable SDDS into our pooled time series cross-sectional model. Next, the dummy variable SDDS is replaced step-by-step by the FPT and MFPT variables respectively. It is important to note that the first model contains every market in the sample data whereas only markets which subscribed to the FPT and MFPT are included the second and the third models.

Table 3 reports the results from estimating our pooled model. Generally, there is a relatively high level of fit for the three examined models since the adjusted R-squared ranges from 66.7% to 77.5%. The significance of the majority of coefficients at conventional levels also indicates the correct selection of explanatory variables.

With regard to Model 1, our variable of interest is the dummy variable SDDS. The coefficient attached to this variable is, as expected, negative and significant at 5%. Accordingly, for countries which subscribed to the Special Data Dissemination Standard, the cross-country sovereign spreads decreases by 23.4%. This is informative of the reduction of premium attributed to investors for holding the debt securities issued by emerging market borrowers. In this schema of things, policy makers will have an interest in improving data transparency to lower borrowing costs. It should be noted that the obtained result is in line with previous findings revealed by, among others, Christofides, Mulder and Tiffin (2003), and Cady (2005).

Contrary to what might be expected, changes in the EMBIG spreads are not at all affected by the country's subscription to the fiscal policy transparency from the view of the coefficient associated with the FPT variable. That is, a better transparency in terms of fiscal policies does not necessarily conduct to lower spreads. For instance, this result is found at least for the countries which are included in the cross-sectional regression. Since the impact of the fiscal transparency on the sovereign spreads has, to our knowledge, not yet been treated in previous literature, there is no study to compare our results with.

Concerning the effect on the EMBIG spreads of the monetary and financial policy transparency, the result shows a positive and significant relationship between two variables of interest. Effectively, we observe an increase of 30.5%

Table 3: Estimation results from the pooled time-series model with fixed effects.

Variables	Model 1	Model 2	Model 3
Budget deficit to GDP ratio (BUD/GDP)	−2.136	−11.764**	−6.688
	(−0.709)	(−2.343)	(−1.037)
Inflation rate (CPI)	0.010*	0.007	−0.081
	(1.719)	(1.012)	(−0.970)
Current account to GDP ratio (CUR/GDP)	0.143	26.470**	−0.906
	(0.058)	(2.452)	(−0.313)
Total external debt to GDP ratio (DEBT/GDP)	0.640**	1.457**	0.530
	(2.941)	(3.174)	(1.291)
Growth rate of GDP (GROWTH)	−1.038	−0.556	−0.179
	(−2.639)	(−1.003)	(−0.231)
Interest to GDP ratio (INT/GDP)	−1.051	−9.602	−29.429**
	(−0.274)	(−1.355)	(−3.588)
Total reserves to total external debt (RES/DEBT)	−2.512**	−3.218**	−4.165**
	(−5.725)	(−4.140)	(−5.420)
Total trade sector to GDP (TRA/GDP)	18.257**	−11.761	29.333**
	(4.813)	(−0.903)	(5.122)
Federal funds rate (USFED)	0.022	0.080	0.401**
	(0.214)	(0.610)	(2.128)
10-year US Treasury bond (USLONG)	−0.572*	−0.405	−0.702*
	(−1.777)	(−1.211)	(−1.751)
Subscription date to the SDDS (SDDS)	−0.234**		
	(−2.947)		
Subscription date to the FPT (FPT)		0.191	
		(1.418)	
Subscription date to the MFPT (MFPT)			0.305*
			(1.691)
Fixed Effects			
South Africa-C	3.798		
Argentina–C	5.431	5.942	7.012
Brazil-C	5.550	6.436	
Croatia-C	6.033		8.407
Ecuador-C	5.472		
Mexico-C	5.340	5.893	6.915
Turkey-C	5.294	4.901	
R-squared	0.791	0.702	0.724
Adjusted R-squared	0.775	0.667	0.686

Notes: This table reports the estimated coefficients from estimating the general pooled model. In Model 1, we relate the evolution of the EMBIG spreads to a set of one dummy variable (SDDS) and 10 explanatory variables which consist of macroeconomic fundamentals. Models 2 and 3 are quite similar to Model 1 with just a small difference. That is, instead of the dummy variable SDDS, we use the dummy variables FPT and MFPT respectively. The number of cross-sections (or countries) is equal to 7, 4 and 3 for Models 1, 2 and 3 respectively, * and ** indicate that the associated coefficient is statistically significant at 10% and 5% respectively. The t-statistics are reported in parentheses.

in the spread levels after the subscription date of one country to the MFPT standard. Clearly, this impact is difficult to interpret. To give an explanation, one may think that the effect of other variables prevails over that of the MFPT subscription during the recent years, and results in the sovereign spreads in most countries reading their highest levels observed during the estimation period.

Like previous works which attempt to analyze the impact of macroeconomic fundamentals on the emerging market spreads, the present study also finds the dominant effect of the liquidity factor (cf. the ratio of total reserves to the total external debt) and the yield on 10-year US Treasury bond. In fact, the coefficient attached to the RES/DEBT variable is negative and highly significant, indicating that the more important is the liquidity, the more the spread will decrease. The same pattern is acknowledged in the case of the USLONG variable. This is explainable because an increase in the yield on the US long-term bond normally leads to lower the yield on bonds of similar characteristics. The other important determinants of the EMBIG spreads include the total external debt to GDP ratio and the total imports plus exports to GDP ratio.

6 Conclusion

The emerging market crises of the 1990s have generated considerable debate about the New International Financial Architecture (NIFA) and were partially attributed to a lack of market information. Improving transparency is considered as the main reform of the NIFA.

This chapter has investigated whether macroeconomic and data transparency standards lead to lower yield spreads in sovereign bond markets. The endogenous variable, sovereign credit spread, is taken from JP Morgan's Emerging Market Bond Index Global. The factor of interest, the subscription to the Special Data Dissemination Standard (SDDS), is represented by a dummy variable that is set to be equal to one for the quarters following the subscription. We also consider the subscription to "The Code of Good Practices on Transparency in Monetary and Financial Policies" and "The Code of Good Practices in Fiscal Transparency". The influence of other factors, mainly macroeconomic fundamentals and external debt variables which have been broadly considered in the literature (Kamin and Kleist, 1999; and Ferrucci, 2003) is controlled.

Using quarterly data and a pooled time-series regression analysis, we found that the macroeconomic and data transparency lead to significantly lower spread levels only when the considered country subscribed to the SDDS. There is a significant response of the spread levels following the subscription to the monetary and financial policy transparency standards. However, the impact is positive and therefore difficult to be interpreted. The adoption of the fiscal policy transparency has no significant impact on the spreads. In addition, macroeconomic fundamentals seem to play an important role in the determination of the borrowing cost in debt markets of emerging countries. The most important factors are the liquidity and the yield on the US long-term bond. In this schema of things, policy makers will have an interest in improving data transparency and liquidity factor in order to lower borrowing costs which reflect the reduction in their country's default risk.

Acknowledgments

We have greatly benefited from comments and suggestions by Georges Pariente, Mondher Bellalah and participants at the 4th International Finance Conference (14–17 March, 2007, Hammamet, Tunisia).

Appendix

Key Standards endorsed by the IMF and World Bank

Subject areas	Key standards	Issuing institutions
Macroeconomic policy and data transparency		
Monetary and financial policy transparency	Code of Good Practices on Transparency in Monetary and Financial policies	International Monetary Fund (IMF)
Fiscal policy transparency	Code of Good Practices in Fiscal Transparency	IMF
Data dissemination	Special Data Dissemination Standard (SDDS)/General Data Dissemination System (GDDS)	IMF
Institutional and market infrastructure		
Insolvency	Principles and Guidelines on Effective Insolvency and Creditor Rights System	World Bank
Corporate Governance	Principles of Corporate Governance	Organization for Economic Co-operation and Development (OECD)
Accounting	International Accounting Standards (IAS)	International Accounting Standards Board (IASB)
Auditing	International Standards on Auditing (ISA)	International Federation of Accountants (IFAC)
Payment and Settlement	Core Principles for Systematically Important Payment Systems	Committee on Payment and Settlement Systems (CPSS)
	Recommendations for Securities Settlements Systems	CPPS and International Organization of Securities Commissions (IOSCO)
Money Laundering	The Forty Recommendations/ 8 Special Recommendations Against Terrorist Financing	Financial Action Task Force (FATF)
Financial regulation and supervision		
Banking Supervision	Core Principles for Effective Banking Supervision	Basel Committee on Banking Supervision (BCBS)
Securities Regulation	Objectives and Principles of Securities Regulation	International Organization of Securities Commissions (IOSCO)
Insurance Supervision	Insurance Core Principles	International Association of Insurance (IAIS)

Source: Financial stability forum.

References

Andritzky, JR, Bannister, GJ and Tamirisa, NT (2007). The impact of macroeconomic announcements on emerging market bonds. *Emerging Market Review*, 8, 20–37.

Arora, V and Cerisola, M (2001). How does US monetary policy influence sovereign spreads in emerging markets?. IMF Staff Papers, 48, 474–498.

Beck, N and Katz, JN (1996). Nuisance vs. substance: Specifying and estimating time-series-cross-section models. *Political Analysis*, 6, 1–36.

Cady, J (2005). Does SDDS subscription reduce borrowing costs for emerging market economies?. IMF Staff Papers, 52, 503–517.

Chortareas, G, Stasavage, D and Sterne, G (2002). Does it pay to be transparent? International evidence from central banks. *The Federal Reserve Bank of St. Louis Review*, July/August 2002.

Christofides, C, Mulder, CB and Tiffin, A (2003). The link between adherence to international standards of good practice, foreign exchange spreads, and ratings. IMF Working Paper, No. 03/74.

Cunningham, A (1999). Emerging economy spread indices and financial stability. *Bank of England Financial Stability Review*, 7, 115–27.

Eaton, J and Gersovitz, M (1980). LDC participation in international financial markets: Debt and reserves. *Journal of Development Economics*, 7, 3–21.

Edwards, S (1984). LDC foreign borrowing and default risk: An empirical investigation. *American Economic Review*, 74, 726–734.

Eichengreen, B and Mody, A (2000). What explains the changing spreads on emerging market debt?. In *The Economics of International Capital Flows*, Edwards, S (eds.), Chicago: University of Chicago Press.

Feder, G and Just, RE (1977). A study of debt servicing capacity applying logit analysis. *Journal of Development Economics*, 4, 25–38.

Ferrucci, G (2003). Empirical determinants of emerging market economies' sovereign bond spreads, Bank of England Working Paper, No. 205.

Gelos, RG and Wei, S-J (2002). Transparency and international investor behavior. NBER Working Paper No. 9260.

Glennerster, R and Shin, Y (2003). Is transparency good for you, and can the IMF help? IMF Working Paper No. 03/132.

Hicks, A (1994). Introduction to pooling. In *The Comparative Political Economy of the Welfare State* Janoski, T and Hicks, A (eds.), Cambridge: Cambridge University Press.

Institute of International Finance, Inc. (2002). Appendix D: Does subscription to the IMF's special data dissemination standard lower a country's credit spread?. *IIF Action Plan Proposals and Dialogue with the Private Sector*, Washington: The Global Association of Financial Institutions.

International Monetary Fund (2004). *Global Financial Stability Report*, Washington: World Economic and Financial Surveys.

Jüttner, DJ, Chung, D and Leung, W (2006). Emerging market bond returns — An investor perspective. *Journal of Multinational Financial Management*, 16, 105–121.

Kamin, SB and Kleist, KV (1999). The evolution and determinants of emerging market credit spreads in the 1990s. Bank for International Settlements Working Paper, No. 68.

Min, H-G, Lee, D-H, Nam, C, Park, M-C and Nam, S-H (2003). Determinants of emerging-market bond spreads: Cross-country evidence. *Global Finance Journal*, 14, 271–286.

Sachs, JD (1981). The current account and macroeconomic adjustment in the 1970s. *Brookings Papers in Economic Activity*, 1, 201–268.

INDEX